The Tunkin Diary and Lectures

Tunkin in naval dress. January 1939. Moscow

The Vinogradoff Institute
Dickinson School of Law
Pennsylvania State University

The Tunkin Diary and Lectures

The Diary and Collected Lectures of G. I. Tunkin at The Hague Academy of International Law

Edited and Compiled, with Translations and an Introduction, by

William E. Butler
John Edward Fowler Distinguished Professor of Law
Dickinson School of Law, Pennsylvania State University
Academician, National Academy of Sciences of Ukraine

and

Vladimir G. Tunkin
Moscow State University

eleven
international publishing

Published, sold and distributed by Eleven International Publishing
P.O. Box 85576
2508 CG The Hague
The Netherlands
Tel.: +31 70 33 070 33
Fax: +31 70 33 070 30
e-mail: sales@budh.nl
www.elevenpub.com

Sold and distributed in USA and Canada
International Specialized Book Services
920 NE 58th Avenue, Suite 300
Portland, OR 97213-3786, USA
Tel: 1-800-944-6190 (toll-free)
Fax: +1 503 280-8832
orders@isbs.com
www.isbs.com

Eleven International Publishing is an imprint of Boom uitgevers Den Haag.

The lectures were originally published in the Recueil des cours and are reprinted with kind permission of the Hague Academy of International Law/Académie de droit international de la Haye.

ISBN 978-94-90947-53-8

Printed in The Netherlands

Contents

The Legal Nature of the United Nations

INTERNATIONAL LAW IN THE INTERNATIONAL SYSTEM

Introduction

The present volume brings together a set of materials unique to the Tunkin family and of considerable interest to historians of international law, legal doctrine, and international diplomacy. The volume opens with the Recollections of Grigorii Ivanovich Tunkin by his youngest son, Vladimir Grigorevich Tunkin. They were prompted by the discovery that Professor Tunkin kept a diary when he traveled abroad. Vladimir Grigorevich was able to relate the diary entries to his own memories of his father and, no less important, to cope with his father's hand, not an easy task to begin with and complicated by the fact that entries were often made in haste while on a moving train or in an aircraft and contained abbreviations and allusions difficult to decipher.

The Diary mentions more than five hundred individuals, nearly all of whom we have been able to identify. In the course of tracing names, Vladimir Grigorevich has been able to re-establish contact with his father's colleagues or their families, all of whom have been unfailingly helpful in the challenge of reconstructing the past. Responsibility for the annotations in the Diary is indicated by the initials of the respective author.

These are followed by the texts of Tunkin's lectures at The Hague Academy of International Law delivered on four occasions between 1958 and 1986. We are grateful to Martinus Nijhoff, Publishers, for permission to republish them. They appear virtually without alterations, not least because there is every reason to believe that Professor Tunkin himself wrote the English version in his own words without the assistance of a translator. The sole adjustment made is that the footnotes are numbered consecutively throughout each of the lectures, which departs from the practice extant at the time of recommencing footnote numbering at the bottom of each page. Citations have been left as in the original, and the style varies from one lecture to another.

The photographs in the book come from the Tunkin Family Archive and have been made available by Vladimir G. Tunkin. There is no indication of by whom they may have been taken, and the family has no means of tracing this. All the original materials used in this volume have since been transferred permanently to the Archive of the Russian Academy of Sciences in St. Petersburg, where they will be available for independent research.

W. E. Butler
V. G. Tunkin

March 2012

RECOLLECTIONS OF MY FATHER, GRIGORII IVANOVICH TUNKIN

Vladimir G. Tunkin

I found myself for the first time in the native village of my father (Chamovo, Vinogradov District, Archangel Region) in 1952. By train to Archangel and after a brief stop to see relatives, we were seated on a boat traversing the route Archangel to Kotlas (a city in the southern part of Archangel Region). A bit more than 300 kilometers along the North Dvina River and we three – father, mother, and I – disembarked at the pier of Konetsgore, which is on the opposite bank of the Dvina from our village. It would be more correct to say this pier was situated there, since boats no longer ply the Dvina.

Chamovo

Birthplace of Tunkin. Chamovo. Northern Russia

On the pier the first cousin of my father, Iakov Ivanovich Varlachev,[1] awaited us with a boat on which we together passed over to the opposite bank. Here on the Dvina are

1 Iakov Ivanovich Varlachev (1908-1983), first cousin of G. I. Tunkin – [VGT].

two long islands which extend one after the other but, happily since the villages of Chamovo and Konetsgore lie opposite one another there is a channel between them lying obliquely to the main channel of the River. We succeeded in traversing the channel, rowing energetically against the strong current in this place. Upon exiting the channel a view of Chamovo opened against the background of the forest, which in wordless silence interrupted sometimes by the sound of birds in flight and an even belt of shade extended from somewhere northward to somewhere southward, creating the impression of a quiet indestructibility.

At home Grandma Daria Efimovna[2] awaited us; Grandpa Ivan Gavrilovich[3] had passed away the year previous. The house was typical of the Archangel Region – the front portion facing the road was an izba, that is, that portion of the house where people live. The two-story household part is a direct extension of the izba, the lower floor a courtyard (dvor) where the livestock and poultry are maintained and the upper floor, a loft. One could pass from the izba to the loft through a corridor. Grain for the livestock and poultry was stored in the loft and, as was true in our home, fishing gear also was stored there. Grandpa was an excellent fisherman and hunter.

Father also was a good angler and hunter and by the age of 13 or 14 years ventured alone into the forest for squirrel, hazel-grouse, and hare. In brief comments on his life written at the age of 15, he wrote that there were days when he brought up to thirty squirrels home. No doubt the squirrel pelts were primarily to be sold. Father's hunting trophies were a great support to the family, for not all grandpa's sisters had married by then and brother Mitia[4] was ten years younger than father.

The house was in the second row of homes, counting from the river. The forest began still farther from the river, a hundred or so meters behind our house. About half way from our house I discovered lying in abundance barbed wire, traces of entrenchment, remnants of logs from a military dug-out. As grandma explained to me, when in 1918 the force of White Guards and interventionists, among which were principally English and Americans, but there were also Canadians, Australians, and French, approached Chamovo, they placed their headquarters in our house – a large house in the center of the village. And on the side facing the forest they organized a semi-circle defense to protect the headquarters.

In the regional museum at Dvina Bereznik – the center of the Vinogradov District, there is a room in which the three primary commanders of the Red Army units are portrayed who operated in these areas. These were Pavlin Vinogradov,[5] who was the first commander of the Dvina Brigade of the Red Army. He organized in the upper areas of the Dvina the siting of cannons on river ships, which then began to be launched downstream with the River current to meet the monitors and gunboats of the interventionists and White Guards. The adversaries met in the region of Dvina Bereznik,

2 Daria Efimovna Tunkina (1884-1976), mother of G. I. Tunkin – [VGT].

3 Ivan Gavrilovich Tunkin (1883-1951), father of G. I. Tunkin – [VGT].

4 Mitia (Dmitrii Ivanovich) Tunkin (1916-1943), younger brother of G. I. Tunkin – [VGT].

5 Pavlin Fedorovich Vinogradov (1890-1918), first commander of the Red Army Dvina Brigade – [VGT].

not far from Chamovo. Sharp battles were waged in these localities. Father related that he saw the battle between the boats of the interventionists and those of the Red Army. Pavlin Vinogradov was killed in September 1918 during the battle where the Vagi River flowed into the Dvina, about twenty kilometers from Chamovo. The district in which Chamovo Village is located was named in his honor.

The second commander of the Red Army represented in the regional museum was A. A. Samoilo,[6] a former general in the Tsarist Army. The force under the command of Samoilo in combination with partisans took the city of Shenkursk in January 1919 and threw the enemy northward for 90 kilometers.

The third commander, Hadji Murat Dzarokhokhov,[7] was an Osetin by nationality and, judging by his name, also Muslim.

In 1919 the White Guards and the interventionists succeeded in advancing along the Dvina almost 100 kilometers. There remained about 800 kilometers to reach Moscow. Having comprehended the utter senselessness of their plan to reach Moscow or to join up with the forces of Yudenich and Kolchak, the interventionists evacuated their units. The White Guards under the command of General Miller[8] remained, but their days were numbered.

It is interesting that the peasants, as father recounted, called the English and the Americans, in any event, among the interventionists "kamans". This was because the sentry standing at his post said to an approaching peasant "come on". Hence the "kamans". In the 1960s, arriving in Chamovo, I met elderly women who called the interventionists "kamans".

The barbed wire left by the interventionists proved to be of use to me and to father when we began to place fishing gear in the River which had been kept in the loft. This was fish-trap gear woven from withe and rather large in size. The basket was fixed to a cord, the other end of which was fastened on the bank. But cords of the necessary length and firmness were not to be found at home, so we gathered the barbed wire itself. It was very inconvenient to work with when placing the gear, but it was necessary to hurry only once, and the next day on the small boat with the assistance of a boat-hook each of the four fish-traps were raised: in three nothing was to be found, but in one, sterlets were found regularly.

This same barbed wire I saw at the same site in 1971 during my regular trip to Chamovo. After this I visited Chamovo only in 2005; the barbed wire and other traces of the sojourn of the interventionists had been removed. At some distance from this place a road has been built travelled by buses from Archangel to Kotlas. And the life of the village in general had changed cardinally; it was no longer a village, but rather a dacha settlement. Only a few winter there, that is, live there year-round. The rest,

6 Aleksandr Aleksandrovich Samoilo (1869-1963), Russian and Soviet military leader, General in the Air Force of the USSR from 1940 – [VGT].

7 Hadji Murat Dzarokhokhov (1874-1945), Commander of cavalry regiment – [VGT]

8 Evgenii Karlovich Miller (1867-1937), Lieutenant-General, Commander in Chief of the White Guards in Northern Russia from 1918 to 1920, kidnapped by Soviet agents in Paris and taken to Moscow in 1937 – [VGT].

who are called dachniki, come for the summer and even during winter holidays from Archangel, Severodvinsk, Petersburg – from those places where fate has cast those descendants of people who were born and lived in this village. Some houses have been trimmed with planks and painted, which imparts to the village a happier view, and not that gray, melancholy sense characteristic of a village which has weathered over time. And no traces of dilapidation and decline.

From the windows of our home the school in the village of Konetsgore on the opposite bank of the Dvina, where father had studied for four years, was visible on a height. As his ability to read and write formed and in what schools he studied he himself related in his notes written at the age of fifteen after he had finished school in Konetsgore. I quote extracts from these notes, preserving the details of the narrative:

"I taught myself to read, I don't know how. Indeed, it was thus: I had an aunt (sister of my father) only seven years older than I. She went to school and taught her older sister at home. I loved to sit there and evidently memorized the letters. And father was somewhat literate and doubtless taught me. I loved to imitate the sexton. I took the prayer-book and a low small bench. I placed the prayer-book on the small bench and read. When I was six years old, I asked to go to school. I was not accepted. I recall that I cried a lot when I left the school.

The next year I was accepted at the school. I studied brilliantly and passed with all fives. I completed the three-year course of study at primary school. I dreamed about travelling to Shenkursk to study. Although a church parish school was six versts away [on the other side of the river in the village of Konetsgore – VGT], one would learn so little there of value that I did not think of enrolling. The year after I graduated from the three-year course this school was re-established as a higher primary school and I enrolled. I studied well. I lived with relatives and in the early years rarely visited my home because I would not go six versts in the winter. I was only eleven years old. The son of my aunt lived with me in the apartment (from the neighboring village of Shuzhogi) and the aunt with whom I lived also had a son. They often hurt my feelings, and I often cried. The school in which I studied (under the reign of the Soviet Republic) was transformed into the II level. Having lived with my aunt for two years, I moved to another apartment with the family of my friend. In all I studied across the river for four years.

I asked my parents what should be my fate thereafter: to go or not to study in Shenkursk. They advised me to go. I confess that I did not want to go far from home.

In the morning I prepared to go into the forest for squirrels. I had put on only one boot as Kolka Fomin[9] entered the izba. He expressed a greeting and said: 'Well, Grishukha, let's go to school'. I was astonished, for he came out of the blue. He left a week and a half ago to study in Shenkursk and suddenly he came. 'You are from where?', I asked. 'From Shenkursk. One is unlikely to find an apartment. We hang about the institutions to no purpose. It was difficult but we did find a private apartment'. 'And where are the others?'" I asked. 'They come from the rear'. Two others came along. I invited them for tea and they did not refuse. They said 'Three by three pupils from

9 Nikolai Fomin, a school friend of G. I. Tunkin – [VGT].

our village have been assigned into two groups'. 'And when do lessons begin?' 'On Thursday we all should assemble'. 'All right, I am coming', I replied. I was delighted, but I preferred not to depart in two days in order to study when soon would be the best time for hunting squirrels. However, one had to go".

Father graduated from the ten-year school in the City of Shenkursk, some sixty kilometers direct from Chamovo on a tributary of the Dvina, the Vaga.

It is interesting that on the labor sheet which corresponds to the modern labor book it is written with respect to social origin – from employees. This is because grandfather served as a buoy-keeper on the Dvina, for which he received an allowance.

After completing the ten-year school father faced the question – what to study further. Naturally for a young man who had grown up in a village where on one side there flows a proper river and on the other is an uninhabited forest, there were two answers to this question: either engage in forestry or with the river. He chose forestry and enrolled in 1925 in a Forestry Tekhnikum (Obozersk Northern Railway Station). He graduated from the Tekhnikum in 1928, after which he worked until 1932 in an organization whose name was changed several times: first it was the Forestry Structure, then Orgles, and finally Sevlesstroi. This organization was located in Archangel. While working in Archangel he lived with his aunt, one of grandpa's four sisters, Anna Gavrilovna Skripova.[10]

When father later worked on his doctoral dissertation "The Korean Question in the Light of International Law" while at a rest home of the Ministry of Foreign Affairs of the USSR, he did so, if weather permitted, in the forest near our dacha, well-removed from the other dachas. For a man for whom the forest is a native element, there was no more convenient place for creative activity. This practice continued, and when a personal dacha came along, it happily was situated beside the forest. Then the trees planted on the dacha plot grew up. On the grassy area beside the dacha a folding table was placed on which an Underwood typewriter stood with a Russian keyboard or a portable typewriter with a Latin keyboard – a work space was thus ready.

One of father's distinguishing characteristics was his firm aspiration to study foreign languages. A small notebook has survived with various entries. On the obverse of the cover there is written: "This book belongs to pupil of the III grade, Konetsgore Higher Primary School. Grigorii Ivanovich Tunkin". The notebook contains entries of several folk songs, for example, the song about Stenka Razin,[11] the song about the cruiser *Varyag*,[12] and so on. They were written in pencil in a hand difficult to decipher. There are also entries of a diary nature, also in pencil. For example: "The year 1921 was a good spring and a dull, rainy summer. I write on Sunday, 31 July, old style. No one is home. Father carried lamps to Shuzhogu, and so on. Grandma went somewhere. Mama left in the morning to gather saffron milk-cap mushrooms in the forest. I am sitting together with my brother. G. Tunkin".

10 Anna Gavrilova Skripova (1899-1990), aunt of G. I. Tunkin – [VGT].

11 Stepan (Stenka) Timofeevich Razin (1630-1671), Cossack leader who led campaign against Tsar Aleksei Mikhailovich – [WEB].

12 A Russian naval cruiser which during the Russo-Japanese War engaged more than ten Japanese cruisers and destroyers (1904) and was finally sunk by the officers and crew – [VGT].

It is interesting that the last phrase and signature were in Latin letters. On the next page French expressions are set out in ink and in a legible hand with translations into the Russian language. Perhaps the French expressions were written out by one of his teachers, someone of whom knew the French language. In the North there were many intelligent people who came to be there other than by their own will. One may assume that father developed at this time an attraction for the study of foreign languages to somehow fill the intellectual vacuum as this made it possible to transcend the limits of the world in which he lived then.

Moscow

But the study of languages did not suffice and in 1932, after four years in forestry, his life underwent a decisive turning point. He travelled to Moscow, where he enrolled in the Moscow Juridical Institute. Many years later, on the eve of his eightieth birthday, he wrote about the decisive changes in his life:

> I fell into diplomacy and the science of international law by a stroke of fate. My teachers in school had me destined for the faculty of physics and mathematics. But from the age of thirteen I was an inveterate hunter and went to a forestry technical school, dreaming to become a forester, and spent entire days in the forest with a rifle. Then the Communist Youth League, gravitation towards the social sciences, philosophy, history, law. Even undertook Hegel but, of course, hr proved to be beyond my capacities. This led me to the Juridical Institute. For days on end I sat in the library reading Thucydides, Plutarch, and other authors of Antiquity. Upon graduating from the Institute, I remained for post-graduate studies on the general history of State and law. I was enraptured by this science. Soon after the defense of my kandidat dissertation, when I was a senior research associate of the Institute of Law, I was directed by decision of the Central Committee of the Communist Party of the Soviet Union to take a position in the People's Commissariat for Foreign Affairs of the USSR. This was in 1939 and decided my future fate, which I do not regret. Work in the Ministry of Foreign Affairs led me to the science of international law. I believed and continue to believe that a diplomat who does not know international law is an incompetent worker. Foreign languages, so essential for the science of international law, I began to study thoroughly at the age of 22 and studied them for virtually my entire life.

As father related, after having worked in Archangel he had enough money not to have to live on a stipend; he sat for hours in the library greedily absorbing knowledge. When his accumulated savings had been exhausted, father proceeded to teach dialectical materialism in one of the technical schools. This was his first attempt at teaching, which he continued after completing his post-graduate studies in 1938.

Teaching, right up to his transfer to the Law Faculty of Lomonosov Moscow State University in 1965, was part-time employment, a second job. During 1939 and 1940, he worked as a docent and then head of the Chair of the Theory and History of State and Law at the All-Union Legal Academy. From 1948 to 1954 (with a break for his sojourn in Korea), he worked as the head of the Chair of International Law of the Moscow Juridical Institute. From 1954 to 1958, as Professor at the Law Faculty of Lomonosov Moscow State University. From 1958 to 1960 – as head of the Chair of Legal Sciences of the Higher Diplomatic School.

Tunkin at Forestry Tekhnikum, May 1928

After the completion of post-graduate studies and defense of a dissertation "Parliamentary Reform of 1832 in England", father was sent to work in the People's Commissariat of the Navy. He worked there in all for half a year, quickly being persuaded that there was nothing for a jurist to do in that people's commissariat. He wrote about this to the highest instance (Central Committee of the Communist Party of the Soviet Union). A valuable acquisition during his brief period in the said people's commissariat was a marine overcoat made of excellent material and very warm in the strong frosts. There is a photograph where father is bundled up in this overcoat with braid on the sleeves corresponding to the rank of captain-lieutenant. The highest instance concurred with the opinion of the captain-lieutenant and transferred him in January 1939 to work at the Institute of Law of the USSR Academy of Sciences, he being allowed to keep his overcoat. There he worked for a brief period, until October of the same year, when he was transferred to the People's Commissariat of Foreign Affairs of the USSR. This transfer was preceded by a chat with the People's Commissar for Foreign Affairs, V. M. Molotov.[13] The chat touched upon his knowledge of foreign languages, and for part of the time they spoke in English and in French. Father successfully passed the examination, but at the end of the conversation asked that his scholarly work not be interrupted. Molotov replied that he would think about the matter. On the following day father was notified that he had been added to the personnel establishment of the People's Commissariat of Foreign Affairs.

Several words should be said about the study of foreign languages by father. One of the methods of studying languages which father used was scattering small cards about the room with a foreign word written on each and a translation into Russian. Father used this system even in 1936, as mother's relatives, with whom father lived together with Mama Itta Efimovna[14] after they were married in 1935, recalled. In the postwar years these cards were scattered about our home when father studied, in particular, Latin with the assistance of this system. In later years when a certain level was reached in the study of the three principal languages necessary to read international legal literature, that is, English, French, and German, father developed the habit of preserving the standard of his knowledge to read literature in these languages before going to sleep. In addition to classical literature, he used detective novels: Simenon,[15] Agatha Christie.[16] Evidently the level of knowledge of these languages was actually achieved. Lev Nikolaevich Smirnov,[17] for many years the former Chairman of the Supreme Court of the RSFSR and then USSR, said that father was greatly respected by the interpreters who worked at the United Nations, saying that he was a person who did not need them. Father also had a command of Italian and Spanish. As regards such languages as Polish, Czech, Romanian, and Hungarian, father read the international legal literature in these languages in the original while using dictionaries. His "excellent" command of the English language was noted by the correspondent of the *Toronto Daily Star* in an interview which father gave to that newspaper on 23 October 1943, being in Canada as the chargé d'affaires.

When the War commenced, father, just as other personnel of the People's Commissariat for Foreign Affairs, applied to go to the front as a volunteer. But he was instructed to go to Iran, to the City of Gorgan, to work as consul. This was because our forces simultaneously with the English had been introduced into Iran. Our sojourn in Iran ended in the summer of 1942.

---

13 Viacheslav Mikhailovich Molotov (1890-1986), sometime People's Commissar (1939-1949) and Minister (1953-1957) of Foreign Affairs of the USSR – [WEB].

14 Itta Efimovna Tunkina (1912-2000), wife of G. I. Tunkin [VGT].

15 Georges Joseph Christian Simenon (1903-1989), Belgian writer of books on the detective Maigret – [WEB].

16 Agatha Marie Clarissa Miller (1890-1976), married name Christie, noted English writer of mysteries – [WEB].

17 Lev Nikolaevich Smirnov (1911-1986), Chairman of the Supreme Court of the USSR from 1972 to 1984 – [VGT].

Tunkin with younger brother, Dmitrii. April 1940

Canada

The next assignment was Canada, where father was to organize the diplomatic mission (until then there had been none there). Possibly when selecting a candidacy to undertake this task a good knowledge of English and French was significant, essential with respect to Canada. We travelled by train to Vladivostok, and waited there for some time for a steamship which had to traverse the Pacific Ocean. Father's brother, Dmitrii Ivanovich, visited us in Vladivostok. Even before the War he had become a naval pilot. In father's papers I found three letters which Dmitrii Ivanovich sent to us in Canada and which returned with us to Moscow. Two letters were sent in 1942, as Dmitrii Ivanovich wrote, from Siberia. The last letter was dated April 1943, written as his unit flew to Europe. As indicated in the communiqué concerning irretrievable losses of the naval aviation group of the Black Sea Fleet, he did not return from a combat mission on 7 July 1943. He was the commander of a flight of torpedo-bombers, second squadron, fifth guards' aviation regiment, and had the rank of guard second lieutenant. When he perished he was not yet 27 years of age.

After Vladivostok, we crossed the Pacific Ocean by ship, spending twenty days in so doing. The Pacific Ocean on this occasion proved to be truly "pacific", and we together with the other personnel of the future mission arrived in the American port of Portland. We then travelled by rail from Portland to New York, and then from New York to Ottawa.

The first to have arrived in September 1942 at Ottawa, the capital of Canada, father occupied himself with a search for and purchase of a suitable house for the diplomatic mission. After lengthy searches, a suitable house finally was found. It was not a new one, but a comfortable detached home on the bank of the Ottawa River, near a park, where the Embassy of the Russian Federation in Canada is presently located, though in a new building. The old one was seriously damaged by fire during the mid-1950s. All this information is contained in father's article "Thirty Years Ago" published in the *Montreal Star*, 17 June 1972 and written at the request of the Canadian side in connection with the thirtieth anniversary of the establishment of diplomatic relations between Canada and the USSR.

Many years after the events described, father related that the mood of part of the Canadian press had changed for the worse with respect to the USSR after the Red Army had begun to acquire supremacy over the Germans. This information was transmitted in good time to Moscow, and the instruction received in reply was to carefully follow this trend as exceedingly important.

My own recollections of the sojourn in Canada are confined only to a single episode. In April 1944 Mama took me to a photo studio in order to stamp my image upon my fourth birthday. The photographer did everything to please the representatives of the Allies. He required me to sit, to stand, to turn my head to one side and then the

Canadian Junior Red Cross presents Tunkin, Chargé d'affaires in Ottawa, with cheque for $20,000 to help Russian children war victims

other, and so on. Ultimately, I stood up, exhausted, and cried, and the photographer exclaimed: "Russian boy! Stalingrad!"

In September 1944 father was instructed by the People's Commissariat for Foreign Affairs to return to Moscow. It was possible by 1944 to return to the Soviet Union by air since the American and Canadian flyers had ferried fighters and transport planes through Alaska to be delivered to the USSR. That father returned to the Soviet Union by air I learned from him only entirely incidentally. During the 1970s, we walked in the park surrounding our home and the conversation turned to the war efforts of America. Father gave it up as a bad job and said: "I know their war efforts, when we flew, the pilot came out in the morning, looked at the sky, and if he saw a cloud, he postponed the flight to the next day". In 2009, when sorting through father's archive for transfer to the Petersburg Branch of the Archive of the Academy of Sciences, I found twenty notebooks with diary entries. On one of the notebooks there are these lines: "I recall when we flew from Washington to Moscow in 1944 on a lend-lease aircraft and spent the night at every aerodrome in the United States and Canada (the flight Washington to Alaska took 10 days, and Alaska to Moscow, where the aircraft was flown by our pilots – 3 days)". Halfway from Washington to Alaska father sent us a postcard, which is before me as I write. The postmark on the postcard reads: 16 Aug. 1944, Great Falls, Mont. The message: "Dear Itta, We departed the 12th from Washington, but for the moment are still in Great Falls – four hours by air from Edmonton. Delays everywhere, and if the same occurs farther on, we will reach Moscow not earlier than autumn. Don't be distressed. We fly without any conveniences. No chairs. Nothing. Kisses. Papa". My mother and I, or rather mother more than me, had to pack things and again undertake the passage by sea across the Pacific Ocean, but in the other direction.

The said diaries were kept from 1962 until the end of father's life. The notebooks containing these diaries are small in format, allowing them to be carried in a jacket pocket. A diary was kept principally during travels abroad. The entries were made in the most diverse places: an evening in a hotel after sessions had finished, in a park, a museum, an aircraft, on a train, and so on. The entries were made in a tiny hand difficult to decipher. Mostly they contain commentaries on the sessions of the United Nations International Law Commission, the Administrative Council of the International Law Association, the sessions of the Institute of International Law, and sessions of other organizations in which father took part. Often father transfers in these diaries to the English or French language. This, evidently, was connected with the fact that, as he writes in a diary, "... when I travel to a country, I begin to think in the language of this country if I know it".

The second time that father was in Canada had to do with the awarding to him in 1990 of the *Encyclopedia Britannica* Prize. He began his speech after being handed the prize as follows: "The last time I spoke to the Canadian public was in 1943". After the address, one of those present approached him and said that he had heard father in 1943.

Tunkin signs USSR-Canada Agreement on Military Deliveries. Looking on are Mackenzie King, Canadian Prime Minister, and V. A. Sergeev, Deputy USSR People's Commissar of Foreign Trade

KOREA

After returning to Moscow, the orientation of father's activity changed abruptly from west to east. From March 1945 until May 1952 he worked as head of the First Far Eastern Section of the People's Commissariat of Foreign Affairs (with a break during his sojourn in the Korean People's Democratic Republic).

On the whole father very rarely and in laconic form touched upon his work in the People's Commissariat, later Ministry, of Foreign Affairs, and if he touched upon something, it was many years after some event to which he was referring. Usually these moments of candor came during a joint walk through the park around our home. I did not put any questions: everything was related in studied laconic form, and silence was enough for what was said. Now I am deciding to relate one of such frank statements. The People's Commissariat of Foreign Affairs during the early postwar years had few staff. During a routine reception in the Kremlin, which happened in this instance à la fourchette, Stalin[18] passed from table to table. Approaching the table where father was and evidently having inquired about his post, Stalin said that he had read his memorandum to the Minister. "You don't know the East", Stalin said. The memorandum contained a proposal to ease the position of the USSR with respect to one of the eastern countries within the ambit of the First Far Eastern Section. Father said that he had only

18 Iosif Vissarionovich Stalin (1878-1953), first General Secretary of the Communist Party of the Soviet Union from 1922 until his death – [WEB].

recently begun to concern himself with the East. Before passing on to the next table, Stalin proposed a toast to the health of Comrade Tunkin.

In 1947 father took part in the work of the Joint Soviet-American Commission for Korea. The Joint Commission met in Seoul and in Pyongyang. Terentii Fomich Shtykov[19] headed the Soviet delegation, a former secretary of the Leningrad Regional Committee of the All-Russian Communist Party (Bolshevik) during the blockade of Leningrad. Father and Shtykov established very warm, friendly relations.

Father went in December 1948 to Pyongyang to organize the embassy of the USSR there. Shtykov was appointed ambassador to the Korean People's Democratic Republic. The following year I with my mother travelled to see father as a guest during the summer holidays. This time we made the trip to Vladivostok not by train, but by air, on an Ilyushin-12. Father lived in a detached house located in the so-called "General's City", evidently so called because Japanese generals had previously lived there. Alongside father's residence was the house in which Kim Il-sung lived with his family.[20] Shtykov's house was somewhat further along. A number of personnel of the Embassy of the USSR in the Korean People's Democratic Republic also lived in the "General's City". The sojourn in Korea is memorable for me because of the large number of chipmunks and large attractive butterflies, one of which I brought to Moscow. As father related to me after his return from Korea, excellent hunting was to be found there during the migration of ducks. Father's hunting skills were of great advantage.

The Korean War began on 25 June 1950. An exchange of messages between Moscow, Peking, and Pyongyang preceded the war as to whether the Americans would intervene in the war or not. Shtykov had still not arrived in Pyongyang, so that father himself had to give what seemed to be the obvious reply to this question; he wrote precisely that the Americans absolutely would intervene. In March 1993 I met father at Sheremetovo Airport upon his return from South Korea. The last year of his life had begun. For some reason on the road home he spoke about the time that had preceded the Korean War. He said that in the Archive of the Ministry of Foreign Affairs they had discovered his memoranda on whether the Americans would intervene in the War or not and the commentaries of personnel who had discovered these documents: "A brilliant mind has been found".

My mother and I learned about the outbreak of the War at the rest home of the Ministry of Foreign Affairs while returning from swimming. The director of the rest home who came to meet us reported in a cheerful and hearty voice: "And war in Korea". We rushed into the reading room, and in all the newspapers it was reported that South Korean forces had crossed the boundary of the Korean People's Democratic Republic and the Republic of Korea; also printed was the photograph of the United States

19 Terentii Fomich Shtykov (1907-1964), military figure, diplomat, and Communist Party functionary – [VGT].

20 Kim Il-sung (1912-1994), Prime Minister (1948-1972) and President (1972-1994), of the Korean People's Democratic Republic, and General Secretary of the Workers Party of Korea – [WEB].

Secretary of State, Dulles.[21] According to the text under the photograph, it was taken in trenches near the boundary of the two Koreas. I cut out the map of the Korean Peninsula from the journal *New Times* [Russian edition – WEB] and noted the line of the front on this map. At the outset the North Korean forces proceeded rather rapidly to almost the southern extremity of the peninsula. Then the American forces landed marines and the line of the front also rapidly began to move northward. Two episodes were related by father about this period, albeit long after the War.

The initial episode was when the Americans were included in the War and their aircraft had begun to bomb North Korea. Shtykov, father, and certain other personnel of the embassy had gone in two vehicles to swim. An American aircraft began to overtake them on the road. The first vehicle in which Shtykov and father rode turned over on the side of the road; people lay on the yard covered by grass and concealed themselves under a green quilt. Those travelling in the second vehicle had fled from it, but not all succeeded in concealing themselves. Colonel Ignatev,[22] of the embassy personnel, was killed.

There is a photograph of the territory of our embassy made after the American bombings. The building of the embassy is in ruins, and immediately in front of the ruins is a small round basin with a statue intact in the middle. The goldfish had been swimming a year before in this basin. The American flyers had bombed precisely.

The second episode was linked with leaving Pyongyang when the American forces approached. Shtykov and father travelled along different roads in the hope that one of them would succeed in departing. One was armed with a colt, the other with a revolver. Happily, both remained alive. In February 1951 father returned to Moscow. When he opened the suitcase and extracted and put on his leather double-breasted jacket, a thick aroma of smoke spread throughout the apartment. It became clear that the Soviet embassy in the People's Democratic Republic of Korea had spent the last months in an earthen cottage.

Father next went to Korea much later, in 1986, during the Sixty-Second Conference of the International Law Association in Seoul. Diplomatic relations with the Republic of Korea still had not been established. He was received as the official representative of a State with which the Republic of Korea wished to establish diplomatic relations, although father said to everyone that he was merely a professor of the Lomonosov Moscow State University. They showed to him, in particular, part of the building of the former Russian mission in Seoul remaining after the Korean War and subsequently repaired. On the territory of the mission the flower beds had been pegged out and several workers were engaged in weeding the flower beds.

21 John Foster Dulles (1888-1959), Secretary of State under President Eisenhower – [WEB].

22 Aleksandr Matveevich Ignatev (1902-1950), Counsellor of the Embassy of the USSR, perished on 23 August 1950 – [VGT].

Stalin watches as Chinese Prime Minister Chou Enlai signs agreement in September 1952. Photo reproduced from Soviet newspapers

LEGAL DIPLOMACY

In May 1952 father became head of the Treaty Law Section of the Ministry of Foreign Affairs of the USSR, and his life began to be closely linked with international law. In 1965 he sought to combine work in the Ministry with being head of the Chair, which he had previously done three times. But then his superiors were others. His superior in 1965 was the Minister of Foreign Affairs, A. A. Gromyko,[23] with whom father had bad relations, about which father expressly wrote in his letter to the highest instance (Central Committee of the Communist Party of the Soviet Union). A Letter of 10 February 1965, No. 220/ДПО, in the name of the Rector of Moscow Lomonosov State University, Academician I. G. Petrovskii,[24] has been preserved; it said "The Ministry of Foreign Affairs of the USSR has no objections to Professor G. I. Tunkin working as a second job as Head of the Chair of International Law of the Law Faculty of Moscow State University". Below is a note made in father's hand "Agreed with the Minister, 9.II.65".

Why was this combination of jobs not realized? The fact is that several days later after obtaining consent, Gromyko reconsidered and refused. Thus, father had to choose between being Head of the Chair and work in the Ministry. Something similar had occurred in October 1939 when he had requested not to be separated from scholarship.

---

23 Andrei Andreevich Gromyko (1909-1989) served in numerous senior diplomatic and governmental posts, having joined the Communist Party in 1931, among them Ambassador to the United States, United Kingdom, and United Nations, Minister of Foreign Affairs, and Vice-Chairman of the USSR Council of Ministers – [WEB].

24 Ivan Georgievich Petrovskii (1901-1973), mathematician, served as Rector of Lomonosov Moscow State University from 1951 to 1973 – [WEB].

But then he did not have the right to choose. In 1965 he in practice had this right, and he chose scholarship and teaching.

The following lines I found in father's diaries: "I write my works on international law not only with my head, but with my heart. I am consoled by the thought that I am thereby doing something for that which is most important: 'the preservation and maintenance of peace'. Often I literally 'agonize' through the theoretical propositions, rethink them dozens of times. Sometimes not months, but years, pass by for this".

Foreign Minister V. M. Molotov signs Joint Declaration of USSR and East European countries, 2 December 1954

Diary of G. I. Tunkin

Transcribed and Edited, with Annotations, by
Vladimir Grigorevich Tunkin
Translated, Annotated, and Edited by
W. E. Butler

1962

8 Aug:
Chamovo: A fine day. A bright sun in the morning, infrequent clouds at intervals. Everyone is haying. Quiet in the village, a slight breeze. Somewhere a calf is mooing, a chicken cackling, a child to whom everything on this planet is new and interesting is singing happily, and again, quiet.

The smooth Dvina peacefully flows, mirror-like, towards the White Sea. Great and mighty, it is aware of its own power and lazily flows on under the rays of the hot sun.

Voltaire. "In spite of the fact that he was an atheist, Voltaire wrote: 'If God did not exist, it would be necessary to invent him'" (W. Durant, *The Age of Voltaire*).

Voltaire. Equality and Freedom. "Equality – natural, when it is limited to rights, unnatural, when it attempts to level goods and power" (W. Durant, *The Age of Voltaire*).

"To be free is to be subject to nothing but the laws" (W. Durant, *The Age of Voltaire*).

24 Oct:
Moscow-London. "Comet" Aircraft: The day before yesterday I was in Kislovodsk, played tennis until I dropped. Yesterday I flew to Moscow and now I am flying to London for a session of the Executive Committee of the Council of the International Law Association. Met an old acquaintance – George Drew, the Canadian High Commissioner in England.[1] We had become acquainted at the 1958 Conference on the Law of the Sea. He was in the USSR with his wife for ten days, at Moscow and Leningrad.

We spoke mostly about Cuban affairs or, more precisely, the actions of the United States with respect to Cuba. I set out our position in detail. The true reasons for the introduction of a "quarantine" by the United States, or more precisely a blockade, are that they want to "smother" Cuba, the first socialist country in America. References to a military

1 George Alexander Drew (1894-1973), former Premier of Ontario, who served as High Commissioner from 1957 to 1964 in London – [WEB].

threat on the part of Cuba are nonsense, camouflage. I demonstrated that the actions of the United States are a flagrant violation of international law, aggression. One must look at matters soberly and recognize peaceful coexistence, recognize the right of every people to freely establish a State and social system. Drew said not one word in justification of the actions of the United States. He listened attentively, expressed regret that the situation had become so aggravated and the hope that everything would be all right. Then we spoke about common acquaintances: Parson,[2] Robertson,[3] Cadier,[4] and others.

Now London. It is already 9:00 in the evening. Comrades from the Embassy met me at the airport and brought me to the Embassy Hotel.

My lecture at University College London is scheduled for 12:00. Before this a coffee party at which the professors of this and other colleges were present, and the legal advisor to the Foreign Office, Vallat.[5] Five minutes before the lecture began the beadle entered the room where we were and announced: "Gentlemen, it is time to proceed to the Theatre" and led us into another building to the lecture hall. The hall was filled to capacity. People sat and stood everywhere possible, even on the window-sills.

The subject was: "The Present and Future of International Law". I spoke from notes. They listened very attentively and applauded warmly. Professor Schwarzenberger – the initiator of the lecture suggested that I submit the text of the lecture for the *Year Book of World Affairs*.[6] I said that I would think about it. The fact was that I had promised to give an article to a new journal of international law and would use the lecture for this.

At the request of Professor Schwarzenberger, I gave a seminar in the evening for post-graduates and professors. In the lecture I touched upon the establishment by the United States of a sea blockade of Cuba. The impression was that England did not support the United States very much in this matter, although of course the Government did so.

It is interesting that when we came to the seminar with Comrade Nesterov (a member of the Embassy of the USSR),[7] Professor Schwarzenberger spoke in the corridor with some American. Then he said to me that this American was from the United States Department of Defense and works in London on some theory. Professor Schwarzenberger told him that everything said at the seminar by Professor Tunkin is off the record and gave him to understand that his presence is "not obligatory". The American did not come to the seminar.

2 Most likely a reference to Lester B. Pearson (1897-1972), former Prime Minister of Canada and Nobel laureate of the Peace Prize – [WEB].

3 Norman Alexander Robertson (1904-1968), Canadian High Commissioner in London and Canadian Ambassador to the United States – [WEB].

4 Possibly a reference to Andrew W. Cordier (1901-1975), United Nations official and President of Columbia University – [WEB].

5 Sir Francis Vallat (1912-2008), Legal Advisor to the Foreign and Commonwealth Office from 1960 to 1968 and Professor of International Law, King's College London, from 1970 to 1976 – [WEB].

6 Georg Schwarzenberger (1908-1991), Professor of International Law at University College London, the founder and editor of the *Year Book of World Affairs* – [WEB].

7 Nesterov [not further identified].

International Law Commission, Geneva. Left to right: Alfred Verdross (Austria); G. I. Tunkin; Georges Scelle (France). 1957

26 Oct:

London: Alarming times. The newspapers are full of news about Cuba: "Cuba – latest news". The newspapers allege that a US invasion of Cuba is imminent, although both the USSR and the United States have agreed to mediation by the acting Secretary General, U Thant.[8]

In the evening there was a session of the subcommittee on the site of the next Conference of the International Law Association. Actually, this was a preparatory session for the Council, and the main question was the fate of the Committee for Peaceful Coexistence.

In comparison with Brussels, the situation had worsened. The Americans three weeks before the Council sent Professor Olmstead,[9] gave 10,000 dollars, and promised more. Professor Olmstead persuaded the President of the Association, Cochaux.[10] They submitted a draft resolution to "discontinue the work of the Committee on peaceful coexistence: to ask the Committee to present a new subject and propose a composition of a new Committee".

On the other hand, Lord McNair,[11] Chairman of the Executive Committee, submitted a proposal to leave the name of the Committee but to cease work on codification

8 U Thant (1909-1974), the Burmese diplomat and United Nations Secretary General from 1961 to 1971 – [WEB].

9 Cecil J. Olmstead (1907-2003), editor of volumes on international drainage basins and on the extra-territorial application of laws; Patron of the International Law Association – [WEB].

10 Maitre Henri Cochaux (1900-19?), international lawyer and member of the Brussels Bar – [WEB].

11 Arnold McNair, First Baron McNair (1885-1975), member of the International Court of Justice (1946-1955) and first President of the European Court of Human Rights (1959-1965) – [WEB].

of the principles and assign the Committee to occupy itself with legal questions connected with the formation of new independent States and non-intervention.

27 Oct:
London: The question of the Committee for peaceful coexistence occupied the Council for two hours. I spoke very gently, in a conciliatory tone, having in mind to speak more sharply if necessary. I said that the ILA had become a world organization. This is consistent with the subject-matter with which it is engaged – general international law. In the text (of the decision) we must be ready to accommodate different trends. It is unequivocally desirable to continue work on peaceful coexistence in order to complete it. Why should this wish not be accommodated?

Others want to study different issues. By all means. One may take up those two questions mentioned by McNair. One may assign everything to one Committee, or one may create an additional Committee.

The Americans insisted on their position. Before the session I spoke with McNair. I said that the situation is serious, but that he might facilitate a resolution. At the session I proposed to take the McNair proposal as the basis, adding from the Brussels resolution a point concerning the drawing up of a list of principles of peaceful coexistence.

My conciliatory speech and proposal were well received. Cochaux de facto disavowed the draft resolution which Olmstead had imposed on him. Seeing the mood, McNair, having spoken with me, submitted a proposal: the Committee to complete work before the 1964 Conference, after which it may be issued. To create a new Committee to study the two questions. The result of the voting: 25 – for, 3 (Americans) opposed.

After the Council there were no sessions. Ended at 16:15 hours. Schwarzenberger invited me to be a guest in Boeg (Denmark).

29 Oct:
London: Front page news: settlement of the Cuban crisis. N. S. Khrushchev[12] stated that the Soviet Union accepts the Statement of the United States that there will be no invasion and a readiness to remove missiles from Cuba. The *Daily Express* writes: "The United States scored an immense diplomatic victory. It is also a victory for peace. Mr. Khrushchev has had the good sense and courage to pull out of a situation which had become untenable".

5 Nov:
Moscow: The "victory" in the Cuban question of which the press of the United States shouts has one consequence which so far no one has noted. The policy of the United States on the Cuban issue has destroyed the myth that the United States does not intend to attack anyone, that they will not begin a war, and so on.

12 Nikita Sergeevich Khrushchev (1894-1971), First Secretary of the Communist Party of the Soviet Union from 1953 to 1964 – [WEB].

26 Nov:
Moscow: I am writing my works on international law not only with my mind, but with my heart. I am comforted by the thought that I can thereby do something of the greatest importance: the preservation and maintenance of peace. Often I literally "suffer through" the theoretical propositions, think them over dozens of times. Sometimes not months, but years, pass.

1963

6 Jan:
The train departed Belorusskii Station at precisely 22:30 hours. The first night passed peacefully. The second was a nightmare. At 01:30 hours (Moscow time) the Polish border guard arrived, thirty minutes later the customs officers, and thirty minutes after them the Czechoslovak border guards and then the customs officers – and upon arrival and departure the Austrian officials at dawn. Every time that I travel by train, I say that this is the last time, as this is tiresome.

Vienna: I suggested to Viktor Ivanovich Avilov[13] that we attend services at St. Stephan Cathedral and then visit the Gallery of Art. Two months ago I went to services at Westminster Abbey – this was interesting. We stay at St. Stephan Cathedral for fifteen minutes and went on to the Gallery. Not bad at all. Many van Dycks, Rubenses. For some reason on this occasion the image of the human form made an especially strong impression on me, not the Titian type, although that too is very expressive, but Rubens – his are completely alive, the blood courses, it breathes.

There are many Italians: Titian, Veronese, Tintoretto, and others; few Spanish. On the whole we both were satisfied. Avilov said that he was in the Gallery for the first time, although he had been in Vienna already for two years.

20 Jan:
Geneva: The weather is diabolically cold. In Moscow temperatures it would be wonderful: minus 12 degrees, but here nothing is adapted for such cold. The hotel is cold, and I am working in a jumper. Snow has fallen for two and a half days, about 25 to 30 centimeters. Outside the windows, the trees in the park are so clothed in snow as rarely happens in Moscow. All of Europe is frozen; in Moscow it is now minus 22 degrees.

In the international arena there is a storm caused by De Gaulle's address last evening. De Gaulle[14] uttered several weighty "nons": (a) supplying France with American Polaris missiles – non, they will do their own; (b) the entry of England into the "Common Market" – non, this would be a step towards transforming the "Common Market" into a tributary of NATO and even greater intensification of American influence.

13 Viktor Ivanovich Avilov (1900-1997) was Ambassador of the USSR to Belgium from 1953 to 1958 and to Austria from 1960 to 1965 – [VGT].

14 Charles de Gaulle (1890-1970), President of France from 1959 to 1968 – [WEB].

For several days before De Gaulle's speech *Le Monde* published a lengthy article which demonstrated that American monopolies are increasingly grasping the economy of Western Europe in their hands by using the "Common Market".

De Gaulle's declaration brought condemnation in all the capitals of the "Common Market" countries and in Washington. Negotiations with England concerning her accession to the Common Market have been broken off because of the position of France.

Many write about the address of N. S. Khrushchev at the Congress of the SEPG in Berlin and the speech there of the representative of the Chinese People's Republic, and that a split between the USSR and the Chinese People's Republic is inevitable.

"Le rendez-vouz des deux vieux messieurs" – this is how the newspaper *La Suisse* (20 January) described the forthcoming meeting between Adenauer[15] and De Gaulle. Adenauer arrives today in Paris.

La Suisse (20 January) reports the death of Theodore Aubert,[16] the lawyer. He defended Conradi,[17] the murderer of Vorovskii,[18] at the trial in 1924.

24 Jan:

Geneva-Vienna Train: Soon Vienna. I am travelling by train. Slept well and rested. Then yesterday I slept five hours in all. I labored for a long time on the article "Le droit international de la coexistence pacifique" for the *Mélanges Rolin*.[19] I had the idea of writing directly in French, but this is difficult. To be sure, this is the second article written in French. The first was "La guerre froide et le droit international" for the journal *Comprendre*.[20] I finished the article only yesterday morning. I had to complete it since I am already late with the article.

I departed Geneva somewhat earlier – the Subcommittee for the Legal Succession of States and Governments was to complete its work on 25 January. But everything had been completed in substance. I hurried since on 31 January the Annual Meeting the Soviet Association of International Law begins, and there will be re-elections.

The Subcommittee for State Responsibility completed work on 16 January, having elaborated the programme for the next rapporteur. Ago[21] was very effective as chairman. The subcommittees, created at my suggestion, have in the general view justified themselves. They have even been noted in General Assembly resolutions.

15 Konrad Hermann Joseph Adenauer (1876-1967), Chancellor of the Federal Republic of Germany from 1949 to 1963 – [WEB].

16 Theodore Aubert (1878-1963), Geneva lawyer who acted as defense counsel for Maurice Conradi – [WEB].

17 Maurice Conradi (1896-1947), a Russian émigré of Swiss descent acquitted in Switzerland of the assassination of the Plenipotentiary Representative of the Soviet Union to Switzerland, V. V. Vorovskii – [WEB].

18 Vatslav Vatslavovich Vorovskii (1871-1923), Soviet diplomatic representative in Switzerland assassinated during the Conference at Lausanne on the Turkish question in 1923 – [VGT].

19 See G. I. Tunkin, "Le droit international de la co-existence pacifique", in *Mélanges offerts à Henri Rolin: Problèmes de droit des gens* (1964), pp. 407-418 – [WEB].

20 See G. I. Tunkin, "La guerre froide et le droit international", *Comprendre*, XXV (1962), pp. 25-32 – [WEB].

21 Roberto Ago (1907-1995), member of the International Court of Justice from 1979-1995 – [WEB].

I am reading Lillian Ross, *Portrait of Hemingway*.[22] He evidently drank a lot, and this is evidence of his discontentedness. One comes to feel sorry for him.

18 May:
Geneva: The third week of our stay in Geneva has commenced. The session of the International Law Commission, to which I came with Itta,[23] began in May. The principal issue is the law of treaties. A very interesting, but difficult question. There is much to read, to think about, and to prepare. On Monday, for example, the invalidity of treaties will be discussed which are contrary to principles of international law having the character of jus cogens. I wrote about this in my monograph Вопросы теории международного права,[24] and this, of course, makes things easier. But all the same one must prepare for the discussion.

The weather has been cold and dry for several days. Today, however, is magnificent. I write these lines in the Perl du Lac Park. Alongside the lake. There is a slight breeze. The famous Geneva fountain spurts water to a height of nearly 100 meters and falls below as rain. Sometimes the wind throws droplets of the fountain far, far away. The enormous chestnuts of Geneva are blooming with white and pink blossoms. The pink ones are very beautiful. There are many flowers, especially tulips.

14 July:
Brussels: Yet another, the XV Session, of the International Law Commission has ended.

Today I flew to Brussels. Stayed in the Hotel Atlanta. Everywhere there is American speech, such that if one closes one's eyes, one may imagine that you are in New York. They always speak loudly, and even those who cannot distinguish them by their pronunciation and now should do so by the language they speak – are not difficult to recognize by this. It is even easier to identify American ladies by their clothing: diversity of color multiplied by an astonishing lack of taste.

I am in Brussels for the third time but have not seen much here. In 1958 I was here for two days, by train en route to The Hague, to deliver lectures at the Academy of International Law. The entire time was devoted to seeing an international exhibition. In August 1962 I was so occupied at the conference of the International Law Association that I succeeded in seeing nothing. To be sure, I was at Erasmus House, where a tea had been arranged. And in 1958 I went to the home of Rubens. But on this occasion I very much wanted to visit a museum of Flemish paintings. Today is Monday, however, and the museum is closed.

·Nationality contradictions are now very exacerbated in Belgium. The French portion has been dominant in the economy and politics. The Flemish presently comprise 51%,

22 Lillian Ross (b. 1927), *Portrait of Hemingway* (1961), a short book which originated as a Profile in the *New Yorker*, 13 May 1950 – [WEB].

23 Itta Efimovna Tunkina (1912-2000), the spouse of G. I. Tunkin – [VGT].

24 G. I. Tunkin, Вопросы теории международного права [Questions of the Theory of International Law] (1962) – [WEB].

and the French about 35% [of the population – VGT]. The Flemish are demanding reforms. There were genuine Four Hundred anti-French pogroms in Flanders recently. Glass windows were broken in French shops. The Government resigned, but the King refused to accept this. It is said that the Government restrained itself only because no one wants elections to Parliament in the summer: holidays are ruined.

16 July:

Amsterdam: The aircraft left Brussels at 17:30 hours. The landing was 15 minutes later in Amsterdam. From here to Moscow nonstop. The last days in Geneva were very intense. The final session of the Editorial Committee; two sessions of the ILC on a single day. In addition, at my suggestion the Committee on Coexistence of the International Law Association was created. There were three sessions, and these too in the last week.

This Committee the Americans attempted to eliminate – they did not like "peaceful coexistence" – but it was kept. The Americans at the October session of the Executive Committee [of the ILA] in London remained in isolation. A draft list of legal principles of peaceful coexistence was prepared at a session of the Committee, that is, the basic principles of international law. An impression – the American position with respect to peaceful coexistence has changed somewhat.

16 July:

Flight from Amsterdam to Moscow: Although Professor Hazard[25] was not at the session of the Committee, the Canadian professor, McWhinney,[26] who is close to the Americans, conducted himself differently from in Brussels in 1962. Something new echoed in the address of Kennedy[27] at The American University in Washington D. C. in 1962. He spoke about coexistence, about the need to strive for cooperation with the USSR, and so on.

A war is being waged against the Kurds in Iraq. The Soviet delegation to ECOSOC raised the question of genocide. The Medical Assistance Programs proposed that this issue be included on the agenda of the next United Nations General Assembly. The member of the International Law Commission from Iraq, Professor Yasseen,[28] was crestfallen. His wife is a Kurd, and the former Minister of Foreign Affairs, Jawad,[29] to whom he was close, is sitting in a concentration camp. Yasseen summoned his wife, children, and father to Geneva. Evidently he did not know what would be done to him after the session.

25 John Newbold Hazard (1909-1995), a leading American specialist on Soviet law – [WEB].

26 Edward Watson McWhinney (b. 1924), Sometime Professor of International Law, Simon Fraser University, Vancouver, Canada, and former President, Institut de droit international; author of several works on peaceful coexistence – [WEB].

27 John Fitzgerald Kennedy (1917-1963), Thirty-Fifth President of the United States – [WEB].

28 Mustafa Kamil Yasseen (1920-1981), Head of the Iraqi delegation to the Vienna Conference on Diplomatic Relations and Ambassador – [WEB].

29 Hashim Jawad (1909-), Permanent Representative of Iraq to the United Nations; Minister of Foreign Affairs of Iraq from 1959 to 1963 – [VGT].

V. M. Molotov and wife and G. I. Tunkin, Vienna Conference on Diplomatic Relations

1964

11 Jan:

Moscow: For several days I have been depressed. I have no desire to do anything, but am worried about legal science in our country, which has become a place for squabbles, intrigues, and other machinations of rogues and careerists. They humiliate Romashkin,[30] Karev,[31] Pavlov,[32] and Aleksandrov.[33] For what? Basically because they have written a great deal and repeated themselves. People are convinced that Chkhikvadze,[34] who is dying to become the Director of the Institute of State and Law of the USSR Academy of Sciences, organized all this. Romashkin has been dragged into seeking the post of Director of the Institute by his friends in the apparatus of the Central Committee [the surnames are abbreviated and difficult to discern – VGT], and Chkhikvadze also is being dragged by his friends in the apparatus of the Central Committee, whom he plies with Georgian wine. They are both people with a brain, although alas not as scholars, but the methods are offensive.

30 Petr Semenovich Romashkin (1915-1975), Director, Institute of State and Law, USSR Academy of Sciences, 1958 to 1964 – [WEB].

31 Dmitrii Stepanovich Karev (1905-1978), Dean of the Faculty of Laws, Moscow Lomonosov State University, from 1956 to 1965 – [WEB].

32 Ivan Vasilevich Pavlov (1909-1972), Deputy Director, Institute of State and Law, USSR Academy of Sciences, from 1951 to 1963 – [WEB].

33 Georgii Nikolaevich Aleksandrov (1902-1979), author and editor of several works on the Nuremberg trials – [WEB].

34 Viktor Mikhailovich Chkhikvadze (1912-2006), Director of the Institute of State and Law, USSR Academy of Sciences, from 1964 to 1973 – [WEB].

Opposing me are Kozhevnikov,[35] Korovin,[36] Zadorozhnyi,[37] Lisovskii,[38] Blishchenko.[39] They write slander to all instances, with signatures and anonymous. This is the third year already. I am accustomed to it, although it is disgusting. A year ago – in January 1963 Korovin and Kozhevnikov failed in the elections to the Executive Committee of the Soviet Association of International Law for these slanders and squabbles. However, they were nominated for membership of the Executive Committee. It was great moral support for me that I received the largest number of votes (secret ballot).

4 June:

Geneva: Again Geneva. The XVI session of the International Law Commission. The draft convention on the law of treaties was before the Commission. Yesterday at breakfast Lachs[40] said: "I consider you to be an example. You represent a great power, one of the two presently existing great powers. But I do not feel in your interventions that you defend the interests of a great power against small countries". I said that I represent not simply a great power, but a socialist power which adheres to the principle of equality. We have, I said, no companies interested in the suppression and exploitation of other peoples.

It was pleasant to hear, as Professor Guggenheim[41] said, that now it is important to know the Russian language, that is, the Soviet science of international law "has become important" ("est devenue importante").

18 Jun:

Geneva: The day before yesterday at breakfast with Briggs[42] (the member of the International Law Commission from the United States) I met with Chayes[43] – the Legal Advisor to the United States Department of State. He came for a couple of days in connection with the Soviet-American negotiations on technical aspects of cooperation in Outer Space. I had seen him in 1961, in the summer when he had just been appointed to this post after Kennedy came to power. This post is a political appointment. Then Chayes had seemed quite young and was very happy and optimistic. Now he looks aged and depressed. He is resigning and preparing to study international law (he is a specialist in corporate law).

---

35 Fedor Ivanovich Kozhevnikov (1903-1998), Member of the International Law Commission (1952-1953) and International Court of Justice (1953-1960) – [WEB].

36 Evgenii Aleksandrovich Korovin (1892-1964), Corresponding Member, USSR Academy of Sciences – [WEB].

37 Igor Pavlovich Blishchenko (1930-2001), head of Chair of International Law at Russian University of Friendship of Peoples – [WEB].

38 Georgii Petrovich Zadorozhnyi (1920-1996), Professor and Head of Chair, Moscow State Institute of International Relations (1961-1987) – [WEB].

39 Vadim Ivanovich Lisovskii (1904-1997), jurist in Ministry of Foreign Trade of the USSR – [WEB].

40 Manfred Lachs (1914-1993), member of the International Court of Justice from Poland – [WEB].

41 Paul Guggenheim (1899-1977), Swiss international lawyer – [WEB].

42 Herbert Whittaker Briggs (1900-1990), Professor at Cornell University and member of the International Law Commission from 1962 to 1966 – [WEB].

43 Abram Chayes (1922-2000), Professor at Harvard Law School – [WEB].

Briggs says that Kennedy was a brilliant man who could inspire people to work with fervor. Now, he said, the situation is otherwise.

Chayes himself hinted that the White House was devoting little attention to foreign policy. Previously the assignments rained down one after another, whereas now this was no longer so.

4 Jul:

Geneva: Yesterday I had breakfast with Schwebel[44] – an Assistant Legal Advisor to the United States Department of State. He was attached to a Department of the United Nations and is concerned with legal issues relating to the United Nations. In 1961 he accompanied me to the Harvard Law School, where before going to the Department of State he was an assistant professor for five years (and before this was engaged in the private practice of law). Schwebel touched upon, *inter alia*, the forthcoming session of the Committee for Principles of Bilateral Relations and Cooperation of the General Assembly, which would meet in session at Mexico from 27 July 1964. From the conversation, the position of the United States seems to be the following (he cautioned that it has not yet been finally formulated):

(a) not to engage in the formulation of principles. To be based on United Nations General Assembly Resolution 1815, where four principles were indicated for study;
(b) to discuss these principles;
(c) to draw up a report in the form of commentaries to each of them, indicating both coinciding and differing views.

Schwebel asked my opinion with regard to the further movement of the questions advanced in the New Year Message of N.S. Khrushchev and, in particular, should not these questions be discussed in connection with the principles. I said that, to be sure, these questions might be touched upon in connection with the principles – but avoided going further.

He also raised the question of the application to the USSR of Article 19 of the United Nations Charter but said nothing new in comparison with the American position well-known to us. He passed on the Memorandum which the Department of State already had transmitted to a number of States. He said that he was unaware whether the Memorandum had been transmitted to the Mission of the USSR attached to the United Nations.

23 Jul:

Vienna: I am sitting in a café near the Imperial Hotel and drinking Gösser Märzen beer. I am returning from Geneva after the session of the International Law Commission.

44 Stephen Myron Schwebel (b. 1929), judge from the United States on the International Court of Justice – [web].

I look at the Imperial and recall May 1955. On 30 April I together with M. G. Gribanov,[45] then the head of the III European Section, flew to Vienna to assist the High Commissar, I. I. Ilichev.[46] The task was not easy – in two weeks to agree and prepare for signature the Austrian Treaty. They met in the building of the Commendant, and then until midnight in the Imperial, where the High Commissar was accommodated; cables were dashed off to Moscow. The signature had been designated beforehand for 15 May. Although every nerve was strained, it would be ready.

The Treaty was agreed with difficulty. The Austrian Minister of Foreign Affairs each day came to the session extremely drunk, but knew his business. The day of signature was a Sunday. A holiday for all Vienna. We went to the Belvedere following Molotov[47] among a thick wall of people and flowers. A fountain pen was ready for each minister. They said that these pens were destined for a museum. But Dulles,[48] having signed the Treaty, placed the pen in his pocket. Confusion reigned. The Austrians ran about, whispered. Then they approached the other ministers and requested them not to keep the pens as a memento.

And now? Austria is dying to join the Common Market – wants to earn money. The streets are full of cars. In the center of a small square is a policeman with a walkie-talkie. He does not hurry, changes the light. But his trained eye seeks any unjustified delay and he immediately intervenes. It is interesting to sit and watch people. How many there are, each having his own life, his own joys and sorrows. There are several tourists with cameras, young, evidently students. They cross the street and stop in indecision: to go to the right or to the left. Evidently for them it does not matter. There is a mother in a bright scarf with a daughter of eight years. The daughter asks something, the mother replies, but plainly does not succeed; her answers obviously raise new questions in the young head of the daughter.

1965

6 Oct:

Moscow-London: I flew to London for the session of the Administrative Council of the International Law Association. An 8:30 departure from Sheremetevo Airport. But 8:30 comes and not a sound. I go to find out, they say the boarding will be announced in all likelihood soon. Indeed, twenty minutes later than announce the boarding. All would be well, but we do not know the secret of the delay and the further adventures awaiting us. It turns out that the Moscow Philharmonic Orchestra is flying to London on this aircraft. They, of course, arrived at the last minute. With them, Kondrashin,[49]

45 Mikhail Grigorevich Gribanov (1906-1987), Ministry of Foreign Affairs of the USSR – [WEB].

46 Ivan Ivanovich Ilichev (1905-1983), High Commissioner of the USSR in Austria – [WEB].

47 Viacheslav Mikhailovich Molotov (1890-1986), Minister of Foreign Affairs of the USSR from 1939 to 1949 and again from 1953 to 1956 – [WEB].

48 John Foster Dulles (1888-1959), Secretary of State of the United States – [WEB].

49 Kirill Petrovich Kondrashin (1914-1981), Russian conductor – [WEB].

Oistrakh,[50] Vishnevskaia,[51] Rostropovich,[52] and a mass of luggage. We were already sitting on the aircraft and suddenly an enormous crowd pours forth from a bus with violins, violas, and so on and crowds into the plane. The departure was again postponed, as a result we arrived two hours late. We arrive in London and await the baggage. An incalculable number of hermetically sealed steel boxes move along the baggage belt, but not all of our things. We wait an hour, more, then they suddenly appear at last.

I was met by a comrade from the Embassy, although I am no longer the Head of the Legal Section of the USSR Ministry of Foreign Affairs. Since 27 August I am the Head of the Chair of International Law at the Law Faculty of Moscow State University. I stayed at the Embassy, called the International Law Association, and said that tomorrow I would be at lunch.

10 Oct:

Westminster Abbey: on the floor stone with a malachite hue in a frame under a beautiful tree (dimensions about 1.5 x 1.8 meters). An inscription: "Remember Winston Churchill. In accordance with the wishes of the Queen and Parliament the Dean and Chapter placed this stone on the Twenty-fifth Anniversary of the Battle of Britain. 15 September 1965".

Alongside stones for Herschel[53] and Darwin.[54] A statue of Disraeli[55] – no grave, evidently because he was a Jew. A statute of Gladstone[56] and his grave and that of his wife. The statues and graves of public figures, scholars, poets, and so on. Here they walk on gravestones, benches stand on them, and some old inscriptions have been completely effaced.

It seems that the day before yesterday a New York correspondent spoke on the radio and commented of the trip of the Pope of Rome to New York. All the heads of delegations were presented to the Pope, it being noted that the conversation with Minister of Foreign Affairs of the USSR, Gromyko,[57] continued somewhat longer than with the others. Wits observed: "It was natural, he had much more to confess".

A luncheon was arranged for 8 October, that is, on the eve of the Executive Council session. A foul luncheon, indeed, at Brooks's, a club on St. James Street.[58] As the

50 David Fedorovich Oistrakh (1908-1974), Russian violinist – [WEB].

51 Galina Pavlovna Vishnevskaia (b. 1926), Russian opera singer – [WEB].

52 Mstislav Leopoldovich Rostropovich (1927-2007), Russian conductor and cellist – [WEB].

53 Sir John Frederick William Herschel (1792-1871), astronomer, mathematician, and chemist – [WEB].

54 Charles Robert Darwin (1809-1882), naturalist – [WEB].

55 Benjamin Disraeli, First Earl of Beaconsfield (1804-1881), British Prime Minister and statesman – [WEB].

56 William Ewart Gladstone (1809-1898), British Prime Minister and scholar of Homer – [WEB].

57 Andrei Andreevich Gromyko (1909-1989), Minister of Foreign Affairs of the USSR from 1957 to 1985 – [WEB].

58 Founded in 1764 and located at 60 St. James' Street, Gaming was historically one of its main attractions – [WEB].

chairman, Lord Wilberforce,[59] said, in the eighteenth century this was a gambling house and Charles James Fox[60] used to play from 6 p.m. til 6 a.m. and then went to Parliament and made an excellent speech there.

We congratulated Jansma[61] (a Dutchman) upon receiving an English decoration. In his remarks Jansma explained the reason for the award as follows. Princess Margaret and her husband recently came to Holland. Jansma was at a luncheon for the Queen of the Netherlands and was seated alongside the Princess, who in turn was alongside the Queen. And Margaret "lost her bag. I tried to pick it up but there were four royal legs and I couldn't". Fortunately, the wife of some ambassador was seated nearby with a lame foot and a cane. Jansma asked for her cane and delivered the bag to the English Princess. He gave us to understand that it was for this "achievement" that he received the decoration. But this was, of course, a joke.

11 Oct:
London: After Churchill's death,[62] some sort of title was conferred on his wife,[63] and she now sits in the House of Lords.

1966

15 Jan:
Monte Carlo: The sessions of the International Law Commission are underway in Monte Carlo. Honestly, I do not like to work here. There is no library, and I cannot even get the *American Journal of International Law.*

Only just returned from Nice with Nechaev.[64] When we come from Monte Carlo, Nice makes an impression of being a very large city and we feel much more comfortable there. Monte Carlo is a tiny city of wealthy idlers. Everything is twice as expensive as in Nice.

Yesterday we visited Le Casino. We met many members of the International Law Commission there. They issued us all a pass giving free entry to Le Casino. Rates from 10 up to 10,000 francs. It is evident that habitués basically play in this season. An attractive young personage attracted our attention. Tiny, somewhat snub-nosed, dark-complexioned face, black hair, and dark clothing. She played with great concentration and even with embarrassment, but the expression on her face did not change whether she won or lost. One may suppose that this young lady left a sick mother at home and came here to make a despairing effort to find money for her care. But this might only seem so. It was

59 Richard Orme Wilberforce, Baron Wilberforce (1907-2003), Lord Appeal in Ordinary – [WEB].

60 Charles James Fox (1749-1806), statesman and Foreign Secretary in England – [WEB].

61 Dr. Kornelius Jansma (1891-1972), a Dutch practitioner and Treasurer of the International Law Association from 1954 to 1972 – [WEB].

62 Sir Winston Leonard Spencer-Churchill (1874-1965), Prime Minister of the United Kingdom – [WEB].

63 Clementine Ogilvy Spencer-Churchill, Baroness Spencer-Churchill (1885-1977), wife of Sir Winston – [WEB].

64 Boris Nikolaevich Nechaev (1922-2006), assistant of Tunkin, later Head of the Treaty Law Section of the USSR Ministry of Foreign Affairs – [VGT].

worth it to watch her, to see how she followed the gambling and how intensively her mind worked, how she calculated the odds and placidly and with determination moved on to play at another table, and it became clear to you that she is an experienced gambler. She sat at a table, having 300 francs, and when after an hour the game at this table had finished and she moved on to another, she had in her hands chips for 6,000 francs. When half an hour later we left, she had chips for 6,500 to 6,700 francs. She continued to play at an empty table, but reduced the odds from 500 to 200-300 francs. Many made notes on the game, evidently to be guided by the laws of probability, but she wrote down nothing.

21 Jan:
Monte Carlo: May a person be simultaneously on the territory of two States? It seems that one may. I was today in this situation, climbing a stairway along which the boundary between France and Monaco passes. The boundary sometimes crosses the house and even rooms in the house.

Monnais Monegasque. Monaco issues four coins: 10 and 20 centimes, and 1 and 5 francs. It is authorized to issue these coins in proportion to the number of such coins in France corresponding to the correlation of the number of citizens of Monaco and France. Virtually none of these coins are in circulation. The tourists make off with them. I have so far only the 10 and 20 centimes.

La langue Monegasque. Yesterday at a breakfast arranged by the Government in honor of the Commission the Secretary General for Culture sat with me. He said that a grammar of the Monegasque language exists and some literature. The language is closer to Latin than any others of the Romance languages. It is rarely spoken. Too few people know it (4,000 citizens in Monaco).

29 Jan:
Paris. Bourget Airport: We are en route back to Moscow. We flew into Paris on 27 January. We left a day before the end of the Session – the forthcoming Annual Meeting of the Soviet Association of International Law, and re-elections. Yesterday evening I took a taxi with Nechaev and went to the Eiffel Tower. I exchanged several phrases with the driver, and then said several words in Russian to Nechaev. The driver also spoke Russian. It turned out that he was a former ensign in the Denikin[65] army; he has worked 40 years as a driver. His son is a French citizen, an engineer. He and his wife are stateless persons. Last year his wife went to Leningrad as a guest of her sister. It was clear that he was very happy to speak. The Tower was already closed, so he took us about Paris for a whole hour, giving commentary.

7 April:
Lagonissi, Greece: An international law conference (4-8 April 1966) was convened by the Carnegie Foundation. 26 persons are taking part: the socialist, capitalist, and neutral countries are represented.

65 Anton Ivanovich Denikin (1872-1947), leader of White Forces against the Bolshevik Revolution in Russia – [WEB].

Professor Tabata (Kyoto University)[66] told me that a student reading circle in his university is studying my book *Völkerrecht des Gegenwart*.

Two questions are being discussed at the conference: *jus cogens* and international rivers. The discussion on the first question was very interesting. All except the Americans (Lissitzyn[67] and Katz[68]) and Schwarzenberger believe that principles *jus cogens* exist.

10 April:

We merely passed through the village of Distomo. The entire population of this village was destroyed during the Nazi occupation.

Now we are having breakfast near the Loukas Monastery in the fresh air. About half of the participants went on the excursion to Delphi.

George Schwarzenberger and G. I. Tunkin at Conference on International Law, Lagonissi, April 1966

66 Probably Shigejirō Tabata (b. 1911), who wrote widely on international law – [WEB].

67 Oliver J. Lissitzyn (1912-1994), Hamilton Fish Professor of International Law and Diplomacy, Columbia University – [WEB].

68 Milton Katz (1908-1995), Henry L. Stimson Professor of Law, Harvard University – [WEB].

6 May:

Geneva: Again a session of the International Law Commission. The last year with this membership. It has just been reported by radio that Francois Mitterand,[69] a former candidate for the office of President of France in the 1965 elections, has formed a "shadow cabinet". Something akin to the English model. So France has become rich – two governments, whereas often there was not even one.

Much noise is being made about our agreement with the Italian firm Fiat about the construction in the USSR of a plant with capacity to produce 600,000 cars. The French are offended. Renault competed for the order. *Le Monde* today devotes an editorial to this issue. But Renault is not losing hope – a delegation from the firm is going to Moscow in a few days. *Le Monde* writes that it is not merely a matter of a plant; roads are needed, repair shops, petrol pumps, and so on.

The withdrawal of France from NATO has shaken this organization to its foundations. And today a new surprise – France is opposing the candidacy of Hallstein[70] – to a post of Chairman of a Common Market commission. A reorganization is in process there and the French are taking advantage of this.

31 May:

Geneva: On this last day of May I went to work in the Parc Barton, across from the Hotel Mon Repos. I saw the green carpet of the lawn and high stout trees along the shore of the beautiful Lake Geneva.

1967

1 April:

London: Magnificent tulips near Kensington Palace, where Princess Margaret[71] lives. I recalled my own tulips of various hues planted at the dacha. The bulbs I brought from The Hague, where in August 1966 I gave a course of lectures at the Hague Academy of International Law.

Today the session of the Executive Council of the International Law Association ended comparatively early. After the session I strolled about with Žourek[72] and Haraszti.[73] In the evening Ambassador M. N. Smirnovskii[74] had invited me to lunch. After the session I was to join Professor Schwarzenberger for lunch, but excused myself, as I could not be with him by reason of the Ambassador's invitation. Tomorrow I will go to Schwarzenberger at the dacha.

---

69 Francois Mitterand (1916-1996), 21st President of France – [WEB].

70 Walter Hallstein (1901-1982), first President of the European Community and author of the Hallstein Doctrine, the foundation of German foreign policy during the Cold War – [WEB].

71 Margaret Rose Windsor, Princess of Great Britain and Northern Ireland (1930-2002) – [WEB].

72 Jaroslav Žourek (1908-1980), a Czech international lawyer – [VGT].

73 György Haraszti (1912-1980), Hungarian international lawyer and member of the International Law Commission from 1948 to 1961 – [VGT].

74 Mikhail Nikolaevich Smirnovskii (1921-1989), Ambassador of the USSR to the United Kingdom from 1966 to 1973 – [WEB].

The Association is experiencing shortages of funds and the Americans are using this. They are seeking "to buy" individual committees by means of donations for their work. Professor Olmstead, who moved from a University to work at Texas Oil Company, is the chief purveyor of this line.

Today, after lunch with Ambassador Smirnovskii, we went for a walk; the Ambassador with his wife, the USSR Minister of Public Health Petrovskii[75] with his wife, who had just flown in to London at the invitation of the Minister of Health of Great Britain, and I. We went on to Bayswater Road. Suddenly someone with a reddish complexion approached and spoke in Russian: "Have you begun to sell some Russian silver?" We tried to go around him, but he followed, continuing to shout. Then Smirnovskii told him that he has in mind evidently the sale of the Tsarist dinner service (referring to a Tsarist dinner service which was sold in London to some restauranteur in March 1967 for 200,000 pounds). "There is not only a dinner service, but also silver" – shouts red-face, pointing a newspaper at us. We turned back and when we approached Kensington Palace Gardens he left, shouting: "Sell Russia to the Jews". Smirnovskii explained to us that this type is a permanent figure and he often confronts ours, and there are grounds to suppose that he is connected with the police. During the visit to London of Chairman of the Council of Ministers of the USSR, Kosygin,[76] he was not in sight, and they no doubt removed him for a period.

The press is full of reports about the disaster with the *Torrey Canyon*, which ran aground off the coasts of England, oil was spilled, and a threat created of pollution of the beaches. At the end of last week it was decided to bomb the tanker and burn the oil. But it seems this did little, since it was late and the oil did not burn well. The incident is interesting and may have consequences in international law. The ship is American, the flag Liberian, chartered by an English company, and the crew and its master – Italians.

20 May:

Stockholm: Fate has brought me to Stockholm. The Swedes have created an Institute for Peace and Conflict Research, and I have been appointed a member of the Learned Council of this Institute. B. S. Krylov[77] has flown in with me.

The sessions were held in a resort locality. I admired the fjord in the evening from the window of the hotel restaurant. A clear sky, sky-blue water, forest-covered mountains around. They say that in every country where a person has visited he leaves a part of himself. But he also receives something from the country, which becomes part of him.

According to the Director of the Institute of World Politics and Economy in Belgrade, Mateos,[78] Yugoslavia a year ago abolished its entry visas for all countries

75 Boris Vasilevich Petrovskii (1908-2004), distinguished surgeon and longtime Minister of Public Health – [WEB].

76 Aleksei Nikolaevich Kosygin (1904-1980), Prime Minister of the USSR from 1964 to 1980 – [WEB].

77 Boris Sergeevich Krylov (b. 1923), specialist in American law and son of S. B. Krylov – [WEB].

78 Leo Mateos (1911-), former Ambassador of Yugoslavia to the United States, Director, Institute of International Politics and Economics, Belgrade, from 1962 to 1972 – [WEB].

as an experiment for one year. Now a law is being considered which provides for the unlimited abolition of visas for so long as the law is in force.

22 May:
Stockholm: Yesterday Prime Minister Erlander[79] gave a luncheon on the occasion of the session of the Council of the Institute. The luncheon was held in a beautiful stately home where the Ministry of Foreign Affairs was accommodated. After lunch, the Prime Minister and our Ambassador, Viktor Fedorovich Maltsev,[80] the French Ambassador, and another dozen or so persons sat in the reception room of the Ministry. Then Erlander rose and said: "I am going to bring here the leaders of both opposition parties". And he brought – the leader of the Conservative Party – an elderly person and … the leader of the Communist Party – a very young person. They were both at the luncheon. Indeed, times are changing.

Today the two-day session of the Council ended. For the moment this entire organization seems not to be solid.

24 May:
Stockholm. National Museum: We strolled with Krylov about the rooms, saw the porcelain and glass. Climbed to the second floor – paintings, but they do not affect one. And suddenly it creeps up on you from behind – paintings by Renoir, Sisley, Cezanne, Monet, Corot, Degas, Gauguin, and several Rodin sculptures. If art does not touch you – it isn't art.

And here is the Swedish Repin, Zorn (1860-1922). The same style. And here a large canvas by Cederström (1845-1933) – the vanquished Charles XII being carried on a litter. A row of troops, mountains on the right, forest on the left, snow. Roslan Alexander (Swede, 1819-1893). A small portrait of a woman whose face is half-covered by a black shawl. How remarkably the face is done!

Rembrandt – about 10 canvases. There is Rubens too, but nothing interesting.

5 June:
Paris: Rue Dupleix – "Defence d'afficher – Loi du 29 juillet 1881". Such inscriptions are numerous in Paris. On me they create a strange impression which I cannot decipher.

After Stockholm, Paris. In Moscow in just a week. Here I am at two UNESCO meetings:

1. A meeting on the occasion of a seminar on international law which is happening in Dar es Salaam from 14 August to 9 September. There I will deliver a lecture on "La function normative de système de UN".
2. A meeting concerning the activities of UNESCO in the domain of international law.

79 Tage Fritiof Erlander (1901-1985), Prime Minister of Sweden from 1946 to 1969 – [WEB].

80 Viktor Fedorovich Maltsev (1917-2003), Ambassador of the USSR to Sweden, India, Finland, and Yugoslavia – [WEB].

The main building of UNESCO is about eight storeys above the ground and four storeys below. Glass and concrete and, they say, diabolically hot in the summer because there are no air conditioners – money ran out.

The major event of the day is, of course, the war between Israel and the Arab countries which began on 5 June. Who started it? Both sides accuse one another. But, evidently, Israel did so. They magnificently battered the Arabs, destroyed many aircraft at airports, and advanced significantly forward.

11 Aug:
Moscow-Paris Train: Yesterday commenced my first trip to Africa. A seminar on international law organized by UNESCO for Africans. The professorial lecturers are: Briggs, El-Erian,[81] Vellas (France),[82] and myself. Tomorrow at 15:00 in Paris and the airplane at 20:00 hours.

I am reading a novel by M. Prilezhaeva «Удивительный год»[83] in a newspaper that publishes novels. An excellent book. But what distinguishes a great writer from an average one? The average one simplifies, takes one or several aspects of life, but not the entire complex of life's problems. A great master takes life with all of its complexities and contradictoriness. The same applies to scholars.

12 Aug:
Already on the East African Airlines aircraft. A magnificent VC-10 Super. Better than the Caravelle. One may write in peace.

12 Aug:
Nairobi: We arrived at about 7:30 hours. Kilimanjaro could not be seen, clouds. The temperature is about 18-20 degrees. I was astonished at what I saw. Landscape like to Northern Dvina: few trees, similar to willows, grass which appears at dry places in Chamovo, and nothing exotic.

The exotic began at the airport. On the aircraft we completed questionnaires which we took with us. At the airport they called out and distributed the surnames. Then they took my passport. We passed through passport control, some other control, and then one had to collect the luggage. I see the customs officials open a suitcase and look at each thing. I approached, made apologies, and said that my airplane leaves within a half hour and that I have a diplomatic passport. They immediately made a mark with chalk on the suitcase and briefcase.

Now it is 8:50 hours. We are headed to Dar es Salaam on an East African Airlines Comet.

---

81 Abdullah El-Erian (1920-1981), member of the International Court of Justice from Egypt – [web].

82 Pierre Vellas (b. 1924), Professor of Public International Law at the University of Toulouse – [web].

83 Maria Pavlovna Prilezhaeva (1908-1983), novelist. Her Удивительный год [A Remarkable Year] was serialized and then published in book form in 1969 – [web].

14 Aug:
Dar es Salaam. Hotel Kilimanjaro: The tropical night is rapidly enveloping the land in its dark embrace. Sunrays still play on the high buildings, but the city is already plunged into darkness. Many sea-going ships in the bay. In the deepening twilight palms somewhat melancholy by day seem to be fairy-tale birds. The view from the balcony of my room is wonderful. The hotel is one hundred meters from the sea. The hotel is magnificent. They say that this hotel belongs to a company, 51% of whose stocks belong to the Government of Tanzania and the rest belong to Israel (private capital, no doubt). A poster hangs in the room leading to the restaurant with the inscription: "Rejoice ye with Jerusalem and be glad with her". In 15-20 minutes it is completely dark.

The seminar of international law for Africans today began with an official ceremony at which the Dean, Chief Justice, and Acting Principal of University College, Friedman[84] (UNESCO) and Hardy[85] (United Nations Legal Department) were present.

15 Aug:
Dar es Salaam: Today I lectured to the seminar on the topic: "Laws of Development of Society and Juridical Organizations", in particular on peaceful coexistence and the sovereign equality of States as basic notions. There were many questions. After 60 minutes of lecture, 30 minutes of replies to questions. And still some remained unanswered.

At coffee an attendee from the Congo who is writing a dissertation at Nancy approached me and said: tribal organization exists in the Congo, and there is no private ownership. The heads of the tribes dispose of common ownership. Are not the socialist States returning to this ownership?"

Now I am sitting in the lecture of Professor Briggs: Law of Treaties – Use of Terms. Capacity.

He said: when the Second World War broke out and England declared a state of war with Germany, Canada declared that it was automatically at war with Germany. But 10 days later they made their own declaration, stating that a declaration of a state of war by Great Britain did not by itself put Canada in a position of a state of war.

16 Aug:
Dar es Salaam: Yesterday the Dean of the Faculty of Law, Professor Weston,[86] invited Briggs and me for lunch. Professor Eörsi[87] from Budapest, who gives the lectures on civil law, also was there. The wife of the dean is local, a black. He himself is from Australia and came to this post when the faculty was organized. This was six years ago. He is 40 to 45 years old. Many say, a great joker. A curious man, said Briggs. Evidently he is divorced from his first wife. Zana – as his present wife is called – is a young, tall,

84 Samy Friedman (b. 1912), French jurist and member of International Council of Social Sciences – [VGT].
85 Michael Hardy, British international lawyer – [VGT].
86 A. B. Weston (1924-2008), Dean of the Faculty of Law, University College, Dar-es-Salaam – [VGT].
87 Gyula Eörsi (1922-1992), a Hungarian comparative lawyer – [WEB].

well-built, attractive black. She does not speak English, he says, because this is the language of the colonizers. But she obviously understands. As Weston said, she believes that Swahili is the most beautiful language in the world. And when I noted that about 100 million people speak Swahili, her eyes widened. There is something child-like in her, but the character is felt.

18 Aug:

Dar es Salaam: A tropical evening is so brief! What a difference with the suburban Moscow evenings. Especially in May and June. I was at the dacha in Perkhushkovo with such pleasure this year, delighting for the first time in how the tulips, lilac, collybia, cherries, and peonies bloomed. For ten years I have spent this time in Geneva, and before that there was no dacha. Now, sitting on the balcony of Hotel Kilimanjaro and observing how the African night falls on the land (there is a song of American negroes – "evening falls, black, just as I"), I already am pining a wee bit for the suburban Moscow evenings.

Yesterday Mr. Mattsson[88] invited us for breakfast. He is the High Commissioner for United Nations Development Programs. His wife is a Spaniard or Latin American – such is the impression. She appeared to welcome the guests before lunch and appeared after, but was not at the breakfast. His villa is on Ocean Road, where good villas are located. Two young negroes served us at the table. Mattsson arrived here several months ago. Before that he was in Indonesia for ten years in the service of the United Nations for rendering assistance.

The seminar went well, the attendees were very active, and put many questions.

21 Aug:

Dar es Salaam: This is difficult to believe, but today, while reading the newspaper after breakfast on the balcony, I was forced to put on a jumper. The wind from the sea was very humid. The local newspaper has the headline: "Russian Jets in Nigeria". The newspaper writes that 15 Antonov aircraft transported jet airplanes and that the delivery is proceeding of airplanes and weapons from other East European countries.

Time is passing. I have been in Dar es Salaam for ten days. I have delivered nine lectures, and must still deliver three. But since El-Erian did not arrive and since I will be here for a third week, I shall deliver two additional lectures and give a seminar. I agreed to deliver a lecture at University College, but do not know what is happening. I have the impression that they are afraid. Weston, the Dean, is in charge, but he said nothing to me about the lecture. The local teacher of international law, Bishota,[89] invited me to deliver the lecture.

---

88 R. Mattson, Chief Science Officer, Tanzania – [VGT].

89 D. M. K. Bishota, Lecturer in Law, University College, Dar es Salaam – [VGT].

As for Weston. He came from Australia with a wife (Canadian). Evidently there were children. Then the family was sent back and he married Zana. She already had a child, and then a joint child appeared. They say Weston has compiled a legal dictionary in Swahili. Many words, of course, they do not have.

I gave two additional lectures at the seminar, 14 in all. The last was on the subject: "Basic Changes in International Law during the Past 50 Years".

On 31 August I gave a public lecture at University College. There were 100 in attendance: students and professors. They listened attentively, although it was evident that international law is badly taught. Professor Bishota had only just begun to teach international law. He studied with Schwarzenberger and at Columbia University. The questions put after the lecture testified to a certain Chinese influence. Question: "You said that contemporary international law is advantageous for developing countries. It would be better if you had created your own law in Europe and let us alone". And during the lectures at the seminar and here they put the question of Soviet intervention in Hungary in 1956.

At the seminar there were about four persons who had graduated from Lumumba University. It was clearly pleasant for them that Tunkin had arrived from Moscow who was, they all said, their professor. They once or twice attended my lectures in Moscow University or were at a report during the Annual Meeting of the Soviet Association of International Law.

On Saturday and Sunday we went to the park to see wild life, as they say here. The park is one of the few in Tanzania. We saw many animals: elephants, rhinoceros, lions, zebras, buffalo, hippopotamus (but he did not leave the water), giraffes, antelopes, and so on. At night we slept in tents. At the advice of Professor Vellas, before lying down we attentively looked over the bedding and space around it to see whether there were snakes or scorpions. One could not fall asleep long with Professor Vellas. At night the snarls of wild bulls were heard, and perhaps lions too. All the same, we slept well. In the morning again on special jeeps with apertures in the roofs for photography. In principle it was not permitted to leave the vehicles. But the lions seemed to be tame. We approached within six meters of them, and they lie about as though they were accustomed.

4 Sept:

Djibouti: Where have I turned up – in Djibouti, Gulf of Aden. They said in Dar es Salaam that after Addis Ababa the aircraft flies to Khartoum, Cairo, Athens, and Rome. It turned out to be Djibouti, Athens, and Rome. I saw an interesting sight in flight: in the distance a beautiful evening sunset, and a black cloud against the background which from time to time is cut by lightning. The cloud is like an atomic explosion. The airplane turns, evidently to avoid it on the left. No, the airplane proceeds towards the cloud, but it evidently will be below us. It is very close and to the left. When the lightning flashes, it seems like a fairy-tale castle in which evil forces create their magic. And the sunset ahead has become purple.

5 Sept:

Rome: The Sistine Chapel. Full of people. The immortal creation of Michelangelo[90] causes trembling with its monumentality, enormity of work, and talent. But one must hurry to see the Borgia Apartment,[91] the works of Raphael,[92] and many, many others. I am sitting on a bench in St. Peter's Cathedral and observe a pigeon in the window. A pigeon is the personification of the Holy Spirit. There is a cupola which Michelangelo began to cover with pictures at the age of 72 and did not succeed in completing. The cathedral is astonishing with its grandeur and magnificence. The church knew how and knows how to impact the psyche of people.

9 Sept:

Nice: I have been here for three days. On Thursday, 7 September, the session of the Institute of International Law opened. I have been elected a member of the Institute. It is regrettable that Žourek was not. We are discussing the termination of treaties and investments in developing countries.

The Institute is so far under the full domination of westerners. And no wonder. Koretskii[93] and I are at a session for the first time. Before this S. B. Krylov[94] took part once. I have become the first Soviet full member of the Institute. Our influence is incomparably greater in the International Law Association. I am thinking of speaking with regard to the law of treaties and in all likelihood on the work program.

It is very interesting to establish personal contact and have the possibility to speak. I became acquainted with Wright,[95] Rolin,[96] with whom I already had correspondence. Charles de Visscher[97] said that soon his book *Les effectivités en droit international public* will appear in which he frequently makes reference to my work *Droit international public. Problemes theorique.*

16 Sept:

Coast of Nice: The session of the Institute ended today at 11:30. Many left earlier: Lachs with his wife and daughter – yesterday; Gros,[98] Rolin, and others. I do not know where the judges hurry to since they all have nothing to do now.

90 Michelangelo di Lodovico Buonarroti Simoni (1475-1564), Italian painter, sculptor, architect, poet, and engineer – [WEB].

91 A suite of rooms in the Apostolic Palace in the Vatican adapted for personal use by Pope Alexander VI (1431-1503), born Rodrigo Lanzol, later known as Rodrigo Borgia – [WEB].

92 Raffaello Sanzio da Urbino (1483-1520), Italian Renaissance painter and architect – [WEB].

93 Vladimir Mikhailovich Koretskii (1890-1984), Ukrainian academician and member of the International Court of Justice from 1960-1970 – [WEB].

94 Sergei Borisovich Krylov (1888-1958), member of the International Court of Justice from the Soviet Union from 1946 to 1952 – [WEB].

95 Philip Quincy Wright (1890-1970), American political scientist – [WEB].

96 Henri Rolin (1891-1973), French international lawyer – [WEB].

97 Charles de Visscher (1884-1973), Belgian international lawyer – [WEB].

98 André Gros (1911-2003), Sometime Legal Advisor to the French Ministry of Foreign Affairs and member of the International Court of Justice from 1964 to 1984 – [WEB].

Koretskii also flew yesterday to The Hague. He must see the President, who is flying to New York, and he remains.

After the scandalous case of Southwest Africa in 1966, things are moving a bit in the Court. One decision: either the President or the Vice President (Koretskii) must be in The Hague. Perhaps this will help. The procedure is being reviewed. But all this is more, it seems, for appearance.

There are no forces there which might really struggle. Koretskii is the best of all our preceding judges, but he too is no "fighter". Lachs never wanted "to spoil relations with the westerners". The representative from Africa, the Senagalese Forster,[99] is in the Institute. He did not say a single word during the entire session, although there were questions, such as investments, which directly affect Africa.

Charles de Visscher – the president d'honneur of the Institute – invited me for breakfast. He proposed that I be the rapporteur on the subject of droit intertemporel. I said that I would think about it. Yesterday I told Bastid[100] that I could not since this topic is beyond the issues with which I am now occupied. De Visscher is about 87 years old. But with an exceptionally lively and alert mind. We spoke about many problems of international law, and he displayed a lively and creative interest.

The discussion was rather interesting, especially on the law of treaties and investments. We adopted a resolution with regard to the first question which did little, and the second was deferred. That which was prepared reflected the interests of the monopolies.

I spoke briefly, but four or five times. The procedures were such that if you spoke in English, a translation into French followed, but there is no translation from the French. The reports were distributed in the French language. Jessup and another twelve persons, including me, proposed that the reports prepared in the French language be disseminated in English. The decision was deferred to the next session. The next session will be in England. Fitzmaurice was elected President – and absolutely delighted.

Last evening in Nice. I was in Nice several times in January 1965, when the International Law Commission was in session nearby in Monte Carlo. Then in May 1965 when there was a Colloquium organized by the Association for the Development of World Law.

17 Sept:

Paris: I am sitting in front of the Palais de Chaillot, admiring the fountains and the Eiffel Tower. Finally I climbed up it. Always there had been no time or the weather was bad. But today is a wonderful day. From the third floor all Paris is clearly visible. How many generations have seen this city, how many events have occurred. The dark Middle Ages with its palace intrigues, and then "emerged the sun of reason", as Engels[101] said critically, and the French Revolution rumbled.

---

99 Isaac Forster (1903-1984), member of the International Court of Justice from Senegal, 1964 to 1982 – [WEB].

100 Suzanne Bastid (1906-1995), member of the International Law Association and Institute of International Law – [VGT].

101 Friedrich Engels (1820-1895), social scientist, philosopher, industrialist, father of Marxist theory with Karl Marx – [VGT].

Accommodated again in the Dupleix, near Av. de Suffran. The hotel is awful, but inexpensive – 35 francs per day. On my own to parade for nothing. But then it is accepted that it is unnecessary to write a report.

Today is Sunday; on Wednesday by train to Moscow. Am so tired of travelling that I want to go home soon.

18 Sept:
Paris: The first half of the day was spent on business. I was at UNESCO, then went to the Embassy, where of course there were many acquaintances. After lunch I rested a bit and then took the metro to the Louvre. Arrived only at 16:00 hours, and it closes at 17:00 hours. Saw the Antiquités égyptiennes. Did this with a guidebook, which I bought many years ago. Reminded me of my bent towards history and was very satisfied.

Now I must travel to Cairo and see the pyramids. Sometime later. Now the situation in Egypt is complex. A plot against Nasser[102] has been discovered. Marshall Amer[103] headed it, who a few days ago ended his life by suicide (while under house arrest, as the newspapers write).

Now I am drinking lemonade at the Café Au Palais Royal, opposite the store Au Louvre. The French are constantly sleeping in cafes. There is a slot machine there. I recall when we flew from Washington to Moscow in 1944 on a lend-lease aircraft and spent the night at every aerodrome in the United States and Canada (the flight from Washington to Alaska took 10 days, and from Alaska to Moscow, where our pilots flew the airplane – 3 days). One of the personnel of the USSR Mission in Canada, Chechulin, who flew with me loved to play these slot machines. And sometimes he won.

The day before yesterday the XXII Session of the General Assembly opened. The Minister of Foreign Affairs of Romania, Manescu,[104] was elected President of the Assembly. For the first time a representative of a socialist country had become the President of the General Assembly. The situation which had existed did not correspond very much to the principle of peaceful coexistence. But, as the *New York Herald Tribune* noted, it was significant for the election of Manescu that Romania on many issues does not agree with Moscow. This is a routine "sop" in order to drive a wedge.

1968

29 March:
Moscow-Cairo: Sheremetevo Airport. I am seated on the aircraft of an Arabian airline. The flight, as announced, will be 4 hours, 50 minutes. When they pushed off, one felt surprisingly at ease. Something has ended, and new concerns have not commenced. Second class is half full, and first class is empty. Some sort of women's delegation is travelling. They let us read Egyptian newspapers in the English language: *Egyptian Gazette* and *Progress Egyptian.*

102 Gamal Abdel Nasser (1918-1970), second President of Egypt from 1956 to his death – [VGT].
103 Abdel Hakim Amer (1919-1967), Egyptian general and political leader – [VGT].
104 Corneliu Manescu (1916-2000), Minister of Foreign Affairs of Romania and President of the United Nations General Assembly – [WEB].

29 March:
Cairo: We arrived at 21:45 hours. A representative of the Egyptian Intourist met me. It seems that recently Professor Ghanom[105] became the Minister of Tourism. So far, as his associate said, there are few tourists. This is understandable. They accommodated me in the Shepheard Hotel. It seems very expensive and in all likelihood I cannot afford it.

It is raining in Cairo. A rare phenomenon and, evidently, one bringing disorganization. We proceeded very slowly – it was slippery.

30 March:
Cairo: At 10:00 the treasurer appeared and gave me 50 Egyptian pounds. This would suffice for five days. The room cost 5.20 pounds. Then the Dean of the Law Faculty and two professors arrived. We went to a sporting club. In the center of the city there are various types of sport, including golf. Earlier, of course, it belonged to the English and Egyptians were admitted only by exception. An associate of the Ministry of Foreign Affairs came for me there, and Ambassador Hadib.[106] They brought me to my hotel, where Judge Brinton[107] awaited me (an American), an interesting and exceptionally pleasant person. He was the judge of the Mixed Court in Alexandria before its liquidation in 1944 (from 1932). Now he is on pension. The Vice President of the Egyptian Society of International Law, he carried on the English portion of the *Revue égyptienne de droit international.* 88 years old, and every day swims in the pool, drives a car. I am aware than I went with him not without apprehension.

He brought me to his place for lunch. He said that his wife had not been warned, but something would be found to eat. His vehicle was a 1946 or 1948 Ford. Everything jingles, but it goes. His wife, it seems, was somewhat upset by the arrival of an unexpected guest. But at breakfast the conversation became lively. She had not been in the United States for nine years. Sometimes she travels to England. Both travel to Beirut, where their son works.

After breakfast the wife proposed that we rest a bit. I sat in an armchair in his office. He supplied me with a packet of books by McDougal,[108] with whom he was very friendly. But I did not read two pages, as I nodded off. I think that he lives in Cairo because he is accustomed and life here is much less expensive than in the United States or in Europe. Next we went to his acquaintance – someone in the Ministry of Foreign Affairs and a former student of Verdross,[109] Miss Fahmi.[110] From there to the pyramids Cheops and Chephren, about 18 kilometers. What enormous structures, an entire mountain from stone.

Today is the Muslim New Year and there are many people there. But what especially astonishes: the mass of healthy people who offer services. Some offer a ride on a camel,

105 M. Ghanom,Director, Cultural Affairs, Alexandria Governorate – [VGT].
106 Hadib, Egyptian Ministry for Foreign Affairs – [VGT].
107 Jasper Yeates Brinton (1878-1973), jurist and diplomatic historian – [WEB].
108 Myres Smith McDougal (1906-1998), Professor of Law at Yale University – [WEB].
109 Alfred Verdross (1890-1980), Professor of International Law, University of Vienna, and Member, International Law Commission – [WEB].
110 Aziza Mourad Fahmi, legal department, Ministry of Foreign Affairs of Egypt, later Deputy Foreign Minister – [VGT].

others on a donkey, yet others simply approach you as unrequested guides, and so on. My lecture has been postponed until tomorrow by reason of the New Year.

31 March:
Cairo: I am in the Egyptian Museum in Cairo. Facing me is an enormous statue of Pharaoh Amenophis III. He is portrayed seated on the throne with a wife. On the sides and between them three of their daughters are portrayed. On the right is something more like a grotto than a sarcophagus – within a semi-statue – a semi-bas relief of Ramses II. What enormous sarcophaguses of the late period. Polished stones with drawings depicting a person who instead of a human head have the head of a beast or a bird. It is one matter to see the monuments of ancient Egypt in the Pushkin Museum in Moscow, in the British Museum, or in the Louvre and here in that very land where they were created. You virtually feel yourself in the I and II millennia before our era.

31 March:
Cairo: The lecture has only now finished, which lasted one hour. 60 to 70 people were present. The Argentine Ambassador was there, with whom I have met at conferences. And from our Embassy – no one. To be sure, the Ambassador, Sergei Aleksandrovich Vinogradov,[111] is now in Moscow.

Dinner at 20:30 hours. They dine late here.

It is interesting that some ministers rarely appear in their office at the Ministry. The former Ambassador to Sweden and other Agib countries, now the head of the office of the deputy Premier, Fawzi,[112] told me yesterday that Fawzi works at home and comes to the office only when there are official meetings. Very decent.

At 12:30 a meeting with Professor Ghanom, who recently became Minister of Tourism. He was very courteous. It turned out that even he was occupied with my ticket. The fact is that my airplane of the Egyptian airline will fly only on Friday. And on Wednesday I must be in Moscow, so that on Thursday I fly to London for a session of the Executive Committee of the International Law Association. On Wednesday there is an Aeroflot plane, but Aeroflot does not accept Egyptian money. Some kind of nonsense. Ghanom, it seemed to me, still does not feel himself to be in his own milieu. He is accustomed to being a professor, and now must resolve various questions.

In the evening (18:00 hours) I was at "tea" with El-Erian's wife. He is in Vienna at a conference on the law of treaties, which began on 26 March. He will return soon. Two large reception rooms (about 50 square meters each). A servant and probably more than one. They have two sons, both very shy. The head of the section for cultural relations of the Ministry of Foreign Affairs and his wife and Miss Fahmi were at the tea. The conversation was lively and unforced. I gave Madam El-Erian a Russian matryoshka doll.

111 Sergei Aleksandrovich Vinogradov (1907-1970), Soviet Ambassador to France from 1953 to 1965 and then to Egypt – [WEB].

112 Mahmoud Fawzi (1900-1981), Prime Minister of Egypt from 1970 to 1972 – [VGT].

2 April:
Cairo: The last evening in Cairo. Already I want to be home. It is always so: travel for a month, the first three weeks one does not think about returning and only in the fourth week wants to go home.

Went once more to the Giza pyramids, which are visible from here to the northwest. Paid 2.5 pounds for the trip. On Saturday I saw the pyramids from the outside and cursorily. Today I climbed into both pyramids, which it was worth doing. It is one thing to read the Guide and another when you climb yourself.

I dictated 6 pages in the morning of the Summary of my lecture to Brinton's secretary. This Summary will be placed in the current issue of the *Revue égyptienne de droit international.* Then I have to do the full text.

Emelianov[113] (counsellor of the Embassy) promised to take me to Memphis, but of course could not go. Engaged with the Minister of Defense, Grechko,[114] who is here now. The newspapers write about the visit in a strictly official tone, if one judges from the *Egyptian Gazette.*

3 April:
Beirut: Departed on an Aeroflot aircraft from Cairo at 8:30. No one accompanied me from among the Egyptians and no one even rang. Strange people. The Beirut airport is near the sea. I am for the first time on the coast of the Mediterranean Sea from the eastern side. The IL-18 takes off; it is not very pleasant to fly on it: much noise and vibration. I read the *Revue égyptienne* – Mr. Brinton sent me the two latest issues.

4 April:
London: I am sitting in a small restaurant on Grosvenor Street. I am drinking Pale Ale and awaiting fried chicken. Red table-cloths on the tables, yellow light, and everything seems unusual. There is no chicken, ordered steak. They bring it rare, and I ask that it be well done.

No one met me, but fortunate that Sofinskii[115] – first Secretary or Counsellor of our Embassy in London – was on the same plane. They met him and took me. Stayed at the recommendation of one comrade from the Embassy in the Kingshill Hotel, not far from Lancaster Gate Station. This is better than the Embassy. A small room, but with bath and very clean.

8 April:
London: I am sitting in a cinema on Leicester Square, viewing "Doctor Zhivago". The film is overdone in a number of places. For example, the number of inhabitants in the

113 Emelianov [not otherwise identified].

114 Andrei Antonovich Grechko (1903-1976), Marshal of the USSR and Minister of Defense – [WEB].

115 Vsevolod Nikolaevich Sofinskii (b. 1924), Counsellor of the Embassy of the USSR in London from 1963 to 1969, later Ambassador of the USSR in several other countries – [VGT].

home of Zhivago's father-in-law, or the scene in the railway car during the departure from Petrograd. The music is very good – Russian motifs.

9 April:

London-Moscow. Tu-104: Well! The trip was useful. I insisted that the report of Professor Pinto[116] on non-intervention devoted principally to Vietnam be discussed not at an official session of the Executive Committee, but at an open session of the Committee with the participation of all who desire, and be multilithed. One of the two Americans present resolutely objected to this. Baxter[117] took a conciliatory attitude. Finally, the East German Branch was confirmed. I was at Schwarzenbergers. He with respect to scholarship is a very informed person and it is interesting to talk with him.

I think that my work gives me satisfaction because I am convinced that I am bringing something, a slight contribution, to the cause of peace. Now it is a *conditio sine qua non* of socialism, communism, human progress, and prosperity. In 1965 the late Spanish Professor De Luna[118] (died in 1967) said to me: "You do not imagine what influence you have on jurists of the West".

6 July:

Grenoble: The day before yesterday I flew into Paris. I had to leave from the dacha at 6:45, and I rose at 3:30. The morning was wonderful, and I did not want to go anywhere. Ate strawberries from the garden, did exercises, and went with Volodya[119] to Sheremetovo Airport.

Paris greeted us with cool weather; before this the heat was up to 37 degrees Centigrade. Yesterday lunched with friends from the France-USSR Society, and then walked to the Louvre. The Conference of Jurists for Vietnam opened today at 9:00 in the evening. Our delegation: L. N. Smirnov,[120] I. I. Karpets,[121] V. F. Grenkov,[122] and myself. Just as soon as we were settled in Olympic Village, Professor Piquemal,[123] from the University of Paris and Secretary of the C.G.T.,[124] saw me and invited me to breakfast with friends from Grenoble.

Now I have added two pages to my address.

8 July:

Grenoble: The Conference is proceeding normally. Yesterday we heard six reports, including mine. I did a legal analysis of the American aggression in Vietnam. Delivered

116 Roger Pinto (1910-2005), French specialist on the law of armed conflict – [WEB].

117 Richard Reeves Baxter (1921-1980), Professor of International Law at Harvard Law School and member of the International Court of Justice – [WEB].

118 Antonio De Luna Garcia (1901-1967), Spanish professor of international law – [WEB].

119 Vladimir Grigorevich Tunkin (b. 1940), the son of G. I. Tunkin and transcriber of this diary – [WEB].

120 Lev Nikolaevich Smirnov (1911-1986), Russian jurist and Chairman of the USSR Supreme Court – [WEB].

121 Igor Ivanovich Karpets (1921-1993), Soviet specialist in criminal law and criminality – [WEB].

122 V. F. Grenkov [not further identified].

123 Marcel Piquemal (b. 1929), author of several works on trade unions. Emeritus Professor of Labor Law, University of Paris X – [WEB].

124 Confederation Generale du Travail – [VGT].

it in French. They chose me to be chairman of the first commission. Today I conducted the session, also in the French language. This pleases the French.

11 July:
Grenoble: It is now 6:00 in the morning. Last minutes in the Olympic Village, consisting of six and fourteen-story buildings. The days, especially the evenings, were diabolically hot and busy. At 5:30 I began work on a resolution, and then followed a lengthy discussion in the Editorial Commission where Rolin presided. Because of the stubbornness of the Vietnamese, Rolin several times prepared to leave. At about 15:30 we found ourselves in a very critical situation: the Vietnamese insisted – "F.L.N. representant du peuple", and Rolin agreed only to "caractère representative". Finally, I proposed to add to the Vietnamese formula "dans la lutte de liberation", and Rolin concurred.

12 July:
Paris: I have long since noticed when I arrive in a country that I begin to think in the language of this country, if I know it. Today I awoke and French phrases revolved in my brain, and not only that which happened in Grenoble or is happening now in Paris, but also that which I will do in Moscow.

Vietnamese friends are very satisfied with the results of the Conference. Yesterday the Resolution of the Conference was handed to representatives of Vietnam at negotiations with representatives of the United States in Paris. Harriman[125] refused to receive the delegation, referring to the fact that he receives no delegations. The French newspapers provided extensive information about the results of the Conference.

2 Sept:
Moscow-London-Edinburgh: Just seated on board an IL-62 aircraft. I have a first class ticket, but there is virtually no one there. We three first-class passengers were allotted two rows (12 seats) at the front of the cabin. It is interesting to fly in an IL-62. I just read the book of the aircraft designer Iliushin,[126] Цель жизни [The Purpose of Life]. Volodya borrowed this book from his scientific supervisor, Sergei Aleksandrovich Akhmanov.[127] A remarkable book. The airplane proceeded smoothly, no vibrations and little noise. Yes, there are no vibrations, but the noise all the same is greater than on the Caravelle. Just departed (14:30 London time) from London airport to Edinburgh. After take-off cottages are seen below us with little gardens, all identical.

125 William Averell Harriman (1891-1986), Personal Representative of the President of the United States in Talks concerning North Vietnam during 1968-69 – [WEB].

126 Sergei Vladimirovich Iliushin (1894-1977), aircraft designer – [WEB].

127 Sergei Aleksandrovich Akhmanov (1929-1991), professor of Physics, Lomonosov Moscow State University and an expert on nonlinear optics – [WEB].

Arrived at Edinburgh at 15:35 hours. The regular session of the Institute of International Law in Edinburgh. Accommodated at the Bruntsfield Hotel. Rested a bit and went for a cocktail with Schachter,[128] the Executive Director of UNITAR. Only a few people, but almost all are acquaintances. All come to shake hands: Quincy Wright, Arechaga[129] with his wife, the Lachses, and Jenkses[130] especially.

6 Sept:
Edinburgh: Just returned to the hotel from a staging of Richard II given in the Assembly Hall. This is a place where annually the clergy of the church assemble. A very curious hall with mezzanines within the large building. Ceilings from thick wood. The stage is similar to one of ancient Greece. They perform magnificently, which we know from Moscow performances. But the heat in the hall is insufferable and I left after the first act.

The work of the Institute is proceeding as usual. I was elected vice-president (second). The Bureau proposed Wengler[131] and me. Fitzmaurice[132] named Wengler first, although according to the alphabet he is the letter "W". There were no objections. After this, the question was decided by secret ballot as to who would be second and who third. I became second, and it seemed to me that Wengler was offended. His ambition, it seems to me, is entirely inordinate.

Edinburgh is an interesting city, many monuments of the past. Tomorrow we go on an excursion.

7 Sept:
Edinburgh: Today we completed a remarkable excursion about the country of Scott[133] and Burns,[134] Loch Lomond and Trossachs. Wonderful landscapes: they do not astonish, as in Switzerland or the Caucasus; they are calming. The mountains are not high, covered by forests and meadows, meadows with fresh green grass; young lambs run about in freedom. Everywhere order, cleanliness, excellent roads.

9 Sept:
Edinburgh: Recently returned after an excursion to the home of Walter Scott. This was very interesting. The guide was the great-great granddaughter of Scott, very beautiful, large, smiling woman, speaking French very well (with a slightly noticeable English accent). The office was a small room and mezzanines. A large room alongside – a library. In the office all the walls have bookcases.

128 Oscar Schachter (1915-2003), United Nations legal counsellor and Professor of international law at Columbia Law School – [WEB].
129 Eduardo Jiménez de Aréchaga (1918-1994), jurist from Uruguay who served on the International Law Commission from 1960 to 1969 and on the International Court of justice from 1970 to 1979 – [WEB].
130 Clarence Wilfred Jenks (1909-1973), British international lawyer – [WEB].
131 Wilhelm Wengler (1907-1995), German international lawyer – [WEB].
132 Sir Gerald Gray Fitzmaurice (1901-1982), member of the International Court of Justice from the United Kingdom for the years 1960 to 1973 – [WEB].
133 Sir Walter Scott (1771-1832), the Scottish writer – [WEB].
134 Robert Burns (1759-1796), the national poet of Scotland – [WEB].

Scott rose early and work several hours before breakfast. They show part of the house: office, library, dining room, and two rooms in which weapons are stored. The remaining part evidently is occupied as the dwelling of the great-great grandchildren.

During the last trips I spoke at length with Vladimir Mikhailovich Koretskii.

11 Sept:

Edinburgh: At 11:00 a photography session was designated on the street, for steps were needed. Rain began, happily not much and we succeeded in being photographed. In the evening there was a reception in the name of Her Majesty's Government. The Solicitor General for Scotland[135] received us. The reception was in the old castle on the hill, the former residence of Scottish kings in a hall filled with weapons and armour. The Scots sacredly keep everything old and constantly emphasize their national distinctiveness. Eustathiades invited me for supper in the evening.[136] He wore me out, spoke for three hours without ceasing. Sometimes he apologized for himself: je suis bavard.

The session of the Institute is approaching the end. I spoke only on two questions: La distinction entre les object militaires et non-militaires et le problem que pose l'existance des armes de la destruction massive (von der Heydte)[137] and on the Andrassy[138] report concerning water pollution.

All ask why I am without my wife; many know her. Guggenheim has aged much. His eyes are not of this world. But Rousseau[139] looks much better than last year.

13 Sept:

Edinburgh Airport: Already on the aircraft. Today at 10:30 the session ended. As always, there were very few people at the last session: everyone has dispersed. Edinburgh I did not succeed in seeing in detail, but I have a general impression of the city.

Upon parting Makarov[140] approached me and said: "Grigorii Ivanovich, we as before love our Motherland and our Leningrad". But this was said with such feeling! It seemed to me that he was always glad when I spoke successfully or when they elected me vice-president.

During the discussion of the draft resolution on pollution I very resolutely opposed the articles on the compulsory jurisdiction of the International Court and voted against. The Poles – Winiarski[141] and Babinski[142] – abstained. Makarov also, and I think only because I had opposed.

135 Ewan George Francis Stewart, Solicitor General for Scotland from 1967 to 1970 – [web].

136 Konstantin Thoukydidon Eustathiades (1913-), Professor of International Law, University of Athens; member of International Law Commission, 1967-1971 – [vgt].

137 Baron Friedrich August von der Heydte (1907-1994), German professor of international law – [web].

138 Juraj Andrassy (1896-1977), Yugoslav international lawyer – [web].

139 Charles E. Rousseau (1902-1993), pre-eminent French international lawyer – [web].

140 Alexander Nikolaevich Makarov (1888-1973), international lawyer who emigrated from the USSR in 1925 – [vgt].

141 Bohdan Winiarski (1884-1969), member of the International Court of Justice from Poland during the years 1946 to 1967 – [web].

142 Leon Babinski (1891-1973), Polish international lawyer – [vgt].

I bought Agatha Christie,[143] *Third Girl*, and now I shall read it. She already had her own publishing house. Among the paper-bound books, the book of A. Kuznetsov,[144] *Babii Yar*, in the English language, 1967. He went to London to collect materials on Lenin[145] and did not return.

14 Sept:

London: I used this day well. In the morning, a Morning Tour of London. Of course an entire hour at the Change of the Guards near Buckingham Palace. When we passed by the British Museum, the guide, in speaking about the library, said: "In this library Marx has written his famous book *Das Kapital*".

Trafalgar Square. The statue of Nelson,[146] which by mistake looks towards the opposite sea. Some sort of meeting is going on, but I cannot decipher the words of the speaker. This is heard: "Old age pensions – this is the subject". 200 people gather at the foot of the statue, where the speaker addresses them from an elevation. People listen, come, leave.

One must visit the National Gallery. At once I go to Rembrandt.[147] The Portrait of Saskia, three portraits of elderly persons, in all about 20 canvases, including the "Belshezzar's Feast" and two self-portraits. Two large canvases of Raphael, "Madonna with Child" and "Jesus on the Cross". Brilliant, striking colors which mark liberation from the darkness of the Middle Ages. Canvas of Leonardo da Vinci[148] "The Virgin of the Rocks". Somber colors, all as though by moonlight. A different manner of writing, vision of the world – but this was not the basis of enmity of these two great artists, one of whom was older (da Vinci) than the other by 30 years.

1970

7 Jan:

Moscow. Sheremetevo Airport: An airplane to Paris at 09:25 hours. I am going for ten to twelve days. An extensive program: the Bureau of the Institute of International Law, Curatorium of the Hague Academy of International Law, a lecture at the University in Nice, then a lecture at the University of Paris and a meeting at UNESCO.

Who may be suggested from our international lawyers to lecture at The Hague Academy: Bogdanov[149] – disarmament; Lukashuk[150] – law of treaties; Morozov[151] –

143 Dame Agatha Christie (1890-1976), noted British crime writer – [WEB].

144 Anatolii Vasilevich Kuznetsov (1929-1979), Soviet writer who defected to the West in 1969 – [WEB].

145 Vladimir Ilich Lenin (1870-1924), Russian revolutionary, lawyer, political philosopher, and founder of the Soviet State – [WEB].

146 Admiral Horatio Nelson, 1st Viscount Nelson, 1st Duke of Bronté (1758-1805), hero of the Battle of Trafalgar – [WEB].

147 Rembrandt Harmenszoon van Rijn (1606-1669), noted Dutch painter – [WEB].

148 Leonardo di ser Piero da Vinci (1452-1519), Italian polymath – [WEB].

149 Oleg Vasilevich Bogdanov (1921-1988), Soviet international lawyer who wrote on disarmament and the United Nations – [WEB].

150 Igor Ivanovich Lukashuk (1926-2007), specialist on the law of treaties – [WEB].

151 Grigorii Iosifovich Morozov (1921-2001), wrote extensively on the legal status of the United Nations – [WEB].

nongovernmental international organizations; Molodtsov[152] – law of the sea; Zhudro[153] – the seabed; Ushakov[154] – sovereignty; Koretskii – codification of international law; Mozolin[155] – private international law. I don't know how Kolodkin[156] is with languages.

7 Jan:

Paris: Again in the Hotel Cayre. It is convenient, in the center of Boulevard St. Germain, 173, not far from the site of the sessions. I disembark from the aircraft and see our Ambassador, Valerian Aleksandrovich Zorin.[157] It turns out that the Minister of Enlightenment of the USSR, Prokofev,[158] flew in. Zorin invited me together with Prokofev to breakfast, where he related much interesting about the situation in France and its foreign policy. De Gaulle in his words is having an impact on policy – he called him a "restraining influence". He lives in an estate more than 200 kilometers from Paris. He has a small secretariat in Paris. The journalists seek after him and what is happening around him. Recently Malraux,[159] who now no longer has a post in the Government, travelled to see him.

I asked how he assessed the New Year messages of Pompidou[160] to Podgornyi,[161] and Nixon.[162] Zorin said that to be sure the difference between these messages to which observers drew attention is no accident. The message to Nixon stressed (implicito) that there exists not only a long, but also a class, friendship between the United States and France.

The activeness of Brandt in developing contacts with the socialist countries is worrying the French. They fear that this may lead to a reduction of the role of France in Europe. The General Secretary of the Ministry of Foreign Affairs of France, Alphand,[163] will soon come to Moscow with the position of France on the European Conference. They, taking a negative position, are lagging behind events. The French refer to the fact that until the settlement of the German Question the Meeting will not happen. Now, when Brandt has agreed to sit at one table with the representatives of the German Democratic Republic, we pointed out to the French the unsubstantiated nature of their objections.

152 Stepan Vasilevich Molodtsov (1919-1998), leading specialist on the continental shelf – [WEB].
153 Andrei Konstantinovich Zhudro (1923-1999), international lawyer from Leningrad and specialist on maritime law – [VGT].
154 Nikolai Aleksandrovich Ushakov (1918-2001), member of the International Law Commission from 1967 to 1986 – [WEB].
155 Viktor Pavlovich Mozolin (b. 1924), specialist in civil law and private international law – [WEB].
156 Anatolii Lazarevich Kolodkin (1928-2011), pre-eminent specialist on the law of the sea – [WEB].
157 Valerian Aleksandrovich Zorin (1902-1986), USSR Ambassador to France from 1965 to 1971 – [WEB].
158 Mikhail Alekseevich Prokofev (1910-1999), Minister of the Enlightenment of the USSR from 1966 to 1984 – [WEB].
159 André Malraux (1901-1976), French author and statesman – [WEB].
160 Georges Jean Raymond Pompidou (1911-1974), Prime Minister and President of France – [WEB].
161 Nikolai Viktorovich Podgornyi (1903-1983), Ukrainian Party and State figure – [WEB].
162 Richard Milhous Nixon (1913-1994), 37th President of the United States – [WEB].
163 Hervé Alphand (1907-1994), French diplomat and statesman – [WEB].

The elderly Tabouis[164] is still bustling about. On 30 December 1969 she was with Zorin, trying to find out our position concerning the withdrawal by the Israelites of five cutters (gunboats) from Cherbourg.

8 Jan:
Paris: Today I went to the restaurant for lunch. J asked for a grapillon rouge as the beverage. I wanted to recall how in 1958 I with Koretskii and Keilin[165] had dined at the Coq d'Or in Geneva and drunk this remarkable beverage. The garcon brought me something in a clay carafe; I tried it – red wine.

The Bolshoi Theater is performing in Paris now with great success. It turns out that Maya Plisetskaya[166] is not among them; she has torn a ligament. Riabinkina[167] is performing here.

10 Jan:
Paris: The sessions have already ended. On 9 January two sessions of the Bureau of the Institute of International Law. The membership of the commissions and the rapporteurs was of some interest. The president d'honneur proposed Žourek on the question of légitime defence. I suggested Chaumont (Paris University).[168] Bastid and Andrassy supported this candidacy and it was accepted. M-me Bastid quietly said that he was in Canada and his position is undetermined. I made as though I did not hear this reply.

Today's session of the Curatorium was much more tense. I met my friends – Yasseen and Ago. All went well if one does not take into account that by 18:00 one's feet promised to drop off from fatigue. Molodtsov will be invited to the Colloquium in 1970 at Teheran; in 1971 Bogdanov on disarmament. Lukashuk is intended in 1972 on the law of treaties, and later Ushakov and Morozov. Not bad. If I had not missed two sessions in 1969, one might have achieved more. A wide door is opening in the international arena for the Soviet science of international law. And now we have something to show.

11 Jan:
Nice: Voici, Côte d'Azur, Nice. Hotel Beau Rivage. Only just flown in, took a shower, rested. Regrettably, it is raining. Nice is beautiful when the sun shines, but in this miserable weather it is completely otherwise. But nonetheless it is pleasant to look upon a dark-blue wave-tossed sea, seemingly dissatisfied with such weather. I recall that a year and a half ago, in September 1967, I swam there each morning. That was superb. And after this I went to the hotel to breakfast with V. M. Koretskii.

---

164 Genevieve Tabouis (1892-1985), French historian and journalist – [VGT].

165 Aleksandr Davidovich Keilin (1894-1970), specialist on Russian maritime law – [WEB].

166 Maya Mikhailovna Plisetskaia (b. 1925), distinguished Russian ballerina – [WEB].

167 Elena Lvovna Riabinkina (b. 1941), Russian prima ballerina at the Bolshoi Theater – [WEB].

168 Charles Chaumont (1913-2001), Professor, Faculty of Law, Free University of Brussels from 1961 to 1971 – [WEB].

My young friend, Charvin,[169] met me in Nice, a very dear and able man, indeed, a communist.

12 Jan:
Nice. Beau Rivage: I am preparing my lecture of today in the University: "L' Accord comme fondement juridique du droit international". In the morning I strolled along the seashore sur le Promenade des Anglais. Empty, not as in the summer. Warm, some 10-15 degrees I believe. The sun appears infrequently. The window of my room looks out on the sea, about 50 to 70 meters away. The window is half-opened. Dupuy[170] arrives at 12:30. We will go to him to dine.

14 Jan:
Paris. Hotel Cayre: The 12 of January in Nice was a tiring day. I prepared my lecture from the morning, then dined with Dupuy, which was very delayed, more accurately my conversation with Dupuy dragged out on the question of the equivalence of diplomas. We had undertaken this work at the assignment of UNESCO: I for the socialist countries and he for the capitalist countries.

Then the lecture. The hall for 250 persons was overflowing. They said that they liked the lecture. Then there were several questions. All this continued for 1 hour, 30 minutes, the lecture itself lasted for one hour. The next day the newspaper *Nice-Matin* gave a detailed report on the lecture. After the lecture, luncheon at which the professors of the Institut de droit de la paix et du development, directed by Professor Dupuy, were present. Again questions during the luncheon. This time the question concerning the events in Czechoslovakia was put. Charvin put the question, a young communist. It seems to me that my reply satisfied him.

Yesterday practically the entire time was spent on the road. The airplane was late. And today much time was lost in a search for Pierre Cot's[171] telephone number. The telephone number I succeeded in finding through his son. Now I must catch Cot. Now I will telephone again. Finally, succeeded in ringing him. He invited me to breakfast on 16 January. Asked whether to invite colleagues. I said that I wanted to talk with him plus tête-à-tête.

15 Jan:
Paris. Hotel Cayre: While in France, I almost all the time think in French. Now, when I take the notebook in hand I was ready to write thus: je viens de revenir de la Faculté de droit. Indeed, just returned after the lecture. It seems the lecture also went well. Unlike Nice, here many of the audience took notes. Twelve to fifteen questions were put. There

169 Robert Charvin (b. 1938), international lawyer and political scientist; Dean, Faculty of Law and Economics, University of Nice, 1977-1980 – [WEB].

170 René-Jean Dupuy (1918-1997), French international lawyer and Secretary-General of The Hague Academy of International Law – [WEB].

171 Pierre Cot (1895-1977) – one of the three chairmen of the International Association of Democratic Lawyers – [VGT].

were no questions on Czechoslovakia. Those present included: Rousseau, Reuter,[172] Bastid, Ténékidès.[173] In my view Rousseau and Bastid, as the organizers of the lecture, were rather satisfied with how the lecture went.

But all the same I am weary. At home in Moscow after a lecture of 80 minutes one is not in condition to work the rest of the day. Here the lecture continued 50 to 60 minutes and then questions. And the lecture was delivered and questions answered in the French language. Now I would wish to stroll about in the park near my home in Moscow, not to mention the dacha in Perkhushkovo.

16 Jan:

Paris: In the morning I met at UNESCO with M. Troper,[174] who talks too much. We spoke about the project concerning the equivalence of diplomas and degrees. This was useful, although far from bringing complete clarity.

Next was a meal with Pierre Cot. I was at his place at 13:30 and spoke almost the entire time about the Czechoslovak question. I set out my conception. In my view he was satisfied with my approach and listened attentively. Stipulating that he would put questions for the purposing of finding "the best resolution of the question for us", Cot said that such an interpretation of the principles of proletarian internationalism is contrary to general international law – jus cogens. I replied no, that is, jus cogens does not interfere and cannot interfere with the establishment of closer relations between States, that is, the process of integration. Then he said that so long as States have not merged into a federation, the principles of respect for sovereignty, equality, and noninterference do not allow deviations. I replied that such an interpretation would mean that general international law prohibits integration, prohibits States from going beyond general international law along the path of strengthening friendship, that is, the process of forming a federation on a world or local scale on the base of socialism, of which Lenin spoke, cannot be completed from today to tomorrow – this is a prolonged process.

He said further that if one allows such an interpretation of the principle of proletarian internationalism, then it, as the leading principle, has priority in the event of a conflict and this may occur on the basis of the consent of all socialist States. To this I commented that all interested socialist States are agreed with such an interpretation. Cot went on, that if one allows such a conception, then the United States might claim to defend the free world. I said that if such norms existed, say, with respect to the United States with other American States, nothing is to be done. General international law does not prohibit this provided that such norms are created on the basis of agreement in compliance with equality and voluntariness. But there are no such norms. He had to agree that there are no such norms. In conclusion, he said that if one acknowledges that the principles of proletarian internationalism allow even the use of force, this undermines such principles as respect for sovereignty, equality, and noninterference. This is

172 Paul Reuter (1911-1990), French specialist on the law of treaties – [WEB].

173 Georges Ténékidès (1910-1990), Greek international lawyer who taught in France – [WEB].

174 Michel Troper (b. 1937), later professor of public law, University of Paris X –Nanterre – [VGT].

very dangerous. Better to apply the doctrine of necessity. I said that I doubt the advisability of referring to the doctrine of necessity and I do not see a danger in my interpretation. We refer to exceptional instances of the possible conflict between a principle of proletarian internationalism and other principles of the processes of integration which remain basic principles of relations of the new type.

Cot replied that he must publish something on this question; otherwise, he would be discredited. A draft article sent to Moscow he is reworking. He is thinking over, in particular, the interpretation of international law of which I spoke. He writes in the article that the situation created in Czechoslovakia and the policy of the imperialist States faced the Soviet Union and other socialist countries with the necessity to take measures. And although there is nothing in international law which would give the right to act, this was extreme necessity. I said that this would mean to treat this question without taking into account the principles of relations between socialist countries.

In the course of the conversation Cot said that the Czechoslovak question would undoubtedly arise at the Congress of the International Association of Democratic Lawyers in July and in order to avoid this it would be advisable to create a round-table conference on this question before the Congress. I confined myself to the comment only that I had little familiarity with the state of affairs in the Association and it would be difficult for me to say something on this issue.

Cot has aged considerably; he is almost 75 years old. In retirement, but he still lectures. This year he gave a course on the "Sociology of International Law", which includes such sections as the Czechoslovak question, the nationalization of foreign ownership in developing countries, and others. Last year he sustained a defeat in elections to the National Assembly, and with his article on the Czechoslovak question he evidently wants to remind himself again.

17 Jan:

Paris: Finally I went to the cinema and saw "Satyricon" by Fellini.[175] Decent nonsense, although one may say that the "decline of civilization" – gluttony, aimlessness, and arbitrariness are shown to some extent. The cinema that screened this film was packed. Tomorrow I intend to visit the Chagall[176] exhibition and a concert at Notre Dame.

18 Jan:

Paris: The exposition of Marc Chagall. An enormous number of works are being shown collected from various countries. Full of people. When one looks at his paintings, one willy-nilly thinks that Chagall is Sholem Aleichem[177] in the paintings. But the subjects are distinctive, although very much of a genre. The pictures of the early period please

175 A 1969 film by Federico Fellini, the Italian director, based loosely on the Petronius novel set in first century Rome – [WEB].

176 Marc Chagall (1887-1985), Russian-Jewish and later French painter – [WEB].

177 Solomon Naumovich Rabinovich (1859-1916), who wrote under the pen-name Sholem Aleichem and whose stories inspired Chagall paintings – [WEB].

me more; they are done with greater care. In the later ones there is much which he might have done better, but "it comes off". To be sure, for a great master, which he undoubtedly is, "it comes off", but it could be better.

In Nice at the Law Faculty in a new building I saw his enormous fresco. Dupuy said that their former dean was a friend of Chagall and he asked him to give something to the Faculty. Chagall gave this fresco. Dupuy said that Chagall was very wealthy.

19 Jan:

Paris. Le Bourget: Finally seated on the aircraft. It was two hours late. Bad weather in Paris, evidently that is why. Yesterday wrote letters to Koretskii and Dupuy. At the Comédie Française they are playing "Le pair offence" by Claudel.[178] Interesting – only six persons perform in the play. Economies, not like we have. Everything looks poverty-stricken. They have rich churches, and we have theaters. The manner of the performance in the Comedie Francaise is somewhat different – declamatory.

At the airport I purchased Simenon, *Un Noël de Maigret*. In Paris I continued to read Maurois, *Les trois Dumas*;[179] I began it in 1967, then laid it aside. Bought *Les trois mousquetaires* for three francs from the bouquinistes.

Today in the morning I visited Zorin and told him about my affairs. He was especially interested in the conversation with Pierre Cot. I set out my conception to Zorin. He said that it might be advisable to publish an article in this spirit quickly. In particular, for the French communists it was now important to find a way out and common ground with the socialists on this issue.

3 May:

The Hague. Hotel du Passage: I flew in here for the session of the Curatorium of The Hague Academy. The session was held yesterday. It usually lasts from 09:30 to 18:00 with a break for lunch. It was decided that Lunts[180] will deliver the general cours on private international law in 1973. Lectures were included in the program from Voicu[181] and Geamănu[182] from Romania.

I arrived on a holiday – the birthday of the Queen, with whom, I recall that in 1943 or 1944 I sat beside at a reception of the Chinese Ambassador in Canada. She was then a Princess.

Our judge, P. D. Morozov,[183] met me together with the First Secretary of the Embassy. During the second half of the day we were at Madurodam – a miniature city in Holland. The weather was very cold and had not Morozov given me a warm coat, I would have been chilled to the marrow. After Madurodam, Morozov and his wife and

178 Paul Claudel (1868-1955), French poet, dramatist, and diplomat – [web].

179 Tunkin refers to André Maurois (1885-1967), *Les trois Dumas*, first published in 1957 – [web].

180 Lazar Adolfovich Lunts (1892-1979), leading authority on private international law – [web].

181 Ioan Voicu, Romanian specialist on the law of treaties – [web].

182 Grigore Geamănu (1903-1985), Romanian international lawyer at the University of Bucharest – [web].

183 Platon Dmitrievich Morozov (1906-1986), diplomat, judge from USSR on the International Court of Justice from 1970 to 1985 – [web].

I went to Rotterdam. We dined in a restaurant on the tower from which the city, and especially the port, could be magnificently viewed. It is enormous, they say the largest in the world. The Maas River breaks up into numerous branches and the ocean-going ships traverse them. Warehouses, cranes, barges. Colossal.

On another day, 1 May, breakfast with V. S. Lavrov.[184] At the breakfast were the cinema producer, Shota Managadze,[185] and script writer, Revaz Tabukashvili,[186] who came in on the same aircraft with me. They made a film about the uprising of Georgian prisoners of war in April 1945 on the Dutch Teksel Island. The both know well Levan Aleksidze.[187]

On 2 May in the evening, that is, yesterday, I visited Lachs. He has a small flat (two floors) and two Polish girls as servants. The judges for three months actually have nothing to do. Although Morozov makes an appearance that he is working. They will continue to work on the rules of procedure; they especially hope to receive an advisory opinion [request] from the United Nations. Fitzmaurice was not elected President, which he aspired to become.

1973

5 Jan:

Orly Airport: I am going to Nice, where there will be a session of the Curatorium of The Hague Academy. I have been sitting here since 13:00 hours and it is now 15:30. I bought a book by A. France,[188] read *France-Soir*, wandered into the buffet and asked for saucisson. What? Saucisson – Hot Dogs. Voila l'américanisation!

5 Jan:

16:30. Paris-Nice Caravelle: We have just taken off. One must reflect on tomorrow's session. At home on the eve of departure I was unexpectedly busy. I finished editing a textbook. Much labor was invested, and I reworked it. Then I wrote 8 pages for the journal *Международная жизнь.*[189] Yesterday the entire evening I prepared a lecture "Sur la nature juridique des organization internationals". I promised to deliver it at Nice and in Paris (Institut des Hautes Études – Ch. Rousseau). I did not finish and will complete it at Nice.

184 Vladimir Sergeevich Lavrov (b. 1919), Ambassador of the USSR to the Netherlands from 1967 to 1973 – [VGT].

185 Shota Managadze (1903-1977), Georgian filmmaker – [WEB].

186 Revaz Tabukashvili (1927-1990), Georgian filmmaker – [WEB].

187 Levan Andreevich Aleksidze (b. 1926), an international lawyer from Tbilisi State University in Georgia – [VGT].

188 Anatole France (1844-1924), born François-Anatole Thibault, French poet, journalist, and novelist – [WEB].

189 Published in an English-language version at Moscow monthly as *International Affairs* . The article was most certainly "The Principle of Non-Use of Force as a Law of International Life", *International Affairs,* no. 4 (1973), pp. 13-15 – [WEB].

Who should be nominated to deliver lectures in 1975, if we will speak about this. I have been given the general cours. Another lecturer is needed for a five-hour cours from the other socialist countries. Perhaps Graefrath[190] – "Droit de l'hommes en pays socialiste"? It is a good idea. He gave a report in the Komitet für Menschenrechte. Haraszti already has lectured or will do so.

6 Jan:

Nice. Hotel West-End: Today as usual we were in session the entire day. And everything was fine, but they smoke such that one breathes nothing else. Rüegger[191] smokes especially actively. All proceeded well but, regrettably, Lachs did not arrive, being ill: mushroom poisoning. Yesterday evening I was at a reception of the Rector of the Académie de Nice and Chancellor of the University. There was a superb dinner in the name of the Mayor, although le Batonnier conducted it. Tomorrow at 15:00 hours a lecture, and on 9 January the second – "Sur la nature juridique des organization internationals". On 10 January a lecture in Aix-en-Provence and on the 11th in Paris.

Ch. De Visscher has died. Very, very sad. Before departing I received his book *L'Equité*. Today I shall send condolences to his son, Paul De Visscher.[192]

7 Jan:

Nice. Restaurant Rivoli: In the morning I rang La Pradelle.[193] He wants me to come to Marseille on the Mistral Train, which arrives that at 16:00 on 9 January. Dinner with him in the evening, at which Hambro[194] will be present. Hambro is giving a lecture on 9 January. In the morning on 10 January La Pradelle wishes to show me about his Aix-en-Provence.[195] I speak with Dupuy, so that my lecture will be in the morning on Tuesday. This would be wonderful – to travel in the afternoon by train from Nice to Marseille.

The Restaurant Rivoli is very pleasant. Beautiful table-cloths, plates and statuettes on the walls. Full of people, one needs to wait. One needs to bring a newspaper with one. I recall that in 1967 Koretskii and I ate in this restaurant more than once during the session of the Institute of International Law. Koretskii was greatly offended when in 1971 at Zagreb they rejected him during the elections for full members. That truly was swinishness. To be sure, when at the session of the Bureau of the Institute I insisted on Koretskii's candidacy, they cautioned me that he might not be successful. But I had reckoned that a former judge, and then the Soviet Union – this would suffice.

190 Bernhard Graefrath (1928-2006), an international lawyer from Humboldt State University in the German Democratic Republic – [WEB].

191 Paul Ruegger (1897-1988), former President of the International Red Cross – [WEB].

192 Paul Marie Albert de Visscher (1916-1996), Belgian international lawyer – [WEB].

193 Paul de Geouffre de La Pradelle (1902-1993), Director, Institute for Political Studies, University of Aix-Marseilles from foundation in 1956 to 1974 – [VGT].

194 Edvard Isak Hambro (1911-1977), Norwegian international lawyer and member of the International Law Commission – [WEB].

195 About 30 kilometers from Marseille – [VGT].

9 Jan:

Nice-Marseille Train: Two lectures for students and a doctorat went, it seems, very well. Dupuy recorded it all. That which I said one may also read in my *Theory of International Law*. But it is in the Russian language. Already translated into the German language, but they do not read German. One cannot say: "New concepts, new theory, new terminology". I tried to use Virally,[196] *L'Organization mondial* (1972). But truly there is very little one can take from this book – Virally's thoughts go in a somewhat different direction.

First Class car. I am alone in the compartment. The tracks pass along the seashore. Yes, heavenly places.

I was accompanied by Zarb.[197] For a long time he was Conseiller Juridique at the World Health Organization in Geneva. I knew him then. Now he is retired. I asked him why he chose Nice as his residence. He said that when retiring in 1962 (he is 74 years old), he wanted to settle in a city where there would be intellectual life, and it would not be such as in Paris. Here he teaches, and this, of course, is a major matter.

Today the Dean of the Faculty of Law arranged lunch at which Dupuy, Zarb, Charvin, and Touscoz[198] were present. The Dean is about 40 years old, a specialist in civil procedure.

The train proceeded slowly and stopped three times.

Charvin is a replacement for a candidate for the Communist Party of France nominated for the French Assembly. A replacement (suppléant) is an interesting institute. If a candidate is elected to the National Assembly, this means his replacement also is elected. If a deputy dies, for example, the replacement takes his seat.

The train is moving faster. Crags and trees are glimpsed through the window. It is almost impossible to read. We arrive in Cannes, Toulon. At 17:00 the train arrives in Marseille.

10 Jan:

Aix-en-Provence. Hotel du Roy René: I was in the hotel yesterday by 19:40 hours. Took a shower and quickly rang La Pradelle, and we dined together. At dinner besides his wife and daughter was Hambro with his son, who is studying here, and his fiancée. La Pradelle is a great patriot of Aix-en-Provence.

11 Jan:

Marseille. Marignanc Airport: I am on the way to Paris. We arrived at the airport one hour in advance and rightly so since it was necessary to reconfirm the Aeroflot ticket Moscow-Paris-Nice and return. But all was arranged. Mr. Bondil (assistant of La Pradelle) was extremely kind. We saw the outskirts of Aix with him, the building of the Law Faculty, and then Marseille. Marseille is situated on hills and very beautiful.

196 Michel Virally (1922-1989), French international lawyer – [WEB].

197 Antoine Henri Zarb (1899-19?), French international lawyer – [VGT].

198 Jean Touscoz (b. 1935), French international lawyer – [VGT].

He can be seen well from the hill where the church Notre Dame de la Garde is located. At the top is a statue to the Mother of God, which seamen call La Bonne Mére.

Yesterday I was completely exhausted. A lecture from 16:30 to 17:40, then a break of fifteen minutes, and questions until 19:00. Then some students wanted to speak, and this lasted until almost 20:00. Then supper with young lecturers. I returned to the hotel at 23:00. But all this was very interesting. The lecture went well, though it was difficult to set out the material in one hour and the audience was a mixture: jurists, political scientists, historians, philosophers, and others. Some came from Toulon. Professor David[199] came, whose book has been published in the Soviet Union. He worked at the Institut de droit comparé in Paris, and three years ago came to Aix and works in the Law Faculty. He says that he preferred a quieter place and is very content that he settled in Aix.

La Pradelle was exceedingly courteous. He has excellent relations with young people. He is the President of the Académie d'Aix. There are about 30 full members in the Academy and a certain number of associates and various specialists. From time to time they assemble and hear reports.

Wassilii Leontev, Nobel Laureate in Economics, and G. I. Tunkin, awarded honorary doctorates at Paris University (I)

11 Jan:

Paris. Hotel Trianon: And so I am for the first time in the Latin Quarter. I have just arrived at the Hotel after a stroll along the Boulevard St. Michel. Many young people. On St. Michel Square in large letters written on a wall: Nixon = Hitler. The Hotel Trianon is a tourist hotel, and there are many youths: English and Scandinavian speech. Paris is cold. Tomorrow I need to buy a sweater, or I shall freeze.

199 René David (1906-1990), the noted French comparative lawyer – [WEB].

13 Jan:

Paris: Yesterday I gave a lecture which lasted for 60 minutes. Then questions and we finished after about 1 hour, 30 minutes. Bastid and Colliard[200] were at the lecture, and about 100 persons in the audience. Supper in the evening: Rousseau, Bastid, Reuter, Žourek, and myself. Žourek said that his wife went to Prague and he is getting ready to travel there.[201] Now he is in Geneva. Judging from everything, he is not living well – he does not have, I understand, a permanent place.

Today in Paris at the Luxembourg Palace during the second half of the day a meeting should open of the leaders of the II International: Mitterand,[202] Kreisky,[203] Golda Meir,[204] Palme (Sweden),[205] Jorgenson (Denmark),[206] and Sorsa (Finland).[207] The newspapers write that if the Prime Minister of Israel arrives, exceptional security measures will be taken and all demonstrations prohibited. At 16:30, when I climbed from St. Michel station upwards towards Boulevard St. Michel, about twenty policemen stood on every corner in helmets. Students stroll about with the appearance of heroes: they are afraid as we are.

At 18:00 I went to stroll about Boulevard St. Michel. The police on motorcycles with sirens tore along (40 persons) first up towards Jardin de Luxembourg and then down. They reminded the students to conduct themselves peacefully.

I stood at the tables on which books were spread out. Bought Camus, *La Peste*.[208]

14 Jan:

Paris. Hotel Trianon: Today in the first half I did an excursion about Paris for tourists on a bus. The trip lasted three hours and I liked it very much, although to be sure I had seen everything before. But, for example, The Cathedral of the Sacred Heart I had not seen for 10 years. I was there once, when Itta and I returned from Geneva and the chauffeur from the Embassy showed us the sights of Paris.

Lunched at the St. Michel Restaurant. Not knowing local restaurants, I came here. The restaurant was full of students. The menu included wine and service, but one might order a la carte. A vegetable soup, entre-cote, ice cream, and coffee. All of miserable quality, meat with some sort of sinews. I recalled luncheon at the Hotel du Roy René in Aix. The entre-cote was four times bigger and of an entirely different quality.

Today in the evening I saw the Fellini[209] film "Les nuits de Cabiria". Cabiria is a prostitute who has a small home. The film begins with her lover confronting her at the river

---

200 Claude Albert Colliard (1913-1991), Dean, Faculty of Law, University of Paris I; Director, Department of International and European Studies from 1971 – [WEB].

201 After the Czechoslovak Events of 1968, Žourek left Czechoslovakia – [VGT].

202 François Maurice Adrien Marie Mitterand (1916-1996), fourth President of France under the Fifth Republic – [WEB].

203 Bruno Kreisky (1911-1980), Chancellor of Austria – [WEB].

204 Golda Meir (1898-1978), fourth Prime Minister of Israel – [WEB].

205 Olof Palme (1927-1986), Prime Minister of Sweden twice – [WEB].

206 Anker Jørgenson (b. 1922), prime minister of Denmark and Foreign Minister – [WEB].

207 Taisto Kalevi Sorsa (b. 1930), Finnish diplomat and sometime Prime Minister – [WEB].

208 Albert Camus (1913-1960), French Algerian philosopher – [WEB].

209 Federico Fellini (1920-1993), Italian film director – [WEB].

and flees, having seized her purse with money. Then a number of episodes, especially religious processions, ecstasy, faith in a miracle. But the miracle does not happen. This is an anti-religious moment. To me the film is profound, philosophical. Fellini shows what man is capable of expecting money and from money.

Indeed "OK" has become embedded here. Today the bus drivers in conversation with one another answered: OK.

17 Jan:

Orly Airport: Yesterday I went to Abrasimov[210] and Oberemko.[211] It is evident that Abrasimov is very satisfied with the trip to Minsk together with Pompidou. He is close to Brezhnev[212] and in general feels himself to be a king. Zorin is much inferior to him.

1974

9 May:

The Hague. Hotel Bali: The hotel which the Academy reserved for me turned out to be unimportant. There was no telephone in the room. P. D. Morozov met me. The Ambassador also was there and met Romanov[213] from the Committee for the Press. Went to the hotel, and then to a reception for the Czechs. Dined at Morozov's.

10 May:

The Hague: Today I went to the Academy in the morning. Wanted to walk to the Peace Palace. But it began to drizzle and I sat on the tram. Arrived at the Academy, and then to the Library. Gave the Chief Librarian the textbook on international law which recently appeared under my editorship. Then sat to look over the literature. Worked diligently, but found nothing interesting.

In the afternoon I with Morozov visited Ambassador, A. I. Romanov.[214] He asked me to speak to workers of the Embassy.

11 May:

The Hague: Today there was a session of the Curatorium. As always we sat in a smoke-filled room until I opened a window. All members were there except Cortina Mauri,[215]

---

210 At this time Petr Andreevich Abrasimov (1912-2009) was the Ambassador of the USSR to France – [VGT].

211 Valentin Ivanovich Oberemko (1926-1980) was the Counsellor-Envoy of the USSR Embassy in France from 1973 to 1980 – [VGT].

212 Leonid Ilich Brezhnev (1906-1982), General Secretary of the Communist Party of the Soviet Union – [WEB].

213 Pavel Konstantinovich Romanov (1913-1992), Chief of the State Committee for the Press of the USSR – [WEB].

214 Aleksandr Iosifovich Romanov (b. 1912), Ambassador of the USSR to Nigeria from 1964 to 1970 and to the Netherlands from 1973 to 1979 – [VGT].

215 Pedro Cortina Mauri (1908-1993), Foreign Minister of Spain from 1974 to 1975 – [WEB].

who had become Minister of Foreign Affairs of Spain. He resigned. Hyde[216] also resigned. Why I do not know. He referred to age. But it seems something is not right. When Castberg[217] (chairman) thanked him and expressed regret, he began to cry a bit.

My absence at two sessions had the effect at least that in 1975 there would be no Soviet professor at the courses. For 1977 I nominated Molodtsov, who at my suggestion was included on the topic of problems of the law of the sea. Then they shoved in such topics as the influence of various religions on the development of international law. Ruegger drags in questions of the law of war, as though this was the most important. He also gravitates towards religion.

I am reading *Le Monde* – incandescence of the second round of Presidential elections is felt to be great. On 7 May our Ambassador, S. V. Chervonenko,[218] visited Giscard d'Estaing,[219] who is a candidate for President from the right. The Communist Party declared that this visit was "inopportune" and "regrettable", that is, may be constructed as support by the Soviet Union for the candidacy of d'Estaing. Mitterand is the candidate of the socialist and the communists. I am reading today in *Le Monde* an article by Jean-Pierre Cot,[220] a socialist deputy. Of course he quarrels with d'Estaing. I recall how he, as a curly-headed youth attended my lectures at The Hague Academy in 1958.

12 May:

Amsterdam. Reichsmuseum: I am sitting with P. D. Morozov before Rembrandt's painting "Night Watch". They say this is not the entire painting, only part. What a combination of hues! What an expression of life!

We decided to go out on a boat along the canals of Amsterdam – the Venice of the North, as the Dutch call it. This truly impresses, sets the city apart from others, since there are no special sights in Amsterdam besides this. What makes the greatest impression – the barges on the canals, old with low living premises fashioned from wood. Some look nice, and others like kennels. They say that there are 50,000 such dwelling barges.

12 May:

The Hague. Hotel Bali: Returned an hour ago with Morozov from Amsterdam. He has a remarkable Cadillac with automatic shift to which he became accustomed in New York. The trip was exceedingly interesting, but P.D. is obviously very weary. I too am tired, but I did not drive the vehicle. For me that would be a bit uncomfortable.

---

216 James Nevins Hyde (1909-1996), practitioner in New York City – [WEB].

217 Frede Castberg (1893-1977), international lawyer from Norway and President of The Hague Academy of International Law – [WEB].

218 Stepan Vasilevich Chervonenko (1915-2003), Ambassador of the USSR to France from 1973 to 1983 – [VGT].

219 Valéry Marie René Georges Giscard d'Estaing (b. 1926), President of the French Republic from 1974 to 1981 – [WEB].

220 Jean-Pierre Cot (b. 1937), Professor of International Law, University of Amiens, later Paris I – [VGT].

15 May:

The Hague: On Monday Arechaga invited me to lunch. Morozov and Lachs also were there with wives. Mrs. Arechaga raised a toast to Mrs. Tunkin. All asked whether she would come in a future year when I would deliver the general cours of lectures at The Hague Academy. What could I reply?

Today Morozov is giving a lunch in my honor. Tomorrow, Waldock[221] – a dinner. Today Gros invited me to lunch, but I said to his secretary that I am taken. Yesterday I met with the legal advisor of the Ministry of Foreign Affairs, Riphagen.[222] Either the Ambassador arranged this or he himself took the initiative, I know not. We met as good old acquaintances and spoke about the forthcoming conference on the law of the sea. He is going as the head of delegation.

I am working intensively in the Library.

17 May:

The Hague: Yesterday I worked in the Library from morning onwards, returned to the Hotel, and at 17:00 hours gave a lecture in the Embassy on the topic "Reduction of Tension and International Law". There were 20 persons present. I scolded our diplomats that they do not know international law well and showed its role. They listened attentively and put many questions.

In the evening, dinner at the Waldocks. Fitzmaurice was there with his Lady, Gros, Onyeama[223] with his wife (Nigeria). The former members of the International Law Commission always greet me with great joy. And in the morning I met with Lachs. We spoke about the program of his visit to the United States.

I selected much material in the Library.

In the evening I strolled along the sea. The weather on the second day is superlative. Today I strolled for two hours. I am trying to spend more time here, but usually an hour and a half. If I had brought sport equipment, I could do exercises by the sea.

Yesterday was lunch with Ambassador Aleksandr Iosifovich Romanov. After lunch he for an hour interrogated me about the law of the sea. We have for a long time been consulting with the major maritime powers: the United States, England, Japan, Italy. A meeting was held in the early days of May in London. V. A. Romanov[224] and A. P. Movchan[225] attended from our side. Molodtsov went to Rome. Our Ambassador received the task of consulting with the Government of Holland and was exploiting me in this connection.

---

221 Sir Claud Humphrey Meredith Waldock (1904-1981), member of the International Court of Justice from the United Kingdom – [WEB].

222 Willem Riphagen (1919-1994), legal advisor to the Dutch Ministry of Foreign Affairs – [WEB].

223 Charles D. Onyeama (1917-1990), member of the International Court of Justice from Nigeria – [WEB].

224 Valentin Aleksandrovich Romanov (1924-2001), international lawyer in the Legal Department of the USSR Ministry of Foreign Affairs – [VGT].

225 Anatolii Petrovich Movchan (1928-1998), Russian diplomat and international lawyer – [WEB].

19 May:

The Hague: I rang Morozov from a common telephone since I have no telephone in my room. This room costs 25 guilders with breakfast and service. We agreed that at 13:00 hours I would lunch with them. Departure tomorrow. Next year the general cours. I was content that I had succeeded in working in the Library so satisfactorily. To be sure, work in the Library in general amounted to 24 hours since luncheons, meetings, and so on cut the time. But I looked over the most recent literature and made copies. Much of this is not in Moscow.

20 May:

Amsterdam. Airport: Yesterday in France Giscard d'Estaing, the Minister of Economy under Pompidou, was elected the President after the death of Pompidou. Mitterand did not succeed. The difference in the number of votes was less than a half million. De Gaullites supported d'Estaing against the socialists and the communists. In general d'Estaing advanced on an anti-communist ticket.

10 July:

Steamship "Lomonosov". Archangel-Chamovo: A landscape well-known and dear to my heart. Superb weather – sun, but a northern wind, humid. My schedule this year is dense. On 8 July I submitted an article to the journal Коммунист [Communist] – "International Law – Basis of Reducing Tension". On 9 July at 15:00 I flew to Archangel, and at 23:00 sat on the steamship. Aunt[226] could not get a cabin on the steamship which departs in the afternoon. On one hand, this is good since I had business in Moscow yesterday, and I could fly only at 15:00 hours. But the steamship arrives at Konetsgore[227] at a very inconvenient time – 01:30 in the morning.

On 19 July I have to be in Moscow since Volodya with his wife Ira[228] are departing for Central Asia and I must be with grandson, Alyesha. To be sure, now there is a child-minder, but all the same I must be there. It is unlikely anything will happen. But in a few days Alyesha dislocated his left arm – it was necessary to convey him to Moscow.

I write on the deck and read Simenon,[229] *Un Noel de Maigret*. I am reading it a second time. I love Simenon, especially Maigret. He writes very sincerely and very French. I also took Hailey's[230] *Airport* and Hamptmann,[231] *Atlantis*. Nothing on international law. Forgotten. Holiday.

The landscape on the whole is old, but the view of the villages which we pass by has somewhat changed. Often large two-story houses are glimpsed, cisterns with petrol, television antennas on the roofs of houses. Motors on the boats.

226 Anna Gavrilovna Skripova (1899-1990), the sister of G. I. Tunkin's father – [VGT].
227 The village and dock on the bank of the Northern Dvina across from Chamovo – [VGT].
228 Irina Petrovna Sazhina (b. 1942), wife of Vladimir Grigorevich Tunkin – [WEB].
229 Georges Simenon (1903-1989), French novelist – [WEB].
230 Arthur Hailey (1920-2004), British/Canadian novelist – [WEB].
231 Gerhart Hamptmann (1862-1946), German writer – [WEB].

15 July:

Chamovo: The third year in a row that I visit Chamovo and each time I experience an oppressive feeling. The elements of this mood are several. Recollections of the past of which little has remained. Conversation with mother which angered me about witchcraft: I ached in my side – this is someone engaging in witchcraft.

Today against I travel with Iakov Ivanovich[232] to fish. Two days ago we caught some fish to prepare "ukha".[233] All to be sure were small, but in the evening the catch was not bad and the mosquitoes were few.

17 July:

Chamovo: I am sitting on the porch. The weather today is overcast, and a light rain is drizzling. Tomorrow I leave. Mother today with all seriousness said to me: You should move to Chamovo, there is work. There are many places, you can build a house. Or this: half a loaf of dried bread. I, she says, dry with sugar. For what? It is unlikely she will not bake bread.

Divorced from reality. Father was not this way – he accepted the new with enthusiasm. Was with Iakov at the cemetery, sat on the grave of Papa.

Today in the morning had breakfast with Iakov Ivanovich. Swept up the room, brought water, wrote a letter to Fedor Mikhailovich in Shuzhega.[234] Now I shall read Maigret, *Sept petites croix dans un carnet.*

Yesterday I photographed Mama – who knows it may be the last time. But I think not; she is still strong. The "samovar" warms itself, but rapidly tires.

19 July:

Chamovo-Archangel. Steamship: So, I am on my way back. I feel relief. I fear only that mother again did not "plot". This witchcraft will not be removed from her by anything. She is tormented by it and torments others. I am travelling in a second-class cabin – a double. The second person is a young man. When I arrived, he was asleep drunk. Now he has left to take the hair of the dog that bit him. My telegram with a booking for a first-class cabin had no effect. Perhaps I sent it late. Today on the airplane. I managed for 10 days.

Yesterday the weather was wonderful. The Dvina was like a mirror, the sun shone. I was conveyed across to the other bank of the Dvina, on the pier by Aleksei Maksimovich Sevastianov[235] (who lives opposite Iakov Ivanovich). The boat is made from duralumin, and the motor a good one. We arrived. Although in one place it was necessary to use the oars.

---

232 Iakov Ivanovich Varlachev (1908-1983), first cousin of G. I. Tunkin – [VGT].

233 "Ukha" is a soup made from fresh fish – [VGT].

234 Fedor Mikhailovich Antushev (1899-1984), first cousin once removed of G. I. Tunkin lived in the neighboring village of Shuzhega – [VGT].

235 Aleksei Maksimovich Sevastianov (1924-1989), a peasant from the village of Chamovo.

28 Dec:

New Delhi. Hotel Ramjit: Here is India. The first striking impression: too many people. There one person is needed, three or four run about.

The Conference of the International Law Association will be held here from 30 December to 4 January. Our delegation: Tunkin, Bogdanov, and Ignatenko.[236] Tomorrow a group of nine tourists is arriving.

I shaved, changed clothes, and was ready to go to lunch, but comrades had just gone to the bank to cash cheques and there was no money yet. Ate a bit of gingerbread, and nothing more.

After lunch we went to stroll about the hotel. What awful poverty! Alongside the hotel behind a fence of old, dusty stalls live families. Small children run about.

It seems they have solved the problem of transport. And it is truly a problem. We are not paid for taxis. We are not permitted to use public transport, that is, buses, as this is dangerous. Europeans do not use them. And it turns out we are far from the site of the conference. A. M. Lozovskii[237] (Deputy Chairman of the Union of Soviet Friendship Societies) helped. The Counsellor of our Embassy, Feliks Nikolaevich Iurlov,[238] is very attentive to us and also promised to assist with transport.

Today the Full Council at 13:00, then at 16:00 a Garden Party given by the President of the Indian Branch. Tomorrow at 10:00 Indira Gandhi opens the Conference.[239]

30 Dec:

New Delhi. Hotel Ramjit: Slept to 05:00. Early. To be sure, went to bed at 22:00 hours. Now it is precisely 06:00. The mullahs in the mosque call the believers to pray with a loudspeaker. It is still dark. Sunrise at 06:30.

31 Dec:

Hotel Ramjit: I am writing in bed. Our tourists invited us to greet the New Year together, but I don't want to and it is not convenient. Intourist is taking care of them. In addition, tomorrow there is an excursion to Agra. At 07:15 we must be at the Hotel Continental. Therefore, Bogdanov and I remained at the hotel. Only Ignatenko, who comports as a tourist although he is a delegate, left for the Ambassador Hotel to the tourists.

Today we quietly buried Sohn's[240] proposal for the Peaceful Settlement of Disputes. It worried me. Two years ago at a Conference in New York the Americans intended to implement it, but we did not permit this. The draft was entirely unsuitable, contrary to the United Nations Charter. Sohn changed it, but all the same it was raw: the basic line

236 Gennadi Vladimirovich Ignatenko (1927-2012), international lawyer at Urals State Legal Academy – [WEB].

237 A.M. Lozovskii [not further identified].

238 Feliks Nikolaevich Iurlov (b. 1932), Counsellor of Embassy of USSR in India, presently at the Institute of Oriental Studies, Russian Academy of Sciences – [VGT].

239 Indira Gandhi (1917-1984), Prime Minister of India from 1966 to 1977 and from 1980 to 1984 – [WEB].

240 Louis B. Sohn (1914-2006), Professor at the Harvard Law School – [WEB].

was the creation in the United Nations of fact-finding conciliation and arbitral procedures, placing new functions on the Security Council, and so on. All this was unnecessary and harmful. Sohn was ill and retired. The draft was buried and the Committee liquidated which had been created for the revision of the United Nations Charter.

1975

02 Jan:

Hotel Ramjit: Today was a difficult day. Two sessions, tea with the President of India from 16:00 to 17:00, cocktails at 19:00, dinner with the Chief Justice at 20:15. Indira Gandhi and the Minister of Foreign Affairs were at dinner. It is interesting that someone of them confused me with Bogdanov, and Bogdanov was seated in the centre and me at the end of the table. To Indira Gandhi I said: "Soviet women admire her. She answered: And I admire Soviet women".

Yesterday the excursion to Agra was interesting. The Akbar Palace is remarkable. Supposedly before his death Akbar's wife took an oath from him that he would not marry and would place a monument to her which the world had never seen. He fulfilled his promise. The monument is a mosque, in the middle of which is the tomb of the Tsarina and alongside the grave of Akbar.[241] The tomb of the Tsarina is in the center, since the mosque was built for her, and Akbar's grave is on the side.

06 Jan:

Hotel Ramjit: The Conference ended on Saturday, 4 January. On Saturday, the President of the Indian Lawyer's Association, Harish Chandra,[242] arranged in our honor a cocktail reception. Yesterday, at the insistence of our Information Center I gave an interview to the correspondent of the Indian Telegraph Agency. I chatted with him for a hour and a half. It was printed in all the central newspapers; some gave the interview in detail, and other a concise version.

Today a lecture at 17:30 in the Indian Society of International Law. I began to prepare the lecture in Moscow. Today I rose at 06:00 and by 07:30 composed the final text.

After the closing of the Conference there was a dinner with our military attaché, Dmitrii Fedorovich Poliakov,[243] and his wife, Nina Petrovna. They are very dear people, as I was told in Moscow. Next I was with the Ambassador, Viktor Fedorovich Maltsev, to whom I reported on the results of the Conference. The Ambassador, with whom I first became acquainted in Stockholm (before this he was Chairman of the Executive Committee in Irkutsk Region), said that when he was Ambassador in Sweden, it seemed to him that there was much work. And now Sweden seemed to him to be a resort.

241 Akbar the Great (1542-1605), Third Mughal Emperor – [WEB].

242 Harish Chandra (b. 1926), Secretary-General, Indian Association of Lawyers; Secretary, International Association of Democratic Lawyers; Judge of High Court of Delhi – [VGT].

243 Dmitrii Fedorovich Poliakov (1921-1988), Major General of GRU (foreign military intelligence), CIA agent for many years, arrested and in 1988, executed – [VGT].

7 Jan:
Delhi Airport: Yesterday too was not easy. Lunch at 13:00. Two members of the Supreme Court were there: Mrs. Gosch – the Secretary-General of the India-USSR Society, and others. Nagendra Singh[244] also was there, who invited me and Bogdanov to tea. After tea, the lecture at the Indian Society of International Law. Singh – the President of the Society – presided. There were few people – 40 to 50. I spoke for 40 minutes and was occupied with so many questions: prohibition of the use of force, the situation in Kashmir, and so on. I gave the library of the Society a copy of my *Theory of International Law*, translated into English by William Butler and published in 1974, and the Textbook, having expressed the hope that soon Indian international lawyers might read it.

We succeeded in seeing Delhi: the home of Nehru,[245] the noted stainless-steel column, the Hindu temple, the Red Fort where Nehru raised the flag of independence of India. Nehru's house, now a museum, was two floors. On the first floor a large guest room and dining room, and an office and bedroom on the second. Nothing magnificent, but also no acesticism.

On Friday at 16:15 was a session of the Conference devoted to the report by Cochaux, who suggested the grandiose project of a Restatement of International Law, or something of that nature. I spoke and emphasized that the projects must be more international than they are. I pointed out that the implementation of such a project, the very work process, would facilitate mutual understanding between jurists of different countries. The speech ended with applause, which happens rarely. Cochaux was very satisfied.

On Saturday at a session of the Full Committee, the Chairman, Lord Wilberforce, congratulated me upon my election as corresponding member of the USSR Academy of Sciences, whereupon this celebration was included on the agenda. How they knew about this I know not, but this was very courteous on their part.

Détente at the Conference was in general felt very strongly.

19 March:
Geneva. Hotel Mon Repos: It is 22:00. I am working but already inclining towards sleep. Last night I slept badly. I awoke at 05:00, began to think how it would be with the International Labor Organization Convention No. 29 on Forced Labor.

Today I was with Itta at a cocktail reception with Valticos,[246] the Director of the Department of Norms. In the afternoon I invited him for lunch in order to speak about what might be done with the comments of the Committee for Convention No. 29. Today with the assistance of Valticos and the rapporteur of the Committee I succeeded

244 Nagendra Singh (1914-1988), member of the International Court of Justice from India, 1973 to 1988, serving as President of the Court from 1985 to 1988 – [WEB].

245 Jawaharlal Nehru (1889-1964), first Prime Minister of India – [WEB].

246 Nicolas Valticos (1918-2003), Assistant Director-General of the International Labour Organisation – [WEB].

in significantly changing the draft comments of the USSR, Belorussian SSR, and Ukrainian SSR on the distribution of students for jobs.

But in general under Convention No. 29 the matter has gone very far, and it seems nothing can be done. It is appropriate to confine oneself to a Statement.

We flew to Geneva on 12 March and will be here until 29 March.

23 March:

Mon Repos: Two sessions almost every day. I wake up at 5:30 to 6:00 and being work. In the evening I also work with the documents. In general, the impression is that the ILO Secretariat drives the experts so that they stamped that which has been prepared by them.

On Monday, 17 March, the session opened of the III United Nations Conference on the Law of the Sea. Our delegation is headed by Deputy Minister of Foreign Affairs, S. P. Kozyrev.[247] He was ill and was to arrive the day after tomorrow. Today in the evening or tomorrow I will meet with Zhudro and learn news about the course of the Conference.

Today there was tea at the Guggenheims. He looks not well – hands and feet tremble – Parkinson's Disease. Rapidly becomes tired. But such a fresh mind.

25 March:

International Labor Organization: Session of the Committee of Experts on the Convention. Now the interpreters are reading the introduction to the document Code Européen de Securité social. The Report and application of this Code the committee is preparing in accordance with an agreement between the Bureau International du Travail and the Council of Europe. All members of the Committee are present. This is the last day of work. There was such a race that it is difficult to imagine. Yesterday was a fight over Convention No. 29 – Forced Labor – with reproaches to the Soviet Union, accusations of the existence of forced labor. Artificial problems created for ideological struggle against socialism. But we have given several pretexts for this.

1976

9 Jan:

Moscow-Paris. IL-62 Aircraft: I am flying to a session of the Curatorium. Have not been in Paris for three years, and missed two sessions of the Curatorium: could not attend in 1974 and in 1975 was in India.

On 15 January I am giving a lecture at the invitation of Virally at the University of Paris II. There is also an invitation to deliver a lecture from Professor Bosc[248] (Catholic University), but it is doubtful that I can accept because of a shortage of time.

247 Semen Pavlovich Kozyrev (1907-1991), Deputy Minister of Foreign Affairs of the USSR – [WEB].

248 Robert Bosc (1909-1979), French jurist and sociologist – [WEB].

11 Jan:
Paris. Hotel Cayre: The secretary of the Consulate met me, M. M. Biriukov,[249] who graduated from the international law faculty of the Institute of International Relations and, of course, knows me.

Yesterday we were in session from 9:30 to 17:00. Castberg is, of course, weak as President and aged (82 years). But in May he will retire. It is said that we will elect Ago, and Lachs, who will be in The Hague as a judge for another 9 years, will be Vice President. The financial status of the Academy is deplorable. If nothing changes, the Academy will be gone by 1978. The American foundations give no money, no doubt they consider it to be a semi-communist organization. The Governments give very little. I proposed to think about how to achieve approval of the activities of the Academy from the United Nations General Assembly. This could help obtain appropriations through, for example, the United Nations University.

At the suggestion of Lachs and myself, the Helsinki issue was included on the list of courses. I insisted that one of the rapporteurs be the Soviet professor, A. P. Movchan, and in place of a Canadian, as was suggested by the Committee, a European. So there will be three rapporteurs: Movchan, Ninčić[250] (Yugoslavia), and Arangio-Ruiz (Italy).[251]

Yesterday evening dinner at the Lavignes.[252] Colliard with his wife also was there. We sat about until midnight.

I was at the Louvre before dinner. As always with reverential trembling I look far ahead down the corridor towards – the Venus de Milo. It is impossible to create anything more perfect. I sit and fall in love. After the Louvre I went to Bastid. She is cheerful, energetic, and, one does not say, soon will be 70. Rousseau and Vignes[253] were there. The Truyols[254] came in. We sat and chatted until almost 19:00.

15 Jan:
Le Louvre: Yesterday before lunch I went to the Pantheon. The Guidebook of ten years ago said the entrance fee was half a franc, and is now five francs. An enormous and impressive building. An inscription on one of the columns: 'A la memoire de Antoine de Saint Exupery. Disparu en cours d'une mission de Reconnaissance airienne. Le 31 juillet 1944". Too bad the Crypt in the basement is closed. Repairs.

In the morning I polished my lecture, which will be delivered today at 19:00. I am now in the Louvre in the hall of Italian painting of the 17-18th centuries. Again I am in

249 Mikhail Mikhailovich Biriukov (b. 1946), Secretary of the USSR Embassy in Paris and now Professor of International Law and Head of the Chair of European Law, Moscow State Institute of International Relations – [VGT].

250 Duro Ninčić (1915-), Deputy Permanent Representative of Yugoslavia to the United Nations; staff member, Institute of International Politics and Economics in Belgrade – [WEB].

251 Gaetano Arangio-Ruiz (1919-), Italian international lawyer – [WEB].

252 Pierre Lavigne (b. 1922), specialist on Soviet constitutional law; Marie Lavigne (b. 1935), specialist on Soviet law and the economy – [WEB].

253 Daniel Vignes (b. 1924), French specialist on the law of the sea – [WEB].

254 Antonio Truyol y Serra (1913-2003), Spanish international lawyer at the University of Madrid – [WEB].

the Galerie Medici.[255] I have not been here for a long time. As is said in the guidebook, "21 tableaux de Rubens à la Galerie de Marie de Medici".

16 Jan:

Orly Airport: Just arrived at Orly from Bourget. Because of fog, Bourget cannot receive aircraft. They sat us in a bus and, not saying a word, conveyed us somewhere. It turned out to be Orly.

Yesterday I gave my lecture on "Le fonctionnement du droit international" at the University of Law, Economy and Social Sciences of Paris (Paris II). The room was packed, about 300 persons. They listened with rapt attention. Colliard, Bastid, Bosc, and Weil[256] as one of the Directors of the Institute, and Virally, who introduced me to the audience, were present from among the professors. Rousseau and Reuter were not there.

After the lecture, Bosc invited me for a meal, and we then went on foot to the Hotel Cayre. He recounted much of interest about the streets of Paris and showed from the outside his Catholic University.

On 14 January the President of the University of Paris II, Prof. Goldman,[257] gave a lunch in my honor. Rousseau. Reuter, Bastid, Weil, and Virally were present. The lunch was magnificent. I had known Goldman for a long time through the International Law Association.

22 March:

Geneva. Hotel Mon Repos: Turned out to be in the same suite with Itta in which we were last year. Tina and Levan Aleksidze met us.

Worked the entire day, although walked twice to the Botanical Garden. Prepared a lecture which I will deliver tomorrow at the Cercle des jurists internationaux. The topic: "The Functioning of International Law". I spoke to this Cercle already, not long after its formation.

I also prepared my address with regard to ILO Convention No. 87.

On Friday I visited Aleksidze. Something ails him – a disturbance of the vegetative nervous system. Evidently from an accident which he suffered in Tbilisi two years ago.

23 March:

Committee Meeting: They are discussing comments on Convention No. 87 concerning Freedom of Association and Harold Kirkcaldy[258] (England) repeated all of the preceding fabrications and I intended to speak rather sharply. Professor Gubinski (Poland) spoke first.[259]

---

255 Galerie Medici, a series of painting by Peter Paul Rubens commissioned by Marie de Medici – [VGT].

256 Prosper Weil (b. 1926), professor of international law at the University of Paris II – [WEB].

257 Berthold Goldman (1913-1993), first President of the University of Paris II from 1974 to 1979 – [WEB].

258 Harold Stewart Kirkcaldy (1902-1976), Montagu Professor of Industrial Relations, Cambridge University – [VGT].

259 Arnold Gubiński (1916-1997), specialist in criminal law from Poland – [WEB].

There were interesting events today. I spoke for half an hour, entirely unusual, with regard to the comments concerning Convention No. 87 on the freedom of association and showed the complete unfoundedness of his discourse once again. There was a skirmish between him and me. There was confusion, since it was evident that Kirkcaldy's suggestions were unfounded. Only the American spoke, saying that the observations are carefully formulated. The chairman (a Nigerian) said that there are no grounds to change anything in the text and that Professor Tunkin may include his statement in the report concerning disagreement, as was done previously. I, of course, did not reckon on more, but think that my address will play its own role in the future.

The Director-General of the ILO, Blanchard,[260] gave a lunch. Before this Valticos informed him what had happened. They had to support Kirkcaldy, and Blanchard in his address very gently spoke of Kirkcaldy and even proposed a toast to his health. In addition, he called upon everyone to conduct themselves properly since the United States might withdraw from the ILO.

Tunkin visits Professor Sir Derek Bowett, Cambridge University

260 Francis Blanchard (1916-2009), Director General of the International Labor Organization from 1974 to 1989 – [WEB].

30 March:

Hotel Mon Repos: Tomorrow is the last day of the Committee's work. Yesterday there was a discussion of the comments on Convention No. 29. The draft submitted by Van der Ven[261] was not bad, but Gubinskii under my arrangement with him proposed to transform the comments into Direct Requests. The Yugoslav supported this, as did the Egyptian. The English and Americans were opposed, but not strongly. The Chairman inclined towards a compromise. A Commission was created of Van der Ven, Vilfan,[262] and Douglas.[263] A compromise draft was obtained.

It is interesting that when after Gubinski's address the discussion unfolded, and I sat and kept silent. Van der Ven conducted himself well, agreeing to the compromise. There is further progress.

14 May:

Moscow-London: I fly to London for a session of the Executive Committee of the International Law Association, and then to The Hague for a session of the Curatorium. I combined the two trips, although initially I thought I would not succeed in doing this. I am going along the line of the USSR Academy of Sciences.

As always before departure there was time trouble. But I did everything and gave the next portion of the Hague cours to the Translation Bureau to type (N. M. Chugunova). I passed the first 54 pages of the textbook on international law to the editor of Progress Publishing House (L. V. Mekhvaladze). They are translating it and are in a hurry. I am writing the introduction – this is necessary for foreigners. We must show our theory of international law. Something has already been dictated. Now the idea has emerged that those points of our conception must be explained which give rise to false interpretations in the West, namely: (1) the basis and superstructure applicable to international law; (2) the concept of peaceful coexistence – two ideologies, two conceptions, and a single international law.

By 20:00 I was already at a dinner at the International Law Association. The time was not specified in the letter; I thought it was 20:00 and was half an hour late. When I arrived, all were at table. Lord Wilberforce – the Chairman of the Council; Ray[264] – the President of the ILA and Chief Justice of India; Lord Hodson,[265] and Edwards[266] rose, approached to greet me, moved over and made a place. Only the American, Olmstead, Vice-Chairman of the Council, did not approach. But later, during desert, he evidently understood that he had not behaved in the best manner and approached. In their

261 Josephus J. M. van der Ven (1907-1988), labour law specialist from The Netherlands – [VGT].

262 Joze Vilfan (1908-1987), Head, Yugoslav Mission to the United Nations after World War II; Deputy Federal Minister of Foreign Affairs; Yugoslav Ambassador to India and Burma; Advisor to President Tito of Yugoslavia – [VGT].

263 William Douglas (1921-2003), sometime Chief Justice of Barbados and labour law specialist – [VGT].

264 Ajit Nath Ray (1912-2010), Chief Justice of India from 1973 to 1977 – [VGT].

265 Francis Lord Charlton Hodson, Baron Hodson (1895-1984), British judge and President of the British Branch of the International Law Association – [WEB].

266 Judge John Edwards (19?-1987), Secretary General, later Honorary, of the International Law Association – [WEB].

addresses Lord Wilberforce and Ray turned not only to the official persons, but also to me. And then they asked me to speak.

16 May:

The session of the Executive Council proceeded in a spirit of amity. They referred to the fact that after dinner everyone said that the ILA needed a new point of departure, a stimulus, in order to enliven its work. I proposed to create the posts of two vice-chairman of the Council: one to be appointed from the socialist countries and the other from the developing countries. This would introduce new forces to the leadership of the Association and help development its activity in various areas of the world. Wilberforce evidenced interest in this proposal. I asked the members of the Council to think about it and to return to this proposal later.

I am in the London Embassy Hotel. Somewhat earlier (I had not been in London since 1968) I stayed in this hotel. But it was still an old hotel. I recall that there was no shower in my room. And now everything is new – a small room, but with all conveniences. Four star hotel, 15 pounds a night.

Haraszti and I, as was agreed yesterday, met at 13:00 in my room in the Hotel, We walked to an Italian restaurant nearby and dined well. Then we went to the National Gallery in Trafalgar Square. I had not been there for a long time. The richest collection of Italian renaissance paintings. We concentrated our attention on them. Haraszti knows the Gallery well and in general is well-schooled in painting. The fact that his wife is an art historian, of course, helped him.

19 May:

London-Amsterdam. KLM Plane: Yesterday I visited our Ambassador in London, N. M. Lunkov.[267] There were four persons from the Administrative Office of the Ministry of Foreign Affairs of the USSR and the Administration for Servicing the Diplomatic Corps. The Embassy is very crowded. The present building of the Embassy was leased until 1980. The English are not giving a plot for the construction of a new building and have dragged this out for fifteen years. The personnel of the Embassy were halved a couple of years ago, 110 persons having been expelled.

The evening yesterday was at the Butlers.[268] There were present: Schwarzenberger with his wife, Brownlie,[269] Higgins[270] with her husband,[271] who is a member of Parliament, and a young bearded man[272] (exile from Rhodesia) with his wife.

267 Nikolai Mitrofanovich Lunkov (b. 1919), Ambassador of the USSR in London from 1973 to 1980 – [WEB].

268 At the home of Professor W. E. Butler, 9 Lyndale Avenue, London NW2, and Darlene Mae Johnson Butler (1939-1989) – [WEB].

269 Sir Ian Brownlie (1932-2010), Chichele Professor of International Law, University of Oxford – [WEB].

270 Dame Rosalyn Higgins (b. 1937), then Professor of International Law at the London School of Economics and Political Science, University of London, and later Judge of the International Court of Justice from 1995 to 2009 and President of the Court from 2006 to 2009 – [WEB].

271 Terence Langley Higgins (b. 1928), Baron Higgins, KBE. British conservative politician – [WEB].

272 Reginald H. F. Austin (b. 1935), Senior Lecturer in International Law, University College London – [WEB].

20 May:

The Hague. Hotel Bali: Yesterday arrived at 12:00. Dropped into the Hotel and had lunch with the Ambassador, A. I. Romanov. He and Galina Vasilevna are very dear people. Next I met with Lachs; we discussed issues of the Academy.

Today in the evening I was at Morozovs. He reunited with his first wife after the death of Nina Nikolaevna. Thus he is twice married to the same woman. A rarity.

22 May:

Hotel Bali: Did exercises along the seashore. The morning was magnificent; I wanted to swim. Now I am in the restaurant, awaiting breakfast. The Curatorium at 09:30.

Yesterday evening Professor Morin[273] of Spain invited me to dinner. A very likeable person, former legal advisor to the Ministry of Foreign Affairs of the Republic, then an immigrant. Worked 26 years at the United Nations, and now (for three years) in his motherland in Barcelona. He is 70 years old, but one might assume 50. Intends to occupy himself with the publication of my book in Spain. Wants to deliver a course of lectures in the Academy.

23 May:

Hotel Bali: Took from the Library J. Spiropoulos, *Theorie générale de droit international* (1930) and recalled the author,[274] who sat beside me in the International Law Commission before departing for the International Court of Justice. What an intelligent and talented man. Small in stature, hunchbacked. He was not, as were many cripples, a pessimist, but a charming man. It seems that the last time I saw him was at The Hague in 1962, when I came to speak to the Court and he invited me and Koretskii for lunch.

I am sitting on a bench opposite that place where in 1975 there was an old expensive hotel, "Dome". Dupuy gave a lunch there. A superb restaurant, reminding one of the Eliseev Store in Moscow.[275] But the Hotel is no longer, and the site is surrounded by a fence. The same fate awaits evidently the Kurhaus Hotel in which the members of the International Court of Justice loved to stay. This Hotel has not operated for several years. Old hotels cannot withstand competition.

27 May:

Hotel Bali: Departure has been deferred for one day. One might fly on a KLM aircraft, but Aeroflot will never agree to this and did not agree this time. The Ambassador says that nothing is to be done. I work the whole time in the Library.

31 Aug:

Madrid. Hotel Conde Duque: International Law Association Conference. Flew in from Moscow to Paris on 28 August. Instead of flying directly to Paris, made a landing

273 Morin [not further identified].

274 Jean Spiropoulos (1896-1972), member of the International Court of Justice from 1958 to 1967 – [WEB].

275 A reference to the Eliseevskii Store founded on Tverskaia Street, in the center of Moscow, by Grigorii Eliseev in 1901 and noted for the vast range of products and its luxurious interior – [WEB].

in Kiev. In addition, a strike of Spanish air traffic controllers (a new phenomenon in Spain), as a result of which we departed from Paris at 22:30, two and a half hours late. Arrived in Madrid, no one meets me. I have no pesetas, only dollars. The taxi driver agreed to take me for five dollars (about 330 pesetas), which is twice as expensive as the meter.

They gave us nice rooms in the hotel. I had thought to arrive on time, take a bath, and sleep as though dead. Not easy to sleep. Movchan said in the morning that he too was weary and could not sleep for a long time.

Yesterday in the morning – Full Council. We terminated the existence of the Committee on Principles of Security and Cooperation. Before the Council, John Hazard approached me. Our opinions coincided, it was necessary to eliminate the Committee and think about the creation of a new Committee on some important general problem. In this spirit we also spoke at the Council. I personally had in view that it was necessary to get rid of Professor Radojković[276] as the rapporteur of the Committee. His reports were basically awful both in orientation and their scholarly level. Second half of the day we both with Movchan delivered prepared reports, and in the evening were at the mayor's reception.

Today at 12:00 I am presiding at the International Water Research Committee. Time to go. Movchan left to walk about the city with Lazarev[277] and Feldman.[278]

I conducted the session. All went well, but two hours is not enough. Moreover, usually at such conferences the schedule is such that two Committees work daily, from 09:30 to 13:00 and from 15:30 to 18:00. But in Madrid there is a siesta from 14:00 to 17:00. Therefore, the two Committees worked in parallel from 09:00 to 11:30 and from 12:00 to 14:00.

On Sunday together with our tourists we saw the city, and from 18:00 to 20:00 were at Corrida. The driver of the tourist bus, Pedro, helped much and gave explanations – a likeable and well-meaning man of forty years. Lazarev translated superbly. They killed six bulls, each every 20 minutes. The entire procedure was strictly regulated. It was interesting to see the noted Corrida. But, it seems, this entertainment did not disturb any of ours.

In the evening a reception at the Ministry of Foreign Affairs. The reception was for a narrow group: one per country, but more Englishmen. The publisher of a South Korean journal, Limb,[279] persuaded the Minister to be photographed with

276 Miloš Radojković (1902-1993), member of the Executive Council of the International Law Association from Yugoslavia; Professor of Public International Law, Belgrade University from 1933 to 1972; Dean of the Faculty of Law from 1956 to 1958 – [WEB].

277 Marklen Ivanovich Lazarev (1920-2008), Russian international lawyer specializing in territorial issues – [WEB].

278 David Isaakovich Feldman (1922-1994), sometime professor of international law at Kazan University – [WEB].

279 Thok-Kyu Limb (b. 1936), Secretary-General and President of the Korean Branch of the International Law Association; editor of journal *Diplomacy* – [WEB].

me. I do not know how enthusiastically he did this. In any event, he placed the wife of Professor Carillo[280] between us. The local correspondent took advantage of this and also made a snapshot.

1977

7 Jan:

Sheremetevo Airport: I am flying to Paris for the Curatorium. I did not book the Hotel Cayre this time since it has become rather expensive and the rooms are terribly gloomy.

Yesterday there was an extraordinary occurrence. Received a passport at the Ministry of Higher Education. The girl noted that the visa was formalized incorrectly – exit before 3 January 1977, and it should be 1978. Waited about until the end of the day.

Tunkin with Prof. Claude-Albert Colliard

7 Jan:

Hotel St. Germain: Paris is a city to visit, but not to live in. What carbon monoxide in the air on the streets. Nonetheless, people go out to stroll. To be sure, the carbon monoxide is high in the center of Moscow. I am saved by the fact that I live near a park and not in the center.

I. A. Paniushkin[281] met me, the son of A. S. Paniushkin.[282] We decided to glance at a small hotel near the Embassy. A small room at the top with a shower cost 107 francs, but in the Cayre one is speaking about 200 francs. And since the Ministry of Higher

280 Juan Antonio Carillo Salcedo (b. 1934), Professor of Private International Law, University of Seville – [VGT].

281 Igor Aleksandrovich Paniushkin (b. 1937), second secretary of USSR Embassy in France – [VGT].

282 Aleksandr Semenovich Paniushkin (1905-1974), Ambassador of the USSR in China from 1939 to 1944, in the United States from 1947 to 1952, and People's Republic of China from 1952 to 1953 – [VGT].

Education gave me not a kopeck, my resources are limited. Now it is time for lunch, which the new President of the Curatorium, Ago, arranged in honor of the departing Castberg.

9 Jan:

Le Louvre: Began as always with the Venus de Milo. What a beauty. Now before me three large paintings by Courbet.[283]

The session of the Curatorium was yesterday. The financial crisis was discussed for two and a half hours. It is surprising that it is difficult to interest the United Nations. Each year a resolution is adopted on expanding knowledge about international law, but the Academy does not exist in their minds.

Rang Lavigne the day before yesterday. She invited me for lunch, also having promised to invite Professor Colliard. She rang in the evening and said that he wants us to come to his home since his wife is not well and cannot leave.

10 Jan:

Hotel St. Germain: In half an hour Igor Paniushkin is coming to take me to the Roissy Airport. I am flying Air France, since our aircraft is full.

The lunch at Colliard's proceeded in a pleasant atmosphere. A misunderstanding was identified. Colliard sent me a telegram with an invitation to deliver a lecture. Therefore, my reply to his question about the lecture was incomprehensible to him because I did not receive the telegram. It was elicited from the conversation that it possibly was not sent since he gave it over the telephone and the girl did not understand, etc. It was agreed that I would give a lecture the following year. Virally with his wife was there. On another day he showed me their library. Professors have access to the stacks: special rooms of journals and United Nations materials. Not bad.

Yesterday I visited Bastid. Such meetings are very useful. Thierry[284] is one of the authors of *Droit international public* (1975), a grandson of the Rothchilds through the mother. According to her, Combacau[285] is the most able of the four authors; he is strong in theory. All the authors are young. This is noteworthy.

We spoke during the entire trip to the airport with Igor Paniushkin, who makes an excellent impression. We recalled common acquaintances among Chinese specialists.

New members of the Curatorium: Riphagen in place of Panhuys.[286] Mosler[287] was elected in May in place of Verdross, who retired. At the last session Waldock was elected in place of Fitzmaurice, and Hambro in place of Castberg. The Dutch member was not elected, but is appointed by the Government of Holland.

283 Gustave Courbet (1819-1877), French realist painter – [WEB].

284 Hubert Thierry (b. 1925), French international lawyer – [WEB].

285 Jean Combacau (b. 1942), Professor of International Law, University of Caen Basse-Normandie from 1973 to 1979; editor-in-chief, *Annuaire francais de droit international*; later Professor of International Law Paris II (Pantheon-Assas) – [WEB].

286 Haro Frederik van Panhuys (1916-1976), Dutch international lawyer – [WEB].

287 Hermann Mosler (1912-2001), German international lawyer – [WEB].

Yasseen now lives in Geneva. I thought that he was again appointed a representative attached to an international organization. It turns out that he left Iraq and sought asylum in Switzerland. The Swiss Government did not want to quarrel with the Government of Iraq and dragged out a reply. Then Ruegger helped him. Lachs says that his wife has oil interests and transferred large funds to Switzerland. His family moved to Switzerland earlier. He feels uncomfortable, but stayed in the Hilton – a very expensive Hotel. He intends, in his words, to occupy himself with children.

Lachs was very content that I proposed his candidacy for the general cours in 1979.

28 Oct:

Sheremetevo Airport: I am on my way to London to a session of the Administrative Council of the International Law Association. I am also delivering a lecture at London University. Yesterday was a difficult day, having learned only in the morning that it was necessary to prepare for departure. On the eve a session was held of the working group for the draft law on international treaties. They reviewed it in light of the Constitution. The draft was ready at the end of June, and I reported on it to the Commission of deputies. To be sure, new ideas emerged after four months. But I think that we shall rapidly complete the work. Reworking the draft law on citizenship is proceeding simultaneously.

London Embassy Hotel: No one met me, the first time in all these years. Although two telegrams were sent by me and by the Academy of Sciences. The room was not booked, and there were no rooms available. Left my things and went to the Embassy – it is nearby. There the Third Secretary, who works in the science section, said that he knew nothing about the telegrams. He says that he knows the hotel manager. We went to the hotel and actually succeeded in finding me a room.

Called Professor Butler in the evening, to whom I gave the telegram yesterday. Then called Professor Schwarzenberger, who sent me a letter to Moscow with an invitation to come to his place.

30 Oct:

London Embassy Hotel: Worked on the lecture in the morning. At 10:00, as agreed, Professor Butler arrived. We visited St Paul's Cathedral, a magnificent church. Services were underway. Then we went to the Temple Church. Selden[288] is buried there. Services also were in progress there: a superb children's choir. Walked along the river bank, took a boat to the Tower. I had never been there, nor had Butler. It was about 13:00. The Tower opened at 14:00, but the queue for tickets was already half a kilometer long. We decided not to stand and went to lunch in a restaurant. Then we strolled about the Tower and see new Ticket Offices opening. Butler is a spry chap, quickly purchased a

288 John Selden (1584-1654), the English jurist and polymath – [WEB].

ticket, and we saw the Tower. Now this is a museum, or, more accurately, several museums. The most interesting is the Museum of Crown Jewels: crowns, swords decorated with gold, scepters, and others. All this, to be sure, does not give an impression as to how the prisoners were kept there, especially Mary Stuart.[289]

Then I went by car outside the city (one hour trip) to Schwarzenberger. Georg showed his collection of early editions of Grotius,[290] Pufendorf,[291] and others.

31 Oct:

London Embassy Hotel: Just returned from Hyde Park – did exercises (50 minutes). Dismal weather, slight rainfall. Now I am shaving, take a shower, eat breakfast, and then a final touch upon my lecture today.

1 Nov:

London Embassy Hotel: Yesterday was a difficult day. Prepared the lecture in the morning. Next the Faculty of Laws, University College London. Lunch with Butler in the student refectory, but in the section for Staff. Nothing hot except coffee. Then administrative formalities – to another building rather far away, receive a cheque, and then to the bank. I received 270 pounds.

Tea before the lecture at 16:30. In 1962 a lecture was a more solemn occasion. A beadle in livery came in, declared that it was time to move into the hall and moved on ahead. Now there was no beadle. About 100 persons at the lecture; in 1962 – 200. The topic of the lecture: "The Contemporary Soviet Theory of International Law".[292] They listened attentively, the students took notes. The task which I put was to create interest in our conception of international law and to show that our modern theory is not Korovin, although I did not mention his name.

In the evening, dinner at the Butlers. Austin and his wife were there.

3 Nov:

London Airport: Butler told me in conversations between us that there had not been such a large audience at a Special University Lecture for a long time as there was at my lecture. He showed me one "marvel". In the building of University College London there is a cabinet in which the body of Bentham[293] is placed. This is not a statue, but a mummy. Because the head began to decay, they replaced it. Everything was done according to his will. He sits in a chair in hat and clothing. During solemn ceremonies, the cabinet is wheeled into the hall and the speakers begin: Mr. Bentham, Mr. President, etc.

289 Mary, Queen of Scots (1542-1587), confined in the Tower and executed for treason – [WEB].

290 Hugo Grotius (1583-1645), an influential writer on the law of war and peace – [WEB].

291 Samuel Freiherr von Pufendorf (1632-1694), jurist and historian – [WEB].

292 G. I. Tunkin, "The Contemporary Soviet Theory of International Law", *Current Legal Problems*, XXXI (1978), pp. 177-188.

293 Jeremy Bentham (1748-1832), political philosopher and jurist – [WEB].

Tunkin in the home of Professor W. E. Butler, London, 19 November 1978

28 Nov:

Budapest. Hotel Gellbert: Arrived in Budapest to receive an honorary doctorate of Budapest University. The degree will be conferred on 29 November. Haraszti met me. The Hotel Gellbert is superb, the very one in which I stayed in 1961, when the delegates to the Conference on Diplomatic Relations came to Budapest from Vienna at the invitation of Ustor[294] for a week-end. Sixteen years have elapsed. Ustor has retired – he was head of the legal section of the Ministry of Foreign Affairs. He invited me for tea on Thursday or Friday. I must ring him. At 15:30 Haraszti comes for me and we go to meet the Rector. They have allocated a car to me.

After the meeting with the Rector, I chatted with Haraszti. He has an attractive office, about 30 square meters, bookshelves to the ceiling. The entrance is through the secretary's office. A mass of literature in the office: bound sets of the *American Journal of International Law, Recueil des cours de droit international*, and others, and no special room.[295] One can work. Then Haraszti's wife arrived, an art historian, works in the Museum of Fine Arts.

I took with me proofs of my Hague lectures which I had received just before departure. Reading them takes much time, although there are not many corrections. I read ten pages in 45 minutes. 220 pages in all. I finish, and will send them at once upon arrival in Moscow.

294 Endre Ustor (1910-1998), Hungarian diplomat and legal adviser – [WEB].

295 In Soviet times certain foreign literature was stored in a special room, access to this literature not being authorized for everyone – [VGT].

Now strolled about for 20 minutes, cold. I think about running tomorrow, all fitted out. We shall see whether the morning is wiser than evening. Bought the Austrian *Die Presse* for 26 November and *Le Figaro* for 24 November.

1 Dec:
Hotel Gellbert: Yesterday I gave a lecture to the students of the University of which I am now an honorary doctor. Gave it in Russian. Veronika Bajaki interpreted,[296] a specialist in State law. She recently defended a doctoral dissertation at the Institute of State and Law of the USSR Academy of Sciences. Delivered without any notes; this is easy with an interpreter. The topic: The Modern Soviet Theory of International Law (not in persons, but in problems). Then conversed in detail with members of the chair of international law.

2 Dec:
Budapest-Moscow Train: The diploma of doctor *honoris causa* they awarded to an Italian – a specialist in ancient Greek philology and translator of Hungarian poetry into Italian, Professor Albini.[297] The ceremony was as follows: Albini and I processed from the office of the Rector to the hall. Then the Rector and Deans of all three faculties of the University: law, philosophy, and natural sciences. Behind them, heralds with maces. Then the Rector opened the session, giving the floor to the Dean of the Faculty of Philosophy. He pronounced an Elegy, which ended with the words: for this I award X the degree of doctor *honoris causa* with all the rights, etc. Then the Dean of the Faculty of Law gave a similar speech with respect to me. Next the floor was given to Albini, who briefly gave thanks, speaking Hungarian. I gave an address for about 20 minutes (without translation) on the subject "The Great October Socialist Revolution and International Law". After this the Rector gave a dinner at the Hotel Intercontinental. There were the deans, the two new doctors, and three or four other persons. The Rector is Professor Adam,[298] a specialist in high neural activity, completed post-graduate studies in Leningrad and speaks Russian fluently.

Yesterday I gave a report at the Institute of State and Law of the Hungarian Academy of Sciences at the invitation of Academician Szabo.[299] Topic: "What Theoretical Problems Have Been Solved and on What Theoretical Problems Soviet International Lawyers are Working". Took 45 minutes with translation, then questions for 30 minutes.

296 Veronika Bajaki (19?-), Hungarian specialist on State law and author of works on citizenship – [VGT].
297 Umberto Albini (1924-2011), Greek philologist and classicist – [WEB].
298 György Adám (b. 1922), Professor of Physiology and Psychophysiology and Rector, Eötvös Lorand University, Budapest, from 1972 to 1978 – [VGT].
299 Imre Szabó (1912-1991), Hungarian legal theorist and comparative lawyer – [WEB].

1978

11 March:

Geneva. Hotel Mon Repos: After breakfast with Valticos, which was interesting, I went to the Library in the Palais des Nations. Met the Bulgarian Dimitrov,[300] who works there, and an old acquaintance, Kasme.[301] Took one book home.

Valticos said that he will soon be 60 years old, the age of retirement, but the Director-General asked him to remain. The Director-General may keep him each time for one year, until age 65. Then it is over.

Freymond[302] retired from the post of Director of the Institut Universitaire, Valticos said, for "reasons not understood". In his stead is the Professor of the University for international law, Dominicé.[303] I do not remember him.

Ténékidès left the post of Director of the School of Political Sciences in Greece. Siotis[304] is applying for his place, not wishing at the same time to leave his post in Geneva. But there are local applicants, and they view Siotis as a foreigner (he told me during a meeting in Moscow in June 1977 that he has lived for 27 years in Geneva).

Batiffol was elected to the Academy.[305] Bastid was elected five years ago.

18 March:

International Labor Organization: Today I invited to lunch a new member from India – member of the Supreme Court of India, Bhagwati.[306] Makes an impression as a progressive and intelligent man. Was in the USSR at the invitation of the Supreme Court, in the German Democratic Republic, and in Czechoslovakia.

Yesterday in the Committee Valticos proposed two working groups: Covenants and Forced Labor. The group on Covenants remains in its former membership (from the socialist countries, Gubinski), and for the Forced Labor group he proposed Ademola[307] as Chairman, Beitzke[308] and Vilfan (Yugoslavia). After the session, I approached Valticos and said that one must not work in this way in international organizations; it is essential to consult before placing on a Committee. I said directly that this question is

---

300 Dimitrov [not further identified].

301 Badr Kasme, compiler of major bibliography on international law – [WEB].

302 Jacques Freymond (1911-1998), Director, Institute of International Relations and Development Studies in Geneva and member, International Red Cross Committee from 1959 to 1971 – [WEB].

303 Christian Dominicé (b. 1931), Swiss international lawyer and member, Institute of International Relations and Development Studies in Geneva – [WEB].

304 Jean Siotis (1931-1994), Professor of International Law, Graduate Institute of International Studies, Geneva from 1967 to 1981; Honorary Professor from 1982 – [WEB].

305 Henri Batiffol (1905-1989), French international lawyer elected to the Academie des sciences morales et politiques – [VGT].

306 Prafullachandra Natwarlal Bhagwati (b. 1921), Chief Justice of the Supreme Court of India from 1985 to 1986 – [WEB].

307 Adetokunbo Ademola (1906-1993), Chief Justice of Nigeria from 1958 to 1972 – [VGT].

308 Günther Beitzke (1909-2004), Professor of International Private Law, University of Bonn; ILO expert – [VGT].

used against the socialist countries, and Vilfan could not be considered a representative of the socialist countries. He immediately agreed with this. He said that Vilfan previously took part in an analogous group and therefore it was not appropriate to remove him. He proposed that I also become a member of his group, and that I need not give a reply at once.

I succeeded in improving the formulation in connection with the possible creation of parallel trade unions with respect to the German Democratic Republic and Mongolia (Direct Requests).

24 March:
Hotel Mon Repos: After breakfast, I went into the city. Passed by the Hotel Metropol and the English Garden. I recalled the I Conference on the Law of the Sea. Our delegation consisted of 25 persons. We often went to the English Garden and there discussed matters which arose in the course of the Conference. The police followed us, evidently afraid of "subversive activity". In the delegation was S. B. Krylov, who died in the autumn of that same year, and A. D. Keilin. In addition, Nikolaev,[309] Zhudro, Molodtsov, and Gusev (oceanographer).[310]

The Hotel Metropol is now closed. 29 years ago it barely hung by a thread, in significant measure thanks to the fact that Soviet delegations stayed there.

1 May:
Sheremetevo Airport: It was convenient to fly on 1 May, although the Curatorium is only on 6 May. Previously there was a flight on Thursday, and this was more convenient. Now on Monday and Saturday. And we are permitted to fly only on Soviet aircraft. On the whole for me it is all the same, as I shall work in the Library.

1 May:
The Hague. Hotel Bali: Consul Aleksandr Aleksandrovich Abramov[311] met me, son of the late ambassador, Aleksandr N. Abramov.[312] In the hotel they gave me the key to Room 31, which I usually occupy. We enter, see someone's belongings there, and nothing has been cleaned. I go to the Reception. They say 10 minutes and all will be ready. 20 minutes pass by, there is no one. Then I place my things in the room, warn Reception, and went with Abramov to the Embassy, since the Ambassador had invited me to lunch. The Trade Representative and his wife, two heads of some of our representations

309 Anatolii Nikolaevich Nikolaev (1915-2004), author of book on the territorial sea who served in Treaty Law Department, USSR Ministry of Foreign Affairs, and Ambassador in Thailand and Sudan – [WEB].

310 Aleksandr Mikhailovich Gusev (1912-1994), oceanographer, famous Soviet alpinist – [VGT].

311 Aleksandr Aleksandrovich Abramov (b. 1937), Head of USSR Consulate in The Hague from 1975 to 1979; Consul in Antwerp from 1989 to 1993 – [VGT].

312 Aleksandr Nikitich Abramov (1905-1973), Ambassador of the USSR to Finland from 1946 to 1948; Sweden from 1949 to 1950; Israel from 1953 to 1958; Cambodia and Laos from 1959 to 1962, Algeria from 1962 to 1964, and Dahomey from 1966 to 1968 – [VGT].

here in Holland with wives, the military attaché with his wife, Judge P. D. Morozov with his wife, and Shokholov's[313] daughter, Svetlana Mikhailovna Sholokhova,[314] were at lunch. I sat down next to her, but did not know who she was by specialty. The ambassador told us. She behaved quietly and modestly.

I arrived at the Hotel at 17:00. Rested and went to the seashore, strolled for one and a half hours. Something made me melancholy. I think that if you work in the Court, you will die of boredom.

3 May:

Hotel Bali: Decided that one must take greater advantage of the sea for purposes of health. I exercise on the piers and about the sea. Yesterday evening I read for two hours on the pier. Naturally I felt like a white crow, for no one reads on the seashore. I read F. S. Northedge, *The International Political System* (1976), a professor at London University.[315] Very little of interest but his criticism of Morgenthau,[316] which was weak. I did not like it on the whole. 1 May was the Queen's Day, 4 May also a holiday, the Library in all being open three days.

5 May:

Hotel Bali: Borrowed six books in the Library and looked them over. They are making me copies of several pages. To economize time, I have agreed with the Librarian, to whom I brought the *Soviet Yearbook of International Law* and a bibliography, that the library personnel will make Xeroxes for me of the pages which I indicate.

In the evening I dined at Lachs. There were no outsiders. They are worried about who will be on the Court from us. Morozov's term is expiring. Elections in the autumn. They wish that it would be me.

7 May:

Hotel Bali: Yesterday the session of the Curatorium. All went well, but G. Morozov was moved to 1980, so next year there will be no one from us. This is a result of the fact that I missed two sessions of the Curatorium. Of course, one cannot work like this.

Yesterday evening dinner at the Waldocks. Morozov and Tarazi (Syria)[317] were there with wives, and Ago.

Today one must rest. Morozov suggested we go to the park of flowers. This is interesting. I was there 20 years ago. In general the week was like a month, looked at so many books and so many meetings.

---

313 Mikhail Aleksandrovich Sholokhov (1905-1984), noted writer and Nobel laureate in literature – [VGT].

314 Svetlana Mikhailovna Sholokhova (b. 1926), journalist and Learned Secretary, M. A. Sholokhov Museum – [VGT].

315 Frederick Samuel Northedge (1915-1985), professor of international relations at the London School of Economics and Political Science – [WEB].

316 Hans Morgenthau (1904-1980), leading theorist of international relations and law – [WEB].

317 Salah El Dine Tarazi (1917-1980), member of the International Court of Justice from 1976 to 1980 – [WEB].

22 May:

Prague. Hotel of the University: The Deputy Head of the Chair of International Law of Charles University, Potočný,[318] and the Secretary of the Chair, Jarka,[319] met me at the Prague Airport. They accommodated me in a hotel for guests of the Rector. A flowering chestnut outside my two windows. It reminded me of my cottage in North Korea. Enormous chestnuts grew alongside, In the autumn the chestnuts fell on a large open balcony on the second floor. The door of my small room opened out on this balcony. I recall how on a hot, cloudy Sunday in July 1950 I was working on my doctoral dissertation. Suddenly a bomb exploded not far away, dropped by an American aircraft. My papers flew off the desk since the door to the balcony was open. The Americans dropped bombs and shelled everywhere, without discrimination. In the morning one is awakened by the chatter of machine guns, quickly jumps up, and stands behind the walls – the house was brick.

24 May:

Hotel of the University: Yesterday Potočný came at 10:00, as agreed, and we went to a meeting with Klusak[320] at the Ministry of Culture. Along the way we saw the Charles Bridge. Were with Klusak, my former post-graduate student, until 12:00. Chatted about everything. He has aged considerably. The Minister gave us carte-blanche in the choice of concerts. In the evening we were at one of the "Prague Spring" concerts. The Czech Philharmonic Orchestra performed the overture to a Weber[321] opera, "The Magic Marksman".

In the afternoon at 16:00 a meeting at the Chair. Potočný put forward two proposals:

1. To write a collective work – a thematic collection of articles on urgent problems of international public and international private law. To be published in Czechoslovakia: articles in the Russian language with an abridged translation into Czech and articles in Czech with an abridged translation into Russian. I approved the idea, saying that it is worth thinking about especially with regard to the problems;
2. To organize a joint symposium with regard to the syllabus of public international law – bilateral, but invite those who wish from other socialist countries.

318 Miroslav Potočný (1925-2001), official at the Czechoslovak Ministry of Foreign Affairs from 1962 to 1967; Head of the Chair of International Law of Charles University from 1990 to 1997 – [WEB].

319 Jarka [not further identified].

320 Milan Klusak (1923-1992), Czech international lawyer and diplomat, arrested by Gestapo in 1942 for participation in the Resistance, released in 1945. Head of CSSR Mission to the United Nations from 1960 to 1961 and from 1965 to 1968. President Svoboda's son-in-law. Minister of Culture in Czechoslovakia from 1973 to 1988 – [WEB].

321 Carl Maria von Weber (1786-1826), German composer – [WEB].

I expressed a positive attitude towards this idea. We have in view to hold a symposium in Moscow during the first half of 1979.

25 May:

Bratislava: In the morning I went with Potočný by train to Bratislava. An old friend, Ján Tomko,[322] met us, a professor and head of the Chair of International Law. The day was overloaded.

A detailed meeting with members of the Chair. We discussed issues of teaching, syllabus, and a number of problems of international law, especially socialist international law. Supper in the evening at the Koliba which the Minister of Trade of Slovakia gave, being, as I understood, a friend of Tomko. Koliba (literally, an enclosure for sheep) is a restaurant stylized like an old Slovak izba. A white Slovak wine, not bad. I drank, of course, symbolically; all the others ate a fair amount.

31 May:

Hotel of the University: Just returned from lunch with the Deputy Minister of Foreign Affairs, Spočil.[323] He completed our Faculty in 1954. Then we met with him "on different meridians".

Yesterday was a difficult one. Prepared a report in the morning until 11:00. At 13:00 a reception with Rector Česhka.[324] He presented me with the medal of Charles University. And immediately after this, at 15:00 a report to the meeting of the Czech Association of International Law. Česhka presided. The topic of the Report: Basic Trends in the Soviet Science of International Law.

Yesterday L. I. Brezhnev arrived here for a visit. Of course, this visit is regarded as a major event.

Now I must consider what I will say tomorrow at the Learned Council of the Faculty of Law. First I thought of my topic being "The Socialist Commonwealth and International Law", but understood from conversations that they are more interested in problems of relations within the socialist commonwealth. This is especially important for them both on the level of the struggle against bourgeois ideology and the practical political level.

2 June:

Prague-Moscow Airplane: Yesterday gave a report at the session of the Learned Council of the Faculty of Law. 40 minutes, without a summary. 30 persons were present. At the session of the Council, the Dean of the Faculty, Delong,[325] awarded me the medal of the Law Faculty. It happened that I was the very first to receive it.

---

322 Ján Tomko (1922-1991), one of the founders and Head of the Chair of International Law at Comenius University in Bratislava from 1957 to 1981; Dean of the Faculty of Law, Comenius University, from 1959 to 1961 – [WEB].

323 Spočil, Deputy Minister of Foreign Affairs of the CSSR – [VGT].

324 Zdenek Česhka (b. 1929), Dean of the Faculty of Law, Charles University, from 1969 to 1973; Rector of Charles University from 1976 to 1990 – [VGT].

325 Vladimir Delong (b. 1925), Dean of the Faculty of Law, Charles University, from 1973 to 1980 – [VGT].

17 Nov:

Sheremetevo Airport: I am flying to London. Flight at 11:50. Never have I been so unready to depart. Only today in the morning did I receive the English visa and went with Volodya to the Consular Administration of the Ministry of Foreign Affairs and received the passport at 09:15. To the airport at once. I should have flown yesterday, but the ticket is for today.

Yesterday Ira[326] invited me to supper. I wanted to go home, but Alyesha asked to sup together, so I agreed. As always, he sat by my side and ate well. He had just come from the children's kindergarten. They say he enjoys it there.

No one met me. This is the second time, and especially in London. Arrived at the Hotel at 14:30. The Conference in London is organized by the International Law Association on State Immunity. The Conference began at 14:30, so it was already late to go there. Rang Butler.

18 Nov:

London Embassy Hotel: Recently returned after a rather stormy session. I opened my Braun in the morning and saw that there was no cord there. Went to the session unshaven. Never thought it would be so unacceptable to be unshaven. After the session, went to a shop and purchased a razor.

At the session of the Executive Council the sharpest discussion revolved around the issue of creating a Committee for the problem "Legal Aspects of the New International Economic Order". This question was put by the Head of the Legal Section of the Ministry of Foreign Affairs of Yugoslavia, Bulajic.[327] He substantiated very well the need to create the Committee. Representatives from Bangladesh[328] and India,[329] Haraszti, and I supported him. The Westerners: O'Connell,[330] Vallat, Lalive (Switzerland),[331] Jaenicke (Federal Republic of Germany),[332] Olmstead (United States) began to object: it was not clear what this Committee would be concerned with, the topic was harmless. I spoke twice. A decision was adopted to create a Study Group under the chairmanship of Chairman Wilberforce. I joined this group.

326 Daughter-in-law of G. I. Tunkin and wife of V. G. Tunkin – [VGT].

327 Milan Bulajic (1928-2009), Yugoslav diplomat from 1949 to 1987; First Secretary of the Yugoslav Embassy in the United States; Legal Advisor, Federal Secretariat for Foreign Affairs; member of Executive Council of the International Law Association from Yugoslavia – [WEB].

328 Judge Syed Mahmud Hossain (1916-1982), Chief Justice of Bangladesh, 1975-1978; member of Executive Council, International Law Association from Bangladesh – [WEB].

329 Maharaj Sri Nagendra Singh (1914-1988), member of the International Law Commission from 1967 to 1972; member of the International Court of Justice from 1973 to 1988 (President from 1985 to 1988) – [WEB].

330 Daniel Patrick O'Connell (1924-1979), Chichele Professor of International Law at Oxford University – [WEB].

331 Pierre A. Lalive (b. 1923), professor at the Institut des hautes études internationals – [WEB].

332 Günther Jaenicke (1913-2008), Professor of International Law at the University of Frankfurt in Germany – [WEB].

Spoke with Wilberforce during the break about my suggestion for two additional chairmen of the Council. He began to avoid taking sides, said that it was necessary to hold a Conference in one of the socialist countries, and then … I said one should act to the contrary. Many have the impression that the International Law Association is a British or Anglo-American organization. I asked that he think about it. Also spoke with Olmstead. He said that perhaps one should have regional vice-presidents. I said that might be so. In a word, the matter was again underway. If the political situation improves, the proposal might go forward.

20 Nov:
London Embassy Hotel: Yesterday in the second half of the day was with Butler at the Museum of London and the British Museum. The Museum of London is devoted to the history of London. Monumental State Coach of the Mayor of London. Beautiful coarse fabric and gold. It is still used on the day of the entry of the new Mayor into office. The Mayor is selected for a year without the right to be re-elected.

Then we went to the Hotel, took a gift from Alyesha for Bradley.[333] Bradley is very affectionate with me, virtually did not move away from me. Taught me how to use a little car which he sent as a gift to Alyesha.

In the morning I was with the Ambassador, N. M. Lunkov. Regrets that the English behave so badly, use any occasion for anti-Soviet propaganda.

21 Nov:
London Embassy Hotel: Conducted a seminar this morning for the students and post-graduates of Professor Butler. The questions put to me concerned principally the following topics: (1) How to explain the existence of general international law from the standpoint of Marxist theory? (2) Socialist international law. (3) The Brezhnev Doctrine.

Conducting this seminar was somewhat tiring for me, but interesting. My exposition of the Soviet theory of international law the majority wrote down.

1979

6 Jan:
Sheremetevo Airport: So I am flying to Paris for a session of the Curatorium. It begins at 09:30 and I am late. Wanted to depart on Thursday – there was no French visa, and on Friday the same. Received the visa only on Saturday afternoon. Wanted to depart on Saturday on the 18:20 Air France flight, but Aeroflot did not permit.

Yesterday morning, that is, on Saturday, rang Colliard, asked to tell Dupuy about my situation and request him to take measures. In all likelihood, this helped, and yesterday

333 Bradley Newman Butler (b. 1973), the youngest son of Professor W. E. Butler – [VGT].

in the middle of the day there was a visa. Evidently there is some "exacerbation" on the part of the French. When I was in India from 20 to 28 December and asked for a visa at the French Embassy, they required me to indicate the address of the inviting organization. This took several days. Earlier this was never requested.

On 10 January I have a lecture at the University of Paris I, with Colliard – "Théorie soviétique des sources du droit international".

7 Jan:

Hotel de Suede: Went from the airport to Hotel Saint-Germain, where I had booked a room. An elderly severe woman says that the room was booked for 5 January and now there is nothing and she does not foresee one become available. I asked permission to leave a suitcase and on to the session. I enter the room where the Curatorium is in session (173 Boulevard Saint-Germain), and they greet me with loud applause. Evidently, Dupuy informed them about the visa difficulties. Yasseen told me later than he had said if I did not arrive because of the visa, he would propose not to hold Curatorium sessions in France. I arrived at the session at 11:45. I missed primarily the question concerning finances.

During the lunch break I go to the Hotel Saint-Germain. A young, likeable woman says that she rang the Hotel de Suede. I might stay there and tomorrow, if I wish, may return to them. I carried the suitcase to Hotel de Suede – not far away – and went to the second session.

7 Jan:

Le Louvre: I am at the Louvre practically each time that I come to Paris. I go there as a believer attends church. When I go to the Louvre, I first proceed to the Venus de Milo. Before me is Delacroix, "La mort de Sardanapal". A spectacular thing.

David – Napoleon's singer. The coronation of Napoleon by Pope Pius VII in Notre Dame. Napoleon took the crown from the Pope and holds it in his hands, having turned to face the public.

La Jaconde has been moved to a large hall. Easier to see it there. In the gallery where it was previously the place was too narrow. Always a crowd about it. Previously one always met Soviet tourists here. Now there are none. Evidently, with a view to economizing the hard currency for tourism has been reduced.

8 Jan:

Hotel Saint-Germain: Was at lunch at the home of Virally. Excellent conversation. I asked about the book by Professor Merle, *Sociologie des relations international.*[334] He said that the book is solid, but relies too much on the Americans. He seeks a person who knows the Russian language. I said that it was desirable to choose a young person.

334 Marcel Merle (1923-2003), French sociologist and political scientist, Institute of Political Studies, University of Paris I – [WEB].

He replied that he seeks a young jurist. Asked me to assist in organizing the sending of literature.

His apartment is in a new modern house. According to our concepts, a magnificent one. Dining room and living room together. The study is two times larger than mine. Two of them live there. The son is an economist who works in a bank. Married, with children. The daughter is a jurist, avocat, married.

Virally knows a lot about arbitration and court cases, and evidently has become weary of them. But these cases give a good income in comparison with professorial activity.

Sat to work on my lecture before bed, but cannot do more. Sleepy. Before nodding off I read *Le Monde*. Most remarkable news – the capture of Phnom Penh by the Patriotic Front of Cambodia. The sanguinary pro-Chinese Government of Pol Pot[335] fled and it is unknown where they are. The newspapers are forced to admit that the capture of the capital was not by Vietnamese forces, but by rebels. Sihanouk[336] announced this. Supposedly flew to Peking from the outskirts of Phnom Penh. Sihanouk declared that he was a prisoner for three years, then he condemns the violations of human rights by the Government of Pol Pot, but considers it to be the legal government and will fight against the aggression of Vietnam.

11 Jan:

Charles de Gaulle Airport: Igor Paniushkin came for me at the Hotel at 09:00. On the road to the airport he showed me the new building of the Embassy, enormous and well done.

Yesterday I was at lunch with Colliard, Lavigne and Carreau[337] (*Droit international economique*) were there, and others. During the stay in France I had the idea of organizing Soviet-French seminars on international law. I expressed it to Colliard. He accepted it with enthusiasm and will speak with Dupuy. He thinks that on their side three universities might take part: Paris I, Paris II, and the University of Nice. In the afternoon I delivered a lecture for his post-graduates (20 persons) – "La Théorie soviétique de droit international". Only a few questions.

On 9 January I dined with Roland Weyl.[338] He as before is lively, says a lot, and is an interesting person. We discussed the general orientation of my article for the *Revue de droit contemporaine*, which he edits.

In the evening on Tuesday I dined with the Lavignes. The French, as Marie Lavigne told me, usually finish dinner parties about 01:00 hours. But I both yesterday and the day before, as the first guest, departed at 23:30 and 23:45.

335 Saloth Sar (1925-1998), known as Pol Pot, leader of Khmer Rouge in Cambodia – [WEB].

336 Norodom Sihanouk (b. 1922), King of Cambodia – [WEB].

337 Dominique Carreau (b. 1939), French specialist on international economic law; Dean of Law Faculty, Paris X from 1972 to 1975; Head, International Law Department, Paris I from 1982 to 1989 – [WEB].

338 Roland Weyl (b. 1919), French legal practitioner, Dean of the Paris Bar; editor, *Review of Contemporary Law* from 1954 to 1991; First Vice-President of the International Association of Democratic Lawyers – [VGT].

Tunkin with Judge Shigeru Oda, Second Hammer Conference, August 1979

11 Jan:
Paris-Moscow Airplane: Three business trips in two months. London, Delhi, Paris. I want to set and work. Have to finish an article concerning the Law on citizenship for the journal Советское государство и право [Soviet State and Law], write on the same subject for Международная жизнь [International Affairs] and for the Revue of the International Association of Democratic Lawyers; hold the annual meeting of the Soviet Association of International Law. Then to the sanatorium.

14 March:
Hotel Mon Repos: Arrived with Itta in Geneva. I have the Committee for the International Labor Organization conventions. Several persons met us, headed by D. N. Kolesnik,[339] who for several months has been the first deputy of the permanent representative, Z. V. Mironova.[340] On 11 March studied the draft report the entire day and on 12 March the working group on forced labor began work. The Secretariat

339 Dmitrii Nikolaevich Kolesnik (b. 1924), international lawyer and Permanent Representative of the USSR attached to the Division of the United Nations and other international organizations in Geneva from 1983 to 1986 – [VGT].

340 Zoya Vasilevna Mironova (1912-1991), Permanent Representative of the USSR attached to the Division of the United Nations and other international organizations in Geneva from 1966 to 1983 – [VGT].

thrust a mass of comments with regard to the socialist countries. The trend is the same: the Secretariat works for the West and against the socialist countries. In Moscow we have no one at present who is occupied with this, and I have no materials for a counter-offensive.

But something has been achieved: (1) the question of the distribution of students, which was mentioned three times, has been practically removed; (2) footnotes to countries will be divided into two parts: (a) States which have ratified; and (b) States which have not ratified; (3) achieved, not without difficulty, that the report will indicate the opinion not only of the majority, but also the minority on disputed issues. This is a very important step forward.

31 March:
Geneva-Moscow Airplane: Completed our three-week stay in Geneva and work in this difficult Committee. At the fifth session of the Committee it was easier, as one knows better what and how. This time did not occupy myself with any scholarly matters, there was no time. My general cours in the Hague Academy has appeared, finally. Received it before departure for Moscow.

Tunkin visits Judge and Mrs. Manfred Lachs, The Hague, May 1979

1980

1 Feb:
Sheremetevo Airport: Am flying to Luxembourg, from there by train to Brussels for a Conference of the International Association of Democratic Lawyers on the question of disarmament in Europe. Members of our delegation: Spokov (Union of Soviet Friendship Societies),[341] Blishchenko, Bogdanov, and myself.

341 Spokov [not further identified].

Alyosha is seven years old today. The birthday will be noted in class. Volodya transported pastries and tangerines there. I have not seen Alyosha for three weeks. I miss him.

3 Feb:
Brussels. Colloquium – Association of Democratic Lawyers: The discussion continues. I spoke twice yesterday after the French Admiral, Sanguinetti,[342] who gave a very interesting address. Soon the Colloquium will end. The Resolution on which the editorial committee worked – MacBride,[343] Salmon,[344] Pavlič (Yugoslavia),[345] Stuby (International Association of Democratic Lawyers),[346] and myself – is almost ready. Worked yesterday from 19:00 to 20:00 and today from 08:30 to 09:30.

3 Feb:
Brussels. Hotel Bedford: The Conference or Colloquium has ended. We had breakfast together in our Hotel, where the food of the delegates was organized at the expense of the International Association of Democratic Lawyers. MacBride offered to meet with our delegation after breakfast. He said that as a friend of the Soviet Union he wanted to say three things:

1. Afghanistan. He does not know whether the introduction of forces was necessary, but if needed, that it would have been possible to do this more skillfully. But this fact was a strong blow against the prestige of the USSR, especially in the developing countries, as the break-down of votes testified in the United Nations General Assembly (104 for);
2. The Sakharov[347] case (exile in the City of Gorkii). You committed a huge mistake. Sakharov helped us. When they spoke about the persecution of dissidents, we replied, look at Sakharov. He even holds press conferences with foreign journalists;
3. Olympic Games. The danger of disruption or detriment through absence is serious. What should be done he does not know, but the chairman of the Olympic Committee is his friend and he, MacBride, is ready to do everything to help us. Perhaps the Soviet Union might declare an amnesty with respect to dissidents, which would ease the situation.

342 Antoine Sanguinetti (1917-2004), joined the French Liberation Army in Africa in 1942, Vice-Admiral from 1974, protested placement of American Pershing and Sovie SS-20 missiles in Europe – [VGT].

343 Sean MacBride (1904-1988), Nobel laureate of the Peace Prize (1974) and Secretary General of the International Commission of Jurists from 1963 to 1970 – [WEB].

344 Professor Jean J. A. Salmon (b. 1931), Free University of Brussels – [WEB].

345 Breda Pavlič (b. 1946), sociologist from Slovenia and long-serving international civil servant in UNESCO – [VGT].

346 Gerhard Stuby (b. 1934), Professor of Law, Bremen University from 1971 to 2000 and in 1980 Secretary-General of the International Association of Democratic Lawyers – [VGT].

347 Andrei Dmitrievich Sakharov (1921-1989), noted Soviet physicist and dissident, Nobel laureate – [WEB].

We thanked him for his candor. Then I asked where he was headed now (he left after breakfast). He said to Monaco to open some Conference. To my next question, whether he was going to Iran, MacBride said that it still was not clear. Waldheim[348] preferred that the international tribunal consist of the representatives of Governments. The Iranians did not agree with this and requested that he be the head of the tribunal consisting of independent people, among which he named also me.

5 Feb:

Hotel Bedford: Yesterday was a heavy day. From 10:00 to 12:00 an interview with the correspondent of the journal *Evenements*. They say this is a new journal claiming great influence. Disarmament, Afghanistan. From 16:00 to 18:00 a conversation with the diplomatic personnel of the Embassy: Colloquium, Afghanistan, China. Conversation with the Ambassador from 18:00 to 19:30, and then dinner. From 20:00 to 22:30 a talk at the Society of Belgian-Soviet Friendship: Afghanistan, Sakharov. So many questions that we could have gone on to midnight. Of course, I spoke the most.

Today delivered a lecture at Louvain University on the topic "The Soviet Doctrine of International Law". I was prepared to speak on "International Law and the Policy of States". When I asked Professor Hans van Houtte[349] which topic interested his students, he replied that he is conducting a seminar on my Hague lectures "International Law in the International System". I already had given lectures on this topic at the London, Paris, and Cambridge universities and therefore began to lecture extemporaneously. Tomorrow a lecture on the same topic at Brussels University with Professor Salmon.

I asked in what language I should lecture, and to my surprise received the reply: better in English. Flemish nationalism. They said that English is the first among foreign languages which they speak. Two years ago the Louvain University, consisting of French and Flemish divisions, was divided into two which territorially are situated in different places. Tomorrow at the French division, of course, I must lecture in French.

6 Feb:

Hotel Bedford: Just returned from a meal with P. De Visscher. An intimate lunch: he, wife, and I. The conversation was very pleasant. He is in a good mood and understands that one must struggle for détente. It seems that Žourek died in Geneva. He was not at the session of the Institute of International Law in Athens and died soon after the session. When I told him that I was surprised that A. P. Movchan again did not get through, he told me frankly that this in significant measure was because I was not at the session. One has to make certain efforts, and my extended absence itself was regarded as the lack of interest in the part of the Soviet side towards the Institute.

348 Kurt Josef Waldheim (1918-2007), fourth Secretary-General of the United Nations. The tribunal at Iran's request would have determined who was the aggressor in the 1980 Iran-Iraq conflict – [WEB].

349 Hans van Houtte (b. 1947), Dutch specialist in private international law – [WEB].

Today I delivered a lecture at Brussels University on the Soviet doctrine of international law, of course, in the French language. There were many questions, then lunch with the professors.

7 Feb:

Hotel Bedford: Today there was a meeting at Brussels University – questions and answers on the topic "Détente". I made a brief address – Détente. Questions: why is the Soviet Union arming itself, Afghanistan, Sakharov, status of Jews. Many questions were malicious, and part of the audience was hostile and that part was the most active. One might form the impression that the entire audience was hostile. But now I have come to a different conclusion. Professor Salmon presided. And when he thanked those present and us, he wisely said that détente begins when different views are heard, and the hall applauded in a very friendly manner.

It is already late and time to sleep. Watched "For Whom the Bell Tolls" on television.

9 Feb:

Hotel Bedford: Yesterday a second meeting with Ambassador S. K. Romanovskii.[350] He gives the impression of being a thoughtful person. Behaves simply, quietly.

A press conference in the morning with representatives of two Spanish newspapers, *El Pais* (Madrid) and a Catholic newspaper in Barcelona on the forthcoming meeting in Madrid. To be sure, I stressed that the main purpose is to rescue détente. Noted the special role of European States.

9 March:

Geneva. Hotel Mon Repos: In Geneva, the Committee on ILO conventions. Came alone. Igor Khokhlov[351] met me. Did not tell Kolesnik and I did not send a telegram. In the hotel they provided a suite – two rooms on Rue de Lausanne.

21 March:

Botanical Garden: Sat for the first time on this bench in 1957, when I was for the first time at the session of the International Law Commission. It was at the end of April. I went by train and slept badly. Came after the trip to this garden, sat, dozed. I slept badly then in general.

Today there were two sessions. An interesting event occurred yesterday. The Report on Migrant Workers was discussed. When I looked it over, I noted nothing special. At the session, looking over the headings once again, I see "Measures against Exploitation". Asked for the floor and said the following: "I am known among my colleagues

350 Sergei Konstantinovich Romanovskii (1923-2003), Ambassador of the USSR to Belgium from 1975 to 1984 – [VGT].

351 Igor Aleksandrovich Khokhlov (b. 1946), Diplomatic Academy of the USSR Ministry of Foreign Affairs; attached to the International Labour Organization from 1976 to 1980 – [VGT].

as a proponent of peaceful coexistence, and it seems to be my mission to raise this problem whenever appropriate. Peaceful coexistence means that we should not introduce into International Law, into international conventions, ideological problems. The term "exploitation" used in this Report reflects an ideological problem. Indeed, according to Marxist-Leninist theory, capital society is based on the exploitation of the working classes by those who own the property. Of course, many in the capitalist world would not agree with that. Let us choose some neutral wording, which would not conflict with either of the two ideologies".

Valticos said that the Convention speaks about "abusive practices" and proposed to return to this question after the coffee-break. They accepted the formula "Measures against Abusive Practices".

29 March:

Geneva Airport: 13:30. Just seated on the aircraft. It should have departed at 12:00. Late arrival from Moscow since they changed a large aircraft for a small one – few passengers. Of the main questions for the Committee, Convention No. 21 remained, and there is little to be done on it. Next year will be Convention No. 87. This is more difficult.

1981

20 Aug:

Charles de Gaulle Airport: Have not travelled abroad since March 1980. Now I am en route to the Fourth Hammer Conference on Peace and Human Rights. I was at the Second in 1979 in Campobello.[352] The Fourth Conference is from 21 to 23 August in Aix-en-Provence. Then the session of the Institute of International Law at Dijon from 23 August to 3 September.

Hammer Conference:

1. To contribute to peace.
2. To be careful – the road to hell is paved with good intentions.
3. I am puzzled. So many divergent opinions, aspects, approaches.
4. The field suggested is enormous. All aspects of human society are interrelated.

Reasonable framework:

5. To form a working group.
6. To ask it to draft a preliminary report to be discussed at a next Conference.

23 Aug:

Aix-en-Provence. Hotel Cezanne: Yesterday an excursion to Marseille. Cruised along the seacoast, visited Chateau d'If – a prison in which A. Dumas[353] wrote in his "Comte

352 Canadian island with home and park of Franklin D. Roosevelt – [VGT].

353 Alexandre Dumas (1802-1870), French novelist – [WEB].

de Monte-Cristo". Then, of course, I climbed up to the Notre Dame de la Garde, had supper, and returned to Aix.

Yesterday I spoke. From the professional standpoint, the Conference is poorly organized. Vasak[354] – the chief organizer – assigned reports to various persons. The devil knows what is in them. As I said in my remarks: there are many ideas, some of them are good, some doubtful, and some are absurd, like a right to death. Today is the last. The matter evidently will be confined to a communiqué of a general nature.

At 12:00 the Conference completed its work. Hammer[355] left at 11:00. Yesterday I spoke with him. Said that we have doubts as to whether to participate in this Conference. But you know how we respect you and the ideas you have proclaimed when organizing this Conference. We were skeptical since Vasak, who organized this Conference, had clearly been moved to the side and "peace" had been moved to the back burner. Hammer said that the main task was to propagandize the idea of not permitting a nuclear war and that conversations about a limited nuclear war were nonsense. It seemed that all these conversations here have no significance, and what he said is the main thing.

Today in the morning they pass to me in the session a packet with a note that Hammer asked me to look at an amendment which he submitted to the draft communiqué. This already was a gesture. Then after the Conference his aide told me that Hammer, in leaving, asked to pass to me all his statements for the press, which he then did. This also was a gesture. He evidently gave Vasak to understand that something, and after the Conference he chatted with us for a long time about future work. We insisted that the next Conference, which would be devoted to the 100th anniversary of the birth of Franklin Roosevelt, be devoted to the basic problem – peace and human rights.

At 13:00 a buffet lunch. The Austrian Minister of Foreign Affairs, Pahr,[356] asked me to give a report to the Austrian Foreign Policy Society, of which he is the chairman. I asked him to pass my greetings to my old friend, President Kirchschläger.[357] Pahr said that when in conversation with Kirchschläger my name always came up and he very warmly recalled me.

Saw the city in the evening. An old city, with many tiny streets. Met Sturua,[358] who spends all his time here. He is arriving on leave from Washington and evidently came here at the invitation of Hammer, with whom he has close relations.

354 Karel Vasak (b. 1929), a French jurist of Czech origin who remained in France after the Czech events of 1968 – [VGT].

355 Armand Hammer (1898-1990), American industrialist who was close to the Soviet leadership – [WEB].

356 Willibald P. Pahr (b. 1930), Austrian Foreign Minister from 1976 to 1983 – [WEB].

357 Rudolf Kirchschläger (1915-2000), Chief of the Legal Department of the Ministry of Foreign Affairs, Foreign Minister, and President of Austria – [WEB].

358 Melor Georgievich Sturua (b. 1928), a Soviet and Russian international journalist – [VGT].

26 Aug:
Dijon. Hotel Frantel: Yesterday the 60th session of the Institute of International Law opened. Spoke with Röling[359] (in Aix) about the 1982 Journal of the Political Science Association. Also spoke with Castaneda, Lachs, Yankov,[360] Colliard, Arechaga. They all expressed interest.

26 Aug:
Salle du Conseil Regional de Bourgogne: The first round of the elections has proceeded. No one from the socialist countries was successful (Movchan, Betanek,[361] Bokor,[362] Degan[363]). I spoke and drew attention to the fact that the Institute must be truly universal and not western European and the need to have just representation of various regions and socio-economic systems.

Now I am working to introduce two amendments to the Statute of the Institute: (1) to increase the number of members to 150; (2) to have an open forum at each session on the great problems of international law. This might be most simply done under the rubric "Rapport de la Commission des Travaux".

In the second round no one received the necessary majority. Now we have voted a third time. I did considerable work for Movchan in advance. Lachs and El-Erian worked actively with me. Schachter (USA) also helped and said that he would explain to the Americans who Movchan was. Agreed with Castaneda and he spoke before the third round and said that, of course, it was necessary to elect in the remaining four places candidates from the countries weakly represented without sacrificing quality: Latin America, Africa, Asia, and the socialist countries.

29 Aug:
Hotel Frantel: Movchan was elected on 26 August: 45 votes was the minimum; he received 46. They congratulated me as though I had been elected. Many said that they voted because he was my student. At the next session we must appear in the full team. To propose to elect Koretsky an honorary member. And of course to propose a new candidacy – perhaps Boguslavskii[364] – from droit international privé. He will succeed; the private lawyers will vote for him.

Yesterday I suggested to M-me. Bastid – the President of the French Society of International Law – to organize bilateral seminars on international law. She and Virally, who came over then, embraced this idea. Decided to think about a topic. To be sure, I stipulated that this is my personal idea. Spoke about the conditions and said that in all probability we could invite them for 1983.

359 Bernard Victor Aloysius Röling (1906-1985), Dutch international lawyer who served as judge at the Military Tribunal in Tokyo from 1946 to 1948 – [WEB].
360 Alexander Yankov (b. 1924), leading Bulgarian international lawyer – [WEB].
361 Betanek [not further identified].
362 Hanna Bokor-Szego (1925-2006), Hungarian international lawyer – [WEB].
363 Vladimir-Djuro Degan (b. 1935), Professor of International Law at the University of Rijeka – [WEB].
364 Mark Moiseevich Boguslavskii (b. 1924), leading specialist on private international law – [VGT].

Yesterday and today discussed the report of Broms[365] "The Effect of Armed Conflicts on Treaties". I "gave it hot" to the draft resolution: it would have been good at the beginning of the twentieth century. Not taken into account was the prohibition against the use of force in international relations. They reworked the entire resolution. Ago supported me on this plane, that the report and draft resolution needed significant polishing. Seyersted[366] also supported this.

I for a long time had propagandized two ideas:

1. to increase the number of Institute members from 132 to 150. Today they submitted a draft change to the Statute. Salmon formalized it.
2. to have a general discussion on the report of the Commission des Travaux. For this it is believed to be necessary also to change the Statute, but Salmon yesterday proposed to discuss the Rapport de la Commission des Travaux. Yesterday this proposal was favored by Lachs at the plenary session, and then by me. Although the idea was mine, Lachs overtook me. But this is of no significance, even better since they relate to my proposals with suspicion.

3 Sept:

Plenary Session: Yesterday we discussed the influence of armed conflicts on treaties. A demonstration of Iranians outside the building demanding that measures be taken against repressions in Iran.

The next session is in England, the President is Professor Jennings[367] (Cambridge). Waldock should have been the President, but he died just before the beginning of the session. Lady Waldock died before him and he, evidently, lost the desire to live. He died on Saturday, 22 August.

1982

5 Jan:

Moscow-Paris Airplane: On the road, on the road, wrote Turgenev.[368] A session of the Curatorium in Paris. Not completely healthy, have a cold, and it is still freezing, yesterday up to minus 30, today minus 12 degrees. Have not been in Paris for three years, to be sure, in August-September 1981 I flew via Paris. An aircraft from Tokyo, two hours late. But there was nothing else. Almost completely full. A mass of Japanese tourists. We are late arriving. Will the Embassy meet me?

365 Bengt Broms (b. 1929), member of Executive Council of International Law Association from Finland – [WEB].

366 Finn Johannes Seyersted (1915-2006), Professor of International Law at the University of Oslo – [WEB].

367 Robert Yewdall Jennings (1913-2004), Judge on the International Court of Justice from 1982 to 1995 – [WEB].

368 Ivan Sergeevich Turgenev (1818-1883), Russian writer of the nineteenth century – [WEB].

6 Jan:

Paris. Hotel Saint-Germain: Thank God they met me at the airport – a comrade from the Representation attached to UNESCO met E. D. Lebedkina[369] and they asked him to meet me too. Lay down to sleep at 02:00 hours. Temperature was 37.2 degrees. Slept well and at 08:20 rang Kuleshov[370] from the scientific section of the Embassy to learn whether all was in order. Nose is still blocked, but no headache. Good there are no sessions today or tomorrow. Plus 8 degrees here, but this is not minus 15 and has a positive effect. Walked about the city for three hours, very interesting to stroll slowly and not travel on the metro: Place de l'Opera, Galeries Lafayette, etc.

As always when in Moscow I prepare to go to France I began to think in French. When I prepare to go to England, I begin to think in English. And usually, especially after reading books in English or French for a long time, I think in these languages automatically. Even after a German book, but less so. Just rang Bastid, Colliard, Virally, Rousseau.

10 Jan:

Hotel Saint-Germain: Le Louvre. Venus de Milo. When I am in Paris, my first visit is to her. Have not been here for three years. How many thoughts come when seeing this statue?

Just returned from lunch with Lavignes. Several years ago, when prices were lower, they purchased a one-room apartment for their son (graduated from the chemistry faculty) and daughter (studies economics and law). The policy of France was close to the policy of the United States. Cheysson[371] was an anti-Soviet, career diplomat. But they say he will not last long. Cot will seek this place, which would be much better.

To my question whether the French understand that the CIA is playing a large role in the events in Poland, he replied firmly that they do not so understand. To the same question yesterday Colliard at lunch said firmly that this is beyond doubt. But he tried to persuade me that Mitterand's foreign policy is the same policy as De Gaulle. And with respect to events in Poland, he considered them to be an internal matter. To my comment that this creates the impression that France is preparing to return to the military organization NATO, Colliard said that this is virtually unlikely.

17 June:

Moscow-Montreal: I am flying to New York for a Special Session of the United Nations General Assembly on Disarmament as a member of the delegation of the International Association of Democratic Lawyers. To arrive in New York it is now necessary to fly through Montreal. President Reagan[372] abolished flights to New York and Washington D. C., forcing tension by all means. So, indeed, did Carter.[373]

369 Elizaveta Dmitrievna Lebedkina (1922-1986), Deputy Head, Department of Foreign Relations, Russian Academy of Sciences – [VGT].

370 Petr Pavlovich Kuleshov (b. 1948), Third Secretary of the Embassy of the USSR in France in 1982 – [VGT].

371 Claude Cheysson (b. 1920), French Minister of Foreign Affairs from 1981 to 1984 – [VGT].

372 Ronald Wilson Reagan (1911-2004), 40th President of the United States – [WEB].

373 James Earl Carter, Jr. (b. 1924), 39th President of the United States – [WEB].

Now I am dining, and then must sleep. I will arrive in New York late, probably not lie down to rest in the hotel before 01:00 hours.

Very important to receive the message of L. I. Brezhnev and speech of A. A. Gromyko. During the flight a man approached me seated across the aisle. Introduced himself – Consul General of the USSR in Montreal, A. S. Ereskovskii.[374] We chatted. He knows me by name, and books, studies at the Higher Diplomatic School in Moscow. At the end of the conversation he said that he was pleased to meet a "legendary individual".

18 June:

New York. Middletowne Hotel: Yesterday Ereskovskii brought me in his car from one airport to the other. He is a very likeable person. E. P. Sviridov[375] met me here, who previously worked in the Treaty Law Section of the Ministry of Foreign Affairs. Today S. M. Beliaev[376] came for me from the Mission and we went to the United Nations. Received a pass there which admits me to the hall of the sessions, but on the second floor. Heard the address by Trudeau[377] (Prime Minister of Canada), then dined at the Mission and in the Hotel. Must rest. Everything is closed at the Mission; Gromyko is there, a member of the Politburo.

19 June:

New York: I still have not read the speech of President Reagan at the General Assembly on 17 June. They say it is very anti-Soviet. Yesterday a commentator on television asked why Reagan spoke so sharply. He replied – because Brezhnev's proposal placed him in a difficult position. It was clearly displeasing to the leader. He said – if Brezhnev proposes, this means this is of advantage to him.

Today the broadcast Christian Aid. Did not proceed without anti-communism. Children – victims of communist oppression: Afghanistan, Ethiopia, South Asia. But not a word about the Near East, Latin America.

21 June:

New York: Met V. A. Kartashkin.[378] Together we with his friend went yesterday to the beach. A bit sunburned. Waded in the sea. Water is still cold. Spent two evenings with Kartashkin. His wife and son went to Moscow. Rested very well. Today at about 12:00

374 Aleksandr Sergeevich Ereskovskii (b. 1936), Consul General of the USSR in Montreal – [VGT].

375 Eduard Petrovich Sviridov (b. 1939), international lawyer and Counsellor of the USSR Representation to the United Nations from 1979 to 1984 – [VGT].

376 Sergei Mikhailovich Beliaev (b. 1953), USSR Mission to the United Nations from 1980 to 1984 – [VGT].

377 Joseph Philippe Pierre Yves Elliott Trudeau (1919-2000), fifteenth prime minister of Canada – [WEB].

378 Vladimir Alekseevich Kartashkin (b. 1934), from 1979 to 1985 special assistant to the Under Secretary-General of the United Nations for Legal Questions – [VGT].

a meeting is scheduled with the legal advisor of the United Nations Secretariat, Erik Suy.[379] Tomorrow must go to Nordman[380] and Bentoumi.[381]

23 June:

New York: Day before yesterday met with Suy. Regrettably, he is unlikely to go to Rio. Says a matter of money, but it seems this is not so. There are rumors that the new Secretary-General, Peres de Cuellar,[382] wants to remove him and send him to Europe as a representative at the Conference on Disarmament. And he already has purchased a villa there.

Yesterday worked the entire day in the Library. There were some things of interest.

Today was at a briefing by Blackaby,[383] the new Director of the Stockholm International Peace Research Institute, of which I learned only here. Recounted the activities of SIPRI. About 200 persons were present.

23 June:

United Nations Ad Hoc Committee: The address of the Chairmen of the Independent Commission, Palme and Edgar Faure[384] (both former premiers) has just finished. Faure proposed the creation of a Conseil Mondial de Conscience. Now Thatcher has begun to speak.[385] She recalled Roosevelt[386] – not a peace at any price. And Churchill – the balance of terror. Nuclear weapons kept the peace for more than 30 years. The main thing is not the nuclear weapon, but the intention to resort to war. Accent on verification. It is a stumbling block. Wars are caused not by armaments, but by ambitions. She spoke for 23 minutes. The sense – one must think not about disarmament, but how to counteract a potential aggressor with adequate force, that is, one must be armed.

24 June:

United Nations General Assembly: Last evening met with Nordman. Looked over, or more accurately he read, the manuscript of the speech. Something underlined, something added. Emphasized, in particular, the reference of defense interests. Added: negotiations – the only route; treaties are not sheets of paper, they contain obligations to comply with the treaty and there is every reason to expect that they will be observed also in the future, especially if the public will be observant. Next was dinner with the Americans and a meeting with the representatives of two American legal associations. There are unresolved issues between the International Association of Democratic Lawyers and American lawyers. Many American lawyers believe, said Nordman, that the

379 Erik Suy (b. 1933), Under-Secretary General and Legal Counsel of the United Nations – [WEB].

380 Joe Nordman (1910-2005), President of the International Association of Democratic Lawyers – [VGT].

381 Amar Bentoumi (b. 1923), first Minister of Justice of Algeria and Secretary-General of the International Association of Democratic Lawyers – [VGT].

382 Peres de Cuellar (b. 1920), Secretary-General of the United Nations from 1983-1991 – [VGT].

383 Frank Blackaby (1921-2000), Director of SIPRI from 1981 to 1986 – [WEB].

384 Edgar Faure (1908-1988), Prime Minister of France in 1952 and 1955 – [WEB].

385 Baroness Margaret Thatcher of Kesteven (b. 1925), Prime Minister of the United Kingdom – [WEB].

386 Franklin Delano Roosevelt (1882-1945), 32nd President of the United States – [WEB].

International Association of Democratic Lawyers is a pro-Soviet organization. Nordman showed the unfoundedness of this view. Spoke well and in detail about practical issues of relations between the International Association of Democratic Lawyers and American lawyers, and also the activities of the IADL, the Secretary-General of which is Bentoumi – the former Minister of Justice of Algeria. Bentoumi arrived at the Hotel at night. Now Nordman approached and gave the text of the speech which was printed this evening.

My proposals relating to the fact that "some say that treaties are scraps of paper" (an express reproach to the speeches of Reagan and Thatcher) he did not incorporate in the text of the speech, although the idea remained in milder form.

Today the representatives of nongovernmental organizations speak. In the hall of the General Assembly the benches of representatives of governments are virtually empty. This is not nice. Now Lord Noel-Baker[387] is speaking: If you want peace, you have to prepare for peace. Nordman's speech went well.

Today O. A. Troianovskii[388] organized a lunch for representatives of nongovernmental organizations. Valentina Vladimirovna Tereshkova,[389] Grechko,[390] Blokhin,[391] and others were present. I sat beside Tereshkova. She impressed me as an attractive and intelligent woman. Comports herself simply and naturally. I told her that, having sat beside her, I as a specialist in international law would devote greater attention to space law.

27 June:

Metropolitan Museum: So far as I can recall, previously on Sundays admission was free of charge. Now it is obligatory to pay. One may pay as much as one pleased. $4 is recommended.

Rembrandt: "Aristotle Before the Statue of Homer". In 1961 the Metropolitan Museum purchased it for $220,000. This was a sensation. We went to see it on the first Sunday. The painting was in the hall under special guard. Now it is in a hall together with the other Rembrandt canvases.

1 July:

Middletowne Hotel: Yesterday brought a visit to O. A. Troianovskii, then lunch with Suy, together with Kartashkin. Suy took us to a fashionable Italian restaurant, expensive, and crowded. I don't like such restaurants – noisy, crowded, but, they say, cuisine.

On Saturday at lunch with Nordman he made several comments: (1) We (Soviet Union) do not devote sufficient attention to unofficial contacts with capitalist countries,

387 Philip John Noel-Baker, Baron Noel-Baker (1889-1982), Nobel laureate – [WEB].

388 Oleg Aleksandrovich Troianovskii (1919-2003), Permanent Representative of the USSR attached to the United Nations from 1976 to 1986 – [VGT].

389 Valentina Vladimirova Tereshkova (b. 1937), first woman in space – [WEB].

390 Georgii Mikhalovich Grechko (b. 1931), Soviet cosmonaut – [VGT].

391 Nikolai Nikolaevich Blokhin (1912-1993), Director of an oncological center in Moscow – [WEB].

except for scientific; (2) the World Peace Council is regarded as the porte-parole of the Soviet Government and therefore its influence is limited.

1 July:

Montreal-Moscow Airplane: With a first class ticket I am flying tourist class since there is no first class. The military attaché in Canada is in the same situation. But the service will be first class. Aeroflot might send first class on the aircraft of other companies, but economizes hard currency.

An interesting event. In Montreal the Vice Consul met me and introduced me to Professor V. V. Passek,[392] Head of the Chair of Foreign Languages of some Moscow Technical Institute. Two weeks ago he flew to the University of Arizona with a group of English language teachers on a course. They were to have spent 56 days there. After a few days the Americans, without making any accusations, asked him to leave the United States within 24 hours. He is distressed. Loutishness.

7 July:

Heidelberg. Hotel Haarlass: First Soviet-West German Colloquium on international law. Heidelberg, Max Plank Institute. Topic: law of the sea.

1. Influence of III United Nations Conference on Law of the Sea on the development of maritime customary law.
2. Concept of the common heritage of mankind.
3. Settlement of disputes.

Delegation: Barsegov,[393] Gureev,[394] Starzhina,[395] Shinkaretskaia,[396] Gitsu.[397]

Yesterday was an interesting exchange of views on two reports. During the opening after Bernhardt[398] I spoke for 20 minutes: put emphasis on the fact that we had created an integral theory of international law. Thereby a blow with regard to reactionary Sovietologists, of which the main one is Meissner.[399] He was present.

---

392 V. V. Passek, Head, Chair of Foreign Languages, Moscow Machine-Tool Institute, from 1955 – [VGT].

393 Iurii Georgievich Barsegov (1925-2008), specialist in territorial, maritime, and diplomatic issues – [WEB].

394 Sergei Aleksandrovich Gureev (b. 1934), Institute of State and Law, Russian Academy of Sciences; Russian specialist on the law of the sea – [WEB].

395 Tatiana Matveevna Starzhina (1939-2004), Russian specialist on the legal regime of the ocean floor; Institute of State and Law, Russian Academy of Sciences – [WEB].

396 Galina Georgievna Shinkaretskaia (b. 1941), specialist on the law of the sea – [VGT].

397 Margarita Alekseevna Gitsu (b. 1940), law of the sea specialist now at the Russian Gubkini University of Oil and Gas – [VGT].

398 Rudolf Bernhardt (b. 1925), pre-eminent German international lawyer and editor of *Encyclopedia of Public International Law* – [WEB].

399 Boris Meissner (1915-2003), Baltic German specialist on the former Soviet Union who founded and headed the Institut für Ostrecht at the University of Cologne – [WEB].

10 July:
Frankfurt Airport: Five days flashed by. The Colloquium was interesting. Our reports were not bad. Gureev spoke in German, Starzhina and Barsegov in English.

Yesterday an excursion. Saw Rothenburg, then to Würzburg, spent the night there and in the morning travelled to Frankfurt. Bernhardt was with us yesterday. Today we were accompanied by Schweisfurth,[400] Hoffmann,[401] and Münch.[402]

General impression: the Germans are rather critical of the Convention on the Law of the Sea. They worry about what will happen if it enters into force. It will collect 60 ratifications. Then what do we do? Ratify? This would be assessed positively by the developing countries. But this would bind us, whereas the United States would not be bound by the Convention. Which is better?

1983

7 Jan:
Sheremetevo Airport: Am flying to Paris. Tomorrow a session of the Curatorium. In three days a joint session of the Bureau of the Institute and the Commission des Travaux. Valticos has introduced an innovation. I am a member of the Commission.

The second time that I am travelling on an employment passport. For 40 years I travelled with a diplomatic one. The Ministry of Foreign Affairs has introduced a new rule – diplomatic passports only for active diplomats. This corresponds to international law.

Now I am weary and rest somewhat. In December I was on leave and became tired properly, that is, I am finishing the book "Law and Force in the International System".

Paris. Hotel Saint-Germain: Rang my acquaintances: Bastid, Lavigne, Colliard, Virally, Rousseau. Rousseau told me that he is coming to the end of his fifth volume. On 9 January I will be at tea with M-me. Bastid, on 11 January at lunch with Colliard, and on 12 January at lunch with Lavigne.

8 Jan:
Hotel Saint-Germain: The session of the Curatorium finished recently. The fact that I was not there in May 1982 had an effect. In general in connection with the fact that I for three years was only at one session instead of six, our professors did not lecture in 1982 or in 1983. In 1985 there will be Sadikov[403] and Feldman in the same year, although he was intended for 1983. Graefrath (German Democratic Republic) was included for 1984. A number of new members in the Curatorium in place of Waldock,

400 Theodor Schweisfurth (b. 1937), German international lawyer – [WEB].
401 Bernd von Hoffmann (b. 1941), member of the Institute of International Law – [WEB].
402 Ingo von Münch (b. 1932), Professor of International and State Law, University of Hamburg – [VGT].
403 Oleg Nikolaevich Sadikov (b. 1925), Russian civilist and private international law specialist – [WEB].

Yasseen, and Sørenson.[404] Vallat in place of Waldock, Boutros-Ghali[405] in place of Yassen, and a Dane in place of Sørenson. Additionally, the former Minister of Foreign Affairs of Mexico, Castaneda, appointed as ambassador to France. Castaneda is very pleased with this appointment.

In conversation with me Boutros-Ghali, Deputy Minister of Foreign Affairs of Egypt, recalled our discussion eight years ago, when he was not yet a deputy Minister. Then he expressed his disagreement with the "unilateral orientation towards the United States" being conducted by Sadat.[406] Egypt, he said, should maintain good relations both with the United States and the USSR. Having recalled this conversation, Boutros-Ghali said that he now adheres to this position and does everything that he can in this direction. I hope, he said, that 1983 will be a turning point. Boutros-Ghali participated in part of the sessions of the Curatorium, being en route to Nicaragua to participate in a Conference of nonaligned countries.

9 Jan:

Hotel Saint-Germain: Rodin Museum. A tremendous number of works. All human experiences embodied in stone: Le Penseur, La Douleur, La Pleureuse, and so on. Three designs for a monument to Balzac,[407] a design for a monument to Hugo,[408] and so on.

During the second half of the day I escaped for one hour to the Louvre and at 17:00 was already at M-me. Bastid. Spoke without noticing until 19:00. Asked her what had happened to J. P. Cot, who left the post of Minister of Cooperation and Development. Bastid related in great detail his disagreements with the Ministry of Foreign Affairs concerning the delimitation of competence and also the substance of relations with various developing countries. For example, he opposed an invitation to Sékou Touré[409] to come to France because he is holding many people under arrest. Cot did not belong to the circle of persons close to Mitterand, who dined with him on Thursdays.

Asked about Raymond Aron.[410] Bastid said that they were recently together at a session of the Institute of International Relations. After the session, Aron offered to give her a ride. He had a magnificent car with a chauffeur. Aron has extensive links in the United States among democrats and is often there.

12 Jan:

Hotel Saint-Germain: Must now go to Mr. Marks from UNESCO. They are preparing to publish my book "Law and Force in the International System", the writing of which I am completing. I promise to give them a table of contents in the English language, more accurately the titles of chapters.

404 Max Sørenson (1913-1981), Danish Professor of International Law, Aarhus University, and editor of UNESCO textbook on international law – [WEB].

405 Boutros Boutros-Ghali (b. 1922), Egyptian international lawyer, Secretary-General of the United Nations from 1992 to 1996 – [WEB].

406 Muhammad Anwar El Sadat (1918-1981), third President of Egypt from 1970 to 1981 – [WEB].

407 Honoré de Balzac (1799-1850), French novelist and playwright – [WEB].

408 Victor-Marie Hugo (1802-1885), French playwright and statesman – [WEB].

409 Ahmed Sékou Touré (1922-1984), President of Guinea from 1958 to 1984 – [WEB].

410 Raymond-Claude-Ferdinand Aron (1905-1983), French philosopher, political scientist, and sociologist – [WEB].

Lunch yesterday with Professor Colliard. I gave him for the Library of Paris I University, of which I am an honorary doctor, our new textbook on international law. He does not read Russian, but asks somebody to translate several passages. We spoke about the French-Soviet Colloquium. He said that one must speak with Bastid about this. I replied that I had chatted with her, but she did not say a word about the Colloquium. Colliard said that tomorrow he will see the new legal advisor at the Ministry of Foreign Affairs (M. Guillaume)[411] and speak with him about this. I am astonished that he said in all probability Virally is obstructing the organization of the Colloquium. Why? It would be inappropriate to ask. He said again that they have disagreement about the possible topics. Bastid believes that the topic should be specific. Colliard himself believes that this is not essential.

13 Jan:
Hotel Saint-Germain: Became acquainted with Michel Lesage,[412] Director of the Institute of Administrative Sciences (Brussels), at a dinner with Lavigne. He made an excellent impression on me. Speaks Russian. Knowledgeable about our affairs. Knows that Kozlov is no longer the Dean.[413] Otherwise, Lavigne spoke more, all about their internal affairs. Marie Lavigne, judging from everything, carries weight. She recounted how many addresses at colloquiums she will have in the socialist and capitalist countries: more than six in 1983. Correspondents often request an interview with her. Now she is preparing an article for *Humanité*.

Colliard came to the Hotel in the evening. Brought Helene Carrère d'Encausse,[414] *L'Empire eclate*. He has spoken about this book yesterday at dinner. She is a Georgian. As Colliard said, when Chikhvadze as Director of the Institute of State and Law had come here in this time, a dinner was arranged in his honor. This woman was invited to the dinner. She spoke with Chikhvadze in Georgian, and he sat beside her and all evening spoke only with her. She is in high esteem, writes anti-Soviet books. She appears on television as a "specialist on the Soviet Union" but has never been in the Union.

Colliard yesterday spoke with Guillaume about the Soviet-French Colloquium. He supports this idea. Spoke about a possible topic. Colliard proposed as a topic: "Principes fundamentaux de droit international". I said that this is a very appropriate topic and in order to take into account the view of those who prefer a specific topic, one might also include a more specific topic, for example: "Principle of Nondiscrimination in International Economic Relations". He concurred. In honor of his 70th birthday, they are preparing to publish a Mélange. He asked my consent to be a member of the organizing committee. We had spoken about this at Dijon and I affirmed my consent.

---

411 Gilbert Guillaume (b. 1930), Director of Legal Affairs, French Ministry of Foreign Affairs from 1979 to 1987 and member of the International Court of Justice from 1987 – [WEB].

412 Michel Lesage (1933-2009), French specialist on Soviet law; Director General, International Institute for Administrative Sciences (Brussels) from 1981 to 1986; Director, Institute of Comparative Studies, CNRS from 1979 to 2001 – [WEB].

413 Iurii Markovich Kozlov (1925-2002), Dean of the Law Faculty of Moscow Lomonosov State University from 1980 to 1982 and specialist in administrative and financial law – [VGT].

414 Helene Carrère d'Encausse (b. 1929), permanent Secretary of the Academie Francaise, historian specializing in Russian history – [VGT].

14 Jan:

Charles de Gaulle Airport: S. M. Rodchenkov,[415] who had assisted me very well, transported me. The trip was full and productive. On 11 January there was a joint session of the Bureau and of the Commission des Travaux of the Institute. Two issues were discussed: (a) methods of work; and (b) the program. The Commission under the chairmanship of Goldberg submitted a report. A lively discussion followed. I said that the Commission (Lachs was a member) had proposed a number of interesting topics: relationship between public international law and private international law, environmental law, and others. But, I said, I preferred to envisage international law in a different dimension. International law is functioning and developing in a certain milieu. It cannot be studied while ignoring the milieu – political milieu. I spoke English: "We have left the problem of the relationship between International Law and its environment, i.e., Juridical System, to political scientists. And the result is that they minimize the role of International Law, and so on".

6 May:

The Hague. Hotel Bali: Once more in my old Hotel. Have not been here since 1979. The First Secretary of the Embassy, A. A. Lapushinskii,[416] a graduate of the Institute of International Relations in 1971, met me. P. D. Morozov is not well and in general has given up. I rang him at home, and his wife said that he had gone to the doctor with an injured hand. I will be with them in the evening.

8 May:

Hotel Bali: Exercised on the seashore, breathing sea air with satisfaction. Everything has greatly changed. A large hotel in place of the old one where wealthy judges lived. Closed and open pools attached to the hotel.

Yesterday at the Curatorium two topics proposed by me in 1986 were adopted, for the moment in preliminary form: "Law and Force in the International System" (Tunkin) and "Principle of Nondiscrimination in International Trade" (Pozdniakov).[417] O. Kunz[418] also is planned for 1986.

10 May:

Hotel Bali: Worked the evening before yesterday on a chapter for the UNESCO textbook; this chapter was submitted in 1980. Insignificant amendments. Next read Lach's book, *The Teacher in International Law*. Survey of doctrines of authors who lived in

415 Stanislav Mikhailovich Rodchenkov (1949-2010), Secretary of the USSR Representation to UNESCO from 1979 to 1984; First Secretary of Embassy of USSR in The Hague from 1986 to 1992 – [VGT].

416 Aleksandr Aleksandrovich Lapushinskii (b. 1948), First Secretary, USSR Embassy in The Hague – [VGT].

417 Vladimir Sergeevich Pozdniakov (1919-1995), specialist in foreign trade law of the USSR and Professor of International Law, USSR Academy of Foreign Trade – [WEB].

418 Otto Kunz (b. 1921), Czech specialist in foreign trade relations; Vice President of the Czechoslovak Branch of the International Law Association – [WEB].

the nineteenth and twentieth centuries, but only authors deceased. Of ours – Korovin, Durdenevskii,[419] Krylov.

Today in the morning at 09:30 I gave a lecture at the Embassy. Topic – "Basic Problems of International Law". Yesterday and today worked a bit in the Library. I love this Library, although far from everything that I need is not to be found here. Yesterday dined with Lachs. Spoke much about theoretical issues. He gave me two of his articles. One on "Good Faith"; I shall use it in a book.

1 Oct:

Sheremetevo Airport: I am flying to Brussels for the Conference of the International Association of Democratic Lawyers on the unlawfulness of siting American Pershing-2 missiles in Western Europe. The beginning is today, possibly the second half of the day. If the first, I am late.

Today the first flight of our aircraft to Brussels after the two-week boycott in connection with the incident with the South Korean Boeing-747 in the Sakhalin area. The United States arranged this provocation so as to facilitate the placement of missiles in Western Europe, against which an extensive movement has developed.

3 Oct:

Brussels. Hotel Bedford: Attended only the second session on 1 October. Two physicists spoke at the first session who recounted how now there are nuclear bombs. It seems that there are already several types with various characteristics. Regret that I was late. With a view to economizing, went nowhere on the fourth day before the Conference. However, I did what I had to do in order to take part in the preliminary preparation of the resolution.

The Conference is in the same Hotel. At the evening session on 1 October they discussed the unlawfulness of a nuclear weapon – on the level of the law of war. Yesterday in the morning commenced the discussion on the siting in Western Europe of Pershing-2 missiles. John Fried (United States)[420] spoke first. An untiring fighter for the prohibition of nuclear weapons. Participant in the Nuremberg Trials, long since on pension.

Next I spoke for 20 minutes. Prepared the speech in Moscow and yesterday before the session got up at 05:00. I spoke about the unlawfulness of a policy of force and anti-communism, violation of the principle of good faith in negotiations in Geneva, and double standards on the siting of missiles.

The entire discussion was in the French language. In general there were too many Belgians and too few foreigners. G. Fischer (France),[421] E. Oeser (German Democratic Republic),[422] Fried, G. Stuby (Federal Republic of Germany), and myself. After lunch

419 Vsevolod Nikolaevich Durdenevskii (1899-1963), Soviet international lawyer – [WEB].

420 John H. E. Fried (1905-1990), lawyer, professor, and human rights activist – [WEB].

421 Georges Fischer (1930-2011), French international lawyer – [VGT].

422 Edith Oeser (1930-2005), Professor of International Law and Head of Department, Humboldt University, Berlin, from 1972 to 1989 – [VGT].

we began to prepare a draft resolution. The first part – unlawfulness – was prepared by the Commission: Salmon, Fischer, and Fried on 1 October in the evening. There were no serious disagreements then. The second part they began to prepare with my participation. There were difficulties with Fischer, but we agreed. At 18:00 the resolution was ready. Fischer and Stuby left.

The plenary session began with half present. Two Belgians, Francois Bailly[423] and Andris,[424] were both well prepared on these issues and spoke against the draft Part II of the Resolution which we had proposed:

1. against express condemnation of United States policy;
2. an attempt to leave a loophole for the use of nuclear weapons in the event of "military necessity";
3. whitewash the Treaty on the creation of NATO by a clever maneuver. Under the Treaty, NATO is a defense organization. Siting the missiles is contrary to the Treaty.

Discussion: I and they, Salmon as an intermediary, were very stubborn. They did not succeed in working in sundry variants of their formulations into point 2. Our formula was adopted in somewhat changed form. I quickly killed their proposals with regard to point 3. Under point 1 we agreed a compromise formulation without mentioning the United States.

Was at the Embassy with the chargé d'affaires, Iu. I. Buzykin.[425] Informed him about the Conference. Buzykin asked me to give a lecture at the Embassy on 6 October at 18:00 hours. Ambassador S. K. Romanovskii is returning from leave tomorrow.

5 Oct:

Hotel Bedford: In the morning prepared the lecture for the Embassy, which will be tomorrow. At 13:00 Mazov (representative of the Union of Soviet Friendship Societies)[426] came for me with Irina and we went to Antwerp. The main thing there – the Rubens Museum. I was in it in 1962, when I spoke at the International Court. This is a palace, albeit small. Architecture in Renaissance style, many statues and bas-reliefs. They say the house was built according to the design of Rubens. Undoubtedly a wealthy person. The Medicis, no doubt, paid him well for paintings which are now in the Louvre. The Flemish call Antwerp the City of Rubens. A good city, although ceding to Brussels.

423 Francois Bailly, Secretary-General, Belgian Association of Democratic Lawyers – [VGT].

424 Andris [not further identified].

425 Iurii Ilich Buzykin (b. 1931), Counsellor-Envoy of the USSR Embassy in Brussels from 1979 to 1986 – [VGT].

426 Vasilii Antonovich Mazov (b. 1922), Lecturer, Chair of International Law, Moscow State Institute of International Relations from 1973 to 1978; representative, Union of Soviet Friendship Societies attached to the Secretariat of the International Association of Democratic Lawyers from 1978 to 1987 – [VGT].

In the evening watched the film "Gandhi". Monumental and, in my view, wholly just. The cruelty of the English is shown and, at the same time, their inclination towards compromise. The role of the policy of resistance without the use of force (non-violent resistance). A strong impression.

6 Oct:

Hotel Bedford: At 11:00 went with Mazov to the Museum of Fine Arts. Was there in all one hour. Many rooms are closed for repair. I was interested mostly in Brueghel[427] (Elder, Younger, and grandson). The Elder is most noted. A few canvases, fewer than in Vienna, but good ones. Were in the Erasmus Museum in Rotterdam. This is the house of the former chanoine in which Erasmus[428] lived for five months as a guest. A tiny museum. There are various editions of "The Praise of Folly". Then we went to dine at the Mazovs. They were so attentive to me, that it was inappropriate that I was the cause to them of so many concerns.

Next I visited the Ambassador, S. K. Romanovskii. I told of our work, the Resolution adopted, and the discussion. He was very satisfied, recalled that I had done much work three years before, requested that I come more often. At 18:00 the lecture in the Embassy. There were about 100 persons. I called the lecture: "International Law and International Policy". They listened attentively. I told them what international law is, what role it plays, how important it is to know it. Used some passages from my book.

Time to prepare for the lecture at the University.

7 Oct:

Hotel Bedford: From 14:00 to 16:00 a lecture at the Law Faculty of the Free University of Brussels (French division). I delivered it instead of Professor Salmon, who also conducted the session. I gave the lecture based on my article for the Mélange Chaumont – "Model du système international généralement reconnu et le droit international". There were about 60 persons.

Dinner in the evening with the leadership of the Belgian Association of Democratic Lawyers.

8 Oct:

Brussels Airport: Yesterday dined with Professor Salmon. The Dean of the Law Faculty, Eric David,[429] also was present at the meal, who works with Salmon and Paulette Pierson-Mathy.[430] She passed to me a letter for the Soviet Committee of Solidarity with

427 Pieter Brueghel the Elder (c. 1525-1569); Pieter Brueghel the Younger (1564/65-1636); Jan Brueghel the Elder (1568-1625) – the celebrated Brueghel dynasty of Dutch painters – [WEB].

428 Desiderius Erasmus of Rotterdam (1466-1536), Dutch Renaissance humanist and theologian – [WEB].

429 Eric David (b. 1943), Professor of Interational Law, Free University of Brussels – [VGT].

430 Paulette Pierson-Mathy (b. 1932), Docent at the Free University of Brussels – [VGT].

the Peoples of Asia and Africa relating to Mozambique. I have known her for a long time. Salmon gave me three volumes of his cours, which significantly increased the weight of my suitcase.

At my Faculty in Moscow we have two lectures on the law of treaties which Rein Müllerson[431] must deliver. On 10 October I will myself be there to lecture. Müllerson leaves on 13 October to Guinea-Bissau to deliver lectures.

1984

6 May:

London Embassy Hotel: Arrived in London for a session of the Administrative Council of the International Law Association. From London to The Hague for a session of the Curatorium. I was not at the last session of the Executive Council, and my arrival clearly gave satisfaction to the leadership of the ILA. They are worried about the authority of the Association, in particular, because their own authority is linked with it. No special decisions were adopted. The main question is the conference in Paris. The Association has virtually not grown. The cause is not moving forward in the developing countries basically, evidently, because of financial difficulties.

I decided today, Sunday, to rest a bit and not think about international law. At the beginning of the day, together with A. K. Zhudro and his wife and G. G. Ivanov,[432] who is in London on a business trip, went to see Windsor Palace. Everything was closed because they do not allow anyone within in the summer. The winter portion of the Palace was accessible to visitors. All the same it was very interesting. In the evening went to the flat of Zhudro. Supper was superlative. Returned to the Hotel at 20:30 and found a message from Butler. He and his wife invite me tomorrow to see the city and dine with them.

9 May:

The Hague. Hotel Bali: On 7 May was a guest of the Butlers. It is cold in their houses; they economize and are used to it. Small children, even tiny ones, in a stroller with head uncovered, and on the street. 7 degrees. At University College London there are four persons from the USSR. Two from the Institute of State and Law (Krylova[433] and Svetlanov).[434] Semiderkin[435] from our Faculty, and one woman from the Sverdlovsk Institute.[436] They were all, except Semiderkin, at the Butlers.

---

431 Rein Müllerson (b. 1944), Professor of International Law, King's College London – [WEB].

432 Georgii Georgievich Ivanov (b. 1931), a Russian specialist on the law of the sea – [VGT].

433 Ninel Sergeevna Krylova (b. 1929), a leading specialist in Commonwealth affairs – [WEB].

434 Andrei Gennadievich Lisitsyn-Svetlanov (b. 1951), specialist in private international law and presently the Director, Institute of State and Law, Russian Academy of Sciences – [WEB].

435 Nikolai Alekseevich Semiderkin (1952-2003), a Russian legal historian in London under The British Council auspices – [WEB].

436 Alla Iurevna Yakusheva (b. 1951), also in England through The British Council and presently Docent at the Chair of History of State and Law, Urals Academy of Law – [WEB].

A. A. Lopushinskii met me at the airport in Amsterdam. Said that tomorrow I have a lecture at the University of Utrecht at 20:00. Now I shall begin to prepare it.

10 May:

Hotel Bali: Spent the entire day on the lecture. Five hours for preparation, one hour of lecture, and one hour of questions. There were about 130 persons. The small room was packed. Ten persons stood in the aisles. Questions were various, but basically not "malicious". The lecture was organized by the Association of Students of International Relations.

Went to the Library in the morning after breakfast, and at 11:30 went to the International Court – announcing the decision in the Nicaragua v. United States case. Television cameras, journalists, all or nearly all the places were reserved. Morozov had reserved a place for me. President Elias[437] very indistinctly read out the Order of the Court about interim measures for one hour and ten minutes. The decision was not bad and struck a blow against Reagan's policies.[438]

12 May:

Hotel Bali: Yesterday worked in the Library from morning. I, as always, saw the Chief Librarian. Passed to him for the Library my book Право и сила в международной системе [Law and Force in the International System]. Asked to instruct his personnel to help me make Xeroxes. He said in conversation: "You are so famous that young people do not think you are alive?" They make me Xeroxes quickly and very accurately. For several hours I gathered numerous materials.

In the evening I dined with Maxwell Cohen,[439] who is a judge ad hoc in the dispute between the United States and Canada on the maritime boundary.[440] Saw many of the judges: Gros, Ago, Ruda.[441] Made the acquaintance of the Chief Legal Advisor of the United States Department of State – Robinson.[442] A spry, young man – son-in-law of Vice President Bush.[443]

13 May:

Hotel Bali: Together with Morozov, visited the house of Peter I[444] in Zaandam. When visiting the house, Napoleon said: "for the truly Great, nothing is small". And above this

437 Taslim Olawele Elias (1914-1991), Member of the International Court of Justice from 1976 to 1991, and President of the Court from 1982 to 1985 – [WEB].

438 The Court found that the United States was "in breach of its obligations under customary international law not to use force against another State", "not to interrupt peaceful maritime commerce" and so on – [VGT].

439 Maxwell Cohen (1910-1998), Canadian international lawyer and statesman – [WEB].

440 Delimitation of the Maritime Boundary in the Gulf of Maine Area – [VGT].

441 José Maria Ruda (1924-1994), member of the International Court of Justice from Argentina from 1973 to 1991 – [WEB].

442 Davis Rowland Robinson (b. 1940), served as Chief Legal Advisor from 1981 to 1985 – [WEB].

443 George Herbert Walker Bush (b. 1924), Vice President of the United States and 41st President of the United States – [WEB].

444 Emperor Peter the Great of Russia (1672-1725), who visited Holland for some time – [WEB].

inscription in French is a poor translation into Russian. Inscriptions have been drawn on the wall of the room where Peter lived. Wanted to see again the house of Rembrandt in Amsterdam, but did not find it. Returned to The Hague, dined with Morozov, then discussed the case of Nicaragua v. United States in the International Court.

Yesterday the Curatorium proceeded well and rapidly. Finished at lunch, which of course pleased everyone. This was not so in the past. In 1985 of ours lectures by Feldman and Sadikov, in 1986, me, and in 1987 (provisionally), Boguslavskii – the general cours on private international law and Galenskaia.[445]

Met with Lachs in the evening. Poland has nominated him for a third term, agreed with Bulgaria that they will not nominate Yankov. This is good. Lachs is a force. Even Morozov acknowledged this time that he is playing a significant positive role.

14 May:

Amsterdam-Moscow Aircraft: Ten passengers in all on the aircraft. But they told me that it is landing in Warsaw, after which it will be full. A. A. Lapushinskii escorted me. He is returning to the USSR in September.

Exercises in the morning by the sea, as usual. Good weather, although humid. La vie est belle meme a mon age. When I sit on an airplane, I often recall the joke: "I love marches – said the General, sitting in an automobile".

29 Aug:

Paris. Hotel Sofitel: Arrived in Paris on 25 August for the 61st Conference of the International Law Association: L. Korbut,[446] M. Lazarev, and myself. G. Starushenko[447] joined us in Paris, having flown here from Geneva.

Spoke on 28 August in the Committee for Legal Aspects of a New International Economic Order. Touched upon a number of general issues.

Today is a non-work day. Excursion to the Saint-Denis Basilica. After that, I read for the second time M. Druon, *Les rois maudits*,[448] which was interesting. Met with Pierre Lavigne in the evening. Rang Colliard, Rousseau; they are not in Paris: holidays.

1 Sept:

Hotel Sofitel: Conference has just finished. At 09:00 the session of the Full Council began. At the first session of the Conference on 26 August I submitted an official proposal (in writing) to create a Committee to draft a Code of Conduct for Nuclear Powers. Indus[449] christened this proposal a "peace bomb", and Professor Brownlie, Director of Studies of the International Law Association, said that I had submitted a proposal

---

445 Ludmila Nikiforovna Galenskaia (b. 1932), private international law specialist in St. Petersburg – [web].

446 Ludmila Vasilevna Korbut (b. 1926) – Secretary of the Soviet Association of International Law from its inception and a specialist on the international law of rivers – [web].

447 Gleb Borisovich Starushenko (1922-2007), Corresponding Member of the USSR Academy of Sciences and specialist in self-determination and international law – [web].

448 Maurice Druon (1918-2009), French writer. The novel referred to first appeared in 1955 – [web].

449 Indus [not further identified].

which cannot be rejected, having in view that some wanted to do so, but this was impossible. After negotiations with a number of delegations, Brownlie agreed to submit the proposal for the creation of a working group of 7 persons in order to prepare the terms of reference for a future Committee on the subject. Today at the Council, the Chairman, Lord Wilberforce himself, submitted this proposal, and Brownlie had somewhat elaborated it. Thus, my proposal was adopted; Lord Wilberforce even thanked me for the initiative displayed.

2 Sept:

Hotel Sofitel: Today we depart. I am content with the results of the Conference. Of course, the resolutions on certain problems were not very satisfactory. I established our disagreement with the resolution on International Terrorism. But the main thing is: the peace bomb exploded. This will be problem No. 1, and the New International Economic Order, problem No. 2. Now it is vital to be at the session of the Executive Council in November. There's the rub. It is unlikely that I will be there, and they will send someone else; this may lead to the collapse of the entire matter.

14 Oct:

Athens. Hotel Priamos: Sunday. Arrived in Athens for the Congress of the International Association of Democratic Lawyers on 12 October. A large delegation. On the aircraft sat beside V. N. Kudriavtsev.[450] Spoke about the forthcoming elections to the Academy of Sciences. The jurists have one place of Academician and this, of course, is for him. Work commenced already on the aircraft: conversations, consultations.

The day passed splendidly. Went by bus in the morning to the Acropolis, saw the ruins of the Parthenon. After the Acropolis, went to the Aegean Sea. Hot, about 33 degrees. Swam superbly. Worked intensively in the morning. Prepared the final draft of the Appeal of the Congress (our draft), edited a number of addresses. Yesterday was my birthday – 78 years old.

19 Oct:

Hotel Priamos: Today was the final session of the Congress. All resolutions were adopted by the General Assembly of the International Association of Democratic Lawyers yesterday and this morning. The main thing: the creation of a commission to draft a code of conduct for nuclear powers (our proposal), on peace and security in Europe (Poland), on sending observers to court trials (Belgium), the inadmissibility of militarization of outer space, the Antonov Case,[451] appeal to the USSR and the United States, appeal to lawyers of the world, and so on. Most of all worries about the two Belgian

450 Vladimir Nikolaevich Kudriavtsev (1918-2007), Director of the Institute of State and Law, USSR Academy of Sciences and Vice President of the USSR Academy of Sciences – [WEB].

451 Sergei Antonov (1948-2007), Bulgarian citizen and representative of the Bulgarian Airline in Rome, arrested and accused of complicity in an attempt against the Pope of Rome, John Paul II – [VGT].

resolutions. Yesterday and today worked principally on these resolutions, carried on negotiations with the Belgians, very difficult negotiations. Most important is that they placed the USSR and the United States on one plane. Succeeded in redoing both drafts and made them acceptable.

648 persons participated in the Congress from 89 countries, 67 draft resolutions, of which 60 were adopted.

21 Oct:

Hotel Priamos: Very weary these days. Yesterday succeeded in resting well. Already read something from the articles given to me here. The Ambassador's chauffeur arrived and brought 10 liters of olive oil and a packet. I spoke with him when he brought us to the Embassy for a reception. A tin of olive oil, five liters, costs 140 drachmas at the Embassy, and 1,450 in the shops. He packed everything for me. Itta urged me to bring it.

Today was a remarkable excursion to the Aegina, Hydra, and Poros islands. Left at 7:15 by coach for Piraeus, then on the boat Hermes. Many of ours spent almost the entire time in the salon, and I with the Minister of Justice of Ukraine, V. I. Zaichuk,[452] outside in the air. Swam on the Aegina and Hydra islands. Read on the eve of sleeping *La patience de Maigret*. At night about 02:00 an unbelievable noise below the windows, I being on the first floor, window open, although the blinds were closed. Learned in the morning that ours returned after an event to which I did not go.

1985

25 Jan:

Delhi: Arrived in Delhi for the Soviet-Indian Seminar on International Law. Sat in the aircraft beside G. B. Starushenko, recently elected a Corresponding Member of the USSR Academy of Sciences.

Soviet-Indian Seminar. India International Center: The seminar opened the day before yesterday. Opened by the Law Minister. I also gave a brief talk. Yesterday morning gave a report on "International Law and the Anti-War Movement". On their side Pathak[453] gave a report. Then from us G. G. Shinkaretskaia and A. A. Rubanov.[454] On their side there were no corresponding reports. Today Iu. G. Barsegov gave a report: "Legal Order and Peace on the Seas".

The plan proposed by the Indian side was very tense. Requested with difficulty time for my press conference in the Soviet Cultural Center. Today I held this press conference. Starushenko was with me. About 15 journalists. Only the *Patriot* published something, but I have not yet seen it. The Embassy asked me to deliver a lecture for our diplomats.

452 Vladimir Ignatovich Zaichuk (b. 1928), Ukrainian SSR Minister of Justice from 1970 to 1990 – [WEB].

453 Raghunandan Swarup Pathak (b. 1924), Judge of the Supreme Court of India from 1978; Chief Justice from 1986; member, International Court of Justice from 1989 to 1991 – [VGT].

454 Avgust Afanasevich Rubanov (b. 1925), Russian specialist on private international law and space law – [WEB].

30 Jan:
Delhi-Moscow Aircraft: The business portion ended on the 25th, that is, lasted for only two days. The remaining time was taken up with a cultural program. Flew to Udalpur in the morning of the 27th. Boeing aircraft, takes off very quickly. Rubanov and Barsegov beside me, and Starzhina, Korbut, and Shinkaretskaia on the other side. Behind them Starushenko and the First Secretary of the Embassy, G. V. Govorin.[455] Miss Manon from the Indian Society of International Law is going with us.

The aircraft made an intermediate landing at Bombay. Several soldiers on duty around the aircraft. They say the situation is tense here, there were attacks on the part of Pakistan.

We stayed in Udalpur at the magnificent Lake Palace Hotel, build by the English as a guest house. Not modern, of course, but smart. Saw the City Palace – an enormous palace – city near a lake. I have never seen such vastness. Also a palace, comparatively small, on an island in the middle of the lake. The Moguls were not here, all these structures of the local maharajah. All this wealth created on the bones of millions, being destroyed, as India lacks the means to maintain them. Next we went outside the city, saw ancient Hindu temples, little ones, like toys.

Were in Ajanta. Exerted ourselves: the bus – and the road – were indifferent. But caves, former monasteries, Buddhist, but with a mixture of Hinduism, were colossal. Frescos, bas-reliefs, land the caves themselves carved into cliffs make a remarkable impression. Each an enormous labor of many masters of their craft. The English discovered them accidentally in 1819. But there is nothing to be removed from here. Statues similar to the Greek or Roman there are none.

In the evening dined with Pathak, a member of the Supreme Court. At 02:45 the flight to Moscow.

22 Aug:
Helsinki. Hotel: Arrived by train in Helsinki for the 62nd session of the Institute of International Law. Have not travelled abroad by train for more than 20 years. Did not enjoy it. In our express car more comfortable. Two births in first class, one above the other. The mattress is hard, sides ache. The Second Secretary of the Embassy, B. V. Ryzhov,[456] met me. On the day of arrival visited A. F. Tishchenko,[457] Counsellor at the Embassy. Very pleasant man. They organized a lecture at the Law Faculty – I will deliver it tomorrow at 10:15 and then will meet with the advocates of peace.

455 Gennadii Vasilevich Govorin (b. 1947), Secretary and then Counsellor of the USSR Embassy in Delhi from 1984 to 1989 – [VGT].

456 Boris Viktorovich Ryzhov (b. 1941), Second Secretary, USSR Embassy in Helsinki, from 1984 to 1987 – [VGT].

457 Anatolii Fedoseevich Tishchenko (1935-2002), Counsellor-Envoy of the USSR Embassy in Helsinki from 1983 to 1988; Ambassador of the Russian Federation to Norway from 1992 to 1995 – [VGT].

The session opened on 20 August at 16:00 in the old building of the University. Koivisto,[458] the President of Finland, was present. The Minister of Foreign Affairs, Paavo Väyrynen,[459] opened the session with a rather pallid speech. Then the acting President, Paul Reuter, spoke (President E. Castren has died) and the Secretary General, Valticos – both with brilliant speeches.

The elections proceeded tautly: four rounds. Hanna Bokor-Szego (Hungary) and Wolfke (Poland)[460] were not elected again.

Today McWhinney invited me to lunch. In his words, the Minister of Foreign Affairs of Canada, Clark,[461] assigned him to travel to Moscow and to meet with a number of our people. Supposedly they seek a way of resolving certain private issues (reunification of families, for example). This is supposedly necessary for Clark in order to justify his certain departures from United States policies. McWhinney leaves for Moscow on 25 August, although the session finished on 29 August. Many are leaving early. About 30 persons after the session are going to Leningrad. Had thorough discussions with Lachs and Yankov.

At 10:15 the lecture at the University. Topic: "International Law and the Anti-War Movement". I spoke roughly as I had at the Congress of the International Association of Democratic Lawyers in October 1984. Then an exchange of views. There were about 15 persons. Among them: Antti Suviranta – Chief Justice of the Supreme Court of Finland;[462] Ekki Ailio – Supreme Court,[463] Professor M. Hidén – Dean of the Faculty of Law.[464]

24 Aug:

Helsinki. Hotel: Yesterday, when at 09:20 I went to the University, Ago told me: I have stunning news – Morozov is retiring as a member of the Court. The President of the Court, Singh, confirmed, saying that when in July he left for Moscow, Morozov's health was poor. So sad for Platon.

Many conversations as to who will be the new Soviet judge. Many said to me that everyone in the Institute would wish that it be me. To this I replied that this will not happen, since I have no desire to be so.

26 Aug:

Helsinki. Hotel: Today was at the morning session of the Administrative Council. The next session will be in Cairo; the Deputy Minister of Foreign Affairs of Egypt, Boutros-Ghali, was elected the President of the Institute.

---

458 Mauno Henrik Koivisto (b. 1923), was the Ninth President of Finland from 1982 to 1994 – [WEB].

459 Paavo Matti Väyrynen (b. 1946), has held several Finnish ministerial posts – [WEB].

460 Karol Wolfke (b. 1915), Professor of International Law, Wroclaw University – [WEB].

461 Joe Clark (b. 1939), Prime Minister of Canada from 1979 to 1980; Secretary of State for Foreign Affairs from 1984 to 1991 – [VGT].

462 Antti Johannes Suviranta (1923-2008), Professor of Labour Law at the Helsinki University from 1967 to 1971, President of the Finnish Labour Court from 1970 to 1982, Chief Justice of the Supreme Administrative Court of Finnland from 1982 to 1993 – [WEB].

463 Erkki Ailio (b. 1922), member of Finnish Supreme Court from 1969 to 1992 – [WEB].

464 Mikael Hidén (b. 1939), Dean of the Faculty of Law, Helsinki University, from 1984 to 1998; Professor of Constitutional and International Law from 1976 to 2004 – [WEB].

At 14:00 the Commission des Travaux. At the suggestion of Schachter and myself (I advanced this at Dijon), they decided that at each session there will be a general discussion at the beginning on the Report of the Commission des Travaux. I submitted the proposal to change the procedure for the discussion of questions at plenary sessions. Now – an introductory word by the rapporteur and after each address the rapporteur replies. I suggested that, with rare exception, the rapporteur should speak at the end of the discussion to sum up. This saves much time. The proposal was accepted.

29 Aug:

Helsinki-Moscow Train: "Tolstoy" is written on each car. This is in honor of Lev Tolstoy. There is another train, the "Repin".[465] On 27 August gave a lecture at the Embassy at the request of the temporary chargé d'affaires, Counsellor A. F. Tishchenko, on the topic "International Law and Diplomacy". Today, the Second Secretary of the Embassy, B. V. Ryzhov, escorted me. In general the Embassy was very attentive.

The sessions finished yesterday. I actively spoke at the sessions on human rights, in the Commission des Travaux, and at plenary sessions on the influence of armed conflicts on international treaties.

The American professors said that they await me. I said that at the beginning of the year I had sent a letter to the Dean of the Harvard Law School asking whether I might plan to come in spring 1986, but received no reply. Schachter promised to take this matter on.

The session was devoted basically to questions of private international law. This was not right. The Report of F. Rigaux,[466] "Legal Consequences of the Dissolution of Marriage", occupied the most time.

1986

25 April:

London Ryan Hotel: Have not flown for more than a year. The last time was India in January 1985. Went by train to Helsinki in August 1985. In London, the Executive Council and the Anglo-Soviet Symposium on International Law. Organizer of the Symposium: W. Butler, University College London. He translated my book, *Theory of International Law.*

Butler met me yesterday. Accommodated in this hotel because our seminar participants will stay here. In general I am accustomed to stay in the London Embassy Hotel near Hyde Park. Early in the morning, having slept until 4:00, I worked on my report.

465 The train was named in honor of Ilia Efimovich Repin (1844-1930), noted Russian painter of historical subjects – [WEB].

466 François Rigaux (b. 1926), French international lawyer – [WEB].

27 April:

London Ryan Hotel: the session of the Executive Council was yesterday. Everything went without complications. The Poles (Makarczyk)[467] proposed that the ILA Conference be held in Warsaw in 1988. This proposal was, in principle, accepted. Representatives of Hungary, Canada, USSR, France, and the Federal Republic of Germany spoke in support.

Today for the first time I did exercises outdoors. Found a quiet square nearby, enclosed by houses, no traffic. With pleasure did them for 40 minutes. Yesterday evening Professors E. T. Usenko[468] and A. A. Rubanov arrived. Regrettably, I. I. Lukashuk did not come. And also regrettable that Usenko leaves on 30 April and we two remain. On television much is being said about the death of the wife of the Duke of Windsor, who in 1936 abdicated from the throne in order to marry a divorced American.

29 April:

University College London: The symposium is proceeding very interestingly. My report: "The Role of Resolutions of International Organizations in the Process of Creating Norms of International Law". On the British side the corresponding rapporteur was Prof. Rosalyn Higgins. The reports of Usenko and Usher[469] on the problems of the relationship between Comecon and Soviet Law and EEC and British Law were combined. Now the report of Professor Merrills[470] on "The Role and Limits of International Adjudication".

3 May:

London-Moscow Aircraft: The day before yesterday travelled with Rubanov to Oxford by coach. Visited the museum, very rich and interesting. Saw a large bookshop – the largest in the world – as a local inhabitant told me, who showed us the way. Then we went to All Souls College to see Professor Ian Brownlie. He showed us the buildings of the library, college, and university. The Librarian[471] brought out Martens' treaty collection, vol. 1, with Martens'[472] inscription, and also my *Theory of International Law*, on which I wrote an inscription at his request. At 19:15 the dinner of the Fellows of All Souls College. They were in black gowns, a mixture of the modern with the medieval.

467 Jerzy Makarczyk (b. 1938), Polish international lawyer – [WEB].

468 Evgenii Timofeevich Usenko (1918-2010), Russian specialist in socialist economic integration – [WEB].

469 Professor John Usher (1945-2008), then Professor of European Law at University College London – [WEB].

470 John Graham Merrills (b. 1942), Professor of International Law at the University of Sheffield – [WEB].

471 John Simon Gabriel Simmons (1915-2005), the greatest British authority on the Russian book and Sometime Librarian of All Souls College – [WEB].

472 Fedor Fedorovich Martens, (1845-1909), legal advisor to the Russian Ministry of Foreign Affairs, diplomat, international arbitrator, and professor of international law at St. Petersburg University – [WEB].

It was a pleasure to meet the Counsellor of the Embassy, K. K. Ivanov, [473] and his wife, Tatiana,[474] daughter of S. T. Bazarov,[475] who entered the People's Commissariat of Foreign Affairs as I did in 1939.

Butler and Ivanov accompanied us. The works at the symposium were adequate. Gave my report and submitted the reports of Lukashuk and Movchan, so that practically I gave three reports.

25 Aug:

Seoul. Hotel Shilla: Flew with L. V. Korbut to Seoul for the 62nd Conference of the International Law Association via Tokyo.

No time. Will be brief. On 23 August we landed in Tokyo at about 11:00 according to local time. Rang the Embassy from the Aeroflot office. Saturday, person on duty, there is no one there. Head of the Aeroflot office sent his associate with us, a Japanese lady, to purchase tickets for the flight on Korean Airlines. They did not sell us tickets since we have no Korean visas.[476] I rang the Embassy – we cannot fly today and must spend the night. I ask that a car be sent to go to the Embassy. At 15:00 the Third Secretary, I. Iu. Nikiforov,[477] rings and says that he is coming for us. We drank coffee at Aeroflot and I nodded off. When I awakened, I spoke with the Japanese lady – let us go and try to purchase a ticket on Japan Airlines. We bought it. About 18:00 Nikiforov arrived. The next day we were convinced that the road to the airport indeed requires 3 hours – traffic jams about the airport. Went to the Embassy, they allotted us two flats for persons arriving. Began to look at the tickets and, how awful, the flight is 23 August and I had requested another day. The time is 22:00. The embassy people say that everything is closed now. Am worried. Korbut went to the duty person and took the Japan Airlines telephone. Rang, explained. No objections. Agreed to the flight of 24 August at 18:00. Rang Seoul, communicated the flight number. Went peacefully to sleep.

The Embassy official, Nikiforov, turned out to be a very dear person. From 10:00 to 14:00 we looked about Tokyo with him. It was exceedingly interesting. Then we quickly dined. The wife of Igor Iurevich is a charming lady. Went to the airport. Five persons met us in Seoul, VIP, no difficulties. Visas, baggage, they did everything. But the suitcases were opened. And in general, it seems to me, their eyes never left us.

---

473 Kirill Konstantinovich Ivanov (b. 1937), Counsellor of the USSR Embassy in London from 1985 to 1990; the first Russian Consul General in Hong Kong and Macao from 1994 to 1998 – [VGT].

474 Tatiana Semenovna Ivanova (b. 1940), Scientific Section of the USSR Embassy in London – [VGT].

475 Semen Tarasovich Bazarov (1914-1985), official of the USSR People's Commissariat for Foreign Affairs who on 8 May 1945 gave to Field Marshal Wilhelm Keitel (1882-1946) for signature the Act of Unconditional Surrender of Germany and also served as USSR Ambassador to Mexico from 1962 to 1968 – [VGT].

476 At this time diplomatic relations had not yet been established between the Republic of Korea and the USSR – [VGT].

477 Igor Iurevich Nikiforov (b. 1952), Secretary of the USSR Embassy in Tokyo – [WEB].

26 Aug:

Hotel Shilla: The Assistant of the Minister of Foreign Affairs, Yong-Gil:[478]

1. A great impression – Gorbachev's speech in Vladivostok.
2. Aspiration to improve relations with the USSR:
   a) economic and other links;
   b) interest in participating in exploiting the wealth of Siberia.

Understand the difficulties for us in connection with North Korea. Set out the position on reunification by means of a gradual improvement of ties with North Korea. Asked to pass this on to Moscow.

In the morning breakfast at the invitation of a Korean. The Filipino Syquia[479] was present with his wife. Syquia – the Gorbachev speech in Vladivostok made a great impression. In particular, his proposal to create in the Pacific Ocean zone a process similar to the Helsinki Process.

At 15:00 the "main" participants of the Conference visited the President of the Republic of Korea, Chun Doo-hwan.[480] There were 9 of us in all. In welcoming us, he specially expressed satisfaction that the famous Professor Tunkin and Professor Avramov[481] from Yugoslavia were present at the Conference. No one else was mentioned.

Soon after the reception Dr. Thok-Kyu Limb approached. Said that the journalists very much want to meet with me, but I asked him to pass on that all my time was occupied. I said that I am a mere professor and not a channel for official communications. Thanked them for the information and said I will see what I can do.

27 Aug:

Hotel Shilla: Our every step is under control. Special duty people on our ninth floor and on the eighth, where Avramov from Yugoslavia lives. Today at 07:30 Professor Lee[482] rang and said that he is inviting me and Korbut to breakfast. I replied that I had not been warned and that we would be ready only at 08:00. After breakfast, he said that my book "Law and Force" is being translated.

Full of invitations. Today the Director of the Institute of Foreign Affairs and National Security, Dr. Oh,[483] gave a lunch. Everything they know and are interested in the Gorbachev proposals made in Vladivostok.

---

478 Yong-Gil [not further identified].

479 Enrique P. Syquia (1930-2005), President of the Philippine Branch of the International Law Association; Honorary Consul of Malta to the Philippines – [WEB].

480 Chun Doo-hwan (b. 1931), twelfth President of Korea from 1981 to 1988 – [WEB].

481 Smilja Avramov (b. 1918), President of the Yugoslav Branch of the International Law Association – [WEB].

482 Yun-Yoong Lee (1923-1992), Professor, Korea University – [VGT].

483 Dr. Jay-Hee Oh (b. 1932), Director, Institute of Foreign Affairs and National Security – [VGT].

Today was a luncheon which the Minister of Foreign Affairs gave. I was weary from the photographing. One after another the Koreans approached and asked to be photographed.

Professor Lee, who translated my *Theory of International Law*, invited me yesterday to deliver a lecture to his students. But there will be no lectures. Means, not authorized. So much the better. I avoid publicity. Tomorrow the Chairman of the International Law Association of the Republic of Korea, Dr. Limb, promised to show me the city. Today after lunch the Deputy Minister of Foreign Affairs, Park,[484] again offered his car and someone to accompany, but I said that I had already agreed with Dr. Limb.

28 Aug:

Hotel Shilla: Today was a free day. At 10:00 I, Korbut, and Dr. Limb drove about the city on an excursion. We visited the place where the house of the Russian Mission had been. The house was destroyed by bombing; they say that all Seoul was destroyed in 1950. Saw the National Museum. Limb summoned his photographer, who snapped us all the time in the Museum. Then lunch in the best hotel in Seoul – Japanese cuisine. Four persons, we three and an aide of the President for relations with States with which Seoul does not have diplomatic relations – Chung.[485] He very insistently attempted to elicit my opinion about how to improve relations with the Soviet Union.

It is clear that they want to improve economic, scientific-technical, and cultural links with us. Asked what I might advise. I said that I am merely a professor, not concerned with these questions, and cannot give any advice. Asked what reflections he has. Chung said that it would be good to arrange air traffic between Moscow and Seoul and to improve scientific and technical, and also cultural exchanges. He said that it may be possible to convent a Conference on Pacific Ocean Problems. Asked me what problems might be put for discussion. I said that the general topic of a Conference might be "The Pacific Ocean Region – Zone of Peace". There are interesting proposals of the Soviet Government set out in Gorbachev's speech in Vladivostok. There might be other proposals. Scholars might discuss them. He was interested in the prospects for a US-USSR Summit. I set out our position. Three Gorbachev proposals especially interested him concerning the background of US policy. He said that he has the Gorbachev speech, but he did not write down these three proposals. In conclusion he passed to me his visiting card and said that his home address was indicated there and if I want to communicate something to him, this might be done privately. Write to him, and he may pass it personally to the President.

In the evening there was a reception at the Olympic complex – magnificent. Again they constantly asked to photograph me and, when all had dispersed, two photographers approached and asked to be photographed with me. First with one, then with the other. In the evening a journalist from a Korean newspaper rang and requested an interview. I said that I am busy and could not.

---

484 Park Yeong-su, Minister of Foreign Affairs, Republic of Korea, from 1998 – [VGT].

485 Chung [not further identified].

31 Aug:
Tokyo. Embassy: On 29 August the Minister heading the Reunification Board arranged a reception. About 20 participants of the International Law Association were there. They sat me to the right of the Minister. Constantly they spoke about reunification. In their words, there were about ten million refugees from North Korea in South Korea. Their position is a step by step approach. Began to speak. Also at the reception of the President they had spoken, that is, all spoke. Then I spoke about the nuclear danger, that the ILA had made a contribution to the progressive development of public international law, and thereby rescued mankind from the nuclear threat. At the Minister's reception I mentioned reunification. I hope, I said, that a next ILA Conference in Korea will be held in a unified Korea.

Tokyo-Moscow Aircraft: Dr. Limb invited us on 30 August to breakfast. About 20 Koreans gathered. I acquainted them with the activity of the Soviet Association of International Law and teaching and scientific research work in the USSR in the field of international law. There were many questions.

Full Council at 09:00. I introduced an amendment to the section on the NIEO,[486] where it was said "unanimous accepted", whereas the Resolution and Declaration were adopted "by consensus". Virally and the Australian presiding in the Committee supported me and the respective amendment was made. Met Owada[487] at the Conference. He invited me to lunch on 30 August in Tokyo. Owada departed on 28 August, and in the evening of 28 August I was rung from the Embassy of Japan in Seoul; they said that Owada had rung them and requested to clarify my flight number for Seoul-Tokyo.

We did not go to the closing session since it was necessary to depart. We went to the airport – VIP, took our baggage and passport. We sit, there remain 30, 20, 15 minutes before departure. Those accompanying us, especially Professor Lee, are nervous. Finally, 10 minutes before take-off we go to the aircraft.

2 Sept:
Moscow. Dacha: Only in Tokyo did we guess what had happened. The Koreans for a long time could not open Korbut's suitcase and were forced to break the lock. I had prudently not closed the lock on my suitcase. Two flats were again allocated to us in the Embassy. We left our things and together with Counsellor G. E. Komarovskii[488] went to the restaurant for lunch with Owada. There I met Yokota,[489] who for four years was a

486 New International Economic Order – [VGT].

487 Hisashi Owada (b. 1932), former legal advisor to Japanese Ministry of Foreign Affairs and member from Japan on International Court of Justice since 2003 – [WEB].

488 Georgii Evgenievich Komarovskii (b. 1933), Counsellor of the USSR Embassy in Tokyo from 1986 to 1991 – [VGT].

489 KisaburoYokota (1896-1993), member of the International Law Commission from 1957 to 1960; Chief Justice of Japan from 1960 to 1966 – [VGT].

member of the International Law Commission at the time when I worked there. Then he was elected Chief Justice. He had only just celebrated his 90th birthday but says that, as before, he plays tennis three times a week.

In brief my address at the Workshop on Peaceful Settlement of Disputes:

1. A threat of nuclear holocaust.
2. The danger of a policy of force and armaments race.
3. The necessity of new thinking.
4. Relations among States must and can be based on negotiation and peaceful settlement of disputes.
5. The role of International Law.

An American professor, Rogers,[490] gave a report. He told me that he comes to Moscow. In the report he briefly described the mood in the United States with respect to the peaceful settlement of disputes – a disappointment.

Prof. Brownlie told me after lunch that he planned this Workshop specially so as not to avoid with silence the Nicaragua-US case. To put this question directly is impossible. Chowdhury[491] (India) gave a good speech against the United States.

Volodya and Alyesha met us in Moscow. Alyesha wandered quite close to the customs point and when I took a luggage cart for the baggage I hear a shout: Didiks (he calls me so). Took Korbut and Alyesha home and arrived at the dacha only at 22:00 hours.

12 Dec:

Paris. Hotel Arcade: Our delegation to the 40th anniversary of the International Association of Democratic Lawyers consists of 11 persons. Among them: A. Ia. Sukharev – chairman of the Association of Soviet Jurists (Ministry of Justice of the RSFSR);[492] S. A. Shishkov – Deputy Procurator General;[493] O. Iu. Ivanitskii – First Deputy Chairman of the Union of Soviet Friendship Societies;[494] P. M. Kuris (Vilnius),[495] and others.

Program devoted to the 40th anniversary of the International Association of Democratic Lawyers:

Nordman – the role of law: protectress and innovator. Judgment of the Court in the Nicaragua-USA case – use of this force;

490 William Dill Rogers (1927-2007), American legal practitioner; Under-Secretary of State for Economic Affairs from 1977 to 1978 – [VGT].

491 Subrata Roy Chowdhury (1923-1994), international lawyer from India; member, International Institute of Space Law from 1989 – [WEB].

492 Aleksandr Iakovlevich Sukharev (b. 1923), Procurator General of the USSR from 1988 to 1990 – [WEB].

493 Sergei Aleksandrovich Shishkov (1915-1989), Deputy Procurator General – [VGT].

494 Oleg Iurevich Ivanitskii (b.1931), First Deputy Chairman from 1986 to 1991, Union of Soviet Friendship Societies – [VGT].

495 Pranas M. Kuris (b. 1938), specialist on State succession and former post-graduate student of Tunkin – [WEB].

Ch. Chaumont – And what purpose has San Francisco served? Spirit of the Conference and realism. Grand alliance of the USSR and USA. Realism – a) limitation of powers, b) provision on the creation of armed forces. Cannot imagine armed forces acting against a Great Power. Idealism – review of ideologies. The Charter has not created an involuntary ideology.

Echeverria[496] – attack against UNESCO is attack against the system of the United Nations. The third world and the socialist countries believe in the purpose of the U.N. The growth of the U.N. and the growth of nuclear weapons.

MacBride – The association of jurists – a peace organization. Sending arms by the United States to South Africa in order to support the colonial regime and resist Angola, Mozambique, Allende, Grenada … Time to face these problems caused by the United States or by the socialist countries (Long ovation). On the whole, the speech was anti-American.

A. Ia. Sukharev – international law is disappearing and is being replaced by a policy of force.

Editor of Mond diplomatique – decline in the role of international law.

Woodir (USA)[497] – aggression against Nicaragua. All jurists should demand the submission of the United States to the decision of the Court.

Zigler (Switzerland)[498] – Law is stopped in the meaning of international relations.

17 Dec:

Hotel Arcade: Today the Franco-Soviet Colloquium "Les Constitutions" began within the framework of the France-USSR Society. My question brought an especially lively discussion: "Dans son excellent rapport Prof. Jean-Pierre Cot nous a explique la cohabitation telle quelle existe a present. Quelle sont les perspectives de cette cohabitation? Comme vous M. Le Prof. Lesage avez pris place du Prof. J. P. Cot j'adresse cette question a vous".

We then were in the Senate. The chairman of the group for assisting the France-USSR Society received us. Saw the Luxembourg Palace built initially by M. Médici.[499] Then the palace was rearranged, rebuilt. Then the Colloquium. Prof. F. L. Hamon:[500] Legal guarantees of the Constitution. As a benchmark (implicitly) the system of the United States. The Constitutional Council. Supervision over the constitutionality of laws is a recent phenomenon.

21 Dec:

Paris-Moscow Aircraft: We are returning. So many events in 10 days that it seemed an entire month elapsed. Had lunch with Colliard. Spoke about the Soviet-French

496 Luis Echeverria Alvarez (b. 1922), Mexican lawyer, law professor, and politician; President of Mexico from 1970 to 1976; Ambassador to UNESCO from 1977 – [VGT].

497 Woodir [not further identified].

498 Jean Zigler (b. 1934), Professor of Sociology, University of Geneva; member, Federal Assembly of Switzerland from 1981 to 1999; Vice President, United Nations Human Rights Council – [VGT].

499 Marie de Médici (1545-1642), mother of King Louis XIII – [WEB].

500 F. Leo Hamon (1908-1993), French lawyer, son of Russian émigrés; Senator from 1946 to 1958 – [VGT].

Colloquium on international law. He is very much "for". Promised to speak with Dupuy, who is now the President of the French Society of International Law. Dupuy was not there, left for holidays. On 19 December dined with Bardonnet.[501] A very pleasant person. Since I will not be at the session of the Curatorium of The Hague Academy, I spoke with him about all matters. I asked that the next session be designated for 9 May. On 2 May I have the Executive Council of the International Law Association in London, and from 4 to 8 – a symposium with the West Germans in Kiel. Next I asked to move my cours from 1988 to 1990, and in place of me recommended Butkevich[502] from Kiev. Also spoke about the Soviet-French Colloquium. He very much approves this idea and also promised to speak with Dupuy.

Before meeting MacBride at the ceremonial session devoted to the 40th anniversary of the International Association of Democratic Lawyers I saw him in Moscow in November 1986 at the "Lessons of Nuremberg". And then I had agreed with him that he would propose to eminent jurists to sign an anti-nuclear appeal. The text was agreed. I included the phrase to strive for the "rule of law in international relations". In Paris his secretary showed me seven signatures. One must have the signature of the Secretary General of the International Commission of Jurists, N. MacDermot.[503] MacBride, Sukharev, and I conversed with him on this occasion. But, finally, he began to object only to the last phrase where it spoke about the need to realize United Nations General Assembly resolutions on general and complete disarmament. The conversation was deferred until morning. The conversation was renewed after breakfast in the Hotel. Sukharev spoke, and McDermot's wife interpreted (she is Russian). I came, listened, but there was no result. Sukharev then left. I spoke with McDermot (a tete reposée) and said: it seems to me that one might not mention General Assembly resolutions but say that the liquidation of a nuclear weapon will be a step towards the final purpose of general and complete disarmament. He agreed and wrote this amendment into the text himself. We agreed that he himself would phone MacBride. I rang MacBride after an hour. He said that he accepted the amendment.

On 14 December I called on Bastid. While at Bastid's (by arrangement with Sukharev) I showed her the text as emanating from MacBride. She, it seemed to me, was somewhat frightened. Began to set out in essence the official French position on the need for France to have a nuclear weapon.

Passed to her our Yearbook of the Soviet Association of International Law. Met Jean-Pierre Cot at the France-USSR Colloquium. He always is very courteous to me, recalls how in 1958 he heard my lectures at The Hague Academy. I promise to pass to him my book "Law and Force", and he, his work – a collection of articles of the United Nations Charter. I am carrying this collection of articles with me. An enormous book, about 1,500 pages.

---

501 Daniel Bardonnet (b. 1931), French international lawyer – [WEB].

502 Vladimir Grigorievich Butkevich (b. 1946), member from Ukraine of European Court for Human Rights – [WEB].

503 Niall MacDermot (1916-1996), Secretary General of the International Commission of Jurists from 1970 to 1990 – [VGT].

Met with Salmon within the framework of the International Association of Democratic Lawyers. Gave him "Law and Force" and the Soviet Yearbook of International Law. We prepared the final text of the Manifesto of the Conference and a cable to Gorbachev and Reagan. Both documents were adopted by the Council on 15 December.

1987

2 May:

London. Thistle Kensington Palace Hotel: This time a lengthy trip: London – 3 days, Kiel – 4 days (Soviet-West German Seminar), and The Hague from 8 to 10 May (Curatorium of The Academy). K. K. Ivanov met me on 1 May at the Airport. Supped at their home.

Today a session until 16:00. Olmstead, who was elected Chairman of the Executive Council of the International Law Association, dragged things out a bit. At the end, more than half of those present had left. Major issues: 1988 Conference in Warsaw and the creation of new committees. Nothing controversial.

4 May:

Thistle Kensington Palace Hotel: Yesterday was in the National Gallery. The Gallery opens at 14:00. I arrived at 12:30. Walked on nearby streets. Purchased Le Carré,[504] *The Perfect Spy*. This, his recent book, is now being widely advertised I am told.

Sat for a long time before the painting by Guido Reni, "Adoration of the Magi".[505] An enormous canvas by Van Dyck, "Charles I on a Horse". The horse's head is very small, but the painting leaves an impression.

On this same day Dr. Limb invited me to dine. Not far away there is a fish restaurant, very good. Gave him "Law and Force".

5 May:

Kiel. Kaufmann Hotel: Flew into Hamburg yesterday. Took a taxi and went to Kiel. Went into a building of the University and found myself in an auditorium. It turned out that this was the Faculty of Economics. Lessons had not yet begun, and the professor courteously took me to his office, rang Professor Wolfrum[506] (Executive Director, Institute for International Law), who is organizing the Seminar. Wolfrum sent his post-graduate student to bring me to the neighboring building to him. Wolfrum was surprised at my early appearance since our Consulate General told him that I would arrive on 5 May.

---

504 David John Moore Cornwell (pseud. John Le Carré) (b. 1931), world renowned writer of espionage novels – [WEB].

505 Guido Reni (1575-1642), Italian painter of high-Baroque style – [WEB].

506 Rüdiger Wolfrum (b. 1941), German international lawyer – [WEB].

Today work has commenced. At the morning session on the reflection of customary international law in national law G. M. Danilenko[507] (Institute of State and Law of the Academy of Sciences) and Rudolf[508] spoke. At the evening session on the influence of resolutions of international organizations on national law: Koenig[509] and I. I. Lukashuk (Institute of State and Law of the Academy of Sciences).

6 May:

Kielen Kaufmann Hotel: Our "youth" have gone into the city – shopping. G. B. Starushenko and I have a free morning. Looked at the *Frankfurter Allgemeine* and the local *Kielen Nachrichten*. At 13:00 went for lunch to Dr. Peter Bendixen,[510] Minister of Education and Cultural Affairs of the State Schleswig-Holstein, in Kielen Schloss.

9 May:

The Hague. Europa Crest Hotel: In the evening dinner at the Kielen Kaufmann Hotel Bernhardt, Wolfrum and Tunkin agreed that:

1. Topic of the next seminar in Moscow – The Law of International Organisations.
2. Materials of the Seminar in Kiel will be published by the University in Kiel. Executive editors: Wolfrum and Tunkin (Korbut later told me that Schweisfurth asked me to write Wolfrum so that Schweisfurth also would be one of the editors).
3. Not only the reports will be published, but also the discussion. They will print the recorded discussion and send to the authors for amendments.

E. T. Usenko and G. G. Shinkaretskaia promised to send Wolfrum their reports. I. I. Lukashuk and G. M. Danilenko already gave me theirs. Both sides expressed their satisfaction with the Seminar. It indeed was interesting.

On 8 May in the morning sailed on a ship along the canals. Then they sat me in a coach and in 30 minutes I was at the Airport. I had already passed through passport control and awaited boarding when Consul Grishanin[511] arrived from the Consulate General. They summoned me to him. I informed him about the Seminar and expressed gratitude for assistance.

Yesterday our Judge, Nikolai Konstantinovich Tarasov,[512] met me in Amsterdam. Tarasov said that I was invited to a reception by Oda,[513] so to say, directly from the ship

507 Gennadii Mikhailovich Danilenko (1955-2001), Russian international lawyer who later emigrated to the United States and taught at Wayne State University in Detroit – [web].

508 Walter Rudolf (b. 1931), German international lawyer – [vgt].

509 Doris Koenig (b. 1957), Head, Chair of Public Law, International and European Law, Bucerius Law School, Hamburg, Germany – [vgt].

510 Peter Bendixen (1943-2007), German politician, Minister of Culture of Schleswig-Holstein *lande* from 1979 to 1988 – [vgt].

511 Grishanin [not further identified].

512 Nikolai Konstantinovich Tarasov (1923-1994), member of the International Court of Justice from Russia from 1985 to 1995 – [web].

513 Shigeru Oda (b. 1924), member of the International Court of Justice from Japan, serving from 1976 to 2003 – [web].

to a ball. Today the session of the Curatorium ended at 12:00. I was not at the sessions since, I believe, 1984. This is of benefit to no one. Lachs has greatly aged. Ago too. Vieillir c'est une seule possibilité de vivre longtemps.

11 May:

Europa Crest Hotel: Yesterday I dined with Tarasov. A very likeable person. Ambassador A. I. Blatov[514] also was there with his wife. At 17:00 met with Lachs. Always interesting to speak with him.

Today from 10:30 to 14:00 worked with satisfaction in the Library. Gave the Library the textbook *International Law* and *Law and Force*. Took three journals to the Hotel.

16 May:

Amsterdam-Moscow Aircraft: This time succeeded in working in the Library for several days. As always, I note the pages and they make copies for me.

Yesterday was lunch with Singh – the President of the Court. He could not come to Moscow for the Soviet-Indian Symposium. We agreed that he would call Delhi and learn when Chief Justice Pathak might come. Then he rang me at the Hotel and said that Pathak might arrive on 29 September and be there until 3 October. The remaining members of the delegation might, if we wish this, stay on. I said that I would consult in Moscow, but think that this will work for us. The reply we will communicate to Delhi.

As a result of my absences at sessions of the Curatorium there will not be any of our lecturers in 1987, 1988, and, no doubt, in 1989. I nominated Kolodkin for the cours "New Trends in the Law of the Sea". The proposal was supported, including by Dupuy. But the next years are already filled up. My cours "Law and Force in the International System" is planned. As I requested, for 1990.

Tarasov escorted me to embarkation on the aircraft. Bought *Le Monde* and the *Herald Tribune* before boarding. Read also an article on the aircraft in the newspaper Московские новости [Moscow News] about Zinovii Peshkov,[515] which was given to me in The Hague. I heard about him from our former Ambassador to China, Petrov,[516] in 1945, when were worked day and night together during negotiations with the Kuomintang. It turns out that this was the brother of Ia. Sverdlov.[517] Maxim Gorky[518] gave Zinovii his surname in order that he, upon the recommendation of

514 Anatolii Ivanovich Blatov (1914-1988), Ambassador of the USSR to Netherlands from 1985 to 1988 – [VGT].

515 Zinovii Peshkov (1884-1966), born Yeshua Zalman Sverdlov to a Jewish engraver in Nizhnii Novgorod, changed his name to Gorky and was christened Russian Orthodox in order to avoid Russian restrictions on Jews living in large cities. Emigrated to Canada in 1904 and later had a remarkable career in French military and diplomatic service – [WEB].

516 Appolon Aleksandrovich Petrov (1907-1949), Ambassador of the USSR to China from 1945 to 1948 – [VGT].

517 Iakov Mikhailovich Sverdlov (1885-1919), Chairman of the All-Russian Central Executive Committee from November 1917 to March 1919 – [VGT].

518 Real name – Aleksei Maksimovich Peshkov (1868-1936), the noted Russian and Soviet writer – [VGT].

V. I. Nemirovich-Danchenko,[519] might enroll in the Theatre Studio of the Moscow Arts Theater. A man of surprising fate: French general, Ambassador of France to China, and then to Japan.

Tunkin with Judge Anatolii Kolodkin, April 1988

1992

25 July:
The Hague. Europa Hotel: Have travelled nowhere for more than a year. Arrived in The Hague for a session of the Curatorium. A brief trip, returning on 29 July.

The Curatorium session proceeded normally. I expressed my misunderstanding with regard to the deferral of the cours of lectures by Boguslavskii and Kolodkin and insisted that their lectures take place as soon as possible. Ago said that the Programme

519 Vladimir Ivanovich Nemirovich-Danchenko (1858-1943), director, dramatist, one of the founders of the Moscow Arts Theater – [VGT].

Committee will take this into account. When discussing the question of the foreign programme for 1993, when a conference should be held in Asia, I proposed that the possibility of holding it in Vietnam be considered.

Visited Lachs. Asked him to help organize the publication of my lectures as a separate book. He rang Martinus,[520] but says the necessary person was not there. Will ring tomorrow.

1993

4 March:

Seoul. Plaza Hotel: Arrived in Seoul for ten days at the invitation of the Seoul Academy of International Law and the Seoul National University. A dinner with Professor Park[521] at a French restaurant in the Seoul National University in the Swiss Grand Hotel. My post-graduate student, Dokju Kim,[522] who was from Seoul National University, met me. They dine early and rise early. Dr. Thok-Kyu Limb, Honorary President of the Korean Branch of the International Law Association, came in the evening. We sat, no doubt, for an hour.

In the morning at 10:30 a meeting with two journalists. After the meeting, went with Kim to see the city and along the way collected Kim's fiancée. Clambered up the mountain, then viewed the Assembly (parliament), library, and office of Kim's father – a member of the National Assembly of South Korea. Three of my books proved to be in the Library of the Assembly: two published in Korea and "Law and Force". An employee accompanied us in the Assembly and gave explanations. Then Kim's father invited us to lunch. At lunch, besides myself, there were Kim with his fiancée and one teacher of the Russian language.

5 March:

Plaza Hotel: Today at 15:00 gave a lecture on "The 20th Century and International Law". Specialists on international law were primarily present, about 50 in all. The lectures lasted about one hour, then questions for 40 minutes. Then a cocktail party and at 18:30 dinner in a Korea restaurant for about 16 to 18 persons. Our Ambassador, A. N. Panov,[523] was there with his wife. A very likeable person, about forty years old. No less than 20 dishes at the dinner. I said that I had learned for the first time what Korean cuisine was.

520 The distinguished Dutch law publishers, Martinus Nijhoff, who have published the *Recueil des cours* of the Hague Academy of International Law since its inception – [WEB].

521 Choon-ho Park (1930-2008), member of the International Law of the Sea Tribunal from 1996 to 2008 – [WEB].

522 Dokju Kim (b. 1965), Professor, Institute of Foreign Affairs – [VGT].

523 Aleksandr Nikolaevich Panov (b. 1944), Ambassador to the Republic of Korea from 1992 to 1993 – [VGT].

Tunkin with Professor Rein Müllerson. April 1988

7 March:

Cheju. Shilla Hotel: Indeed I have "come a long way for nothing". Flew with Kim to Cheju on 6 March at 13:00, dined at the airport, then an hour plus in a taxi to the Hotel. Here it is raining. The sea is merged with the clouds. The Hotel is superb, better than the Plaza. Gorbachev stayed here when he met with Roh Tae Woo.[524] After supper went to my room and chatted for more than an hour. Kim said that he wanted to be a lecturer in public international law. This pleased me. Then we strolled with Kim to a garden and saw a tablet where it was written that in April 1991 Presidents Gorbachev and Roh Tae Woo walked along this path.

Everything is wonderful. There is never enough time for these strolls in the park and a nap.

524 Roh Tae Woo (b. 1932), thirteenth President of Korea – [WEB].

8 March:

Seoul. The Swiss Grand Hotel: Arrived by air from Cheju at 13:00. A strike of restaurant workers in the Hotel, confined ourselves to a sandwich and coffee. At 17:00 the Counsellor-Envoy of our Embassy, G. D. Toleraia,[525] came to me for consultations with regard to our property in Seoul. The Koreans do not want to return the land plot to us which belonged to the Tsarist diplomatic mission and since 1907 to the consulate. I have some advice. Toleraia makes the impression of a very knowledgeable person.

Toleraia said that since Eltsin[526] promised to transfer documents to the Koreans about the outbreak of war in 1950, these documents are being studied in the Archive of the USSR Ministry of Foreign Affairs. He also took this up with Goncharov[527] and saw documents signed by me. Goncharov, in his words, said: that was one bright man, Tunkin, who understood everything correctly.

10 March:

The Swiss Grand Hotel: Yesterday at 11:00 gave a lecture to students in the second year of the Seoul National University on "Sources of International Law". Gave it in English, but there was a translation. Professor Park said after the lecture that when a foreign professor delivers a lecture, there are about 100 to 150 persons present. At my lecture, in his view, there were about 500 persons.

Today I lectured at the Institute of Foreign Affairs and National Security. This is in the nature of our Diplomatic Academy. There were 30 persons. I spoke for 50 minutes on "International Politics and International Law". Then questions and speeches. Together with conversations before and after, this took up three hours.

Tomorrow the entire day is occupied: lunch at 12:00 with Dr. Limb. After this, he invites me to his office for an interview with the journal *Diplomacy*.

12 March:

Seoul-Moscow Aircraft: Kim escorted me to the aircraft. Yesterday after lunch Dr. Limb and I went to the journal *Diplomacy*. Dr. Limb interviewed me for an hour. At 19:30, supper, given by Professor Park. There were 12 persons, mostly young lecturers. Before supper at about 18:00 met with Kim's father. A pleasant man in his fifties. Evidently a person well-off – a wholesale trader in medical goods.

---

525 Georgii Davidovich Toleraia (b. 1956), Counsellor-Envoy of the Russian Embassy in Seoul from 1993 to 1998 – [VGT].

526 Boris Nikolaevich Eltsin (1931-2007), first President of the Russian Federation – [WEB].

527 Sergei Nikolaevich Goncharov (b. 1955), scientific worker, Institute of Far East, USSR Academy of Sciences from 1982; official, Russian Ministry of Foreign Affairs from 1992; author of *Uncertain Partners: Stalin, Mao, and the Korean War* (1994); Counsellor-Envoy, Embassy of Russian Federation in Beijing from 2001 to 2006; representative of Rosneft in Asian-Pacific Region since 2006. In March 2012 VGT corresponded with S. N. Goncharov, who wrote: "In 1992-93 I, together with another Korean specialist, was assigned to prepare documents for declassification concerning the eve and first beginning of the Korean War. We worked rather a long time in the Presidential Archive (formerly, Politburo Archive) and were probably the first persons to become acquainted with these documents. During this stage of the work, the analytical reports with [G. I. Tunkin] prepared in summer-autumn 1949 made a deep impression (as I recall, he was chargé d'affairs with the departure of Ambassador Shtykov). He succeeded to foreseeing a great deal in these materials. I take off my hat to the highly professional standard and genuinely gentlemanly character of your Father".

I am reading Simenon, *Le charretier de "la Providence"*. We are flying at 850 kilometers per hour. I think about the Korean professors. Not strong. And from where. Studied in the United States, where the science of international law does not shine. Except for English, they do not know other languages. The teaching of public international law has only practical, narrowly practical purposes. They understand very little of theory.

My former post-graduate student, Kim, was with me the entire time. A dutiful young man. I want him to become a great specialist. Of course, this depends mostly upon him. So far he has done little. Often travelled from Moscow to Korea. Spoke well with him. Discussed everything. In the summer he is prepared to go to the United States, Illinois, where there are supposedly many materials on Russia. I thought and said to him on another day: why are you going to the United States and studying materials about Russia. You must study international law, and for this it is better to go to The Hague, attend courses on public international law, work in the Library. And it was decided so. Professor Park gave good advice: give Kim an assignment to prepare a synopsis in the Russian language on individual problems. I already gave him an assignment to prepare two synopses by April on the topics: (1) theory of bringing wills into concordance; (2) the system of contemporary law.

18 May:

Moscow-Paris Aircraft: I am flying to Paris to take part in the ceremony of awarding a Peace Prize to The Hague Academy. On 21 May I must be in The Hague, and on the 22nd at the session of the Curatorium. Many concerns with obtaining a French visa. The French required that the inviting organization indicate that it is paying expenses on the territory of France and guaranteeing medical insurance. Bardonnet in a telegram did not mention medical insurance. Had to ask for a new telegram to be sent with a mention of medical insurance.

19 May:

Paris. Hotel de Suede: La vie est belle. Just had breakfast in the room. Wonderful coffee, not the instant coffee which we drink. Yesterday at 15:30 went from the Hotel to UNESCO, where the awarding took place of the Félix Houphouët-Boigny Peace Prize to The Hague Academy. The ceremony was fixed for 15:00, then carried over to 16:30 and commenced at 17:10. The Queen of the Netherlands, President Francois Mitterand, and the President of Portugal were present. Next cocktails in the UNESCO building, followed by dinner given by Houphouët-Boigny in his palace in Paris.[528] Houphouët-Boigny is the President of the Ivory Coast and also present at the ceremony, where he spoke.

The palace is magnificent; he purchased it in Paris recently. A hundred persons were present at the reception. I sat beside an Ambassador, the representative of the Ivory Coast to UNESCO and asked him: It seems that your President is very wealthy? He replied to me: very wealthy. At the end of the dinner I was completely épuisé. But the dinner was superb. Having listened to the address by Houphouët-Boigny, which was

528 Félix Houphouët-Boigny (1905-1993) played a leading role in the decolonization of Africa – [WEB].

read out by one of his acolytes, I left. Slept until 11:45 and got up in a wonderful mood. It seems that my sore is better (a consequence of irradiation).

Today I must obtain a Dutch visa and purchase a ticket. The Dutch Consulate spoiled my mood. Did not give a visa. Rang Bardonnet. He rang the Ministry in The Hague. Agreed that I will receive the visa at the Amsterdam Airport. Tomorrow morning I will buy a ticket.

20 May:

Hotel de Suede: Yesterday agreed with Bastid that I will visit her at 16:30. And we chatted until 19:00. Rousseau died two months ago. Yesterday she was at the ceremony but did not attend the dinner. Of course, our situation in Russia no one even begins to understand. Indeed, we ourselves do not understand it well.

To my surprise the Bon Marche was open. I went in and purchased Machiavelli,[529] *Le Prince.*

21 May:

The Hague. Europa Hotel: I do not know whether an instruction about my visa was at the Airport or not. Paid 79 guilders and in forty minutes they gave me a visa. Spoke on the telephone with Margarita Aleksandrovna.[530] Tarasov will be at work until 19:00. Margarita Aleksandrovna says that the judges have a lot of work and they are hurrying to complete it within the period. Decided to move the meeting to tomorrow.

22 May:

Europa Hotel: Exercises in the morning on the seashore. Yesterday the Curatorium proceeded normally. For some reason they are delaying with Boguslavskii and Kolodkin. I insisted that this be in 1996 or 1997. Postponed until January. Elected: Skubiszewski[531] in place of Lachs and Vargas[532] (Colombia) in place of Castaneda, who has retired. Vallat is Vice President, and Visscher – chairman of the Drafting Committee.

Went to the lakes with Tarasov. Had never been there. The trip was remarkable. Large glade or, more accurately, several glades near the lake. Returned to the Hotel at 18:30. Am now listening to the BBC broadcast of the conductor Stokowski,[533] who last conducted at the age of 95 in 1977.

23 May:

Seaside: 19:00 hours. Superb weather. Have been sitting for an hour and a half, reading Machiavelli, *Le Prince.* I seek ideas, omit examples. Am persuaded that the current

529 Niccolò di Bernardo dei Machiavelli (1469-1527), Italian political philosopher, diplomat, and humanist – [WEB].

530 Margarita Aleksandrova Tarasova, the wife of Judge of the International Court of Justice, Nikolai Konstantinovich Tarasov, who served as Judge from 1985 to 1995 – [VGT].

531 Krzysztof Skubiszewski (1926-2010), Polish international lawyer and Minister of Foreign Affairs – [WEB].

532 Diego Uribe Vargas (b. 1931), Colombian international lawyer – [WEB].

533 Leopold Anthony Stokowski (1882-1977), British-born, naturalized American orchestral conductor – [WEB].

impression of him as a purveyor of the policy of force and amorality is not correct. Just as Schwarzenberger and Morgenthau, he does not believe that the dominance of force is good, but says that such is the reality. He does not say one should act amorally, which is good, but that the amoral persons succeed. From their point of view, this is to be expected. And this is so. And then there is hesitation. In my Politica[534] I am speaking somewhat differently about Schwarzenberger and Morgenthau.

27 May:
Europe Hotel: Worked these days somewhat in the Library. Looked over all the journals on international law. So many of them in the United States! An enormous range of problems. Not the case in Russia. Virtually every university in the United States publishes a journal of international law. In any event, the view that political science has almost supplanted international law is untrue.

Today I am going from the Library to the Peace Palace to see Tarasov and suddenly hear: "Professor Tunkin". I look, and Oda is waving his hand from the third floor. He asks: "Are you not going to Tarasov? Yes, I too am going there". Chatted for an hour and a half. Then Tarasov invited me to lunch with Schwebel. We are old acquaintances.

534 A work in progress by G. I. Tunkin but not completed before his death – [VGT].

Co-Existence and International Law*

Introduction

Starting our lectures we have, according to the old tradition, to define the subject matter of these lectures. To say "coexistence and international law" is not really to say much.

Co-existence (we mean, of course, co-existence of States) has always been present since States appeared. States not only existed parallelly, they co-existed in the sense that there have always been relations between States. States have never been isolated from each other. The scope and volume of these relations changed. From regional relations in ancient history and also, to a very great extent, during the middle ages, they have become nowadays universal. There has also been an enormous increase in the volume of these relations. The history of co-existence in this sense coincides in fact with the history of international relations.[1]

We shall make a closer approach to contemporary conditions if we envisage co-existence of States having different economic and political systems. Such is certainly the case in our days, but it was also the case in the past, in certain periods of history (e.g. in the period of transition from feudalism to capitalism). To state that at present we have co-existence of States belonging to two different economic systems would be to state only half of the truth. Co-existence of States in our epoch has specific features; it is a co-existence of States belonging to two *diametrically* different economic systems. One system is based on private property in the means of production, the other on common property.

To this division correspond two diametrically different ideologies: one of socialism and communism, i.e. the Marx-Lenin theory of reconstruction of society and building a new society based on common property in the means of production, envisaging elimination of social classes and extinction of the State; the second, propounding principles of existing capitalist society based on private property. Profound differences of ideologies reflect differences between economic systems, not vice-versa.

---

* This lecture was originally published in Recueil des cours, Tome 95 (1958), pp. 1-82 and is reprinted with kind permission of the Hague Academy of International Law/Académie de droit international de la Haye.

1 In this sense the term "co-existence" has been used in the widely known judgment of the Permanent Court of International Justice in the *"Lotus"* case: "Les règles de droit liant les Etats procèdent de la volonté de ceux-ci, volonté manifestée dans des conventions ou dans des usages acceptés généralement comme consacrant des principes de droit et établis en vue de règler la coexistence de ces communautés indépendantes ..." Recueil des Arrêts, Sérle A, No. 10, p. 18.

To deal with present day problems of international law it is necessary to take co-existence as it is now. This means that we ought to consider not co-existence of States in general, not even co-existence of States with different economic and political systems, but co-existence of States belonging to two diametrically different economic systems. The specific character of co-existence in our times can hardly be denied and still it is usually overlooked when dealing with the problems of international law.

Nobody can contest that the event of primary historic significance in the 20th century was the Great October Socialist revolution in Russia, the creation of a new economic system diametrically different from the then existing system, the appearance of the first socialist State and, 30 years after, the appearance of a number of new socialist States.

In our epoch the development of society as a whole, the development of international relations and international law, are generally conditioned by the course and by the results of the competition between two existing social systems.

The subject of co-existence and international law falls necessarily into two parts: co-existence and international law, international law and co-existence.

The first group of problems relates to the influence of coexistence on international law. What are the main changes which have taken place during the period of co-existence in the general international law, that is in the law recognized by all States and regulating relations between them? What main developments are taking place in the general international law now? What are the forces at work bringing about those changes?

There is a second group of problems. International law as well as internal law exercises influence upon social relations it is called to regulate. What is the character of this influence and its scope? What is the role of international law in ensuring peaceful co-existence in the conditions of to-day?

Those are problems of primary importance to the theory of international law; they are of no less significance from the point of view-how can international law best serve the cause of international peace?

Chapter I Creation of General International Law Norms

In examining the influence of co-existence of States belonging to two diametrically different *economic* systems on international law we have to start with the problem of modes of creating *its* norms. We ought to study, as it is usually put, "formal sources" of international law, or *in* other words the processes by which the norms of this specific law come into being. This approach affords the possibility of basing conclusions not on some purely logical categories but on the very facts of international life, bearing in mind that the first condition of every scientific investigation *is* to take facts as they are. The study of modes of creating norms of international law may pave the way to examining the substance of these norms and also to discovering social forces which determine the main characteristics of international law.

1. International Treaty

In international law we see first of all norms created by treaties concluded between States. An international treaty as a means of creating international law norms is a clearly expressed agreement between States concerning recognition of this or that norm as a norm of international law, changing or abrogating existing norms of international law. So a conventional norm of international law is a result of an agreement between States expressed *in* a specific form-in the form of an international treaty. As to the division of treaties into so-called law-making treaties and other treaties, the importance of this problem seems to have been greatly exaggerated. Anyhow this problem goes beyond the framework of this study. What is necessary to establish here *is* that norms of international law may be created by treaties.

This norm-creating quality of an international treaty has always been recognized by internationalists, with the exception of those who considered that States do not create norms of international law at all, and that different sources of international law constitute merely an outward expression of pre-existing law.

2. Custom

Everyday observation shows that a considerable part of general international law consists of customary norms. States refer to such norms in their mutual relations and nobody has ever contested that there are customary norms of international law.

But as soon as we approach the problem of the main characteristics of customary rules and especially the problem of the essence of such norms a considerable difference of opinion becomes evident. Professor J. Basdevant in his course of lectures at the Hague Academy of International Law in 1936 said about the problem of customary international law: "Depuis que l'on écrit sur le droit international ce problème a été envisagé sans que l'on soit arrive á se mettre d'accord."[2] It is no less true now than it was over 20 years ago.

There may hardly be any doubt that the problem of customary international law is one of the most important and also one of the most difficult of all the problems of international law. Upon the solution of this problem depends to a very great extent the whole concept of international law. It is therefore no wonder that this problem has been under constant consideration by international lawyers. Certainly the fact that no unanimity of opinion has been reached and the problem of customary international law is still far from being solved should not discourage further study. Customary norms of international law grow out of international practice. What are the main elements of this practice resulting in the formation of a customary rule of international law?

First of all there is an element of repetition. Historically a customary norm of international law arises out of repeated actions of States. Continuity, that is an element of time, usually plays an important role in a process of formation of a customary norm. But an element of time may scarcely be accepted even as merely creating a presumption in favour of the existence of a customary norm, still less may it be considered as legally required that a customary rule should be "ancient" or of long standing.[3]

The characteristic of a rule as "ancient" may be a positive as well as a negative factor. Along with the meaning that it has been in use for a considerable time and therefore proved by life, this very characteristic may give rise to some doubts as to whether a rule of such an ancient origin corresponds to the present circumstances. But the most important thing in relation to the time element is that though time plays historically, as a matter of fact, a considerable role in the process of formation of a customary rule of conduct, it is juridically irrelevant.

As has rightly been pointed out by many authors, not every repetition creates a customary norm of international law. A continuous habit of doing certain actions may not result in forming a norm of conduct, and if a norm of conduct has been formed this norm may not necessarily be a legal norm. This may be a norm of international morality or a norm of *comitas gentium*.

Some writers express the opinion that international practice leading to the formation of a customary rule must have been continued and repeated without interruption of continuity.[4] This suggestion is untenable. No rule of international law has ever been created by practice "without interruption" of continuity.[5]

2 58 Recueil des Cours (1936, IV), p. 505.

3 In this sense see J. Basdevant, *Règles générales du droit de la paix, 58* Recueil des Cours (1936, IV), pp. 513, 518; J. Kunz, *The Nature of Customary International Law,* 47 American Journal of International Law (1953), p. 666.

4 See, for instance, J. Kunz, *loc. cit.*

5 See J. Basdevant, *Règles générales du droit de la paix,* 58 Recueil des Cours (1936, IV), p. 518.

Let us take as an example a principle of non-intervention in the internal affairs of a State which is a universally recognized principle of the modern international law. This principle first appeared in international law in the time of the American and French revolutions in the 18th century. It gradually gained strength, though at times there were considerable set-backs; the 19th century, and especially the first half of it, saw many interventions contradicting to the principle of non-intervention: Napoleonic wars, the Holy Alliance, which made a policy of intervention its official policy, etc. In spite of all these facts the principle of non-intervention had, up to the second half of the 19th century, become a principle of the general international law as it was understood at that time.

But at the same time it would be incorrect to assert that interruption may not influence the formation of a customary rule of conduct. It may really destroy a customary norm which is still in the process of formation. All depends on what kind of interruption we have before us. Though again the most important point is that non-interruption as well as the time element is not decisive in itself.[6]

The question of whether a customary rule may be established only by positive actions or by abstention from certain actions as well gave rise to some controversy. Prof J. Basdevant pleading for France in the affair of *Lotus* before the Permanent Court of International Justice in 1927 had expressed an opinion which was often cited afterwards. He said as follows: "L'attitude adoptée par les Etats de s'abstenir de poursuivre les ressortissants étrangers supposés coupables d'avoir provoqué un abordage en haute mer constitue une règle coutumière internationale."[7]

Contrary opinion was expressed by the representative of Turkey and by Judges Nyholm and Altamira who held the view that negative facts were unable to form a customary norm.[8]

A customary rule of international law grows out of international practice. Practice of States may be that of taking actions in certain circumstances or taking no action. Of course it is usually much easier to ascertain the existence of a customary rule in a case of positive acts, but there is no reason whatsoever to deny the possibility of creating a customary rule by way of a negative practice. The continued habit of not taking actions in certain situations may certainly lead to the formation of a rule of conduct which may be a legal rule. And it goes without saying that all that has been said before concerning the element of repetition and time applies as well to the negative practice.

---

6 See Ch. de Visscher, *Coutume et traité en droit international public,* Revue Genéral de Droit International Public, 1955, p. 358.

7 Publications de la Cour Permanente de Justice Internationale, série A, III Arrêt 9, p. 25. In this sense see also Y. Gouet, *La coutume en droit constitutionnel interne et en droit constitutionnel international,* Paris, 1932, p. 73; M. Sorensen, *Les sources du droit international,* Copenhagen, 1946, p. 98-101; A. Ullon, *Derecho International Publico,* Vol. 1, Madrid, 1957, para. 48.

8 See Publications de la Cour Permanente de Justice Internationale, Série C, XII session, p. 112; Série A, IV Arrêt 9, p. 59; Série A, III, Arrêt 9, p. 96 the same opinion is expressed by G. Gianny, *La coutume en droit international,* Paris, 1931, p. 126; K. Strupp, *Regles générales du droit de la paix,* 47 Recueil des Cours (1934, I), p. 307.

Many principles and norms of international law contain to a smaller or greater extent an obligation on States to abstain from certain actions in the relations with other States. The principle of respect of sovereignty, for instance, obliges the States to refrain from any act which may constitute an infringement of the sovereignty of another State. According to the principle of nonintervention in the internal affairs of other States every State is under the obligation to refrain from all acts which constitute an interference with the internal affairs of another State. Even such a principle as the principle of the freedom of the high seas, positive in itself, contains an obligation of a negative character, namely to refrain from all acts which may prejudice "the interests of other States in their exercise of the freedom of the high seas".[9] How might such principles have come into being if there had not been a continuous practice of States of abstaining from certain actions?

All the elements of a customary norm of international law stated before come under the heading of "usage". But it is generally accepted, and with good reason, that "custom in its legal sense means something more than mere habit or usage".[10]

It has already been pointed out that a rule of conduct, if any, created by repetition of certain actions or continuous abstentions of States from doing certain actions may not necessarily be a legal rule. Only a recognition on the part of States of such a rule as legally binding, i.e. recognition of such a rule as a rule of international law, has a decisive influence and consummates the process of creating a customary norm of international law. In this sense Article 38 of the Statute of the International Court of Justice expressly speaks of "international custom, as evidence of-a general practice accepted as law" *("reconnue comme étant de droit").* A certain ambiguity in this formula gave rise to different interpretations and criticism.[11]

In our opinion Article 38 of the Statute of the Court defines a customary norm of international law first of all as evidence of a general practice. But this general practice is not sufficient to create a customary norm. The general practice, or rather a rule of conduct which is a product of this practice, becomes a customary norm of international law only if it has been accepted or recognized by States as legally binding, as a rule of law.[12]

What does recognition or acceptance by States of a certain rule of conduct as legally binding, as a legal norm, mean? What is the essence of this recognition? Recognition or acceptance by a State of a certain international practice as a rule of law means an expression of a will of a State, it is a consent to consider this customary rule as a rule of international law and therefore as a juridically obligatory rule.

At the same time such a recognition or acceptance implies an offer to other States to accept this rule as a norm of international law. It is a tacit offer, there are no conferences

9 Convention on the high seas of 29 April, 1958, Art. 2.

10 J. Brierly, *The Law of Nations,* 1955, p. 60. See also A. Verdross, *Völkerrecht,* Wien, 1955, p. 119; J. Kunz. *The Nature of Customary International Law,* 47 American Journal of International law (1953), p. 667.

11 See for instance Ch. Rousseau, *Principes généraux du droit international public,* Paris, 1944, p. 120.

12 See G. Tunkin, *Fundamentals of Contemporary International Law* (in Russian), Moscow, 1956, p. 13; *International Law,* Academy of Science of the USSR, Institute of Law, Moscow, 1957, p. 8.

or negotiations; this offer is implied in actions of State constituting its recognition of a certain rule as a legal norm.[13]

If such an offer to consider a certain rule as legally obligatory is accepted by some other States, i.e. that these States show by their actions that they recognize this rule as legally binding, in this case a customary norm of international law has made its appearance.

The conclusion that agreement is the essence of custom as a mode of creation of norms of international law is not a self-evident truth. It is a scientific abstraction, reflecting in a general way the realities of life and making it possible to understand more fully the essence of creating a customary norm of international law.

If a customary norm of international law is produced by agreement between States and therefore there is an expression of wills of the States, the sphere of validity of a customary norm is confined to relations of those States which recognized this norm as a norm of law, i.e. which are parties to a tacit agreement.

The sphere of validity of a customary principle or norm of international law may expand by and by, and it is usually in this way that some customary norms have become universally recognized. In many cases a start has been given to a customary norm by a declaration of a single State. Many principles of international law have been proclaimed, for instance, by a revolutionary France in the 18th century, such as respect for the sovereignty of a State, non-intervention in the internal affairs of a States, the principle that military operations should be directed only against military objects and not against civilian population, etc. Or a prohibition of aggressive wars, a principle enunciated by the Soviet State in its Decree on Peace of 8 November, 1917.[14]

All those principles have gradually won recognition on the part of other States, recognition which found its expression in different ways. These principles are now universally recognized principles of international law.

The principle of prohibition of aggressive war, for instance, came into international law as a conventional principle of the Paris Pact of 1928. In relations between the parties to the treaty this principle replaced the former principle jus *ad bellum*. Gradually the new principle had been recognized by other States, either by adhering to the Paris Pact or in a customary way, so that for some States it was conventional, whereas for others a customary principle of international law. In this way the principle of prohibition of aggressive war has become a universally recognized principle of international law replacing the old principle *jus ad bellum*. It has been further developed by the Charter of the United Nations which speaks already of the prohibition of the threat of force and of the use of force in international relations (Art. 2, para. 4 of the Charter) and with this new content it has been universally recognized by States and is now a principle of general international law.

Starting with the facts of international life we have come to the conclusion that the essence of the customary process of creating norms of international law is agreement

13 See in this sense K. Strupp, *Règles générales du droit de la paix*, 47 Recueil des Cours (1934, I), p. 306.

14 See *Documents of the USSR Foreign Policy*, Vol. I, Moscow, 1957, pp. 11-14 (in Russian).

between States. And now coming back to the facts, armed with this general idea, we may say that juridically relevant are all those facts which contribute one way or the other to forming an agreement giving rise to a customary norm of international law.

There are many writers who reject the concept of the *pactum tacitum* but are of the opinion that "recognition" or "acceptance" of, or "consent" to consider a rule as legally binding constitute a decisive element in the process of creation of a customary norm of international law. So M.J. Basdevant states that customary norms "qui naissent spontanément des exigences de la vie internationale reçoivent un caractére positif du fait qu'elles sont reconnues par ceux qui sont en situation de leur assurer une certaine force d'application dans la vie internationale".[15]

Professor Ch. de Visscher in his somewhat vague definition expresses himself in the following terms: "Dans les rapports internationaux, une coutume se forme quand une pratique, par ses applications concordantes, paraît suffisament implantée pour que l'on puisse y voir l'expression d'un equilibre et d'une stabilisation au moins provisoire des interêts en présence, par conséquent comme l'élément d'un ordre juridiquement accepté par la généralité des Etats".[16] And a few lines below he adds: "II est donc bien vrai que le fait précède ici chronologiquement la qualification légale; mais celle-ci seule reste décisive, et jamais de la seule uniformité ou de la régularité extérieure de certaines attitudes il n'est permis de conclure à la normativité."[17]

These authors speak at the same time of the *opinio juris* as of an indispensable element of customary norms. In the judgment of Professor J. Basdevant the *opinio juris* means that "telle règle est reconnue comme faisant droit."[18]

Professor Ch. de Visscher considers the *opinio juris* as "reflètant l'attitude du pouvoir à l'égard d'une pratique donné".[19] Such an understanding of the *"opinio juris"* practically amounts to recognition.

Usually, however, the term *opinio juris* is given a meaning quite different from that indicated above. And here starts the real trouble with this notion of *opinio juris*. Professor Kunz defines the *opinio juris* as follows: "The practice must have been applied in the conviction that it is legally binding."[20]

At the same time Professor Kunz rightly envisages difficulties to which this concept of the *opinio juris* gives rise. He says that on the one hand it is said that usage plus *opinio juris* leads to a customary norm, but on the other hand, in order to lead to such

15 J. Basdevant, *Régles générales du droit de la paix,* 58 Recueil des Cours (1936, IV), p.:116.

16 Ch. de Visscher, *Coutume et traité en droit international public,* Revue Générale de Droit International Public, 1955, p. 356.

17 *Ibid.,* p. 357.

18 J. Basdevant, *Op. cit.,* p. 513.

19 Ch. de Visscher, *Théories et réalités en droit international public,* Paris, 1955, p.188.

20 J. Kunz, *The Nature of Customary International Law,* 47 American Journal of international Law, (1953), p. 667; see also A. Verdross, *Völkerrecht,* Wien, 1955, p. 119: "Nur jene Übung Gewonheitsrecht begriindet, die yom Rechtsgefiihl oder Rechtsbewusstsein *(opinio juris vel necessitatis)* begleitet wird"; L. Kopelmanas, *Custom as a Means of the Creation of International Law,* British Year Book of International Law, 1937, p. 129, describes the *"opinio juris"* as a "feeling on the part of the States that in acting as they act they are fulfilling a legal obligation".

a norm, the States must already practice the first cases with the *opinio juris.* And he adds: "Hence the very coming into existence of such norm presupposes that the States acted in legal error."[21]

Really the *opinio juris* understood in this sense implies that States should act in the conviction that the corresponding norm of international law already exists and that therefore such a norm had come into being, not out of the practice of States but has existed irrespective of this practice. This reasoning inevitably leads to a conclusion that a norm envisaged by the concept of the *opinio juris* is not at all a customary norm growing out of the practice of States but a kind of a "natural law" norm.

A leading argument advanced against the concept, according to which the essence of custom as a specific mode of creation of international law norms is an agreement between States, is that allegedly a customary norm of international law binds States irrespective of "recognition" or "acceptance" of this norm on the part of these States. The States, says Professor J. Basdevant, "ne reconnaissent pas al'Etat nouveau la faculte d'accepter ou non la regle coutumiere; ils Ie considerent comme soumis de plein droit au droit coutumier. La doctrine de la *Vereinbarung* se trouve ici en presence d'un difficulte qu'elle a cherche a tourner en faisant appel a une fiction. . .".[22]

Professor H. Kelsen asserts that "international customary law could be interpreted as created by a consent of the States only if it were possible to prove that the custom which evidences the existence of a norm of international law is constituted by the acts of all the States which are bound by the norm of customary law, or that a norm of customary law is binding upon a State only if this State by its own acts participated in establishing the custom in question".[23] And continuing the same line of thought Kelsen says that since customary norms of general international law are binding upon all the States, it would be necessary to prove that all the States have consented to all the customary norms of general international law by their actual conduct, by participation in the establishment of the custom which evidences the law. According to Kelsen such a proof is not required by international law. Customary norms of international law, according to Kelsen, are created not by "the common consent of the members of the international community" but by "a long established practice of a great number of States, including the States which, with respect to their power, the culture, and so on, are of certain importance".[24]

---

21 J. Kunz, *Op. cit.*, p. 667. See also P. Guggenheim, *Traiti de droit international public,* Vol. I Geneve, 1953, p. 47; G. Gianni, *La coutume en droit international,* Paris, 1931, p. 157.

22 J. Basdevant, *Regles generales du droit de la paix,* 58 Recueil des cours (1936, IV) p. 515; A. Verdross (*Völkerrecht,* Wien, 1955, p. 119) expresses the same opinion on the doctrine of "*pactum taciturn*" in the following terms: "Sie wird schon dadurch widerlegt, dass sich die Staaten häufig auf Regeln berufen, die sie selbst oder der Staat, von dem etwas gefordert wird, noch nicht geübt haben." In this sense also J. Kunz, *Op. cit.*, 47 American Journal of International Law (1953) p. 666; P. Guggenheim, *Traité de droit international public,* Vol. I, Geneve, 1953, p. 49; G. Morelli, *Nozioni di diritto internazionale,* (3 ed.), Padova, 1951, para. 19; M. J. Sierra, *Tratado de Derecho Intemacional publico* (2 ed.), Mexico, 1955 p. 25.

23 H. Kelsen, *Principles of International Law,* New York, 1952, pp. 311-312.

24 H. Kelsen, *Op. cit.*, p. 313.

The foregoing arguments advanced by various authors against the concept of agreement applied to custom are not valid. It does not follow from the concept of agreement that all States should participate in creating every specific customary norm of international law. It is not necessary at all that "practice" should be universal. A customary norm of international law may be created by the practice of a limited number of States and in fact it may become first a customary norm with a limited sphere of application. But to become a norm of international law of universal application it should be recognized by all the States. This extension of the sphere of validity is in some respects analogous to what we may observe in the case of conventional norms of international law. Really, norms of a certain international treaty very often have not been created by all the States parties to this treaty. Those States which have adhered to this treaty did not take part in establishing the norms of this treaty.

Now as to the allegation that a customary norm established by long practice of "a great number of States" is binding upon all other States irrespective of their attitude to this norm, the point is of the gravest importance. Such an assertion can not be accepted either from the theoretical standpoint or on practical considerations.

The above mentioned thesis is, in fact, based on the assumption that the majority of States in international relations may dictate norms of international law binding upon all the States. This idea has been recently developed to its logical limit by Professor R. Quadri. Explaining his concept of "collective or social will" *(volontà collettiva o sociale)* Professor Quadri maintains that a will, a decision of a group of States, may create in international relations legal norms binding upon all States, i.e. create norms of universal international law. According to Quadri international law is based on the "decision of the overwhelming force in the international community".[25] In his other work published in the *Recueil de Cours* the author explains what he means by the "overwhelming force". He says: "II suffit la volonté, la décision et l'action commune d'un ensemble étant en mesure d'imposer le cas échéant son autorité."[26]

This concept is in complete contradiction with the fundamental universally recognized principles of international law, and especially with the principle of equality of States. There is no doubt that the attitude of the majority of States, including States of both social systems, and especially the position of great powers, is of primary importance in the process of creation of universally recognized norms of international law. It is a factual situation. Juridically wills of different States in the process of creating norms of international law are equal. In international relations the majority of States cannot create norms binding upon other States; this is an immediate consequence of the principle of sovereign equality of States.

In practically all cases when it is necessary to find out that a specific customary norm belongs to a body of rules of general international law the normal procedure consists in investigating whether there is the "general practice" accepted as law and whether this acceptance or recognition has been given by all the States.

25 R. Quadri, *Diritto internazionale publico,* Palermo, 1956, p. 89.

26 R. Quadri, *Le fondement du caractère obligatoire du droit international public,* 80 Recueil des Cours (1952, I), p. 625.

Of course a general recognition of a certain rule as a legal norm may be a good reason for assuming that this norm is universally recognized, but it is only a good reason for a presumption, not for a final conclusion.[27] It goes without saying that it is not always possible, and may even in most cases be impossible, to state with mathematical precision that a specific norm is recognized by all the States as a norm of international law, but we may say that it is a usual case in social problems, and that difficulties which may arise in the process of calculation may not be considered as undermining the rule itself.[28]

This way, as we understand it, has been followed by the International Law Commission. In dealing with the problem of privileges and immunities of administrative, technical and service staff of a diplomatic mission the Commission has found out that some States (the U.S.A., the United Kingdom, the Soviet Union and others) include, on the basis of reciprocity, members of the administrative and technical staff, and some even members of the service staff, among the beneficiaries of the privileges and immunities, though there are considerable differences in the scope of those privileges and immunities granted to different categories. And the Commission has easily come to the conclusion that there is no rule of international law on the subject, as there is no general practice on the subject.[29]

On the problems of exemption from customs duties on articles for the personal use of a diplomatic agent, the Commission stated that "as a rule, no customs duties are levied on articles for the personal use of the diplomatic agent or members of his family belonging to his household, including articles intended for his establishment". Thereby the Commission came to a conclusion that the practice of exemption is general. But then the Commission added, and with good reason too, that "this exemption has been regarded rather as based on international comity".[30]

The doctrine according to which customary norms recognized as such by a considerable number of States are binding upon all the States implies a considerable danger in the epoch of coexistence. This point should be specifically emphasized in view of the fact that this doctrine is widely accepted by western writers, and some judgments of the International Court of Justice maybe interpreted in favour of this doctrine.

This doctrine may certainly encourage a definite group of States to try to impose upon new States, for instance upon socialist States or newly born States of Asia and Africa, some norms which may be considered by this group of States as norms of

27 See in this sense Strupp, who says that when a norm is applied by any considerable number of States "il y a une presumption normale, *presumptio juris,* donc refutable, enfaveur de la validiteté la norme pour tous les Etats..." (K. Strupp, *Regles générales du droit de la paix,* 47 Recueil des Cours (1934, I), pp. 301-02).

28 See e.g. J. Brierly who says: "This test of general recognition is necessarily a vague one; but it is of nature of customary law, whether national or international, not to be susceptible of final formulation." *(The Law of Nations,* Oxford, 1955, p. 62.)

29 See Report of the International Law Commission covering the work of its ninth session, 1957, Commentary to Art. 28.

30 Report of the International Law Commission, 1957, Commentary to Art. 27.

general international law but which have never been accepted by the new States and which may prove, partly or wholly, inacceptable to these new States. Of course such a tendency to dictate norms of international law in the present circumstances is doomed to failure, but the situation which may be a result of that tendency may lead to serious international complications.

3. Treaty and Custom in General International Law

International treaty and international custom are two modes of creating norms of international law. The essence of both of these modes is agreement between States on the subject of recognition of a certain rule as a norm of international law. It means that the binding force of conventional and customary norms of international law is the same.

In relation to the place occupied by customary norms and conventional norms in general international law, there is a concept widely accepted in western literature on international law. According to this concept an international treaty is not a source of general international law, i.e. a conventional norm can not be a norm of general international law. Partisans of this doctrine consider that general international law is exclusively customary law. One of the leading representatives of this opinion, Prof. H. Kelsen outlines the said doctrine in the following terms: "General or common international law is customary law valid for all States belonging to the international community. (Customary law is law created by the habitual practice of States.) Particular international law is valid for some States only, and comprises especially norms created by treaties valid only for the contracting parties".[31]

There are some other authors who, while being essentially of the above stated opinion, admit exceptionally the existence of conventional norms of general international law. So, for instance, Professor A. Verdross considers that general international law is substantially customary law but, at the same time, he points out that some multilateral treaties are also part of general international law. He specifically refers to the Briand-Kellogg Pact of 1928, the Statute of the League of Nations and to the Charter of the United Nations.[32]

The concept according to which general international law is exclusively customary law, though quite correct in the time of Vattel,[33] is obsolete; it does not reflect the real present day situation as to the sources of international law. The existence of a considerable number of multilateral international treaties to which all or almost all States are parties (i.e. general or universal international treaties) and also extensive efforts in the field of codification of international law have led to a situation when international treaties become a direct means of changing, developing and creating new norms of general international law.

---

31 H. Kelsen, *Principles of International Law,* New York, 1952, p. 19; see also J. Kunz, *General International Law and the Law of International Organisation,* 47 American Journal of International Law (1953) p. 457.

32 A. Verdross, *Volkerrecht,* Wien, 1955, p. 83.

33 See E. Vattel, *Le Droit des Gens, Preliminaires,* para. 24.

We should also not lose sight of the fact that with the enormous growth in the number of international treaties the amount of conventional norms in the whole network of international law is increasing. This also tends to increase the indirect influence of international treaties on general international law.

An international treaty possesses a quality which makes it especially fit to be a means of creating norms of international law in the epoch of coexistence: it is an express agreement between States. This is of considerable importance for proving the fact of an agreement and also the contents of this agreement. It should also be taken into consideration that in an age of rapid changes in every sphere of life international treaty is a more suitable means of creating norms of international law than custom.[34]

The concept that international custom constitutes a primary and the most important means of creating norms of international law was certainly correct for the 19th century, but in view of the changes indicated above it no longer reflects the present day situation in international law. In contemporary conditions the principal means of creating norms of international law is a treaty. This is the point of view held by the great majority, if not by all, of the Soviet authors who have treated this subject.[35]

4. The Problem of General Principles of Law

The problem of general principles of law has been a subject of animated discussion, especially in connexion with Article 38, 3 of the Statute of the Permanent Court of International Justice and now of the Statute of the International Court of Justice.

The great majority of western authors, following Lord Phillimore's definition, hold the opinion that the general principles of law are principles of national legal systems common to all "civilized nations".

But as to the relation to these principles to international law there is a great variety of opinions. The representatives of the new doctrine of natural law see in general principles of law justification of their concept. According to M. L. Le Fur, though the general principles of law are not directly principles of natural law which are few in number, "les principes généraux découlent directement du droit naturel ou objectif Tous deux en effet puisent leur fondement dernier dans cette notion de justice et de moralité qui est

34 This has rightly been pointed out by Ch. Visscher, see his *Coutume et traité en droit international public,* Revue Générale de Droit International Public, 1955. He says that, in the present day international relations there is no such, as he calls it, "degree of passivity" *(degrée de passivité)* which has played a substantial role in the formation of customary norms of international law. In these conditions international custom may play only a subordinate role in comparison with treaty ("... le coutume ne saurait tenir qu'un rôle subordonné"), p. 359. It seems, though, that the author considers it a negative development (see his *Théories et réalitiés en droit international public,* Paris, 1955, p. 196).

35 See *International Law* (edited by Prof. V. Durdenevsky and Prof. S. Krylov), 1947, p. 21; *International Law* (edited by Prof. E. Korovin), 1951, p. 16; F. Kojevnikov, *Soviet State and International Law,* 1948, p. 220; G. Tunkin, *Fundamentals qf Contemporary international Law,* 1956, p. 12; *International Law* (edited by Prof. F. Kojevnikov), 1957, p. 8.

universelle et qu'on peut dire naturelle chez l'homme". These principles should find their positive expression in the municipal law of "civilized States".[36]

According to Professor Verdross general principles of law as they are understood in Article 38, 3 of the Statute of the Court are principles of natural law which have found their positive expression in the existing national legal systems. General principles of law are based on the common legal consciousness of the peoples. They should be distinguished from general principles of international law as general principles of law do not find their expression in treaties or in international custom. They constitute therefore a separate source of international law. General principles of law, according to Verdross, constitute a foundation of the whole international law, being at the same time an integral part of it.[37]

There are other authors who consider that general principles of law if understood as being principles of national legal systems have nothing to do with international law. In the opinion of M. D. Anzilotti the general principles of law indicated in paragraph (c), Article 38 of the Statute of the Court, are first of all general principles of international law and, in the second place, principles universally recognized in the legislation of different countries. If the former, though having originated in national legal systems, have been recognized as principles of international law, the latter, remaining principles of national legal systems, do not belong to international law and may be used only as building materials for framing a norm of international law.[38]

Quite a number of other authors hold the opinion that the general principles of law in the sense of Article 38, 3 of the Statute of the Court are only those principles of national legal systems which have entered international law by way of custom or treaty. Professor P. Guggenheim says that general principles of law "reposent soit sur Ie droit conventionnel, soit sur le droit coutumier".[39] Dr B. Cheng, while insisting that "the essence of general principles of law is the fact of their being common to all legal systems"[40] admits that "international custom or customary international law, understood in a broad sense, may include all that is unwritten in international law, i.e. both custom and general principles of law".[41] The authors holding the opinion that principles of national legal systems as such form part of international law refer usually to the decisions of international courts and tribunals. We are going to deal with the role of those decisions in the creation of norms of international law later on. At present it will suffice

36 L. Le Fur, *La coutume et les principes généraux du droit comme sources du droit international public,* in Recueil d'Études sur 1es Sources du Droit en l'honneur de François Gény, Vol. III, 1937, p. 368; see also his *Règles générales du droit de la paix,* 54 Recueil des Cours (1935, IV), p. 205.

37 A. Verdross, *Völkerrecht,* Wien, 1955, pp. 12, 23, 124 *et seq.* See also his *Les principes generaux du droit comme source du droit de gens,* Recueil Gény, 1937, Vol. III, p. 385-88.

38 D. Anzilotti, *Corso di diritto intemazionale,* Roma, 1928, p. 106-07; G. Morelli considers that application of a particular general principle of law in international law may mean that this principle has entered international law through custom or treaty and that Art. 38, 3 does not make "general principles of law" norms of international law. And he adds: "non resta che considerare quei principi come semplici criteri ai quali, nella constatata assenza di norme consuetudinarie 0 convenzionali applicabili al caso, dovevano conformarsi Ie singole decisioni della corte ..." *(Nozioni di diritto internazionale,* Padova, 1951, p. 29).

39 P. Guggenheim, *Traire de droit international public,* Vol. I, Geneve, 1953, p.152.

40 B. Cheng, *General Principles of Law as applied by International Courts and Tribunals,* London, 1953, p. xv.

41 *Ibid.,* p. 23.

to say that there is no general practice on the subject, in the sense, it should be understood, in the time of co-existence, and there is no recognition of such a situation as legally binding by the States belonging to both economic systems of today.

Principles of municipal law of various States exercise a profound influence on international law, but this does not mean that these principles may be, as such, also principles of international law. The juridical and class nature of the principles of national legal systems differs from that of principles of general international law. Principles of municipal law express the will of the ruling class of one State. They may be changed by the State, so that a principle considered to be "common" to all legal systems today may lose this tomorrow. Principles of national legal systems may be binding only in the framework of municipal law, as one State cannot create norms binding upon other States in international relations.

The fallacy of the doctrine indicated becomes especially striking in the light of the co-existence of States belonging to two diametrically different economic systems. General principles of law which may be found in the legal systems of States belonging to those two systems, though sometimes containing technically similar rules, are of different juridical and class nature, i.e. are different as legal norms. There are therefore no general principles "common to all States". There may be common legal notions reflecting general features of legal phenomena, but not common legal norms. But in spite of this, general principles of different national legal systems are of importance to international law. They exercise a general influence on the development of international law and they influence it also in a direct way, being a material for creating norms of international law through custom or treaty. This transformation of principles of national legal systems leads to a creation of corresponding principles of international law, which may be technically similar to those of the municipal law of various States, but as legal norms these are different.

From the point of view of a scientific classification of modes of creating norms of international law Article 38, 3 of the Statute of the Court cannot be accepted as denoting a separate mode of creating norms of international law. It may be interpreted as indicating the historical origin of a certain category of principles recognized as norms of international law. Therefore "general principles of law" can only be principles of international law. This point of view on the subject of "general principles of law" is generally accepted in the Soviet literature on international law, though there is some difference in interpretation of this general idea by several authors.[42]

5. The Role of "Auxiliary Sources" of International Law

The norm-creating process in international law is a very complicated one. International treaty and international custom are two modes which consummate the process

42 See (in Russian): V. Korezky, *General Prindples of Law in International; Law,* Kiev, 1957, p. 45; V. Durdenevsky, *Five Principles,* International Affairs, 1956, No.3, p. 45; *International law* (edited by V. Durdenevsky and S. Krylov), 1947, pp. 26-27; *International Law* (edited by E. Korovin), 1951, p. 17; G. Tunkin, *Fundamentals of Contemporary International Law,* 1956, p. 4; *International Law* (edited by F. Kojevnikov), 1957, p. 8.

of creating norms of international law and therefore bring into being norms of law. However, in addition to these two modes there are other forms which play a certain role in the norm-creating process taken as a whole.

These forms constitute definite stages in the process of creating, developing, altering and annulling norms of international law, i.e. are stages in the process of moulding agreement between States on these questions. Moreover, some of them help to establish the fact of the existence of norms of international law and play a not minor role in their interpretation. Considering the role of these forms they may be called "auxiliary sources" of international law. These auxiliary sources include resolutions of international bodies, decisions of international courts and arbitral tribunals, national legislation and decisions of municipal courts, opinions and resolution of different non-governmental organizations and "teachings of the most highly qualified publicists of the various nations" (Art. 38 of the Statute of the Court).

Decisions of international bodies, especially decisions of the General Assembly and of the Security Council of the United Nations, adopted in conformity with the provisions of the Charter, play an important role in the process of forming new principles and norms of international law, corroborating, consolidating and interpreting existing principles and norms of international law. They do not, however, create norms of international law. The United Nations is not a world government and is not empowered to dictate rules of international law. According to the Charter, decisions of the General Assembly on different questions regarding relations of States may not go beyond recommendations, and therefore are not legally binding upon States, though decisions of this body adopted by the votes of States belonging to both existing systems, including great powers, possess a great moral authority.

As to the Security Council, it may adopt decisions binding upon States. Article 25 of the Charter stipulates that all Members of the United Nations should abide by the decisions of the Security Council, adopted in accordance with the provisions of the Charter, and carry them out. However, a decision of the Security Council is an act relating to a specific case only and, therefore, does not create a norm of international law. It is an act of application, but not one of creation, of law.

What has just been said about the United Nations is still more justified with regard to any other general international organization.

Decisions of international courts and arbitral tribunals play an important role "as subsidiary means for the determination of "rules of law" (Art. 38 of the Statute of the Court). The decisions of the International Court of Justice, for instance, are usually referred to as corroborating or denying the existence of a certain rule of international law. So the Court in its judgment of 9 April, 1949 in the *Corfu Channel* case corroborated the existence of the principle of the sovereignty of the coastal State over its territorial waters.[43] On the contrary, in its judgment of 18 December, 1951 in the *Anglo-Norwegian Fisheries* case the Court expressed the opinion that the so-called 10 mile rule, according to which gulfs and bays enclosed by the land of one and the same State may be

43 See Reports of Judgments, Advisory Opinions and Orders, 1949, pp. 18, 23, 36.

considered as internal waters of this State only in the case when their entrance from the sea is not more than 10 miles, is not a rule of general international law.[44]

But the opinion of Judge H. Lauterpacht can hardly be accepted. This is what he says, referring to decisions of the international courts: "They state what the law is. Their decisions are evidence of the existing rule of law. That does not mean that they do not in fact constitute a source of international law. For the distinction between the evidence and the source of many a rule of law is more speculative and less rigid than is commonly supposed ... In so far as they show what are the rules of international law they are largely identical with it."[45] This statement gives rise to objections. To say that international courts "state what the law is" and that "their decisions are evidence of the existing rule of law" is not quite accurate. This concept, rooted as it is in the municipal systems of common law countries is not applicable to international law. To ascribe to international courts a role as the mouthpiece of international law is going too far. According to the Statute of the International Court of Justice decisions constitute only one of the "subsidiary means for the determination of the rules of law" (Art. 38 of the Statute). And Article 59 of the Statute of the Court expressly provides that "the decision of the Court has no binding force except between the parties and in respect of that particular case". To assert that, though the decisions of the Court are not binding either upon States or upon the Court, yet "no written provision can prevent them from showing authoritatively what international law is, and no written rule can prevent the Court from regarding them as such",[46] is not in conformity with the above-mentioned provisions of the Statute of the Court. If the Court regarded its own decisions as "showing authoritatively what international law is", that would mean that it considered them as binding upon itself and upon States. But it is just the contrary of what Articles 38 and 59 of the Statute of the Court provide.[47]

Having no desire whatsoever to underrate the authority of the decisions of the International Court of Justice, especially those decisions which have been adopted unanimously, we ought to state that no other authority may be ascribed to the decisions of the Court except that provided for in the Statute of the Court itself. The International Court of Justice is an international body and like every international body it owes its existence to an international agreement. This agreement is the Statute of the Court. No international body may acquire greater authority than that provided for in the international agreement which has agreement between States, which in some cases may be also a tacit agreement.

National legislation and decisions of municipal courts may also be means of ascertaining what the rules of international law are. This role of the above-mentioned means of ascertainment derives from the fact that norms of international law are created by

44 See Reports of Judgments, Advisory Opinions and Orders, 1959, p. 131.

45 H. Lauterpacht, *The Development of International Law by the International Court*, London, 1958, p. 21.

46 H. Lauterpacht, *The Development of International Law by the International Court*, London, 1958, p. 22

47 Former judge Prof. S. Krylov says: "The Court has no right to create a norm not known to International Law in force" (S. Krylov, *The International Court of Justice*, Moscow, 1958, p. 65 (in Russian)).

agreement between States and national legislation, as well as decisions of municipal courts, may be considered in some instances as expressing acceptance or recognition by a certain State of this or that rule as a rule of international law. The municipal courts are organs of the State and as has rightly been pointed out by Judge H. Lauterpacht "their decisions within any particular State, when endowed with sufficient uniformity and authority, may be regarded as expressing the *opinio juris* of that State".[48]

But one point ought to be specified. Judicial decisions, even though regarding the matters of international relations, may still be only expressing *opinio juris* in the framework of internal law. To be relevant to international law they should express, as suggested by M. K. Strupp,[49] *opinio juris gentium,* i.e. should imply recognition of a certain rule as a norm of international law. This equally applies to national legislation and to various official declarations of States.

Writings of international jurists may also be one of the means of ascertaining the rules of international law. The Statute of the International Court of Justice enumerates, alongside judicial decisions, also "teachings of the most highly qualified publicists of the various nations, as subsidiary means for the determination of the rules of law" (Art. 38 of the Statute). Considering specific difficulties proceeding from the multitude of instruments and sometimes also from a considerable ambiguity, especially of customary norms of international law, the doctrine of international law is of considerable help. But at the same time it is true that with the growth of practice of States, evidenced by widely accessible records and reports, and of decisions of international organizations and tribunals reliance on the authority of writers as means of ascertaining norms of international law tends to diminish.[50]

Opinions and resolutions of social, scientific and other organizations, both international and national, may playa considerable role in the process of development and application of international law. They constitute a kind of subsidiary means for ascertaining the existence of various norms of international law and their interpretation. They may also be very valuable from the point of view of the progressive development of international law as very often they contain suggestions in this respect.

While paying due regard to the importance of the above mentioned auxiliary sources, it should, however, be emphasized that norms of general international law come into being solely as a result of the completion of the international norm-making process, which takes place either in the form of a treaty or in the form of an international custom.

48 H. Lauterpacht, *The Development of International Law,* p. 20.
49 See K. Strupp, *Règles générales du droit de la paix,* 47 Recueil des Cours (1934, I), pp. 307-08.
50 See in this sense opinion of H. Lauterpacht in *Oppenheim's International Law,* Vol. I, 1955, para. 19 b.

Chapter II The Foundation of Contemporary International Law

1. Juridical Nature of Agreement as the Means of Creating Norms of International Law

Norms of general international law are created different processes of forming an agreement between States, which is the essence of the various modes of creating those norms. Two modes culminate the process of creation bringing into life norms of international law: treaty and custom.

The concept according to which agreement between States is the only means of creating norms of international law was widely accepted in international law literature in the second half of the 19th century and in the beginning of the 20th century. It may be said that at that time it was a dominant doctrine of international law. This doctrine usually started with the fact that in international relations we have to do with independent and equal States and then came to a logical conclusion that in these circumstances the only means of creating norms binding upon subjects of law might be an agreement between those subjects.[51]

The partisans of this doctrine may be found in the western literature on international law also after the Second World War, but they are not so many.[52]

What is an agreement as a means of creating norms of international law? How is it being formed and what is its substance? These questions are of primary importance to

---

51 In relation to a "positive" international law the concept of agreement was proclaimed already by H. Grotius, *De Jure Belli ac Pacis,* L.I.C.I., para. 14 *et seq.;* also E. Vattel, *Le droit des gens ou principes de la loi naturelle, 1758, Preliminaires,* para. 27; R. Phillimore, *Commentaries on International Law,* London, 1879, p. 38; Ph. Martens, *Contemporary International Law of Civilized Nations,* Vol. I, Petersburg, 1882, p. II (in Russian). In relation to international law as a whole see H. Triepel, *Völkerrecht und Landesrecht,* Leipzig, 1899, pp. 32, 75, 83 etc; D. Anzilotti, *Corso di diritto internazionale,* Vol. I, Roma, 1928, pp. 43, 63, etc; T. Perassi, *Teoria dommatica delle fonti di norme giuridiche in diritto intemazionale,* Rivista di diritto internazionale, 1917, p. 220; L. Oppenheim, *International Law,* London, Vol. I, 1928, para. 12; S. Séfériadès, *Aperçus sur la coutume juridique international et notamment sur son fondement,* Revue générale du droit International Public, 1936, p. 131 *et seq.;* K. Strupp, *Règles générales du droit de la paix,* 47 Recueil des Cours (1934, I), p. 307.

52 See, for instance, Ch. Hyde, *International Law,* v. I, 1945, p. 4; Cli. Rousseau, *Droit international public,* Paris, 1953, p. II;0. Svarlien, *An Introduction to the Law of Nations,* New York, 1955, pp. 65-66; Manuel J. Sierra, *Tratado de Derecho Internacional publico,* Mexico, 1955, p. 24.

the theory of international law. The study of these problems will enable us to find out a link which exists between international law and other social phenomena and will open the way to the real foundation of international law.

The classical doctrine of agreement as a means of creating norms of international law adequately reflected one aspect of reality: that agreement between subjects of the law of nations is the only means of bringing into being norms of this specific law. But a purely dogmatic approach to the subject could not lead to an understanding of the essence of juridical phenomena. In fact such an approach implied a refusal beforehand even to investigate that very problem of the essence of these phenomena.

Triepel, transferring notions of municipal law into the field of international law, started with a logical presumption that in international law only a higher will, standing above the wills of individual States, could create norms of law binding upon States. This higher will is a common will *(Gemeinwille)* of States and is a result of fusing identical wills of various States.[53] Therefore, according to Triepel, in forming an agreement *(Vereinbarung)* identical wills of States are fused into a "common will" which is the source of a norm of international law.

According to Anzilotti, agreement is the declaration of a united will *(concorde volontà)* of States, which creates a norm of international law. This "united will" is, as with Triepel, also a result of melting together wills of individual States. But, as was emphasized by Anzilotti himself, he, in contradistinction to Triepel, does not seek the explanation of the *vis obligandi* in a higher "common will" as standing above the wills of particular States, but in a "basic norm" which according to him is the norm *pacta sunt servanda.*[54]

This classical concept was closely connected with the ideas of the liberalism which was characteristic of the pre-monopolistic stage of development of the capitalist society. It was an immediate outcome of the ideas of equality of States, it was inspired by the idea of a "rule of law" in international relations, which were of course understood as relations between "civilized States" only.

The classic doctrine of agreement contained a rational kernel, namely that agreement between States is the sole means of creating norms of international law. This rational kernel should be taken over from the classical concept, which was basically democratic.

But interpretation of agreement itself as being a result of a "concurrence of wills" of States, as expressing their "common will", is inadequate. This inadequacy becomes obvious specifically when the doctrine is confronted with the realities of contemporary general international law, which is a law regulating relations between States belonging to two diametrically different economic systems.

Agreement, as a means of creating norms of contemporary international law, is the result of the co-ordination of wills of different States, which in fact are the wills of their ruling classes.[55] Let us see what is going on in the process of forming an agreement

53 See H. Triepel, *Völkerrecht und Landesrecht,* Leipzig, 1899, p. 32, 52.

54 D. Anzilotti, *Corso di diritto intemazionale,* Vol. I, Roma, 1928, pp. 43, 63, 64 *et seq.*

55 See G. Tunkin, *Fundamentals of Contemporary International Law,* Moscow, 1956, p. 4 (in Russian).

between States in the case of establishing norms of general international law? First, the process of concluding international treaties. In the modern conditions of the coexistence of States belonging to two different social systems the process of conclusion of general international treaties shows that there we have a collision of different positions on problems of international law, a collision of wills of States. Then we witness the process of co-ordinating those wills by negotiation. The result of this process, fixed in a treaty, is usually more or less different from what each particular State has originally suggested. In the process of creating a customary norm of international law there are no negotiations as such, but as we have shown previously, the essence of this process consists also in framing an agreement between States on the question of recognizing or accepting this or that norm as a norm of international law. This agreement is reached, not by the way of formal negotiations, but by, figuratively speaking, negotiations conducted in the language of facts and actions.

Co-ordination of wills of States refers both to the contents of a particular norm and to its recognition as a norm of international law. This co-ordination of wills of the States in the process of creating norms of general international law does not signify their merging into some kind of "common will" or "single will". To explain that these wills cannot fuse, it is sufficient to say that their class natures, expressed in the aims and tasks of the States concerned, are different and even antagonistic (the wills of socialist and capitalist States). In an agreement these wills are, however, co-ordinated and aimed at establishing a certain rule as a norm of international law.

The norms of general international law are therefore expressing not a "single will", but "co-ordinated wills" of States, i.e. wills equally directed towards a definite aim – recognition of the given rule as a norm of international law.

Agreement presupposes that the wills of States are not only "co-ordinated" in relation to recognition of the given norm as a norm of international law, but are also mutually conditioned. Let us suppose that there are two States, each of which recognizes a definite norm as a norm of its conduct; such a recognition, such a "co-ordination" of the wills of these States does not create in their mutual relations a norm of international law, i.e. a norm on the basis of which one State may legally demand of another State to fulfil certain obligations deriving from this norm. There is no agreement. Agreement between States includes a mutual conditioning of wills, the substance of which is that the assent of one State to recognize a particular rule as a norm of international law is conditional on analogous assent by the other State. This "interconditionality" is the thread which links the wills of different States in the process of shaping (developing or annulling) or extending the sphere of operation of a norm of international law. This "inter-conditionality" is characteristic of an agreement as the mode of creating norms of international law.

The norms of general international law are, therefore, expressing not the "co-ordinated and inter-conditioned wills" of the States belonging to two existing economic systems.

The norms of general international law reflect not only community of interests, but also contradictions between them; not only co-operation, but also a struggle. The less, therefore, can we, in contemporary conditions, regard such an agreement as an expression of ideological identity.

2. Inadequacy of "Basic Norm" Doctrines

As to the problem of the foundation of international law, two approaches are characteristic of international law literature, leaving aside international law literature in socialist countries. There is one group of doctrines which considers international law as something self-sufficient and tries to find the foundation and explanation of international law within international law itself. Another group of doctrines seeks the foundation of international law in other social phenomena, trying to find a link between those social phenomena and international law.

Into the first category fall different positivist theories representing international law as developing by itself and through itself. This is a direct consequence of the main idea of positivism, namely that each norm of law may exist only because there is another norm which constitutes a basis for the validity of the first norm. It is inevitable that this juridical construction leads to at least one norm, the "basic norm" *(Grundnorm, norma-base),* which is considered to be the foundation of the whole structure of international law or even of law in general.[56]

Thus for Kelsen norms of law are such because "their validity is derivable from a higher, i.e., more general norm, as the particular is derivable from the general" or because these norms have been created "through acts by those individuals who have been authorized by a higher norm to create norms".[57] In all cases "der Grund fur die Geltung von Normen immer wieder nur eine Norm sein kann".[58] Starting with "the lowest norm within international law" Kelsen comes, as far as conventional norms of international law are concerned, to a "basic *norm" – pacta sunt servanda.* This norm is a norm of general international law which is created by custom. "The basic norm of international law, therefore, must be a norm which countenances custom as norm-creating fact, and might be formulated as follows: The States ought to behave as they have customarily behaved."[59] This is according to Kelsen "une norme supposee ou hypothetique".[60]

According to M. T. Perassi, who refuses to go beyond the confines of juridical "dogmatics", each norm, traced back to the "source", presupposes another norm on which the juridical significance of the first norm is based. In the final analysis, there should be at least one norm on the "norm-creating process" *(sulla produzione giuridica).* This is the final point beyond which one cannot go without transgressing the limits of

56 See T. Perassi, *Teoria dommatrice delle norme giuridiche in diritto internazionale,* Rivista eli diritto internazionale, 1917, p. 197; D. Anzilotti, *Corso di diritto internazionale,* Vol. I, Roma, 1928, p. 49, new edition, Padova, 1955, pp. 43-44; H. Kelsen, *Principles of International Law,* New York, 1952, pp. 408-18.

57 H. Kelsen, *Principles of Intemational Law,* pp. 409-10.

58 H. Kelsen, *Das Problem der Souveranitiit und die Theorie des Volkerrechts, 1928,* p. 105.

59 H. Kelsen, *Primiples of international Law,* p. 417-18.

60 H. Kelsen, *Thiorie du droit international public,* 84 Recueil des Cours, (1953, II), p. 129; in this sense see also G. Morelli, *Nozioni di diritto internazionale* (3rd ed.), Padova, 1951, paras. 5, 6, 17; J. Humphrey, *The Foundations of international Law,* 39 Americanjournal of international Law (1945), p. 242.

international law. This "basic norm", according to Perassi, belongs to international law; it is a legal norm.[61] The "basic norm" of international law, for Perassi, is a norm which considers agreement as a "source of the juridical norms". Norms of international law are created by agreement between States, but why agreement is apt to create norms a jurist is unable to say, as any explanation of this fact does not belong to legal science. This is a postulate which is necessary for building up the juridical conception. And at the same time it is a logical deduction from the principle according to which for juridical dogmatics "l'ordinamento jiuridico eun postulato".[62]

Anzilotti, who like Perassi is a partisan of the "agreement theory", considers that binding force of international law "is based on the principle according to which States should observe treaties entered into--*pacta sunt servanda*". He also states that this principle "is not susceptible of further substantiation from the point of view of norms themselves: it should be accepted as an objective absolute value, in other words as an initial hypothesis which cannot be proved". But he adds that it does not mean that this principle cannot be proved from the ethical, political or other points of view; this, however, goes beyond the limits of the science of international law.[63]

The positivism in international law literature has been subjected to severe criticism by many western writers. Recently Professor R. Ago has asserted that every concept of international law which reduces all international law to "positive law" "as opposed to all forms of abstract and ideal law, or law created only by thought" leads to a "vicious circle from which legal positivism cannot escape".[64] Though this criticism is wholly justified as far as "positivist doctrines" are concerned, it would be going too far to extend it to any concept which does not recognize any other international law except that created by agreement between States. But the real trouble with positivism is the fact that it approaches the main problems of international law, and first of all the problem of the foundation of international law, with the notions of formal logic. The problem of the foundation of international law stands, therefore, before positivism as a scholastically insoluble "problem"-which came first, the chicken or the egg? But the problem of the foundation of international law goes far beyond the possibilities of formal logic.

The concept according to which each legal system is based on a "basic norm", accepted as a postulate, does not correspond to the reality. The study of the development of society as a whole makes it evident that all efforts to find a final explanation of law in general, and international law in particular, within law itself, are futile. This impossibility has been shown by the positivist school itself when it was forced to admit a "basic norm" which cannot be juridically explained. The doctrine of a "basic norm" is a purely logical construction which is wholly unable to explain the historical development of

61 T. Perassi, *Teoria dommatica delle fonti di norme giuridiche in diritto internazionale,* Rivista die diritto internazionale, 1917, pp. 917-98.

62 *Ibid.,* pp. 201 *et seq.*

63 D. Anzilotti, *Corso di diritto internazionale,* Vol. I, Cedam-Padova, 1955, pp. 43-44.

64 R. Ago, *Positive Law and International Law,* 51 American Journal of International Law (1957), pp. 700-02.

international law, and the actual relationship between its different norms and between international law and other social phenomena.

Norms of international law are created by agreement between States, but this does not mean, as has been usually asserted, that international law is based on the principle *pacta sunt servanda* as on some basic, initial norm. In reality the development of international law does not proceed from any kind of "basic norm". As far as the principle *pacta sunt servanda* is concerned, this principle has developed as a customary norm alongside other norms of international law. And this principle is very closely tied up with such principles of international law as the principle of respect for the sovereignty of a State, non-intervention in the internal affairs of a State, the principle of equality of States. These and other fundamental principles of contemporary international law are inter-dependent.

All these principles juridically reflect one of the main features of the existing international situation, namely that international relations are first of all relations between sovereign States.

3. Modern Natural Law Doctrines

The doctrines which dominate international law literature in western countries now are those which are characterized by a revival of concepts of natural law in one form or another. Despite different interpretations of the notion "natural law", representatives of these doctrines generally agree that alongside "positive" international law there is another part of international law, which is, in contradistinction to the first component, not "man-made" law,[65] but a "natural law". This natural law is not only a part of international law, but also its foundation.

As to the essence of this natural law part of international law the divergency of opinion between partisans of this school is very considerable.

For Le Fur natural law is based in the final analysis on notions of justice and morality "which are natural to man". According to Le Fur "Ie droit naturel, en effet, ne comprend qu'un très petit nombre deprincipes irréductibles qu'on pourrait presque réduir á deux: le respect des engagements honnêts et librement consentis, et l'obligation de réparer le dommage injustement causé". In fact, according to Le Fur, natural law is not only a part of international law, but it influences international law mainly through general principles of law which "découlent directement du droit naturel ou objectif". These general principles of law, which are the direct emanation of natural law, do not immediately become part of international law. "Pour que les principes généraux de droit puissent être considérés comme du droit international objectif, il faut encore qu'il se retrouvent dans les législations internes positives de la presque totalité des Etats civilisés; en d'autres termes, il faut que ces principes soient reconnus par Ie droit positif

65 See J. Kunz, *The Nature of Customary International Law,* 47 American Journal of international Law, (1953), p. 665.

des Etats." Therefore, says Le Fur, these principles enter international law from municipal legal systems.[66]

Thus, in the opinion of Le Fur, international law is based on notions of justice and morality. This assertion proceeds from the presumption that law is what is considered just and moral. But we know perfectly well that notions of justice and morality differ considerably from country to country and in the capitalist society notions on many problems of justice and morality differ considerably from one social class to another. From which notions of justice and morality can international law emanate? Of course we may speak of international morality and, first of all, consider as contrary to this morality all actions which endanger, or may endanger, international peace. No doubt, in the opinion of millions and millions of people, international law should correspond to the precepts of this morality. But to say that international law should live up to the precepts of international morality and to say that international law flows out of morality are two completely different assertions. There is certainly a link between international morality and international law, but it does not mean that international morality constitutes a "basis" of international law. International practice shows that it is not a rare case when certain rules of international morality become rules of international law, but it would be far from reality to assert that all rules of international morality are *ipso facto* norms of international law or vice versa. Morality or a notion of Justice do not constitute the "basis" of international law, though they certainly exercise a definite influence in the process of the development of international law. Morality, as well as law, is, as we are going to show later on, an element of the superstructure of a society; morality and law both have their roots in the economic structure of a society.

Professor A. Verdross, proceeding from the Hegelian conception, seeks the basis of natural law and international law as a whole in an "idea of law" *(Rechtsidee),* which is in fact a purely logical construction, derived not from the realities of life but from another logical construction. According to Verdross, the aim of every legal order is a peaceful order, i.e. a prohibition of the use of force. This is the basic "common value" *(gemeine Werte).* The legal expression of this "common value" is "idea of law", the essence of which is the idea of a peaceful order. Referring to Aristotle and Acquinas, Verdross says that in its development *Rechtsidee* acquires a wider meaning, becomes an idea of moral society, because the prohibition of the use of force between the members of the community is not sufficient for securing "durable peace"; for this purpose it is also necessary that fundamental rights of the members of the community should be assured—otherwise they will be compelled to resort to force in the fight for their rights. *Rechtsidee* is, in the opinion of Verdross, the basis of every legal order, and at the same time it is a kind of standard to which norms of international law should conform. "Legal norms," he says, "may be considered as binding only to the extent to which they do not transgress the limits which are put on them by the idea of a reasonable and

66 L. Le Fur, *Règles générales du droit de la paix,* 54 Recueil des Cours, (1935), pp. 205-05; see also his *La Coutume et les principes généraux du droit comme sources du droit international public,* in *Recueil d'Études sur les sources du droit,* Recueil Geny, Vol. III, 1937, p. 368.

moral community." Along with this, the *Rechtsidee* has an immediate application so far as "each legal order is imperfect".[67]

In Verdross's concept the relationship between the *Rechtsidee* and natural law is not quite clear. It may, however, be surmised that natural law is considered by Verdross as derived directly from the *Rechtsidee.* But at the same time he states that "natural law" is not an "ideal law", but it is a law which corresponds to the "moral nature of man as he exists in the world of reality". But as some features of the moral nature of man remain constant and others change, it is impossible to construct immutable and perfect systems of natural law.[68] Similarly to Le Fur's conception, Verdross pictures natural law as being very closely connected with general principles of law. But in contra-distinction to Le Fur, Verdross seems inclined to consider that principles of natural law are more numerous than they are according to Le Fur. As to the relationship between natural law and international law, the opinion of Verdross is very close to that of Le Fur. Natural law constitutes a basis of international law as a whole and as a part. Natural law also influences international law through general principles of law, which are not directly principles of natural law, but principles of natural law which have already found their positive expression in national legal systems.[69] As to the "positive" international law, it requires a coincidence of legal conceptions. According to Verdross, such a community of legal notions is to some extent always present, because the community of legal consciousness is based on a common human nature.[70]

Some other followers of the new school of natural law seek the foundation of international law in "reason" *(Rechtsbewusstsein)* which certainly is not far from "justice", "morality", "idea of law", etc. So M. E. Kaufmann asserts that "la seule veritable 'source' de laquelle le droit découle et dans laquelle il a son origine, la 'source' au sens matériel, est la Raison objective. . ..".[71]

A century ago K. Marx and F. Engels, criticizing Hegelian philosophy with its "objective idea", pointed out that in this philosophy the relationship between reality and ideas was put the other way round. So it is also the case with those authors, who instead of proceeding from the facts of international life to ideas, which in substance are nothing more than a reflection of those facts, a reflection more or less right or more or less wrong, start with an idea as conceived by each individual author and from this idea proceed to reality.

The *Rechtsidee,* as representing "order" in general, or "peaceful order" in general, does not correspond to reality. Here we will only say that the main characteristic of law is that it is not neutral, but is a system of norms expressing the will of the ruling class of a State (the relation of this will to the will of the people depends on the class nature of the State),

67 A. Verdross, *Volkerrecht,* Wien, 1955, p. 13 *et seq.*

68 A. Verdross, *Volkerrecht,* Wien, 1955, p. 16.

69 *Ibid.,* p. 17.

70 *Ibid.,* p. 17; see also L. Nelson, *Die Rechtswissenschaft ohne Recht,* Leipzig, 1917, p. 236.

71 E. Kaufmann, *Regles generales du droit de la paix,* 54 Recueil des Cours (1935), p. 319: H. Drost, saying that every law exists in the legal consciousness of a human community, considers that "Uber Bestand und Inhalt jeder Volkerrechtsnorm entscheidet demgemass das in dieser Rechtsgemeinschaft herrschende Bewusstsein" (H. Drost, *Grundlagen des Volkerrechts,* Miinchen & Leipzig, 1936, p. 40).

a system designed to contribute to maintaining and developing a social order beneficial to the ruling class. When law ceases to be an expression of the will of the ruling class, it will cease to be law. That will be a social phenomenon completely different from law.

To seek the basis of international law in "reason", "justice", "morality", "idea of law", "common legal consciousness", etc. means to seek this basis in something which is common to all nations, in fact, in a common ideology. There is a logical inconsistency in all these efforts. As has been aptly pointed out by M. A. Ulloa and supported by M. A. Bustamante, if reason dictated imperative criteria, there would exist a complete agreement concerning the principles of international law, but this agreement is obviously lacking.[72]

There is also a practical, political aspect of this problem, which should not be overlooked. Proclaiming "natural law" as a basis and a part of international law, different new doctrines of natural law open, *volens nolens,* an opportunity for those who would like, in justification of their actions contravening "positive" international law, to refer to abstract principles, such as principles of so-called natural law, derived from "human nature", "idea of justice" etc. Proceeding from those theories it is logically easy to reduce the international law in force to a kind of second-grade law. So at the time when Hitler broke one international treaty after another, pushed aside all principles of international law, pretending that there are principles which stand above the principles of positive law, a German jurist, E. Kaufmann, said from this rostrum the following: "Le vice dont le droit injuste est entaché exige que, si les possibilités légales de le modifier ont été épuisées ou sont restées futiles, l'Etat ait le droit de s'en délier en temps utile. Les Etats sont liés aux idées êternelles du droit et de la justice; il ne Ie sont pas au contenu tempore! du droit." And then Kaufmann used all his eloquence to praise war and unilateral acts as a means of changing international law and creating new law.[73]

Indeed, "the road to hell is paved with good intentions", or at least with good words. In the world of today different doctrines of natural law may, in real life, only be detrimental to international law. It is characteristic of the present situation that the partisans of "power politics" usually prefer to invoke abstract principles of "justice", rather than principles of international law.

4. The Economic Structure of Society as a Real Foundation of International Law

People who from generation to generation have been familiar with a certain social phenomenon are inclined to consider this phenomenon as inherent in the society. Such is the case with law. The formula *"ubi societas ibi jus"* has been for centuries accepted in bourgeois international law literature as an axiom. And still it is erroneous.

History shows that there was a time when human society did not have State as well as law, though there also were some rules of human conduct. The development of

72 A. Ulloa, *Derecho Internacional publico,* Vol. I (4th ed.), Madrid, 1957, para. 2 a. A. Bustamante, *Derecho internacional publico,* t. I, Habana, 1933, para. 67.

73 E. Kaufmann, *Règles générales du droit de fa paix,* 54 Recueil des Cours (1935, IV), p. 520.

productive forces led to the appearance of private property in the means of production, which, with the increase in productivity of labour could be used to exploit other men's labour. The appearance of private property in the means of production constituted a ground for growing economic inequality between different groups of members of society, i.e. for splitting society into social classes, which are characterized mainly by their different positions in relation to the means of production. With all these appeared the State as an organ of the economically most powerful class, as an effective means of class domination. And with the State appeared law, which distinguished itself from rules of conduct in the pre-state society essentially by the fact it did not represent the will of the whole society but the will of the ruling class, being directed to maintain and develop not an order in general but such social order as was as advantageous as possible to this ruling class, the norms of this law being enforced, whenever necessary, by organs of the State.

When there was no law at all there could not be international law. As law appeared as the result of this division of human society into classes, as the result of class contradictions, it could be initially only national law. On the basis of national law emerged international law. The same basic causes which led to the origin of national law led also to the inception of international law.

International law, like national law, is a characteristic of a class society. But a class society, as was proved by K. Marx, represents only a certain stage in the development of human society. There was human society where there were no classes, and with the high development of productive forces there will be a classless society. The same is true of law in general and of international law in particular. There was a society which did not know law, and there will be a society which will have no law and, of course, no international law as well. It does not mean that in this future society there will be no rules of conduct. The existence of human society and especially a highly organized human society necessarily implies the existence of rules of conduct. But the nature of these rules will be quite different from that of law. The future society, a communist society, will certainly have rules of conduct, but they will not be legal rules.

The real basis, i.e. the causes which led to the origin of this social phenomenon and which condition its development, should not be sought in "human nature" or in the "idea of justice" and so on. The point made by many western scholars that without some kind of identity between people law in general and international law in particular would be impossible is simply a generality and explains nothing, signifying merely that without a definite identity between people, human society and, of course, law, would be impossible. The basis of law and of international law in particular cannot be anything else but the basis of society as a whole, as law is only one of the social phenomena. This basis is the economic structure of society, which itself is conditioned by the development of the productive forces of the society. The economic structure of society is the basis on which all other social phenomena develop and in this sense these other social phenomena, taken together, are called in the Marx-Lenin theory, a superstructure, meaning a superstructure over the economic basis of the society. The economic basis of society, and therefore the laws of its development, generally condition. the development of all other social phenomena, including, of course, international law.

In seeking to trace the influence exercised by the economic structure of society upon international law, or upon any other social phenomenon, the problem should not be over-simplified. The economic structure determines the main features of the superstructure in general and international law as a part of superstructure in particular. But the influence of the economic structure and of the laws of its development makes its way through a complex pattern of other influences: different elements of superstructure mutually exercise influence upon each other and they also influence the development of the economic structure itself

As regards international law, its basic features are conditioned by the economic structure of the society at a given stage of development of that society. But at the same time international law is influenced by the other parts of the superstructure: politics, national law, philosophy, morals, religion, etc. Here we have a complicated interplay of varying phenomena, in which international law, being subjected to the influence of the economic structure and also to the influence of other parts of the superstructure, itself influences these other parts of the superstructure and the economic structure of society. The influence exerted by the economic structure of society and its laws is expressed in the process of creating norms of international law through the will of the State, since the contents of this will is determined basically by the economic conditions of the ruling class of the given State. Through this will, influence is also exerted on international law by the other parts of the superstructure: the internal law of the State (which itself is an expression of the will of the same ruling class), morals, religion, philosophy and so on.

The process of creating norms of international law is a complicated one in which various influences are exerted through the will of States. The laws of development of the economic structure of a society, which determine the main features of the superstructure as a whole, exercise a decisive influence in this process, not only by "direct" action, but also through other categories of the superstructure, the influence of which, naturally, cannot go beyond the limits determined by the economic structure of that society. The economic structure of the international society at present is characterized by the existence of the two diametrically different economic systems. Each of these systems exercises its influence on the development of international law, the main features of this influence being conditioned by the very nature of a given system.

Economic systems of to-day are not separated by insurmountable barriers; they are connected with each other by different economic ties. International economic relations exercise an immediate and very extensive influence on the development of international law.[74] This means that furthering economic relations between countries and first of all increasing international trade is of the greatest importance to the position of international law.

---

74 See on the subject (in Russian) R. Bobrov, *On the Problem of the Objective Foundation of International law,* Vestnik Leningradskogo Universiteta, No. 5, 1956 (Seria ekonomiki, philosophii i prava); I. Lukashuk, *International Relations and International Treaty,* Uchenye Zapiski Saratovskogo Juridicheskogo Instituta, vipusk VI, 1957.

Laws of development of the economic structure of society, which are of course also basic laws of development of society as a whole, should not be confused with law in a juridical sense. In his study on the problem of formal sources of international law almost a quarter of a century ago, Professor G. Scelle, proceeding from the main idea of the solidaristic school, *solidarite sociale,* as a basis of society, stated that the laws of development of society (we leave aside here the problem of the substance of these laws) constitute "objective law" *(droit objectif),* which is law in a juridical sense. Objective law, according to Scelle, is a basis, and part, of law. He expressed himself in the following terms: "La validité du droit positif réside dans sa conformite aux 'lois causales' d'existence de la société. Ce fond juridique premier, nous l'avons appelé droit objectif, parce qu'il ne peut être entaché d'aucune subjectivité, n'étant encore ni capté, ni traduit, ni voulu par une intelligence humaine. A partir du moment, aú contraire, oú se produit l'intervention humaine, celle-ci ne se contente pas de capter et de traduire; elle apprécie, elle s'efforce de diriger et d'utiliser la source du droit, et l'élément subjectif s'introduit. L'élément volonte s'ajoute a l'élément nécessité, le finalisme à la causalité, et, sans doute, l'erreur á la découverte. Tout droit positif est en quelque mesure une déformation du droit objectif et, par conséquent, une production juridique imparfaite. II se peut même que la source devienne si corrumpue par la subjectivité de ses interprêtes, qu'elle cesse d'être le droit, devienne le non-droit: le droit positive peut être anti-juridique."[75] In his *Cours de droit international* of 1948, Professor Scelle is less explicit on the subject and, we may say, much more cautious. He does not assert any more that causal laws are "law" in a judicial sense. He says that the material source of law is a "potentiel juridique" of a society, which corresponds to the "nécessité sociale". From this material source emerge rules of law. International law may be explained only as proceeding from social facts of international life, which themselves are the result of "lois causales".[76]

Laws of development of society, i.e. first of all, laws of development of economic structure of society, do exist irrespective of the will of people, irrespective of whether people like them or not. People may come to understand these laws and to use them for their own benefit as far as possible, but they are unable to abrogate them. Laws of development of society exercise a decisive influence on law and on international law in particular, but they are not themselves rules of a legal system.[77] Law in the juridical sense is a system of obligatory norms, which express the will of the ruling class of a State, or as in the case of international law, the coordinated. wills of States, i.e. of the ruling classes of those States; these norms are always connected with enforcement measures undertaken by a State or, as in international law, also by several States jointly.

To confuse laws of development of society with law in the juridical sense is to assert what does not exist.

75 G. Scelle, *Essai sur Les sources formelles du droit intemational,* Recueil Gény, 1937, Vol. III, p. 401.

76 G. Scelle, *Cours de droit international public,* Paris, 1948, p. 9.

77 See S. Kechekyan, *Norms of Law and Legal Relations,* Soviet State and Law (in Russian), 1955, No. 2, p. 29.

Chapter III Co-existence and General International Law

1. The New "Doctrine of Agreement" and Co-existence

The scientific value of any theory is determined by the extent to which that theory corresponds to the objective laws of development of a specific social phenomenon.

The previously-outlined concept of agreement as the sole way of creating norms of general international law reflects the peculiarities of the latter. International law is a law *sui generis*. It regulates mainly relations between sovereign States and, therefore, there is no legislative body which might lay down norms binding upon the subjects of this law; nor is there a centralized apparatus similar to that in the framework of internal law which could, if necessary, compel the subject of the law to abide by it.

The basic features of international law are determined by the laws of historical development, namely those laws which condition the existence of sovereign States, belonging to two diametrically different economic systems. The point is not that governments do not desire to part with sovereign powers; this lamentation is often presented by jurists. The existence of sovereign States is determined by fundamental laws of the development of society in our epoch.

It is evident that after the First and in particular after the Second World War, there has been a well defined tendency towards the growing competence of international organizations. However, it would be quite wrong to appraise this development as indicating the development towards a world state. The laws of historical development, which call forth the tendency to increasing competence and widening functions of international organizations put, at the same time, a certain limit to this growing competence.

It has already been pointed out that the State is not something which is inherent in human society. The State is a form of organization existing only during a certain stage of development of human society. With the growth of productive forces, alteration of the economic structure of society and the extinction of social classes, States will disappear. On this road to a stateless society, the creation of a world federation may be possible only when the society as a whole has considerably advanced in the direction of a classless, i.e. stateless, society.

In the present epoch of co-existence, the limits to the extention of competence of international organizations are set forth by the fact of co-existence of sovereign States. These limits are, at the same time, emphasized by the fact that this co-existence is a co-existence of States belonging to two diametrically different economic systems.

All plans tending towards organizing a world state or something close to that are, therefore, Utopian, as they do not correspond to the laws of historical development in our epoch. A plea for creating a world state and liquidating state sovereignty is, and we should not disguise this fact, detrimental to international law, because it leads openly or by implication to a depreciation of fundamental principle of international law, such as respect for the sovereignty of States, non-intervention in the internal affairs of a State, etc.

If, however, the existence of sovereign States is a fact determined by the laws of historical development in our epoch, the norms of law which might be binding upon these sovereign entities can be only the outcome of agreement between them. Agreement between States on the basis of equality as the essence of norm-creating processes in general international law is specifically characteristic of the present epoch of co-existence of States belonging to two different social systems, that of socialism and capitalism. If in the past cases were not rare when powerful States dictated norms of international law to small States, at the present day all efforts of any group of States to proclaim norms which are welcome to them as norms of general international law binding upon other States are not only legally null and void as being contrary to fundamental principles of international law, but also futile.

The new concept of agreement as delineated above corresponds, in our opinion, to the laws of historical development in our epoch, which is characterized by the existence of States belonging to two diametrically different social systems.

2. Peaceful Co-existence and General International Law

Is general international law possible in the age of co-existence of States belonging to two diametrically different economic systems? And if so, is the basis of this law getting wider or narrower?

In our times these questions have become particularly acute in international relations and are far from being only theoretical questions of international law. Two different approaches to international law have become evident: one approach, which constitutes an integral part of the "position of strength" policy, practically denies the possibility of the existence of general international law; the second is the policy of peaceful co-existence which is intimately related to the idea of the necessity of general international law.

The scientific reply to the question about the possibility of the existence of general international law may be given only in the light of the laws of development of modern society, in the light of real factors and forces which are at work in international relations.

The possibility of the existence of general international law in our times is determined eventually by the possibility of the peaceful co-existence of States of two systems. This relationship between peaceful co-existence and general international law can hardly be contested. Peaceful co-existence includes collaboration between States; without collaboration peaceful co-existence can not be conceived of. States, as we have already pointed out, have never existed in isolation from each other. Each State finds itself from its very inception in a system of States. Nowadays relations between States are so extensive and multi-sided that problems which arise out of co-existence are numerous and important. For settling these problems which arise in international relations daily, collaboration between States of different systems is indispensable. If such a collaboration is lacking, the problems which arise will find no solution and will lead to growing international tension and even eventually to war.

Of course, collaboration between States has never excluded competition or struggle between them, but what it is essential to state now is that peaceful co-existence presupposes collaboration. Meanwhile, collaboration between States presumes a certain degree of agreement between them. But agreement between States belonging to two existing systems is exactly what is indispensable for making the existence of general international law possible. So the possibility of peaceful co-existence of States belonging to two diametrically different economic systems includes the possibility of the existence of general international law. Social forces which act in the direction of peaceful co-existence are, therefore, also forces which contribute to developing and strengthening general international law.

This thesis should not, however, be misinterpreted. It may be suggested that insofar as there is not, at present, a sufficient degree of collaboration between States, and specifically between great powers belonging to two systems, general international law is impossible. But is it a permanent situation, are there no possibilities of collaboration?

Let us turn now to those objective and subjective factors which condition the possibility of peaceful co-existence of States of two existing diametrically different social systems and which, therefore, ensure the possibility of existence of general international law. Peaceful co-existence of States of two systems in our age is the process in which States of those two systems come in to contact, the process in which takes place a collision between opposing historical laws of social development relevant to each of those systems, a collision between different social forces. As far as socialist States are concerned, common property in the means of production, and the liquidation of classes which concentrated this property in their hands and used it as a means of exploitation of other men's labour, have created a solid basis of peaceful policy of socialist States. Peaceful foreign policy is, therefore, not a temporary policy, but it is a general line of policy of these States which finds its foundation in the new economic structure of their society. On the other hand, the economic causes of wars continue to exist in the capitalist society but, at the same time, the development of capitalist society has brought into being powerful forces which are strongly opposed to aggressive wars.

The growing influence of objective as well as subjective factors for peace makes it possible to avoid wars and to solidify peaceful co-existence. The development of productive forces in contemporary society creates a situation when no country can successfully develop without economic and cultural relations with other countries. Normalization of international economic relations is therefore an objective economic necessity. But development of economic relations is development of peaceful relations.

So the growing level of productive forces of society necessitating extensive economic relations between different countries creates economic tendencies towards peaceful co-existence.

We should not, however, overlook the fact that specific features of capitalist society bring about the tendency which is contradictory to that stated above. This contradictory tendency may, in certain periods and in certain directions, outweigh the tendency towards international economic co-operation. This is certainly the case now so far as relations between some capitalist countries, on the one hand, and socialist countries, on the other hand, are concerned.

The growing power of all the forces striving to strengthen international peace is of primary importance for ensuring peaceful co-existence. In our opinion, the real significance of factors working in the direction of solidifying the peaceful co-existence of States belonging to the two existing social systems has greatly increased and it is going to increase still further. This means that the social basis of general international law is getting stronger and that possibilities of its development become wider. Considering these factors, Soviet international lawyers are of unanimous opinion that general international law, regulating relations between all the States irrespective of their social systems, not only can exist, but has good prospects of progressive development. At the same time Soviet lawyers fully realize that to utilize these possibilities would require considerable efforts on the part of all those who are willing to preserve and to strengthen international peace.[78] It seems that international lawyers in other socialist countries hold generally the same view on the perspectives of the progressive development of general international law.[79]

In the meantime the opinion is often expressed in the western international law literature of recent years that in the present day division of the world into two diametrically different systems, general international law is going to disintegrate into separate regional systems or at least that the ground on which it may exist has become narrower. This conclusion usually proceeds from a completely erroneous assumption that every law, and therefore international law as well, is based on a community of ideology. From this it follows that since there is no such common ideology between States of the socialist and capitalist systems, general international law has no basis for its development

78 See (in Russian) *International Law* (ed. By V. Durdenevsky and S. Krylov), Moscow, 1947; F. Kojevnikov, *Soviet State and Intemational Law,* Moscow, 1948; S. Krylov, *The USSR Struggle for Fundamental Principles of International Law,* "Uchenye Zapisky" of the Academy of Social Sciences, Moscow, 1949, pp. 19-33; V. Durdenevsky, *Five Principles,* International Affairs, 1956, No.3, pp. 44-49; E. Korovin, *Five Principles-Foundation of Peaceful Coexistence of Peoples and States,* International Affairs, 1956, No. 5, p. 45-53; G. Tunkin, *Fundamentals of Contemporary International Law,* Moscow, 1956; G. Tunkin, *Peaceful Coexistence and International Law,* Soviet State and Law, 1956, No.7; V. Korezky, *General Principles of Law* in International Law, Kiev, 1957; *International Law* (ed. by F. Kojevnikov), Moscow, 1957.

79 See, for instance, M. Lachs, *System of Collective Security and Questions of Ensuring Security and Peace,* in Problems of Collective Security in Europe (translated into Russian), Warsaw, 1955, pp. 44-118; C. Berezovsky, *(Treaties of Mutual Assistance in the System of Collective Security),* in Problems of Collective Security in Europe, Warsaw, 1955, pp. 119-76; M. Genovsky, *Fundamentals of International Law* (in Bulgarian), Sofia, 1956.

and even for its existence. So, according to Professor Leibholz, in order to be able to speak of an "international legal community" *(Völkerrechtsgemeinschaft)* it is necessary to have "some minimum of homogeneity of *Weltanschauung*" which does not exist at present.[80] Serious apprehension as to the fate of general international law is expressed by Professor Q. Wright, in whose opinion "international law tends to split into opposing ideologies of Western and Soviet international law".[81]

Prof. K. Wilk, in his elaborate article entitled *International Law and Global Ideological Conflict,* also comes to extremely pessimistic conclusions as to the prospects for general international law. He starts with the assumption that "for law to be accepted within any group some common understanding of values within that group is indispensable".[82] And then Wilk puts a very grave question, whether at present there exist "regular relations and shared standards pertinent to the observance of international law"?[83] The acceptance of an obligation, says Wilk, which means the validity of international law "depends upon the minimum of human relationship across national frontiers that admit of and call for international regulation, and upon a minimum of values that are understood or understandable across national frontiers and that may serve as standards for such regulation. On this assumption, the area of the dominion of international law extends as far as such regular relationship and commonly understood or understandable values extend."[84]

The author says that factual international relations do exist and therefore there is necessarily "relationship across national frontiers". But as to "some shared standards" he is doubtful whether they exist at all in international relations, because there are "conflicting beliefs as to what are . . . the underlying standards of the law".[85] With good reason Wilk states that unity of beliefs is not indispensable for international law. Emphasizing this point, the author says that even "national societies live under law without achieving comprehensive or fundamental unity of belief in values, or even agreement as to what values are fundamental ones". Referring to international law he states again that "there is no reason to consider wider or more basic agreement internationally the prerequisite of international law. To expect it of global law, international or supranational, is Utopian."[86] And still, in the opinion of Professor Wilk:, there is looming on the horizon a spectre of the disintegration of general international law. The profound differences between the principal Powers has not destroyed all common standards on which different States can and do agree, but in relation to some of them, and namely in relation to those which are the most important, there is an "emphatic disagreement". According to the author, all this does not exclude the "universal validity of

80 Leibholz, *Zur gegenwärtige Lage des Völkerrechts,* Archiv des Völkerrechts, I, 1948-1949.

81 Q. Wright, *International Law and Ideologies,* 48 American Journal of International Law (1954), p. 617.

82 K. Wilk, *International Law and Global Ideological Conflict,* 45 American Journal of International Law (1951), p. 657.

83 *Ibid.,* p. 663.

84 *Ibid.,* p. 658.

85 *Ibid.,* p. 663-64.

86 *Ibid.,* p. 667.

international law" but "fewer opportunities remain for agreements . . . the agreements are revealed as verbal rather than substantial". This impedes the development of new norms of general international law. "It promotes the further growth of non-universal, or particular, international law among those States which are bound by a community of special interests reflected in common standards that reach beyond the universally accepted minimum and are held to express more fundamental values." Continuing the same line of thought Wilk: draws a very gloomy picture of the development of general international law. "Universal agreement would no longer survive on matters that used to be governed by universal international law. Carried to its extreme, such a development could break up the universal system of international law, as it has come down to us, into regional or other partial systems, with no international legal rules to govern the actions of States across the frontiers of the various systems." This would be "a state, if not of virtual isolation, then of extreme hostility".[87]

We have dealt at some length with the views of Professor Wilk only because he has drawn all the logical conclusions from the thesis now popular in western international law literature concerning the so-called "crisis" in international law.[88] In a less extreme form doubts as to the possibility of the progressive development of general international law have been expressed after the Second World War by quite a number of western authors.

The gist of this conception is that the ground for development of general international law has become narrower as a result of the appearance of socialist States and of new States in Asia and Africa. So, for instance, Professor Verdross expresses the opinion that contemporary international law which has originated in the "Christian western community", has expanded throughout the world in consequence of coming to America, Australia and South Africa of the European colonists who brought with them "Christian European principles"; at the same time a considerable part of the non-European world represented colonies and spheres of influence of the European States and, therefore, also accepted principles of European law. The Great October revolution in Russia and the organization of new States from former colonies, according to Verdross, represent a tendency towards narrowing the basis of general international law. He substantiates this thesis by saying that the Soviet Union has not accepted all the norms of the then existing international law, and new States, which have appeared as a result of gaining independence by "coloured peoples", "have never belonged to the western Christian circle and therefore partly represent legal views which distinguish themselves from the western legal ideas".[89]

We cannot possibly agree with this view, but we are glad to indicate that Professor Verdross is far from being pessimistic about the prospects of general international law. Considering that "positive" international law can develop only if there are "certain

87 *Ibid.*, p. 668-70.

88 See, for instance, H. Smith, *The Crisis in the Law of Nations,* London, 1947; J. Kunz, *La crise et le transformation du droit des gens,* 88 Recueil des Cours, (1955, II).

89 A. Verdross, *Völkerrecht,* Wien, 1955, p. 44.

common legal notions of different peoples" he comes to the conclusion that a basis for such a development is present, because "as a result of the common nature of man a minimum of common values will always be recognized".[90]

The western authors we mentioned above raise in fact two questions. One is whether co-existence of States belonging to two diametrically different economic systems, co-existence as such, leads to a disintegration of general international law into regional systems? The answer to this question has already been given. We have shown that so far as agreement between States of two systems is possible, so far as peaceful co-existence of these States is possible, there is a solid ground for the existence and development of general international law.

Difference of ideologies has always existed. True, this difference at present is profound. But when States agree on recognition of this or that norm as a norm of international law they do not agree on problems of ideology. They do not try to agree on such problems, for instance, as what is international law, what is its social foundation, its sources, what are the main characteristics of a norm of this law, etc. They do agree on rules of conduct. And Wilk is quite right in pointing out that even in one and the same State there is often much disagreement on ideological questions. For thousands of years jurists have not been able to agree on what is law. And still throughout all this time law existed. So States may profoundly disagree as to the nature of norms of international law, but this disagreement does not create an insurmountable obstacle to reaching an agreement relating to accepting specific rules as norms of international law.

After forty years of co-existence this question is no more a matter for abstract speculation. The answer to this question has been given by life itself. Four decades of co-existence have shown that peaceful co-existence, and therefore also general international law, are possible.

It is curious enough that up to now in western international law literature it is very often alleged that the legal opinion in the Soviet Union does not recognize the existence of general international law regulating relations between all the States and binding upon them. To our regret opinions have occasionally been expressed in the Soviet literature which might give some ground for these allegations. Such opinions were, in particular, stated by Professor E. Korovin in 1924-1926,[91] and even after the Second World War. So in his article published in 1951[92] Korovin developed the idea that to the States of one "social structure" are inherent certain "international law principles and norms", whereas to the States of another "social structure" are inherent other international law principles and norms and universally recognized principles and norms of international law are "identical norms of various legal super-structures". Such opinions of Professor E. Korovin, which afterwards were recognized as erroneous by himself,

90 *Ibid.*, pp. 11-12.

91 See E. Korovin, *International Law of Transitional Period* (in Russian), Moscow, 1924; also by *him: Contemporary Public International Law* (in Russian), Moscow, 1926.

92 See E. Korovin, *Universally Recognized Norms of International Law*, Soviet State and Law, 1951, No. 9.

are frequently interpreted in western literature as signifying that Soviet international lawyers do not recognize general international law.[93] But as a matter of fact the overwhelming majority of Soviet international lawyers never shared these views expressed by Professor Korovin. On the contrary, these views were strongly criticized by many lawyers.[94]

The thesis about the impossibility of the existence of general international law leads objectively to a justification of the "position of strength" policy and of the "cold war". The partisans of this policy, as we know, try to justify it by the allegation that agreements between capitalist and socialist countries are impossible, that such agreements are of little value and that nowadays only the language of force is of any use in international relations.

The second question is whether the emergence of socialist States and the new States of Asia and Africa has brought about a limitation of the field of general international law? In our opinion this view takes into consideration only one aspect of the problem, overlooking another, a more important one.

It is true that the Soviet Union did not accept all the norms which at the time of her emergence were considered as norms of general international law. But the Soviet Union refused to recognize only reactionary norms such as norms relating to colonial domination, spheres of influence etc. V. 1. Lenin said "We reject all provisions sanctioning international robbery and oppression, but all provisions relating to good-neighbourly relations we willingly accept, we cannot reject them."[95] These words express the attitude of the socialist State to international law in general.

It is not therefore inaccurate to assert that with the appearance of the Soviet State some norms of the then general international law, rejected by the Soviet State, ceased to be norms of general international law, but it is of importance to add that this limitation took place at the expense of reactionary norms of international law. As to democratic norms of general international law, the Soviet Union never rejected them. On the contrary, the Soviet Union has always supported democratic norms of international law and exercised continuous efforts to ensure their further development and strict observance by States.[96]

But there is another aspect of the problem which, as we have just pointed out, is overlooked by the partisans of the before mentioned concept.

The Soviet Union and now also other socialist States have consistently fought and are continuing to fight for the introduction into general international law of new

93 See, for instance, H. Kelsen, *The Communist Theory of Law,* New York, 1955, p. 156; W. Kulski, *Les tendances contemporaines dans le droit international soviétique,* Révue de droit internationale de sciences diplomatiques et politiques, 1953, p. 272; Ch. Visscher, *Théories et réalites en droit international public,* Paris, 1955, pp. 305-07; A. Ulloa, *Derecho internacional publico,* Vol. I, Madrid, 1957, para. 12.

94 See *Soviet State and Law,* 1952, No.7, pp. 67-77.

95 Lenin, *Works* Vol. 26, p. 223 (in Russian).

96 See S. Krylov, *Les notions principales du droit des gens; la doctrine soviétique du droit international,* 70 Recueil des Cours (1947, I), pp. 441 *etseq.;* R. Bobrov, *The Great October Revolution and International Law* (in Russian), Pravovedenye, 1957, No. 1.

principles and norms, which are of vital importance for strengthening international peace and developing friendly co-operation between States (prohibition of the use office in international relations, the principle of self-determination, the principle of peaceful co-existence; efforts for introducing into international law norms concerning the reduction of armaments, the prohibition of nuclear weapons etc.). Such a position of socialist States with regard to international law is a direct outcome and a part of their peaceful policy, generally determined by a new social order.

The new States of Asia and Africa, which have come into existence as a result of gaining independence by the colonial peoples, also as a rule support democratic norms of general international law and their progressive development and are taking an active part in the efforts to introduce into international law new democratic principles and norms. They bring their own valuable contribution to the progressive development of international law, always mindful of the fact that previously they not only could not take part in creating norms of international law, but that this law was used as an instrument of colonial oppression of their countries.

The rise and consolidation of the socialist States and the emergence into the international arena of new States of Asia and Africa, far from signifying the collapse of general international law or narrowing its field, are factors of quantitative increase of principles and norms of general international law and deepening of their democratic content.

We do not deny that the threat of the disintegration of contemporary general international law exists. But this threat proceeds not from the fact of co-existence of States belonging to two diametrically different economic systems, as such. It comes from the "position of strength" policy, the policy of arms race.

3. Fundamental Changes in General International Law in the Period of Co-existence

The norms of international law created in the process of cooperation and struggle between States are the result of the clash and co-ordination of the wills of the ruling classes of different States, which on the international arena appear as wills of corresponding States. These norms are created by sovereign States. The wills of these States which come in to contact in the process of creating norms of international law are juridically equal. But it goes without saying that the actual influence exercised by those wills in the process of moulding norms of international law is not at all identical. The scope of this influence depends on the role played by the particular State in international relations and also on the nature of the principles advanced by this State. Contemporary international law develops under the ever-growing influence of the socialist States and the other States pursuing the policy of peaceful co-existence in international relations, under the growing influence of all the forces of peace.

It is not surprising, therefore, that when we survey the development of the general international law in the decades of co-existence of States belonging to the two existing diametrically different economic systems we will find no traces of degradation or falling back. On the contrary, we get a clear picture of the passing away of reactionary institutions and the strengthening and developing of principles and norms aimed at ensuring peace, peaceful co-existence and free national development for all peoples.

Owing to the disintegration of the colonial system, the sphere of applications of international law has greatly expanded. The peoples of colonial countries which previously were deprived of the opportunity of taking part in international relations create their own national States. These States appear in the international arena as equal subjects of the law of nations. As a result of this process only since the Second World War over 20 new States have come into being. International relations have definitely gone beyond the framework of relations between States populated by the peoples of the white race and are becoming really universal.

International law becomes more and more universal, not only in the traditional sense of universal application of its norms. What is much more important, it becomes more and more universal in the process of creating its norms. International law formerly was created by a handful of States. Other countries, having the major part of the population of the globe, had no means of having their say in the development of international law, or their influence in this process was very insignificant (e.g. States of Asia which were, in fact, not considered as equal to European States). Now, having formed their own States, they take an active part in the progressive development of international law.

As a result of the struggle waged by all the progressive forces there have arisen new important principles which constitute an enormous progress in international law.

It can hardly be contested that the most important of these new principles is the principle of prohibition of the use of force in international relations.[97] International law before the Great October Socialist revolution recognized *jus ad bellum,* in accordance with which a State might resort to war in each case when it considered that its rights were violated by another State. In other words, war was considered as one of the legal means for settling international disputes, though an ultimate means *(ultima ratio).*

The principle of the prohibition of aggressive war was introduced into international law in the period between the First and the Second World Wars. The new Soviet State was the first which officially raised the question of the international prohibition of aggressive war, stating its position in the sense that aggressive war should be considered unlawful. In its Decree on Peace, which was adopted by the supreme organ of revolutionary Russia-the All-Russian Congress of the Soviets-on the 26 October (8 November), 1917, the Soviet State declared that aggressive war constituted "the greatest crime against humanity".

The Covenant of the League of Nations did not prohibit aggressive war, though it restricted the right of Member States to resort to war and provided for sanctions against a Member which would "resort to war in disregard of its Covenant".

97 See (in Russian) K. Baginyan, *Aggression-the Gravest International Crime,* Moscow, 1955; G. Sharmazanashvili, *The Principle of Non-Aggression in International Law,* Moscow, 1957.

Only the Paris Pact of 27 August, 1928, contained express provisions prohibiting aggressive wars. Article I of the Pact reads as follows: "The High Contracting Parties solemnly declare in the names of their respective peoples that they condemn recourse to war for the solution of international controversies, and renounce it as an instrument of national policy in their relations with one another." The Pact also provided for an obligation to settle all disputes or conflicts by peaceful means.

According to Kelsen, the Paris Pact did not prohibit war waged in defence of violated rights. Kelsen says: "Thus a war which is a reaction against a violation of international law, and that means a war waged for the maintenance of international law, is considered as an instrument of international, and hence not of national, policy."[98] Referring to the above-mentioned opinion of Kelson, Professor Verdross rightly pointed out that, if such had the case, the Paris Pact would not have introduced anything new in comparison with the classic doctrine, according to which a State might resort to war whenever its rights were violated by States.[99]

The Charter of the United Nations constitutes a further progress in this field. The Charter does not stop at the prohibition of aggressive war, but prohibits "the threat or use of force against the territorial integrity or political independence of any State, or in another manner inconsistent with the Purposes of the United Nations" (Art. 2, 4). At the same time the Charter contains the obligation to settle international disputes "by peaceful means in such a manner that international peace and security, and justice, are not endangered" (Art. 2, 3). According to the Charter, the resort to force in international relations may take place only in two cases. First is the case of taking "collective measures for the prevention and removal of threats to peace, and for the suppression of acts of agression or other breaches of peace" (Art. 1, 1). These measures may be effected by the decision of the Security Council adopted, naturally in conformity with the provisions of the Charter. As to the use of force by individual States against other States, this, according to the Charter, may take place only in the case of "individual or collective self-defence if an armed attack occurs" (Art. 51).

These, as well as other, provisions of the Charter regarding relations between States have become principles of general international law. Eighty-one States are now members of the United Nations. All other States which have not yet been admitted to the United Nations, and this fact may only be regretted, have on many occasions confirmed their adherence to the principles of the Charter. The principles of the Charter should, in our opinion, be regarded as universally recognized principles of international law. We, therefore, emphatically reject the assertions made by some of the western authors to the effect that the provisions of the Charter of the United Nations constitute no more than principles of particular international law in contradistinction to general international law; proceeding from this assumption, they make far-reaching conclusions, especially as far as the prohibition of the use of force is concerned. So, for instance,

98 H. Kelsen, *Principles of International Law,* New York, 1952, p. 43.

99 A. Verdross, *Völkerrecht,* Wien, 1955, p. 358.

Kelsen, considering the foregoing provisions of the Charter regarding the prohibition of the use of force as being only the provisions of the "law of the United Nations" makes an allegation that general international law does not prohibit the use of force or war, and that therefore according to general international law a State may resort to war if it considers that its rights have been violated by another State. "General international law," says Kelsen "authorizes the State, i.e. the individual member of the international community, to resort, in the case of a violation of its rights, to reprisals or war against that State which is responsible for the violation."[100] And in his *Principles of international Law* he states: "If reprisal and war typical measures of self-help-are not considered as legal sanctions because a minimum of centralization is considered to be an essential element of the law, the social order we call general international law cannot be regarded as law in the true sense of the term."[101]

The foregoing interpretation is juridically untenable and is in clear contradiction to the general trend of development of international law.

The consolidation of the principle of the prohibition of the use of force, or in other words the principle of non-aggression in the interpretation of the Charter of the United Nations, as a principle of general international law, has been, as we have already pointed out, the major achievement in international law. Not so long ago two states of relations between States were considered as being on the same footing in international law: the state of peace and the state of war. Now a state of war cannot be considered as "equal" to a state of peace. The starting of war constitutes, according to contemporary general international law, the gravest breach of international law involving, side by side with the responsibility of a State which resorts to such war, also personal responsibility of the perpetrators of the war.

One of the most important developments in the field of international law in the period of co-existence has been the emergence of the principle of self-determination of nations.[102] As is well known, the inception of this principle took place in the time of bourgeois revolutions. With the "principle of nationality" the class of bourgeoisie then rising to power fought for the creation of national States in Europe. But the "principle of nationality" was not a generally recognized principle of international law, even within the framework of European international law.[103]

The Soviet State, in accordance with the provisions of the Programme of the Communist Party concerning national self determination, had given a new meaning to

100 H. Kelsen, *Collective Security and Collective Self-Defence under the Charter if the United Nations*, 42 American Journal of international Law (1948), p. 783.

101 H. Kelsen, *Principles of International Law*, New York, 1952, p. 36; see in this sense also P. Guggenheim, *Les principes de droit international public*, 80 Recueil des Cours (19521, I), p. 169; also by him *Traité de droit international public*, Genève, Vol II, 1954, p. 93-94; R. Quadri, *Diritto internazionale publico*, Palermo, 1956, p. 221.

102 See L. Mojoryan, *The Concept of Sovereignty in International Law* (in Russian), Soviet State and Law, 1955, No. 1; S. Molodzov, *Disintegration of Colonial Systems and its influence on International Law* (in Russian), Soviet State and Law, 1955, No.5.

103 See V. Danevsky, *Systems of political equilibrium and legitimism and the principle of nationality in their mutual relationship*, Petersburg, 1882, p. 267 *et seq.* (in Russian).

the principle of national self-determination. Having accepted this principle as a principle of its municipal law, the Soviet State advanced it as a principle of international relations.[104] This principle, as understood by the Soviet State, is a principle admitting of no national oppression whatsoever and including the right of nations freely to determine their own political destiny. In the opinion of the Soviet State this principle should be applied not only to the "civilized States", as it was understood before, but to all the nations equally.

Now we find the principle of self-determination of peoples in the Charter of the United Nations and it is to be considered as a principle of general international law (Articles 1, 55, 76 of the Charter). Later on this principle was confirmed and developed in the General Assembly resolutions of 5 February and 16 December, 1952. It follows from the principle of self-determination of peoples that sovereignty of the State cannot be based at present on the suppression of the right of peoples to self-determination, but should be based on the respect of this right.[105]

A new page in the development of general international law constitutes the principle of peaceful co-existence.[106] This principle is in fact at the very basis of the United Nations. Really, this world organization was instituted to comprise the States of both systems, and to ensure their peaceful co-existence. The primary aim of this organization is "to save succeeding generations from the scourge of war"; States are called upon "to practice tolerance and live together in peace with one another as good neighbours" (Preamble of the Charter). Article 1 of the Charter imposes upon the States an obligation "to maintain international peace and security", "to bring about by peaceful means, and in conformity with the principles of justice and international law, adjustment or settlement of international disputes or situations which might lead to a breach of the peace" and "to develop friendly relations among nations" etc.

The principle of peaceful co-existence has been confirmed in many bilateral and multilateral international documents, such as the well known Chou En-lai/Nehru Declaration of June, 1954, Final Communique of the Bandung Conference of April, 1955, Resolution of the General Assembly of 14 December, 1957, etc.

The principle of peaceful co-existence includes the obligation for each State to use only peaceful means and methods in its relations with other States, to develop friendly relations with other States, to follow such a foreign policy as would contribute to strengthening peaceful co-existence, and to refrain from any action which might endanger peaceful relations between States. The principle of peaceful co-existence goes far beyond the principle of non-aggression. It requires that States not only should refrain from the threat or use of force in international relations, but also from pursuing a policy which might eventually lead to war.

104 See Decree on Peace of 8 November, 1917. *Documents of the USSR Foreign Policy*, Vol. 1, Moscow, 1957, pp. 11-14 (in Russian).

105 G. Tunkin, *Fundamentals of Contemporary International Law*, Moscow, 1956, p. 17 (in Russian).

106 See V. Durdenevsky and M. Lasarev, *Five Principles if Peaceful Coexistence* (in Russian), Moscow, 1957; S. Ivanov, *The Principle if Peaceful Co-existence* (in Russian), Moscow, 1958.

The process of creating new progressive principles and norms of international law is continuing. Vital significance should be attached to the formation of international law norms concerning the reduction of armaments and the banning of nuclear weapons, the use of which is contrary to already-existing principles of international law, to the efforts to secure a universally recognized definition of aggression, universal recognition of norms prohibiting war propaganda, etc.

At the same time we witness the continued development and strengthening of the old democratic principles and norms of international law: the principles of respect for State sovereignty, non-interference in internal affairs, equality of States, and others.

Chapter IV International Law and Peaceful Co-existence

1. Foreign Policy and International Law

International law, as well as national law, influences the social relations which it regulates. This influence is exercised in the complex conditions of the co-existence of States belonging to two diametrically different social systems.

The influence of international law, as of any other law, on social relations is exercised through the rules influencing the behaviour of the subjects of international law, i.e. chiefly States, influencing the foreign policy of States.

The relationship between foreign policy and international law has its own features, distinct from those of the relationship between policy and national law. These features derive chiefly from the fact that the principles and norms of international law are created by agreement between States and for this reason are not an expression of the will of the ruling class of one State, but an expression of the co-ordinated wills of different States, in other words the wills of their ruling classes. In creating norms of national law or in sanctioning customary norms as norms of law, the ruling class of a State can, generally speaking, adequately reflect its policy in law. Yet in establishing norms of international law there is a collision of wills of the ruling classes of various States, wills frequently contradicting one another, with the result that the norms of international law, as a rule, do not adequately express the policy of each particular State.

Further, the will which is expressed in national law is the supreme will which knows no juridical limitations. But even a national law, which is aimed at consolidating and developing social relations advantageous to the ruling class, may from time to time, in some parts come into contradiction with policy. Here, however, the contradiction between policy and law can, in principle, be easily overcome, since the State can, if it so wishes, change its law.

But in international law a single State cannot change legal norms at will, so that here, much more frequently than in national law, we see a contradiction between law and policy, in other words, between foreign policy and international law.

Contradictions between the foreign policy of a State and international law should be decided, of course, in favour of international law, in so far as every State has to comply with its obligations under international law. Rules of international law created by agreement between States can be changed only by a new agreement between them. This is a fundamental principle of contemporary general international law.

Here we come to the doctrine according to which war, which is but a continuation of the policy of States by different means, is an instrument of changing international law. The partisans of this doctrine assert that war plays in international law the same role as revolution in municipal law. As successful revolution legally justifies itself by introducing new law, so successful war justifies itself by creating new norms of international law.[107]

This doctrine should be most emphatically rejected.[108] Theoretically this concept is completely wrong, i.e. does not correspond to the present-day reality. It could be right, to some extent at least, in the conditions which have already gone. But in the contemporary epoch of co-existence witnessing the enormous growth of all the forces of peace, which are at the same time forces supporting international law, such a theory does not reflect the reality. Politically this doctrine is nothing else but the reiteration of well-known concepts consecrating the domination of force and propounding the "progressive role" of wars in international relations.

A State alone cannot change international law, though it can influence its development. But a State may use international law as a means of its external policy. As a matter of fact, States very often support their claims on other States or justify their actions by referring to international law. Present-day general international law is the aggregate of norms created by agreement between the States of the two systems and it can be used as an instrument of the foreign policy of these States. The norms of international law express the co-ordinated wills of the ruling classes of States and are instruments of their policy.

This, of course, does not mean that international law can be an instrument of any policy. The norms of international law can be used as instruments of the policy of States only within the limits determined by their substance, i.e. the substance of the agreement between States, which have brought those norms into being.

2. "State of Intermediacy" or Peaceful Co-existence

The present day international tension and "cold war" have brought about a suggestion to change existing international law by introducing a "third status", the so-called "intermediate status". For centuries international law had known two legal states of international relations: a state of peace and a state of war. Now it is suggested to accept a third state of relations.

Professor Ph. Jessup who has very elaborately outlined this idea, gives the following three characteristics of a state of intermediacy:

(a) There would be between the opposing parties a basic condition of hostility and strain. Referring to Turkey's practice up to the middle of the 18th century not to make treaties of peace, but only armistices with the Christian States, because the Koran forbade making treaties of peace with the infidels, Jessup, in fact, suggests making this practice one of the elements of the "state of intermediacy".

107 See, for instance, E. Kaufmann, *Regles generales du droit de la paix, 54* Recueil des Cours (1935, IV), p. 520; R. Quadri, *Diritto intemazionale publico,* Palermo, 1956, p. 222.

108 See in this sense H. Kelsen, *Principles of International Law,* New York, 1952, p. 36.

(b) The issues between the parties would be so fundamental and deep-rooted that no solution of a single issue would terminate them.
(c) An absence of intention or at least of a decision to resort to war as the means of solving the issues.

Jessup suggests introducing this state in international law, placing it between "peace" and "war". He admits that the introduction of such a state would require the re-examination of the Charter of the United Nations.[109]

Professor L. M. Quintana, also approving of the idea of introducing in international law a "third status", suggests naming it a "neutral status", i.e. a state of relations when there is "neither peace nor war".[110]

The partisans of this concept are trying to justify their suggestion by referring to the necessity to "square the law with the facts".[111]

The first point which should be made clear is that existing international law does not recognize any "intermediate status". The opinion expressed by Professor M. McDougal that according to international law in force "there is not one stage of intermediacy, but countless stages" between "peace" and "war",[112] may be true only in the sense that relations between various States differ and therefore their legal relations are also not identical. But it does not follow that there are in general international law intermediate stages between peace and war.

We are in full agreement with Professor Lachs who states that "international law does not recognize any intermediate status between war and peace."[113]

But how does this question present itself in the light of development of international law and also in the light of ensuring international peace?

There is no doubt that international law should not alienate itself from the realities of life. But it does not mean that international law should adapt itself to any practice of the various States in international relations. And it is very important to find out what is the practice which would be legally consecrated by introducing in international law the suggested "status of intermediacy", irrespective of the intensions of the authors of this suggestion.

The acceptance of the proposal to introduce in international law this "third status" would result in legally consecrating the situation of international tension -and "cold war", which have been created after the Second World War by the "position of strength" policy.

It may appear that an introduction in international law of a "state of intermediacy" might be advisable because such a "status" would be in any case better than war. But

109 Ph. Jessup, *Should International Law Recognize an Intermediate Status between Peace and War,* 48 American Journal of international Law (1954), p. 100-02.

110 Lucio M. Moreno Quintana, *El Tercer Estado del Derecho Intemacional,* Biblioteca Grotiana, Vol. II, München, 1954, pp. 38-39.

111 Ph. Jessup, *Op. cit.,* p. 102.

112 See M. S. McDougal, *Peace and War: Factual Continuum with Multiple Legal Consequences,* 49 American Journal of International Law, (1955), p. 67.

113 M. Lachs, *Geneva Agreements of* 1954 *on Indo-China* (Russian translation), Moscow, 1956, p. 180; see also A. Verdross, *Völkerrecht,* Wien, 1955, p.83; G. Tunkin, *Peaceful Collaboration or "State of Intermediacy",* New Times, 1956, No. 25.

a "status of intermediacy" with its international tension and hostility is a dangerous status which may easily lead to war.

The introduction in international law of the suggested "status of intermediacy" would be a step back. In fact it would mean that peaceful co-existence, which is a normal state of relations according to contemporary international law, would be replaced by a "state of intermediacy" or, in other words, by the state of "cold war", which would be legally accepted as a normal status of international relations.

The interests of preserving and consolidating international peace require a different approach to this problem. Peaceful co-existence-this is the only way by which peoples can evade a new destructive war.

3. International Law as a Means of Ensuring Peaceful Co-existence

Contemporary general international law regulates relations between States belonging to the existing systems, in other words, regulates relations between all states. Its primary aim is to ensure peaceful co-existence of these States.[114]

This is not a logical presupposition or "wishful thinking", but a mere statement of fact. In the age of co-existence of States belonging to socialism and to capitalism norms of general international law may only be those norms which correspond to the objective of strengthening peaceful relations between States irrespective of their social and economic systems. As far as this objective is concerned there is no other ground for agreement between socialist and capitalist States.

The value of international law is determined in our times primarily by the role which it plays and can play in ensuring peaceful co-existence.

The "position of strength" policy and the "cold war" which is the outcome of this policy, have undoubtedly diminished the role of international law in international relations since the end of the Second World War.

In these circumstances, we find in western literature on international law nowadays not a few pessimistic assessments concerning the real role of international law in international relations. We have already spoken of the concepts according to which the ground for development of general international law is getting narrower and that general international law is going to disintegrate into separate regional systems. We have also spoken of suggestions for introducing into international law the so-called "intermediate status".

But probably the most widespread view at present is the view that international law in its present state is embrionic, primitive law, and that only the establishment of a "world state" or the greatest possible approximation to it can make international law into "real" law. This concept is outlined with excellent clarity by Professor Lauterpacht.

114 H. Rolin stated at the XLIVth Conference of the Inter-Parliamentary Union in 1955: "Le droit international a, en effet, essentiellement pour mission de definir les regles du maintien de la paix. C'est dire qu'il est intimement lie ace probleme de la coexistence pacifique . . ." *Compte Rendu de la XLIV Conference de l'Union Interparlementaire,* Geneve, 1956, p. 719; see also G. Lyon-Caen, *Le droit international et la coexistence pacifique des Etats relevant des systemes Politiques opposes,* Journal du Droit International, 1952, p. 54.

In his last edition of Oppenheim's *International Law* he states: "The historic idea of a 'general international organisation' – an idea prominent in the legal and political thought of the last three centuries – connotes an association of States of potentially universal character for the ultimate fulfilment of purposes which, in relation to individuals organised in political society, are realised by the State. The achievement of these purposes, which are outlined below, is as essential to the Law of Nations as it is to the internal law of the State. Failing their accomplishment, or an attempt at their accomplishment, International Law must be deemed to dwell in the realm of a twilight existence in which its very claim to be considered as a system of law is precarious and controversial. To that extent, which is fundamental in its scope and nature, the course of International Law is identical with that of a general political organisation of mankind as distinguished from organs of international administration and co-operation for particular purposes. For it is only under the shelter of and through such general organisation endowed with overriding and coercive power for creating, ascertaining and enforcing the law that International Law can overcome its present imperfections."[115]

Were we to accept this view, the prospects for international law would be gloomy indeed. Really, according to this view international law may become a "real" law only as a result of creating a world state. We have already pointed out that the idea of establishing a "world state", a "world government" and so on, as things are today, is not realistic – it is out of tune with the laws of social development in our times.

It is characteristic of this view that its partisans approach international law simply with the notions accepted in municipal law. But such an approach is scientifically untenable inasmuch as it does not take into consideration the specific features of international law. International law is a law *sui generis*, and so long as international law exists its specific features will exist. The main peculiarities of international law derive from the fact that it regulates, first of all and mainly, relations between sovereign entities, i.e. States. And it has been pointed out with good reason by many authors that establishing a "world state" would mean the end of international law, as this law would be replaced by the internal law of a "world state".[116]

We have already had an occasion to explain that the concept of a "world state" is not only Utopian in the present day conditions of co-existence, but also detrimental to international law. We may add to this that from this concept there is but a step to

115 L. Oppenheim, *International Law* (edited by H. Lauterpacht), Vol. I, 1955, para. 166; see also H. Kelsen, *Problem der Souveränität und die Theorie des Völkerrechts*, Berlin, 1928, p. 320; H. Kelsen, *Principles of International Law*, New York, 1952, pp. 108-10; Ph. Jessup, *A Modern Law of Nations*, New York, 1948, pp. 2-3; G. Schwarzenberger, *A Manual of International Law*, 1947, p. 144; G. Perrin, *Le Fondement et les Limites du Droit des Gens*, Schweizerisches Jahrbuch für Internazionales Recht, 1955, p. 53.

116 See, for instance, A. Verdross, *Völkerrecht*, Wien, 1955, pp. 5-8; G. Sperduti, *Osservazioni sulle basi sociali dell'ordinamento intemazionale*, Rivista di diritto internazionale, Vol. XXXVIII (1955), pp. 3-16; H. Smith, *The Crisis in the Law of Nations*, London, 1947, p. 22; H. Kelsen himself states in this respect: "If, however, the centralization of the organization, especially the centralization of the power to create general legal norms binding upon the members, exceeds a certain degree, the international community is transformed into a national community, a state, and the law created by the central organ ceases to be international law; it assumes the character of national law." (H. Kelsen, *Principles of International Law*, New York, 1952, p. 366.)

affirming the hopelessness of any attempt to consolidate and develop general international law as it is today, and the recognition of the rule of force in international relations.

Enhancing the role of international law in ensuring peaceful co-existence should be sought, not by establishing a world state and abolishing State sovereignty, by creating a "new international law", etc. but primarily by encouraging the activities of all the forces of peace in their struggle for peace, international co-operation in all fields of life, for consolidating, developing and consistently observing the generally recognized principles and norms of international law in force. As many of the most important principles of general international law are inscribed in the Charter of the United Nations the strict observance of the provisions of the Charter is of primary importance. And here come first the well known Five Principles of peaceful co-existence, which constitute nothing more than principles already contained in the Charter, but given a more precise formulation.[117]

Exceptional importance should be attached to the elaboration and introduction in international law of principles and norms aimed at reducing armaments, banning the tests, use and manufacture of nuclear weapons, prohibiting war propaganda, defining aggression, and other norms aimed at preserving peace, furthering friendly relations and co-operation between sovereign. and equal States.

The basic condition of effectiveness of contemporary general international law is a recognition by all the States of the situation when capitalist and socialist States exist side by side, and the rejection of any attempt at changing this situation by force. Professor P. Bastid has rightly stated that besides a clear renunciation of any interference in internal affairs, it is essential for ensuring the possibility of agreements between States and of their observance (and therefore ensuring the effectiveness of international law) to have "a renunciation of any idea of crusade".[118]

Contemporary general international law, which regulates relations between States for the purpose of ensuring their peaceful co-existence is, therefore, objectively directed against "*Machtpolitik*", against any policy which is harmful to friendly cooperation between States. And because of this very quality of contemporary general international law, it may be used as a means of ensuring peaceful co-existence. But the effectiveness of international law depends on the might and activity of those social forces which are fighting for peace and for developing friendly relations between States.

117 See (in Russian) V. Durdenevsky and M. Lazarev, *Five Principles of Peaceful Co-existence,* Moscow, 1957; V. Durdenevsky, *Five Principles,* International Affairs, 1956, No.3; E. Korovin, *Five Principles-Basis of Peaceful Coexistence .of States and Peoples,* International Affairs, 1956, No.5; G. Zadorojny, *International Law Principles of Peaceful Coexistence of States,* Soviet State and Law, 1955, No.8; S. Ivanov, *The Principle of Peaceful Co-existence,* Moscow, 1958; *International Legal Forms of Peaceful Co-existence of States and Nations,* Institute of International Relations, Moscow, 1957; D. Levin, *Peaceful Co-existence of the two World Systems and International Law,* Pravovedenye, 1958, No. 1; A. Movchan, *U.N. and Peaceful Co-existence,* Moscow, 1957.

118 P. Bastid, *Les principes juridiques et moraux de la coexistence,* Bulletin Interparlementaire, 1955, No. 1, p. 4; see also H. Rolin's speech at the XLIVth Conference of the Inter-Parliamentary Union, Compte Rendu de la XLIV Conference, pp. 718-28; M. Bartos, *Aspect juridique de la coexistence pacifique active entre Etats,* Report of the Forty-Seventh Conference of the International Law Association (1956), pp. 17-39; M. Lambilliotte, *La Coexistence pacifique et la Paix,* Syntheses Revue Internationale, fevrier, 1957, pp. 337-39.

The Legal Nature of the United Nations*

Chapter I The Basic Laws of Development of Society and the United Nations

1. International Organisation as an Element of Superstructure

Any contemporary international organisation (intergovernmental) is created by States by means of concluding an international treaty for the purpose.

A treaty creating an international organisation, usually called charter, statute, etc., like any other international treaty, is the result and an expression of the coordinated wills of participating States.

It seems on the surface that States can, therefore, establish whatever international organisation they wish. And the question arises, why States do not create a more perfect international organisation than the United Nations. Most jurists would answer this question in a formal manner. There is, they would say, State sovereignty. States should relinquish their sovereignty in favour of a world organisation. It is the desire of States and statesmen to keep their prerogatives that bars the way to a more efficient international organisation.

But does such an answer explain anything? Not at all. What is behind the wills of States when expressed in an international treaty establishing an international organisation?

Here one cannot limit oneself to a purely legal analysis of the Charter of a particular international organisation, of the various amendments proposed at the international conference where the Charter has been discussed and adopted. One must find out the actual causes of the legal position taken up by States in the process of creating this international organisation.

There one will find a great variety of inter-acting social phenomena. To understand these complex relationships one must differentiate between primary influences and secondary ones, between decisive influences and less important ones.

A jurist is confronted here with basic laws of society which govern these relationships and exercise through them the decisive influence on international organisation.

* This lecture was originally published in Recueil des cours, Tome 119 (1966), pp. 1-68 and is reprinted with kind permission of the Hague Academy of International Law/Académie de droit international de la Haye.

According to the Marxist theory the initial general cause of various transformations which take place in society is the growth of productive forces of society. Productive forces consist of material (means of production) and human elements. To produce things men improve means of production and at the same time improve themselves.

In the process of production men inevitably enter into relations with each other which are called relations of production. The nature of these relations is conditioned by the level of productive forces.

For instance, when modern industry started to develop, the forms of relations between men which existed in the feudal society became inadequate. In England, which was one of the countries which led the way to the capitalist society, Adam Smith tried to persuade the ruling classes of the country of the advantages of free labour as compared with slave labour and appealed for the removal of various feudal restrictions on the movement of men and goods. The feudal relations of production had been eliminated, and the new capitalist relations took their place.

Corresponding to different stages of development of material forces of production relations between men in the process of production took various forms by which we distinguish societies based on slave labour, feudal society, capitalist society and socialist society. In each of these societies relations of production are different.

Social relations in the process of production constitute the economic structure of society, a basis for all other social institutions, such as State, law, ideology, art, etc., which constitute the superstructure of society.

When forces of production have grown considerably the old economic structure becomes inadequate; then social revolution comes and destroys this old economic structure and creates a new one. With the transformation of an economic structure a whole superstructure changes more or less rapidly.

The conclusion therefore is that the development of the superstructure is determined in its main features by the development of the economic structure which itself is conditioned by the development of productive forces.

The development of international organisation as an element of superstructure is a convincing corroboration of the Marxist theory. The very emergence of modern international organisations was due to the growth of productive forces which have brought about the enormous expansion of international intercourse that necessitated the creation of permanent international bodies to handle various problems arising out of this intercourse.

2. Two Opposing Social Systems and the United Nations

At present there are two main economic systems, two diametrically opposite economic structures. As the nature of superstructure is determined by economic structure there corresponds to each economic structure a specific superstructure. There seems to be therefore a contradiction in the statement that in spite of the existence of two opposing economic structures there are common elements of a superstructural character, e.g. general international organisation.

This contradiction is, however, only apparent.

Superstructure is not a kind of mirror reflection of economic structure. Various elements of superstructure influence each other and make the picture much more complicated, though it should be stressed that the impact of economic structure is a decisive one. Economic structure sets a general framework within which this interaction of various elements of superstructure takes place.

Common international elements of a superstructural character spring from the relations which exist between these two systems. If the world of today is split into two diametrically opposite systems it does not mean that they are isolated one from the other. Even in the early history of mankind States did not live in isolation. In the contemporary world with its highly developed economy and world-wide division of labour isolation of one group of States from another group of States is unthinkable. There are economic relations between States belonging to various social and economic systems. There must therefore be some superstructural elements corresponding to these relations.

It should, however, be kept in mind that international economic relations are of a derivative character with regard to primary economic structures. But still they are of a structural and not of a superstructural character.

There are other relations between States of different systems: political, cultural, scientific, etc., which are of a superstructural character. As international economic relations they are also not primary ones but derivative in relation to superstructures of a primary nature which are proper to each of the systems.

The split of the world into opposing systems did not stop the objective process of development of productive forces of the society and, with it, the growth of international division of labour, which intensifies international economic relations. And with the growth of economic relations other relations between States also develop.

Of course the emergence of the Socialist system has brought into international life many new elements. The Soviet State proclaimed new principles of international relations, such as principles of equality of all peoples without distinction as to race, colour, religion, etc., self-determination of peoples, peaceful coexistence of States irrespective of their social systems, prohibition of aggressive war, etc. It refused to recognise all reactionary principles of the old international law and started its struggle for their elimination with the view to introducing into international law such new principles and rules as would make it a real instrument of peace and liberation of colonial peoples.

The October Revolution marked the end of the "golden age" of colonialism. The solution of the nationalities problems in the Soviet Union on the basis of the Marx-Lenin theory set an inspiring example. The Soviet State in its activities in the international arena did not conceal that it considered the colonial system unjust and contrary to international law and has consistently supported the struggle of colonial peoples for independence. The upheaval of the national liberation movement, in the course of a few decades, has brought the colonial system to complete disintegration.

Among socialist countries a new type of international relations has developed which exercises an ever-increasing influence on international relations in general.

Meanwhile the objective process of the growth and expansion of international relations continues. This fact has an immediate impact on international organisation. With the expansion of inter-State relations the number of international problems which cannot be dealt with on a bilateral or a regional basis is constantly increasing.

Problems which cannot be satisfactorily solved simply by the conclusion and application of multilateral treaties stipulating rights and obligations of States are becoming more numerous. Such problems call for the creation of international organisations which are permanent bodies to handle specific matters entrusted to them by States.

The expanding scope of such problems and the ever-increasing need to deal with them expeditiously bring about the growing competence of international organisations.

The United Nations itself is a convincing example: its competence is much wider than the competence of the former League of Nations.

So, the growth of productive forces intensifies the international division of labour and through it international economic relations. This leads to the expansion of international relations in general and to the emergence of international organisation.

However, this is only one aspect of the influence of the laws of development of the society on international organisation. If this aspect alone is taken into consideration, the conclusions drawn may be completely wrong. The important problem is, what is the social content of international relations in a specific epoch.

Contemporary international relations are loaded with acute conflicts between States. The main conflict in today's international relations is the conflict between States belonging to the two opposing social systems: between socialist and capitalist States.

It is useless and even harmful to the cause of international peace to close one's eyes to this fact or to minimise its importance. This conflict does not result from the ill will of anybody but is rooted in the struggle of the new and the old economic and social systems. It does not mean, of course, that ill will may not influence relations between States or that all the existing tensions may be attributed to the basic conflict between the two main systems. All we would like to stress is that the basic conflict is there and that it is not casual.

A new social system based on collective ownership of the means of production came into being half a century ago, and it is gradually replacing the old economic and social system. History shows that old social systems have never given way to new social systems without resistance. A new economic and social system always destroys the privileged position of the ruling classes of an old system and these classes try to destroy, or at least to hamper, the development of a new system.

In the period of transition from the capitalist to the socialist society this struggle is much more intense than it was in the former periods of transition from one social system to another. In the transitional periods of the past the question was only which class would dominate the society economically and politically. But the institution of private ownership of the means of production remained, and the exploitation of man by man was not in question.

Socialist revolution tends to destroy the very foundation of the old society, i.e. the private ownership of the means of production and the exploitation of man by man. Thereby it strikes the ruling classes of the old society a much heavier blow.

In the period of the bourgeois revolutions and especially during the French revolution of the 18th century the ruling classes of the feudal society reacted very strongly against the new social system.

Due to the facts we have just indicated the reaction of the ruling classes of the capitalist society against the socialist system was much more violent and the struggle between the two systems much more intense.

What is the impact on international organisation of the coexistence of States belonging to two diametrically opposite systems? This fact leaves the only possible basis for creating a general international organisation. This basis is peaceful coexistence of States having these systems which, in brief, means that an inevitable struggle between States of two diametrically opposite systems should be pursued by peaceful means only and cooperation between them in all fields developed.

The second World War had greatly contributed to the understanding of the importance of peaceful coexistence of States of the two opposing systems for the future of mankind. The United Nations has been created as an organisation of peaceful coexistence of States belonging to different economic and social systems.[1]

The Charter of the United Nations, though not using the term "peaceful coexistence", embodies the idea in all its main provisions. In the Preamble of the Charter Members of the United Nations expressed their determination "to save succeeding generations from the scourge of war", "to practise tolerance and live together in peace with one another as good neighbours" and to unite their "strength to maintain international peace and security, and to ensure, by the acceptance of principles and the institution of methods, that armed force shall not be used, save in the common interest".

The Charter obligates the Organisation and its Members to maintain international peace and security and to settle international disputes by peaceful means, to develop friendly relations among nations based on respect for the principle of equal rights and self-determination of peoples, to develop international cooperation in various fields.

Created as an organisation of peaceful coexistence, the United Nations was intended to function on the basis of agreement between States with different social and economic systems. This basic requirement of peaceful coexistence has found its expression principally in the rule of unanimity of the great powers in the Security Council.[2]

3. SOVEREIGN STATES AND THE UNITED NATIONS

One of the basic laws of development of present-day society which has an immediate bearing upon international organisation is the existence of sovereign States.

1 See M. Lachs, The United Nations and Peaceful Coexistence, "Polish Perspectives", N 4, 1960, pp. 3-10; G. Tunkin, Die rechtlicheNatur der UNO und der Weg zur Festigung der intemationalen Organisation, "Vereinte Nationen" Bonn, August, 1965; The United Nations and Vital Contemporary Problems (Ed. V. Zorin, G. Morozov), Mocsow, 1965, pp. 66-91.

2 See N. Ushakov, The Principle of Unanimity of the Great Powers in the United Nations, Moscow, 1956 (in Russian), p. 39 et seq.

We are still living in an epoch when the State as a social institution cannot be done away with.

This institution is, however, not inherent in human society. It is wrong to assume that human society cannot exist without States.

There was no State in primitive society. Another form of social organisation existed; this was the clan organisation.

Only with the growth of productive forces of the society which led to the emergence of private ownership of the means of production, to the increasing economic inequality between men and to the split of society into classes was clan organisation replaced by or rather converted into State.

The State was not only a new institution but an institution radically different from clan organisation as far as the social content and also the form of organisation were concerned.

Clan organisation represented society as a whole because there were as yet no social classes in existence. And although the State which had replaced clan organisation also claimed to represent the whole society, it was actually, as Lenin put it, an organisation in the hands of a class which occupied the commanding position in the economic field and which through the State affirmed itself also as the politically dominating class.

The State is a social institution inherent only in the class society. There was a time before social classes had come into being when the State did not exist. And on a very high level of development of the human society with the disappearance of private ownership of the means of production and social classes the State will give way to another, more perfect form of social organisation.

The existence of about 120 States is not, therefore, fortuitous. It is a manifestation of one of the basic laws of the development of present-day society.

But if this is so, international organisation should be framed on the basis of this assumption. The analysis of the Charter of the United Nations reveals that this situation was duly taken into account by its framers. As Article 2 of the Charter says: "The Organisation is based on the principle of the sovereign equality of all its Members". Art. 2, para.7, states the principle of non-interference in matters which are essentially within the domestic jurisdiction of a State.

These principles which are closely linked also find their expression tin the provisions of the Charter regarding relations between States and the United Nations, the competence of various organs of the Organisation, the legal force of its decisions, etc.

The general conclusion therefore is that the United Nations is an inter-State, not a super-State organisation.[3]

3 Fore a more extensive dicussion of the subject see G. Morozov, The United Nations, Moscow, 1962, pp. 160-221 (in Russian); R. Bobrov, Regarding the Legal Nature of the United Nations, "Soviet Yearbook of International Law, 1959", Moscow, 1960, pp. 229-240; The United Nations and Vital Contemporary Problems (Ed. V. Zorin, G. Morozov), Moscow, 1965, pp. 11-19.

4. Disintegration of the Colonial System and the United Nations

Decolonization is one of the fundamental laws of the development of society in our epoch. The colonial system could not persist very long in the new era opened by the Great Socialist October revolution, in the era of general upheaval against exploitation of man by man of which the colonial system was the most ugly manifestation.

To what extent has this basic law found its expression in the Charter of the United Nations? It is well known how colonial powers opposed the inclusion in the United Nations Charter of the proposals made by the Soviet Union regarding colonial problems. These proposals were, generally speaking, intended to fortify the principle of self-determination of peoples and to provide for means of realisation of their rights by the peoples of the colonies and other dependent territories.

A very important proposal was made by the Soviet Union during the discussion on the United States draft chapter relating to trusteeship. The Soviet Union proposed to provide in the Charter that the object of the trusteeship system was "a speedy achievement of full State independence".

As a result of the opposition of colonial powers this amendment was not adopted. However, a provision was adopted to the effect that one of the objectives of the trusteeship system was the progressive development of the peoples of the territories placed under the trusteeship system "towards self-government or independence as may be appropriate to the particular circumstances of each territory and its people. . ."[4]

On the proposal of the Soviet Union Article 1 of the Charter was supplemented by a provision stating that principles of equal rights and self-determination of peoples were basic principles for developing friendly relations among nations. Insufficient though they were, the provisions of the United Nations Charter regarding decolonization represented a substantial step forward in comparison with the situation in international law which existed prior to the Charter. They have been used afterwards by all who fought for the independence of colonies and first of all by the colonial peoples themselves.

Although the Charter contained some progressive provisions, especially those relating to the right of self-determination, it would be an exaggeration to assume that the Charter adequately reflected the historical law of decolonization. As a result, some "over-cautious" provisions of the Charter on the subject have been superseded by subsequent developments due to the struggle of colonial peoples for independence, and the support given to this struggle by all progressive forces in the world.

5. The Mechanism of Influence of the Basic Laws on International Organisation

Basic laws of the development of society exercise their decisive influence on the nature of an international organisation from the very moment of its creation.

4 Art. 76.

As has been indicated before, international organisations are established by States through the medium of international treaties. The will of each particular State participating in such a treaty is in its main features determined by the whole complex of conditions in which the ruling class of this State finds itself, or in a socialist State, where there is no ruling class, by the conditions in which the people as a whole finds itself. These conditions include not only internal but also external conditions.

It has already been stated that the economic structure of society plays a decisive role in framing these conditions. The basic laws of development of society determine the development of the economic structure and also that of the superstructure. They determine therefore in their main features the conditions which influence the will of a State in the process of creating an international organisation. Through these channels the laws of history influence international organisation.

This influence makes itself felt and through the same channels also in the course of further development of each particular international organisation.

All this, however, does not mean that the nature of any international organisation inevitably corresponds to the laws of development of society. These laws are not robots that act by themselves and make every international organisation conform completely to them.

In present-day society with its antagonistic classes there are social forces which act contrary to the laws of history, because its normal progress is not in their interest. And there are other social forces which consciously or unconsciously act in harmony with these laws and thereby assure the progress of society.

History shows that in the long run the progressive forces have always been victorious and assured the progressive development of human society. But this line of general progress has not been even. As Lenin said, it would be an oversimplification to picture the history of society as a constant progressive development without serious retrogressions. Of course these retrogressions do not set aside the basic laws of development of society which ultimately prevail.

The same applies to the international organisation. The basic social laws make themselves felt and always prevail in the final analysis, whether by bringing about a situation when an international organisation has a sufficient degree of conformity with these laws or assuring the collapse of an international organisation which comes into serious conflict with these laws.

Chapter II The Charter as the Legal Basis of United Nations Activities

1. The Charter as an International Treaty

The Charter of the United Nations is an international treaty. It passed the usual stages of the conclusion of treaties, including its ratification by States. As a statute of an international organisation the Charter is a treaty *sui generis*.

In contradistinction to an ordinary treaty a statute of an international organisation creates an international institution which functions on its basis. Organs of an organisation have specific powers assigned to them by its statute and provisions of this type are implemented, primarily not by States as such but by the organs of an international organisation. In other words, a statute of an international organisation sometimes gives birth to a very complex international machinery which is lacking in ordinary treaties.

A statute inevitably regulates relations not only between States parties to such treaty but also establishes the competences of the various organs of an organisation and their relationship, and it governs relations between the organisation and member-States.

Generally speaking a statute of an international organisation is a more complex phenomenon than an ordinary international treaty and its life is also richer than the life of an ordinary treaty.

It should also be borne in mind that the Charter of the United Nations stands out among statutes of international organisations as an instrument of the highest authority. It is a statute of an international organisation which has been put by States in a predominant position with regard to all other international organisations. Its competence includes practically all the most important questions of international relations and especially those relating to the maintenance of international peace and security. Other general international organizations "having wide international responsibilities"[5] are brought into some relationship with the United Nations.

The Charter puts the United Nations in a superior position with regard to regional organisations of collective security and gives it wide powers over actions of those agencies, especially as to the use of force.[6]

The Charter is also above all other treaties concluded by the members of the United Nations.[7]

5 Article 57 of the Charter.

6 Articles 53 and 51.

7 Article 103.

And, last but not least, the Charter embodies fundamental principles of contemporary international law.

But in spite of all this the Charter is an international treaty, although a treaty *sui generis*. With regard to the application of the rules of the law of treaties to treaties which are constituent instruments of international organisations the International Law Commission stated in. Article 4 of its final draft on the Law of Treaties: "The application of the present articles to treaties which are constituent instruments of an international organisation or are adopted within an international organisation shall be subject to any relevant rules of the organisation".[8]

There are no rules (and there cannot be any rules) in the United Nations which exclude the application to the Charter of the basic rule of the law of treaties–*pacta sunt servanda*.

The rule *pacta sunt servanda* means, as the International Law Commission stated in its draft articles on the Law of Treaties, that "every treaty in force is binding upon the parties to it and must be performed by them in good faith".[9]

It further means: that States parties to a treaty may not be legally required to do more than they are obliged to do under the terms of the treaty.

In its application to treaties which are statutes of international organisations it also means that the provisions of such treaties regarding the competence of their organs should be complied with.

It should be stressed therefore that the Charter of the United Nations with those modifications which have been lawfully introduced into it is the only legal basis of the activities of the United Nations.

2. The Theory of "Inherent Competence" of International Organisations

The practices of the United Nations under the influence of some Western powers have in many instances amounted to flagrant violations of the fundamental provisions of the Charter.

The most important of them were the so-called "Uniting for Peace" resolution[10] and the practices with regard to the United Nations military forces.

It was evident that such practices could not be justified on the basis of the Charter. This situation has given birth to various theories which tended to give such legal interpretations as to justify deviations from and grave violations of the Charter of the United Nations. In saying this we are far from suggesting that such theories are always adopted by their authors intentionally, in order to justify certain policies.

8 Report of the International Law Commission on the Work of its Eighteenth Session, 1966, Doc. A/CN.4/191. The view that the Charter is a kind of constitutional document which finds itself completely or to a great extent outside the law of treaties (see, for instance, Sh. Rosenne, The Constitution of an International Organisation an International Treaty? in "Comunicazioni et Studi", vol. XII, p. 46), in our estimation, has never been substantiated on the basis of the international law in force.

9 Art. 23 of the final Draft, Report, 1966.

10 Resolution 377/V/ of November 3, 1950.

One of the theories which falls within this category is the theory of "inherent competence" of international organisations.

In its extreme manifestations this theory asserts that according to contemporary international law each international organisation has "inherent competence" vested in it as such to take all "sovereign" actions subject only to specific limitations contained in its constituent instrument, if any.

The basic argument advanced by a few proponents of this extreme view is that the practices of the United Nations as well as of other international organisations indicate that their activities go beyond the express provisions of their respective statutes.

The theory of "inherent competence" of the United Nations has found its expression, for example, in the advisory opinion of the International Court of Justice on *Certain Expenses of the United Nations* The Court stated that ". . .when the Organisation takes action which warrants the assertion that it was appropriate for the fulfilment of one of the stated purposes of the United Nations, the presumption is that such action is not *ultra vires* of the Organisation".[11]

Referring to this presumption the Soviet Judge V. Koretzky has rightly pointed out in his dissenting opinion that admission of such a presumption would mean coming back to a maxim condemned by history–the aim justifies the means.[12]

A Norwegian jurist, F. Seyersted, who is one of the most ardent proponents of this theory, defines its substance in the following terms: "It is submitted that any organisation which satisfies the criteria listed above[13] is, on the basis of general international law, *ipso facto* a general subject of international law, in the sense that it, like States, has the inherent capacity to perform any act of international law which it is in a practical position to perform, subject to the two negative restrictions listed under 111(3) to the extent that these might be considered to have an external effect in respect of (States and) intergovernmental Organisations".[14]

Rightly stating that the activities of international organisations in many instances go beyond the provisions of their respective statutes, the proponents of this theory draw from this fact conclusions which not only cannot be substantiated on the basis of international law but run counter to its fundamental principles.

The first problem which presents itself is whether these practices are sufficient to prove the existence of a norm of general international law according to which international organisations may perform any acts within the limits of their purposes.

How could such a norm come into existence? It is true that customary norms of international law emerge from the practice of States. Repetition of certain actions by States in analogous circumstances may lead to the formation of a rule of State conduct. But such a repetition may equally not bring about the formation of any rule of conduct and may be considered as mere expediency. Even if as a result of such repetitive actions a rule

11 I.C.J. Reports, 1962, p. 168.

12 Ibid., p. 268.

13 These criteria actually come to one–the factual existence and functioning of the organisation.

14 F. Seyersted, Objective International Personality of Intergovernmental Organisations, "Nordisk Tidsskrift for International Ret", vol. 34, 1964, p. 55.

of conduct has emerged it may not necessarily be a legal rule. It may be a simple usage connected with no obligations whatsoever, or a rule of international morality which imposes moral obligations. There is quite a number of such rules in international relations.

The existence of a certain State practice is not a sufficient proof of the existence of a customary rule of international law corresponding to this practice. Practice is only one element in the process of formation of a customary rule of international law.

The second indispensable element of a customary rule is its acceptance by States as a rule of law. In other words, a rule of conduct is not a legal rule until it has been recognized as such by States. When such recognition has been achieved or, as is usually said, an *opinio juris* has been formed, a formation of a customary rule of international law is completed and the rule is there."[15]

There is, however, no evidence at all that the practice of international organisations to develop their activites beyond provisions of their respective statutes has been accepted by States as a rule of general international law. The same is still more true of the alleged rule of general international law to the effect that international organisations may perform any acts within their purposes.

Such a rule, if it existed, would be in open conflict with fundamental principles of contemporary international law, and would contradict the very nature of present-day international organisations and of the United Nations in particular.

The United Nations is an inter-State organisation, States have created it for certain purposes, they have prescribed certain means for the realisation of its objectives, and the Organisation may not go beyond these limits without their consent.

The alleged rule of an "inherent competence" of international organisations would also be inconsistent with a basic principle of international law – *pacta servanda sunt.*

The proponents of the theory of "inherent competence" of inter-national organisations actually represent them as entities which might exist independently of States-members. It is obvious, however, that this is not the case.[16]

The theory of "inherent competence" of international organisations also misrepresents the nature of international treaties, ascribing to a statement of purposes which is usually found in the preamble of a treaty a magic force taking these purposes from the context of a treaty and making them independent of the coordinated wills of States of which the treaty as a whole is an expression.

3. The Theory of "Implied Competence" of International Organisations

The theory of "implied competence" of international organisations has the same origin as the theory of "inherent competence". But by comparison with the latter this one is not so far-reaching, claiming only that an international organisation has not only the

15 Cf., G. Tunkin, Droit international public. Problèmes théoriques, Paris, 1965, pp. 76-89.

16 See Chapter 3, para. I below. Professor L. Gross says that the theory of "inherent competence" "inverts the basic principle of international organisation: under international law an organization has no plenitude of powers like sovereign states. . ." (L. Gross, Expenses of the United Nations for Peace-Keeping Operations, in "International Organization", vol. XXVII, Number I, 1965, p. 9).

competence explicitly provided for in its statute but also such additional competence as is implied in the provisions of the statute.

This theory has found its formulation, for instance, in the advisory opinion of the International Court of Justice in the *Reparation for Injuries Case*. The Court stated:

> "Under international law, the Organisation must be deemed to have those powers which, though not expressly provided in the Charter, are conferred upon it by necessary implication as being essential to the performance of its duties"[17]

Of course, practice has abundantly shown that no statute of an international organisation and, especially of such a multifunctional organisation as the United Nations, can contain specific provisions for all its activities. When drafting a statute of an international organisation representatives of States always assume that some secondary problems which may arise in the course of its functioning will be settled later on the basis of the provisions of the statute.

Thus far we may speak of an implied competence. The implied competence is not a rule of general international law; it is a problem of interpretation of the statute of a particular international organisation.

The advisory opinion of the International Court of Justice which we have just quoted goes beyond the interpretation of the provisions of the Charter of the United Nations, alleging a rule of international law to the effect that additional powers "essential" for the performance of the duties of an international organisation are always implied. This seems to be the opinion of many writers influenced by the Court's pronouncement.[18]

The separate opinion of Judge Hackworth is of interest in this context although it cannot be accepted without reservation. He stated:

> "There can be no gainsaying the fact that the Organization is one of delegated and enumerated powers. It is to be presumed that such powers as the Member States desired to confer upon it are stated either in the Charter or in complementary agreements concluded by them. Powers not expressed cannot freely be implied. Implied powers flow from the grant of expressed powers, and are limited to those that are "necessary" to the exercise of powers expressly granted".[19]

As the problem of implied competence of international organisation is a problem of interpretation of constituent treaties and supplementary agreements, generally accepted rules on interpretation of international treaties should apply in a case where the question of implied competence arises.

17 I.C.J. Reports, 1949, p. 182.

18 See, for instance, P. Reuter, Institutions internationales, Paris, 1962, p. 210; Ingrid Defter, Law Making by International Organisations, Stockholm, 1965, p. 31.

19 I.C.J. Reports, 1949, p. 198.

The International Law Commission stressed in its draft on the Law of Treaties that the provisions of a treaty should be interpreted in good faith in accordance with the ordinary meaning to be given to its terms in the context of the treaty. The interpretation should be given in the light of the objects and purposes of the treaty, but this does not mean that these objects and purposes can be an independent source of rights and obligations.[20]

It is also possible that the statute of an international organisation or some less formal agreement or understanding may contain provisions regarding the interpretation of the statute.

As to the interpretation of the Charter of the United Nations, the question was discussed at the San Francisco Conference in 1945. The Report of Committee 2 of Commission IV approved by the Conference contained the following statement: "It is to be understood, of course, that if an interpretation made by any organ of the Organization or by a committee of jurists is not generally acceptable it will be without binding force".[21]

So the "implied competence" of an international organisation may be admitted in each particular case only to the extent to which it may be considered as actually implied in the provisions of the statute of the organisation but not on the basis of a specific rule of international law on the implied competence.

4. United Nations Practice and the Charter

The role of United Nations practice in developing or modifying the provisions of the Charter has become one of the major legal and political problems.

Alongside the theories of "inherent competence" and "implied competence" of international organisations, a thesis has also been advocated with some insistence that UN practice as such may amend the Charter.

It has already been stated that State practice may lead to the emergence of a rule of conduct which, to become a rule of international law, needs to be accepted by States as legally binding.[22]

In the present case, however, the problem is, what effect the practice of the organisation may have on the Charter of this organisation. There is no reason to deny that the rules of international law regarding the role of practice in modifying multilateral treaties are applicable to treaties which are constituent instruments of international organisations, in this case to the Charter of the United Nations.

The problem, however, has not been sufficiently studied in spite of the abundant literature which has appeared in the last 15 years. Most of the Western jurists seem to take the position that the problem is very simple, and more and more they speak of the practice, almost forgetting that there is the Charter.

20 Art. 27, Report. . . ,1966.

21 UNCIO Documents, vol. 13, p. 710.

22 Cf., Chapter II, para. 2 above.

They describe the events, mix together licit and illicit decisions of the United Nations organs and come to conclusions more or less similar to that of Professor Leland Goodrich who states:

> "In actual practice, the structure of power and influence in the United Nations has been quite different from what was initially envisaged. The Charter itself has not been amended. The composition, functions, and powers of organs have remained the same on paper. But in the course of the day-to-day interpretation and application of these provisions, a quite different system of power relationships has emerged from that which was anticipated at the time the Charter was approved in San Francisco".[23]

However, the assumption that the real law of the United Nations is not the Charter but the practice, whatever it may be, is not only legally unjustified but also very dangerous politically.

From a very general point of view there is always interaction between conventional and customary rules of international law. The binding force of both is the same. The legal basis is also identical – explicit or tacit agreement between States. This means that modification of an international treaty by the parties through practice accepted as a rule of law is not excluded. In such a case a new, customary rule intended to modify provisions of the treaty embodies the new agreement which is substituted for the original one. With regard to the provisions of the treaty concerning its amendment, such a simplified form of modification would constitute an exception which the parties to the treaty may make by mutual consent.

Coming back to the Charter of the United Nations we may say that modifications may be brought about by way of practice if certain conditions are present.

Certainly a great deal of caution should be exercised when admitting this method of modification, first of all because it usually presents some difficulties in ascertaining the actual expression of the will of the parties, and secondly because it is an exception to the provisions of the Charter regarding its amendment.

The International Law Commission while admitting the possibility of modification of a treaty by subsequent practice of the parties in the application of the treaty stated that only such practice does matter in this respect as establishes the agreement of the parties to modify the provisions of the treaty. The Commission said in Article 38 of its draft on the Law of Treaties: "A treaty may be modified by subsequent practice in the application of the treaty establishing the agreement of the parties to modify its provisions".[24]

The practice, therefore, should be accepted by all or almost all the members of the United Nations as a legal rule developing or modifying certain provisions of the Charter.

In any event it cannot logically be admitted that the customary way of modifying the Charter may fall short of its express provisions as to the number of the parties

23 L. Goodrich, The United Nations, New York, 1959, p. 115: See also M. Virally, L'ONU d'hier à demain, Paris, 1961 where the author says: ". . . dispositions essentielles/de la Charte/sont restees lettre morte ou sont constamment violées" (p. 21). And he states: "des chapitres entiers ont disparu ou ont été remplacés sous l'action de la pratique, par l'effet d'une coutiime constitutionnelle. ." (p. 27).

24 I.L.C. Report, 1966.

whose consent is required for formal amendments of the Charter. The Charter provides that amendments to it may be adopted either by the General Assembly or by a General Conference of the Members of the UN by a two thirds vote and that any amendment shall come into force when ratified by two thirds of the Members of the UN, including all the permanent members of the Security Council.

So, a very important requirement for a practice to be considered as modifying the Charter is that such a practice should establish the agreement of all the permanent members of the Security Council to that effect. The specific significance of this requirement stems from the fact that it is a reflection of one of the aspects of the nature of the United Nations as an organisation of peaceful coexistence of States belonging to different social and economic systems.[25]

There is one more safeguard which is dictated by the relationship between the ordinary and customary way of modifying a treaty. It is that the principal provisions of a treaty should not be considered as susceptible of amendment in the customary manner. This seems to be a legal conclusion which may be drawn from the anaysis of the practice of States.

5. The Development of the Charter

As the UN Charter is a treaty, an amendment of it may be effected only by a subsequent agreement of the parties according to the provisions of the Charter itself or, as far as non-substantial modifications are concerned, by way of practice as indicated above.

It may be argued that the principles we have stated for possible modifications of the Charter by way of practice are too rigid and prevent the adaptation of the Charter to changing international life.

However, those are not only express legal requirements but also the requirements dictated by the very nature of the United Nations.

It was clear from the very beginning that the United Nations as an inter-State organisation and as an organisation of peaceful coexistence of States belonging to different social and economic systems might be effective and might successfully develop only on the basis of consensus among member States and first of all that of the great powers.

The tendency to impose upon the United Nations certain practices in violation of the basic provisions of the Charter and the efforts to present them as modifications of the Charter in spite of strong opposition from certain members of the UN, including a permanent member of the Security Council, have in no way contributed to the adaptation of the Charter to the new needs of international society. They have caused great tensions and brought the Organisation to the verge of a breakdown. They have made the adaptation of the United Nations to the ever changing international situation much more difficult, being as they are attempts to make the United Nations serve the aggressive policies of the imperialist powers.

On the contrary, the respect for the Charter and compliance with the principles of international law bearing on the development and modification of the Charter would create an atmosphere of goodwill and mutual confidence which would make much easier the development of the United Nations as an instrument of peace.

25 Cf., Chapter I, para. 2.

Chapter III The Legal Nature of the United Nations and Its Structure and Functioning

1. Member States in the United Nations

Much has been said of the United Nations as an autonomous entity and subject of international law.

Of course, the United Nations, although created by States, is a social phenomenon distinct from States members of the Organisation. The United Nations has been endowed with certain features which make it a subject of international law.

International organisations may possess various degrees of international personality, such as may have been allotted to them by States in corresponding constituent instruments or complementary agreements.

A constituent instrument of an international organisation is binding upon States parties to it or, in other words, upon members of the organisation, although nothing prevents any other State from accepting expressly or tacitly the international personality of the organisation, of which it is not a member.

The United Nations possesses the largest degree of international personality, by comparison with other general international organisations.

When speaking of the international legal personality of international organisations we should, of course, keep in mind that they may not be put on the same level as States – original subjects of international law.[26]

International legal personality of international organisations is of a derivative character. The most important element inherent in the original subjects of international law – States, viz. the element of sovereignty, is lacking in the case of international organisations.

We are not going to dwell upon this point at any great length. There is actually no controversy at present so far as general recognition of the United Nations as a subject of international law is concerned. The controversy begins beyond that.

Under the influence of the "cold war" practice of imposing the will of one group of States upon the United Nations in violation of the basic principles of the Charter there emerged a well defined tendency to misrepresent the real relations between

26 As the International Court of Justice has rightly stressed in its advisory opinion on the Reparation for Injuries, I.C.J. Reports, 1949, p. 179.

States members and the United Nations, and to divorce the Organisation from its membership.

This tendency is felt in the advisory opinions of the International Court of Justice proceeding from the theories of "implied" or even "inherent" competence of international organisations.

In line with these pronouncements of the Court some authors draw too far-reaching conclusions from the very fact that the United Nations is a subject of international law. As a matter of fact, they maintain that because the United Nations is a subject of international law it is a completely independent entity developing by itself.

So, for instance, Sir Gerald Fitzmaurice is of the opinion that "the personality and capacities of the Organisation have their origin in an instrument contractual in form, but once created and established they come to assume an objective, self-existent character for all the world".[27]

A Norwegian jurist, F. Seyersted, goes still further, saying that as soon as an international organisation has been established it is a subject of international law and as such has the same capacities under general international law as any other subject of international law– unless it is precluded by special rules from performing certain acts.[28]

Such conclusions are true with regard to States which are *ipso facto* subjects of international law.

However, there is no such rule of general international law regarding international legal personality of international organisations.

If under general international law a State is a subject of international law possessing certain rights and obligations, the position of international organisations is different.[29]

The legal personality of an international organisation is on the contrary based on its constituent instrument.

And with regard to the statutes of international organisations it should be stated that there is practically none which would contain carte-blanche provisions concerning the legal personality of a particular international organisation.

The case is actually the converse. A constituent instrument of an international organisation provides for certain rights and capacities of the organisation which lead to the conclusion that the organisation possesses a certain degree of international legal personality.[30]

---

27 Fitzmaurice, The Law and Procedure of the International Court of Justice: International Organizations and Tribunals, 29 B.Y.I.L. (1952), p. 1, at p. 14.

28 See F. Seyersted, International Personality of Intergovernmental Organizations; Do their Capacities Really Depend on their Constitutions? The Indian Journal of International Law, v. 4, N 1, January 1964, pp. 66-67.

29 See G. Tunkin, Fundamentals of International Law, Moscow, 1956, pp. 17-18 (in Russian); P. Pescatore, Les relations extérieures des comrnanutés européennes, Recueil des Cours, v. 103 (1961), p. 29.

30 See in this sense Parry, The Treaty-Making Power of the United Nations, in British Yearbook of International Law 26 (1949), p. 110; Zemanek, Das Vertragsrecht der intemationalen Organisationen, Wien, 1957, S. 47; Kasmé, La capacité de l'Organisation des Nations Unies de conclure des traités, Paris, 1960, p. 26.

Very little attention has generally been paid to the nature of the United Nations. It has already been pointed out that the United Nations is an organisation of sovereign States and an organisation of peaceful coexistence of States belonging to different social and economic systems. These are, as we have seen, not casual characteristics. They reflect the basic laws of development of the society.

These specific features make themselves felt in the structure of the Organisation, its competences and activities as set forth in the Charter.

The important organs of the United Nations having the power of decision, such as the General Assembly, the Security Council, etc., are composed of the representatives of States who act according to their governments' instructions, expressing the wills of their respective States.

The powers of the Organisation and its organs have been established by agreement between States as set forth in the Charter and may be modified only by agreement between member States.

States make the machinery of the United Nations function and the UN activities depend on the policies of the member States.

Of course it would be an over-simplification, as has rightly been pointed out by Professor M. Virally,[31] to consider the United Nations only as a meeting place for representatives of States, an instrument of diplomatic negotiations, a kind of diplomatic conference.

The United Nations has all these features but it also has something more.

It is true that when one finds oneself at a session of the General Assembly, one may well forget that it is not a diplomatic conference but an organ of the United Nations. Delegations, proposals, amendments, negotiations and other diplomatic activities, etc.; all that is also typical of a diplomatic conference.

These elements are also present to some extent in the Security Council, although not all the States members are represented there, and this organ may pass decisions binding upon the members of the United Nations.

But both of them are organs of an international organisation which function in a certain permanent framework and interrelationship.

The decisions of the organs of the United Nations, although expressing the coordinated wills of members represented on them, as is the case with a diplomatic conference, the procedure of adopting these decisions and their effect are governed by the provisions of the Charter. The procedure of adopting decisions by the organs of the UN differs from that of a diplomatic conference, especially in the Security Council. As to the legal effects of the decisions of the UN organs, they are also different in many respects from those of a diplomatic conference.

It is, therefore, inaccurate to assume that the United Nations is an entity independent of its member States.

---

31 M. Virally, L'ONU d'hier à demain, Paris, 1961, p. 25.

2. Legal Nature of United Nations Decisions

The legal nature of the United Nations has found its manifestation, inter alia, in the methods of adopting decisions by its organs and in the legal character of these decisions.

a. Resolutions of the General Assembly

In spite of the abundant literature on the subject many controversial issues have remained unresolved and the problems involved have sometimes been further obscured.

The method of adopting resolutions of the General Assembly has much in common with that of a diplomatic conference.

Decisions on important questions are adopted by a two thirds majority of the members present and voting. Decisions on other questions are adopted by a majority of the members present and voting.[32] The adoption of resolutions by the committees of the General Assembly is made by a majority of members present and voting.

Under the influence of the United Nations it has become customary for diplomatic conferences to adopt rules of procedure which prescribe the same voting procedure for the plenary meetings and for the committees as is used in the General Assembly of the United Nations.

The resolutions of the General Assembly as well as resolutions of a diplomatic conference are the expressions of the coordinated wills of States which have voted for them.

In the case of diplomatic conferences most of the decisions relate to the adoption of texts of international treaties. Such decisions do not represent the final coordination of the wills of States.

The process of the conclusion of a treaty is the process of coordination of wills of States which terminates in relation to each particular State participating in it with the deposit of its instruments of ratification, and as to the treaty as a whole with its entry into force.

The adoption of the text of a treaty by a diplomatic conference is only one of the stages in this process. The same is true with regard to the resolutions of the General Assembly on the adoption of texts of international treaties.

Resolutions containing recommendations to States or to international organisations are also sometimes adopted by a diplomatic conference. So the first conference on the Law of the Sea in 1958 adopted 8 resolutions of this nature.[33]

In this case the coordination of wills of States is final. The legal effects of such resolutions have not raised any controversy: they are considered as not binding upon States, even those which have voted for them.

Most of the resolutions of the General Assembly are not concerned with the texts of international treaties but with problems of international peace and security,

32 Art. 18 of the Charter.

33 See, United Nations Conference on the Law of the Sea. Official Records (A/CONF.13/38), vol. II, pp. 143-145.

disarmament, international cooperation in various fields, and also financial and administrative questions.

Here the coordination of wills of States which have voted for them is final. The legal effects of these decisions are determined by the Charter and they are more diverse and complicated than in the case of decisions of a diplomatic conference.

Most of the controversy centres around the problem of the binding force of the resolutions of the General Assembly. Some confusion and wishful thinking which have often been introduced into the discussion of this problem were due, to a considerable degree, to disregard of the legal nature of the United Nations.

It has recently been suggested by Mr. E. Schwelb that the difference between international treaties and resolutions of international organisations is diminishing and the dividing line between them becoming blurred.[34] Prof. Schwelb maintains that there has emerged a third category of international instruments which comprises the resolutions of international organisations. They are not international treaties and they are not "not binding".[35]

The legal force of the decisions of an international organisation is determined by the act or acts on the basis of which the international organisation exists and functions.

According to the Charter of the United Nations there are two categories of resolutions of the General Assembly: binding resolutions and recommendations.

The first category of decisions comprises resolutions relating to: the admission of States to membership in the United Nations (Art. 4); the suspension of the exercise of rights of membership (Art. 5); the expulsion of States from the United Nations (art. 6); the budget of the Organisation (Art. 17); the election of non-permanent members of the Security Council (Art. 23); the election of members of the Economic and Social Council (Art. 61); the approval of agreements concluded by ECOSOC with specialised agencies (Art. 63), etc.

As far as this category of resolutions is concerned, the provisions of the Charter are in most instances clear, and in principle all States are in agreement that such resolutions if adopted in accordance with the Charter are binding upon all the members, viz, binding also upon those States which have voted against them.

The difference of opinion exists primarily with regard to the second category of resolutions relating to a very wide range of other questions, including questions of cooperation in the maintenance of international peace and security, in the political, economic, social, cultural, etc., fields.

According to the Charter the General Assembly may make recommendations on all questions except those which are on the agenda of the Security Council (Art. 10). These recommendations may be addressed to States, the Security Council or both (Art. 10).

The language of the Charter leaves no doubt that the resolutions of the General Assembly falling into the second category have as a rule no binding force although some

34 E. Schwelb, Neue Etappen der Fortentwicklung des Völkerrechts durch die Vereinten Nationen, "Archiv des Völlerrechts", 13. Band, 1. Heft, Mai, 1966, S. 44.

35 Ibid., S. 25-26.

of them may have great political and moral influence and play an ever-increasing role in the formation of rules of international law.[36]

It is a matter of course that when we speak of the resolutions of the General Assembly we mean decisions adopted in accordance with the Charter. Resolutions adopted in violation of the Charter – and there are, unfortunately, some which are – are *ultra vires* the Organisation and therefore non-existent.

There are, however, resolutions of the General Assembly which may be considered wholly or in part as an interpretation of the provisions of the Charter.

Although the Charter itself provides for no exceptions with regard to such resolutions, the Report of Committee 2 of Commission IV of the San Francisco Conference relating to the interpretation of the provisions of the Charter to which we have already referred actually contains such an exception.

The conclusion which may be drawn from this Report is that unanimously adopted resolutions of the General Assembly constituting an interpretation of the provisions of the Charter, to the extent that they constitute such an interpretation, are binding upon the members of the United Nations.[37]

There are also some other resolutions of the General Assembly which should be singled out. We have in mind resolutions which sum up recent developments in the field of international law and contain statements to the effect that certain legal rules are rules of international law in force.

According to the Charter such resolutions may not be anything more than recommendations.

However, they have quite different weight in the framework of the customary process of formation of norms of international law. They are in fact declaratory of the existing rules of international law. Such pronouncements are binding upon those States which have voted for them. However, in this case it is not a resolution of the General Assembly as such which is binding. The resolution is a corroboration of a pre-existing customary rule of international law which itself embodies a tacit agreement between States. It therefore states and confirms explicitly this pre-existing agreement.

But as customary rules of international law are very often not sufficiently precise, such resolutions may well contain elements of progressive development of international law. They may also be for some States the first expression of their *opinio juris* with regard to rules of international law embodied in it.

This role of the General Assembly's resolutions falls outside the Charter and belongs to the customary process of formation of norms of international law.

As far as this process is concerned, the resolutions of the General Assembly may also start the process of formation of customary rules, accelerate this process or be a certain stage in it. But they never finalise this process.

---

36 See, for instance, M. Lachs, Le rôle des organisations internationales dans la formation du droit international, Mélanges Rolin, Paris, 1964, pp. 165-166; C. A. Malinin, Criteria of the Legality of Resolutions of the General Assembly of the U.N., "Pravovyedenie", N 2, 1965, pp. 113-123; M. V. Janovsky, Legal Force of Resolutions of the U.N. General Assembly, "Sovjetskoye Gosudarstvo i Pravo", N 9, 1965, pp. 120-124.

37 See UNCIO, Document 933, IV/2/42, vol. 13, p. 710.

If in the case we have just examined a resolution of the General Assembly appears to finalise the process of formation of a customary rule, in fact what really matters is not the resolution but certain actions of States belonging to the customary process of formation of rules of international law, for which the resolution is only an instrument. These acts may well be performed outside the resolution, say through a special declaration made by a State to the same effect.[38]

The fact that on the most important questions falling within the competence of the United Nations the General Assembly may adopt as a rule only recommendations but not binding decisions is one of the significant manifestations of the nature of the United Nations.

Indeed, if the General Assembly could make decisions on important problems of U.N. activities binding upon States which would be a kind of international legislation, such a supra-national authority of the United Nations relating to matters of primary importance would be inconsistent with the nature of the United Nations as determined by the laws of development of society.

b. The Principle of Unanimity of the Great Powers in the Security Council

The Security Council consisting originally of 11 members and now of 15 members of the United Nations out of the total membership now amounting to 122 States is a comparativaly small body.

If the competence of the General Assembly covers all matters within the scope of the Charter, the Security Council deals essentially with problems relating to the maintenance of peace and security. This is therefore an organ designated to act in the field of the main objectives of the United Nations.

The Security Council has specific powers and responsibilities some of which exclusively belong to it. It has "primary responsibility for the maintenance of international peace and security"[39] and powers to determine, for the purpose of taking action, the existence of any threat to peace, breach of the peace or act of aggression.[40]

It is the only organ empowered to take measures for maintaining or restoring international peace and security.

And finally the Security Council may pass binding decisions (of course in accordance with the Charter). As stated in Article 25 of the Charter, "the members of the United Nations agree to accept and to carry out the decisions of the Security Council in accordance with the present Charter".

In view of the magnitude of the role of the Security Council in the United Nations system it is only logical that the nature of the Organisation has manifested itself here most vigorously.

It is well known that it was not easy to find an adequate solution. Such a solution had to satisfy the need for prompt and efficient action, take into account the principle

38 See G. I. Tunkin, Droit international public. Problèmes théoriques, Paris, 1965, pp. 109-111.

39 Art. 24 of the Charter. 15.

40 Art. 39 of the Charter.

of sovereign equality of States and their actual unequal role in international relations and be generally consistent with the nature of the Organisation.

Two extreme solutions were both inadequate. The unanimity rule which existed in the League of Nations would have had the same paralysing effect in the framework of the United Nations as it had in the League system.

The majority rule might have formally seemed the simplest way of securing prompt and efficient action. It might also appear as best corresponding to the principle of sovereign equality of States. Actually, however, the majority rule would not have assured efficient action of the Organisation or corresponded to the principle of sovereign equality of States members and to the nature of the Organisation in general.

The Yalta formula was founded on the unanimity of the permanent members of the Security Council.[41]

According to Article 27 of the Charter decisions of the Security Council on procedural matters shall be made by an affirmative vote of seven (now nine) members. The decisions on all other matters shall be made by an affirmative vote of seven (now nine) members, including the concurring votes of the permanent members.

The Yalta formula relating to the veto power of the permanent members has been constantly attacked on the ground that it allegedly barred the effective functioning of the Security Council.

We shall see in the course of further discussion that this criticism is unfounded and has been dictated either by legal formalism or by political tendencies having nothing in common with the aims and purposes of the United Nations.

The very institution of the permanent membership in the Security Council was due to the recognition of the fact that in spite of the legal equality of States members as sovereign entities their respective roles in international affairs and especially in matters relating to the maintenance of international peace and security which constituted the primary objective of the United Nations were not at all equal. It was also due to the tacit acceptance of the idea that the United Nations should never become an instrument of States of one social system directed against States of another system.

The function of the Security Council consisting primarily in taking measures to maintain international peace and prevent or suppress acts of aggression required the presence of all the great powers and of a certain equilibrium between States of the two systems.

The rule of unanimity of the permanent members of the Security Council permitted the escape from the paralysing effect of the complete unanimity rule.

This rule reflects at the same time the reality that the UN may be an effective international organisation only on the basis of agreement among the great powers belonging to different economic and social systems.

On the other hand it presented an alternative to a majority rule which, as we have already stated, contradicted the nature of the United Nations and would have made the Organisation unworkable.

---

41 See on this subject, N. Ushakov, Op. cit., pp. 34-76; V. Fedorov, The Security Council, Moscow, 1965, pp. 58-60 (in Russian).

The rule of unanimity of the permanent members of the Security Council has also been severely criticised on the ground that it has established the hegemony of the great powers.

This assertion, however, does not correspond to the actual situation. In fact the right of veto prevents the hegemony of some great powers in the Security Council and thereby in the United Nations in general.

Indeed, if the unanimity rule did not exist the Security Council might easily become an instrument in the hands of the Western great powers which have a majority of votes there. This principal organ would be used not in the interests of all members but to serve the policies of these powers. And instead of being an organ of a general international organisation based on the agreement of States with different economic and social systems, it might become a tool of one block against the rest of the members.

The analysis of the actual use of the veto reveals the important role it has played in preventing the Security Council from being used in this way.

It is appropriate in this context to mention a widely accepted legend that the use of the Soviet veto paralysed the work of the Security Council preventing it from taking decisions on many occasions, whereas the United States has never used the veto and therefore has never interfered with the normal functioning of the Security Council.

The Soviet veto prevented many actions harmful to international peace and cooperation initiated by the Western powers in pursuit of their "cold war" policies against socialist countries and also against developing countries.

As to the United States refraining from using the veto, Professor John Stoessinger, of the City University of New York, has rightly stated: "One of the most persistent myths surrounding the United Nations concerns the use of the veto power by the Soviet Union and the United States. It is an established fact that by late 1965 the Soviet Union had vetoed 103 Security Council resolutions, whereas the United States had yet to cast its first veto. Hence it is said that the Soviet Union's frequent use of the veto has hampered and weakened the United Nations by preventing it from acting, while the United States has exercised remarkable self-discipline by never using the veto at all."[42] And the author goes on: "To say that the United States has not used the veto power is literally correct, but highly misleading in a broader sense. The implication would be that one superpower had selfishly put national interest above international considerations while the other had unselfishly subordinated national interest in order to further international co-operation. The fact of the matter is that the United States has not used the veto because it has been able to protect and promote its national interest in other ways. By obtaining majority votes against resolutions it opposes, the United States has never been forced to cast a veto. The key to this America "hidden veto" is, of course, the composition of the Security Council. It is a fact that a majority of the members of the Council have regularly been military allies of the United States".[43]

42 J. G. Stoessinger, The United Nations and the Superpowers, New York, 1965, p. 3.

43 J. G. Stoessinger, The United Nations and the Superpowers, New York, 1965, pp. 13-14.

The unanimity rule of the permanent members of the Security Council has proved to be indispensable for protecting the sovereign rights of all the members of the United Nations and preserving in the Organisation the principle of peaceful coexistence of States belonging to two opposing social systems. The principle of unanimity of the great powers in the Security Council is the most important manifestation and guardian of the nature of the United Nations.

3. The Legal Nature of the United Nations and the Secretariat

The Secretariat of the United Nations as a principal organ of the Organisation is quite distinct from the other principal organs of the UN. It has already been emphasized that other organs of the United Nations, with the exception of the International Court of Justice, are composed of representatives of States and act on the basis of agreement between them reached in accordance with the rules of procedure of a corresponding organ.

The Secretariat, on the contrary, consists of a Secretary-General and the staff who do not represent the member States but are "international officials responsible only to the Organisation" (Art. 100).

Secretariats of international organisations, as principal organs thereof, have emerged and developed in the course of the last 50 years. Up to that time permanent secretariats of international organisations had practically been non-existent. Small secretarial services of various international organisations, such as the International Telegraphic Union (1865) or the Universal Postal Union (1874), were usually composed of national officials lent to the international organisation.

The growth of international organisations, the extension of their activities and their increasing role in dealing with international problems have inevitably brought about the emergence and expansion of permanent secretariats composed of international officials.

Recent decades have also witnessed the growing role of secretariats in the activities of international organisations. This has also been the case of the United Nations.

But although these tendencies are inevitable and generally contribute to the proper functioning of international organisations they have given rise to some dangerous trends within the United Nations.

There are two problems of consequence from the point of view of the nature of the United Nations: a/ the role of the Secretariat of the United Nations and especially of the Secretary-General in the United Nations system; b/ the composition of the staff of the Secretariat.

According to the Charter the Secretary-General is "the chief administrative officer of the Organization" (Art. 97). The language is explicit. He is not a chief executive officer but a chief administrative officer.

The Secretary-General acts in this capacity in all meetings of the General Assembly, of the Security Council, of the Economic and Social Council, and of the Trusteeship Council. He also performs such other functions as may be entrusted to him by these organs (Art. 98).

The Secretary-General may bring to the attention of the Security Council any matter which in his opinion may threaten the maintenance of international peace and security (Art. 99).

The expansion of the functions of the Secretary-General in the course of the history of the United Nations is evident. The reasons are twofold. The first is the growth of the Secretary's functions, with the increasing activities of the United Nations. The Charter provides that the principal organs of the Organisation, such as the General Assembly or the Security Council, may entrust to the Secretary-General new functions. And it is natural that with the expanding activities of the United Nations in many fields the scope of the activities of the Secretary-General has also increased.

The problem lies elsewhere, and that is the second point. In many instances the Secretary-General, under the pressure of the Western powers, has been given such functions as the Charter assigns to other organs of the Organisation, especially the Security Council.

Thus the role assumed by the Secretary-General with regard to the UN military operations constituted an encroachment upon the functions and responsibilities of the Security Council and the Military Staff Committee.

Such a development was not at all due to the normal evolution of the Organisation but was imposed upon it by the Western powers and especially by the United States which until the election of the present Secretary-General considered the Secretariat the easiest organ to use for their own ends. The following statement of Professor Stoessinger is very revealing. He says: "In 1950, the United States, eager to circumvent the Soviet veto, persuaded the General Assembly to pass the Uniting for Peace Resolution, which broadened that organ's mandate in peace and security matters. The United States saw its interest better served in an Assembly that its allies controlled than in a veto-bound Security Council. In 1956, again as a result of American initiative and, significantly, after the first increase in membership, the locus of power moved from the Assembly to the Office of the Secretary-General. The large influx of new members in the Assembly that had been actively sought by the Soviet Union had cost the United States its automatic majority. Hence, the United States encouraged the passage of broadly conceived resolutions that invested the Secretary-General with increasing policy-making responsibilities."[44]

The violations of the Charter with regard to the functions of the Secretary-General and the encouragement he received from the Western powers have led some former Secretaries-General to look upon their post as an office of chief executive of the United Nations almost similar to that of the chief executive in the United States.

The developments we have just referred to are evidently in contradiction with the legal nature of the United Nations and the express provisions of the Charter. They have been nothing but manifestations of tendencies to use the Organisation as an instrument of a group of powers but not as a general international organisation.

44 J. Stoessinger, Op. cit., pp. 170-171.

As to the composition of the staff of the Secretariat, the Charter provides that "the paramount consideration in the employment of the staff and in the determination of the conditions of service shall be the necessity of securing the highest standards of efficiency, competence, and integrity. Due regard shall be paid to the importance of recruiting the staff on as wide a geographical basis as possible" (Art. 101).

These two criteria should evidently be the guiding principles in the recruitment of the personnel of the Secretariat, and there is no need that one should give way to the other.

If the high standards of efficiency, competence, and integrity are of greatest importance, especially from the technical point of view, the second criterion is of major significance from the point of view of the nature of the Organisation.

As a matter of fact the geographical distribution of the staff of the Secretariat disguises, first of all, its allocation among States belonging to different social systems. The actual importance of the problem can be realised only if one looks at it in the light of this reality.

Attempts have frequently been made to minimize the importance of the second criterion in recruiting the staff of the UN Secretariat.

It is true that the Charter stipulates that "in the performance of their duties the Secretary-General and the staff shall not seek or receive instructions from any government or from any other authority external to the Organization, and that they shall refrain from any action which might reflect on their position as international officials responsible only to the Organization" (Art. 100).

Let us assume that all these requirements are strictly complied with. Still we have to admit that members of the staff have different ideologies, different concepts of international relations and also of international law. This would influence their approach to the various problems they are confronted with, even if they personally want to be perfectly objective.

The degree of this influence would differ, depending on the character of the problems in question. It is a fact that documents issued by the United Nations Secretariat sometimes reflect these differences of approach. Of course at present the predominant influence is exercised in the Secretariat by the members of the staff from the Western countries, and the documents which reflect Socialist and Afro-Asian concepts, say, in international law, are rare.

If high standards of professional ability of the members of the staff are necessary for the efficiency of the Secretariat, proper geographical distribution of the staff is no less indispensable.

The various influences mentioned above, when properly balanced, would constitute a substantial guarantee that the Secretariat always acts objectively in accordance with the provisions of the Charter, which is the primary condition of the proper functioning of the Secretariat.

Chapter IV The Legal Nature of the United Nations and the Problem of the UN Military Forces

1. The Basic Provisions of the Charter

To maintain international peace and security and to take collective measures to restore international peace – these are the primary objectives of the United Nations. "We the Peoples of the United Nations determined to save succeeding generations from the scourge of war. . ." – these are the opening words of the Charter of the United Nations.

But the United Nations is not a military affiance intended to be put in operation when a *casus foederis* arises. It is an organisation created to deal with the problems of international peace and security in all their complexity.

The primary causes of war are deeply rooted in the social system of the class society based on private property and the exploitation of man by man. With these original causes of war as a social phenomenon the United Nations cannot deal directly, as the social systems of various States are internal matters outside the authority of the United Nations.

But there are innumerable immediate factors of international tensions and armed conflicts where United Nations activities have been envisaged by the Charter.

The purposes of the United Nations include in particular the development of friendly relations between nations and the settlement of international disputes by peaceful means. The Organisation has also been endowed with powers to use a whole range of coercive measures, including military force to maintain or restore international peace and security.

The authority of the United Nations to use military force is unique. States are permitted to use military force against other States only in virtue of their right of individual or collective self-defence in case of an armed attack, and only until the Security Council has taken measures necessary to maintain international peace and security (Art. 51).

The same applies to regional organisations which, except in the case of collective self-defence as provided in Article 51 of the Charter, can take no enforcement action without the authorisation of the Security Council (Art. 53).

The nature of the United Nations manifests itself very strongly throughout the provisions of the Charter relating to the composition and use of the United Nations military forces.

The Security Council has been given exclusive powers to determine the existence of any threat to the peace, breach of the peace, or act of aggression, and to take appropriate measures in each particular case (Art. 39).[45]

The Military Staff Committee has been set up to advise and assist the Security Council on all questions relating to the composition and use of armed forces and other military requirements of the Security Council (Art. 47).

It should be noted in this context that the Charter does not envisage the creation of a permanent United Nations military force. It prescribes that all members of the Organisation shall make available to the Security Council armed forces and facilities whenever the Security Council calls upon them (Art. 43).

But the Security Council cannot freely dispose of the armed forces of the States members of the United Nations. The Charter provides that a special agreement must be concluded between member States and the Security Council which would specify the numbers and types of forces, their degree of readiness and general location, and the nature of the facilities and assistance to be provided (Art. 43).

The Security Council cannot impose such agreements on the members. They should be freely consented to by the States concerned, and the Charter provides that such agreements "shall be subject to ratification by the signatory states in accordance with their respective constitutional processes" (Art. 43).

All these provisions of the Charter are of primary importance and constitute the manifestation of the nature of the United Nations. The Charter provisions concentrating in the hands of the Security Council all questions relating to the use by the Organisation of extreme measures, i.e. the use of military force, are the most important guarantee that the United Nations does not degenerate into a military block of States belonging to one social system directed against States of another social system.

2. The "Uniting for Peace" Resolution and the Charter

a. The Origins

The official Western version of the origins of the "Uniting for Peace" Resolution is probably best related in the book by Professor L. Goodrich to which we have already referred. The full effectiveness of the Security Council, he says, was premised on two conditions neither of which materialised: 1. the availability to the Security Council of military forces and facilities under the terms of agreements concluded between the Council and Members; 2. the effective cooperation of the permanent Members of the Council in dealing with threats to the peace, breaches of the peace, and acts of aggression. The Military Staff Committee could not provide the consensus on the substance of agreements to be concluded under Article 43 of the Charter. The effective cooperation

45 See G. Morozow, Op. cit., pp. 104-105; V. Sobakin, Collective Security, Moscow, 1962, p. 188; E. Krivchikova, United Nations Armed Forces, Moscow, 1965, pp. 64-72; V. Kopal, Otázka ozbrovenijch sil OSN, Praha, 1961.

of the permanent members of the Security Council has not materialised. The Council was deadlocked by the use of the veto.[46]

In these circumstances, continues Professor Goodrich, "to fill the gap in the United Nations system of peace and security caused by the impotence of the Council. . ." the course has been adopted "to develop the General Assembly as a substitute for the Council and thus create a modified United Nations system which would be more effective under the conditions that have existed since the War than that set out in the Charter".[47]

This explanation is evidently an oversimplification. It does not go to the root of the problem.

Actually the "Uniting for Peace" Resolution was an outcome of the "cold war" policy, of the Western powers' intention to use the United Nations as an instrument of their domination in the world. As Professor Goodrich himself admits, when the United Nations was being created the Western Powers expected that it would be dominated by the West, as formerly the League of Nations had been.[48]

The rule of unanimity of the permanent members in the Security Council stood in the way of realization of this expectation. Five years of the existence of the United Nations had shown that this was a major obstacle at the time. In the General Assembly the Western powers had a secure majority which never failed to vote for whatever proposals the Western powers wanted to be adopted. But in the Security Council the Soviet veto stopped all attempts to use this organ as freely as they might use the General Assembly.[49] And the Western powers decided, as has already been pointed out, to shift the powers from the Security Council to the General Assembly.

This was the real origin of the "Uniting for Peace" Resolution.

b. Was the "Uniting for Peace" Resolution an Interpretation of the Charter?

Under the terms of the "Uniting for Peace" Resolution adopted by the General Assembly on November 3, 1950,[50] whenever the Security Council as a result of the absence of unanimity among the permanent members of the Council, is unable to adopt a decision, in case of alleged breach or of threat to the peace, the General Assembly may take up the matter and make to the Members of the U.N. recommendations including recommendations relating to the use of military force. If the General Assembly is not in session, a special session may be convened within twenty-four hours.

The widely accepted concept among Western international lawyers is that the "Uniting for Peace" Resolution was based on the interpretation of the Charter.

Professor Goodrich considers the case to be a "liberal interpretation" of the Charter[51] but admits at the same time that it was a modification of the existing United Nations system.[52]

46 L. Goodrich, The United Nations, New York, 1959, pp. 164-176.
47 L. Goodrich, The United Nations, New York, 1959, p. 176.
48 Ibid., p. 41.
49 Cf. Chapter III, 2 (b).
50 Resolution 377 (V) of November 3, 1950.
51 Goodrich, Op. cit., p. 168.
52 Ibid., p. 167; in this sense also Jiménez de Aréchaga, Derecho Constitucional de las Naciones Unidas, Madrid, 1958, pp. 204-205.

His argument is as follows: The Charter provides that the General Assembly may discuss any questions within the scope of the Charter or relating to the powers and functions of any organ and make recommendations. Following the reasoning of the "Uniting for Peace" Resolution he maintains that the General Assembly "has at least a "residual responsibility" of its own.[53]

Meanwhile the provisions of the Charter to which Professor Goodrich addresses himself provide that the General Assembly may discuss any question within the competence of the United Nations and make recommendations, with the exception of those questions which are on the agenda of the Security Council. But there is no hint whatsoever of any "residual responsibility" of the General Assembly for taking "actions" to maintain international peace and security. Nor may any trace of such "residual responsibility" be found in the documents of the San Francisco Conference (*Travaux preparatoires*).

Professor Goodrich admits, of course, that in Article 11 there is another limitation on the power of the General Assembly to make recommendations. This Article provides that the General Assembly shall "either before or after discussion" refer any question on which "action is necessary" to the Security Council.

To circumvent this difficulty, he says that "action" is an enforcement action under Chapter VII and that only binding decisions of the Security Council are meant in this case. "This interpretation"–he proceeds–"would not necessarily exclude recommendations by the General Assembly after the Security Council has failed to take action and has removed the matter from its agenda".[54]

This argument has been taken up by the International Court of Justice which in its advisory opinion on the case of *Certain Expenses* of the United Nations stated that "the kind of action referred to in Article 11, paragraph 2, is coercive or enforcement action."[55] The word "action" must mean, according to the Court, such action as was solely within the province of the Security Council, namely that indicated by the title of Chapter VII: "action with respect to threats to the peace, breaches of the peace and acts of aggression". The Court stated that "the last sentence of Article 11, paragraph 2, has no application when necessary action is not enforcement action".[56] The general conclusion of the Court was that Article 11, paragraph 2, authorises the General Assembly to take action including the establishment of military forces which are not intended for "coercive or enforcement action".

The following arguments may be advanced against this reasoning.

There is no justification in the Charter for the contention that the term "action" in Article 11 (2) means only "coercive or enforcement action."

Of course the term "action" in Article 11 (2) was not intended to cover all actions of the United Nations. Article 11 (2) deals only with "questions relating to the maintenance of international peace and security" and stipulates that "any such question

53 Ibid., p. 177.

54 Goodrich, Op. cit., p. 177.

55 I.C.J. Reports, 1962, p. 164.

56 I.C.J. Reports, 1962, p. 165.

on which action is necessary shall be referred to the Security Council by the General Assembly either before or after discussion".

Neither in the Charter itself nor in the documents of the San Francisco Conference is there any evidence supporting the Court's contention that the term "action" in Article 11 (2) was used to cover only "coercive or enforcement action". The idea was that whatever "action" is required to maintain international peace and security, it is only the Security Council that may take such action.

But even if we admit that the term "action" in Article 11 (2) means only "coercive or enforcement action", it would cover the use of military force.[57] The use of military force by the United Nations for "peace-keeping operations" is also a measure of pressure by force and therefore a "coercive or enforcement action".[58] Thus, even according to this interpretation, the United Nations military force may be established and used only under the provisions of Chapter VII which is, as the Court itself admitted, the sole province of the Security Council.

The only question which does arise with regard to Article 11, paragraph 2, is whether the General Assembly when referring the question requiring "action" to the Security Council may or may not make recommendations to the Security Council. As Article 11 was intended not to limit the general scope of Article 10, it may be admitted that the General Assembly may make in such cases recommendations to the Security Council. This would leave the final decision concerning "action" to be taken with the Security Council.

The Court[59] and some writers[60] also suggest that Article 14 of the Charter may be considered as a source of the General Assembly's authority to adopt recommendations on the creation of the U.N. military forces. This assumption is, however, completely artificial.

Article 14 says that "subject to the provisions of Article 12, the General Assembly may recommend measures for the peaceful adjustment of any situation, regardless of origin, which it deems likely to mpair the general welfare or friendly relations among nations. . .". If we compare this Article with Article 11 (2) there would hardly be any doubt that Article 11 (2) deals with the competence of the General Assembly in matters relating to the maintenance of international peace and security whereas Article 14 envisages different problems, namely those relating to "the general welfare or friendly relations among nations". Military force may be used by the United Nations only for maintaining or restoring international peace and security and therefore Article 14 has no bearing upon this matter.

It has also been suggested that the General Assembly might establish military forces in virtue of the authority given to it under Article 22. This Article reads as follows: "The General Assembly may establish such subsidiary organs as it deems necessary for the performance of its functions".

57 See H. Kelsen, The Law of the United Nations, London, 1951, p. 962. A. Verdross, Idées directrices de l'Organisation des Nations Unies, "Recueil des Cours, vol. 83 (1953), p. 54.

58 See in this sense Dissenting Opinion of Judge V. Koretzky, I.C.J. Reports, 1962, p. 259.

59 Advisory opinion on the case of Certain Expenses of the United Nations, I.C.J. Reports, 1962, p. 172.

60 See, for instance, Bowett, United Nations Forces, London, 1964, p. 286.

Professor L. Sohn of Harvard University does not hesitate to suggest that once ". . . it has been accepted that mediators or commissions, appointed by the Assembly to supervise a truce agreement or the observance of the Resolutions of the Assembly, might need additional personnel for the exercise of their functions, there seems to be no logical limit to the number of persons needed. Similarly, if military personnel are added to the United Nations missions and guards are sent to defend the personnel and the property of such missions, it is difficult to draw the line between permitted and prohibited types of personnel. . ."[61]

The inaccuracy of this contention is, however, evident. The language of Article 22 is exactly the same as that of Article 29 relating to the authority of the Security Council to establish its subsidiary organs, but nobody has ever suggested that it was intended to cover the authority of the Security Council to establish military forces.

It follows, in our opinion, that the "Uniting for Peace" Resolution may not be construed as being an interpretation of the Charter.

As the International Law Commission has stated in Article 27 of its draft on the Law of Treaties, "a treaty shall be interpreted in good faith in accordance with the ordinary meaning to be given to the terms of the treaty in their context and in the light of its object and purpose".[62]

The "Uniting for Peace" Resolution which envisaged a completely different system from that provided in the Charter cannot be considered as being its interpretation.

c. Have the "Uniting for Peace" Resolution and the Practice Based Upon It Modified the Charter?

It has been admitted by some authors, at least by implication, that the "Uniting for Peace" Resolution and the practice developed on the basis of this resolution constituted an amendment of the Charter through practice.[63]

We have examined the problem of the modification of a treaty through subsequent practice and have come to the conclusion that practice and logic dictate some caution.

The fundamental condition is that the provisions of the treaty may be modified by subsequent practice only if such practice establishes the agreement of the parties to modify its provisions.

The question is therefore whether the "Uniting for Peace" Resolution and the practice based upon it have been accepted as a modification of the Charter by all or nearly all or at least by the majority needed for formal amendments of the Charter in accordance with Chapter XVII of the Charter.

Mr. G. Castañeda, of Mexico, proceeding from the above-mentioned assumption, tries to substantiate the conclusion that the practice based upon the "Uniting for Peace"

61 L. Sohn, The Authority of the United Nations to Establish and Maintain a Permanent Force (1958), 52 A.J.I.L., p. 234; also G. Schwarzenberger, Report on Problems of a United Nations Force, International Law Association. Report to the 49th Conference, Hamburg, 1960, p. 140.

62 Report of the International Law Commission, XVIII session, 1966, Doc. A/CN.4/191.

63 See, for instance, Goodrich, Op. cit., p. 176; Virally, Op. cit., p. 27; Arechaga, Op. cit., p. 204.

Resolution has been accepted by all the members of the United Nations and therefore has brought about the modification of the Charter.

This is what he says: "The thesis which will be here sustained is that the Uniting-for-Peace resolution could not, by itself, have the legal consequences of altering the collective security system of the Charter, but that it was the starting point, as well as the nucleus of a rule shaped during the subsequent years, through the conscious and repeated acquiescence to it, either tacit or stated, of all groups of the United Nations Members; and that by virtue of this rule, the legal situation prevailing at present as regards the collective security system of the United Nations is different in an appreciable degree and in several aspects, from the original Charter's system".[64]

The arguments submitted by the author are substantially the following: the "Uniting for Peace" Resolution has been adopted by the General Assembly by votes of all the members with the exception of socialist States. On the other hand, on the question of the intervention of Great Britain, France and Israel in Egypt in 1956 the socialist countries voted for a number of resolutions adopted by the General Assembly. Only Israel voted against the principal resolution. As far as the States which voted against or abstained on the resolutions relating to the intervention in Egypt formally voted for the "Uniting for Peace" Resolution, it may be sustained that after the Suez crisis there remained no members of the United Nations which in one case or the other have not approved the "Uniting for Peace" Resolution and therefore have not accepted its legal implications.[65]

However, the facts are not accurately stated here. The Soviet Union voted only for those resolutions of the General Assembly which called upon the parties to the Suez conflict to agree upon the cease-fire or contained recommendations to the members of the United Nations to refrain from delivering arms to the region of armed conflict,[66] appeals to Israel, Great Britain and France to withdraw their military forces from Egyptian territory,[67] etc.

The Soviet Union abstained on the resolutions relating to the establishment of the United Nations Emergency Force and their functioning[68] but did not vote against them, not because it accepted them as legally justified, but because the State which was the victim of the armed attack considered the establishment of such forces expedient.

The Soviet Union made its legal position absolutely clear. The delegate of the Soviet Union, V. Kuznezov, stated at the 567th meeting of the First Emergency Session of the General Assembly on 7 November 1956 the following:

> "As regards the creation and stationing on Egyptian territory of an international police force, the Soviet delegation is obliged to point out that this Force is being created in violation of the United Nations Charter.

64 G. Castañeda, Certain Legal Consequences of the Suez Crisis, "Revue Egyptienne de Droit International", vol. 19 (1963), p. 3.

65 G. Castañeda, Op. cit., p. 9.

66 Resolution 997 (ES-I).

67 Resolution 1002 (ES-I).

68 Resolutions 998, 1000, 1001 (ES-I).

> "The General Assembly resolution on the basis of which it is now proposed to form this Force is inconsistent with the Charter. Chapter VII of the Charter empowers the Security Council, and the Security Council only, not the General Assembly, to set up an international armed force and to take such action as it may deem necessary, including the use of such a force, to maintain or restore international peace and security".

There was therefore neither explicit acceptance nor acceptance by acquiescence. On the contrary it was clearly stated that the "Uniting for Peace" Resolution was inconsistent with the Charter and that the practice based upon this resolution was illegal.

The rejection of the "Uniting for Peace" Resolution and the practice based upon it by the Soviet Union alone is sufficient to deprive them of any legal effect with regard to the Charter, as even for introducing formal amendments to the Charter the ratification of not only of two thirds of the Members is required but also the ratification by all the permanent members of the Security Council.

The conclusion to be drawn is that the "Uniting for Peace" Resolution and the practice based upon it have not modified the relevant provisions of the Charter.

And the next conclusion is that this resolution and the corresponding practice constitute grave violations of the fundamental provisions of the Charter bearing upon the very nature of the Organisation.

The fundamental provisions with regard to the United Nations military forces remain as follows:

- the United Nations military forces may be established and used only under the terms of Chapter VII;
- only the Security Council is authorised to act under the terms of this Chapter;
- the United Nations military forces may be established and used only by a decision (recommendation or binding decision) of the Security Council;
- there is nothing in the Charter and in the travaux própаratoires to substantiate the thesis that it was intended to give the General Assembly the authority to make recommendations with regard to the establishment and use of aimed forces; no additional agreement has ever been made to give the General Assembly such an authority;
- the assumption that the United Nations military forces may be established and used except by authority of the Security Council is contrary to the express provisions of the Charter and to the legal nature of the United Nations.

3. The Problem of Expenses for the Upkeep of Military Forces

The problem of expenses for the upkeep of military forces has sprung into prominence in connection with expenses incurred in maintaining the United Nations Emergency Force in the Middle East and the United Nations operations in the Congo.

Much has been said about a financial crisis of the Organisation. But the crisis, if one may speak of a crisis, is deeply rooted. The very nature of the Organisation is in question.

Here we propose to deal with only one, but a decisive, aspect of the problem: do such expenses fall within the competence of the Security Council or that of the General Assembly?

As the Security Council is the only organ competent to determine the existence of any threat to the peace, breach of the peace, or act of aggression (Article 39), to adopt a decision to use military force (Art. 42), to determine which States should participate in the action (Art. 48) and with what armed forces (Art. 43), it seems logical that the problem of expenses for such action should also be within the competence of the Security Council.

The Charter is, however, not explicit on this subject, and this has given rise to a controversy.

The supporters of the "Uniting for Peace" Resolution maintain that it is within the competence of the General Assembly, divorcing thereby the establishment and use of armed forces from their financial implications.

What are the provisions of the Charter on this point?

Article 43 provides for the conclusion of agreements between the Security Council and member States concerning armed forces, and the assistance and facilities which each member State or a group of member States shall make available to the Security Council when it calls upon them to do so.

Article 49 provides that the members of the United Nations shall join in affording mutual assistance in carrying out the measures decided upon by the Security Council.

And Article 50 stipulates that if preventive or enforcement measures against any State are taken by the Security Council any other State which finds itself confronted with special economic problems arising from the carrying out of those measures shall have the right to consult the Security Council with regards to a solution of those problems.

To clarify the situation reference should be made to the documents of the San Francisco Conference. The provisions dealing with the contribution of the members of the United Nations to the maintenance of international peace and security (Chapter VIII, Section B), including the financing of United Nations armed forces, were referred to Committee 3 of Commission ITT–the Committee which drafted the present Chapter VII of the Charter.

A proposal was made in this Committee to the effect that the expenses of enforcement measures against an aggressor State should be borne by that State. The Committee recognised the validity of the proposal that "the expenses for enforcement action carried out against a guilty State should fall upon that State" and declared itself "satisfied with the provisions of paragraphs 10 and 11" (Articles 49 and 50 of the Charter).[69] This opinion of the Committee was approved unanimously by the plenary Conference.

The reference in the Committee's report to Articles 49 and 50 of Chapter VII of the Charter is of importance to substantiate the view that the expenses for the upkeep of

69 UNCIO, b. 12, p. 513.

the United Nations military forces were regarded by the Committee as coming under the provisions of Chapter VII, and not under Article 17 of the Charter.

Indeed, for many years nobody questioned the view that expenditures for armed forces do not fall within the scope of Article 17 and do not constitute part of an ordinary budget to which this Article refers. In their commentaries on the Charter of the United Nations Goodrich and Hambro then stated that expenses referred to in Article 17 do not include expenses for enforcement action.[70] And, as has been stated above, to maintain that the use of armed force maybe anything else but a "coercive or enforcement" measure, is completely wrong.

There is therefore ample evidence for the view that the expenses of the United Nations for the upkeep of military force fall within the competence of the Security Council and that they should be covered either by an aggressor State or by States in accordance with agreements concluded with the Security Council under Article 43 of the Charter or in some other way as decided by the Security Council under Article 50.

70 L. Goodrich, E. Hambro, Charter of the United Nations. Commentary and Documents. Second and revised edition. Boston, 1949, p. 184.

Chapter V The Legal Nature of the United Nations and Strengthening the Organisation

1. The Problem of a World State

The tendency to regard a world State as the most desirable objective of the development of the United Nations is very strong among Western international lawyers.

A world State or a supra-national organisation which is as close as possible to a world State is considered by many the only means of making wars impossible and international law a real law.

The idea is not new. It has been expressed in the course of history by many great philosophers and statesmen beginning with Plato. It also has many supporters today.

Professor Hans Kelsen, almost 50 years ago, soon after World War I, expressed the view that only civitas maxima can give force to international law.[71]

Professor J. Kunz is of the opinion that the progressive development of international law cannot be effected exclusively by way of international treaties but requires some sort of supra-national action.[72]

Professor H. Lauterpacht asserted that international law can develop from its present status when, as he puts it, the very existence of it is precarious, to an actual law only through an international organisation vested with powers to create and apply international law, i.e. through a world State.[73]

Professor Ph. Jessup, now a Judge at the International Court of Justice, says in his book "A Modern Law of Nations": "Until the world achieves some form of international government in which a collective will takes precedence over the individual will of the sovereign state, the ultimate function of law, which is the elimination of force for the solution of human conflicts, will not be fulfilled. There must be organs empowered to lay down rules (a legislature); there must be juridical organs to interpret and apply those rules (a judiciary); and there must be organs with power to compel compliance with the rules (a police force)".[74]

71 H. Kelsen, Das Problem der Souveränität und die Theorie des Völkerrechts, Berlin, 1928, p. 320.

72 J. Kunz, Sanctions in International Law, A.J.I.L., v. 54 (1960), p. 347.

73 L. Oppenheim, International Law (Edited by H. Lauterpacht), Vol. I, London, 1955, para. 166.

74 Ph. Jessup, A Modern Law of Nations, New York, 1948, pp. 2-3.

Professor Hans Morgenthau, in his recent publication, states that "L'ordre et la paix entre les nations ne seraient assures que daps le cadre d'un Etat universel englobant toutes les nations de la terre".[75]

From the theoretical point of view the main weakness of these conceptions results from ignoring the basic laws of development of society bearing upon the nature of international organisations and of the United Nations in particular.

The proponents of a world State base their conclusions and expectations not on these basic laws but on certain aspects of contemporary international relations only. They refer, for instance, to the growing interdependence of States. This growing interdependence, as we have tried to show above, important though it is, constitutes only one aspect of international relations.[76]

Many plans have been drafted to modify the United Nations into a kind of world State. One of them has been presented by two American jurists, G. Clark and L. Sohn.[77] Whatever the intention of the authors, the plan they have presented is nothing more than a constitutionalisation of United States domination in the United Nations.

The problem is whither to go.

It should be noted, first, that the claim of the protagonists of a world State as being more progressive than those who take a more realistic approach is absolutely unfounded, as the following discussion will, in our opinion, show.

It is also indispensable to dissipate another misconception, viz. that the Soviet Union and Soviet jurists are against the idea of a world State, and therefore against an effective international organisation, whereas the Western powers and Western jurists are in favour of a world State and therefore of an effective international organisation.

Our approach to the problem of a world State is based on the Marxist theory of State.

It has already been indicated that the State as a social institution is not inherent in human society but exists only during a certain period of human history. In the early days there was no State, and on a very high level of development of society the State will give way to a new form of social organisation. It will be a world-wide organisation but not a world State because the State as an institution will not exist any more. On the road to such a stateless organisation different forms of unions of socialist States are possible, including regional federations and even a world federation.

The creation of a world federation or some other form of world State can therefore be envisaged only in the framework of Socialist revolution, liquidation of private ownership of the means of production and of social classes, and the development of society to a stateless organisation. In his famous publication on the problem of a United States of Europe Lenin said: "United States of the World (not United States of Europe) constitute a form of union of States which we link with socialism–until the complete victory of communism brings about a complete disappearance of any, including a democratic State".[78]

75 Hans Morgenthau, L'Etat universel et les institutions supra-nationales, Comprendre", 23-24, 1962, p. 61.

76 See Chapter I.

77 G. Clark and L. Sohn, World Peace through World Law, Harvard Univ. Press, 1960.

78 Lenin, Complete Works, v. 26, p. 354 (in Russian).

Various theories or plans of a world State in present-day circumstances constitute wishful thinking. Unfortunately they are not harmless. The tendencies inspired by these theories which have manifested themselves in the United Nations, especially with regard to such problems as relative competence of the Security Council and the General Assembly, the creation and functioning of United Nations military forces, financing the United Nations military operations, etc., have done great damage to the Organisation.

The development of the United Nations towards a world State is neither feasible nor desirable.

Professor M. Bourquin, analysing the number of studies on the United Nations made in various countries, has stressed that in most of these studies the authors have come to the conclusion that in the present situation a thorough reconstruction of the United Nations intended to increase its powers was impossible and that to follow this way would entail great dangers to the world organisation.

Professor Bourquin has particularly emphasized the following points: It is often forgotten that the powers would be vested not in a homogeneous organ representing the common interests of the international community but in an association of States each of which would be guided primarily by national considerations and would try to use for the purposes of its own policies the facilities of the organisation. In law, the authority of the organisation as such would be increased. But this would be appearance only. The powers of the organisation would be used by the majority and first of all by the powers around which such majority would be built. In the present-day world so deeply split, it would be actually putting in their hands a very dangerous weapon, which might lead to a collapse of the Organisation, instead of strengthening it.[79]

Professor Q. Wright, stating that it is highly improbable that the United Nations would develop into something which might be called a world federation, rightly says that the basis of world order should be the Charter of the United Nations based upon the principle of sovereign equality of States.[80]

Professor Hans Morgenthau, though considering, as has been pointed out, that in principle only a world State can assure international peace, states that "The contemporary advocacy of world government contains an element of perfectionist escapism. Actually, even if it were possible to establish world government tomorrow, the facts of political life will still be with us".[81]

The conclusion can only be that attempts to push the development of the world organisation in the direction of a world State are contrary to the nature of the United Nations and harmful to it; the development of the United Nations as an instrument of international peace and cooperation should be envisaged in the framework of its nature, i.e as a development of inter-governmental organisation, an organisation of peaceful coexistence.

---

79 M. Bourquin, L'Etat souverain et l'organisation internationale, New York, 1959, p. 32; See also Ch. Chaumont, Les rôles respectifs de l'Assemblée Générale et du Conseil de Sécurité, "Revue de droit contemporain", N 2, 1965, pp. 24-25.

80 Q. Wright, Op. cit., p. 60, 54-55.

81 Hans Morgenthau, Politics in the Twentieth Century, Vol. I, The Decline of Democratic Politics, The University of Chicago Press, 1962, p. 315.

2. Strengthening the World Organisation

The thesis according to which nuclear weapons have made the Charter obsolete and that therefore the United Nations should be completely reorganised finds no justification, either in theory or in practice.

Actually none of the proponents of a cardinal revision of the Charter has ever presented any convincing argument that the emergence of nuclear weapons has made it either possible or advisable to proceed with a reconstruction of the United Nations.[82]

The experience of the United Nations testifies to the contrary. The threat of a nuclear war urgently requires that the nature of the United Nations should be thoroughly respected and the principles of the Charter complied with.

At present any serious violation of the Charter and especially one which encroaches upon the nature of the Organisation is too dangerous by reason of the existence of those terrific instruments of destruction.

If the nature of the United Nations as embodied in the Charter corresponds to the laws of development of contemporary society, then the principal condition of strengthening the United Nations is: back to the Charter. Numerous violations of the Charter should be discarded and the full power of the provisions of the Charter restored.[83]

In this respect it is of great importance to restore the balance between the General Assembly and the Security Council as established by the Charter. The present-day situation tending to majority rule is contrary to the nature of the United Nations and incompatible with its fundamental provisions.

Legal principles, such as the principle of respect of sovereignty and the principle of the equality of States, which are often adduced to substantiate the claim for supremacy of the General Assembly over the Security Council should be viewed in the real context of the United Nations and international relations in general.

The idea of the supremacy of the General Assembly may seem favourable to small States which have a majority of votes in the General Assembly. However, in actual fact if the power of decision and action on major problems relating to the maintenance of international peace were shifted from the Security Council to the General Assembly, a new situation would present dangers, first of all, for the small powers.

The door would be thrown wide open to the imperialist powers to use various combinations to pursue their old policies of divide et impera from which small powers have suffered so much in the past.

Such combinations might also be resorted to against a great power, and this might be the end of the Organisation.

The basic consideration is that such a situation would be in flagrant contradiction with the nature of the United Nations. This very contradiction would open the way to

82 A very interesting analysis of the problem is given by G. Castañeda, Mexico and the United Nations, New York, 1958, p. 121 et seq.

83 As the Government of the USSR stated in its Memorandum, "to enhance the effectiveness of the United Nations in keeping the peace means first of all putting an end to violations of the Charter. . ." (Doc. S/5811 of 10 July, 1964).

a degeneration of the general international organisation into an organisation of States belonging to one social system or to one military block, and this would be fatal to the United Nations.

With regard to the United Nations armed forces, the present situation should be brought into conformity with the Charter. We do not consider justified the pessimistic assessments that a return to the provisions of the Charter in this field is impossible.[84]

The first condition is that all questions relating to the establishment and use of military forces should be dealt with by the Security Council. Some recent developments may be encouraging. The Security Council has been revived.

Whether it will be a lasting situation is open to question. We have quoted Professor Stoessinger who has rightly pointed out that to assure their domination in the United Nations the United States in 1950 pressed to shift power from the Security Council to the General Assembly controlled by its allies, and in 1956, when the situation in the General Assembly had changed as a result of the increase in membership, the United States constantly tried to move the locus of power to the Secretary General.

It well may be that the present position of the United States with regard to the Security Council is due, at least to some extent, to a new situation in the Secretariat after Hammerskjöld and of course also to the increasing influence of socialist States and new States in the General Assembly.

The problem of the composition of United Nations forces is one of importance.

In the world of today, when members of the United Nations belong to different social systems, to different political orientations and to different military affiances, the keeping of a proper balance in the composition of the United Nations forces is one of the substantial guarantees that these forces are used in the real interests of international peace and security, in accordance with the principles and purposes of the United Nations. It means that alongside elements from Western and non-aligned countries elements from socialist countries should take part in the United Nations military forces.

It also seems high time to revive the Military Staff Committee and to make it proceed with its duties as defined in the Charter.

Agreements provided for in Article 43 of the Charter should be concluded between the Security Council and various members of the United Nations to specify the numbers and types of forces to be kept in readiness, and the nature of the facilities and assistance to be provided.

A problem of major importance from the point of view of strengthening the United Nations is the universality of the Organisation. The mere fact that some Western powers have made it impossible up to now for the People's Republic of China to be represented in the United Nations has already done great damage to the United Nations and to the cause of international peace.

Next comes the adaptation of the Charter and the Organisation to ever-changing life. As we have stated earlier, there are two ways for such adaptation: formal amendments

84 See, for instance, Virally, who says: "Le retour au système de 1945 s'avérant impossible, l'idée de sécurité collective doit être abandonnée" (Virally, Op. cit., p. 67).

in respect of all major changes, and adaptation through practice accepted by members, including permanent members of the Council, to modify or develop some less important provisions of the Charter.

In dealing with the problems of the United Nations one thing should always be kept in mind: the United Nations is not an entity independent of States; the activities and the very existence of the United Nations depend on the policies of States members and, above all, of the great powers.

It would be inaccurate to hold that the United Nations in its turn does not influence the policies of member States, including the great powers. Examples of such influence are many. However, this influence is exercised in the final analysis by States acting collectively as the United Nations.

The influence of the United Nations on the policies of States is not decisive and cannot be decisive in virtue of the nature of the Organisation. For instance, aggressive policies, such as the United States intervention in Vietnam, are directed against the very basis of the United Nations.

The original objective, therefore, is to make States bring their policies into conformity with the United Nations Charter. To achieve this objective, a supreme effort is required in and outside the United Nations.

Strengthening the United Nations as an instrument of peace and international cooperation urgently requires that all practices constituting violation of the Charter are abandoned. It also requires that the development of the Organisation is approached in the light of its nature.

International Law in the International System*

Part I
General Theory

Chapter I Marxist-Leninist Theory of Society and International Law

1. The General Laws of Societal Development

International law is a normative subsystem of the international system which in its turn is a component of human society as a whole. That is why the laws of societal development also determine in general the development of the international system and international law.

The society develops according to certain historical laws – this is one of the principal premises of the Marxist-Leninist theory of society.

Principal laws of societal development were formulated by Marx as follows:

> "In the social production of their life, men enter into definite relations that are indispensable and independent of their will, relations of production which correspond to a definite stage of development of their material productive forces. The sum-total of these relations of production constitutes the economic structure of, society, the real foundation, on which rises a legal and political superstructure and to which correspond definite forms of social consciousness. The mode of production of material life conditions the social, political and intellectual life process in general. It is not the consciousness of men that determines their being, but, on the contrary, their social being that determines their consciousness. At a certain stage of their development, the material productive forces of society come in conflict with the existing relations of production, or – what is but a legal expression for the same thing with the property relations within which they have

* This lecture was originally published in Recueil des cours, Tome 147 (1975), pp. 1–218 and is reprinted with kind permission of the Hague Academy of International Law/Académie de droit international de la Haye.

> been at work hitherto. From forms of development of the productive forces these relations turn into their fetters. Then begins an epoch of social revolution. With the change of the economic foundation the entire immense superstructure is more or less rapidly transformed."[1]

Assessing the significance of these laws of societal development, V. Lenin wrote:

> "The historical materialism was a great achievement in scientific thinking. The chaos and arbitrariness that had previously reigned in views on history and politics were replaced by a strikingly integral and harmonious scientific theory, which shows how, in consequence of the growth of productive forces, out of one system of social life another and higher system develops – how capitalism, for instance, grows out of feudalism."[2]

What is meant by laws of societal development? Any law, societal or law of nature "expresses an objective, necessary, stable connection between phenomena, between processes. Similarly, the laws established by historical materialism and other social sciences express a necessary, stable and recurrent connection between social phenomena and processes".[3]

According to the Marxist-Leninist theory, the laws of societal development are objective laws as well as the laws of nature. At the same time the socio-historical laws differ radically from the laws of nature. This is expressed in the definition of societal development as a "natural historical process". Natural historical process of the societal development is a process that does not depend on men's will and consciousness, but in fact determines that will and consciousness. At the same time, unlike the process of nature, the natural historical process is a result of the activity of people themselves. Engels wrote:

> ". . History is made in such a way that the final result always arises from conflicts between many individual wills of which each in turn has been made what it is by a host of particular conditions of life. Thus there are innumerable intersecting forces, an infinite series of parallelograms of forces which give rise to one resultant – the historical event. This may again itself be viewed as the product of power which works as a whole unconsciously and without volition. For what each individual will is obstructed by everyone else, and what emerges is something that no-one willed. Thus history has proceeded hitherto in the manner of a natural process and is essentially subject to the same laws of motion. But from

1 Marx, "A Contribution to the Critique of Policial Economy", Karl Marx and Frederick Engels, *Selected Works*, Vol. I, Moscow 1969, pp. 503-504.

2 V. I. Lenin, *Selected Works*, Moscow 1968, p. 21.

3 *The Fundamentals of Marxist-Leninist Philosophy*, Progress Publishers, Moscow 1974, p. 281.

> the fact that the wills of individuals – each of whom desires what he is impelled to by his physical constitution and external, in the last resort economic, circumstances (either his own personal circumstances or those of society in general) – do not attain what they want, but are merged into an aggregate mean, a common resultant, it must not be concluded they are equal to zero. On the contrary, each contributes to the resultant and is to this extent included in it."[4]

Some societal laws operate at all stages of societal development. These include the laws of the determining role of the social being in relation to social consciousness; the determining role of the mode of production in relation to the particular structure of society; the determining role of the productive forces with regard to economic relations; the determining role of the economic basis in relation to the societal superstructure; the dependence of the social nature of the individual on the sum-total of social relations and so on. These are general sociological laws that operate at all levels of societal development.

Besides these general laws there are others that are valid only for certain socio-economic formations, such as the law of the division of society into classes and the law of the class struggle as a driving force of history which operate only in socio-economic formations characterised by the existence of the antagonistic classes.

2. The Socio-Economic Formations and Historical Types of International Law

According to the Marxist-Leninist theory the system of all societal relations decisively depends on "the mode of production of material life". This mode of production is characterised by the forces of production and relations of production. "The productive forces are the forces by which society influences nature and changes it."[5] The societal forces of production comprise two quite different elements: means of production created by society and above all the instruments of labour, and people who put them into operation.

In creating material goods people enter into various relations with one another. These relations may be either production – technical or social. Social relations of production are characterised by the distribution of means of production in the society or, in other words, by the ownership of the basic means of production. Production relations comprise not only the relations in the process as such of production of material goods but also the relations of exchange of goods, services, etc.

Productive forces and relations of production are two inseparable aspects of social prbduction. They are in constant interaction. Historical law of this interaction

4 K. Marx and F. Engels, *Selected Works*, Vol. 3, p. 488.
5 *The Fundamentals of the Marxist-Leninist Philosophy*, p. 305.

is the correspondence of the relations of production to the character and level of development of forces of production. It should, however, be emphasised that it is not a one-way influence of the forces of production upon relations of production; it is an interaction between them in which relations of production exercise their influence on the development of forces of production as well. The equilibrium between these two social phenomena is relative. Forces of production constitute a more fluent element. The evolution of the forces of production makes the existing relations of production more and more inadequate and, as Marx put it, "from forms of development of the productive forces they turn into their fetters". A social revolution becomes unavoidable in order to change the inadequate relations of production and create new relations of production which would correspond to the changed character and level of the productive forces.

Revolutionary change in relations of production which constitute "economic foundation of the entire immense superstructure" leads more or less rapidly to a drastic change in the whole superstructure. A new socio-economic formation emerges.

Each socio-economic formation is a specific "social organism" which distinguishes itself from another socio-economic formation by the character and level of productive forces by the nature of the relations of production, or in other words, by the economic structure of society. Each socio-economic formation has its specific superstructure distinct from the superstructures of other socio-economic formations.

The history of society is the development and change of socioeconomic formations. According to the Marxist-Leninist theory there are five socio-economic formations: primitive communal, slave, feudal, capitalist and communist of which the first stage is socialism.

The sequence of these formations is not a rigid pattern to which the history of each country must strictly obey. Some people are held up in their development, while others may by-pass a whole socio-economic formation. In the course of history there have also been various transitional or mixed forms.

History reveals that the development of society was on the whole progressive.

"The history of mankind, despite its contradictions, temporary periods of stagnation and regression, is ultimately an ascent, a movement from the old to the new, from the simple to the complex. As it develops, mankind creates more powerful productive forces, a more effective economy, more perfect forms of political administration, expanding in varying degrees the limits of man's opportunities and freedom."[6]

The historical progress is an objective law of societal development. However the problem of historical progress should not be oversimplified. Warning against such an over-simplification, Lenin said: ". . . It is undialectical, unscientific, and theoretically wrong to regard the course of world history as smooth and always in a forward direction, without occasional gigantic leaps back ."[7]

6 *The Fundamentals of Marxist-Leninist Philosophy*, pp. 375-376.
7 V. I. Lenin, *Collected Works*, Vol. 22, p. 310.

Historical progress would be unthinkable without continuity, a relative continuity in the history of society. Productive forces, cultural values, etc., created by one generation usually pass on to another generation and so on.

Historical progress is particularly evident in the replacement of one socio-economic formation by a new, a higher socio-economic formation. Law in general and international law in particular first emerged when private property, social classes and the State came into being. Social content of the rules of law was different from that of the rules of conduct which existed in the primitive communal system and from which rules of law developed. Bourgeois theories of law usually define law as an aggregate of rules of conduct. Such a definition ignores the essence of law. Rules of conduct are indispensable for any human society whereas law is not. Law is an institution of a class society.

Law is an aggregate of rules of conduct which have a class character; they express above all the will of the economically and politically dominant class of the society and defend primarily the interests of this class. With the elimination of private property and classes the class character of law will gradually diminish and in the end disappear. Rules of law will be transformed into rules of conduct which will not be a class institution, but will express the will and equally defend interests of all members of the community.

The law of each socio-economic formation as an element of superstructure is distinct from the law of another socio-economic formation in spite of the continuity of the history of law. So we distinguish the law of the slave-owning society, the feudal law, the bourgeois law and the socialist law.

International law, as well as national law, is part of a superstructure the principal features of which are determined by the economic structure of society. That means that international law of one socioeconomic formation is distinct from international law of another. Accordingly we distinguish the following historical types of international law: international law of the slave-owning society, feudal international law, bourgeois international law and contemporary international law which is the law of the period of transition from capitalism to socialism, a law of coexistence of States having diametrically different socio-economic systems (see below Chapter II, 4).

The development of international law has been as a whole a progressive development. This has taken place in the form of passing over from one type of international law – to another, a more progressive and developed one and also in the development of international law in the framework of one socio-economic formation and one type of international law.

At a certain stage of the development of a socio-economic formation, when the relations of production (economic structure of society) proper to this formation become inadequate, international law of this formation also becomes a harassment to progress. The replacement of the old socio-economic formation by a new one leads to the replacement of the old international law by a new international law. In such a way the bourgeois international law replaced the feudal international law, and in its turn gave way to contemporary international law.

The principal features of each type of international law are determined by its basis, that is by economic structure of the society at a certain stage of its development. Engels wrote:

> ". . The economic structure of society always furnishes the real basis, starting from which we can alone work out .the ultimate explanation of the whole superstructure of juridical and political institutions as well as of the religious, philosophical, and other ideas of a given historical period."[8]

The relationship between economic structure of society and superstructure, a part of which is international law, is not a simple one. It is an interaction which takes place in a very complex system of society, where the influence of economic structure upon superstructure, although decisive, is not the only one. Therefore the thesis that economic structure of society conditions the character of superstructure does not mean that all the details of superstructure or of its various elements can be deduced from the character of economic structure. Criticising those who attempted to interpret the Marxist theory this way, F. Engels wrote almost a hundred years ago:

> ". . According to the materialist conception of history, the ulti mately determining element in history is the production and reproduction of real life. More than this neither Marx nor I have ever asserted. Hence if somebody twists it into saying that the economic element is the only determining one, he transforms that proposition into a meaningless, abstract, senseless phrase. The economic situation is the basis, but the various elements of the superstructure – political forms of the class struggle and its results, to wit: constitutions established by the victorious class after a successful battle, etc., juridical forms, and even the reflexes of all these actual struggles in the brains of the participants, political, juristic, philosophical theories, religious views and their further development into systems of dogmas – also exercise their influence upon the course of the historical struggles and in many cases determine mainly their form. There is an interaction of all these elements in which, amid all the endless host of accidents . . . the economic movement finally asserts itself as necessary. Otherwise the application of the theory to any period of history would be easier than the solution of a simple equation of the first degree.
> We make our history ourselves, but, in the first place, under very definite assumptions and conditions. Among these the economic ones are ultimately decisive. But the political ones, etc., and indeed even the traditions, that haunt human minds also play a part, although not the decisive one."[9]

8 F. Engels, *Anti-Dühting*, Moscow 1969, p. 37.
9 K. Marx and F. Engels, *Selected Works*, Vol. 3, Moscow 1970, p. 487.

This means also that superstructure possesses a relative independence in relation to its basis, and is an active force influencing all aspects of social life, including its own basis.

International law is a part of superstructure. But to say this is not enough. It is an international element of superstructure. This means that international law is influenced by economic structures of various States, and, at present, by economic structures of different socioeconomic formations (see below Chapter II, 2).

3. THE THEORY OF THE CO-ORDINATION OF THE WILL OF STATES

The theory of the co-ordination of the will of States which originated in 1956-1958[10] has since become the leading theory in the Soviet science of international law. It has been considerably developed and the sphere of its application, which at first was limited to the process of creating norms of international law, extended.[11] The theory of the co-ordination of the will of States is now successfully applied also in analysing the processes of formation of other norms of the international juridical system, the functioning of international law and of international organisations.

The fundamental premise of this theory is that in an international system consisting primarily of sovereign and equal States there is no other means of creating rules of law binding upon these States except by the co-ordination of the will of States regarding the contents of the rules and their recognition as legally binding.

It is evident that this theory is closely connected with the bourgeois theory of agreement which was a dominant theory during the second half of the 19th and the beginning of the 20th centuries. This theory also proceeded from the assumption that in a system of sovereign States agreement between them is the sole mode of creating norms of international law.

The Soviet theory of the co-ordination of the will of States has taken from the bourgeois theory of agreement a rational core, namely the proposition that in the society of sovereign States the co-ordination of the will of States, of which agreement is the principal form, is the only means of creating norms of international law.

10 See G. Tunkin, *Fundamentals of Contemporary International Law*, Moscow 1956 (in Russian); German translation – in "Drei Sowjetische Beiträge zur Völkerrechtslehre", Hamburg 1969, pp. 1-57; "40 Years of Coexistence and International Law", *Soviet Yearbook of International Law*, 1958.

11 See, for instance, J. Baskin and D. Feldman, *International Law, Problems of Methodology*, Moscow 1971; R. Bobrov, *Principal Problems of Theory of International Law*, Moscow 1968; C. Ignatenko, *International Law and Social Progress*, Moscow 1972; D. Levin, *Current Problems of Theory of International Law*, Moscow 1974; I. Lukashuk, *International Legal Regulation of International Relations*, Moscow 1975; G. Tunkin, *Questions of Theory of International Law*, Moscow 1962 (translations: German – *Völkerrecht der Gegenwart. Theorie und Praxis*, Berlin 1963, French – *Droit international public. Problèmes théoriques*, Paris 1975. There are also translations into Polish, Hungarian and Arabic); *idem – Ideological Struggle and International Law*, Moscow 1967 (translations: German-in "Drei Sowjetische Beiträge zur Völkerrechtslehre", Hamburg 1969. There is also a Japanese translation); *idem – Theory of International Law*, Moscow 1970 (revised editions: German – *Völkerrechtstheorie*, Berlin, Verlag, 1972; American – *Theory of International Law*, Harvard University Press, Cambridge, Mass., 1974; British – *Theory of International Law*, George Allen & Unwin Ltd., London 1974).

The bourgeois theory of agreement was a formalistic theory which has not uncovered the essence of the norm-creating processes in international law and has passed over the processes of struggle and cooperation which take place in the international system.

The theory of the co-ordination of the will of States is a new theory. It is based on the Marxist-Leninist theory of society and theory of law. It is characterised by the following main features.

The theory of the co-ordination of the will of States considers the process of creating norms of international law as one of the aspects of the functioning of an international system. Therefore the process of norm-creating is the process of the struggle and co-operation between States.

The bourgeois theories of agreement, in accord with the bourgeois theory of State consider the wills of States as the wills of certain abstract entities, divorced from their class content. The Marxist-Leninist theory of the co-ordination of the wills- of States maintains that the will of a State participating in the process of creating norms of international law reflects the class nature of the State. The will of a capitalist State is primarily the will of the economically and politically dominant class of that State. The will of a socialist State is a will of the entire people under the guidance of the working class.

It is of primary importance to find out by which factors the will of a State is conditioned. In this respect the theory of the co-ordination of the will of States proceeds from the Marxist-Leninist thesis that the will of a ruling class is conditioned by all the circumstances in which this ruling class finds itself. In the system of these circumstances the major role play economic conditions or in other words economic structure of society.

The economic structure of society has a decisive influence on the contents of the State's will and this influence is exercised in two ways: directly and through other media.

Directly, as the maintenance and development of the existing economic structure of society is always the primary interest of a ruling class, because this economic structure ensures the dominant position of this class in society and in the State. The primary aim of the foreign policy of any State is, therefore, to ensure favourable external conditions for the maintenance and development of the existing economic structure of society. This consideration plays a decisive role in forming the content of the will of a State regarding norms of international law, especially those connected with fundamental problems of foreign policy.

Economic structure of society exercises its influence on the contents of a State's will also indirectly through other media. They include external economic, scientific, technical, cultural and other relations, internal law, philosophy, internal class struggle, etc. In other words the whole system of society influences the contents of a State's will. If, however, the decisive influence on the whole structure of society is exercised by its economic structure this indirect influence on the content of the State's will operates generally within the framework determined by the economic structure.

Thus through the will of States the economic structure of society exercises a decisive influence on the development of international law.

Some critics of the Marxist-Leninist theory attempted to assert that this theory is unable to explain the existence of general international law in the period of the co-existence of the two different economic structures of society. Professor E. McWhinney, for instance, said that the "main dilemma" of the Soviet doctrine of international law is "how can radically different (Capitalist and Communist) economic bases yield the same superstructure of international law".[12] He maintained that the Soviet theory of international law "has signally failed to explain, in consistently Marxist philosophic terms, the existence of a common international law that is supposed to be binding on Capitalist and Communist States at the present day".[13]

The misfortune of such critics is that they do not understand the Marxist-Leninist theory and in thinking that they criticise it, they actually deal with the fruits of their own imagination.

The present-day Soviet theory of international law is the only theory that offers an adequate explanation for the existence of general international law in the world divided into two radically different socioeconomic systems and ideologies.

Indeed most of the Western theories of international law, proceeding from a widely accepted thesis that law is an expression of common ideology, has long been at a loss regarding which position to take with regard to international law. And many eminent internationalists in the capitalist countries have been led to the conclusion that there is no basis for the existence of general international law as there is no common ideology any more, and that the existing international law has a tendency to disintegrate into regional systems.[14]

International law is not a mirror reflection of the economic structure of society. The existing economic structures influence international law, but they do not create rules of international law. They affect the development of international law through the wills of States.

The co-ordination of the will of States which produces norms of international law is a process objectively determined by the laws of societal development. States belonging to different socio-economic systems do not and cannot live in isolation. There are economic, political, scientific and other relations between them, the scope and the role of which in the life of society is growing. These relations require legal norms to maintain and develop them.

That is why, in spite of the division of the world into diametrically different socio-economic systems, there exists such a common superstructural element as general international law. It may also be added that there are other common superstructural elements, such as international morality, equity, etc.

We would not, however, like to create an impression that the Marxist-Leninist theory of international law was ready the next day after the Great October Socialist Revolution. It has required a long time and the joint effort of many Soviet internationalists to properly apply the Marxist-Leninist theory of society to the study of international law and to create the Marxist-Leninist theory of international law. Now we have such

12 E. McWhinney, *"Peaceful Coexistence" and Soviet-Western International Law*, Leyden, 1964, p. 46.

13 *Ibid.*, p. 39.

14 For further details see G. Tunkin, *Theory of International Law*, Harvard University Press, 1974, pp. 22-35.

a theory and the Soviet experts on international law, who are many, jointly with the international lawyers of other socialist countries are developing it further.

The theory of the co-ordination of the wills of States considers the norm creating in contemporary international law as a complex process comprising various parts and stages. It reveals the essence of the process of the co-ordination of the will of States which is so important for understanding the nature and functioning of contemporary international law.

For the emergence of a norm of international law two conditions are necessary: the co-ordination of the wills of States regarding the content of a rule and the co-ordination of the wills of States regarding its recognition as legally binding.

The wills of States participating in the process of creating norms of international law must therefore be directed toward the creation of a legally binding rule of conduct of the subjects of this legal system. This is what these wills have in common.

The co-ordinated wills of States may, however, differ in class nature, as is the case in the process of creating norms binding upon States of different socio-economic systems. The difference in the class nature of the wills involves inevitably a difference in the ultimate aims of the States concerned.

In the process of forming long-term aims of a capitalist State the interests of the ruling class exercise an overwhelming influence, pushing to the second plan truly national interests and the common interests of mankind.

In a socialist State, on the contrary, where there are no social classes which could use the State for their own benefit, national interests, as the interests of the entire people, play a decisive role in determining the long-term aims of the State. As the interests of the people of a socialist State are not essentially different from the interests of working people in other States, the long-term aims of a socialist foreign policy accord with the basic interests of mankind as a whole.

There are also purely objective factors which influence the longterm aims of States. They are many and growing in importance. One might name the internationalisation of economic and other aspects of life, the threat of war with the use of nuclear and other weapons of mass destruction, the need for preservation of the environment, etc.

As a result of the operation of such factors, States belonging to different socio-economic systems more and more often succeed in coming to an agreement on long-term aims, in spite of the existence of opposing long-term aims determined by their opposing class nature.

The Charter of the United Nations is the principal, although not the sole, example. The Charter sets forth the following purposes which should be pursued by the Organisation and its members:

1. "To maintain international peace and security, and to that end: to take effective collective measures for the prevention and removal of threats to the peace, and for the suppression of acts of aggression or other breaches of the peace, and to bring about by peaceful means, and in conformity with the principles of justice and international law, adjustment or settlement of international disputes or situations which might lead to a breach of the peace;

2. To develop friendly relations among nations based on respect for the principle of equal rights and self-determination of peoples, and to take other appropriate measures to strengthen universal peace;
3. To achieve international co-operation in solving international problems of an economic, social, cultural, or humanitarian character, and in promoting and encouraging respect for human rights and for fundamental freedoms for all without distinction as to race, sex, language, or religion; and
4. To be a centre for harmonising the actions of nations in the attainment of these common ends."[15]

These are the common aims of all the States Members of the United Nations embodied in the legal norms binding upon them.

One of the important features of the norm-creating process in international law is that the wills of States are mutually conditioned. The co-ordination of the wills of States concerning the content of a rule and its recognition as a norm of an international law on the condition that the other State or States also recognise it as such.

A rule recognised as binding in international relations by one State only is not yet a norm of international law. The State may abide by such a rule as it abides by rules of its domestic law, but it can at any moment deviate from it without incurring international responsibility.

There are at present three forms of co-ordination of the will of States which produce norms of international law, namely: international treaty, international custom and legally binding resolutions of international organisations. The two first are traditional forms, whereas the third is relatively new. The legally binding resolutions constitute also a more complex phenomenon, as in this case the coordination of the will of States results in an act of international organisation (see below, Chapter XII).

The theory of the co-ordination of the will of States is applicable also to the process of creating recommendatory resolutions of international organisations and international understandings (see below, Chapter IV).

15 Article I of the Charter.

Chapter II The Emergence of Contemporary International Law

1. The International Legal Principles of the Great October Socialist Revolution

The Great October Socialist Revolution opened a new era in the history of mankind. A new socio-economic formation emerged and a period of transition from an old to a new formation began. Such transitional periods also existed in the past. However in this case the transitional period basically differed from those in the past, when a new socio-economic formation came to replace an old one, but both of them were based on private property of the means of production and both were characterised by the existence of antagonistic social classes.

The October Revolution gave birth to a new socio-economic formation based on common property of the means of production, and the liquidation of the exploitation of man by man. Socialist relations of production, i.e., the economic structure of society are diametrically different from those in capitalist society. This has led to a reconstruction of a whole superstructure.

The international legal ideas and principles of the Great October Socialist Revolution reflected the basic principles of a new emerging socio-economic formation in the field of international relations.

These ideas and principles can be divided into three basic closely interconnected groups:

(a) principles of socialist internationalism in relations between socialist States;
(b) principles of equality and self-determination of nations and peoples whose spearhead was aimed against the system of colonialism as well as against any national oppression and inequality;
(c) principles of peaceful coexistence in relations between States with different social systems.

a. The Principles of Socialist Internationalism

The Principles of socialist internationalism correspond to a new type of international relations, to the relations between socialist States. Historically these principles are routed in the principles of the international workers' movement.

The guiding principle of the international workers movement has always been the principle of proletarian internationalism which signifies the fraternal friendship, close co-operation and mutual assistance of the working classes of various countries in the struggle for their social liberation.

Other principles of working-class policies have also been moulded together with the principle of proletarian internationalism. They applied to relations with the working classes of various countries and their parties and also to relations between nations and States.

With the emergence of the first socialist State these principles became basic principles of its internal as well as external policy. They were embodied in relations between nations and between the Soviet Republics formed on the territory of the former Russian empire after the October Revolution. Of course the relations between these republics were not completely international, but they had an international aspect too.

The foreign policy of the new socialist State has always been based on the principles of socialist internationalism. The Soviet State has always acted in the international arena, taking into account principles of the proletarian internationalism in the sense that it always took into consideration its duties with regard to the working class and the oppressed peoples of other countries.

The newly born Soviet State had a sincere intention of establishing its relationship with the revolutionary regimes in Germany and Hungary in 1918-1919 on the principles of proletarian internationalism. However these revolutions were soon smashed by the united forces of imperialism.

Relations with Mongolia which were established soon after the October Revolution are an example of relations based upon the principles of proletarian internationalism. After the people's revolution in Mongolia the Mongolian People's Republic, with the fraternal assistance of the Soviet State, has achieved great economic and cultural successes and bypassing the capitalist stage of development has proceeded to the construction of socialism.

After the Second World War socialist revolution took place in some other countries and a socialist commonwealth of nations was formed. The principles of proletarian internationalism became basic principles of relationships between the socialist States, and in this capacity they are usually called the principles of socialist internationalism.[16]

b. The Principles of Equality and Self-Determination of Peoples

Among the leading principles proclaimed by the Great October Socialist Revolution were principles of equality and self-determination of peoples and nations. As these two principles are so intimately connected with each other they are sometimes considered as a single principle.[17]

16 See Chapter V, 8.

17 See, for instance, Declaration of Principles of International Law of 1970.

The origin of these principles dates back to the period of the bourgeois revolutions. Later under the banner of the "principle of nationality" the bourgeoisie, striving to establish its predominance, struggled in the 19th century for the creation of independent national States in Europe. The "principle of nationality", however, was not generally recognised even within the framework of European international law.

V. I. Lenin and the Bolshevist Party gave a new revolutionary content to this principle. In the Decree on Peace of 8 November 1917 V. I. Lenin gave a classical definition of this new revolutionary content of the principle. The Decree on Peace said:

> "In accordance with the legal consciousness of democrats in general and of the working classes in particular, the government conceives the annexation or seizure of foreign lands to mean every incorporation of a small or weak nation into a large or powerful State without the precisely, clearly and voluntarily expressed consent and wish of that nation, irrespective of the time when such forceable incorporation took place, irrespective also of the degree of development or backwardness of the nation forcibly annexed to the given State, or forcibly retained within its borders, and irrespective, finally, of whether this nation is in Europe or in distant overseas countries. If any nation whatsoever is forcibly retained within the borders of a given State, if, in spite of its expressed desire – no matter whether expressed in the press, at public meetings, in the decisions of parties, or in protests and uprisings against national oppression – it is not accorded the right to decide the forms of its State existence by a free vote, taken after the complete evacuation of the troops of the incorporating or, generally, of the stronger nation and without the least pressure being brought to bear, such incorporation is annexation, i.e., seizure and violence."[18]

The Soviet State gave an example of a foreign policy based on the principle of self-determination. It broke completely and immediately with the colonial policy of tsarism and repudiated all treaties of Tsarist Russia having a colonial annexationist, unequal character. In the treaty between the RSFSR and Persia in 1921 the parties emphasised "the right of each people to the free and unimpeded resolution of its own political fate".[19] The Treaty between Russia and Turkey of 16 March 1921 proclaimed the "principle of the fraternity of nations and the right of peoples to self-determination".[20]

The principle of self-determination was embodied also in some other treaties with neighbouring countries such as China.

A new principle of international law – a principle of self-determination of peoples and nations started its long but victorious way in the world.

---

18 V. I. Lenin, *On the Foreign Policy of the Soviet State*, Progress Publishers, Moscow 1973, p. 12.

19 *Documents of Foreign Policy of the USSR*, Moscow, Vol. 3, p. 538 (in Russian).

20 *Ibid.*, p. 597.

c. The Principles of Peaceful Coexistence

The first word of a socialist State born by the October revolution was "peace". The Decree on Peace declared:

> "The workers' and peasants' government, created by the Revolution of October 24-25 and basing itself on the Soviets of Workers, Soldiers and Peasants Deputies, calls upon all the belligerent peoples and their governments to start immediate negotiations for a just, democratic peace."[21]
>
> This was an expression of the basic principle of the foreign policy of the socialist State – the principle of international peace. This principle is deeply rooted in the nature of the new socio-economic formation, and in the class nature of the socialist State, as a State representing, for the first time in history, not the interests or mainly the interests of a ruling class, but the interests of the people.
>
> The policy of peace laid down by Lenin was based on two fundamental premises: (a) the rejection of war as a means of spreading socialist revolution; (b) the nature of the socialist system and socialist State. Lenin wrote that it was always the people's blood that was spilled in wars, always the working classes that suffered the most. Saying that civil wars of the working classes against oppressors and national liberation wars as well as defensive wars were justified and progressive, Lenin stressed that "socialists have always condemned wars between nations as a barbarous and brutal thing".[22] Accordingly a socialist State could not but follow a policy of peace in international relations.
>
> Closely connected with the principle of peace was the idea of the unjust and criminal character of aggressive wars. They were also put forward in the Decree on Peace that said: "The government considers it the greatest of crimes against humanity to continue this war over the issue of how to divide among the strong and rich nations the weak nationalities they have conquered . . . ."[23]

The Great October Socialist Revolution proclaimed the principle of peaceful coexistence of States with different socio-economic systems.[24] Since then this principle has ever been a leading principle of the foreign policy of the Soviet Union and also other socialist States in their relations with the States of another socio-economic system.

But the Soviet State proclaimed the principle of peaceful coexistence not only as a principle of its foreign policy, but also as a legal principle of relations between States of different socio-economic systems. Since its first days the Soviet socialist State has consistently tried to obtain the consent of the capitalist States to develop their mutual

21 V. I. Lenin, *On the Foreign Policy of the Soviet State* (1973), p. 11.

22 Lenin, *Complete Works*, Vol. 21, p. 299.

23 V. I. Lenin, *On the Foreign Policy of the Soviet State*, p. 12.

24 See Chapter III, I.

relations on the basis of the principle of peaceful coexistence which at that time had only just started on its thorny way in international relations.

Principles of peaceful coexistence, prohibition of aggressive wars, criminality of aggressive wars, self-determination of peoples, socialist internationalism and other principles, proclaimed by the Great October Socialist Revolution, have exercised a profound influence on the development of international law.

As a result of the consistent struggle of the Soviet Union and other socialist States, new States born in the process of the disintegration of the colonial system and all the progressive forces in the world, the international legal principles of the Great October Socialist Revolution detonated the most fundamental new principles of contemporary international law, such as the principles of the prohibition of aggressive wars, non-use of force, self-determination of peoples and many other principles of general international law which have emerged on the basis of these principles. The principles of socialist internationalism have become guiding international legal principles in relations between the socialist States.

If the development of international law in the 19th century was marked by the preponderant influence of the international legal ideas and principles of the bourgeois revolutions, and above all of the French bourgeois revolution, the development of international law after the Great October Socialist Revolution has been dominated by the international legal ideas and principles of this revolution.

2. The Laws of Societal Development of Our Epoch Having Immediate Bearing Upon International Law

A reference was made earlier to such basic laws of societal development as the decisive role of the productive forces with regard to production relations and the determining role of economic basis with regard to societal superstructure and international law as part of this superstructure.

Here we propose to analyse some other laws of societal development which have immediate bearing upon the development of international law today and determine principal processes in the present day international law, namely the internationalisation of economic and other aspects of life; the existence of sovereign States; the coexistence of States belonging to diametrically different socio-economic systems; decolonisation. Of course, the influence of these laws on the development of international law should be viewed within the framework of an international system and of the general process of the present day societal development which is in the process of transition from capitalism to socialism.

a. The Internationalisation of Economic and Other Aspects of Life

The development of productive forces of society, enormously accelerated by the scientific and technological revolution leads to the growing internationalisation of the economic life of society, to the growing economic interdependence of nations. The increasing internationalisation finds its expression above all in the expanding international division of labour.

International division of labour means intensification of all kinds of economic, scientific and technological ties between countries. However, one should not forget that the international division of labour and international economic links are relations of production which, with regard to relations of production existing in each State, are of a secondary nature. The character of the international division of labour and of international economic relations depends on the character of national complexes of relations of production.

There are at present two diametrically different types of relations of production: the socialist relations of production and the capitalist relations of production, in other words, the socialist and the capitalist economic systems. To them correspond two types of international division of labour and international economic relations. It seems that one can speak of a specific type of international division of labour within the framework of the developing countries. Besides these types of international division of labour there is a global division of labour, global economic ties.

International division of labour takes place on different levels: in the framework of a socio-economic system and on the world-wide scale.

International economic relations constitute the principal developmental base for other international relations: political, cultural and others. All this leads to the growing volume of international relations and to increasing their relative importance with regard to other social relations. The process of internationalisation means that many aspects of life: economic, political, scientific, cultural, etc., are increasingly tied up with the analogous aspects of life in other countries. This leads to growing interdependence of nations in different spheres of life.

The expansion of international relations widens the scope and increases the role of international law which is indispensable for regularising and developing these relations.

The intensification of international relations and the growing interdependence of nations produce an increasing number of international problems which cannot be dealt with only by concluding international treaties between States. They call for the creation of international bodies which would be constantly busy with these problems and which would facilitate the co-operation between States. This leads to the increasing role of international organisations in the international system.

b. The Existence of Sovereign States

The existence of sovereign States is one of the most important laws of the development of mankind in our time which has direct relation to international law and international organisations.

We are still living in an epoch when the State as a social institution cannot be done away with. The State was born when the growth of productive forces of society led to the emergence of private ownership of the means of production, to the increasing economic inequality between men and to the splitting of society into social classes. After that the former clan organisation of society was replaced or rather converted into a State. The State is a class organisation and it is inherent in the class society. So before social classes came into being, the State did not exist. And on a very high level of development of human society, with the disappearance of private ownership of the means of production and social classes, the State will give way to another more perfect form of social organisation. But whilst private ownership of the means of production and social classes exist, the State will also exist.

However another question may be put forward: if the existence of the State is inevitable why must States be sovereign, why cannot a world federation be created? There is a theory according to which the growing internationalisation of various aspects of life brings about a new situation requiring the creation of a supranational authority. The stress is usually laid upon the growing economic interdependence of nations. Seeing that in the light of the laws of societal development the theories of world federation are based mostly only on one of these laws – the law of internationalisation. They do not take into consideration other laws of societal development which act in a different direction.[25]

The existence of sovereign States is of capital importance for the present-day international law and international organisations. Above all it makes it inevitable that the present-day international law and international organisations are based on the co-ordination of the will of States.

c. Coexistence of States with Diametrically Different Socio-economic Systems

Coexistence of States belonging to the two diametrically different socio-economic systems is an objective phenomenon of our epoch, of transition from capitalism to socialism. This coexistence has two aspects so far as international law is concerned. First – the split of the world into two opposing systems makes it in general more difficult to reach agreement between States belonging to different systems in the process of creating norms of international law. It should also be stressed that if the existence of States belonging to different socioeconomic systems is, generally speaking, an obstacle to agreements between them, it is not an unsurmountable obstacle. Theory and practice have shown that if there is a sincere desire on both sides agreement may be reached between the capitalist and socialist States on all international problems.

The second aspect is that the Great October Socialist Revolution and the emergence and the growth of the socialist system have brought about a new situation beneficial to the development of international law.[26]

d. The Break-Up of the Colonial System and the Emergence of New States

The chain of events that have followed the Great October Socialist Revolution, which gave a great impetus to the national liberation movement in the colonies, has finally brought about the complete collapse of the colonial system. An international system, for the first time in history, has become global. New States now represent a very important part of the international system. The emergence of many new States has considerably changed the international system as a whole. This change has had, in general, a beneficial effect on the development of international law.

25 See G. I. Tunkin, *Theory of International Law* (1974), pp. 366-380.

26 See below Chapter II, 3.

(e) The Interaction of the Laws of Societal Development
The laws of societal development mentioned above exercise a decisive influence on the development of international law in our time. They are in constant interaction, the main features of which are the following:

These laws often act in different directions. So the internationalisation of economic and other aspects of life operates in the direction of the widening and deepening ties between States, the increasing interdependence of nations which leads to the expansion of the sphere of application of international law and the increasing role of international law and international organisation.

The existence of sovereign States, although a precondition of the very existence of international law, puts, on the contrary, certain limits to the process of development of international law conditioned by internationalisation.

One and the same law can exercise conflicting influences on the development of international law. The coexistence of States with different socio-economic systems, for instance, operates in the same direction as internationalisation, as it leads to the growth of the forces of peace and progress and thereby strengthens the social basis of the progressive development of international law. At the same time it operates partially in the same direction as the existence of sovereign States, because the profound differences in the economic structure and class nature of States belonging to different socio-economic systems make the co-ordination of the wills of such States in the process of creating norms of international law, generally more difficult in comparison with the co-ordination of the wills of States belonging to one socio-economic system.

Different laws usually affect different aspects of the development of international law. Internationalisation, for instance, affects principally the sphere of operation and role of international law. Meanwhile the coexistence of States with the diametrically different socio-economic systems has led primarily to a profound change in the nature of international law.

The disintegration of the colonial system and the emergence of new States is contributing to the transformation of the nature of international law.

3. THE PRINCIPAL CHANGES IN INTERNATIONAL LAW SINCE THE GREAT OCTOBER SOCIALIST REVOLUTION

The history of international law since the October Revolution has been of continuous struggle between the international legal principles of socialism proclaimed by the Socialist Revolution, developed and enriched afterwards by the socialist States, and principles of the bourgeois international law, which have become out of date.

The growth of the socialist system, the increasing strength of the working-class movement, the growing influence of all democratic forces on foreign policies of the capitalist States, the national liberation movements in the colonies and dependent countries changed the situation more and more in favour of progressive development of international law.

The very core of international law – its fundamental principles – has radically changed. Important transformations have also taken place in various branches of international law.

The history of international law after the October Revolution is clearly divided into two periods by the Second World War.

The outstanding event in the course of the first period was the emergence of the principle of the prohibition of aggressive war (Pact of Paris of 1928) and gradual, although not complete, acceptance by the capitalist countries of the principle of peaceful coexistence of States belonging to two diametrically different socio-economic systems.

Hitlerite Germany tried by force of arms to replace international law by a "new order" based on the concept of racial superiority and domination by the German people, brutal subjugation and enslavement of other peoples.

On the part of the Anti-Hitlerite coalition the struggle against Hitlerite Germany was objectively, and on the whole, the struggle against the most reactionary forces for further progress of international law.

A historic document that crowned the victory of the Allied powers, the victory of all mankind, over Hitlerite Germany and imperialist Japan was the Charter of the United Nations. The Charter constituted a remarkable achievement in the progressive development of international law.

The Charter goes beyond the Pact of Paris of 1928, prohibiting not only aggressive war, but also the threat or use of force in international relations. At the same time the Charter contains an obligation to settle international disputes "by peaceful means in such a manner that international peace and security and justice are not endangered".

In spite of the resistance of the colonial powers the principle of self-determination of peoples was embodied in the Charter, although in somewhat general terms. At the San Francisco Conference in 1945 the USSR delegation proposed to supplement Article I of the Charter by stipulating that one of the purposes of the Organisation is the development of friendly relations among nations "based on respect for the principle of equal rights and self-determination of people".[27] This amendment was adopted.

References to the right of self-determination in the Chapter on trusteeship, suggested by the USSR delegation, were partly rejected and partly accepted by the Western powers.

Notwithstanding the imperfections of the wording of the Charter, it constitutes a turning point in the development of the principle of self-determination. It became a firmly established principle of international law which is now recognised by all the States. Later on it has been concretised and developed in such important documents as the Declaration on Granting Independence to Colonial Countries and Peoples and the Declaration on the Principles of International Law adopted by the General Assembly of the United Nations, respectively in 1960 and 1970.

27 *Documents of the United Nations Conference on International Organization*, Vol. III, p. 622.

The process of formation of the principle of self-determination is a convincing example of the influence of a changing situation in the world on the contents of the wills of States in the process of formation of norms of international law. The world-wide struggle against the aggression and barbarism in the course of the Second World War, in which the Soviet socialist State played a leading role, brought about a tremendous increase in the activities of all democratic forces in the world and a new rising of national liberation movements in the colonies and dependent countries. In this situation, at the San Francisco Conference in 1945, the colonial powers had to make some concessions on the problem of self-determination. The result was the co-ordination of the wills of States on the subject giving birth to the correspondent stipulations of the Charter.

However the intention of the imperialist powers was to make this principle non-operative. That is why later on they objected to a more precise formulation of the principle of self-determination. In 1952 they voted in the General Assembly against a draft article on self-determination intended for inclusion into the Convenants on human rights. They also voted against the Declaration on Granting Independence to Colonial Countries and Peoples in 1960.

Up to 1966 when the General Assembly of the United Nations adopted the Covenants on human rights, the colonial system actually collapsed. From its ruins many new States emerged and became members of the United Nations. In this situation the opposition of the colonial powers to the principle of self-determination relaxed somewhat and when the article on self-determination of the Covenants on human rights was voted on, only a few Western powers (USA, Great Britain, New Zealand and Norway) voted against it. Twenty other States, mostly Western, abstained. Four years later, when the General Assembly adopted the Declaration on Principles of International Law which contained a still more elaborate text on the principle of self-determination, no Western power objected to it.

The principle of equality and self-determination of peoples, which meant at first the right of a people to freely decide its political future, has since greatly developed. Its contents nowdays include the prohibition of colonialism, the right of peoples to freely choose and develop their social, economic, political and cultural institutions, sovereignty of the people over their natural resources, prohibition of racial discrimination and apartheid. These aspects of the principle may well be considered as separate principles. There is, however, still much to be done to make these new aspects of the principle, or these new principles, generally accepted, but they are certainly gaining strength.

One of the most important developments in international law of the post-war period was the general acceptance of the principle of peaceful coexistence of States belonging to different socio-economic systems as a principle of international law. The co-operation of States of the two systems during the Second World War indicated that such cooperation might go much further than it was expected by any of the parties concerned. The principle of peaceful coexistence was tacitly accepted as a foundation of a new international organisation. Although the term "peaceful coexistence" is not used in the Charter of the United Nations, the principle of peaceful coexistence runs throughout the Charter of this international organisation. The preamble of the Charter speaks of the determination "to save succeeding generations from the scourge of war", "to establish conditions under which justice and respect for the obligations arising from treaties and other sources of international law can be maintained". States are called upon "to practise tolerance and live together in peace with one another as good neighbours". Article I of the Charter obligates States "to develop friendly relations among nations" to take "other appropriate measures to strengthen universal peace", "to achieve international co-operation in solving international problems of an economic, social, cultural or humanitarian character and in promoting and encouraging respect for human rights and for fundamental freedoms for all without distinction as to race, sex, language or religion". Finally the United Nations Charter says that this international organisation must "be a centre for harmonising the actions of nations in the attainment of these common ends" having in view first of all the harmonised actions of States of different social systems. The Charter proceeded therefore from the assumption that the States of all existing socio-economic systems should co-operate peacefully and that the new world organisation should be a means of developing such co-operation.

The "cold war", however, slowed down the further development of the principle of peaceful coexistence for a long time. The very use of the term "peaceful coexistence" was considered in some Western countries as subversive propaganda.

With the end of the "cold war" and international détente gaining strength the explicit recognition of the principle of coexistence has been gradually coming. This recognition was expressed in the practical policy of developing co-operation of the Western powers with the USSR and other socialist States, in the words of many international documents. Among them a number of bilateral declarations and treaties, such as: "Principles of relations between the USSR and France" of 1971, the 1970 Treaty between the USSR and the Federal Republic of Germany, entered into force in 1972, Treaties between the People's Republic of Poland and the Federal Republic of Germany, between the Germany Democratic Republic and the Federal Republic of Germany and many other bilateral documents.

It is worthy to note that in the "Basic principles of mutual relations between the Union of Soviet Socialist Republics and the United States of America" signed in Moscow on 29 May 1972 by L. I. Brezhnev for the USSR and Richard Nixon for the United States of America it is stated as follows: "1. They will proceed from the common determination that in the nuclear age there is no alternative to conducting their mutual relations on the basis of peaceful coexistence."

The most powerful capitalist State, which opposed peaceful coexistence longer and more resolutely than other capitalist States, has at last explicitly accepted the principle of peaceful coexistence.

Since the early sixties the principle of peaceful coexistence may be found in various United Nations documents and international multilateral treaties concluded under the auspices of the United Nations. The wording of these principles varies in different documents, but the essence is practically the same. The Vienna Convention on diplomatic relations of 18 April 1961 says in its preamble: "Believing that an international convention on diplomatic intercourse, privileges and immunities would contribute to the development of friendly relations among nations, irrespective of their differing constitutional and social systems". The Vienna Convention on consular relations of 24 April 1963 uses the same formulation.

The Convention on special missions adopted by the General Assembly of the United Nations on 8 December 1969 speaks of "the development of friendly relations among nations whatever their constitutional and social systems".

The Vienna Convention on the law of treaties of 23 May 1969 speaks of "developing peaceful co-operation among nations whatever their constitutional and social systems".

The Declaration on Principles of International Law Concerning Friendly Relations and Co-operation among States in Accordance with the Charter of the United Nations of 1970 expresses this idea by saying that "States have the duty to co-operate with one another, irrespective of the differences in their political, economic and social systems".

The principle of "peaceful coexistence" as such has been for the first time named in the "Charter of Economic Rights and Duties of States" adopted by the General Assembly on 12 December 1974. Among 15 principles by which "economic as well as political and other relations among States shall be governed", there is the principle of "peaceful coexistence" (Chapter I of the Declaration).

An opinion is often expressed in Western literature on international law that the principle of peaceful coexistence is only a political principle, but not a principle of international law. So Professor Ch. Rousseau says:

> ". . . The so-called principle of peaceful coexistence is nothing more but a simple statement of the fact, and namely the taking into consideration the existence in the framework of the international community of States having different, even opposite, political, economic and social systems. The taking into consideration of a situation existing in interstate relations is not the same as the formulation of a legal principle, even if one implies the will of mutual tolerance."[28]

One may hope that the evolution of the Western science of international law with regard to the principle of peaceful coexistence will be the same as it was with regard to the principle of self-determination of peoples. Until recently the majority of Western international lawyers did not recognise the existence of the principle of self-determination as a legal norm, but further development of international law proved without any shadow of doubt that such a principle does exist and at present there are very few Western international lawyers who do not admit it.

The principle of peaceful coexistence although a very broad one has a legal content. The principle of peaceful coexistence of States with different socio-economic systems also presupposes the existence of other important principles of international law, such as the non-use of force, respect for sovereignty, non-interference in internal affairs, equality of States and peoples, self-determination, fulfilment in good faith of international obligations of States and others. It reflects their content in a generalised form, adding to that some general normative elements.

28 Rousseau, *Droit international public*, t. I, Paris 1970, pp. 391-392.

The principle of peaceful coexistence requires, first of all, not only the renunciation of the use or threat of force against other States but also the renunciation of policies which could lead to war and to international tension. It includes an obligation to pursue policies which contribute to the strengthening of international peace and security and developing international co-operation. The 1970 Declaration on Principles of International Law points out that all States shall "strive to adopt appropriate measures to reduce international tension and strengthen confidence among States".

The principle of peaceful coexistence includes the obligation of States to recognise and respect different socio-economic systems existing in various States. It is well known that after the October Revolution Western powers refused to recognise the legality of a new socioeconomic system in Russia based on collective property of the means of production. Such attempts should be considered as contrary to contemporary international law.

The principle of peaceful coexistence includes the obligation of a State not to attempt to impose its own system on another State with the aid of force. A recent example of such an attempt is the economic blockade of Cuba by the United States. This blockade may be considered not only as the use of economic force against territorial integrity and political independence of a State, but also as an attempt to liquidate the socio-economic system in Cuba.

The principle of peaceful coexistence includes also the obligation of States to co-operate with one another irrespective of the differences in their socio-economic and political systems.

It seems that this component of the principle of peaceful coexistence is becoming a separate principle of international law. It has been singled out in the Declaration on Principles of International Law of 1970 which says:

> "States have the duty to co-operate with one another, irrespective of the differences in their political, economic and social systems, in the various spheres of international relations, in order to maintain international peace and security and to promote international economic stability and progress, the general welfare of nations and international co-operation free from discrimination based on such differences."

This formula is of primary importance. It means that a State has an obligation not to refuse to co-operate with other States on the ground of the difference in their socio-economic systems.

The post-war period of the development of international law has also been marked by the emergence of such new principles of international law as the principle of disarmament, respect for human rights, prohibition of war propaganda and so on. These new principles are gradually gaining strength.

Side by side with the formation of important new principles of international law we have witnessed the further development and strengthening of the old democratic principles of international law, such as the principles of respect for State sovereignty, non-interference in internal affairs, equality of States, *pacta sunt servanda*, and others.[29]

The important changes which have occurred in various branches of international law are above all the sequence of the change in the fundamental principles.

In the domain of international responsibility of States, whose importance in the system of international law it is difficult to overestimate, there has been an extension of responsibility upon the war and its consequences.

There has also emerged a new important institute of international law: the responsibility of individuals for crimes against humanity, as they have been defined in the Statute and Judgment of the International Military Tribunal in Nuremberg.

Significant changes have taken place in the law of treaties. Contemporary international law declares void the treaties imposed upon a State through the unlawful use of force or those which contravene norms of international law having the character of *jus cogens* and recognises a special status for treaties concluded with regard to an aggressor State.[30]

New subjects of international law have emerged – international intergovernmental organisations and also peoples fighting for their independence.

International custom has surrendered its place as the principal source of international law to international treaty. Resolutions of international organisations, and especially of the United Nations, are playing a larger and larger role in the process of forming norms of international law.

More or less significant changes have taken place in all other parts of international law.

The intensification and deepening of international ties has led to the emergence of new areas of international legal relations and new branches of international law.

4. Contemporary International Law – A New Historic Type of International Law

Under the influence of the growing might of the forces of socialism, of the new independent States which emerged from the ruins of the colonial system and of all the forces of democracy and progress, international law has undergone, as has been shown earlier, fundamental changes since the Great October Socialist Revolution.

International law before the Great October Socialist Revolution, or in other words bourgeois or classical international law, was essentially the law of the strong. It permitted the use of force and the recourse to war in international relations, and legally sanctioned what was acquired by force, thereby legitimising the rule of force in international relations.

Contemporary international law prohibits the resort to war, the use or threat of force and obligates States to settle their disputes by peaceful means only. The recourse to war is an international crime. Victory gives no rights according to contemporary

29 For greater detail see G. I. Tunkin, *Theory of International Law*, pp. 49-87.

30 See Articles 52, 53 and 75 of the 1969 Vienna Convention on the Law of Treaties.

international law. The consequences of war are governed primarily by the norms of international law concerning the international responsibility of States.

Contemporary international law is a law of peace, a law aimed first of all at ensuring international peace which is the greatest common interest of all mankind.

The classical international law contained norms and institutes which were an instrument of colonial subjugation of peoples. Inequality of nations, division of all the peoples into "civilised" and "non-civilised", the right of "civilised" States to occupy the territory of "non-civilised" peoples and to establish on these territories regimes of colonial subjugation, were part and parcel of classical international law.

Contemporary international law is in its essence anti-colonial. It is a law of equality, self-determination and freedom of peoples.

International law today is a law of international co-operation. According to classical international law States were under no obligation to co-operate among themselves. According to contemporary international law States have the duty to co-operate with one another in resolving international problems.

Contemporary international law, reflecting changes that have taken place in the society after the Great October Socialist Revolution, has turned its face to the human being. The problem of international cooperation in ensuring respect for human rights has become one of the principal problems of contemporary international law.

Not only the normative content of international law but also its social nature has been transformed.

Norms of general international law are the result of the co-ordination of the will of all States, including, therefore, the socialist and capitalist States. This means that norms of contemporary general international law cannot be socialist, since agreement on this basis between socialist and capitalist States is impossible. On the other hand, they cannot be capitalist, and still less an embodiment of an imperialistic policy, since agreement between socialist and capitalist States also is impossible on this basis.

The principles and norms of contemporary general international law are of general democratic character: this is the only basis for agreement between States of the two diametrically different socio-economic systems. The notion of being generally democratic, however, is a very broad concept. The degree of the democratic nature of specific norms of international law is determined by the influence which has been exerted on the creation and development of such norms by the forces which favour the progressive development of international law and the forces which impede such progress.

Particular norms of international law may have the same social nature as the norms of general international law or a different one. Particular norms which operate in relations between socialist and capitalist States are of the same nature as norms of general international law. Particular norms in relations between capitalist States may have a bourgeois (capitalist) nature, whereas particular norms in relations between socialist States – a socialist nature.

All this means that a revolutionary change has taken place in international law as a result of a revolutionary change in society. Contemporary international law differs substantially from the bourgeois (classical) international law. It is a new historical type of international law – the international law of the period of transition from capitalism to socialism, the law of coexistence of States with diametrically different socio-economic systems.

The concept of a new international law does not mean that all or even the majority of norms of the present-day international law are completely new. Contemporary international law has emerged as a result of gradual accumulation of quantitative changes which have been turned into qualitative changes. These qualitative changes as we have seen have taken place in the most important parts of international law. They constitute a profound transformation of the main characteristics of international law including its social nature, the character of its influence on the development of the international system and so on.

Some Western lawyers interpreted the concept of a new international law as an attempt to transform the existing international law into a new one. So Professor Francis Vallat, at the time the chief legal adviser to the British Foreign Office, referring to my lecture at the University College, London, in 1962, wrote:

> "His theme seemed to be that we now have or will soon have a 'new international law', that this was or would be the gift of the Soviet Union and their friends and that the new international law embraced and was founded on the Soviet concept of 'peaceful coexistence'."[31]

This statement was made quite a time ago and might be forgotten if the same idea did not continue to appear in the Western writings. In his review of my book Theory of International Law Professor John Hazard of Columbia University says: "Remoulding international law in a socialist image has been a major aim of Professor Gregory I. Tunkin for something over two decades."[32]

Actually the concept of a new international law has nothing to do with the remoulding of the present-day international law. It is not an appeal to change the international law in force. It is an assertion that as a result of fundamental changes the bourgeois (classical) international law has been transformed into a new historic type of international law.

One may, of course, agree or disagree with this concept of contemporary international law, but that is another matter.

Contemporary general international law can be defined as international law of the period of coexistence of States belonging to diametrically different socio-economic systems, the norms of which are created by the co-ordination of the will of States and have a general democratic character, regulate relations between States in the process of struggle and co-operation in the direction of ensuring peace and peaceful coexistence, freedom and independence of peoples, which are enforced, when necessary, by coercive measures taken by States individually or collectively or by international organisations.

The concept of a new international law does not imply that the existing international law is perfect.

It is evident that in our age of rapid change international law must constantly develop to keep pace with the development of international relations.

31 Sir Francis Vallat, "International Law – a Forward Look", in the *Year Book of World Affairs* (1964), p. 248.

32 *Harvard Law Review*, Vol. 88 (1975), p. 1044.

Chapter III Peaceful Coexistence, Ideological Struggle and International Law

1. Lenin's Notion of Peaceful Coexistence

Proceeding from the theory he had formulated that capitalism developed unevenly in different countries, Lenin came to the conclusion that a socialist revolution could not take place simultaneously in all developed countries, and that at first it should occur in one or several of them only. It followed that a more or less protracted period of the parallel existence of the two diametrically different socioeconomic systems was inevitable.

What would this period of coexistence be like?

Lenin rejected Trotsky's concept of "permanent revolution" according to which the socialist revolution can win only if it takes place in all developed countries more or less simultaneously. Lenin called this concept "absurdly left".[33]

Lenin proceeded from one of the main postulates of Marxist theory that socialist revolution in a country, although closely linked with the world proletarian movement, was an affair of the people of that country. In June 1918 Lenin said:

> "Of course, there are people who maintain that a revolution can take place in some other country by an order or by an agreement. They are either madmen or provocateurs. We have had in the course of the last 12 years two revolutions. We know that they cannot be made neither by an order nor an agreement, and that they take place when tens of millions of people come to the conclusion that it is impossible to live any longer as they live at present."[34]

Lenin, therefore, also opposed Trotsky's thesis of "revolutionary war" as a war intended to expand the socialist revolution to other countries by the force of arms. In an article "Strange and Monstrous", published in the Pravda on 28 February and 1 March 1918, V. I. Lenin wrote appealing to the authors of a resolution adopted by the Moscow Regional Party Bureau:

> "Perhaps the authors believe that the interests of the world revolution require that it should be given a push and that such a push can be given

33 See Lenin, *Collected Works*, Moscow, Vol. 20, p. 346.

34 Lenin, *Complete Works* (in Russian), Vol. 36, p. 457.

> only by war, never by peace, which might give the people the impression that imperialism was being 'legitimised'? Such a 'theory' would be completely at variance with Marxism, for Marxism has always been opposed to 'pushing' revolutions, which develop with the growing acuteness of the class antagonisms that engender revolutions."[35]

In spite of the opposition of some leftist groups, Lenin's view prevailed in the party.

From these theoretical conclusions followed a certain line of foreign policy of a socialist State with regard to capitalist States. The thesis that socialist revolution is a result of internal conditions in the country concerned, that it is a matter for the working people of that country to decide, and the rejection of the concept of a "revolutionary war" against the capitalist States to expand upon them the socialist revolution which has occurred in Russia, led inevitably to a practical policy of peaceful coexistence between States belonging to the old capitalist system and the new socialist system.

And indeed the Soviet socialist State proposed a policy of peaceful coexistence in its very first legislative act – the Decree on Peace of 8 November 1917. In this Decree it condemned imperialistic, aggressive wars as "the greatest of crimes against humanity" and urged the belligerent States to stop the slaughter and immediately negotiate "a just, democratic peace".[36]

The idea of peaceful coexistence of the socialist State with the capitalist countries was clearly expressed by Lenin in his concluding remarks on the Decree on Peace at the Second All-Russian Congress of Soviets on 8 November 1917. Speaking of the treaties of Russia with other countries Lenin said:

> "The secret treaties must be published. The clauses dealing with annexations and indemnities must be annulled. There are International Law in the International System various clauses, comrades – the predatory governments, you know, not only made agreements between themselves on plunder, but among them they also included economic agreements and various other clauses on good-neighbourly relations.
> We shall not bind ourselves by treaties. We shall not allow ourselves to be entangled by treaties. We reject all clauses on plunder and violence, but we shall welcome all clauses containing provisions for good-neighbourly relations and all economic agreements; we cannot reject these."[37]

That was a proposal to the capitalist States to develop good-neighbourly relations, that is relations of peaceful coexistence between States of different socio-economic systems.

---

35 V. I. Lenin, *On the Foreign Policy of the Soviet State* (1973), p. 43.

36 *Documents of the Foreign Policy of the USSR*, Vol. 1, Moscow 1958, pp. 11-12.

37 Lenin, *On the Foreign Policy of the Soviet State*, p. 17.

At that time nobody yet used the term "peaceful coexistence". For the first time a term close to that appeared in a note of the People's Commissar of Foreign Affairs of the RSFSR to the German Consul-General on 19 September 1918. The note stated:

> "The Workers and Peasants' Government desires with full resolve the observance of good-neighbourly relations and peaceful cohabitation with Germany despite all the differences in the system of both States, and it is convinced that the German Government also wishes to live together peacefully with it; whilst living together it shall remain as it is as also the German Government, and it expects that the latter as itself will take into account all consequences of these differences which, however, have not precluded the establishment between both States of good-neighbourly relations corresponding to the true and deeply rooted interests of both sides."[38]

So at that time not the term "peaceful coexistence", but rather the term "good-neighbourly relations" was used. Occasionally, however, the term "peaceful coexistence" also appeared. In his report to a session of the all-Russian Executive Committee of the Soviets on 17 June 1920 the People's Commissar of Foreign Affairs, G. V. Chicherin, said:

> "Our slogan was and remains one and the same: peaceful coexistence with other governments, whatever they are. The very reality has led us and other States to the necessity of establishing long-term relations between the workers' and peasants' government and the capitalist governments. These lasting relations are resolutely imposed upon us by economic realities."[39]

At the same time Lenin foresaw that the ruling classes of the capitalist States would hardly accept this peaceful offer of a newly born socialist State. Referring to the history of the French bourgeois revolution of the 18th century, Lenin warned the Party and the Russian workers and people in general that the ruling classes of the capitalist countries would not leave the socialist State alone and would use every means at their disposal, including military force, to smash the new socialist system, the very existence of which they considered a threat to their position as ruling classes of society. In his report on the problem of peace at the Second All-Russia Congress of Soviets Lenin said: "The governments and the bourgeoisie will make every effort to unite their forces and drown the workers' and peasants' revolution in blood."[40] The Seventh Congress of the Russian Communist Party, held in March 1918, stated in its resolution on war and peace: "In the present initial period of the era of socialist revolution, repeated military incursions

38 *Documents of the Foreign Policy of the USSR*, Vol. 1, p. 488.
39 *Documents of the Foreign Policy of the USSR*, Vol. 2, p. 639.
40 Lenin, *On the Foreign Policy of the Soviet State*, p. 15.

by the imperialist States (from West and East) against Soviet Russia are historically inevitable."[41]

These prognoses soon came true. Shortly after that the Soviet State was attacked by the armed forces of 14 capitalist States. Despite hunger, the devastation of the economy, counter-revolutionary uprisings inside the country, the Soviet State stood firm against the overwhelming forces of the invaders. In the midst of this struggle Lenin said in his report to the Eighth Congress of the Russian Communist Party on 18 March 1919:

> "We are living not merely in a State, but in a system of states, and it is inconceivable for the Soviet Republic to exist alongside the imperialist States for any length of time. One or the other must triumph in the end. And before that end comes there will have to be a series of frightful collisions between the Soviet Republic and the bourgeois States."[42]

This and some of Lenin's other statements on this question have been quoted time and again by the opponents of peaceful coexistence in their vain efforts to prove that Lenin held peaceful coexistence of States belonging to the two opposing systems impossible and that, in his opinion, the new, socialist State would go to war against the capitalist States in order to spread socialism.

In advancing such allegations the most reactionary forces in the capitalist countries tried to justify their armed attack against the Soviet State, i.e., their military intervention in Russia soon after the October Revolution to destroy the emerging socialist system and restore capitalism in Russia. Now such allegations are intended primarily to discredit the Soviet policy of peaceful coexistence by presenting it as a tactical manoeuvre.

These allegations have been proved false by the whole history of the Soviet foreign policy. As has been stated above the very first step of the Soviet State was to propose to the capitalist States peace and friendly relations. Lenin considered wars between the Soviet State and the capitalist countries inevitable only because he was sure that the capitalist States would attack the Soviet State. Those who try to pervert Lenin's policy of peaceful coexistence, proclaimed on the very first day of the existence of the Soviet State, have to prove that it was not the capitalist countries that attacked Soviet Russia but that it was Soviet Russia that attacked the capitalist countries. The facts of an armed attack by the capitalist States against Soviet Russia- are, however, too well known.

At the end of the intervention, in November 1920, Lenin summed up the developments in the following terms:

> "We are now in a position of having won conditions enabling us to exist side by side with capitalist powers, who are now compelled to enter into

41 *The CPSU in Resolutions and Decisions of Congresses, Conferences, and Plenary Meetings of the Central Committee*, Moscow 1953, Part 1, p. 404.

42 Lenin, *Collected Works*, Moscow, Vol. 29, p. 153.

> trade relations with us ... We have something more than a breathing-space: we have entered a new period, in which we have won the right to our fundamental international existence in the network of capitalist States."[43]

Lenin repeatedly underlined the Soviet desire to live in peace with the capitalist countries and to develop economic and other relations with them. So, in 1922, referring to Soviet Russia's relations with Britain and France, Lenin told correspondents of two British newspapers, the Observer and the Manchester Guardian: "We believe fully friendly relations with both powers to be quite possible, and that is our aim. We believe that the interests of Britain and France, rightly understood, will likewise operate in that direction."[44]

There is much confusion in the Western legal and political literature with regard to the notions of "coexistence" and "peaceful coexistence". Coexistence of States belonging to the two diametrically different socioeconomic systems is an inevitable parallel existence of such States during the period of translation from capitalism to socialism. It is an objective fact. Peaceful coexistence of States with different socio-economic systems is a desirable state of relations between these States, which is not automatically available, but requires certain efforts to be achieved, maintained and developed.

However there are powerful objective factors that tend toward peaceful coexistence and the influence of which is growing. They make peaceful coexistence more and more an objective necessity for present day society. Lenin's theory of peaceful coexistence was based on objective laws of the development of society. Growing internationalisation of economic as well as other aspects of life is a powerful factor for peaceful coexistence. More than half a century ago, referring to this factor, Lenin said: "There is a force more powerful than the wishes, the will and the decisions of any of the governments or classes that are hostile to us. That force is world general economic relations, which compel them to make contact with us."[45]

The growing might and influence of socialism, the emergence of many newly independent States, the rising power of the working class and of all democratic forces in the capitalist countries are the most important social factors operating in favour of peaceful coexistence.

The emergence of the weapons of mass destruction making any eventual great war a catastrophe, leaves but one reasonable way for humanity – the way of peaceful coexistence.

That is why the Soviet Union spares no effort to develop peaceful coexistence between socialist and capitalist States. In his report to the 25th Congress of the CPSU, approved by the Congress, the General Secretary of the Party, L. I. Brezhnev, said: "The struggle to consolidate the principles of peaceful coexistence, to assure lasting peace, to reduce, and in the longer term to eliminate, the danger of another world war has been, and remains, the main element of our policy towards the capitalist States."[46]

---

43 Lenin, *On the Foreign Policy of the Soviet State*, pp. 287-288.

44 Lenin, *On the Foreign Policy of the Soviet State*, pp. 386-387.

45 Lenin, *Collected Works*, Vol. 33, p. 155.

46 L. I. Brezhnev, *Report of the CPSU Central Committee and the Immediate Tasks of the Party in Home and Foreign Policy*, Moscow 1976, p. 20.

Two aspects of Lenin's theory of peaceful coexistence are all important: (a) the inevitable struggle between States belonging to different socio-economic systems must be pursued by peaceful means only; (b) co-operation, normal and as far as possible friendly relations between them must be developed.

Contrary to an erroneous idea maintained by many sovietologists in the West, the Communist party of the Soviet Union and the Soviet Government have never understood "peaceful coexistence" as meaning a simple parallel without war existence of States belonging to two opposing socio-economic systems. Soviet understanding of peaceful coexistence has always included the co-operation of these States in various fields. Developing Lenin's theory of peaceful coexistence and outlining various aspects of it, the Programme of the CPSU (1961) says that peaceful coexistence implies renunciation of war as a means of settling international disputes, and their solution by negotiation; equality, mutual understanding and trust between countries; consideration for each other's interests; non-interference in internal affairs; recognition of the right of every nation to solve its problems by itself; strict respect for the sovereignty and territorial integrity of all countries; promotion of economic and cultural co-operation on the basis of complete equality and mutual benefit.[47]

The question is often put forward, why do we consider the struggle between States belonging to the opposing socio-economic systems as part of the notion of peaceful coexistence. The answer is that the notion of peaceful coexistence should not, in our opinion, be a pure desideratum, but a scientific notion based on realities of life, whether we like them or not. History shows that there has always been a struggle among States, the roots of which are hidden in the class nature of society.

How can one expect that peaceful coexistence of States belonging to the two diametrically opposite socio-economic systems could exclude struggle between States? It would be hypocrisy or lack of understanding. The struggle between States of different socio-economic systems is a reality and it will continue, whether we speak of it or not. We have to present things as they are and not to hide them from the people.

We should also not lose sight of the fact that many of those who accuse us of including struggle between States in the notion of peaceful coexistence wage a relentless struggle against the socialist countries, while hypocritically declaring that they reject peaceful coexistence because it includes struggle among States.

The struggle between States of different socio-economic systems as part of the notion of peaceful coexistence embraces all spheres of their relations: economic and political relations, ideology, etc. But what is of paramount importance is that this struggle is not meant as pure confrontation; it exists side by side with co-operation among the same States. The struggle and co-operation between States interpenetrate. Of course struggle can eliminate co-operation, but co-operation among States cannot eliminate struggle between them. When States belonging to opposed socio-economic systems co-operate with each other, there is always an element of competition, i.e., struggle in the wide sense of this term.

47 See *Programme of the Communist Party of the Soviet Union*, Moscow 1961, p. 56.

In fostering peaceful coexistence the task is, therefore, not to exclude struggle between States. In accepting peaceful coexistence the socialist States do not abandon the Marxist-Leninist theory of class struggle, the struggle between socialism and capitalism as well as the ruling classes of the capitalist countries do not abandon their struggle against socialism. But the acceptance of peaceful coexistence by both parties means that they are bound to pursue this struggle by peaceful means only and in such a manner that it would not hamper the development of co-operation between them.

There is, however, one more element that is often not taken into consideration. Peaceful coexistence of States with opposing socioeconomic systems is something that is not so easy to achieve and to ensure. There are powerful forces in the world which oppose peaceful coexistence. The struggle against such forces is indispensable so as to make peaceful coexistence a reality.

The Soviet doctrine of peaceful coexistence singles out ideological struggle and with good reason. Of course the primary requirement of peaceful coexistence that the struggle must be pursued by peaceful means only, covers ideological struggle as well.

But if in the field of political, economic, technical, etc., relations there are possibilities for compromise and these compromises are indispensable for peaceful coexistence, in the field of ideology there is no place for compromise as the communist and bourgeois ideologies are irreconcilable. But such a compromise is not necessary for peaceful coexistence.

The struggle between States of opposing socio-economic systems is a specific form of the class struggle between socialism and capitalism. It is a class struggle because it is a struggle between States of a different class nature. The foreign policy of a State is always a class policy, a policy determined by a ruling class or ruling classes of the State. We have already discussed the problem of how class will of the State is determined by the sum-total of conditions in which the ruling class finds itself at a certain time. In contemporary international relations there is a clash, first of all, between foreign policies of the socialist and the capitalist States which have opposing class natures. It is a class struggle between socialism and capitalism.

At the same time this is a specific form of class struggle. It is not a direct confrontation of opposing social classes; the struggle is going on between States and therefore through States and in a specific sphere of societal relations – in interstate relations.

2. Peaceful Coexistence and the Development of International Law

As has been indicated above, peaceful coexistence means above all that the inevitable struggle between States is pursued by peaceful means only and co-operation between them enhanced.

It is easy to see that peaceful coexistence is propitious to the progressive development of international law. Indeed the climate of co-operation and peaceful settlement of international differences is essential for the development of international law as well as for its effectiveness. More than that. Peaceful settlement of differences and the development of co-operation among States inevitably lead to the creation of new norms of international law and to its progressive development in general.

This is true with regard to general international law as well as with regard to local international legal norms. The co-operation between the Allies in the Second World War made it possible to create the Charter of the United Nations which is the basic document of contemporary international law. The relaxation of tension in recent years has been marked by the conclusion of a number of important international treaties and adoption of other international normative documents of major importance, such as the Treaty on the Non- Proliferation of Nuclear Weapons of 1970, Declaration on Principles of International Law concerning Friendly Relations and Co-operation Among States in Accordance with the Charter of the United Nations of 1970, Treaty on the Prohibition of the Emplacement of Nuclear Weapons and other Weapons of Mass Destruction on the Seabed and the Ocean Floor and the Subsoil Thereof of 1972, Convention on the Prohibition of the Development, Production and Stockpiling of Bacteriological (Biological) and Toxic Weapons and on Their Destruction of 1972, Final Act of the Helsinki Conference on European Security and Co-operation of 1975 and many others.

As to the development of local international legal norms a striking example is the present relations between the Soviet Union and the United States since 1972. The détente in these relations resulted in the conclusion of dozens of Soviet-American agreements.

All this makes it possible to maintain the thesis this author advanced in his lectures at the Hague Academy in 1958, namely: "The possibility of the existence of general international law in our times is determined eventually by the possibility of the peaceful coexistence of States of two systems."[48]

Peaceful coexistence as well as the progressive development of international law are characterised by the co-operation and struggle between States. Although peaceful coexistence and the development of international law both take place in interstate relations, outside this sphere a great variety of social forces is involved in the struggle and co-operation on problems of peaceful coexistence and the progressive development of international law. These activities of social forces exercise their influence on the interstate processes.

There is one important relationship between the struggle for peaceful coexistence and the efforts for the progressive development of international law. States and social forces that fight for peaceful coexistence are also fighting for the progressive development of international law, whereas reactionary forces opposing peaceful coexistence also oppose the progressive development of international law.

As a result of the influence of the forces that fight for peaceful coexistence, the main requirements of peaceful coexistence have been embodied in principles and norms of contemporary general international law. General international law which is the foundation of the whole system of international law has acquired one of its main characteristics, namely it has become a law of peaceful coexistence.

The functioning of contemporary general international law is generally directed to ensuring normal functioning of the international system and above all to ensuring peaceful coexistence of States with diametrically different socio-economic systems.

48 G. Tunkin, "Coexistence and International Law", *RCADI*, 1958, p. 58; see also "Peaceful Coexistence and International Law", *Soviet State and Law*, 1956, No. 7, p. 6.

Part II
International Law and International Juridical System

Chapter IV International Juridical System

1. The System Approach to International Law

There is no generally accepted definition of the notion of "system". The present day Marxist-Leninist philosophy defines "system" approximately as a number of interrelated elements, an entity, having integral qualities and constituting a relatively separate unity in its relations with the environment.[49]

A system approach to the study of social phenomena means, therefore, that an object of study is considered as a unit of components in organic interaction and development. At the same time the system under study should also be considered in its interaction with other social phenomena outside the system, in other words, with the environment. Each system possesses a system quality resulting from various kinds of interactions. This quality differs from the sum-total of the qualities of its components. On the other hand each component of the system acquires a system quality which it does not have outside the system.

The system approach sets out an arduous task of taking into consideration an infinite number of variables that influence international relations and international law.

System approach has always been a basic premise of the Marxist-Leninist theory – dialectical materialism. F. Engels called dialectics "the science of universal interconnection".[50] Lenin characterised the most essential features of dialectics, particularly emphasising "the interdependence and the closest and indissoluble connection between all aspects of any phenomenon (history constantly revealing ever new aspects), a connection that provides a uniform and universal process of motion, one that follows

49 See V. S. Tuchtin, *Reflection, Systems, Cybernetics*, Moscow 1972, pp. 11-12; V. N. Sadovsky, *Fundamentals of the General Theory of Systems*, Moscow 1974, pp. 83-84.

50 F. Engels, *Dialectics of Nature*, Moscow 1972, p. 17.

definite laws . . ."[51] K. Marx widely applied the system approach in his famous treatise Das Kapital.

Modern system theories, although not essentially new, have added some useful methods and techniques to increase the effectiveness of scientific research.

System approach is not intended to replace the methods of normative analysis. Normative analysis is indispensable for legal science.

Marxist-Leninist science of law has, however, never considered normative analysis as sufficient for legal science. It has always studied law in general and international law in particular in its interaction with other social phenomena, especially with the economic structure of society and politics. That means that the Marxist-Leninist legal science has always applied the system approach.

The application of the modern system approach, based on the Marxist-Leninist theory, to the study of international relations and international law, which is now at its initial stage, presents new possibilities for the study of international phenomena.

2. The Contemporary International System

Subjects, the activities of which transcend national frontiers are diverse: States, intergovernmental organisations, non-governmental national and international organisations, individuals, private corporations, etc. Do all these subjects and relations between them constitute a system – an international system?

Although it is primarily a problem of the science of international relations, one or the other solution of it is of paramount importance to the science of international law.

In Western literature on international relations and international law there is a strong tendency to consider the international system as including all social relations transcending national frontiers. This is the notion on which Professor Ph. Jessup based his concept of "transnational law". Jessup wrote: "Transnational situations . . . may involve individuals, corporations, States, organisations of States or other groups."[52] Accordingly he is of the opinion that "instead of 'international law' the term 'transnational law' to include all law which regulates actions or events that transcend national frontiers" should be used.[53]

R. Aron considers that there are at present an "international society" and an "international system". The first, according to him, includes non-interstate relations, such as commercial exchanges, migration of persons, organisations which transcend national frontiers and so on, whereas the latter is a system of interstate relations.[54]

Professor W. Friedmann in his book *The Changing Structure of International Law* presented a somewhat different notion of international relations. According to him international relations are today developing on three levels, international, transnational

51 V. I. Lenin, *Collected Works*, Vol. 21, p. 54.

52 Ph. Jessup, *Transnational Law*, New Haven 1956, p. 3.

53 *Ibid.*, p. 2.

54 R. Aron, *Paix et guerre entre les nations*, Paris 1962, p. 115.

and supranational.[55] "International society", says Friedmann, is represented by the traditional system of interstate diplomatic relations, the relations of "coexistence".[56]

"Transnational society is represented by the increasing volume and scope of international co-operation in matters of common concern. The principal agents of these transnational relations are the States, using their instrumentalities of multilateral or bilateral international conventions, in such fields as international transport and communication, health, conservation of fisheries, meteorological standards and the alike. An important proportion of these transnational relations is, however, carried and promoted by semi-public and private groups dealing directly with each other."[57]

There are finally, says Friedmann, also important beginnings of a "supranational society, i.e., a society in which the activities and functions of States or groups are merged in permanent international institutions."[58] Taken together these three types of relations constitute the present day international relations.

A Soviet Academician N. Inozemzev gives the following definition of "international relations":

> "International relations, which reflect basic and superstructural relations inside States, constitute the sum-total of the economic, political, ideological, legal, diplomatic, military and other ties and interrelations between States and groups of States, between the main social classes, principal social, economic and political forces, organisations and social movements acting in the international arena, that is relations between peoples in the widest sense of this term."[59]

This is also a very wide definition which probably needs further elaboration and diversification as it includes the elements of a different nature.

A Soviet sociologist of international relations, E. Pozdnyakov, speaks of a system of global socio-economic relations (macrosystem) and a system of interstate relations as one of its subsystems. However he does not define the limits of the global system of socio-economic relations.[60]

There are evidently very close ties between interstate relations and relations between private individuals, corporations, etc., of different countries, as the latter also transcend State frontiers. Interstate relations decisively influence other transnational relations through international conventions governing such relations or other means. There is also a certain interaction between interstate and non-interstate relations, so that the latter exercise their influence on interstate relations.

55 W. Friedmann, *The Changing Structure of International Law*, London 1964, p. 37.
56 *Ibid.*, p. 37.
57 *Ibid.*, p. 37.
58 *Ibid.*, p. 38.
59 N. Inozemsev, "The Unity of Theory and Practice in the Leninist Policy of Peace", *Communist*, No. 18, 1975, p. 44.
60 See E. Pozdnyakov, *System Approach and International Relations*, Moscow 1976, pp. 36-37.

However, the nature of the elements and the nature of relations between them included in these definitions of "international system" are so different, that the question inevitably arises whether they constitute a single system, or whether we are faced with several, although interrelated, systems. This problem, as it seems, has not yet been solved by the science of international relations.

For the purpose of studying international law one has sufficient justification for envisaging the international system in a narrow sense of this term, as a system of global interstate relations. Such a system really exists. It includes States and state-like entities; peoples and nations, fighting for their independence, which are actually States in the process of formation; intergovernmental organisations and other associations of States; relations between these elements. It also comprises international law and other social norms operating in international relations.

It is hardly necessary to emphasise that the present day international system is a complex phenomenon. It is an international system of the period of transition from one socio-economic formation to another – from capitalism to communism, of which the initial stage is socialism.

It comprises States belonging to diametrically different socio-economic systems, States of a different class nature, big and small, States on different levels of economic development, etc. There are also contradictions between States of which the most deeply rooted are contradictions between the States belonging to diametrically different socioeconomic systems.

International relations are societal relations and therefore in the present day a specific form of the relations of classes, as States are class organisations. Struggle and co-operation. among States are therefore always present in the international system. The nature of the struggle and its intensity, the degree of co-operation, vary in space and time.

It is of paramount importance to keep constantly in mind that the main components of the international system – States – exist above all outside this system. This fact makes the relations between the international system and its environment quite specific. The specific character of these relations has its repercussions not only on the development and functioning of the international system, but also on the development and functioning of international law as part of the international system.

3. The Notion of International Juridical System

The growth of the forces of production and of international division of labour, accelerated by the revolution in science and technology, result in the rapid increase of internationalisation of economic and other aspects of life. This means ever-widening and deepening relations between countries which has led to the diversification of the normative means of regulating and developing these relations.

Alongside international law there have emerged new international norms, which are not norms of law but contain some legal element. These new norms are the recommendations of international organisations and international understanding like those embodied in the Final Act of the Conference on European Security and Co-operation of 1 August 1975.

If such is the case, there are good reasons for considering that international law, recommendations of international organisations and international understandings constitute one system of international norms, which may be named as international juridical system. Such a system would include not only legal, but also semi-legal norms, closely interrelated. All of them result from the co-ordination of the wills of States and are addressed to States. All of them are either fully or partially legal. All these features differentiate them from other social norms which may operate in the international system and, still more, from other components of this system.

There is also a specific part of the international juridical system – the internal law of international organisations which will be discussed separately.

It should, however, be emphasised that if all these three categories of international norms have some common element and constitute one system of such norms, they differ one from the other. This difference is especially great between norms of international law and the norms of two other categories.

Norms of international law embody full-size legal obligations of States resulting from the co-ordinating of their will. They constitute the basis of all other legal phenomena in the international system, including the legal element in the resolutions-recommendations and international understandings.

It is entirely wrong to assume that the difference between international law and the two other categories of international norms is disappearing. One can, for instance, hardly accept the view of Professor R. Falk when speaking about the United Nations General Assembly resolutions where he asserts: "The main point is that the traditional dichotomy between what is obligatory and what is permissive is crumbling and that therefore international lawyers need a more adequate . . . theory of legal obligation . . . ."[61] Professor E. Schwelb is of the opinion that the difference between treaties and resolutions of international organisations is being obliterated.[62]

The actual situation is that international law remains international law, but beside it there have emerged new international norms which are only partially legal and which are on the whole a less effective means of stabilising existing relations between States or creating new ones, but which are more flexible and therefore easier to agree upon or even in some instances better suited to the situation, than norms of international law.

4. Recommendations of International Organisations

Many of the resolutions of the present-day international organisations contain norms addressed to States. These resolutions may be binding upon the States members or may be resolutions-recommendations. Resolutions-recommendations are not legally

61 R. A. Falk, "New Approaches to the Study of International Law", *AJIL*, LXI (1967), p. 487.

62 E. Schwelb, "Neue Etappen der Fortentwicklung des Volkerrechts durch die Vereinten Nationen", *Archiv des Volkerrechts*, XIII (1966), p. 44.

binding upon States and member States "themselves determine their attitude to these resolutions".[63] These resolutions-recommendations are certainly the most numerous and very important acts of international organisations, especially of the United Nations.

The volume of these recommendatory norms that constitute a new phenomenon in international life is steadily growing. And there is hardly any doubt that these norms exercise a certain influence on the framework of the international system. They also play an increasing role in the process of the creation of norms of international law – a problem to be discussed later.

There is extensive literature on resolutions of international organisations, above all those of the General Assembly of the United Nations. But in our opinion an adequate solution to the problem has not yet been found.

The problem with which we are concerned now is whether the norms of recommendatory resolutions of international organisations contain some legal element, and if so, what it is.

There seem to be three main schools of thought on this problem which have found their expression primarily with regard to the resolutions of the United Nations General Assembly, namely: resolutions-recommendations of international organisations or at least some of them are legally binding upon member States; they have only political and moral significance; they possess a certain legal element.

The first view is expressed mainly by some African and Asian jurists. It reflects the tendency of many Afro-Asian States in the United Nations to increase the role of the General Assembly where they have a preponderant "numerical power".

Professor Elias, now a judge at the International Court of Justice, says as follows:

> "It seems clear that, as far as General Assembly recommendations in respect of the nine specifically enumerated matters in Article 18 (2) are concerned, its 'decisions' in the form of 'recommendations' are binding upon all concerned once they have been adopted by a two-thirds majority. As regards all other matters within the competence of the Assembly, a simple majority is all that is required by Article 18 (3) of the Charter."[64]

The reference to Article 18 (2) of the Charter in this case is, however, unjustified. Article 18 (2) deals not with the legal force of the resolutions, but only with the problem which questions are considered important and therefore resolutions on these questions require a two- thirds majority. Among the important questions mentioned in Article 18 (2) are both those regarding which the General Assembly takes binding decisions and those regarding which it may only adopt recommendations. The inference that all recommendations adopted by a two-thirds majority are binding is entirely wrong.

63 Memorandum of the USSR Government to the International Court of Justice, *ICJ Pleadings, Oral Arguments, Documents, Certain Expenses of the United Nations*, 1962, p. 274.

64 T. O. Elias, *Africa and the Development of International Law*, Leiden 1972, p. 71.

But Judge Elias goes much farther stating as follows:

> "If there is unanimity in the Assembly during the vote, all are bound, provided that the subject falls within its competence. If the vote is divided, then those States that vote for a particular resolution by the requisite majority are bound on the ground of consent and of estoppel. Those that abstain are also bound on the ground of acquiescence and tacit consent, since an abstention is not a negative vote; while those that vote against the resolution should be regarded as bound by the democratic principle that the majority view should always prevail where the vote has been truly free and fair and the requisite majority has been secured."[65]

The result of this reasoning is that all resolutions of the United Nations General Assembly are binding upon the members of the United Nations provided that the matters dealt with in these resolutions are within the competence of the Assembly. But the author forgets the Charter of the United Nations and in the name of democracy rejects the most important democratic principle of international relations *pacta sunt servanda*. The Charter is an international treaty and according to international law "every treaty in force is binding upon the parties to it and must be performed by them in good faith".[66] Indeed the author makes not even the slightest effort to base his conclusions on the provisions of the Charter.

Professor Asamoah, in discussing the legal significance of the declarations of the General Assembly of the United Nations, has come to the conclusion that they are agreements between States and as such binding upon those member States which have voted for them.[67] As Declarations are also resolutions and the Charter makes no distinction between them this reasoning refers by implication to all the General Assembly resolutions.

The basic assumption of the author that the declarations of the United Nations General Assembly are agreements is, as will be shown later, unfounded.

An Indian author, P. Menon, maintains that the General Assembly of the United Nations is an organ representing sovereign States and, therefore, representatives of States in the Assembly can bind their States. If these representatives approve a resolution, the States represented by them become "parties to the code of conduct resolved by the Assembly".[68]

The mistake of the author is evident. The General Assembly of the United Nations is a representative organ of States. But it is not a world parliament. The competence of this representative organ is defined by the States members themselves in the Charter of the United Nations. Therefore legal force of the decisions of this organ depends on the Charter, but not on abstract considerations regarding the representative character of the organ.

65 T. O. Elias, *op. cit.*, pp. 74-75.

66 Article 26 of the Vienna Convention on the Law of Treaties.

67 See O. Asamoah, *The Legal Significance of the Declarations of the General Assembly of the United Nations*, The Hague 1966, pp. 66-67.

68 P. K. Menon, "U.N. Special Committee and Decolonization", *The Indian Journal of International Law* (1969), p. 27.

The second school considers that the resolutions-recommendations possess no legal element at all and have political and moral significance only. So A. Verdross says: "If the General Assembly on the basis of the United Nations Charter may direct only recommendations to States, such resolutions may be neither binding nor quasi-binding".[69]

Professor S. Bastid is of the opinion that the resolutions-recommendations of international organisations "have only political significance".[70]

According to the third school the resolutions-recommendations of the United Nations General Assembly have some legal element, but there is a considerable divergence of opinion as to what this element actually is.

To clarify the situation three principal questions should be examined: is there any legal aspect to a rule of conduct enunciated in the norms of recommendatory resolutions; whether such norms have functions and if so what is their nature; whether such norms constitute a legal foundation for voluntary actions of States (the problem of legitimation).

To prove the legal character of the recommendations A. Malintoppi suggested the following: there is a basic obligation of each member of an international organisation to co-operate in achieving its goals. Recommendations are adopted exactly for this purpose. The member that does not comply with a recommendation does not fulfil this general obligation.[71]

Professor Virally says that the recommendation is first of all a diplomatic instrument.

> "This does not mean, however, that a recommendation has no legal significance at all. International organisations are created to promote international co-operation and on becoming members of these organisations the States undertake obligations to develop this co-operation and act accordingly (see, for example, Article 56). The recommendations constitute an instrument of this cooperation and consequently a means for the States members to fulfil their constitutional obligations by complying with the recommendations."[72]

Professor P. Vellas, of Toulouse University, is of the opinion that the recommendations of specialised agencies "possess a considerable socio-juridical power of applicability".[73]

Lauterpacht suggested another idea regarding legal aspects of recommendations. In his individual opinion on the South West Africa case in 1955 he argued that a resolution of the United Nations General Assembly is a "legal act" of a principal organ of the United Nations and that "all members of the organisation are obliged to consider it with respect due to a resolution of the General Assembly".[74]

---

69 A. Verdross, "Kann die Generalversammlung der Vereinten Nationen das Völkerrecht weiterbilden", *Zeitschrift für ausländisches öffentliches Recht und Völkerrecht*, XXVI, 1966, p. 693.

70 S. Bastid, *Droit international public. Le droit des organisations internationales*, Paris 1969-1970 (mimeo), fasc. 1, p. 91.

71 See A. Malintoppi, *Le raccommandazioni internazionali*, Milan 1958, p. 49 et seq.

72 Virally, *L'Organisation mondiale*, Paris 1972, p. 187.

73 P. Vellas, *Droit international public; institutions internationales*, Paris 1967, p. 214.

74 *ICJ Reports* 1955, p. 120.

There are specific provisions in the statutes of some international organisations connected with the resolutions-recommendations. The constitution of UNESCO says in Article IV, 4:

> "Each of the Member States shall submit recommendations or conventions to its competent authorities within a period of one year from the close of the session of the General Conference at which they were adopted."

Article VIII stipulates:

> "Each Member State shall report periodically to the Organisation, in a manner to be determined by the General Conference, on its laws, regulations and statistics relating to educational, scientific and cultural life and institutions, and on the action taken upon the recommendations and conventions referred to in Article IV, paragraph 4."

The constitution of the International Labour Organisation which was the first to contain such provisions goes a little further imposing upon its members by Article 19, 6, the following obligations:

(a) to bring the recommendation before the authority or authorities within whose competence the matter lies for the enactment of legislation or other action;

(b) to inform the Director-General of the International Labour Office of the measures taken in accordance with this Article to bring the recommendation before the said competent authority or authorities with particulars of the authority or authorities regarded as competent and of the action taken by them;

(c) to report to the Director-General of the International Labour Office at appropriate intervals as requested by the Governing Body the position of the law and practice in their country in regard to the matters dealt with in the recommendations showing the extent to which effect has been given or is proposed to be given to the provisions of the recommendations.

Somewhat analogous provisions exist in the constituent instruments of the World Health Organization and FAO.

With regard to such provisions of constituent instruments of international organisations there is one important nuance which is usually overlooked. These provisions belong to two different categories. The first category of constitutional provisions contains obligations of member States to perform certain acts in case a resolution-recommendation is adopted.

Such are the obligations of member States to bring the recommendations before the competent authority and to inform the Director-General that this has been done and also of the measures taken by the competent authority. In this case the norms of the resolution-recommendation do not function, the recommendation is a simple fact putting into operation relevant legal norms in force in the organisation.

Quite different seems to be another category of norms of constituent instruments of some international organisations stipulating that member States have to report to the organisation the position of the law and practice in their countries in regard to the matters dealt with in the recommendations showing the extent to which effect has been given or is proposed to be given to the provisions of the recommendations.

In this case the norms of the resolutions-recommendations operate as soon as States have to compare their laws and practices with these norms and to report the results. Such constitutional provisions therefore grant some legally binding force to the norms of resolutions-recommendations.

With regard to the existence of sanctions related to the norms of resolutions-recommendations different opinions have been expressed. A. Malintoppi considers that such sanctions exist and they are "social sanctions" which constitute a reaction of a social group against a State that refused to comply with the recommendations.[75]

Lauterpacht considered that there was a legal sanction with regard to the United Nations General Assembly resolutions although his reasoning was somewhat vague. He said that the State in its attitude towards the recommendations of the General Assembly, especially those adopted almost unanimously, crossed an imperceptible line dividing impropriety and illegality, between discretionary and arbitrary, between exercising a legal faculty not to comply with the recommendation and the abuse of this faculty and may find itself exposed to the consequences in the form of a legal sanction.[76]

Castañeda is of the opinion that although it is generally admitted that recommendations lack sanction in the juridical sense and that their value is political and moral, the distinction is neither obvious nor clear. "... The means of pressure", he says, "employed by international bodies to achieve the execution of a typically political, non- mandatory recommendation, are the same as those used to impose the compliance of juridical obligations."[77]

The problem of sanctions is closely related to the implementation of the resolutions-recommendations because measures taken by international organisations to put into effect such resolutions very often imply some pressure upon member States.

Indeed, very often international organisations, above all the United Nations, exercise some pressure upon a State that does not comply with its recommendation. This pressure may have different forms and degrees. It may take a form of a renewed invitation to States concerned to comply with the recommendation. And these invitations embody different degrees of pressure. The General Assembly of the United Nations has used in its resolutions such terms as: "invites all States", "requests member States", "appeals to the States", "calls upon all States", "urges the States", etc.

On important problems dealt with in its resolutions the General Assembly appointed special committees with the view to studying situations and report to the General Assembly for further action.

75 A. Malintoppi, *op. cit.*, pp. 49 et seq.

76 *ICJ Reports* 1955, *loc. cit.*, p. 120.

77 G. Castañeda, *Legal Effects of United Nations Resolutions*, New York and London 1969, p. 11.

As to the problem of legitimation, H. Lauterpacht expressed the following opinion on the United Nations General Assembly resolutions-recommendations "... Although on proper occasions they provide a legal authorisation for Members to act upon them individually or collectively, they do not create a legal obligation to comply with them."[78]

In discussing the resolutions-recommendations of international organisations we have in mind only those resolutions which are in conformity with the statute of each particular organisation, as the resolutions adopted in violation of the statute are legally non-existent.

In Soviet literature on international law there is complete agreement as to the political and moral influence of the resolutions-recommendations of international organisations, above all those of the United Nations General Assembly, if such resolutions have been adopted by the votes of States belonging to all existing principal political groups. As to the legal element of these resolutions, divergent opinions have been expressed, ranging from the assertions that they are legally binding to the opinion that they have political and moral significance only.[79]

The problem of the nature of the resolutions-recommendations of international organisations can be properly solved only if it is examined in the light of general theoretical propositions.

A resolution-recommendation of an international organisation is a result of the co-ordination of the wills of States members. The process of the co-ordination takes place on the basis of the constituent instrument of a particular organisation and produces an act of the organisation – a resolution-recommendation. The nature of such a resolution depends on the provisions of the constituent treaty and such supplementary agreements (express or tacit) of the members on the basis of the constituent instrument that can emerge in the course of the activities of the organisation.

A normative resolution-recommendation of an international organisation embodies the co-ordination of the wills of the States members with regard to the content of the rules of conduct.

However, resolutions-recommendations do not stop at that. They differ from the resolutions of international organisations by which they adopt texts of international treaties. In the latter case the co-ordination of the wills of States concerns the content of the rules of conduct embodied in the draft treaty, plus a tacit recommendation to the States to sign and ratify the treaty adopted. There is no invitation to apply immediately the provisions of the treaty.

In the case of recommendations of international organisations the co-ordination of the wills of States concerns the content of the rules of conduct fixed in the recommendation plus an invitation to the member States to comply with these rules of conduct.

This appeal may have a different degree of insistency. All this, however, does not convey to a resolution-recommendation any element of legal obligation to comply with its norms.

78 *ICJ Reports* 1955, p. 115.

79 See for a detailed analysis M. Yanovsky, *The General Assembly of the United Nations*, Kishenev 1971.

It seems that Malintoppi and Virally are, in principle, right that a legal element of the resolutions-recommendations stems from the following: international organisations are created to promote international co-operation and member States are under a general obligation to act accordingly; resolutions-recommendations constitute one of the instruments of this co-operation and consequently a means for the member States to fulfil this principal obligation by complying with the recommendations.

There are also specific provisions in the constituent instruments of some international organisations (UNESCO, ILO, WHO, FAO) to which we have referred earlier that imply some legal force of the recommendations.

It is necessary to emphasise that we speak of an element of legal obligation only, which may be different in different cases. It depends above all on the legal rules in force in the organisation concerned.

It seems at the same time that such circumstances, such as the character of a resolution, the statement of a State concerned regarding the illegality of the resolution and so on, may be relevant in each case.

Measures taken to ensure compliance of member States with the resolutions-recommendations or in case of non-compliance also have some legal element. They are not only "social sanctions".

Social sanctions really exist in the international system and they play an increasingly important role with regard to the norms of international law and other social international norms. But the existence of a social sanction does not in itself make an international norm a legal norm, or confer upon it some element of legal character. Social sanctions exist in the case of moral norms also and their presence is, therefore, not an indication of a legal element of the resolutions-recommendations.

A norm of international law, being a norm of law, is connected with legal sanctions applied in case of its violation. A legal sanction, in contradistinction to social sanctions related to moral norms, is a measure taken by States or international organisations as an organ of States on the basis of law.

The measures taken by the international organisations come, in some cases, very close to legal sanctions. They are intended to exercise pressure upon States to make them comply with the recommendations. They are taken by the international organisations on the basis of legal norms. They have, therefore, a legal element, although they are not legal sanctions.

Summing up we may say that the resolutions-recommendations of international organisations constitute a new category of international norms which are not norms of international law, but have some legal element, and therefore, should be considered part of the international juridical system.

5. International Understandings

The Final Act of the Conference on European Security and Co-operation, signed at Helsinki on 1 August 1975, has aroused vivid discussion among international lawyers as to what kind of a document it was.

It is evidently not an international treaty. This follows from the text of the Final Act and no representative of the States participating at the conference interpreted it as a treaty.

The document is called the Final Act. Of course, the denomination of a document has no legal significance.[80] Still there is good reason to believe that in this case the title of the document had been chosen with a view of not giving the impression it is an international treaty.

According to international practice a Final Act of Conference is a document stating formally which States participated at the Conference, what were its organs, what documents have been adopted and so on. However, in this case the Final Act is not a document of this sort, it is a normative document.

The Final Act carefully avoids the terminology used in international treaties, especially in its preamble and in the final provisions. In the preamble the formula "have accepted the following" has been used instead of a customary treaty formula "have agreed as follows" or "have agreed on the following".

Another indication that the participating States did not intend to conclude a treaty is the provision of the Final Act to the effect that, although the Final Act will be sent to the Secretary-General of the United Nations, it was not subject to registration under Article 102 of the Charter of the United Nations.

If the Final Act of the Helsinki Conference is not an international treaty, the problem does arise as to what kind of norms it contains.

The Final Act comprises at least two categories of norms. First of all there are principles embodied in the Declaration on Principles Guiding Relations between Participating States. These ten principles are principles of general international law binding these States independently of the Final Act. However, in comparison with the Declaration on Principles of International Law adopted by the United Nations General Assembly in 1970, the wording of the same principles in the Final Act is somewhat different.

This part of the Final Act may be considered as a concretisation and interpretation of the principles of general international law with regard to the relations between the participants of the Final Act.

What is the legal force of this part of the Final Act? This depends on the co-ordination of the wills of States the result of which is the provisions of the Final Act. There may be two possibilities.

The first one is to consider that as soon as the States embodied in this part of the Final Act generally recognised legally binding principles, the co-ordination of their wills with regard to this part comprised the legally binding force of such concretisation and interpretation also.

There are some indications, although not conclusive, in the Act itself militating in favour of this conclusion. This is first of all the title of the "Declaration on Principles Guiding Relations between Participating States". The preamble to the part entitled "Co-operation in the Field of Economics, of Science and Technology and of the Environment" emphasises that "their co-operation in this field should take place

80 See Article II of the Vienna Convention on the Law of Treaties.

in full respect for the principles guiding relations among participating States as set forth in the relevant document".

The alternative to this may be an interpretation that the Final Act is a unity and everything new it contains in the Declaration of Principles as compared with the existing norms of international law has the same nature as other parts of the Act.

The final answer to this question may give the practice of States only.

However, here we are concerned not with the Declaration of Principles but with the rest of the norms of the Final Act. With regard to the nature of these norms divergent opinions have been expressed.

Professor S. Malinin, of the University of Leningrad, is of the opinion that the Final Act "may be equated to regional agreements".[81] According to him the Final Act contains binding and recommendatory norms, both being norms of international law.[82]

Professor G. Ignatenko, of the Sverdlovsk Juridical Institute, considers that the Final Act is a complex document comprising ordinary norms of international law and also programme-declarations and recommendations. All of them are, however, norms of international law although norms of different kinds.[83]

Jean-Francois Prevost, of the University Paris X, suggested the following conception.

> "Having no legal force of a treaty, the Final Act possesses a specific legal force . . .[84] According to Prevost, the Final Act contains specific legal norms which he calls droit directif, viz, a law indicating direction. This law, says the author, "defines the goals which the States set forth and methods of their actions, being somewhat similar to general principles which must sustain and direct actions. We have to do here with somewhat similar to defining parameters of future actions of States".[85]

In spite of the difference between these three opinions all of them come generally to the same conclusion: norms of the Final Act, which we are discussing, are norms of international law, although they differ from the ordinary norms of this system of law.

An opposite point of view has been expressed by Professor I. Lukashuk, of the University of Kiev. According to him these norms are "political norms". He defines political norms as follows:

> "International political norm is a politically binding rule of conduct in international relations, which is created, implemented and enforced by political means. From the politically binding force of such kind of norms

---

81 S. Malinin, "The Conference of Helsinki (1975) and International Law", *Pravovedenie*, No. 2, 1976, p. 27.

82 *Ibid.*, p. 23.

83 G. Ignatenko, "The Final Act of the European Conference at Helsinki", *Pravovedenie*, No. 3, 1976, pp. 93, 97, 102-103.

84 Jean-Francois Prévost, "Observations sur la nature juridique de l'Acte final de la conférence sur la securitée et la coopeération en Europe", *Annuaire français de droit international*, 1975, p. 142.

85 *Ibid.*, p. 153.

> stems political responsibility. Political responsibility is a duty of a State to act in accordance with a political norm. Non-compliance with the norm leads to the application of sanctions against a delinquent State. Among political sanctions the principal place belongs today to measures depriving the delinquent State of the benefits connected with the association with the given political system."[86]

The idea is of interest, although it is not new. The primary thing of course is not the name to be given to these norms but their nature, what distinguishes them from the norms of international law and what is the nature of their binding force. The formula suggested by Professor Lukashuk does not specify this distinction and is therefore not convincing. Indeed, to say that political norms are created, implemented and enforced by political means, does not mean to distinguish them from the norms of international law as exactly the same may be said about the latter.

To define the nature and place of the norms in question we have again to consider them in the light of the process of the co-ordination of the wills of States, as this nature is determined in the course of this process.

Viewed against the process of creating norms of international law by means of international treaty, the Final Act of the Helsinki Conference covers, first of all, the first stage of this process: the co-ordination of the wills of States with regard to the content of the rules of conduct.

However the Final Act is more than the first stage in the norm- creating process. The first stage of the norm creating in international law ends with the adoption of the text of a multilateral treaty by an organ of international organisation or by an international conference. The co-ordination of the wills of States in this case does not contain an element of the invitation to comply with the rules adopted. A resolution by which an organ of international organisation adopts the texts often contains an invitation to the States to sign and ratify the treaty. So the General Assembly of the United Nations resolution 2200 (XXI) on International Covenants on Human Rights of 16 December 1966 said that the General Assembly "expresses the hope that the Covenants and the optional protocol will be signed and ratified or acceded to without delay and come into force at an early date".

The norms of the Final Act are binding norms. The General Secretary of the CPSU, L. I. Brezhnev, has rightly emphasised: "We consider the Final Act of the European Conference as a code of international obligations the sense of which is to ensure lasting peace."[87] Other participating States have also stressed the binding nature of the provisions of the Final Act.

What is the nature of these obligations? If the participating States had had the intention to give the norms in question the force of legal norms they would not have so carefully avoided creating an impression that the Final Act is an international treaty.

86 I. Lukashuk, "International Political Norms in the Period of Détente", *Soviet State and Law*, No. 8, 1976, pp. 107-108.

87 *Pravda*, 19 January 1977.

Above all the obligations embodied in the norms of the Final Act are of a moral character. The co-ordination of the wills of participating States went further than simply fixing the content of the rules of conduct. The text of the Final Act contains, inter alia, the following provisions: "have solemnly adopted the following"; "declare their resolve, in the period following the Conference, to pay due regard to and implement the provisions of the Final Act of the Conference"; "declaring their determination to act in accordance with the provisions contained in the above texts".

It may therefore be assumed that in this case the co-ordination of the wills of States included mutual intention, mutual promise, a word of honour to comply with the norms of the Act. It means that, first of all, the norms of the Final Act contain moral obligations.

There is also some legal element to these obligations. From the text of the Final Act and the statements of the participants at the Helsinki Conference it may be inferred that the wills of the participating States have been also co-ordinated to the effect of not divorcing the provisions of the Act from international law. The intention of the parties was, rather, to formulate on the basis of the principles of international law enunciated in the Declaration of Principles and in the light of the existing situation in Europe new norms which would be not only moral in character, but also to some extent legal norms. The co-ordination of the wills of the participating States has not brought these norms up to the level of the norms of international law. The legal element in these norms is less pronounced, they are less rigid than the norms of international law. These norms are therefore more flexible than the norms of international law.

The next problem is whether the norms of the Final Act have sanctions. In other words whether there has been the co-ordination of the wills of the participating States with regard to such sanctions. We have stated before that a full-size international legal sanction is proper to the norms of international law only.

In this case there are first of all purely "social sanctions" to the provisions of the Final Act. A violation of these provisions would certainly entail very strong public pressure upon the delinquent State. With the enormous growth of international and national non-governmental organisations this pressure is, nowadays, of the greatest importance.

Are there also other sanctions? The Final Act is silent on this subject. However there is hardly any doubt that, as soon as the coordination of the wills of the participating States included a specific binding force of the provisions of the Final Act, it also included measures against a State or States which do not comply with these provisions. These measures, as it seems, may be of two kinds (1) moral pressures; (2) some coercive measures similar to those applied in cases of the violations of the norms of international law.

The conclusion is that the norms of the Final Act (with the exception of the principles) which are often called "understandings", are of a semi-legal nature, and there are therefore sufficient reasons to consider them as part of the international juridical system.

Discussing the nature of international understanding we have taken as an example the norms of the Final Act of the Helsinki Conference. It is evident, however, that international understanding may be also bilateral, and they are many.

6. Internal Law of International Organisations

Internal law of international organisations as it is understood here[88] is also part of the international juridical system. However this component of the system is so specific, its nature depends so much on the nature of contemporary international organisations, that the analysis of the subject is left to the part of this work dealing with international organisations.

88 See Chapter XI.

Chapter V Some Problems of the Present System of International Law

1. Preliminary Remarks

The problem of a system of contemporary international law has been much neglected during the last decades. It is true that considerable research has been made on some important problems relating to the system of international law, such as *jus cogens*, general principles of law, fundamental principles of international law, and principles of socialist internationalism. But the problem of the system of contemporary international law as a new historic type of international law has been studied very little.

Some new conceptions in the capitalist countries concerning the system of international law have brought much confusion into this subject. This confusion stems mainly from the tendencies to present private corporations and individuals as subjects of international law.

These tendencies reflect the interests of the big business corporations, especially multinational corporations, which are, to use the words of R. Barber, "The colonisators of the XXth century".[89]

Now they want to have a full-size legal personality in public international law which would certainly open for them new possibilities of profit-making. But to demand the place of subjects of international law for private corporations only, whose activities are looked upon by the peoples with increasing anxiety, would be very awkward politically. Therefore the problem of the individual as subject of international law has been pushed to the first plan to camouflage the principal issue.

Such is the substance of the situation, although probably the majority of the proponents of the idea of international personality of individuals and private corporations are guided by different motives.

The above-mentioned tendencies take shape in different conceptions such as "transnational law", or the like, which put together norms of public international law, private international law and partially of municipal law of States.

Problems of the system of international law are many. We are discussing in this chapter some of them only.

89 R. Barber, *Le pouvoir américain*, 1972, p. 337.

2. Is There a System of International Law?

According to a theory which prevailed in the German doctrine of international law in the second half of the 19th century, a system of law is possible only if there is a supreme authority which creates such a system. As soon as international law has no such authority there can be no system of international law.

H. Heller maintained, for instance, that there was not and could be no system of international law. "A system of law", he wrote, "presupposes the sovereignty; it exists only there where there is a universal decision and executive authority which makes the system of law and ensures its operation".[90]

Theories of this kind exist even today in a disguised form. In our opinion, the Lasswell-Macdugal theory is basically a theory of this type. Indeed, they strongly attack the idea that the present-day international law is a universal system. They say that "the discrediting of claims to universality which are in fact false is thus a first necessary step toward clarifying the common goals, interpretations and procedures essential to achieve an effective international order. . . ."[91] "Obviously today", they say, "it is more accurate to speak of international laws or multinational law than of international law."[92]

Such an approach to a system of international law is a logical sequence of their theory that in fact fuses international law with policy and presents it as a simple tool of policy. Professor Anderson of the University of California has rightly pointed out that Macdugal "denies the normative quality of the rules of international law and decides questions of 'legality' under the law of nations by primary reference to extra-legal sources".[93]

Professor Barkun asserted that "all manner of conceptual confusion lies" in the notion of international law "as a coherent body of law".[94] He stressed this point by saying further that "the view that international law constitutes an external standard to which States should be held . . . serves only to blur our understanding of what actually occurs in international relations".[95]

We reject as completely divorced from reality this pessimistic and dangerous assessment which opens the Pandora's box of power politics. A system is not something imposed upon a social reality from outside. It is a reality itself.

International law is a unit, an aggregate of legal norms in interaction. A change of one element of this system inevitably influences in greater or smaller degree other elements of the system. So the cardinal change of fundamental principles of international law which has taken place after the Great October Socialist Revolution has influenced other parts of international law. The elimination of the "right of a State to wage war"

90 H. Heller, *Die Souveranität*, Berlin 1927, p. 136.

91 M. Macdugal and H. Lasswell, "The Identification and Appraisal of Diverse Systems of Public Order", in *International Law in the 20th Century*, New York 1969, p. 173.

92 *Ibid.*, p. 178.

93 *AJIL*, Vol. 57 (1963), p. 378.

94 1972 *Proceedings of the American Society of International Law*, p. 41.

95 *Ibid.*, p. 42.

and the emergence in international law of the principle of the prohibition of aggressive war has led to the liquidation of the "right of the victor", the institute of conquest and to the expansion of the principles of State responsibility to the field of war. According to old general international law war was permitted and therefore there could be no responsibility for planning, preparation and initiation of war. As soon as aggressive war was prohibited there appeared in international law a responsibility for an aggressive war.

States have sufficiently clearly demonstrated that they consider international law as a system of legal norms and that international law should be taken as a unit, each element of which is interrelated with other parts of the unit. This position is demonstrated by every day practice of States and has found its expression in the Declaration on Principles of International Law adopted by the General Assembly of the United Nations in 1970 which says: "In their interpretation and application the above principles are interrelated and each principle should be construed in the context of the other principles."

Then, international law is a separate unity in its relations with the environment which is the international system. It is a specific component of the international system which must not be confused with other components of the system.

The emergence in international law of peremptory norms (*jus cogens*) as indicated in Article 53 of the Vienna Convention on the law of treaties of 1969 has certainly contributed to the coherence of the system of international law.

It must, however, be stressed that we speak of the system of international law which should not be confused with the notion of national legal systems.

3. The Unified System of Contemporary International Law

It has been stated earlier that as a result of fundamental changes the bourgeois international law has been transformed into a new historical type of international law – contemporary international law.

The question arises as to what has become of the principal division of international law into two parts: the law of peace and the law of war, which was characteristic of the previous historical types of international law.

This division was proper to international law when recourse to war by States in their relations was permitted. According to this international law States had a choice between peaceful relations and war.

Such a situation exists no more. Recourse to war and even to the threat or use of force in international relations is forbidden. States, therefore, have no choice between peace and war. The only state of relations among States that corresponds to international law is the state of peace and co-operation. There is, therefore, no division in the present-day international law into the law of peace and the law of war.

However to prohibit the recourse to war does not mean to abolish wars. Wars still occur and the rules of international law regarding the conduct of hostilities and related questions are necessary. There is no adequate denomination for this small part of international law. It is often called "the law of armed conflicts".

Professor W. Friedmann has suggested a new division of contemporary international law into two principal parts: the law of coexistence and the law of co-operation. In his essays The Changing Structure of International Law Friedmann formulated "the principal thesis" of his views in the following terms:

> "... In international law it is today of both theoretical and practical importance to distinguish between the international law of 'coexistence', governing essentially diplomatic interstate relations, and the international law of co-operation, expressed in the growing structure of international organisation and the pursuit of common human interests."[96]

The primary difference between contemporary international law and "traditional", in Friedmann's view, lies in the fact that a new important part, which he calls "co-operative international law" has emerged. The "traditional" part of contemporary international law is predicated on the conflict of national interests, whereas "co-operative international law" requires a community of these interests.[97]

Friedmann comes to a very pessimistic, but happily erroneous, conclusion: "'International law' can no longer be regarded as one body of principles, rather is it a general description of various patterns and levels of international legal relations, which are only to a limited extent governed by the same principles."[98]

Friedmann pointed out some important developments in international law, but failed to notice other important innovations. He is right when he speaks of the increasing importance in contemporary international law of the principles and norms relating to the co-operation of States in various fields. It may be even said that there are norms of international law which put stress on international co-operation whereas others concern primarily the struggle among States. So, the principle of the non-use of force concerns, first of all, the struggle among States prohibiting to use force as a means of this struggle. At the same time, however, this is one of the most important principles of international co-operation. The principles of sovereign equality of States and non-intervention are intended not only to keep the struggle among States within a certain framework, but they are also a very important legal basis of international co-operation. Therefore, the division of international law into the "law of coexistence" and "law of co-operation" proposed by Friedmann is artificial.

Friedmann is right when he says that there is a diversity in contemporary international law, even when he maintains that this diversity is growing. But he is wrong in generalising this tendency to the point that the present-day international law "can no longer be regarded as one body of principles".

It seems to us that the transformation of international law and the emergence of contemporary international law as a new historical type of international law, has

96 W. Friedmann, *The Changing Structure of International Law*, London 1964, p. xiii.

97 *Ibid.*, p. 367.

98 *Ibid.*, p. 367.

brought about a greater unity of international law on the universal level and greater diversity on a regional level.

The laws of societal development and other sociological factors which have determined the greater unity of general international law are mainly the following: the internationalisation of economic and other aspects of life; the emergence and growth of the socialist system; the disintegration of the colonial system; the growing importance of global problems.

The greater unity of general international law manifests itself first of all in the following features of contemporary international law.

There is no longer the division of international law into the law of peace and the law of war. There is a unified international law of peace and international co-operation, the last being the most important prerequisite of peace.

There is no more a legal difference of the status of States and peoples in international law, which existed in the old international law. According to contemporary international law all States and all peoples are equal.

The emergence and the growing number of the principles of *jus cogens* is also contributing to the unity of international law.

In spite of the division of the world into diametrically different socio-economic systems, the prevailing tendency is the growing unity of general international law and the expansion of it upon new fields of international relations.

At the same time there is a growing diversity of international legal norms on a regional level. This is determined mainly by the fact that the processes of internationalisation are more pronounced in the framework of each socio-economic system and regional groupings. The examples may be, on the one hand, the socialist international legal norms operating in the relations among socialist States, and, on the other hand, legal norms operating in the European Economic Community. Each of these groups of norms constitutes regional international legal norms. They differ from each other both in social and normative contents.

4. Universalism And Regionalism, in the System of International Law

The unity and diversity in international law, as has been indicated earlier, relate mainly to the two levels of international law: universal and regional. International law as a whole comprises general international law and particular international legal norms.

Norms of general international law result from the co-ordination of the wills of all or almost all States, therefore, States belonging to different socio-economic systems. As there is no central legislative authority in international law, particular norms created by the co-ordination of the wills of two States or a group of States have in principle the same legal foundation as the norms of general international law and should be considered as belonging to the *corpus juris gentium*.

Norms of general international law are created only by States whereas particular norms can be created also by other subjects of international law.

Most of the particular norms are conventional norms, or norms of resolutions of international organisations. In the bourgeois doctrine of international law the prevailing view is that general international law consists of customary norms only. However, recently, some leading authors in the West[99] have already rejected this view.[100]

It is true that a hundred years ago general international law consisted exclusively, or almost exclusively, of customary norms. But nowadays, with the increasing number of general multilateral treaties used to codify and to develop international law, general international law becomes more and more conventional international law. In many instances, however, norms of present day general international law are mixed norms, viz, norms that have become binding upon some States by the process of treaty-making, whereas for some others by the customary process.[101]

The role of particular norms in international law is very great. The situation in the international system is such that norms of general international law are in many instances not sufficient to properly govern relations between individual States having particular problems to be solved. In such cases especially in bilateral relations specific legal norms are required. When relations between two States develop satisfactorily the number of bilateral treaties between them is always growing. It is also true of local multilateral relations. Particular norms are therefore indispensable for the development of relations among States.

Particular norms are also of great importance for the proper functioning of norms of general international law. In a decentralised legal system such as international law the effective functioning of norms of general international law in many instances depends upon the creation by the States concerned of particular norms based on norms of general international law. These particular norms usually specify the rights and obligations of the parties in the light of the situation, thereby making norms of general international law more effective.

Although norms of general international law and particular legal norms have the same legal basis – the co-ordination of the wills of States – the distinction between them is of great importance. This distinction is in many instances not fully realised.

If norms of general international law result from the co-ordination of the wills of all States and particular norms from the co-ordination of the wills of some of them only, then the relationship between these two categories of norms should be considered in the light of the corresponding provisions of the Vienna Convention on the law of treaties of 1969. Article 41 of the Vienna Convention says:

> "1. Two or more of the parties to a multilateral treaty may conclude an agreement to modify the treaty as between themselves alone if:
> (a) the possibility of such a modification is provided for by the treaty; or
> (b) the modification in question is not prohibited by the treaty and;

99 C. De Visscher, H. Lauterpacht, Ch. Rousseau, A. Verdross, W. Friedmann.

100 For greater detail see G. Tunkin, *Theory of International Law*, pp. 137-147.

101 See Chapter VIII.

> (i) does not affect the enjoyment by the other parties of their rights under the treaty or the performance of their obligations;
> (ii) does not relate to a provision, derogation from which is incompatible with the effective execution of the object and purpose of the treaty as a whole."

With the exception of *jus cogens* other norms of general international law do not prohibit such modification that is the creation of particular norms between some States and binding upon these States only. But such particular norms cannot infringe upon the rights of other States.

5. *Jus Cogens*

In recent years the problem of *jus cogens* has attracted much attention from the experts on international law. This is mainly due to the discussions in the International Law Commission and at the Vienna Conference of 1968-1969 on the problem of the invalidity of treaties conflicting with peremptory norms of international law (*jus cogens*).

The controversy centres principally on the following questions: are there norms of international law from which States are not competent to derogate via treaty arrangement inter se; if there are such norms, what is their legal nature; which principles of international law of today may be considered as having the character of *jus cogens*.

For the partisans of natural law the problem is a simple one: there is a natural law, independent of the wills of States, binding upon them. Grotius stated that the natural law is so unshakeable that it cannot be changed, even by God.[102]

Vattel speaking of an "indispensable law of nations", said, "as this law is unshakeable and obligations imposed by it indispensable and unavoidable, nations cannot introduce into it any alterations by their agreements and cannot liberate themselves from these obligations either by unilateral act or by mutual consent".[103]

The contemporary school of natural law maintains the thesis that positive law is based on natural law, independent of the wills of States. This logically leads to the acceptance of principles from which States cannot deviate by an agreement.[104]

The normativist school, on the contrary, is inclined to deny the existence of principles of *jus cogens* and maintains that there is no legal limit to the freedom of States to create, by particular treaty arrangements, mutually binding legal norms.

In discussing the problem of whether norms of general international law have the character of *jus cogens*, Kelsen thinks that no clear answer to this question can be found in the traditional theory. Some writers maintain, he says, that there exists a complete, or almost complete, freedom of contract, while others maintain that treaties which are at

102 Grotius, *De Jure Belli Ac Pacis*, L.I.ch.1,X,5 (Russian translation), Moscow 1956.

103 Vattel, *Le droit des gens*, preliminary remarks, para. 9 (Russian transl.), Moscow 1960.

104 See, e.g., A. Verdross, *Völkerrecht*, 12, 14, 22, 130 (1964); Antonio Truyol y Serra, *Fundamentos de Derecho internacional Publico* 62 (1955); Antonio Marin Lopéz, *La Fundamentación Moderna del Derecho Internacional* 130 (1963).

variance with universally recognised principles of international law are null and void. And he adds the following pragmatic remark: "But they do not and cannot precisely designate the norms of general inter national law which have the character of *jus cogens*, that is to say, the application of which cannot be excluded by a treaty".[105] Nevertheless, he admits that a treaty by which two or more States release one another from the obligations imposed upon them by the norm of general international law prohibiting occupation of parts of the open sea, would be declared null and void by an international tribunal competent to deal with this case.[106] So Kelsen gives no positive answer to the question, but is disposed to think that all norms, of general international law have the character of jus dispositivum, whereas peremptory norms are only particular norms. This point of view has been much more emphasised in the second edition of his Principles of International Law.

The concept that there are no norms of *jus cogens* in international law was definitely laid down by Professor Guggenheim about 20 years ago when he wrote: "Norms of public international law do not possess the character of *jus cogens*. Therefore, according to international law, the treaty may have a content without any limitation whatsoever".[107] Meanwhile in the second edition of his treatise, Guggenheim comes out against principles of *jus cogens* much more cautiously. He says:

> "Bien qu'il n'y ait pas de raison d'ordre logique de ne pas admettre des principes d'un '*jus cogens*', il existe certaines difficultés d'accepter le '*jus cogens*' dans le cadre de la procédure actuelle de la création du droit des gens. La principale difficulté provient du fait que le droit international contemporain ne contient pas de règles générales qui entraineraient de plein droit la nullité de certaines normes conventionnelles qui lui seraient opposées."[108]

Generally, opponents of *jus cogens* base their arguments on the assumption that such principles are possible only in a well-organised and highly effective system of law. As international law does not represent such a system of law, it cannot contain principles having the character of *jus cogens*. This sort of argument has been most clearly stated by Professor Schwarzenberger:

> "Unlike municipal law, international customary law lacks rules of *jus cogens* or international public policy, that is, rules which, by consent, individual subjects of international law may not modify. In fact, *jus cogens*, as distinct from jus dispositivum, pre- supposes the existence of an effective de jure order, which has at its disposal legislative and judicial machinery, able to formulate rules of public policy, and, in the last resort, can rely on overwhelming physical force."[109]

105 H. Kelsen, *Principles of International Law*, 460 (1967).
106 H. Kelsen, *Principles of International Law*, 483 (1967).
107 P. Guggenheim, 1 *Traité de droit international public*, 57 (1953).
108 P. Guggenheim, 1 *Traité de droit international public*, 128 (1967).
109 G. Schwarzenberger, *A Manual of International Law*, 29-30 (1967).

However, the dominant point of view among Western international lawyers is that although most of the norms of general international law have the character of jus dispositivum, there are some norms from which States cannot derogate by a treaty arrangement inter se.

Lord McNair, maintaining that there are rules of public policy in any legal system, says "It is difficult to imagine any society, whether of individuals or of States, whose law sets no limit whatever to freedom of contract".[110]

Professor Verdross is also of the opinion that, "in any legal order there are certain basic rules which belong to the ordre public and thereby constitute its *jus cogens*".[111]

Professor Ch. Rousseau, comparing international law to internal law, says: "In international law, where there is no authority superior to subjects of law and where the creation of law depends upon these subjects, the existence of super-conventional public order is not so easy to conceive."[112]

According to Quadri, there are principles in international law which are the direct expression, ". . . de la volonté du corp social international". These principles are "primary norms" and as such they have a "superior force" with respect to all other norms.[113]

To Professor Dahm, there are some peremptory principles in international law, but they are rare.[114]

The opinion that the present-day international law contains some principles of *jus cogens* has prevailed also among the Western members of the International Law Commission.

It is worthwhile to point out that in spite of divergent opinions on the origin and essence of *jus cogens* expressed in the International Law Commission by the Western and Socialist representatives, the thesis that there are certain principles in international law which cannot be modified by an inter se agreement has been accepted by all the members of the Commission. This acceptance has led to the insertion in the Draft Articles on the law of treaties prepared by the Commission of Article 50 under the title, "Treaties conflicting with a peremptory norm of general international law (*jus cogens*)",[115] which later became Article 53 of the Vienna Convention on the law of treaties of 1969.

Professor Lauterpacht, in his report on the law of treaties presented to the International Law Commission in 1953, proposed an article whereby a treaty, ". . . is void if its performance involves an act which is illegal under international law. . . ."[116] In his commentary on this article, Lauterpacht said that the voidance of a treaty is due to an inconsistency with such overriding principles of international law which may be regarded as constituting principles of international public policy (ordre international public)".[117] To him these principles might be principles of law as well as principles ". . . expressive of rules of international morality".[118]

110 Lord McNair, *The Law of Treaties*, 213-14 (1961).

111 A. Verdross, *Völkerrecht*, 130 (1964).

112 Ch. Rousseau, *Droit international public*, tome I, Paris 1970, p. 150.

113 Quadri, "Cours général de droit international public", 113 *RCADI* 335 (1964).

114 I. Dahm, *Völkerrecht*, 6 (1958-1961).

115 (1966) 2 *ILC Yearbook*, 247.

116 Lauterpacht, "First Report on the Law of Treaties (1956)", 2 *ILC Yearbook* 154.

117 *Id.*, at 155.

118 *Id.*

Sir Gerald Fitzmaurice expressed a similar point of view in his third report on the Law of Treaties in 1958. He wrote:

> "It is essential to the validity of a treaty that it should be in conformity with or not contravene, or that its execution should not involve an infraction of those principles and rules of international law which are in the nature of *jus cogens*."[119]

The fourth rapporteur of the Commission on the law of treaties, Sir Humphrey Waldock, followed his predecessors and in his report of 1963 presented an article to the effect that a treaty is void, "... if its object or its execution involves the infringement of a general rule or principle of international law having the character of *jus cogens*".[120]

The special rapporteur's proposal met with the general approval of the Commission, although the wording of the article presented considerable difficulties. The text of the article as adopted by the Commission in 1963 reads as follows:

> "A treaty is void if it conflicts with a peremptory norm of general international law from which no derogation is permitted and which can be modified only by a subsequent norm of general international law having the same character."[121]

This draft article was discussed in the Commission for the second time in 1966 when the Commission had before it comments by governments and, opinions expressed by various representatives in the Sixth Committee of the United Nations General Assembly.

The final wording of the article (Article 50) adopted by the Commission was identical to the text of 1963.[122]

The Commission did not present a list of principles of *jus cogens*. After some discussion the Commission came to a justified conclusion that enumeration of such principles was outside the scope of the articles on the law of treaties. The present author stated in this connection that unequal treaties, inter alia, should be considered as void under this article.[123]

The discussions in the Sixth Committee of the General Assembly in 1963, 1966 and 1967 on the preliminary, as well as on the final Draft Articles on the law of treaties and the comments of governments, revealed a substantial measure of support for the article on *jus cogens*.

However, the comments by the Governments of the United States, the United Kingdom, France and some other countries, and the remarks made by the representatives of these governments in the Sixth Committee indicated that these governments

119 Fitzmaurice, "(Third) Report on the Law of Treaties (1958)", 2 *ILC Yearbook* 26.

120 Waldock, "(First) Report on the Law of Treaties (1963)", 2 *ILC Yearbook* 52.

121 *Id.*, at 198.

122 (1966) *ILC Yearbook* 247.

123 Tunkin (1963), 2 *ILC Yearbook* 69.

were actually against the article on *jus cogens*. Although not openly opposing the article, they pointed out that the lack of the enumeration of the principles and the absence of a provision for compulsory jurisdiction made the article unacceptable to them. In the present day situation regarding compulsory jurisdiction in international relations and the obvious impossibility of agreeing at the conference on a list of principles of *jus cogens*, such a position was tantamount to a rejection of the article.

The Government of the United States, in its comments on the Preliminary Draft Articles, recommended to the International Law Commission that it, "reconsider the provisions of that article and all aspects of the matter in which it might be applied, particularly the question as to who should decide when the facts justify application of the rule".[124]

The position was more explicitly stated in a note from the Permanent Representative of the United States to the United Nations on 2 October 1967. The note said that if, ". . . careful and meticulous delineation of existing peremptory norms is not carried out Article 50 might have a most disastrous effect upon international co-operation and harmony. . .".[125]

The United Kingdom representative in the Sixth Committee of the General Assembly stated in 1967 that the concept of *jus cogens* was still so underdeveloped that it was not ripe for inclusion in the codification of the law of treaties.[126]

The same trends with regard to the article on the principles of *jus cogens* may be traced through the debates on this subject at the Vienna Conference on the law of treaties of 1968-1969.

The delegations of the Socialist States and most of the delegations of Afro-Asian countries firmly supported the article concerning the principles of *jus cogens*. The representative of Mali, Mayga, in his intervention at the Conference on 7 May 1968 stated that the rules of *jus cogens* were a cornerstone of the progressive development of contemporary international law and they were essential for the stability of international relations and constituted one of the most effective instruments of peaceful coexistence of States with different economic and social systems.[127]

The delegations of principal capitalist countries opposed the adoption of this article. The United States delegation proposed a new wording of the article which differed considerably from that adopted by the International Law Commission. According to the American proposal, in order for a legal principle to be considered a principle of *jus cogens* it should be accepted as such by national and regional legal systems.[128] This actually meant that each State would be authorised to make its own legal system the supreme criterion for accepting or rejecting a particular principle as a principle of *jus cogens*.

The American amendment reflected the 19th-century German doctrine of "external State law". As the delegate of Cuba, Alvares Tabio, said, the United States amendment

124 1 *Comments by Governments* (23 Feb. 1965/UN Doc. A/CN.4/175).

125 UN Doc. A/6827/Add.2/1967.

126 22 *GAOR* (1967) Sixth Committee SR, 967 Meeting, para. 4.

127 UN Conf. on the Law of Treaties (1968), Doc. A/C.1/SE.56. 128.

128 *Id.*, Doc. A/6827/Add.2.

would subordinate the rules of *jus cogens* of international law to national and regional legal systems and would enable a State to thwart any rule of *jus cogens* by invoking its domestic legislation.[129] The delegate of Spain, de Castro, stressed that the effect of the United States amendment would be to revive the ultra-nationalist idea of what might be described as an external State law incompatible with the concept of real international law and that this would be a retrograde step in international law.

The United States delegation voted for the text of the article presented by the International Law Commission with insignificant alterations introduced at the Conference. At the same time the United States delegate, Kearney, in explaining his vote, made it abundantly clear that he did not expect that this article would actually operate. Expressing his concern over the article he said that instant declarations and paper resolutions did not establish customary international law for which a considerable body of unambiguous State practice is required.[130] The implication was that such a practice was still non-existent.

The British delegation, although recognising the existence of the principles of *jus cogens*, opposed the adoption of the article. The British delegate, Sinclair, stated, that he would not dispute that international law now contained certain peremptory norms, in the sense in which that term was used in the article proposed by the International Law Commission, but international society and international law had not yet developed to a stage where it was possible to define where the borderline between peremptory and other rules of international law lay.[131] The British delegation was among those that abstained during the vote on this article.

The article on *jus cogens* was adopted by 87 votes to 8 with 12 abstentions.

The text of the adopted article which became Article 53 of the Vienna Convention differs from the text of the International Law Commission only in wording and is as follows:

> "A treaty is void if, at the time of its conclusion, it conflicts with a peremptory norm of general international law. For the purposes of the present Convention, a peremptory norm of general international law is a norm accepted and recognised by the international community of States as a whole as a norm from which no derogation is permitted and which can be modified only by a subsequent norm of general international law having the same character."[132]

The discussions at the Vienna Conference on the problem of *jus cogens* constitute sufficient evidence of recognition by all or almost all States of the existence of principles having the character of *jus cogens* in contemporary international law. The text of Article 53 of the Vienna Convention defines the content of these principles. All this

129 52 UN Conf. on the Law of Treaties (First Session 1968) O.R.
130 39 UN Conf. on the Law of Treaties (1968), Doc. A/SR.20.
131 53 UN Conf. on the Law of Treaties (1968), O.R. (First Session).
132 UN Doc. A/Conf.39/27; 63 AJIL 875, 891; 8 Int'l Leg. Materials 679, 698 (1969).

may be considered as an important contribution to the progressive development of international law in response to some basic developments in international relations.

With the growth of economic, scientific, technical and other relations between States and the existence of weapons of mass destruction the number of international problems the settlement of which cannot be left to bilateral or local multilateral arrangements has increased and is constantly growing. These problems are of interest to many or all the States and the establishment of legal norms with regard to such problems by a group of States may damage interests of other States. The fact that principles of *jus cogens* grow in number and importance constitutes one of the reflections of these basic developments in the field of international law.

The legal nature of the *jus cogens* principles is also a source of continuing controversy. Some writers maintain that these principles are independent of the wills of States. Many of the Western jurists claim that the nature of *jus cogens* cannot be explained on the basis of the theory of the co-ordination of the wills of States.

Actually norms of general international law having the character of *jus cogens* may be created and are actually created by the co-ordination of the wills of States as are other norms of international law. The content of the *jus cogens* principles differs from that of other rules of international law. This means that the co-ordination of the wills of States which brings into being a principle of *jus cogens* differs in its content from that which creates "ordinary" norms of general international law.

All norms of international law are binding upon respective subjects of international law. A violation of any norm of international law involves international responsibility of a delinquent subject of international law. However, in most cases, States are competent to replace inter se norms of general international law by other rules of conduct different from the norms of general international law.

The content of each norm of *jus cogens* embodies the result of the co-ordination of the wills of States to the effect that no derogation from such a norm is permitted and that a derogatory agreement will be void. In other words, principles of *jus cogens* are created in the same manner as other norms of general international law, i.e., by treaty or custom. Lord McNair is right in saying that principles of *jus cogens* consist of "rules which have been accepted either expressly by treaty or tacitly by custom . . . ."[133]

Many norms of general international law are created jointly by treaty and custom.[134] This is also true with regard to principles of *jus cogens*. The principles of the Charter of the United Nations, which are principles of *jus cogens*, may seve as an example. For States that are members of the United Nations, they are conventional principles, whereas for States that are not members, they have become binding by way of custom.

It seems that in most instances, some existing norms of general international law acquire in the course of time the character of *jus cogens*. But this does not rule out that a principle of *jus cogens* may possess this character from its very inception.

133 Lord McNair, *op. cit.*, pp. 213-214.

134 See Chapter VIII.

There is a strong tendency to view the principles of *jus cogens* as principles based on international morality. It is true that certain principles of *jus cogens*, remaining legal norms, have acquired also the character of moral principles because they enjoyed strong moral support. It is also possible that principles of international morality become parallely principles of general international law with a character of *jus cogens* by way of the co-ordination of the wills of States to that effect.

Nevertheless, international law and international morality are different systems of social norms and in spite of a close connection between principles of *jus cogens* and principles of international morality, a Principle of general international law is a principle of *jus cogens* on the basis of international law, not on the basis of international morality.

An excellent example is the Niirnberg principles which, in my opinion, have the character of *jus cogens*. The norms relating to war crimes are old norms which have acquired the character of *jus cogens*. Norms concerning crimes against peace are relatively new and yet have had the *jus cogens* character from the very beginning. Norms regarding crimes against humanity have been mainly norms of international morality which have recently become norms of international *jus cogens*.

Article 53 of the Vienna Convention on the law of treaties deals only with the relationship between international treaties and principles of *jus cogens*. But the same problem does arise with regard to international local customary norms. It seems logical that the rule embodied in Article 53 should also apply to such norms.

As to international treaties, there is one problem which has not been adequately covered by the text of Article 53. International practice leaves no room for doubt that for some time general multilateral treaties have played an increasingly important role in creating norms of general international law, including rules of *jus cogens*. In principle, therefore, the problem of a conflict between such treaties and the peremptory norms of general international law does not arise, or if it may present itself in some instances it has quite a different nature. Article 53 may actually be applicable in its entirety only to local treaties, i.e., to bilateral or non-general multilateral treaties.

The problem of *jus cogens* is closely linked with the progressive development of international law and with the existence of regional legal norms. If principles of *jus cogens* are to exist they cannot bar the establishment of general or local norms which go beyond them in promoting peaceful and friendly relations among nations, corresponding to higher stages of international integration. Principles of *jus cogens* can also not prohibit the establishment of local norms which are different from them in their social contents.

6. Fundamental Principles of International Law

There is not a clear cut dividing line between principles and norms of international law. Broadly speaking principles are the most important and general norms of international law. Those principles which are of primary importance are often called fundamental principles of international law. The term is current in the present-day diplomatic practice and in the writings on international law. However, the Charter of the United Nations as well as the Declaration on Principles of International Law of 1970 speak of "principles" only. It is clear, however, that they deal with the most important principles of international law. The meaning seems to be that the term "principles" implies the primary importance of these norms.

The laws of societal development find their expression first of all and more markedly in fundamental principles which constitute the core of the present system of international law.

The nature of fundamental principles of international law determines the general character of a system of international law. Since the Great October Socialist Revolution there has been, as we have indicated previously, a substantial change first of all in the field of fundamental principles of international law. Some age-old principles of international law such as the right of a State to wage war and many others have disappeared and new principles such as prohibition of aggressive war and later on non-use of force have taken their place.

The process of the formation of new important principles of international law continues. Accordingly, we may often find a situation in international law when a new principle has already appeared, but continues to be in the process of formation. This may mean that the content of the principle has not yet been fully developed or that it has not acquired recognition by all States. Such is now, for instance, the position of the principles of disarmament and respect for human rights. The principle of disarmament does exist in contemporary international law, but its content comes down to the obligation of States to refrain from an arms race and to strive for disarmament by concluding an international agreement. It lacks therefore the most important element: the obligation of States to disarm or to reduce their armaments. But even in its present form the principle of disarmament is an important step forward in the development of international law. The obligation to strive for disarmament, reduction of armaments or for reducing or stopping the armament race has found its realisation in many international treaties such as the 1968 Treaty on the Non-Proliferation of Nuclear Weapons, the 1972 Convention on the Prohibition of Bacteriological Weapons, the Soviet-American strategic arms limitation agreements and many others.

As to the principle of respect for basic human rights the Charter of the United Nations has introduced this principle into international law. This principle, now accepted by all States, although lacking in precision as there is no enumeration of basic human rights, is of primary importance. It contains a very general obligation of States to respect basic human rights. It remains to specify which rights should be respected and how. This is being done, especially in the Covenants on human rights which have recently entered into force and in many collateral conventions such as the Convention on the Prevention of the Crime of Genocide (1948), the Convention on the Political Rights of Women (1953), the Convention on the Nationality of Married Women (1957), the Convention on the Elimination of all Forms of Racial Discrimination (1965) and many others. The situation with regard to this principle is therefore such that it has already been recognised by all States, but as to the content it has been specified in many international conventions to which not all the States are parties.

There is no general agreement as to the number of fundamental principles in contemporary international law. The Declaration of 1970 names seven principles, but it does not pretend to be exhaustive.

The Committee on Peaceful Coexistence of the International Law Association under the Chairmanship of Mr. H. Cochaux in which the present writer took an active part, approved the list of principles of international law that included 16 principles.[135]

The recent Soviet manual of international law presents the following system of fundamental principles:

I. The principle of peaceful coexistence.
II. Principles relating to the maintenance of international peace and security:
   (a) the principle of non-use of force and the threat of force;
   (b) the principle of peaceful settlement of international disputes;
   (c) the principle of collective security;
   (d) the principle of disarmament;
   (e) the principle of the prohibition of war propaganda.
III. General principles of international co-operation:
   (a) the principle of respect for State sovereignty;
   (b) the principle of equality of States;
   (c) the principle of non-intervention;
   (d) the principle of equal rights and self-determination of peoples;
   (e) the principle of co-operation;
   (f) the principle of respect for human rights;
   (g) the principle of fulfilment of international obligations.[136]

What is the position of the fundamental principles in the system of international law? Whether all fundamental principles are principles of *jus cogens*?

During the discussion of the seven principles in the Special Committee on Principles of International Law of the General Assembly some delegates expressed the opinion that these principles were of the nature of *jus cogens* (the delegate of Venezuela), whereas some others held that they were not *jus cogens* (the delegate of the United States).[137] Therefore, some writers are inclined to think that the principles enumerated in the Declaration of 1970 could not be considered as principles of *jus cogens*.[138]

It is doubtful that the position of those delegates in the Special Committee on Principles of International Law which refused to recognise the *jus cogens* character of these principles may be justified on the basis of the existing international law. The principles

135 See *Report of the Fifty-First Conference of the International Law Association*, Tokyo 1964.

136 See *International Law* (ed. G. Tunkin), Moscow 1974 (in Russian).

137 *Special Committee Report*, 1970, paras. 109 and 254.

138 See, for instance, A. Magarasevié, in *Principles of International Law concerning Friendly Relations and Co-operation* (ed. M. Sahović, Belgrade 1972, pp. 215-216).

stated in the Declaration of 1970 are principles of the Charter of the United Nations. As we have emphasised earlier, Article 103 of the Charter stipulates that in the event of a conflict between the obligations of the members of the United Nations under the Charter and their obligations under any other international agreement, their obligations under the Charter shall prevail. Although this formulation does not fully correspond to the notion of *jus cogens* it embodies a considerable part of this notion. It seems, however, that the practice of States which may be considered as recognised by States as legally binding, has gone farther in accepting the principles of the Charter as *jus cogens*. This is one of the reasons why the refusal to recognise the character of *jus cogens* with the principles enumerated in the Declaration of 1970 should be considered as incompatible with international law.

The second argument in favour of the *jus cogens* nature of these principles is that the International Law Commission after a thorough study had come to the conclusion that principles of *jus cogens* are part of the international law in force. Therefore Article 53 of the Vienna Convention on the law of treaties of 1969 is not an innovation but a statement of existing law. But if principles of *jus cogens* do exist in the present-day international law, then certainly they shall be looked for, first of all, among the fundamental principles of the contemporary international law. That means that the position according to which none of the fundamental principles enumerated in the Declaration of 1970 is a principle of *jus cogens*, is incompatible with international law.

There is, of course, a different question, namely whether the formulation of these principles in the Declaration has a force of *jus cogens*, or simply a binding force at all.[139]

The opinion generally accepted by the Soviet international lawyers is that all fundamental principles of the present-day international law are principles of *jus cogens*. However, no sufficient research has been made to prove whether all fundamental principles are peremptory or as it may be supposed some of them are only partially peremptory.

If the fundamental principles have the character of *jus cogens* then their position in the system of international law is clear: they are higher norms than other norms of international law. But regardless of whether a fundamental principle is *jus cogens* or partially *jus cogens* or not at all, it always differs legally from other norms of international law, at least as far as the responsibility for the violation of norms of international law is concerned. The violation of a fundamental principle which deals with vital international relations entails higher sanctions.

However, it is hardly justified to speak of these principles as "constitutional principles of the international society".[140] Such a concept is due to the natural law doctrine and also means the application of the notions of national legal systems to international law, which usually leads to confusion.

It should be stressed that fundamental principles of contemporary international law are more determined by the laws of societal development than other norms of

139 See Chapter X.

140 See, for instance, A. Verdross, *Völkerrecht*, pp. 20-21.

international law. They may be considered as an expression of these laws, which themselves are not legal phenomena, in the system of international law. But fundamental principles of international law are legal principles and as all other norms of international law they are created by the co-ordination of the wills of States.

7. General Principles of Law

The extensive Western literature on "general principles of law" is based mainly on Article 38 of the Statute of the Permanent Court of International Justice and on the travaux preparatoires of the Commission of Jurists of the League of Nations.

Meanwhile the Statute of the International Court of Justice is a new international treaty. This treaty has been concluded in conditions different from those under which the Statute of the Permanent Court of International Justice had come into being, the parties to these two treaties are different, and therefore the supposition that articles of the Statute of the International Court of Justice identical in formulation to articles of the Statute of the Permanent Court of International Justice mean always the same thing, is not justified.

For the interpretation of Article 38, I, c, of the Statute of the International Court of Justice, the intentions of the framers of the Statute of the Permanent Court of International Justice are mainly of historical interest, although in some instances they may be of importance according to the rules of interpretation of international treaties. It is generally accepted that the drafters of the Statute of the PCIJ, representing various systems of the bourgeois law, had it in mind to widen the possibilities of the Court in deciding contentious matters by giving it the right to refer to the principles common to the national legal systems of bourgeois States.

However, the interpretation of Article 38, I, c, of the Statute of the International Court of Justice cannot be based on this understanding. In interpreting this provision we have first to find out the intentions of States that took part in the San Francisco Conference of 1945 where this Statute was adopted. It is further indispensable to examine whether there has been subsequent practice of the implementation of this provision accepted by all the parties to the Statute as adding new elements to the interpretation of the said paragraph.[141]

The last question may be answered first: such practice in our view is non-existent.

As to the original meaning of Article 38, I, c, of the Statute of the ICJ attention should be drawn to a very important amendment adopted at the San Francisco Conference on the proposition of the delegation of Chile, namely – "whose function is to decide in accordance with international law such disputes as are submitted to it". And although Professor Bishop quite accurately specifies that this is the only difference between Article 38 of the Statute of the ICJ and Article 38 of the Statute of its predecessor[142] this "only difference" means quite a lot. It invalidates the understanding

141 See on this point G. Tunkin, "The Legal Nature of the United Nations", *RCADI*, Vol. III, 1966 (an offprint), pp. 25-28.

142 W. Bishop, *International Law. Cases and Materials*, Boston-Toronto, 1962, p. 22.

of Article 38, I, c, that was prevailing in the Commission of Jurists in 1920. It seems that this transformation of the meaning of Article 38, I, c, has been to a considerable extent responsible for an inconsistency of the practice of the ICJ with regard to the "general principles of law". In some instances the Court seems to have meant under this term fundamental principles of international law, such as respect of sovereignty;[143] or principles "common" to national legal systems;[144] or some legal postulates generally accepted, such as *res judicata*,[145] etc.

This amendment makes impossible the interpretation of Article 38, I, c, according to which "general principles of law" are simply principles "common to all civilised nations". It clearly defines that "general principles of law" are principles of international law.

It should be pointed out that the concept according to which "general principles of law" are principles common to legal systems of civilised nations has, quite independently of the intentions of its proponents, been used and is still being used, as an argument against socialist States and also against some developing countries, especially in cases of nationalisation of foreign property. Usually in such cases fundamental principles of national legal systems of the leading capitalist countries, such as the doctrine of acquired rights, adequate compensation for nationalised property of foreigners, etc., are presented as general principles of law of "civilised nations" binding upon all the States. The intention is to use the notion of "general principles of law" to make some principles of the bourgeois system of law "obligatory for all States".[146] Such attempts are legally without foundation and politically they may only lead to aggravating relations between States.

It is highly doubtful that the opinion of Abi-Saab on the subject corresponds to the reality. Concerning general principles of law he says as follows: "This source of international law is very important from the point of view of the newly independent States. It is through it that they hope their legal systems will contribute to the development of international law."[147] Experience of the International Law Commission, the Sixth Committee of the United Nations General Assembly and of various international conferences rather indicates that the newly independent States attach in this respect primary importance to the international treaty as a means of developing and changing international law.[148]

Attempts to justify these claims by references to the decisions of international courts and tribunals are unfounded. The practice to which such references are made is but a practice of certain bourgeois States. It is not general in the sense in which this should

143 Cf. *ICJ Reports* 1949, p. 35.

144 *ICJ Reports* 1955, p. 23.

145 Cf. *ICJ Reports* 1954, p. 53.

146 Cf. V. Koretzky, "General Principles of Law" in *International Law*, Kiev 1957 (in Russian).

147 G. M. Abi-Saab, "The Newly Independent States and the Rules of International law: an Outline", *Howard Law Journal*, Washington, Vol. 8 (1962), p. 109.

148 See in this sense R. Ago, "La codification du droit international et les problèmes de sa réalisation", *Mélanges Guggenheim*, p. 100.

be taken nowadays, and it has not been accepted as a rule of international law by States of different social and economic systems.

Taking into consideration the amendment adopted at the San Francisco Conference, general principles of law according to Article 38, I, c, of the ICJ Statute constitute a part of international law. It follows therefrom that the existence of similar principles in legal systems even of all the States does not mean that such principles are ipso facto general principles of law. To be applicable in international law they have to become part of this legal system.

However Article 38, I, c, of the Statute of the ICJ does not speak of the "general principles of international law" but of the "general principles of law". The direct logical consequence is that what is meant here are principles of law in general, principles common to all the existing law, to all the existing systems of law, i.e., common to national legal systems and to international law.

One may, to a considerable degree, accept the opinion of Professor Ch. Rousseau who submits that the general principles of law are "principles considered as constituting unavoidably part of any legal system".[149]

If, according to Article 38, I, c, of the Statute of the ICJ, "general principles of law" are principles common to national legal systems and to international law two questions arise: (a) are there actually principles common to national legal systems of States belonging to diametrically different social and economic systems, common to socialist law and to bourgeois law?; (b) are there principles common to a national legal system and to international law?

Kelsen says:

> "It is doubtful whether such principles common to the legal orders of the civilised nations exist at all, especially in view of the ideological antagonism which separates the communist from the capitalist, and the autocratic from the democratic legal systems."[150]

According to Professor Verdross,

> "nombre des principes généraux applicables aux relations internationales a subi une réduction par suite de la division des conceptions juridiques entre les Etats socialistes et les autres. Mais on peut penser que le développement des relations commerciales et culturelles entre eux va renverser ce mouvement".[151]

It should be stressed that there are no normative principles or norms common to two opposing systems of law: socialist and capitalist law. Rules of these systems of law, even when they appear identical, are basically different. Rules of law are not "pure" rules of

149 Ch. Rousseau, *Droit international public*, tome I, para. 517.

150 H. Kelsen, *Principles of International Law* (ed. by Tucker), 1967, pp. 539 bis 540.

151 A. Verdross, *op. cit.*, *Mélanges Guggenheim*, p. 525.

conduct, they are social rules, having social content. Norms of the socialist law and norms of the capitalist law are socially different: they embody different class wills, their aims are different as well as the roles they play in these two societies.

This, however, does not mean that there is nothing in common between norms of these opposing types of law. The content of a legal norm includes three elements: rule of conduct as such, aim, that always has social character and actual influence on social relations. The last two elements of the content of norms of socialist law and norms of capitalist law are always different, more than that – they are diametrically different. But the first element is very often the same.

This common element of the content of norms of different social types of national law has a considerable impact on the development of norms of international law. The existence of norms in various national legal systems which have this element in common, in other words norms that contain the same rule of conduct (although their social aims and actual influence may be different) may lead to the formation of corresponding principles and norms of international law (through treaty or custom). Such is the case of the principle of respect of sovereignty, of the State sovereignty over territorial sea, of many rules of the Covenants on Human Rights, etc.

These principles and norms of international law, i.e., principles and norms whose emergence in international law was due, or to a certain degree due, to the existence of the said common element in the content of norms of various national legal systems, are not "general principles of law" but simply principles and norms of international law. Being an integral part of international law such principles share, as has rightly been pointed out by Professor Bartos, the destiny of the system of international law.[152]

Principles and norms of national legal systems exercise a considerable influence on the development of international law, but through this they do not become part of international law. Principles and norms of a national legal system are the expression of the will of a ruling class (in a socialist State – of the whole people), whereas the class content of norms of international law is different: they are the result of the co-ordination of wills of States. Norms of domestic law may be changed by States, so that principles which are common to some national legal systems today may cease to be "common" tomorrow. Norms of a national legal system are binding only within the framework of this system, as one State cannot create norms binding upon other States.

A certain similarity of one element (rule of conduct) of the content of some norms of international law and norms of socialist and capitalist systems of law does not mean that these norms are identical. Two other elements of the content of these norms (social aims and actual influence on social relations) are different. Norms of national legal systems can be the "raw material" for the creation of norms of international law. But norms of international law made of this "raw material" and in some instances having apparent similarity with corresponding norms of national legal systems are actually different legal norms.

152 M. Bartos, "Transformation des principes généraux en regles positives du droit international", *Mélanges Andrassy* (an offprint), p. 2.

The answer to the two questions put forward above is therefore as follows: there are no norms of law that are common to the socialist and capitalist systems of law; there are no norms of law common to the contemporary international law and national legal systems.

There are, however, certain legal notions, legal postulates, rules of logic, rules of legal technique, that are often called "principles". They are used in application and interpretation of the rules of law – international and national, socialist and capitalist. They are actually not norms of law, they do not fix rights and obligations of subjects of law, but are in some instances indispensable for understanding the relationship of legal norms, their proper application, their contents, etc.

Few examples will suffice to demonstrate what these "principles" are like: lex specialis derogat generali, lex posterior derogat priori, nemo plus juris transfere potest quam ipse habet, *res judicata*, etc.

The much-discussed question of whether "general principles of law" constitute a separate source of international law is the question of how these principles enter international law. If they become part of international law through treaty or custom, they are not a source of international law. If they emerge in the system of international law by some other way, then the question arises – how? Those who entertain the latter point of view usually come volens nolens to the theory of natural law.

In the opinion of Professor Verdross, "general principles of law" are similar provisions which underlie national legal systems of civilised nations. They are the expression of natural law; they are not, however, principles of natural law as such, but principles of natural law as expressed in existing legal systems of States.[153] "General principles of law" are based on common legal conscience. They are distinct from general principles of international law, as "general principles of law" are not expressed in international treaties or custom.[154] "International law", says Professor Verdross, "is not only conventional and customary law; these two categories should be supplemented by general principles of law."[155]

We are not going to repeat here our criticism of various theories of natural law.[156] They confuse law with other social phenomena, introduce into law social phenomena which are not law.

Another point of view expressed in a widely quoted commentary by Lord Phillimore is that principles common to national legal systems, accepted in foro domestico constitute a reservoir from which the International Court may borrow, whenever necessary, and apply directly or use as material for creating norms of international law.[157]

153 A. Verdross, *Völkerrecht*, Vienna 1964, s. 23-24.

154 *Ibid.*, s. 147.

155 *Ibid.*, s. 151. See in this sense also Le Fur, "La coutume et les principes généraux du droit comme sources du droit international public", *Recueil Geny*, v. III, 1937, p. 368.

156 See G. Tunkin, *Voprosy teorii mezhdunarodnogo prava*, Moscow 1962, pp. 163-164. (French translation: *Droit international public. Problèmes theoriques*, Paris 1965, pp. 131-132; German translation: *Völkerrecht der Gegenwart*, Berlin 1963, ss. 133-134).

157 D. Anzilotti, *Corso di diritto internazionale*, Rome 1928, pp. 106-107; G. Morelli, *Nozioni di diritto internazionale*, Padova 1967, p. 46; S. Nahlk, *W step do nauki prawa miedzynarodowego*, Warsaw 1967, s. 382.

Meanwhile if the International Court were competent to borrow legal norms from national legal systems, it would mean that the Court had norm-creating functions. But the ICJ has no competence to create rules of law.

At the same time it can hardly be accepted that Article 38, I, c, means the inclusion into the system of international law of all principles "common" to various national legal systems. A number of norms of national legal systems which according to this concept should be considered as common to these systems are absolutely unacceptable in international law (for instance, the right of individuals to apply to courts, etc.). If not all common principles of national legal systems are included in international law, the question does arise who can choose and what are criteria for this choice. There is no answer to this question in this theory.

Even legal notions, postulates, etc., common to national legal systems cannot always be applied in international law. For instance such maxim generally accepted in national legal systems as *nemo judex in sua causa* is not applicable in international law; there is in principle no compulsory jurisdiction.

"General principles of law" are such "principles" which are common not only to national legal systems but at the same time also to international law. The fact that a certain notion, postulate, etc., is common to all national legal systems is not enough to consider it a "general principle of law", i.e., law in general. The evidence is necessary that such a "principle" exists also in international law. If this evidence is available the "principle" may be considered common to any system of law, "general principle of law".

How can legal notions, postulates, etc., common to national legal systems become applicable in international law? Evidently through their recognition by States as applicable in international law, i.e., through international treaty or custom. In the latter case the practice of the International Court of Justice may be of considerable importance.

In interpreting Article 38, I, c, of the Statute of the ICJ attention is usually concentrated on the first part of the paragraph and the second part – "recognised by civilised nations" is not duly taken into consideration. To become "general principles of law", legal notions, postulates, etc., common to national legal systems should be recognised by States as applicable in international law.

Therefore, in our opinion, "general principles of law" are legal notion, legal postulates, rules of logic and legal technique applied in national legal systems and in international law in the process of interpretation and application of rules of law. They enter the realm of international law through the co-ordination of the wills of States.

Our opinion on the subject seems to be very close to that of Professor Ch. Rousseau who says:

> "By custom or by treaty States themselves determine the content of their rights and obligations. But they may also recognise by a common accord that certain legal principles which already exist in other spheres of law will also be applied in their mutual relations."[158]

158 Ch. Rousseau, *Droit international public*, tome I, p. 371.

That means that Article 38, I, c, of the Statute of the ICJ contemplates a specific part of international law.

There is a strong tendency in contemporary Western doctrine of international law to magnify unduly the role of these "principles" common to national legal systems in international law. According to Professor Verdross, "general principles of law", being principles of natural law posed in national legal systems, are the basis of the whole system of international law.[159] Professor Waldock says that "general principles of law" constitute "the common law" of the international community[160] is of the opinion that principles common to national legal systems "give us the basic foundations of a universal system of international law", while the solution of this problem may require "a generation or a series of generations".[161] Professor Friedmann considers that general principles of law constitute "the principal source from which the new bodies of international law are being developed".[162]

The actual development of international law, especially in the postwar period, gives, in our opinion, no basis for such conclusions.

As to the role of "general principles of law" in the resolution of international disputes the difference of opinion is again considerable. According to one school of thought "general principles of law" are applicable only in instances when there are neither conventional nor customary rules of law available.[163] The others consider that in such situations the applicable law is derived from the "general principles of law".[164] Some authors are in favour of complete discretion of the Court in applying "general principles of law".[165]

In our opinion "general principles of law" as we understand them cannot be the sole legal basis for a court's decision, but in the process of interpretation and application the rules of international law may be referred to whenever circumstances so require.

8. The Principles of Socialist Internationalism

As was stated earlier[166] the principles of socialist internationalism derive from the principles of proletarian internationalism which were formed by the theory of Marxism-Leninism and by the practice of the workers' movement. In fact the principles of socialist internationalism constitute adaptation of the principles of proletarian internationalism to a new sphere of relations – relations between socialist States. They also represent a further development of the guiding ideas of the principles of proletarian internationalism.

159 A. Verdross, *Völkerrecht*, s. 22.

160 H. Waldock, "General Course on Public International Law", *RCADI*, Vol. 106 (1962), p. 54.

161 W. Jenks, *The Common Law on Mankind*, London 1958, p. 106.

162 W. Friedmann, "The Uses of 'General Principles' in the Development of International Law", *AJIL*, Vol. 57 (1963), p. 282.

163 E.g., A. Verdross, *Völkerrecht*, s. 148.

164 E.g., Lord McNair, Separate Opinion, *ICJ Reports* 1950, p. 148.

165 E.g., H. Lauterpacht, "Règles générales du droit de la paix", *RCADI*, Vol. 62 (1937), pp. 163-169.

166 See Chapter II, I.

Until the formation of a world socialist system after the Second World War the development of the principles of socialist internationalism as principles of interstate relations was limited. A full-scale development of these principles began after the Second World War with the emergence of a number of socialist States in Eastern Europe. As mutually accepted political principles of relations among socialist States they have acquired also legal character and become the guiding international legal principles of relations among socialist States.

The principles of socialist internationalism constitute a system of legal principles among which the principle of socialist internationalism stands out as a guiding principle. They include, also, other socialist principles, such as the principle of respect for State sovereignty, equality of States, mutual non-interference in internal affairs and mutual benefit.

The principle of socialist internationalism is a very broad principle meaning above all close co-operation and fraternal mutual assistance of socialist States. At the same time this principle requires that cooperation among socialist States be developed on the basis of principles of respect for sovereignty, equality, non-interference in internal affairs and mutual benefit. So with regard to the development of their economic co-operation the States members of the Council for Mutual Economic Assistance declared in 1971 the following:

> "The further extension and improvement Of co-operation and the development of socialist economic integration by the CMEA member-countries shall continue to be implemented in accordance with the principles of socialist internationalism, on the basis of respect for State sovereignty, independence and national interests, non-interference in the internal affairs of countries, complete equality, mutual advantage and comradely mutual assistance. Historical experience has fully confirmed the viability of these Marxist-Leninist principles of interstate relations of a new type, which fully comply with the objective requirement of strengthening socialist construction in every country, satisfy the conditions for the development of the socialist world system and help to create a firm basis for extensive and fruitful international cooperation."[167]

The principles of socialist internationalism are closely inter-related and no one of them may be considered in isolation. The principle of socialist internationalism as the basic principle of socialist interstate relations penetrates and unites all other socialist international legal principles.

The socialist principles of respect for State sovereignty, equality of States and non-interference in internal affairs differ fundamentally from the corresponding principles of general international law. They go further than principles of general international

167 *Comprehensive Programme for the Further Extension and Improvement of Co-operation and the Development of Socialist Economic Integration by the CMEA Member-Countries*, Moscow 1971, p. 15.

law in reflecting closer co-operation and greater friendship which exist between the socialist States than in global international relations.

The specific nature of these principles stems from the fact that they embody the co-ordination of the wills of socialist States. As a result their social content is different in comparison with the social content of the corresponding principles of general international law: they aim at strengthening and developing relations of the fraternal commonwealth of socialist countries, at ensuring the construction of socialism and communism, and at protecting the socialist States from the infringements of forces hostile to socialism.

Their normative contents also differ from that of the corresponding principles of general international law. For instance, the principle of respect for State sovereignty in general international law means the obligation to respect external independence and internal exclusive jurisdiction of States. Both relate to law, only, not to a factual situation, so that, even without the violation of this principle, weak States may actually be very much restricted in the exercise of their sovereign rights, because they find themselves under economic and other pressures from powerful States.

The socialist principle of respect for State sovereignty goes beyond purely formal respect for sovereignty. As a result of the influence of the principle of socialist internationalism, the socialist principle of respect for sovereignty includes the obligation of mutual assistance to ensure respect for State sovereignty.

Another example. The principle of equality of States in general international law means equal rights and obligations of States as subjects of international law. This is also a very important principle of general international law, but it provides again only for purely legal equality. It does not concern economic, political, military, etc., inequalities among States which are very great and which make themselves felt strongly in international life. This principle, therefore, cannot always ensure the realisation of equal in law rights of small and weak States in their relations with large and powerful States.

The socialist principle of equality of States, under the influence of the principle of socialist internationalism, again goes further than the principle of equality of States in general international law. Alongside, with respect for legal equality of States, it requires mutual assistance in the realisation of these equal rights, so that regardless of power or the level of economic development these equal rights could be used by every socialist State. This socialist principle goes still further and requires the exercise of mutual efforts and mutual assistance to achieve factual equality of socialist States, especially in economic development. One of the principal aims of economic co-operation between the socialist States set forth in the programme of socialist economic integration of 1971 is the "evening of their economic development levels".[168]

All this should not be interpreted as in any way minimizing the role and importance of the fundamental principles of general international law; their observance is the primary condition of the normal functioning of the international system. The intention is

168 *Comprehensive Programme for Further Extension and Improvement of Co-operation and the Development of Socialist Economic Integration by the CMEA Member-Countries*, Moscow 1971, p. 14.

only to show that the socialist international legal principles go beyond the minimum laid down by the general democratic principles of general international law and that they are socialist principles reflecting the nature of a new type of international relations – the socialist interstate relations.

There is no contradiction between the principles of socialist internationalism and the principles of general international law. The observance of the principles of socialist internationalism includes the observance of the principles of general international law.[169]

There is a growing number of other socialist international legal norms created in relations among the socialist States. These norms are created mainly by treaties, bilateral or multilateral, and concern various fields of relations among socialist States.[170]

The situation with regard to relations among socialist States is such that there function two types of norms: the socialist principles and norms and the general democratic principles and norms of general international law. According to the maxim lex specialis derogat generali, whenever there are socialist principles and norms they function first and where there are no such norms, norms of general international law do apply.

169 For a detailed analysis of the problem see E. Usenko in *The Council for Mutual Economic Assistance* (ed. E. Usenko), Moscow 1975, pp. 87-121.

170 See W. Seiffert (ed.), *Sozialistische Oekonomische Integrationrecht*, Berlin 1976.

Part III
The Process of Forming Norms of International Law

We are going to discuss in this part problems relating to the so-called "sources of international law". This term has been rightly criticised as inadequate. Indeed it does not reflect the fact that the formation of norms of international law is a process. However, as soon at the term "sources" is widely accepted in legal literature we use it sometimes as denoting, according to our understanding, not only final results of the process of forming international law norms, but the process as well.

Various theories regarding sources of international law reflect the differences of opinion concerning the nature of international law itself. Natural law theories, positivist theories, sociological theories of international law present different interpretations of sources of international law.

The theory of sources exposed here, although to some extent resembling each of the above-mentioned theories of sources, differs from them essentially. It is based on the Marxist-Leninist theory in general and on the Marxist-Leninist theory of international law in particular.

The immediate basis of our theory of sources of international law is the theory of co-ordination of the will of States.

Norms of international law originate and develop in international system. As an international system functions permanently the process of forming international law norms is also a permanent process.

That means that international law is in a process of constant change. There is nothing new in this statement, but still it poses some problems and, first of all, the centuries-old problem of stability and change.

The constant dynamism of international law does not mean, however, that one cannot define what are norms of international law at a certain moment.

Professor M. McDougal proclaims actually a complete uncertainty of international law. He states: "In the process of decision making in the world arena the technical rules that constitute the lex lata are continually being defined and redefined in the application of policy to ever changing facts in ever changing contexts."[171] This theory, based on the common-law countries internal practices, is completely alien to international

171 M. McDougal, "International Law, Power and Politics: A Contemporary Conception", *RCADI*, Vol. 82 (1953), p. 156.

law. If applied to international law it would mean – law is practice and practice is law. That would be a complete negation of international law. Professor R. Falk is right when speaking of McDougal's theory, he states:

> "... A stress on openness accentuates the potentiality of possible manipulation of legal rights and duties by powerful, anarchistic or desperate States. At the same time such openness impairs the capacity of legal criteria to provide the organised international community with impartial yardsticks by which to measure its response to crisis and conflict, and thereby to legitimise its own role in resolving international disputes and to make possible a clear decision achieved after minimum debate ... The McDougalian image is at once too complex and too vague to provide guidance either to national actors or to global institutions."[172]

The statement that international law is in constant change should not be understood as meaning that each norm of international law is in a process of continuing change. A norm of international law that has emerged as a result of the co-ordination of the wills of States or other subjects of international law, is a specific social phenomenon which is distinct from factual relations between subjects of international law. The change in factual relations does not automatically bring about change in international law. The change in international law can be effected only through legal processes of forming and changing norms of international law based on the co-ordination of the wills of States and other subjects of international law. This legal process is ignored by McDougal which leads him to equalising factual relations, State practice and policy with international law. In the McDougal's conception international law is destroyed, it disappears as a specific social phenomenon.

The formation and development of contemporary international law norms comprise three interrelated processes: treaty process, customary process and legally binding resolutions of international organisations. The last process is a new one that has emerged with the growth of international organisation. Its importance is growing although treaty and custom remain the only sources of general international law.

We do not discuss here the different processes of interpretation of norms of international law which influence the norm-creating process, but do not belong to it as such: judgments of the International Court of Justice and other international courts, decisions of international arbitral tribunals. International lawyers should overcome a confusion created by insistent efforts of Anglo-American lawyers to introduce into international law their domestic common-law practices with regard to the role of the courts' judgments in the development of law.

The science of international law influences the process of norm- creating by its contribution to forming a general approach to international law as well as by its concrete findings. But it is also outside the process of norm-creating.[173]

172 R. Falk, *The Status of Law in International Society*, Princeton 1970, pp. 47-48.

173 The author has discussed these subjects in his *Theory of International Law*, pp. 184-190.

Chapter VI The Treaty Process

Recent decades have witnessed a number of new developments in the treaty process of forming norms of international law. Due to the growth of international organisation new subdivisions of treaty process have emerged. If some 50 years ago treaties between States or semi-state entities were the only international treaties, now there are, in addition to them, also treaties between States and international organisations and treaties between international organisations. Of course, treaties between States remain the most important part of the treaty processes. Only these treaties of all the international treaties can create norms of general international law.

1. Treaties Between States

Treaties between States have grown immensely in number and now play the major role in the development of international law.

International organisations are taking an increasingly active part in the process of concluding treaties between States. More and more these treaties are concluded within the framework of international organisations especially that of the United Nations and specialised agencies.

Diversification, and in many instances simplification of forms of treaties, is also apparent.

The present day process of forming norms of international law by way of treaties between States may be divided into three stages: preparatory stage; the co-ordination of the States' wills concerning the contents of the rules of conduct; the co-ordination of States' wills concerning recognition of the rules of conduct as legally binding.

The preparatory stage plays a very important role in concluding multilateral treaties. It has many variations. In some rare instances this function is fulfilled by a non-governmental organisation like the International Maritime Committee, sometimes by Secretariats of international organisations. But in most cases the preparatory work is done by various committees and groups, acting as subsidiary organs of international organisations. They may be composed of independent experts, like the International Law Commission of the United Nations or of governmental representatives or experts.

The work of the International Law Commission composed of independent experts from various countries is not, however, divorced from the influence of governments. Candidates, from whom the General Assembly of the United Nations elects members of the Commission, are proposed by governments. Each year the Commission reports on its work to the General Assembly of the United Nations. This report is discussed in the Sixth Committee, an appropriate resolution is passed by the General Assembly on the suggestion of the Sixth Committee. The International Law Commission is bound to take into consideration these resolutions as well as the opinions expressed in the Sixth Committee. When draft articles on some subject are ready, they are circulated by the Secretary-General of the United Nations to the member States for their comments. Observations on the draft received from the governments are discussed in the Commission. The Commission, of course, is not bound by these observations. After that the Commission prepares the final draft of the articles. This final draft is presented by the Commission to the General Assembly which decides whether to convene a diplomatic conference for the elaboration of a convention on the basis of this draft or to instruct one of its Committees to discuss it and present a draft convention to the General Assembly for final approval.

Therefore, in this procedure there is some sort of participation of governments in the elaboration of the text of a treaty, but this participation can hardly be considered as a process of the co-ordination of the wills of States.

The other, more numerous, type of bodies dealing with the elaboration of preliminary texts of treaties comprises various commissions composed of the representatives of governments: the UN Commission on Human Rights, the UN Committee on Peaceful Uses of Outer Space, the UN Commission on Internatiohal Trade Law and also many ad hoc committees.

As soon as such bodies are composed of the representatives of States their work presents the co-ordination of the wills of States regarding the content of the corresponding rules of conduct, but is a preparatory one. They do not establish a final text of the treaty and, as a rule, not all interested States take part in such bodies.

The first stage of the co-ordination of the wills of States in the process of concluding multilateral treaties usually starts at a conference of plenipotentiaries, or in an organ of an international organisation. This stage terminates with the adoption of the text of a treaty as final.

The rules according to which the text is adopted by the conference are determined by the rules of procedure of the conference. In the past the dominant rule was that of unanimity. Later on, especially after the Second World War, two rules were usually applied: a simple-majority rule in a conference committee and a two-thirds majority rule in the plenary. The two stages of the adoption of the text afforded additional possibilities for the co-ordination of the wills of participating States. The space of time between the adoption of the text by the Committees and the voting in the plenary may be used for further negotiations, reconsideration of positions and the co-ordination of the wills of States. That is why, even in a case when the subject-matter cannot be divided between several committees of the conference, a committee of the whole is instituted to maintain the two stages of discussions first in the committee and second in the plenary.

Recently, a very useful innovation has been introduced, that of dividing an important international conference into two or more parts with a considerable lapse of time between them. Such a procedure was adopted for the Diplomatic Conference on the Law of Treaties, the first part of which took place in 1968 and the second in 1969. This procedure presents new opportunities for a deeper study of problems involved, for reconsidering positions in the light of all the circumstances. The time between the first and the second stages of the conference makes it possible for each government to consider carefully the results of the first stage of the conference, to have consultations with other governments and to introduce necessary changes into its position as formulated for the first stage of the conference. All this creates more favourable conditions for the co-ordination of the wills of States.

The third conference on the law of the sea has introduced a number of innovations. Two principal aspects of this conference may explain its specific features: the paramount importance of the problems involved; the majority of the participants being new States eager to exercise their influence and unwilling to entrust the preparation of a draft convention to any international body with limited membership. As a result there was actually no preparatory stage, although a preparatory committee was set up by the General Assembly of the United Nations. But almost all States participated in the work of this committee, a fact which has certainly greatly delayed the work and made it impossible to draft any text of an eventual convention. Actually that was a conference, not a preparatory stage of the conference.

When the Third Conference on the Law of the Sea officially opened in Caracas in 1974 there were no draft articles to discuss and no text was adopted by the Conference. So when the second session of the Conference started in Geneva in 1975 there was again no draft before it. At this session the Conference also failed to adopt any text: the Chairmen of the three committees of the Conference were each instructed to produce a single negotiating text intended to reflect the main tendencies of the conference. At the end of the third and fourth sessions of the Conference the same procedure was followed and new single negotiating texts were produced by the chairmen of the committees of the Conference.

Another important innovation with regard to the adoption of the texts of treaties by conferences and by organs of international organisations is the tendency to achieve general agreement and to adopt the text by consensus. This tendency has found, for the first time, its reflection in the Rules of Procedure of the Third Conference on the Law of the Sea. According to these rules all efforts should be made to achieve a consensus. Taking a vote is not excluded, but is considered as an extreme action to be avoided as far as possible.

Another important new rule in the Rules of Procedure of the Third Conference on the Law of the Sea is the majority of votes required for the adoption of a text. According to the rules commonly followed by international conferences of recent decades the text is adopted by a two-thirds majority of the representatives present and voting. The phrase "representatives present and voting" means representatives present and casting an affirmatve or negative vote. Representatives who abstain from voting are considered as not voting. In some instances it led to a peculiar situation when an article might be adopted by a very small number of votes because the majority of the representatives abstained. Considering the importance of the questions the Rules of Procedure of the Third Conference on the Law of the Sea provide that in the case of voting the required two-thirds majority should include not less that one-half of all the States participating in the Conference.

However, the rules of procedure of the Conference on the Representation of States in Their Relations with International Organisations which took place in the beginning of 1975, follow the old pattern of a two-thirds majority of the representatives present and voting.

If the elaboration of the text of a treaty takes place in an organ of an international organisation, the co-ordination of the wills of States proceeds according to the rules in force in the corresponding international organisation.

The first stage of the co-ordination of the wills of States, that is the co-ordination of the wills regarding the content of the rules of the treaty, terminates with the adoption of the text by an international conference or an organ of international organisation. The rules are already there, but they are still not norms of international law.

The second stage of the co-ordination of the wills of States, as has been pointed out earlier, is the co-ordination of these wills with regard to the recognition of the rules adopted by a conference or by an organ of an international organisation as legally binding.

The second stage consists of the individual actions of States such as signature, ratification, depositing or exchange of the instruments of ratification, etc.

The consent of a State to be bound by a treaty does not mean that the norms of the treaty become immediately binding upon that State. The co-ordination of the wills of States includes their mutual conditioning, their reciprocity. A State gives its consent to consider a treaty as binding on the condition that other State or States do the same.

In bilateral treaties, norms of the treaty become binding upon both participants simultaneously, either from the date of signature, exchange of the instruments of ratification, or on any other date specified in the treaty itself.

If a treaty is subject to ratification the ratification constitutes final consent of the State to be bound by the treaty as far as internal law of the State is concerned. However, on the international scale, the final act of the State is the exchange of or the depositing of the instruments of ratification.

In multilateral treaties the number of the instruments of ratification deposited with the depositary, required for its entry into force, is specified in each treaty. It cannot be less than two. In local multilateral treaties sometimes ratification by all the signatories is required. In general multilateral treaties open to participation of all States this figure varies, but it never includes all the signatories. The greatest number of ratifications required in existing treaties seems to be 35, as for instance in the International Covenants on Human Rights and in the Vienna Convention on the Representation of States in Their Relations with International Organisations of Universal Character of 1975. That means that many years may pass from the date when a State performed its final act in the process of the co-ordination of the wills of States and the date when the corresponding treaty enters into force and its provisions become binding upon this State.

The minimum of two ratifications required for the entry into force of an international treaty may be found in a number of international labour conventions.

The depositing of the last instrument of ratification required by the provisions of the treaty for its entering into force terminates the process of co-ordination of the wills of States and the provisions of the treaty become international legal norms. However, this process is terminated only for the parties to the treaty. It may, however, continue with regard to other States which may become parties to the treaty later on.

This is the normal way of forming norms of international law by way of treaties. In practice there are many deviations from this pattern. Very often, for instance, a treaty enters into force not immediately after the process of co-ordination of the wills of States has been completed, but some time later. Norms of international law emerge in this instance with the termination of the process of concluding the treaty, but until its entry into force they are in a latent state. Sometimes the situation is reversed. A number of treaties, bilateral as well as multilateral, provide that they would enter into force provisionally before the process of concluding the treaty is completed.[174]

The practice of some specialised international organisations has produced some simplified forms of concluding treaties between States and even some new forms of interstate treaties. For instance, according to the Constitution of the International Labour Organisation, a convention adopted by the ILO General Conference is signed by the President of the Conference and the Director-General of the Organisation. Then the text of the convention is circulated to member States for ratification. After ratifying a convention the government of the respective State notifies the Director-General of this fact. Signature of the convention by States and depositing of the instruments of ratification are dispensed with. An analogous simplified procedure of concluding international treaties is provided for by the UNESCO Constitution.[175] The Constitution (as also the constitutions of certain other specialised agencies) provides for the possibility of convening by decision of the General Conference of UNESCO, international conferences to discuss and adopt corresponding international conventions.[176]

The activities of international organisations have also produced new forms of interstate treaties which combine elements of unilateral acts of international organisations with those of international treaties, being in substance interstate treaties. We have in mind regulations adopted by some specialised international organisations, mainly on technical questions. The speedy progress in science and technique makes it indispensable to change some regulations quickly for which the classical procedure of concluding treaties is too slow.

As we have stated there are different procedures used but the most far-reaching is this: norms are adopted by an organ of an international organisation and they become binding upon all members of this organisation which have not informed the organisation that they do not accept them.

For instance, according to the constitution of the International Civil Aviation Organisation technical rules called standards adopted by the council of the Organisation

174 For examples see G. Tunkin, *Theory of International Law*, p. 100.

175 See Article 4.

176 See Article 4.

become effective for all members of the Organisation which have not notified their disagreement with them.

Sanitary and other regulations adopted by the World Health Organisation become binding upon all member States within a prescribed period (usually from 3-9 months) "except for such Members as may notify the Director-General of rejection or reservation".[177] The question of the acceptability of reservations is decided by the World Health Organisation Assembly which may reject reservation if it is incompatible with the character or purpose of the corresponding regulation. In this case the regulation does not apply to the State which made a reservation.

Some authors have suggested that such regulations constitute international legislation.[178] The emergence of such regulations reflects the increasing role of international organisations including that of their normative function. These regulations have two aspects. On the one hand, they are unilateral acts of international organisations, especially in those cases where such regulations are adopted not by plenary conferences of international organisations but by councils with limited participation of member States. On the other hand, they are international treaties. And this aspect is decisive. Indeed, they become binding upon a State only with its consent. It is true this consent is a tacit one, but it is present. Each member State when he receives such a regulation has to make a decision: to accept or to reject it. If it accepts the regulation, no action on its part is required. But no action in this case is an expression of the will of a State to accept the regulation. So to make the regulation binding upon the State this State has to remain silent, thereby giving its consent to be bound by the regulation. This is a specific way for a State to express its will, but the expression is there as well as the co-ordination of the wills of States. Such regulations therefore constitute a specific group of international treaties which are essentially treaties between States, but at the same time acts of international organisations.

2. Treaties with the Participation of International Organisations

Treaties concluded between States and international organisations or between international organisations themselves become more and more numerous as a result of the growing role of international organisations in international life.

They are international treaties. The validity of such treaties is determined on the basis of international law, primarily on the basis of the charters of the corresponding international organisations. Questions arising in connection with the operation of these treaties do not fall within the scope of the municipal law of States, unless the treaty itself provides otherwise, and are resolved on the basis of international law.

Treaties between States and international organisations and between international organisations create norms legally binding upon the parties to such treaties.

177 Article 22 of the Constitution of the WHO.

178 See, for instance, W. Friedmann, *The Changing Structure of International Law*, p. 280; I. Detter, *Law-Making by International Organisations*, Stockholm 1965, p. 321; P. Guggenheim, *Traité de droit international public*, t. I, 1967, p. 284; C. Colliard, *Institutions des relations internationales*, Paris 1974, p. 598.

All this does not mean however that such treaties can be equated to treaties between States. The specific nature of international organisations as interstate organisations affects the treaties which they conclude. Norms of these treaties are of a secondary nature. Their principal legal basis constitutes charters of international organisations.

The International Law Commission, when discussing articles on the law of treaties, rightly decided to formulate first draft articles relating only to the treaties between States. At the same time the Commission "recognised that international organisations may possess a certain capacity to enter into international agreements and that these agreements fall within the scope of the law of treaties".[179]

At the same time it should be emphasised once more that the legal nature of the process of forming norms of international law by way of concluding treaties between States or between States and international organisations or between international organisations is in essence the same – the co-ordination of the wills of subjects of international law. That means that the basic legal features of all these treaties are the same. Professor P. Reuter, special reporter of the International Law Commission on the subject of treaties concluded between States and international organisations or between two or more international organisations, is right in stating that "the actual bases of the Vienna convention on the law of treaties are common to treaties between States, treaties between States and international organisations and treaties between two or more international organisations . . ."[180]

There certainly exists a difference between treaties concluded between States and international organisations and between international organisations themselves. But how important is this difference? Professor Reuter's opinion is as follows: "It is therefore possible and even certain that in the case of certain specific problems it will be necessary to draw a distinction between the two categories mentioned above."[181] However, he suggested to the Commission not to separate these two categories of international treaties as soon as basic rules of the Vienna convention on the law of treaties are applicable to both these categories of treaties.[182]

Such a proposal seems reasonable, as there is no doubt that many rules will be the same for both categories of treaties and to separate them would lead to repetition. Still, these are two categories of treaties: there is a difference between them as regards participating subjects and, in most cases, also as regards objects of the treaties. It may be expected that these differences will lead in the course of time to increasing legal differentiation between these two groups of treaties.

179 *ILC Yearbook*, 1962, II, p. 161.

180 P. Reuter, Third report on treaties concluded between States and international organisations or between two or more international organisations. Doc. A/CN.4/279, 1974, paragraph 6.

181 Third report, paragraph 5.

182 *Ibid.*, paragraphs 6, 7.

Chapter VII The Customary Process

The essence of the customary process of forming norms of international law has been a matter of controversy for centuries. Various bourgeois theories on the subject may be divided into two major groups.

To one group belong theories which maintain that customary norms of international law are formed independently of the wills of States.

The second group comprises theories which consider that customary norms of international law have the same legal basis as conventional norms, that they result from the wills of States (agreement, consent, acquiescence, etc.). As has been pointed out earlier this type of theory was dominant in the West in the pre-imperialistic period of capitalism and reflected generally the ideas of bourgeois liberalism. In the period of imperialism the influence of these theories was gradually diminishing, giving way to neo-naturalist theories. In the period of coexistence of the two diametrically different socio-economic systems and especially after the Second World War, under the growing influence of the new sociological theories, the influence of the said theories has further diminished.

At present only a few Western international lawyers consider customary norms of international law as depending on the wills of States. So Professor Charles Chaumont has emphasised in his lectures at the Hague Academy of International Law that with regard to customary norms "one cannot escape the logic agreement".[183] Professor I. Brownlie is of the opinion that "ultimately custom depends on the consent of States".[184]

As has been indicated earlier the Marxist-Leninist theory of law in general and the Marxist-Leninist theory of international law in particular is a sociological theory. It does not divorce law from other social phenomena. They are all considered as parts of the system of society which are in constant interaction. At the same time the Marxist-Leninist theory does not confuse law with other social phenomena.

According to our theory the essence of the process of forming customary norms of international law is the same as that of the treaty process – the co-ordination of the wills of States. But at the same time the customary process is in many respects different from the treaty process.

And all that has been said earlier[185] concerning the States' wills being determined by various social phenomena applies to this process.

183 Ch. Chaumont, "Cours général de droit international public", *RCADI*, Vol. 129, p. 440.

184 I. Brownlie, *Principles of Public International Law* (2nd ed.), Oxford 1973, p. 10.

185 See Chapter I.

Customary norms of international law are formed in the course of State practice. As a rule customary norm emerges gradually as a result of the repetition of certain actions by States. Such a rule is a usage that is a rule of conduct usually followed by States. It does not imply legal obligation to observe it. Such a rule may remain a usage for years and may never become a norm of international law. In this case the process of international norm creating is terminated and a norm thereby created would belong in the category of specific international norms – usages, which are not legal.

But if the customary process of norm-creating continues then the usage would amount only to the first stage of the formation of customary norms of international law, which is the co-ordination of the wills of States with regard to the rules of conduct. The element of legal obligation usually grows gradually. The impetus may be given by one State only advancing the idea that a certain usage entails legal obligation. However, the process of co-ordination of the wills of States regarding recognition of a certain usage as a norm of international law starts only when at least one more State behaves in the same sense.

The gradual recognition of a usage as a norm of international law goes two intermingled ways. One is the growing intensity of the recognition of the usage as a norm of international law. Another is the increase in the number of States recognising the usage as a norm of international law.

Let us quote one example relating to the emergence of one of the most important norms of contemporary international law – the principle of sovereign equality of States. The usage to respect the sovereignty of a State had existed for thousands of years before becoming a norm of international law. This usage was dictated by very powerful reasons: each State exercised supreme power over its territory and population and other States had to take this into consideration. And although there was no legal obligation, States usually respected the sovereignty of other States as contrary behaviour would lead to retaliatory actions on the part of injured States and would also facilitate the violation of their own sovereignty. So the violation of this usage might have factual consequences for an offender, but there were no legal consequences connected with the violation of norms of international law.

There existed, however, particular treaties, mostly bilateral, containing legal obligations to respect the sovereignty of each other, but there was no norm of international law to that effect more or less generally accepted. Only in the period of transition from the feudal to the capitalist system powerful economic reasons led to the transformation of the usage to respect State sovereignty into the norm of international law. The development of international trade required orderly relations between States which were impossible without mutual respect for State sovereignty. The usage to respect State sovereignty was elevated to the level of fundamental principles of international law through gradual recognition by States of its legal character.

The second example is the emergence of the principle of the self- determination of peoples. First proclaimed in its narrow content by the American and especially by the French bourgeois revolutions, it received support from a certain part of public opinion and of national liberation movements. However, it was rejected by the majority of

States. The ruling classes of the United States and of France themselves some time after the revolutions also abandoned this principle. The result was that the principle of self-determination of peoples did not succeed to become a generally recognised principle of international law.

As a much wider and deeper principle it was proclaimed by the Soviet State in its Decree on peace of 8 November 1917. The proposal of the Soviet State to consider the principle of self-determination of peoples as a basic principle, of international law was soon accepted by some, mostly Eastern, States. President Wilson had to include this principle into his "Fourteen points" programme. Many gallant words were said about the "civilizatory mission" of the Western States with regard to colonial peoples, but actually, however, the principle was rejected: it did not appear in the Statute of the League of Nations.

Only in a new situation in the course of the drafting of the Charter of the United Nations did the colonial powers reluctantly agree to include it into this document. However, the principle was formulated in somewhat vague terms, so that representatives of some colonial powers as well as some Western authors tried to deny that this principle was a principle of international law.

Meanwhile the colonial peoples were successfully fighting, supported by the socialist States and other progressive forces in the world, for the realisation of this principle, for their independence. The principle was, in spite of the opposition of the colonial powers, more and more strongly voiced in various international documents, especially in the resolutions of thc United Nations General Assembly. Under pressure from different forces the colonial powers were gradually giving up. Recognition of the principle as a norm of general international law has been growing. Now it is one of the generally recognised fundamental principles of international law.

Thus the process of forming customary norms of international law consists of two stages. The first stage is the co-ordination of the wills of States with regard to the rule of conduct – the formation of a usage. The second stage is the co-ordination of the wills of States with regard to the recognition of a usage as a norm of international law.

Sometimes, although rarely, the first and the second stage of the process take place simultaneously. This happened, for example, with certain norms of space law. In such rare cases it appears as if the first stage was non-existent. On the basis of analysis of the origin of norms of space law B. Cheng came to the conclusion that "international customary law requires only the single constitutive element, namely the opinio juris of States".[186] One cannot, however, accept this view. Even in those instances when the first and second stages take place simultaneously, they nevertheless, strictly speaking, do not blend and it is necessary to distinguish them. In the majority of instances these, two stages are distinctly demarcated.

The leading theories in the Western doctrine of international law are inconsistent as far as the role of States in the process of creating customary norms of international law

186 B. Cheng, "United Nations Resolutions on Outer Space: 'Instant' International Customary Law?", *IJIL*, V (1965), p. 45.

is concerned. They consider that there are two elements of custom – usage and opinio juris – and still maintain that customary norms of international law are formed independently of the wills of States. In fact the opinio juris means that a State considers or recognises a certain rule as a norm of international law. But the recognition by one State of a certain rule as legally binding does not create a norm of international law. There should also be the recognition of such a norm on the part of one or more other States. This is the co-ordination of the wills of such States regarding recognition of a certain rule of conduct as a norm of international law. The result of this co-ordination of the wills of States may be considered as tacit agreement. However, this term is somewhat misleading as it may be interpreted as meaning that in this case the process is the same as in the case of The treaty process, whereas the customary process is a specific process of norm-creating.

Rejecting the tacit agreement as a basis of the customary norms, Western writers maintain that such a thesis is not corroborated by practice and if accepted would lead to enormous difficulties.

H. Kelsen expresses himself as follows:

> "Since general international law is customary law and since it is binding upon all States of the international community, it would – according to the theory that custom is a tacit consent – be necessary to prove that all the States of the international community have consented to all the norms of general international law by their actual conduct, by participation in the establishment of the custom which evidences the law. Such a proof is not required by international law and is in all instances excluded where general international law is applied to States which never had the opportunity to participate in the establishment of the law-creating custom."[187]

Such reasoning is, however, fallacious because what it is necessary to prove, namely that customary norms are binding upon States even without their consent, is taken as proved.

Professor Ch. Rousseau advances against the theory of tacit agreement approximately the same arguments. He says that this theory cannot explain why new States are considered in practice bound by customary international law although they have not participated in its creation. He further asserts the following:

> "... The voluntarist theory ignores the evolutionary character of customary law. To accept it would mean that it is necessary to base each modification of international custom on a pre-existing tacit agreement between the interested States concerning this modification. The completely unrealistic character of this explanation is sufficient to dismiss it."[188]

187 H. Kelsen, *Principles of International Law* (2nd ed. revised and edited by R. Tucker), 1967, p. 444.
188 Ch. Rousseau, *Droit international public*, t. 1, Paris 1970, p. 313.

International practice and above all the practice of the International Court of Justice to which the Western writers usually refer, is contradictory.

The first question is what is the meaning of the phrase "general practice accepted as law".[189]

As soon as there is no authority above States that might dictate norms of international law to States, States only may accept practice as law. In its judgment in the Asylum case the International Court of Justice has rightly stated with regard to local customary norms:

> "The Party which relies on a custom of this kind must prove that this custom is established in such a manner that it has become binding on the other party . . . that the rule invoked by it is in accordance with a constant and uniform usage practised by the States in question, and that this usage is the expression of a right appertaining to the State granting asylum and a duty incumbent on the territorial State."[190]

The question is whether the criteria of acceptance or consent applicable to a local customary norm should also be indispensible in case three, five or more States are involved? It seems that an affirmative answer is the only possible one. In the society of sovereign States no State can decide for another, and therefore the practice can be accepted as law only by each State individually. That means that acceptance or recognition, the essence of which is the co-ordination of the wills of States with regard to the recognition of certain rules as norms of international law, is a decisive element in the formation of customary norms. This view is corroborated also by the judgment of the International Court of Justice in the Anglo-Norwegian Fishery case when the Court recognised that the ten-mile rule for the aperture of bays could not be applied to Norway in particular because Norway always had objected to this rule.[191]

The requirement of consent does not mean that "general customary law should be a myth", as D'Amato puts it.[192] The requirement of the consent of all States for a usage to become a norm of general international law does mean either that all States have to participate by their actions in the formation of such a norm, or that it should be proved by precedents that each State recognised such a norm as a norm of international law.

A customary norm may be created by the practice of a limited number of States. The recognition of this norm by other States may gradually lead to its incorporation into the corpus of general international law. Expansion of the operative sphere of a customary norm is to some extent analogous to that which takes place with regard to conventional norms of international law. Norms of an international treaty are created very often by only a few of the States parties to this treaty. Those States which subsequently

189 Article 38 of the Statute of the International Court of Justice.

190 *ICJ Reports* 1950, pp. 276-277.

191 *ICJ Reports* 1951, p. 131.

192 D'Amato, *The Concept of Custom in International Law*, p. 246.

accede to the treaty have not participated in creating the norms of this treaty. However, if the accession to a treaty means explicit consent to be bound by the treaty, the acceptance of a customary norm as legally binding is not always explicit and it is not required to be always explicit. Lack of protest or acquiescence may in certain cases amount to the acceptance of a usage as a norm of international law. Indeed the usually long period of the formation of a customary norm gives to a State enough possibilities to make its choice: to express its opposition to the emerging customary norm or to accept it by acquiescence or otherwise.

The problem of the universality of customary norms has been widely discussed. Western international lawyers usually maintain that customary norms of international law recognised by a significant number of States must be considered ipso facto binding upon all States. Such a thesis actually means that the majority of States may dictate norms of international law to other States. This assumption is contrary to the basic principles of contemporary international law. According to the principle of sovereign equality of States no State or group of States can create norms of international law binding upon other States. The actual state of international relations nowadays would make it futile for any group of States to attempt to dictate rules of conduct to other States.

How is this problem solved on the basis of the theory of the coordination of the wills of States? According to this theory universal customary norms of international law are based on the co-ordination of the wills of all States. It is true that in most instances it is impossible to determine that a particular customary norm has been recognised as such by all States without exception. Therefore for practical purposes it is considered that if a customary norm is recognised by the overwhelming majority of States (by different ways, including acquiescence) it is tacitly accepted as a norm of international law by the rest of the States. This assumption, however, can be contested by a State. Such a State has then to prove that it has never accepted the customary norm in question, or acquiesced in it.

However, a purely quantitative characteristic of an "overwhelming majority" is at present not sufficient. There are three groups of States which differ from each other qualitatively: the socialist, capitalist and so-called developing States. If the States of two groups, making eventually an overwhelming majority of States, have accepted a customary norm as binding, would this situation justify an assumption that the rest of the States, in this case belonging to a different socio-economic system, have tacitly accepted this norm? Evidently there is no sufficient reason for this. At present an "overwhelming majority of States" should include States belonging to different socio-economic systems which may be considered as sufficiently representative of the corresponding groups of States.

The theory of the co-ordination of the wills of States does not however stop at that. As we have mentioned above the Marxist-Leninist theory of law is a sociological theory. The formation of customary norms of international law takes place in a social environment which influences this process. The analysis of the legal aspect of this process does not fully explain it. Legally the wills of States participating in the norm-creating process is equal. This legal equality of States is of great importance. Actually, as has been stated before, the influence of various States in the norm-creating process is different. The second aspect Which is worth mentioning is that the position of the majority of States, including States of different socio-economic systems does exercise a strong influence on the position of those States which still hesitate to accept an emerging customary norm of international law. There are, therefore, important sociological factors in favour of a legal assumption that if an overwhelming majority of States including States of different socio-economic systems, recognised a customary norm the rest of the States may be considered as having tacitly accepted such a norm if there is no proof to the contrary.

Chapter VIII The Interaction Between Treaty and Customary Processes

1. The Predominant Role of the Treaty Process in the Development of International Law

The accelerated tempo of life and the enormous expansion of international relations have made the international treaty a primary means of developing international law. The treaty process of creating norms of international law has several advantages in comparison with the customary process. The customary process is slow and uncertain. The treaty process is much faster and the co-ordination of the wills of States is more explicit. The treaty process presents very important opportunities for discussing the problems involved, understanding each other's positions making mutual concessions and reaching results satisfactory to all the participants. These aspects are almost non-existent in the customary process. The treaty process is a much more effective way of changing relations among States and improving their co-operation.

The Soviet doctrine of international law has always considered the treaty as the principal source of international law. Now more and more Western writers are coming to the same conclusion. Thus Professor Ch. De Visscher, pointing out that in the modern era of rapid change there is no "degree of passivity" which was important for the formation of custom, maintains that the international treaty now plays the principal role in the development of international law "leaving only a subordinate role to custom".[193]

Professor A. Verdross says that the old thesis according to which custom only could produce norms of general international law has been rejected by the recent practice of concluding codifying treaties. And he concludes: "With this codification treaty law has come to the foreground as compared with customary law."[194]

Professor W. Friedmann writes: "It is obvious that in the fast-moving articulate and complex international society of today the international treaty increasingly replaces custom as the principal source of international law."[195]

However, many Western international lawyers still maintain that international custom is the primary source of international law. According to them general international

193 Ch. De Visscher, "Coutume et traite en droit international public", *RGDIP*, 1955, p. 359.

194 A. Verdross, *Die Quellen des universellen Völkerrechts*, Freiburg 1973, p. 38.

195 W. Friedmann, *The Changing Structure of International Law*, London 1964, pp. 123-124.

law is customary law only and treaties always create particular norms of international law. As general international law constitutes the basis of the whole system of international law, therefore, according to this reasoning international custom as the only source of this law must be considered the principal source of international law. So G. Fitzmaurice asserts that international custom both now and in the future will be the basis for the development of international law. He maintains that international treaties are not in principle capable of influencing the future of international law as lex generalis however much they may, as lex specialis, add to its content.[196]

This is an old theory. Vattel wrote: "Since it is obvious that a treaty binds only the contracting parties, the conventional law of nations is not universal, but special law."[197]

The concept that general international law is exclusively customary law and therefore international custom is the primary source of international law was correct before or even in the 19th century. Now, however, this concept is obsolete and does not reflect contemporary international reality.

It is evident that at present when tens of thousands of international treaties, bilateral and multilateral, are in operation, conventional norms constitute a far greater proportion of the corpus juris gentium than customary norms.

At the same time general multilateral treaties have become a direct means of creating, modifying and developing norms of general international law. Professor Lauterpacht wrote some 20 years ago:

> "Universal international law is created when all or practically all the members of the Family of Nations are parties to these treaties . . . many law-making treaties have been concluded which contain general international law because the majority of States, including the leading powers, are parties to them . . ..[198]

General international treaties now play a special role in the development of general international law. These are treaties relating to questions which are of interest to all States and are intended to create norms binding all States – that is norms of general international law.

The notion of general multilateral treaties has been included by the International Law Commission in its draft articles on the law of treaties in 1962. It reads as follows: "General multilateral treaty means a multilateral treaty which concerns general norms of international law or deals with matters of general interest to the States as a whole."[199]

This notion implied that such treaties should be open to all States. Because of this the Western powers objected to this notion. At that time they insisted upon a discriminatory formulae intended not to admit the participation in such treaties of

196 G. Fitzmaurice, "The Future of Public International Law and of the International Legal System in the Circumstances of Today", Institut de droit international, *Livre du centenaire*, 1873-1973, p. 200.

197 E. de Vattel, *Pravo narodov*, Moscow 1960, p. 33.

198 Oppenheim, *International Law* Vol. I, 1955, p. 28; see also Dahm, *Völkerrecht*, B. 1, Stuttgart 1958, p. 21.

199 *ILC Yearbook*, 1962, II, 161.

some socialist States (German Democratic Republic, Korean People's Democratic Republic, Democratic Republic of Vietnam). Under pressure from the Western members the majority of the International Law Commission abandoned the notion of a general multilateral treaty. The proposals of some socialist and non-aligned States at the Vienna Conference on the Law of Treaties to introduce the idea of a general multilateral treaty into the Vienna Convention were not accepted because of the opposition of the Western powers.

Since the end of the Second World War, mostly under the auspices of the United Nations, many general multilateral treaties have been concluded. These treaties belonged to two groups: one group consists of codifying treaties and the other of treaties covering new spheres of international relations.

Codifying treaties should not, however, be understood as simply emboding existing international law. The experience of the International Law Commission has proved that drafting a codifying convention does not mean simply reflecting existing international law. It also includes its progressive development.[200] The element of progressive development of international law may differ from one article to another and from one convention to another, but it is always present.

To this group of treaties belong, inter alia, such conventions as the four Geneva conventions on the law of the sea of 1958, the Vienna convention on diplomatic relations of 1961, the Vienna convention on consular relations of 1963, the Vienna convention on the law of treaties of 1969, the Vienna convention on the representation of States in their relations with international organisations of a universal character of 1975, and many others.

The second group of general multilateral treaties comprises treaties covering new fields of international relations. Such treaties contain mostly new norms of international law. To this group belong, inter alia, such general multilateral treaties as the treaty banning nuclear weapons tests in the atmosphere, in outer space and under water of 1963, the treaty on principles governing the activities of States in the exploration and use of outer space, including the moon and other celestial bodies of 1967, the treaty on the non-proliferation of nuclear weapons of 1968, the treaty on the prohibition of the emplacement of nuclear weapons and other weapons of mass destruction on the seabed and ocean floor and in the subsoil thereof of 1971, the convention on the prohibition of the development, production and stockpiling of bacteriological, biological and toxic weapons and their destruction of 1971, and many others.

There are also general multilateral treaties which are intermediate between the two groups. They contain a considerable element of codification as well as of progressive development, and it is difficult to say which element prevails. Such seem to be the international covenants on human rights of 1966, the international convention on the elimination of all forms of racial discrimination of 1965, and some other general multilateral treaties.

200 See A. Movchan, *Codification and Progressive Development of International Law* (in Russian), Moscow 1972.

As regards the relationship of general multilateral treaties and general international law there is always the problem of participation in such treaties. The fact is that none of the above-mentioned general multilateral treaties has acquired the universal participation of States. On this fact usually insist those who deny the role of general multilateral treaties as a means of directly creating norms of general international law.

As will be shown later one should not completely separate treaty process and customary process as a means of developing general international law. In many instances customary process is added to the treaty process and the two of them jointly lead to the creation of norms of general international law.

2. The Development of Customary Norms by Treaty Process

Whatever is the respective role of treaty and custom in the development of international law, conventional and customary norms have the same legal basis and equal legal force. The legal basis of both types of norms is the co-ordination of the wills of States.

It means that a customary norm may be changed or abrogated by means of a treaty and vice versa. Now, when the intensive process of codification and progressive development of international law is going on, modification of customary norms by means of treaty has become an every-day practice.

In the beginning a new treaty norm always embraces a narrower group of States than the old customary norm. The problem of respective spheres of operation of a new treaty norm changing an old customary norm and this customary norm must be settled according to the provisions of the Vienna convention on the law of treaties. The old customary norm remains binding upon the States which are still not parties to the treaty and between States parties to the treaty and the States not parties to the treaty. As between the States parties to the treaty, they are bound in their mutual relations by the new treaty norm. With the increasing number of States parties to the treaty the sphere of operation of the old customary norm will diminish. When all States become parties to the treaty, or some of them become parties to it and the others recognise the treaty norm as legally binding by way of custom, the customary norm becomes replaced by a new conventional norm.

An important example of such a process is the emergence of the principle of the prohibition of aggressive war which replaced an old customary norm – "the right of a State to resort to war" (*jus ad bellum*). The pact of Paris in 1928 was the first general multilateral treaty establishing the principle of the prohibition of aggressive war. With the increasing number of parties to this pact and with the aid of custom this new principle gradually acquired the character of the generally recognised principle of international law that superseded the old norm.

3. The Development of Treaty Norms by Customary Process

The development of treaty norms by customary process is a much more delicate problem than the development of customary norms by treaty process. In this case an explicit agreement is superseded by a tacit one which is much less certain. And also the modification of the treaty norms by means of custom is less common since the treaties as a rule provide a procedure for their amendment or denunciation.

There is, however, little doubt that in the course of the implementation of treaties, bilateral as well as multilateral, they are frequently "adapted" to changing circumstances. In many instances it may be an interpretation. A legal norm may be applied to different situations as it is intended to cover a variety of analogous situations. In the course of the treaty's functioning the situations covered by the treaty may change considerably, although remaining within the sphere of application of its provisions. The question may arise how to apply these provisions to the new circumstances. This is a problem of the interpretation of the treaty.

If the treaty does not contain specific provisions regarding its interpretation, and most of the treaties do not, each contracting party may interpret the treaty. But the only interpretation binding upon the parties is, of course, that made by express or tacit agreement of all the parties concerned or by an international organ to which interpretation of the treaty has been entrusted by the agreement of the parties.

However, in many instances the practice of application of international treaties goes beyond their interpretation and amounts to their amendment.

The special rapporteur of the International Law Commission on the subject of the law of treaties, Professor H. Waldock, has cited two cases when bilateral treaties have been amended by subsequent practice of the parties. The first case was that of a treaty between Cambodia and Thailand concerning the boundary between the two States in the area of the Preah Vihear Temple. The International Court of Justice in its Judgment of 15 June 1962 concerning the dispute between Cambodia and Thailand over this question concluded that since both parties actually had recognised a boundary line other than that stipulated in the treaty over a long period of time, the result of this practice was a modification of the treaty.[201]

The second case mentioned by Waldock was an arbitral award of 22 December 1963 (R. Ago (President), P. Reuter, and H. P. de Vries) in the dispute between the United States and France over the interpretation of a 1946 agreement on air transport services between these countries. The award indicated that a specific practice of the parties was evidence of a "tacitly concluded agreement", which is an "independent agreement supplementing the agreement of 27 March 1946 and reflecting the same general principles".[202]

Waldock presented a draft article intended to cover such situations. As a result of the discussion the following article (Article 38) was included into the final draft presented by the Commission to the General Assembly of the United Nations: "A treaty may be modified by subsequent practice in the application of the treaty establishing the agreement of the parties to modify its provisions."[203]

201 *ICJ Reports* 1962, p. 33.

202 "Sentence arbitrale du 22 décembre 1963", *Revue générale de droit international public*, XXXVI (1965), p. 258.

203 *ILC Yearbook*, 1966, 11, p. 236.

The text of this article contains two elements. First, that subsequent practice should show the co-ordination of the wills of the parties concerning creating a new legal norm amending or replacing the norm of the treaty. That would mean that a new agreement has been formed, this time by the customary process. Second, that this new agreement should embrace all the parties to the treaty.

It should be emphasised that admitting the amendment of the treaties by the customary process entails certain risks. The Commission went, probably, too far in admitting that any provision of a treaty may be modified by the customary process. In any case Article 38 of the Commission's draft was not adopted at the Vienna Conference on the Law of Treaties. As a result the problem, which actually exists, remained unsolved.

4. The Extension of the Sphere of Application of Conventional Norms by the Customary Process Mixed Norms

The problem of whether a treaty norm can become binding upon States which are not parties to the respective treaty by the customary process, is of considerable theoretical and practical interest. With the increased number of general international treaties intended to be generally binding, the problem of means for attaining universality becomes vital. An analysis of data on the course of ratification of such treaties shows that after a particular general treaty has obtained ratification by a majority of States, the ratification process slows down. The question is, whether the extension of the binding force of such treaties upon States which have not ratified them and therefore are not parties to them by the customary process is possible?

According to the theory of the co-ordination of the wills of States, both treaty and customary norms result from and embody the coordination of the States' wills. The extension of the sphere of recognition of a treaty by the customary process would mean that the treaty process of the co-ordination of the States' wills is supplemented by the customary process of such a co-ordination.

The International Law Commission provided for such a possibility. Examining the problem of treaties and third States, the Commission included in its final draft the following article: "Nothing in Articles 30 to 33 precludes a rule set forth in a treaty from becoming binding upon a third State as a customary rule of international law" (Article 34).

This text might be interpreted as admitting a gradual extension of the recognition of the binding force of treaties by the customary process. However, such an interpretation was not the only one possible. As most of the Western international lawyers still take the view that "customary norm" is a norm of general international law, whereas "conventional norm" is always a particular norm of international law, they may well interpret this article as meaning that a treaty norm may become binding upon third States only in a case when it, by way of custom, has become generally binding. The possibility of such an interpretation has been increased at the Vienna Conference on the Law of Treaties by adding to the Commission's draft the words "recognized as such" (Article 38).

Indeed such was an interpretation given to Article 38 of the Vienna Convention on the Law of Treaties by the International Court of Justice in its Judgment of 20 February 1969 in the case of the North Sea Continental Shelf. In examining the argument put forward on behalf of Denmark and the Netherlands to the effect that the equidistance principle embodied in Article 6 of the Geneva Convention on continental shelf has become "a rule of customary international law binding upon all States", the Court stated:

> "In so far as this contention is based on the view that Article 6 of the Convention has had the influence, and has produced the effect, described, it clearly involves treating that Article as a norm-creating provision which has constituted the foundation of, or has generated a rule which, while only conventional or contractual in its origin, has since passed into the general corpus of international law, and is now accepted as such by the *opinio juris*, so as to have become binding even for countries which have never, and do not, become parties to the Convention. There is no doubt that this process is a perfectly possible one and does from time to time occur: it constitutes indeed one of the recognised methods by which new rules of customary international law may be formed."[204]

This judgment contains a number of implications and not all of them are justified. It proceeds from an obsolete assumption that contemporary general international law is customary law only. It embodies the idea of Article 38 of the Vienna Convention on the Law of Treaties that a conventional norm may become binding upon third States by the customary process. At the same time it interprets the text of this Article in such a way as to exclude intermediary stages in the process of a treaty norm becoming generally recognised with the aid of the customary process.

The process of recognition of a treaty norm as binding upon States which are not parties to the treaty is a gradual one. Not all the States recognise such a norm as legally binding upon them on the same date; the number of these States grows gradually until the moment when the assumption becomes justified that all States have recognised it as a norm of international law. The Court said: "is now accepted as such by the opinio juris, so as to have become binding even for countries which have never, and do not become parties to the Convention." But such an opinio juris cannot appear as deus ex machina all over the world at a certain moment. What is the situation, if the opinio juris has formed in some States non-parties to the treaty only, whereas others still linger? There is no answer to this question in the Court's pronouncement.

Logically, as has been already stated it is possible, as soon as both treaty and customary norms have the same legal basis, that a norm of a treaty becomes binding by customary way upon some States only who recognised it as binding by the customary process.

---

204 *ICJ Reports* 1969, p. 41.

As an example of treaty norms which have become binding on many States not parties to a treaty is the Vienna Convention on diplomatic relations of 1961. Most of the norms of this Convention are, of course, declaratory of existing international law. However there are important innovations. The Convention, for instance, has extended diplomatic privileges and immunities, with some exceptions, to members of administrative and technical staff of diplomatic missions together with their families. Members of the service staff of diplomatic missions have also been granted some privileges and immunities which they did not enjoy before. The Convention entered into force in 1964. At present all States respect the provisions of the Convention and it may well be said that even those which have not ratified it consider it legally binding. This is an example where the norms of a convention have become generally binding through the combination of the treaty and the customary process. This process has taken some time. As the process of recognition might be only gradual, at any moment before the completion of the process the Convention might be considered binding for those States only which up to that moment had recognised it as legally binding either by the way provided in the treaty itself or by the customary process.

When, at a certain moment, conventional norms become binding upon the parties to the treaty, on one side, and, by the customary process, upon all or not all States, which are not parties to the treaty, the situation is such that for the States parties to the treaty these norms are binding as conventional norms, whereas for the States not parties, as customary norms. Such norms may be called mixed norms, that is treaty-customary norms.

Chapter IX Binding Resolutions of International Organisations

Resolutions of international organisations constitute a new method of creating norms of public international law, a new source of this law. In all well-developed international organisations there are certain categories of resolutions of their organs which are legally binding not only upon its organs but also upon States members of these organisations. Among them are normative resolutions such as rules of procedure of various organs, United Nations Regulations relating to the registration of treaties, etc. Such resolutions play an important role in creating norms of the law of international organisations as part of public international law (see Chapter XI).

As will be discussed below, not all binding resolutions of international organisations belong in public international law; some of them create norms of internal law of international organisations which is a separate part of the international juridical system (see Chapter XI).

Chapter x Resolutions-Recommendations and the Creation of Norms of International Law

Resolutions of international organisations, above all those of the United Nations exercise an ever-increasing influence upon the development of international law, commensurate to the growing importance of international organisations in the international system.

Although all resolutions of international organisations may exercise some influence on the development of international law within the framework of the norm-creating process of primary interest they are normative resolutions.

The influence of a resolution of an international organisation on the development of international law depends, first of all, on its content: how much it is in harmony with the laws of societal development, to what extent it reflects the aspirations of the peoples of the world and what is the correlation of the forces of peace and progress and the forces of reaction.

The process of forming norms of international law and the process of forming recommendatory international norms are two different processes. Their legal basis, however, is essentially the same – the coordination of the wills of States. Norm-creating in international law is primarily an inter-state process. Creating recommendatory international norms is also essentially an inter-state process. Resolutionsreconimendations are, as a rule, adopted by organs of international organisations composed of representatives of States and therefore result from the co-ordination of the wills of member States.

However the final result of the co-ordination of the wills of States in both cases is different. In the first case it is a norm of international law (conventional or customary). In the second case it is an act of international organisation containing recommendatory norms.

Further development of a recommendatory norm into a norm of international law can take place by way of treaty or custom.

1. Resolutions-Recommendations and the Treaty Process

Some resolutions of international organisations may constitute part of the treaty process of creating norms of international law. Such is the position of those resolutions by which international organisations adopt texts of multilateral treaties.

The position of normative resolutions-recommendations is different. The adoption of a resolution-recommendation by an international organisation terminates the process of the co-ordination of the wills of States resulting in the appearance of recommendatory norms.

Recommendatory resolutions serve sometimes as a basis for the treaty process of creating norms of international law. The Universal Declaration of Human Rights adopted by the United Nations General Assembly on 10 December 1948 was a starting point for a treaty process which resulted in the adoption by the General Assembly in 1966 of two treaties – the International Covenants on Human Rights.

The case was the same with the Declaration on the Elimination of All Forms of Racial Discrimination adopted by the General Assembly in 1963. The text of the Convention on the Elimination of All Forms of Racial Discrimination was adopted by the General Assembly three years later.

On 13 December 1963 the General Assembly adopted the Declaration of Legal Principles Governing the Activities of States in the Exploration and Use of Outer Space. In a separate resolution the General Assembly stated that "consideration should be given to incorporating in international agreement form, in the future as appropriate, legal principles governing the activities of States in the exploration and use of outer space".[205]

In the practice of the International Labour Organisation recommendations are very often adopted with a view to transforming their norms in the future, with possible modifications, into conventional norms legally binding upon member States.[206]

The treaty process in such cases is not a continuation of the process of forming recommendatory norms. The latter does not become part of the treaty process. The treaty process starts with the first stage of the co-ordination of the wills of States, i.e., the co-ordination of the wills concerning a rule of conduct.

The parties to a treaty process are not legally bound by a resolution-recommendation which constitutes a starting point for the elaboration of a treaty. The transformation of a recommendatory norm into a treaty norm entails a basic change of its status: it becomes legally binding upon States. It is, therefore, natural that States approach this process with much greater care than that of the formation of recommendatory norms.

If one compares the provisions of the International Covenant on Human Rights of 1966 with the provisions of the Universal Declaration of Human Rights of 1948, the difference is not difficult to see. It is true that in this case the difference is due not only to the fact that in the first instance the States Members of the United Nations created recommendatory norms whereas in the second legally binding norms of international treaties. In an interval of almost 20 years the situation in the world in general and within the United Nations changed considerably. The correlation of forces in the United Nations in 1966 was essentially different from that of 1948. The membership of

205 Resolution 1963 (XVIII).

206 See N. Valticos, *Droit international du travail*, Paris 1970, p. 250.

the Organisation has doubled since 1948 to 1966, mainly because of the influx of new States born in the process of the liberation of colonial and dependent countries.

As a result of this new situation, the right of self-determination, of which there is no mention at all in the Declaration of 1948, occupies the first place in the Covenants on Human Rights. The provisions of the Covenants regarding the right of self-determination constitute a considerable development of the contents of this principle in comparison with the Charter of the United Nations.

At the same time, the fact that in the second case legally binding norms were being formed also made itself felt. The Western capitalist States agreed, for instance, to include into the Declaration of 1948 social, economic and cultural rights, such as the right to work, the right to education, the right to social security. However, they were hesitant to make these recommendatory norms full-size conventional norms. The cause of their hesitation was manifest. If to take the principal of these rights – the right to work, there are no conditions in the capitalist society to ensure the realisation of this right. The Western powers, therefore, insisted on separating the provisions regarding economic, social and cultural rights into a separate treaty. An escape clause was included into this Covenant to the effect that no immediate realisation of the rights recognised in the Covenant is required, but that each State party to the Covenant "undertake to take steps . . . to the maximum of its available resources with a view to achieving progressively the full realisation of the rights recognised in the present Covenant . . .."[207]

This example is cited to prove that the process of creating conventional norms on the basis of recommendatory norms starts with the beginning, that is with the co-ordination of the wills of States with regard to the contents of rules of conduct; this process is not the continuation of the process of creating recommendatory norms and the parties to the treaty process are not legally bound by the recommendatory norms constituting the starting point for a treaty process.

The above is true with regard to all universal international organisations. However, the situation and the role of the recommendations adopted by international organisations depends in each case on the provisions of the constituent instrument of an international organisation. The Statute of the Council of Mutual Economic Assistance of 1959 states in Article IV: "The recommendations accepted by the Member Countries of the Council shall be enforced by a decision of the governments or competent bodies of these countries in conformity with their legislation."

It does not state explicitly whether "acceptance" of a recommendation creates or does not create international obligations. The practice has, however, developed to the effect that in cases when a recommendation is intended to establish rights and obligations of States, the acceptance of such a recommendation by States makes a recommendation an international treaty binding for States which accepted it.[208]

---

207 Article 2 of the International Covenant on Economic, Social and Cultural Rights.

208 For more detail see *The Council of Mutual Economic Assistance. Fundamental Legal Problems* (ed. by E. T. Usenko), Moscow 1975, pp. 220-228.

Such recommendations are of a somewhat different nature. The process of creating them is primarily a treaty process. On the other side, it seems reasonable to maintain that although such a recommendation gives birth to a treaty, it continues to exist as a recommendation alongside with the treaty it has brought about.[209]

2. Resolutions-Recommendations and the Customary Process

The relationship between resolutions-recommendations and the customary process of forming norms of international law differs considerably from the relationship between such resolutions and the treaty process.

The comparison of the resolutions-recommendations with different stages of the customary process reveals some interesting features. The first stage of the customary process brings about the emergence of a usage which is a norm, a rule of conduct, although not an international law norm. The co-ordination of the wills of States with regard to a rule of conduct as such is terminated. In contrast to the treaty process it results in the emergence of a living norm, a norm which operates, although it is not a norm of law. The second stage consisting of the co-ordination of the wills of States regarding the recognition of this rule as legally binding, i.e., as a norm of international law may follow or may not.

Resolutions-recommendations (normative) terminate the process of the co-ordination of the wills of States resulting in the emergence of the recommendatory norms, which, like usages, are living norms. But there is a difference between these two types of norms. A usage is the reflection of States' practice, it is a rule which already operates. Resolutions-recommendations, as a rule, do not result from States' practice; they are recommendations for the future.

As rules of conduct are fixed in a resolution-recommendation, what can take place afterwards by customary process is the recognition by States of these rules as legally binding. The process of the co-ordination of the wills of States with regard to the recognition of such rules as legally binding does not exclude the possibility of changing these rules. But as the customary process, in contradistinction to the treaty process, does not include negotiations among States, the actual possibility of changing rules fixed in recommendatory resolutions is not greater than the possibility of changing already existing customary norms of international law.

Professor Verdross expressed an opinion that when a resolution-recommendation becomes part of customary international law by way of practice, there emerges first an opinio juris embodied in the resolution and afterwards a norm of law, whereas as a rule the process is vice versa.[210]

As it seems, it is not the case. From the above analysis it follows that if norms of recommendatory resolutions become norms of international law by customary process, such resolutions as a rule, take place of the first stage of the customary process of

209 See *ibid.*, p. 225.

210 A. Verdross, *Die Quellen des Universellen Völkerrechts*, p. 116.

creating norms of international law. There is still no opinio juris. It comes later in the course of practice when States gradually recognise a norm contained in a resolution-recommendation as legally binding.

There are many instances when some norms of the United Nations General Assembly's resolutions have become or are becoming customary norms of international law. To this category belong certain provisions of the Universal Declaration of Human Rights, certain norms of the United Nations General Assembly resolutions concerning the prohibition of colonialism, racial discrimination, apartheid, etc.

There is no problem when norms of resolutions-recommendations become norms of international law in a traditional customary way, i.e., by way of States' practice. One remark is, probably, pertinent: if a State acts in accordance with the provisions of a normative resolution-recommendation, this fact does not make such a resolution legally binding upon this State.

The problem is whether the voting for a resolution of an international organisation may make it legally binding, in other words may elevate it to the status of norms of international law.

In voting for a resolution-recommendation members of an international organisation create an act of the organisation the legal force of which depends on the provisions of the constituent instrument of this organisation. Such an act has a recommendatory nature. Recognition by States of recommendatory norms as legally binding is a special process not connected with the voting on the resolution and goes beyond the limits of the organisation.

This is a generally accepted view.[211] Even those exceptional authors who consider that by voting for a resolution a State may legally bind itself, if such was its intention, admit that it is not voting as such, but a different act of a State which may make a resolution legally binding upon it. F. Vallat, for example, says:

> "Delegations acting without special authority from their governments are limited by the provisions of the Charter. They cannot bind their governments except so far as the Charter allows. If by their votes or their speeches they purport to bind their governments, they do so not by virtue of their position as delegates to the General Assembly but by virtue of some extraneous authority from their governments."[212]

Emphasising the fact that actions of States as a result of which a resolution-recommendation may become binding upon them, Bindschedler points out:

> "When an obligatory character is acquired by a recommendation, we have before us two different legal phenomena, the act of the United Nations remains a recommendation and, more specifically, a not obligatory

211 For further details see G. Tunkin, *Theory . . .*, pp. 165-169.

212 F. A. Vallat, "The Competence of the United Nations General Assembly", *RCADI*, 97 (1957), p. 230.

> recommendation. The States have no power to change the legal character of the acts of the Organisation. However, to the recommendation, the nature of which does not change, is added a second act, which is a contractual or unilateral acceptance of binding character and which constitutes an obligation. This juridical act of the State member is the foundation of the binding character."[213]

However, to say this is not enough. It is true that States, whether members of the organisation or not, may recognise some norms of recommendatory resolutions of this organisation as legally binding by customary process and that these actions of States are different from their vote on the resolutions in question. It is, at the same time, of considerable importance to state that this procedure is outside the respective international organisation. It is based not on the constituent instruments of these organisations, but on general international law.

3. The Problem of Declaratory Resolutions of the United Nations General Assembly

It seems that the name of a resolution does not of itself change the legal status of the resolution. There are no indications in this respect in the UN Charter or in the generally accepted practice of the United Nations. There is no doubt, however, that only those resolutions are named declarations which are considered to be of specific importance, and the intention is to emphasise this importance. But this denomination does not change the recommendatory character of a resolution.

The real problem is posed by those resolutions which are declaratory of existing international law. The declaratory character of a resolution should be expressed in the resolution itself with sufficient clarity. In the Declaration on Principles of International Law concerning Friendly Relations and Co-operation Among States in Accordance with the Charter of the United Nations of 1970 it is done in the following terms: "The principles of the Charter embodied in this Declaration constitute basic principles of international law . . ."

The term "declaratory" for such a resolution conveys but a general character of it. Nobody contests that the seven principles stated in the Declaration belong to the basic principles of contemporary international law. But at the same time, the contents of these principles have never been specified in such detail before. There is, therefore, a considerable element of innovation in the Declaration of 1970.

The problem is whether the declaratory character of a resolution makes it binding upon States which voted for it. The situation is this: in the case of a unanimous vote in the General Assembly there is the co-ordination of the wills of member States with

213 R. Bindschedler, "La délimitation des compétences de l'ONU", *RCADI* (1963), Vol. 103, pp. 349-350; see in this sense also Ph. Manin, *L'Organisation des Nations Unies et le maintien de la paix*, Paris 1971, p. 271.

regard to the recognition of the content of the resolution as expressing international law in force. The question is what is the legal significance of this co-ordination of the wills.

The first possibility is that as soon as the process of the co-ordination of the wills of member States has taken place on the basis of the Charter, it produces those results which are provided for in the Charter, i.e., a recommendation. The content of such a recommendation addressed to the States members would be an appeal to consider the principles as formulated in the Declaration as principles of existing international law, therefore as binding upon States.

The interpretation according to which the Declaration on principles of international law of 1970 is a recommendation has been suggested by some authors.[214]

Another interpretation is based on the assumption that the Declaration is an interpretation of the UN Charter. Indeed, the report of the Committee 11/2 of the San Francisco Conference which raised no objections at the Conference, contained the following statement: "It is to be understood, of course, that if an interpretation by any organ of the organisation or by a committee of jurists is not generally acceptable it will be without binding force."[215] The inference is that an interpretation of the Charter, if generally accepted, is binding upon the members of the United Nations.

Proceeding from this, Professor M. Sahovic comes to the conclusion that the Declaration is legally binding as it constitutes an interpretation of the Charter. He says:

> "Since this is the first document after the adoption of the Charter to elaborate its basic principles and fully reaffirm their universal legal force the unanimous adoption of the Declaration places it in the category of official interpretative acts, whose binding force derives from consensus of all the members of the United Nations."[216]

Such a statement is justified to a certain extent, as the Declaration constitutes an interpretation of the principles of international law embodied in the Charter. But the Declaration, as is evident from its text, goes far beyond the interpretation of these principles. The UN General Assembly resolution of 1962 (1815 (XVII)) concerning a study to be undertaken of the seven principles, emphasised that this was to be done "with a view to their progressive development and codification".

The Declaration is a considerable development of the principles embodied in the Charter of the United Nations. In this fact resides its force and its weakness. If the Declaration were a simple interpretation, i.e., explanation of the principles of the Charter it would be of much less value. Actually the Declaration develops these principles and formulates many new important concrete norms. In this consists the historical

214 See, for instance, G. Abi Saab, "The Third World and the Future of the International Legal Order", *Revue égyptienne de droit international*, Vol. 29, 1973, p. 48.

215 UNCIO, Vol. XIII, pp. 710-711.

216 M. Sahovic, "Codification of the Legal Principles of Coexistence and the Development of Contemporary International Law", in *Principles of International Law concerning Friendly Relations and Co-operation* (ed. by M. Sahovic), Belgrade 1972, pp. 48-49.

significance of the Declaration and this makes it apt to become "a landmark in the development of international law".[217]

The main problem is whether the voting for such a resolution may have an effect in the framework of the customary process of creating norms of international law. There are, indeed, two elements required for a customary process: the co-ordination of the wills of States with regard to the rules of conduct; and the co-ordination of the wills with regard to the recognition of these rules as norms of international law (opinio juris).

Logically it may be considered that the voting for a declaratory resolution, i.e., for a resolution stating that the norms enunciated in it are norms of international law in force, may be considered as binding.

That is what Professor M. Virally assumes. He says that "a declaration unanimously adopted constitutes, if its content permits that, that consent of the international community which is indispensable for the emergence of a customary norm".[218]

Professor A. Colliard is, however, more cautious. Discussing the problem of declaratory resolutions of the UN General Assembly, he says:

> "One may consider, especially when they have been adopted unanimously or with a few abstentions contrasted with a heavy majority in favour, that they express, at a certain moment, a consensus of the States members of the international community on a question."

They resemble, therefore, the international custom of which they borrow one element.

The declaratory force is less than an obligatory force of the treaty, but it still exists."[219]

There is much truth in these statements. Indeed, it would be absurd if a State voting for a resolution stating that certain norms are norms of international law in force would afterwards express a different opinion.

But to make it legally impossible there should be a general practice accepted as a norm of international law to the effect that the voting in the General Assembly of the United Nations produces an effect outside the Charter, as soon as according to the Charter even such declaratory resolutions are also recommendations. In other words there should be a norm of international law according to which the voting for such resolutions in the UN General Assembly alongside the results it produces on the basis of the UN Charter, has also other consequences, that is the consequences within the framework of the customary process of creating norms of international law.

There seems to be insufficient evidence at present to maintain that such a norm is in the process of formation, still less that it has already emerged. The practice of the application of the Declaration. on Principles of International Law of 1970 will demonstrate the position of States on the subject and thereby resolve the problem one way or the other.

217 Resolution 2625 (XXV) of 24 October 1970.

218 M. Virally, *L'Organisation mondiale*, Paris 1972, p. 330.

219 A. Colliard, *Institutions des relations internationales*, Paris 1974, p. 276.

Part IV
International Law and International Organisations

Chapter XI International Organisations in the International System

1. Intergovernmental and Non-Governmental International Organisations

There are two categories of international organisations: intergovernmental (or more precisely interstate) international organisations and non-governmental international organisations. The latter category greatly outnumbers the former.

The difference between these categories of international organisations is essential. Intergovernmental international organisations only constitute part of the international system as defined earlier. Non-governmental international organisations are outside this system. Intergovernmental international organisations only can be subjects of international law, take part in its development and functioning.

Non-governmental international organisations do influence the development and functioning of international law, and this influence is important, but it is not direct. It is exercised through States or intergovernmental international organisations.

That is why intergovernmental international organisations (later – international organisations) only are dealt with here.

2. The Laws of Societal Development and the Nature of International Organisations

Earlier (see Chapter II, 2) four laws of societal development having immediate bearing on the development of international law and international organisations were indicated: internationalisation of economic and other spheres of life; the existence of sovereign States; coexistence of States with different and even diametrically different socio-economic systems; the break-up of the colonial system and the emergence of a great number of new States having a colonial heritage.

The influence of various laws of societal development on the development of international organisations is contradictory, a fact we have noticed when discussing the same problem with regard to international law.

The principal law of societal development determining the growth of contemporary international organisations is the internationalisation of economic and other spheres of life of contemporary society. The process of internationalisation is greatly accelerated nowadays by the scientific and technological revolution. Internationalisation makes itself felt in the speedy development of economic, political, scientific, cultural and other ties between States, in increasing the interdependence of States. The number of problems which involve various interests of a number of States, or of all States, is rapidly growing. These problems require for their solution not only concerted actions of several, or all States, but new forms in their co-operation – specific permanent systems of co-operation international organisations. Internationalisation is the main objective foundation of the growth of international organisations. At the same time the traditional means of international cooperation such as negotiations, bilateral and multilateral treaties, etc., remain and grow in importance as well.

The existence of sovereign States is, as has been indicated earlier, a law of the development of a society divided into social classes. The existence of sovereign States as basic elements of the international system makes it inevitable that international organisations are interstate entities and cannot possess any substantial supranational powers. This law puts, therefore, certain limits on the growth of international organisations dictated by the law of internationalisation.

The coexistence of States belonging to the diametrically different socio-economic systems is the most important characteristic of the period of transition from the capitalist system to the socialist system of society. It introduces into the international system and into international organisations composed of States belonging to different systems an element of class struggle. Previously struggle or competition between States also existed. But it was the struggle between States of the same socio-economic system or between States of different socioeconomic systems, but all based on private property and exploitation (as in the period of transition from feudalism to capitalism). The States represented therefore identical or similar socio-economic systems and the struggle between States was in essence the struggle between different national groups of the same class or between similar classes.

The law of coexistence exercises a two-fold influence on international organisations. The struggle between States with diametrically different socio-economic systems is essentially a specific form of class struggle between opposing social classes. It makes peaceful coexistence between States of diametrically different socio-economic systems more difficult, which is indispensable for the very existence of all international organisations comprising States of different socio-economic systems. This strengthens the tendency rooted in the existence of sovereign States.

On the other side, it operates in the direction of expanding the sphere of activity and the jurisdiction of international organisations. This is due to the growing influence of the socialist States in the international system. The constant policy of socialist States is the policy of peaceful coexistence of States belonging to different socio-economic systems. The socialist States favour, therefore, the development of co-operation between the States of the different socio-economic systems and also between all States, and the creation for this purpose of international organisations. The socialist States spare no efforts to make international organisations, especially the United Nations, more effective instruments for ensuring international peace and co-operation in various fields to satisfy the essential needs of the peoples.

The influence of the law of decolonisation upon international organisations can be divided into two stages. The first stage embraces the period of the steady growth of national liberation movements after the Great October Socialist Revolution up to the emergence of the bulk of the newly independent States in the 1960s. During this stage national liberation movements, as an expression of this law of societal development, exercised their influence upon international organisations mostly from "outside". A relatively small number of independent States emerged during this period as a result of the liberation of colonies and entered international organisations. The principal proponents of anti- colonialism in the international organisations were the socialist States.

The second stage started with the major break-up of the colonial system in the 1960s and the influx into the international organisations of the growing number of newly independent States. This marked the beginning of a new era in the life of the international organisations.

The appearance in the universal international organisations of a great number of newly independent States has changed many aspects of the universal international organisations. It has changed the composition of the universal international organisations. The newly independent States now constitute a majority in all the universal international organisations. These organisations are becoming truly universal.

The co-relation of forces in international organisations has changed materially. As most of the new States pursue a policy of peaceful coexistence and energetic fight against colonialism, apartheid, racial discrimination, against continuing exploitation of the underdeveloped countries by the capitalist monopolies, their appearance in the international organisations meant strengthening the forces struggling in the international organisations for international peace and co-operation. This exerts a salutary influence upon the international organisations.

The laws of societal development determine the social nature and principal legal characteristics of the international organisations. The principal ones, but of course not all. The laws of societal development make themselves felt in the complex system of society as overriding tendencies. The principal legal characteristics of contemporary international organisations are, therefore, not casual, but are determined by objective laws of societal development which people cannot change at will.

3. Multisocial and Monosocial International Organisations

The existence of different socio-economic systems means that alongside the global laws of societal development proper to the present day society as a whole there are laws of societal development proper to each of the differing socio-economic systems.

That is why it is of primary importance to distinguish two types of international organisations: international organisations comprising States belonging to different socio-economic systems which may be called multisocial international organisations and international organisations comprising States of one socio-economic system only which may be called monosocial international organisations.

The multisocial international organisations develop primarily under the influence of the global laws of the societal development of those systems which determine the class nature of the corresponding States and which, in its turn, determines generally the main features of the foreign policy of these States.

The monosocial international organisations develop, on the contrary, under the decisive influence of the laws of societal development of the corresponding socio-economic systems, although the global laws of societal development also exercise their influence upon these organisations. So, the organisations of capitalist States develop under the decisive influence of the laws of societal development proper to the capitalist system, whereas the international organisations of socialist States develop under the decisive influence of the laws of societal development of the socialist system of society.

The multisocial international organisations include universal (general) international organisations and also such regional (local) international organisations which are comprised of States of different socio-economic systems.

As monosocial international organisations are comprised of States of one socio-economic system, they can be only of regional (local) character.

4. The International Organisation as a System

An international organisation is generally defined as an association of States based on an international treaty and having permanent organs. Each international organisation is a system within the framework of an international system. Components of such a system are States members, organs of an organisation, comprising representatives of member States and a secretariat. The basic components are evidently States. The system of an international organisation includes also specific elements, namely interactions between the components, norms of international law and some other norms of the international juridical system.

The international organisation as a system is characterised by its components, first of all its principal components, which are not only sovereign States but States belonging either to different socio-economic systems or to one (in this case to which one) of the existing systems, States with differing interests, non-equal powers, etc., and by the interactions between its components.

At the same time each international organisation is a subsystem of the international system which constitutes an environment with regard to an international organisation. To understand the functioning of an international organisation one should take into consideration not only the interactions between its components, but also the interactions between an international organisation and its environment.

Interaction between States within the framework of a system of international organisation has a decisive influence on the functioning of an international organisation. Specific features of this interaction in comparison to those outside the international organisation are of primary interest.

States belong only partially in the system of an international organisation. They are principal actors of this system and at the same time principal actors of the international system as a whole.

Professor M. Virally has emphasised the complexity of the problem saying:

> "What is disquietening and puzzling with the World Organisation is . . . that internal and external milieus merge. The World Organisation presents itself as a social structure inside of which all the States of the world have taken or are supposed to take their places. At the same time it acts as an autonomous actor in the framework of international global society ."[220]

In an international system where sovereign States are principal actors they are inevitably also principal actors in such subsystems as international intergovernmental organisations. Co-operation and struggle which exist in their relations outside international organisations are to a certain extent brought into the international organisations.

However, interactions between States inside and outside the international organisations differ not only as regards their form, but also as regards their qualitative aspects.

Interactions between States inside international organisations are more complex than their interactions outside international organisations. In an international organisation these interactions are effected through a more or less sophisticated mechanism of this organisation with other elements of the system, such as organs and a secretariat, which are always involved.

Decisions inside international organisations are reached usually by somewhat different legal methods than those outside international organisations. A decision of an international organisation may be contrary to the will of a State member. It is a decision of an organisation.

Then an international organisation as a system possesses of itself a system quality. Activities of international organisations depend on the policies of member States, but States act somewhat differently within a system of international organisations. The result of the actions of individual member States within an international organisation is an act of organisation which is not simply a sum-total of the actions of individual members.

The interaction between an international organisation and its environment also influences the functioning of the organisation. The environment that is an international system influences international organisations mostly through States which are

220 M. Virally, *L'Organisation mondiale*, Paris 1972, p. 30.

principal components of both systems. At the same time an international organisation as a subsystem influences its environment, i.e., an international system also mostly through States: decisions of international organisations are implemented primarily by States and the system quality acquired by member States in international organisations is not without influence on their policies outside the organisation. But there is also an interaction between an international organisation as an entity and its environment, i.e., an international system where the organisation as an autonomous entity is in relationship with other components of the international system.

A striking example of a system quality as manifested in the system of the United Nations is the position of colonial powers on problems of decolonisation. The important changes in the international system such as the surge of the national-liberation movement, the increasing pressure of the socialist States and other progressive forces, were decisive in forcing the colonial powers to agree to the independence of the colonies. But the system of the United Nations has also influenced the position of the colonial powers and accelerated the process of de-colonisation. There can hardly be any doubt that without the United Nations the process of decolonisation would have been more painful and prolonged.

International organisations, first of all the United Nations, have introduced a qualitatively new element into the international system. The importance of this change should not be underestimated. With international organisations appeared a whole network of permanent mechanisms greatly facilitating co-operation among States and influencing States' conduct.

International organisations are drawing to themselves more and more questions which were previously dealt with in the course of direct contacts between States. When an international organisation is created to take care of these questions this fact does not, of course, change the interstate character of the involved questions. But in such a case an international organisation is as though it were standing between the States, and the relationship between States with regard to corresponding questions pass through the more or less complex mechanism of this international organisation.

However, the functioning of an international system as a whole and of international organisations as subsystems of it depends primarily on the interactions between sovereign States, which are principal components of an international system and of international organisations as its subsystem.

5. International Organisations and International Law

International organisations exercise an ever-growing influence upon the development and functioning of international law.

International organisations have changed considerably the process of the formation of norms of international law. Progressive development of international law being an objective necessity, international organisations are instrumental in making, at least to a considerable extent, this objective necessity a reality.

Establishing permanent and active channels of communication between States, international organisations have greatly widened the possibilities of the co-ordination of the wills of States including that necessary for the formation of norms of international law.

Largely due to the international organisations, first of all to the United Nations, considerable progress in codification and progressive development of international law has been achieved. Resolutions of international organisations have become an important means of progressive development of international law.

International organisations play a more and more important role in the functioning of international law as they expand their activities into new fields of international relations and become more efficient in enforcing norms of international law.

At the same time international law is the legal basis for the existence and activities of international organisations. When States create international organisations they are bound by international law. So, for instance, an international organisation with aggressive purposes would be illegal under the present-day international law.

International organisations are bound in their activities by international law in two ways: (a) States, as the principal components of international organisations on the policies of which depend primarily their functioning, are bound in their actions within the framework of the international organisations, not only by the norms of respective constituent treaties of these organisations, but also by norms of general international law; (b) international organisations as subjects of international law are bound by this law.

6. The Law of International Organisations. The Internal Law of International Organisations

The term "law of international organisations" is widely used. However, as to the meaning of this notion opinions differ considerably.

The law of international organisations is a comparatively new phenomenon. Earlier the distinction was between the national legal systems of sovereign States and the system of international law. Now new autonomous entities have appeared in the international system, entities quite different from States. The legal norms which govern the activities of these entities really present a problem.

According to one concept the law of international organisations is a part of international law which "should embrace the totality" of international organisations or, in other words, "the institutional framework of the world community".[221] Jenks divided "the law of international institutions" into the following subdivisions: the constitutional law of international organisations, the parliamentary law of international organisations, the administrative law of international organisations and the law governing the mutual relationship of international organisations.[222]

221 W. Jenks, *The Common Law of Mankind*, London 1958, p. 22.

222 *Ibid.*, p. 23.

Jenks thought that constitutional law covers the membership, structure, competence, powers, basic procedures and legal status of international organisations, the general principles governing their mutual relations and their relations with States and individuals, and the arrangements for the modification and interpretation of their constitutions. The parliamentary law would include rules of procedure and "parliamentary practice". The administrative law of international organisations, according to Jenks, "includes the law governing their financing and financial administration and the law governing their relationships with their staffs".[223]

Professor G. Morozov defines the law of international organisations as follows: "The law of international organisations is an organically interrelated aggregate of legal principles and norms ensuring the existence and activities of international intergovernmental organisations".[224] According to him the law of international organisations comprises three groups of legal norms. The first group includes norms governing the activities of international organisations as such, status of the staffs, questions of finance, administrative questions. He calls this group the internal law of international organisations. The second group consists of legal norms governing the status of international organisations in international relations. These norms are embodied in the agreements of international organisations with States or other international organisations. This group he calls "external law" of international organisations. To the third group he allocates the norms governing the normative activities of international organisations. The law of international organisations as a whole is considered by Professor Morozov as a part of public international law.[225]

So Professor Morozov's concept of the law of international organisations covers generally the same norms as the concept suggested by W. Jenks, although the subdivisions of this law are different in each case. And according to both concepts the law of international organisations is part of international law.

According to another concept not all the legal norms governing the activities of international organisations are part of international law. They should be divided into two groups corresponding to the two types of the activities of international organisations: internal and external. In the opinion of F. Durante, internal activities of an international organisation consist of acts whose effects do not extend beyond the organisation. External activities, on the contrary, consist of acts, whose effects go beyond the entity, into the sphere of relations of an international organisation with other actors on the international arena. The internal activity of an international organisation is aimed at ensuring its normal functioning so as to achieve the proper results of its external activities for which the organisation has been created.[226]

Two sets of legal norms correspond to these two parts of the activities of international organisations. As soon as external activities of international organisations, says

223 *Ibid.*, pp. 23-25.

224 G. Morozov, *International Organisations. Some Problems of Theory*, Moscow 1974, p. 261.

225 *Ibid.*, pp. 259-261.

226 See F. Durante, *L'ordinamento interno delle Nazioni Unite*, Milan 1964, pp. 41-45.

Durante, produce legal relations with subjects of international order, they are governed by international law, general or particular. Internal activities of international organisations operate inside the organisation only and therefore are governed by legal norms that constitute an internal legal order of the organisation.[227]

The internal legal order of an international organisation consists of legal norms of different origin. It embraces, inter alia, corresponding norms of the statute of an international organisation, rules of procedure of its organs, normative resolutions of the respective organs concerning the creation of subsidiary organs and of their statutes, regulations relating to the staff of the organisation, etc. The internal legal order of an international organisation is not, according to Durante, part of international law, but is connected with it and is in a certain way subordinated to international law.[228]

Professor W. Morawecki also takes the view that "norms relating to the internal functioning of an international organisation are usually defined as internal law of the international organisation".[229] But in contrast to the previously quoted authors Morawecki is of the opinion that the norms of the internal law of international organisations partly belong to international law and partly do not. "Only those norms that immediately govern relations between States or relations between States and the international organisation may be considered norms of international law".[230] Morawecki does not answer the question as to what is the position of the rest of the internal law of international organisations, to where it belongs.

There are grains of truth in all these concepts of the law of international organisations and the internal law of international organisations. However it seems that in this case alongside with the norms of international law there is a new phenomenon that does not fall into two types of law: internal law of States and international law.

The basic assumption of the first concept that all legal norms relating to international organisations are international, is correct. International character of these entities penetrates all spheres of their activities and conveys an international nature to all legal norms governing these activities.[231] However, some of the norms included, according to this concept into the law of international organisations, certainly do not belong to public international law as will be shown later.

Another concept as presented by Durante is very tempting. Indeed, there is an internal functioning of an international organisation as a system, and relations between this system and its environment – the international system. One should certainly distinguish between legal norms governing the internal functioning of an international organisation system and legal norms governing interaction between this system and its environment. But one should not equate international organisations to States and

227 *Ibid.*, pp. 45-46.
228 *Ibid.*, pp. 69-70.
229 W. Morawecki, *Funkcje organizacji miedzynarodowej* (Russian translation), Moscow 1976, p. 164.
230 *Ibid.*, p. 168.
231 See in this sense W. Jenks, *The Proper Law of International Organisations*, London 1962, p. 3.

a set of legal norms governing internal functioning of an international organisation to internal law of States.

One can hardly accept the view taken, though very cautiously, by Judge H. Mosler. In his Hague lectures he says:

> "The question had been raised as to whether the internal legal order of international organisations is part of international law or whether it forms a separate legal order analogous to the legal systems of States. As international organisations are also members of international society . . . it might be expected that the latter theory would be correct."[232]

International organisations are not sovereign like States. They are international and international law penetrates them, whereas it does not in principle penetrate the sphere of State sovereignty.

In spite of the fact that international organisations are autonomous entities within the international system, subsystems of the international system States which are the principal components of international organisations are also the principal component of their environment – the international system. International organisations represent in essence another form of the interaction between States in comparison to the international system. That is why the interaction between States within an international organisation and within the international system as a whole is governed by the same law – international law.

So, what are the legal norms governing activities of international organisations and do all of them belong to the law of international organisations?

There are norms of general international law binding all subjects of international law including international organisations which are such subjects. These norms are part of a general international law, not of the law of international organisations.

Legal norms relating specifically to the activities of international organisations may be divided into the following groups:

1. Norms of the statutes of international organisations. These are the basic legal norms for any international organisation.
2. Norms of treaties concluded between States and governing the status, privileges and immunities of international organisations, etc. To this category of treaties belong the Convention on Privileges and Immunities of the United Nations of 1946, the Convention on Privileges and Immunities of Specialised Agencies of 1947, the Vienna Convention on the Representation of States in Their Relations with International Organisations of a Universal Character of 1975 (not yet in force).

The International Law Commission is working now on draft articles relating to treaties concluded between States and international organisations or between two or more

232 H. Mosler, "The International Society as a Legal Community", *RCADI*, Vol. 140 (1973), p. 216.

international organisations. As the special rapporteur of the Commission on the subject Professor P. Reuter explained:

> "the aim of the draft articles is not to formulate a system of uniform law based on a comparative study of the law peculiar to each international organisation, but to identify and formulate the rules necessary for the consolidation and development of a solidly based practice recognising the legal value of the treaties of international organisations, irrespective of the special features which may characterise each organisation".[233]

The idea of the rapporteur seems to be that the binding force and the regime of the treaties of international organisations can rest only on general international law. Therefore he sees the aim of the Commission in adapting whenever required the law of treaties, as part of general international law embodied in the Vienna Convention on the Law of Treaties of 1969, to treaties of international organisations.[234] That may well be the first international convention covering all international organisations which possess the capacity to conclude international treaties.

With the processes of internationalisation going on this tendency may develop and bring about an expanding set of legal norms covering all or almost all international organisations.

3. Norms created by international organisations themselves on the basis of their statutes intended to govern their internal activities, such as the rules of procedure of their organs, norms regarding the allocation of seats in various organs to States of different geographic regions, etc.
4. Norms of the treaties concluded by international organisations with States or other international organisations.
5. Norms created by international organisations and relating to their staffs.

Norms of the first four groups govern relationships between States Members of the international organisation or between States and the organisation or between the organs of the organisation, or between international organisations. They are, therefore, on the interstate level, and are part of international law. These norms constitute the law of international organisations, as a set of norms of international law intended specifically to regulate the activities of international organisations.

From the above analysis it follows that there is at present no general law of international organisations, i.e., law binding upon all international organisations. The law of international organisations comprises norms of regional (in the sense that they cover several international organisations) or bilateral treaties, but mostly norms proper to each individual international organisation.

233 P. Reuter, *Third Report on Treaties Concluded Between States and International Organisations or Between Two or More International Organisations*, 1974, Doc. A./CN.4/279, p. 23.

234 *Ibid.*, paragraphs 7, 8.

In many instances all these norms are similar for many international organisations. However, it is a mistake to consider such norms as norms common to all or many international organisations.[235] They are similar but not common: norms of one international organisation similar to some norms of another international organisation are valid in the framework of this organisation only. They cannot be considered as norms binding several international organisations also because each organisation is free to change such norms and the existing similarity may disappear at any moment.

The law of international organisations may be divided into two groups of norms: the norms whose sphere of application is within international organisations and those governing relations between various international organisations as subjects of international law and between these organisations and States outside the internal framework of international organisations. The first group may be called to use Jenks' term, but giving it a different meaning, "the proper law" of international organisations, meaning that such law is also international and that each organisation has its own law.

There is at the same time within each international organisation a specific category of legal norms. These are regulations regarding employment, salaries, holidays, pensions, working hours and many other questions of the organisation of the work of the secretariat. These legal norms are created mainly by the organisations. They are international norms in the sense that they are based in the statutes of the organisations, operate within international entities and do not belong to any national legal system.

But these are specific sets of legal norms. They govern relations between the international organisation and its employees. Compared with national legal systems this law may be considered as including norms of different branches of law: labour law, social security law, administrative law. Such norms although international in a certain sense, are not part of international law. They form a separate aggregate of international legal norms which may be called the internal law of international organisations. This law is not part of the law of international organisations, which is part of international law. Internal law of international organisations is a specific part of the international juridical system.

235 Such a mistake is made by Professor G. Morozov. See Morozov, *International Organisations. Some Problems of Theory* (in Russian), Moscow 1974, pp. 258-261.

Chapter XII The Principal Legal Characteristics of Contemporary International Organisations

1. The Co-ordination of the Wills of States and International Organisations

The basic legal characteristic of the contemporary international organisations deriving from the laws of societal development in our epoch is this: the co-ordination of the wills of States is the legal basis of the creation and activities of international organisations.

If the internationalisation of the economic and other aspects of life makes the creation of international organisations imperative, the only way of creating such organisations is an agreement between States. Such agreements terminate the process of the co-ordination of the wills of States and embody its results.

States members of an international organisation remain sovereign. International organisations being autonomous entities within the international system and subjects of international law are not above the States. They are organs of co-operation between States. As has been pointed out in the Declaration on the occasion of the Twenty-Fifth Anniversary of the United Nations adopted by the General Assembly on 24 October 1970, the United Nations is "one of the centres for the co-ordination of the activities of Nations".

If the very existence of international organisations depends on the co-ordination of the wills of States as embodied in their constituent instruments, the operational activities of international organisations are as a whole also based on the co-ordination of the wills of the member States. In creating international organisations States do not let them free to live a life of their own. States are the principal components of an international organisation system and the interaction between States within an international organisation has, as stated earlier, a decisive influence upon the functioning of that organisation. As a rule all major decisions are taken by the organs of international organisations composed of the representatives of the member States and the co-ordination of the wills of these States underlies these decisions.

Modalities of the functioning of international organisations differ to some extent from one organisation to another, but the basic feature of this functioning is the same – the co-ordination of the wills of member States.

As each international organisation is a system the result of the coordination of the wills of member States, that is the result of their interaction is not a simple arithmetical total of these wills. A system quality makes itself felt.

The result of the co-ordination of the wills of States members of an international organisation is not just a collective act of States members. It is an act of international organisation.

2. The Creation of International Organisations

Contemporary international organisations are created, as has been stated above, by the co-ordination of the wills of States, which usually takes the form of an international treaty, i.e., "an international agreement concluded between States in written form and governed by international law".[236]

Exceptionally, however, the co-ordination of the wills of States may be embodied not in the form of a treaty, but in less formal agreements. H. Schermers quotes several examples of international organisations created by international agreements not in the form of a treaty. The Nordic Council has been established by parallel decisions of the parliaments of the respective States. He rightly points out that also in such cases there is an agreement between States.[237]

In this case, speaking more precisely, the decisions of the parliaments were internal acts. The international agreement resulted from the concerted actions of the respective States that have created the international organisation and participated in its activities.

The Council of Mutual Economic Aid was also established without a formal treaty. The basic legal provisions of this organisation were adopted at the Moscow economic conference of the six socialist States (Bulgaria, Hungary, Poland, Roumania, USSR and Czechoslovakia) in January 1949. Although not a treaty the results of this conference constituted an international agreement embodying the co-ordination of the wills of the participating States with regard to the establishment of an international organisation. This co-ordination of the wills of States also fixed fundamental legal principles of the Council of Mutual Economic Aid.

The activities of the Council of Mutual Economic Aid were developing in the course of the first ten years of its existence on the basis of the principles adopted in 1949, additional international agreements between member States and the practices of the organisation accepted by its members. In December 1959 a formal international treaty – the Statute of the Council of Mutual Economic Aid was approved by a session of the Council, signed by the representatives of States, ratified by member States. It entered into force on 13 April 1960.[238]

There are, however, certain new phenomena in the field of the creation of international organisations. The expansion of the functions of international organisations

236 Vienna Convention on the Law of Treaties, Article 2.

237 H. Schermers, *International Institutional Law*, Vol. I, Leiden 1972, p. 7.

238 For more detail see *The Council of Mutual Economic Aid* (ed. E. Usenko), Moscow 1975 (in Russian).

makes inevitable the establishment of numerous subsidiary organs which in a number of instances operate to a certain extent as autonomous international organisations although subordinated to the international organisations which created them.

Such is the case of the United Nations Industrial Development Organisation. The decision to establish this organisation was taken by the United Nations General Assembly at its twentieth session.[239] The next session of the General Assembly adopted the Charter of the UNIDO.[240] According to these resolutions, the United Nations Industrial Development Organisation "established as an organ of the General Assembly, shall function as an autonomous organisation within the United Nations . . ." .[241]

The General Assembly resolution establishing the first of this kind of international organisations – the United Nations Conference on Trade and Development – was less explicit on the autonomous character of the organisation.[242]

These organisations are, therefore, subsidiary organs of the General Assembly and at the same time autonomous international organisations. This is an innovation that should not be overlooked. But despite the peculiarities of the creation of these international organisations, it would be incorrect not to note the treaty basis of these organisations. They are international organisations of a secondary order, subsidiary organs of the existing international organisations created by international treaties. The fundamental legal basis of these international organisations established by the resolutions of the primary international organisations, are treaties by which these primary international organisations had been created. In all these cases it is the Charter of the United Nations. The existence of such subsidiary international organisations depends completely upon the existence of this basic international treaty and the United Nations which has given birth to these subsidiary international organisations.

In creating international organisations States are legally free to choose different modalities of such organisations within the framework of international law. These legal possibilities are often confused with actual possibilities. This confusion is at the basis of all the numerous plans of a world government presented by philosophers, politicians and jurists in the capitalist countries. They maintain that the existence of sovereign States is a source of wars and that to make wars impossible it is necessary to create a world State. They draft various plans of such a world State.[243]

The main mistake of most of these plans consists in ignoring the laws of societal development altogether or taking into consideration the internationalisation of economic life only and ignoring other laws of societal development.[244]

States are legally free not to create international organisations at all. But the force of circumstance compels them to establish various international organisations.

239 Resolution 2089 (XX) of 20 December 1965.
240 Resolution 2152 (XXI) of 17 November 1966.
241 *Ibid.*
242 Resolution 1995 (XIX).
243 See, for example, G. Clark and L. B. Sohm, *World Peace Through World Law*, 3d ed., Cambridge, Mass. 1966.
244 For a detailed analysis of this problem see G. Tunkin, *Theory of International Law*, pp. 366-380.

States are legally free to dissolve all existing international organisations. However they cannot do this.

States are legally free to create a world federation, but actually they cannot do this.

It is because, in the process of creating international organisations, which is a process of the co-ordination of the wills of States, the contents of these wills are determined, as stated above, by the existing situation, that is in the final analysis by the laws of societal development.

3. Constituent Instruments of International Organisations as International Treaties Sui generis

It has been stated above that contemporary international organisations are created by agreements between States usually in the form of an international treaty. The treaty origin of the constituent instruments of international organisations is not contested.

As to the functioning of these treaties there is a theory according to which constituent instruments of international organisations have a completely different life from the ordinary multilateral treaties. The basic idea of this theory is that as soon as a constituent treaty creates an autonomous international entity, it ceases to be an international treaty and becomes a constitution of this entity. It evades the holding of the parties to the constituent treaty and the organisation itself may amend it as a State may amend its constitution.

This idea underlay a United States draft resolution which later became resolution 377 (V) of 3 November 1950 of the General Assembly, named, contrary to its content, "Uniting for Peace". This resolution tended to amend some basic provisions of the UN Charter by a decision of an organ of this organisation. There were at the time some other instances of the adoption by the UN General Assembly, under the pressure of the Western powers which had a majority in the General Assembly, of similar resolutions on some other questions.

Some Western international lawyers take these practices as law without giving thought to whether they are legal or not. Strenuous efforts were made to justify these practices which caused considerable harm to the United Nations. Out of these efforts the above-mentioned theory was born and it is usually called constitutional theory.

Professor Jimenez de Arechaga in his book Derecho constitucional de las Naciones Unidas, published in 1958, referring to resolution 377 (V) wrote as follows:

> "This constitutional development shows that the Charter is an international document which is not static and which has demonstrated that it possesses to a high degree the quality of a constitution in adapting itself to unexpected changes and new circumstances. It is possible to assert that few national constitutions have undergone in the process of their application such important and rapid changes as has the United Nations Charter . . . ".[245]

245 E. Jiménez de Aréchaga, *Derecho constitucional de Las Naciones Unidas*, Madrid 1958, p. 204.

Undoubtedly influenced by the constitutional practices in the United States, Professor W. Friedmann also accepted the constitutional theory with regard to the Charter of the United Nations. He wrote:

> ". . . As formal amendments of an international constitutional document, such as the UN Charter, are almost impossible to achieve, the adjustment generally proceeds by the consolidation of practice or by de facto revision. Thus a whole body of parliamentary law has been developed in the United Nations, a formalised interplay between the various named organs of the United Nations, and the Committees set up by them. The text of the Charter would, for example, entirely fail to account for the de facto shift in the relative competences of the Security Council and the General Assembly . . . The Uniting for Peace Resolution of 1950 can be regarded as an indirect amendment of the Charter, transferring certain functions from the Security Council to the Assembly without the complex process of amendment provided by the Charter itself . . . ".[246]

And clarifying still further his tendency to equate the Charter to a State constitution, Friedmann stated: "National constitutions, notably that of the United States, have also been greatly moulded by the interplay of social change, legal practices, and legal interpretations".[247]

The legal argument in justification of the constitutional theory was, at the time, worked out most thoroughly by S. Rosenne who maintained that the law of treaties was basically inapplicable to the constituent instruments of international organisations.[248]

Recently the constitutional theory has again been brought to the fore by Professor G. Schwarzenberger who entitled his book International Constitutional Law.

He writes:

> "Thus, at first sight, it is more likely that if there is any international constitutional law, this is not one coherent body of constitutional law but a multitude of competing and fragmentary sets of laws, comparable to the hundred and fifty or more fragmentary constitutional laws of sovereign States."[249]

The fundamental assumption of the constitutional theory equating constituent instruments of international organisations with national constitutions is based on ignoring or giving a wrong interpretation to the legal nature of contemporary international organisations.

246 Friedmann, *The Changing Structure of International Law*, New York 1964, p. 153.

247 *Ibid.*, p. 154.

248 S. Rosenne, "Is the Constitution of an International Organisation an International Treaty?", *Communicazioni e studi*, XII, 1966. For a criticism of his argument see G. Tunkin, *Theory of International Law*, pp. 232-326.

249 G. Schwarzenberger, *International Constitutional Law*, London 1976, p. 117.

As stated above, contemporary international organisations are associations of sovereign States. International organisations, although autonomous entities in the international system differ basically from States, which are the main components of the international system. International organisations, in contrast to States, are based on international law. As a result of all these peculiarities of international organisations as components of the international system, although autonomous, but not equal to States, international law penetrates the internal structures and activities of international organisations. Their constituent instruments remain treaties under international law.

As a result, one should proceed from the assumption that all basic provisions of the law of treaties are applicable to the constituent instruments of international organisations, in a number of instances with some modifications. The Vienna Convention on the Law of Treaties is explicit on this point. It states: "The present Convention applies to any treaty which is the constituent instrument of an international organisation and to any treaty adopted within an international organisation without prejudice to any relevant rules of the organisation" (Art. 5).

Thus the Convention states, first of all, that the constituent instruments of international organisations are international treaties. It states further that the provisions of the Convention apply to such treaties. And at last it provides that if there are specific norms relating to the subject-matter in force within this or that international organisation these norms as lex specialis have priority. This last provision applies actually to any international treaty.

The Vienna Convention on the Law of Treaties refutes, therefore, the constitutional theory of the constituent instruments of international organisations. It affirms the basic proposition that the constituent instruments of international organisations are treaties and the fundamental norm *pacta sunt servanda* is applicable to them. This norm has been formulated in the Vienna Convention as follows; "Every treaty in force is binding upon the parties to it and must be performed by them in good faith" (Art. 26). The constitutional theory maintaining that an international organisation could change by the decisions of its organs its constituent treaty implied that the norm *pacta sunt servanda* was inapplicable to the constituent instruments of international organisations. Judge Alvarez declared in 1948: "The fact should be stressed that an institution, once established, acquires a life of its own, independent of the elements which have given birth to it, and it must develop not in accordance with the views of those who created it, but in accordance with the requirements of international life."[250]

In qualifying the constituent instruments of international organisations as international treaties, the Vienna Convention is in accord with the Charter of the United Nations. Article 103 of the Charter provides: "In the event of a conflict between the obligations of the Members of the United Nations under the present Charter and their obligations under any other international agreement their obligations under the present Charter shall prevail." The words "under the present Charter and their obligations

250 *ICJ Reports* 1948, p. 68.

under any other international agreement" leave no doubt that according to the terms of the Charter even this constituent instrument is an international agreement.

The International Court of Justice which during the "cold war" in some instances tended in its practical conclusions to depart from this fundamental idea, has never dared to deny it expressis verbis. Thus, in its advisory opinion on the question of Certain Expenses of the United Nations, the Court, although moving far away from this proposition in its conclusions, had to reiterate it stating the following:

> "On the previous occasions when the Court has had to interpret the Charter of the United Nations, it has followed the principles and rules applicable in general to the interpretation of treaties, since it has recognised that the Charter is a multilateral treaty, albeit a treaty having certain special characteristics."[251]

The constitutional theory has actually referred not to all constituent instruments of international organisations, but only to the Charter of the United Nations. It is appropriate to emphasise at this place that the Charter stands out among all other constituent instruments of international organisations. It is a constituent instrument of an international organisation, the importance of which for humanity is far above that of any other international organisation. It is an almost universal, and certainly soon will be a completely Universal, international organisation. The Charter contains the fundamental principles of contemporary international law and is, therefore, the principal document of contemporary international law. The binding force of the provisions of the Charter is above that of all other international agreements. All this makes the United Nations Charter a unique constituent treaty. But still it is a treaty like all other constituent instruments of international organisations, although a treaty *sui generis.*

Another aspect of the problem is – what means *sui generis*? How far go the peculiarities of these treaties? Generally speaking the constituent instruments of international organisations are more complex phenomena than ordinary treaties. In contrast to the ordinary multilateral treaty, the constituent instrument of an international organisation creates a permanent autonomous international entity which functions on its basis. Such a treaty defines not only rights and duties of States parties to the treaty, but also the structure of the organisation, its competence, the functions and competence of its organs, the mutual relations between the organisation and the member States, and so forth.

The basic conclusion just made that the constituent instruments of international organisations, in spite of their specific characteristics, are international treaties, implies that the peculiarities of these treaties do not go far enough to substitute the basic characteristics of international treaties.

The constituent instruments of international organisations distinguish themselves from ordinary multilateral treaties to some extent as far as their functioning, interpretation and amendment are concerned. The degree of these distinctions varies from one constituent instrument to another.

251 *ICJ Reports* 1962, p. 157.

It is common to all the constituent instruments of international organisations that their functioning, the implementation of their provisions differ considerably from those of ordinary multilateral treaties.

However this difference is mostly factual, political, not legal. In the case of ordinary multilateral treaties their functioning depends primarily on the actions of individual States parties to the treaties. In the case of constituent instruments of international organisations their functioning takes the form principally of acts of the organs of international organisations. However these organs do act mainly because States members act within international organisations.

As to interpretation, the constituent instruments of international organisations may usually be interpreted by organs of the organisations. But such interpretation is, as in the instance of ordinary multilateral treaties, not binding upon member States, unless they accept it. The rules of interpretation of the constituent instruments of international organisations are, as has been rightly pointed out by the International Court of Justice[252] the rules applicable in general to the interpretation of treaties.

The problem of amendment of the constituent instruments of international organisations is of specific importance. As has been stated earlier, the constitutional theory denies the treaty nature of the constituent instruments of international organisations mostly because according to it, these instruments may be amended by international organisations themselves, as constitutions of States may be changed by States.

The amendment of the constituent instruments of international organisations has certain peculiarities distinguishing it from the amendment of the ordinary multilateral treaties.[253] In both cases, however, according to international law, the modalities of introducing amendments into a treaty may be fixed in each particular treaty.

In the case of ordinary multilateral treaties, amendments are usually adopted by a conference or through negotiation in which each one of the contracting States has the right to take part.[254] Amendments to the constituent instruments of international organisations are, as a rule, adopted by plenary organs of the organisations in which all member States are represented. In both instances an amendment adopted embodies a new co-ordination of the wills of States parties to an original treaty. This new co-ordination of the wills of contracting States supersedes the original one, a new agreement abrogates the original agreement.

At this moment, however, a considerable difference begins between the two types of treaties.

In the case of ordinary treaties, the amending agreement does not bind any State party to the treaty which does not become party to the amending agreements.[255] As a result, when the parties to the amending treaty do not include all the parties to the

252 *ICJ Reports* 1962, p. 157.

253 See R. Zacklin, *The Amendment of the Constitutive Instrument of the United Nations and Specialized Agencies*, Leiden 1968.

254 Article 40 of the Vienna Convention on the Law of Treaties.

255 Article 40 of the Vienna Convention on the Law of Treaties.

original one, the original treaty remains in force between the States parties to it, which have not become parties to the amendment, and between them and the rest of the parties to the original treaty; the amended treaty binds only those States parties which expressed their consent to be bound by the amendment.[256]

In the case of international organisation the situation is, as a rule, different. An amendment to the constituent instrument of an international organisation which has been adopted and comes into force in accordance with the rules of the organisation, becomes binding upon all members of the organisation. And it is logical. An international organisation can hardly function normally if there are different legal regimes within the organisation. Actually, however, the uniformity of the legal-regime within an international organisation, although always desirable, is indispensable only as far as substantial matters are concerned. Therefore, in some international organisations, certain categories of the amendments to the constitutional instruments enter into force for those member States only which ratified them (ICAO, IMCO).

Another difference between the ordinary multilateral treaties and the constituent instruments of international organisations relates to the mode of expressing the consent to be bound by an amendment. In the case of the ordinary multilateral treaties a decision of a conference to amend the treaty is not binding. After that follows the signature, ratification and depositing of the instruments of ratification. In some international organisations, first of all in the United Nations, the procedure is the same. In some other international organisations, however, the procedure is different, at least with regard to less important amendments.

Such is the case of the UNESCO and the Food and Agricultural Organisation. Article 13 (I) of the constituent instrument of the UNESCO reads:

> "Proposals for amendments to the Constitution shall become effective upon receiving the approval of the General Conference by a two-thirds majority; provided, however, that those amendments which involve fundamental alterations in the aims of the Organisation or new obligations for the Member States shall require subsequent acceptance on the part of two-thirds of the Member States before they come into force."

The fundamental peculiarity of the amendments to the constituent instruments of international organisations therefore is that an amendment duly adopted becomes binding upon all the parties to a constituent instrument, including those which opposed it.

But this difference between constituent instruments of international organisations and ordinary multilateral treaties, although important, does not destroy the treaty nature of the constituent instruments. In the final analysis no amendment to a constituent instrument of an international organisation can become binding upon a member State without its consent, explicit or tacit.

256 Article 30 of the Vienna Convention.

Indeed, if the objecting State does not consider it possible to acquiesce in an amendment to the constituent instrument of an international organisation it has the right to withdraw from the organisation. This is, of course, a legal possibility, which in many instances is not an actual possibility. Circumstances may be such that a member State prefers to remain in the international organisation, in spite of the entering into force of an amendment to the constituent instrument which this State had opposed. The wills of States are determined. But whatever the reasons, if a member State remains in the organisation, that means that it has given its consent to be bound by the amendment.

The conclusion is, that in spite of important specific characteristics of the process of amending the constituent instruments of international organisations, the basis of the process is the same as that of the ordinary multilateral treaties – the co-ordination of the wills of States. No amendment to a constituent instrument of international organisation can bind a member State without its consent to be bound by this amendment.

The possibility of amending constituent instruments of international organisations by the customary process, that is mostly by the subsequent practice of the organisations is controversial. The International Law Commission has tried to solve the problem by including in the draft articles on the law of treaties Article 38 as follows: "A treaty may be modified by subsequent practice in the application of the treaty establishing the agreement of the parties to modify its provisions."[257]

This provision would apply to all treaties including the constituent instruments of international organisations, and probably first of all to these instruments. The practice of international organisations indicates that instances are not rare when this practice, on the basis of the coordination of the wills of member States, amplifies the constituent instruments of organisations, or even amends them. In the United Nations two outstanding instances may be cited. First, the amendment of Article 27 of the Charter by a subsequent tacit agreement that the abstention of a permanent member of the Security Council does not mean a veto and does not prevent the adoption of a resolution which requires "the concurring votes of the permanent members". This new rule proved more flexible and useful.[258]

Another example presents the increased powers of the Secretary-General of the United Nations. The fact is well known. It is not an amendment of the Charter, but the development of its provisions in some instances on the basis of the co-ordination of the wills of all the member States, while in some others without this co-ordination, and therefore illegally.

The following conclusion may be drawn from the above discussion: the constituent instruments of international organisations emerge as international treaties and remain international treaties in spite of the fact that in many instances they differ from ordinary treaties, although not basically. That is why the constituent instruments of international organisations should be considered as international treaties *sui generis*.

257 *ILC Yearbook*, 1966, II, p. 236.

258 For further detail see G. Tunkin, *Droit international public. Problèmes thèoriques,* Paris 1965, pp. 94-95.

4. The Powers of International Organisations

a. The Legal Basis of Powers

It is of considerable importance to distinguish between the foundations of the legal powers of States in international relations and those of international organisations. It is also of importance to comprehend that the powers of an international organisation comprise two indivisible parts: powers relating to the purposes of the organisation, including the sphere of its activities and its aims, and powers relating to the means for attaining these aims (jurisdictional powers). These two parts of the powers are inseparable as each action of an international organisation relates to a certain sphere of interstate relations, is intended to achieve a certain aim and is exercised with certain means.

States are "natural" or original legal persons in international law. They are sovereign entities. They create norms of international law and establish international organisations. The existence of sovereign States, deeply rooted in the form of society divided into social classes, is one of the laws of societal development in our epoch. This is, as has been stated earlier, one of the main factors determining the nature of the present international system and international law. States have, therefore, the legal powers to act in the international system for all purposes and with all the means not prohibited by international law, created by them.

The position of international organisations is different. They are created by States by way of concluding international agreements which define the purposes of an organisation and set forth rules relating to the means of its action.

International organisations have, therefore, only those powers which are granted to them by States and which are fixed in constituent instruments or other agreements between States members. These powers are always limited. These limitations relate to the purposes as well as to the means to be used by the international organisation. International organisations have no power to extend powers granted to them by States.

This situation is not casual, it is a reflection in international law of the present state of the international system determined by the laws of societal development. An international organisation possessing powers to act in all the spheres of international life and jurisdictional powers limited only by the norms of general international law, and also having the power to extend its own jurisdiction, would be in many respects, a super-state. This, however, is contrary to the laws of the present-day societal development.

That is why there is at present no international organisation the powers of which are not limited with regard to its purposes as well as with regard to the means to be used for the attainment of these purposes. Even the United Nations belongs to this type of international organisation. The purposes of the United Nations as formulated in Article I and in some other articles of the Charter are very wide, but not all- embracing. They do not include, for instance, international co-operation in the field of telecommunications, meteorology, or public health. The jurisdictional powers granted to the United Nations are also limited factually and legally. The factual situation is that the United Nations, as any other international organisation, has no territory or population and, as a result, its own physical power. This factual situation is reflected legally in the Charter of the United Nations. The Charter contains certain obligations of the member States to contribute to the implementation of the decisions of the Organisation.

One example of the limitation of the jurisdictional powers of the United Nations may be sufficient to demonstrate how important these limitations are. There is no need to argue that disarmament and limitation of armaments are essential for the fulfilment of the principal purposes of the United Nations, viz. "to maintain international peace and security". However, all that the United Nations can do in the field of disarmament is to adopt recommendations to the States, to exercise certain moral and political pressures upon them and to facilitate the reaching of agreements between them on different aspects of the matter.

In the "cold war" period when there was a tendency on the part of some Western powers to use their majority in the organs of the United Nations to deviate from the provisions of the Charter, the theory was advanced according to which all actions of the Organisation, appropriate for the fulfilment of its purposes, are to be considered as within the limits of its power. In his oral statement before the International Court of Justice in the Certain Expenses of the United Nations case the United States representative A. Chayes went as far as to maintain that the UN General Assembly "might have chosen to raise the force by direct recruitment . . . It is hard to see what would prohibit the Organisation from raising such a force . . . ."[259]

Two points of this statement must be emphasised: first, that the General Assembly might raise the military force even by direct recruitment as soon as such a force was needed for the fulfilment of its purposes. Second, it might do so because the Charter contains no prohibition to this effect. With regard to the second proposition Professor Leo Gross has rightly pointed out that:

> "it inverts the basic principle of an international organisation: under international law an organisation has no plenitude of power like sovereign States; on the contrary, being an 'artificial person' it has only such powers and competences as are conferred upon it by its constitution, which is a multilateral treaty."[260]

The International Court of Justice gave its benediction to the above-mentioned theory, which is sometimes called the theory of "institutional effectiveness"[261] in its advisory opinions in 1949 and 1962. In the Reparation for Injuries case the Court said the following concerning the powers of the United Nations: "It must be acknowledged that its Members, by entrusting certain functions to it, with the attendant duties and responsibilities, have clothed it with the competence required to enable those functions to be effectively discharged."[262]

259 *ICJ Pleadings, oral arguments, documents, Certain Expenses of the United Nations*, 1962, p. 424.

260 Lee Gross, "Expenses of the United Nations for Peace-Keeping Operations", *International Organization*, Vol. XVII (1963), No. I, pp. 9-10.

261 See dissenting opinion of Judge Bustamente, *ICJ Reports* 1962, p. 298.

262 *ICJ Reports* 1949, p. 179.

In the Certain Expenses of the United Nations case the Court said in part: "... When the Organisation takes action which warrants the assertion that it was appropriate for the fulfilment of one of the stated purposes of the United Nations, the presumption is that such action is not *ultra vires* the Organisation."[263]

Both these dicta have been widely hailed in the Western doctrine of international law as contributing to the strengthening of the United Nations. In fact both were legally wrong and reflected the position of strength policy followed at the time by some Western powers.

The theory backed by the Court is not in conformity with the nature of contemporary international organisations, which as interstate entities created by States possess only those powers which have been given to them by member States and which are fixed in their constituent instruments or other agreements.

The presumption as formulated in the Court's opinion of 1962 is unwarranted because it is based on one part of the powers of international organisations ignoring another. However, as stated earlier, two dimensions of powers, one relating to the purposes and another relating to the means are inseparable and each action of an international organisation concerns both of them.

The theory discussed now is also inconsistent with the norms of treaty interpretation. Article 31 of the Vienna convention says in part: "A treaty shall be interpreted in good faith in accordance with the ordinary meaning to be given to the terms of the treaty in their context and in the light of its object and purpose." Putting undue emphasis on purposes of the treaty the theory of institutional effectiveness contradicts this basic rule of the interpretation of international treaties.

There is no doubt, of course, that States creating an international organisation mean to make it effective. But it is absurd to suggest that they have an intention to give it powers to take any action for the fulfilment of its purposes not prohibited by the constituent instrument. That would be a kind of a superstate. The intention of the States in such cases always is to grant to an organisation certain powers only, as agreed between them and fixed in the constituent instrument of this organisation, or in supplementary agreements of the members on the subject.

Each State member of an international organisation is under an obligation to act in such a way as to make the organisation effective, to enable it to discharge its duties. But at the same time each member State is bound to act in accordance with the agreement or agreements which govern the activities of the organisation. Accordingly the Charter of the United Nations says in paragraph 5 of Article 2: "All Members give the United Nations every assistance in any action it takes in accordance with the present Charter...."

b. The Problem of Implied Powers

The problem of implied powers is linked to the theory of institutional effectiveness.[264] However, if the theory of institutional effectiveness must be totally rejected as legally

263 *ICJ Reports* 1962, p. 168.

264 See Ch. Rousseau, *Droit international public*, tome II, Paris 1974, p. 471.

erroneous and practically harmful, the question of implied powers presents a problem which, if properly resolved, may serve a useful purpose.

The Western doctrine of implied powers has developed during the last quarter of the century under the influence of the advisory opinion of the International Court of Justice in the Reparation for Injuries case. The Court then stated: "Under international law, the Organisation must be deemed to have those powers which, though not expressly provided in the Charter, are conferred upon it by necessary implication as being essential to the performance of its duties."[265]

Along the same lines the Court said: "Whereas a State possesses the totality of international rights and duties recognised by international law, the rights and duties of an entity such as the Organisation must depend upon its purposes and functions as specified or implied in its constituent documents and developed in practice."[266]

As usual this opinion of the Court was accepted by the majority of Western international lawyers as the most authoritative interpretation of the UN Charter. Professor M. Virally says that the Court has formulated "a very interesting and far-reaching theory" which constitutes a practical means to extend the powers of the United Nations "beyond the limits formally set forth in the texts – that is to apply an extensive interpretation, normally excluded for the texts of treaties limiting the sovereignty of the parties".[267]

For Professor R. Bindschedler, implied competence means that "the Organisation is capable of receiving new formal competences if by that the realisation of its purposes is facilitated . . . ."[268]

Commenting on the opinion of the Court G. Castafieda says:

> "The doctrine of implied powers means, then, that the Organisation has the legal competence to carry out certain activities neither expressly provided for in the Charter nor prohibited by it, when these are indispensable for the fulfilment of its purposes and functions, and to the extent to which this may be necessary."[269]

He also points out that:

> "according to the Court, it is not necessary that certain purposes and functions be explicitly enumerated in the Charter in order to give rise to a correlative power; it is sufficient that such purposes or functions be implied in the Charter. Moreover, the terms used by the Court mean 'that the quality and degree of these implied powers also depend on the measure and

265 *ICJ Reports* 1949, p. 182.
266 *ICJ Reports* 1949, p. 180.
267 M. Virally, *L'Organisation mondiale*, Paris 1972, p. 211.
268 R. Bindschedler, "La délimitation des compétences de l'ONU", *RCADI*, Vol. 103 (1963), p. 351.
269 G. Castañeda, *Legal Effects of United Nations Resolutions*, New York 1969, pp. 35-36.

> condition in which the purposes and functions that form their basis are 'developed in the practice (of the Organisation)'."[270]

Referring to the opinion of the Court H. Schermers says: "We may suppose that tasks attributed to a particular organisation imply a competence without which those tasks could not be performed in a reasonable and useful manner."[271]

The theory of implied powers as proclaimed by the International Court of Justice and interpreted by the majority of the international lawyers in the capitalist countries may lead to a conclusion made by Goodrich which is as follows:

> "When we look at the extent of the changes that the United Nations has experienced, we cannot but be impressed by the flexibility that the Charter has been shown to have. The record clearly demonstrates that it is in a real sense a living thing, capable of growth and adaptation. This has been clearly shown by the view widely held that any necessary and generally desired changes in the United Nations system can be achieved under the provisions of the existing Charter without any need of formal amendment or even the holding of a review conference with that possibility in view."[272]

Such a theory of implied powers has no foundation in international law. The legal objections which may be levelled against this theory are basically the same as those given before with. regard to the theory of institutional effectiveness. The theory of implied powers as outlined above implies a refusal to respect international treaties and its practical application would lead to chaos in international relations and aggravation of international tensions.

A much more reasonable interpretation of the implied powers is given by Professor Ch. Chaumont. He defines "implied powers" as follows:

> "By implied powers are understood those powers, which while not textually provided for by the creators of the organisation, have been recognised or accepted by member States within a certain period of the life of the organisation as auxiliary or subordinate means to accomplish the permanent ends for which the organisation was founded."[273]

However, the formula suggested by Professor Chaumont may contain, depending on circumstances, two elements: (a) implied powers and (b) powers which may derive from supplementary agreements of the member States.

270 G. Castañeda, *Legal Effects of United Nations Resolutions*, New York 1969, p. 35.

271 H. Schermers, *International Institutional Law*, Vol. I, p. 156.

272 L. Goodrich, "The Changing United Nations", in *Transnational Law in a Changing Society. Essays in honour of Philip C. Jessup*, New York 1972, pp. 263-264.

273 Ch. Chaumont, "La signification du principe de spécialité des organisations internationales", *Mélanges Rolin*, p. 59.

Still more restrictive and containing more truth is the definition of "implied powers" given by Judge Hackworth in his dissenting opinion in the Reparation for Injuries case. He stated:

> "There can be no gainsaying the fact that the Organisation is one of delegated and enumerated powers. It is to be presumed that such powers as the Member States desired to confer upon it are stated either in the Charter or in complementary agreements concluded by them. Powers not expressed cannot freely be implied. Implied powers flow from the grant of expressed powers, and are limited to those that are 'necessary' to the exercise of powers expressly granted."[274]

"Implied powers" is not a norm of general international law. According to international law, there are no other powers of an international organisation, except those granted to it by an agreement between States establishing this organisation or by complementary agreements between them. These powers may be stated expressly or implied as logically following from the powers expressly granted. An international organisation has no other powers but "statutory powers".

The problem of "implied powers" is, therefore, a problem of interpretation. This thesis is accepted by many Western authors. Most of them, speaking of implied powers, ignore, however, that the powers of an international organisation are composed of two inseparable parts: powers relating to the purposes of the organisation and powers relating to the means for fulfilling these purposes and base their conclusions with regard to implied powers on purposes of the organisation only.

The theory of "statutory powers" of international organisations as exposed above, corresponds to the fundamental principles of contemporary international law and, as aptly stated by Professor P. Radoynov, "proceeds from the position of strict international legality".[275]

5. Decision Making

Decision making in international organisations is and will remain different from decision making inside States because international organisations are entities essentially different from States.

The overriding feature of decision making in contemporary international organisations is that all important decisions, binding or recommendatory, result from the co-ordination of the wills of member States as sovereign and equal entities. The co-ordination of the States' wills takes place in accordance with the rules of the constitutional instruments. This basic characteristic of international organisations is

274 *ICJ Reports* 1949, p. 198.

275 P. Radoynov, *The Law-Making Functions of International Organizations*, Sofia 1975, P. 328 (in Bulgarian).

determined by the nature of the present-day international system which in its turn is determined by the laws of societal development.

The necessity of making international organisations more effective has given birth, especially in the course of the last decades, to many new phenomena that have made decision making in international organisations very diversified and complex. However the basic feature remains unchanged – all important policy decisions in international organisations result from the co-ordination of the wills of member States.

a. The Composition of Decision-Making Organs

In all general international organisations, with the exception of the International Labour Organisation, policy decisions are taken by organs composed of the representatives of member States. However there are some deviations from and variations of this basic characteristic.

In the International Labour Organisation all the principal organs comprise, alongside with the representatives of States, the representatives of workers and employers. Each State delegation to the General Conference of the ILO consists of two government representatives, one representative of the workers and one representative of the employers. The composition of other ILO organs is based on the same tripartite principle. The Administrative Council of the ILO, which is a very important body, consists of 48 members of which 24 represent governments, 12 represent the employers and 12 the workers.

There was a certain tendency on the part of the principal capitalist powers after the Second World War to weaken the ties between the administrative councils of international organisations and member States and to increase thereby the possibilities of pressure on individual members of the councils. So, up to 1954, members of the Executive Board of the UNESCO, although elected by the General Conference from among the delegates appointed by the member States, acted in their personal capacity. In 1954, however, the constitution of the UNESCO was amended, so that since then a member of the Executive Board represents the government of the State of which he is a national (Article V, A, I of the Constitution). This new status of the members of the Executive Board is much more in accord with the nature of international organisations.

In the World Health Organisation the World Health Assembly, as the highest organ of the WHO, elects a number of States members corresponding to the number of members of the Executive Board of the Organisation and each of these States designates one member of the Board. Members of the Executive Board act in their personal capacity. However, as each State member can recall its representative and appoint another one, the provision that members of the Board formally act in their personal capacity makes not much difference.

The situation with regard to the composition of the decision-making organs is also somewhat different in international financial organisations, like the International Monetary Fund. The supreme organ of this organisation – the Board of Governors – consists of the representatives of participating States. More restricted and subordinate to the Board of Governors organ – the Executive Directors – is composed in a different way, viz. from 20 directors 6 represent the States having the largest quotas of the capital of the Fund and others are elected by the rest of the member States and represent those States.

Deviations from the basic characteristic, namely that major decisions in international organisations are taken by their organs consisting of the representatives of member States, are the greatest in the European Economic Communities. However, the EEC is an international organisation with the participation of the capitalist States only. The Commission of the EEC, which is a rather important decision-making organ, consists of persons, although designated by common accord of the member States, but not representing the governments of their respective countries. However, even in the EEC, all major policy decisions are taken, not by the Commission, but by an organ consisting of the representatives of States – the Council, on the basis of the co-ordination of their wills.

According to the principle of sovereign equality of States, all member States of an international organisation take part in decision making as far as plenary organs of international organisations are concerned. But plenary organs resemble international conferences from which international organisations have developed. The practice has long proved that such a method of decision making alone cannot ensure the effectiveness of international organisations. This necessitated the creation of restricted decision-making organs – administrative or executive councils or boards which now exist in all general international organisations and in most of the others.

To make international organisations effective it has further been necessary in the composition of such restricted bodies. to take account of the actual involvement of various member States in the sphere of activities of each particular international organisation. In the composition of the restricted decision-making organs of practically all general international organisations preference is given to member States whose activities are greatest in the respective spheres.

In the United Nations – the principal international organisation – of the 15 members of the Security Council, 5 powers which played the major part in defeating the aggressors and creating the post-war order, are permanent members. The Security Council of the United Nations is, of course, a specific decision-making organ which cannot be put on the same level as the councils of other international organisations. It has "primary responsibility for the maintenance of international peace and security" (Art. 24 of the Charter).

The constituent instruments of other international organisations do not name member States which have permanent seats on the councils of these organisations, but usually allocate a number of seats for the member States which are particularly involved in their respective fields of operation (the Intergovernmental Maritime Consultative Organisation, the International Labour Organisation, the International Atomic Energy Agency), or ensure a preferential representation of such member States through other means (for example, the International Civil Aviation Organisation). In international organisations whose constituent instruments contain no provisions to this effect, the custom has been established rather firmly according to which the most important States in the field of operative activities of the respective organisations are usually elected members of their councils.

As only a minority of member States can sit on the council of an international organisation, it is of importance that the members of the Council should at least represent all the important groups of States. As a result a legal principle has developed providing for the equitable representation on the councils of international organisations of different regions of the world. As Schermers rightly points out "the words 'region' and 'regional' should not necessarily be understood in their strict geographical sense".[276] And he further points out that the composition of regions may differ depending on the purposes of various organisations.[277]

b. The Process of the Co-ordination of the Wills of States

The decision-making process in the international organisations is in most cases begun by one member State or a group of States. Each member State has an equal right to present proposals and thereby initiate this process.

The secretariats of international organisations also have the right to initiate the decision-making process. In many international organisations this right is rather wide. The right of the Secretary-General of the United Nations is conceived, for instance, in these terms: "The Secretary-General may bring to the attention of the Security Council any matter which in his opinion may threaten the maintenance of international peace and security."[278] He may also initiate the decision-making process on many other questions, especially those relating to the internal problems of the organisation. According to the constituent instrument of the UNESCO the Director-General "shall formulate proposals for appropriate action by the Conference and the Board, and shall prepare for submission to the Board a draft programme of work for the Organisation with corresponding budget estimates".[279]

It is common knowledge that the factual influence of the secretariats of international organisations in the decision-making process is constantly growing at the expense of the organs composed of the representatives of member States. This tendency is encouraged by the leading capitalist countries. Their citizens, or people ideologically close to them, constitute a majority of the staff of the secretariats of the universal international organisations and through them they exercise a considerable supplementary influence on the activities of these organisations. This tendency is in contradiction to the very nature of the international organisations and the provisions of their constituent instruments and poses a very serious problem.[280]

There are within international organisations numerous subsidiary organs of experts not representing governments. These organs may also present their proposals to the decision-making organs and initiate the decision-making process.

276 H. Schermers, *International Institutional Laws*, Vol. I, Leiden 1972, p. 108.
277 *Ibid.*, pp. 109-110.
278 Article 99 of the UN Charter.
279 Article VI, 3, a.
280 See, for instance, V. Sobakin, *UNESCO: Problems and Perspectives*, Moscow 1972, pp. 100-117.

All this mostly represents the legal aspect of the decision-making process. In actual life, the initiatives of member States, in many instances, may be of secondary character, being prompted by original initiatives of non-governmental international or national organisations, private corporations, etc.

The decision-making process is a process of interaction between various components of the system of an international organisation. It is mainly a process of interaction between member States which are the principal components of the system.

The decision-making process within international organisations is in a decisive manner influenced by the environment, mainly due to the fact that the principal components of international organisations – States are also the principal components of a wider system – the international system and also parts of society as a whole. The contents of the wills of States, participating in decision-making, is determined mainly by the factors which are outside the international organisations.[281]

The process of decision making as a process of the co-ordination of the wills of States members of an international organisation reflects to a lesser or greater degree, depending on the issues involved, the global or regional situations in the international system. It reflects the struggle and co-operation which exists in the international system. In the international organisations of socialist States the decision-making process reflects the basic features of the new socio-economic formation, the principles of socialist internationalism.

The final stage of the co-ordination of the wills of member States in the decision-making process is the adoption of a decision which is a decision of an international organisation.

c. Voting Systems

The "one State, one vote" model is used in most international organisations, first of all in the United Nations and its specialised agencies with the exception of the International Labour Organisation, and international financial organisations. The "one State, one vote" model is a sequence of the principle of sovereign equality of States which in its turn reflects one-aspect of the factual situation in the international system, namely that the States are sovereign, independent of each other and in this sense equal.

However, the "one State, one vote" model is in contradiction with the factual inequality of States which is very great and also with the real involvement of various member States of international organisations in the respective spheres of their activities. This creates certain tensions between the legal situations and the factual situation.

Many arguments have been presented in favour of weighted voting in international organisations, such as the great difference in population and in real interests and activities of various member States in the spheres of operation of international organisations, etc. However, in spite of many objections which may legitimately be levelled against the "one State, one vote" model it is based on the existing structure of the international

281 See also Chapter I, 3.

system, reflecting through the equality of States equal rights of peoples to participate in international life and serving best the cause of peace and international co-operation.

That is why the principle of sovereign equality of States and as its consequence the "one State, one vote" system constitutes one of the basic characteristics of the contemporary international organisations and this system is applied in almost all general international organisations, as well as in regional international organisations.

However, to alleviate tensions resulting from the application of this voting system in the conditions of actual inequalities among States, a certain adaptation of the system was accepted with regard to decision making in the Security Council of the United Nations. The overriding importance of the Security Council, which has power to adopt binding decisions on many important questions and which can use force, made the adaptation imperative. According to the Charter decisions of the Security Council on all non-procedural matters are made by an affirmative vote of seven members (now nine members), including the concurring votes of the permanent members.[282] This meant that important decisions of this organ may be adopted only if all the powers involved in the field of the principal activities of the United Nations, do not object to them.

In many international economic and financial organisations various models of weighted voting are applied. Weighted voting exists, for instance, in the International Monetary Fund, where every member State has 250 votes, and one additional vote for each part of its quota, equivalent to 100,000 US dollars. As a result, the United States has 51,850 votes and Haiti or Sierra Leone 400 votes each. In the International Bank for Reconstruction and Development every member has 250 votes and one additional vote for each share of stock held. The result is as follows: the United States has 63,750 votes, the Netherlands 5,750, Sierra Leone, 400. The analogous system is used in such regional development banks as the Inter-American Development Bank, where the United States has 41.8 per cent, of the votes, in the African Development Bank, where the inequality of voting power is less pronounced (the Arab Republic of Egypt has 3,629 votes and the weakest State (Togo) 725 votes); in the Asian Development Bank where the United States and Japan hold 17.7 per cent, of the votes and the weakest State (Western Samoa)-0.74 per cent.[283]

The system of weighted voting is also used in such international organisations as the International Coffee Council, the International Tin Council, the International Sugar Council, etc.

In the European Economic Communities a system of weighted voting is used in two ways. In the Assembly different member States have different numbers of representatives and decisions are adopted by an absolute majority, or by a two-thirds majority, of the votes cast. In the Council of the Communities France, the Federal Republic of Germany, Italy and England have 10 votes each; Belgium and the Netherlands have 5 votes each; Denmark, Ireland and Norway 3 votes each and Luxembourg 2 votes.

282 Article 27 of the UN Charter.

283 See H. Schermers, *op. cit.*, Vol. II, pp. 332, 333.

All these international organisations were originally established by the capitalist States which adopted the organisational form of a stock company.

The situation is quite different in the international economic and financial organisations of the socialist States. As with all other international organisations of the socialist States these organisations, reflecting a new type of interstate relationship, are based on the principles of socialist internationalism. In the Charter of the Council for Mutual Economic Assistance, which is the principal international economic organisation of the socialist States it is stated:

> "The Council for Mutual Economic Assistance is based on the principle of the sovereign equality of all the Member Countries of the Council. Economic, scientific and technological co-operation among the Member Countries of the Council shall be implemented in accordance with the principles of socialist internationalism, on the basis of respect for State sovereignty, independence and national interests, non-interference in internal affairs of countries, complete equality of rights, mutual advantage and reciprocal comradely assistance."[284]

Accordingly the one State, one vote system is used in the Council for Mutual Economic Assistance. The same system is also used in the international financial organisations of socialist States: the International Bank of Economic Co-operation and the International Investment Bank The Councils of these banks, which are the highest organs of these organisations, consist of the representatives of all member States and each State has one vote, irrespective of its share in the capital of the respective bank.[285]

In most of the general international organisations decisions are adopted by a majority of votes. However, even when the "one State, one vote" system is used, as is the case generally, a majority rule, whatever the majority required, poses some problems. Usually the decision of an international organisation, either legally binding or not binding, is operative for all the member States. Of course, the nature of decisions taken by an international organisation depends on its constituent instrument, which is an international treaty embodying the results of the co-ordination of the wills of States on the basis of sovereign equality. But the application of the voting system according to which a decision adopted by a majority is operative also for those States which voted against it, created certain tensions.

The greater the majority required the less the tension between the voting system and the principle of sovereign equality of States and that aspect of the international system which it reflects. This tension disappears when the unanimity rule is applied.

But at the same time, the greater the majority required, the greater the tension between the voting system and the actual inequality of States and their real involvement

284 Article I, 2 of the CMEA Charter.

285 Articles 26 and 21 respectively of the Statutes of these banks.

in the activities of international organisations. This tension reaches its highest point when the decision-making system is based on unanimity.

Practically in all international organisations with a considerable number of member States having divergent interests, a majority system is used: as a rule, a two-thirds majority for important matters and a simple majority for other matters. Such a voting system does not totally eliminate any of the tensions mentioned above, but makes these organisations function. In the restricted organs of international organisations the institution of permanent or quasi-permanent members helps to alleviate the second kind of tension, increasing somewhat the first one. But as the tension between the legal principle of equality and the factual inequality of States members, and different degrees of their involvement in various fields of activities of international organisations, is of very great importance for the functioning of international organisations, different devices are used to minimise this kind of tension.

In the Security Council of the United Nations, in addition to the institution of the permanent membership in the Council, there is a specific system of voting. No simple majority rule in the strict sense of the term is applied. Decisions of the Security Council on procedural matters are adopted by an affirmative vote of nine members (formerly seven). Decisions on all other matters are made by an affirmative vote of nine members also, but this time these nine votes must include "the concurring votes of the permanent members."[286]

This is a principle of qualified unanimity, of the unanimity of those member States whose real involvement in the field of international peace and security is the greatest. As the Security Council is vested with the primary responsibility in this sphere, the rule of unanimity of permanent members of the Council lessens the tension between the legal and factual situation as far as these matters are concerned.

A very flexible voting system has been used in the Council for Mutual Economic Assistance since its establishment in 1949. The Charter of the Council adopted in 1959 says:

> "All recommendations and decisions in the Council shall be made only with the consent of the interested Member Countries of the Council, and each country shall be entitled to indicate its interest in any matter before the Council.
> Recommendations and decisions shall not apply to the countries which profess to have no interest in a given matter. Each of these countries, however, may subsequently join the recommendations and decisions adopted by the other Member Countries of the Council."[287]

This system combining unanimity with the interestedness, helps to solve the problem of tension between the sovereign equality of member States and their involvement in

286 Article 27 of the Charter.

287 Article IV, 3 of the CMEA Charter.

the different fields of activities of the Council. E. Ushtor has rightly pointed out in his Hague lectures that the principle of unanimity:

> "coupled with the principle of interestedness . . . has proved to be a satisfactory basis for the smooth functioning of the CMEA for nearly a quarter of a century. The two together form a principle of qualified or relative unanimity, safeguarding on the one hand the sovereign rights of the member States and excluding the right of veto on the other."[288]

It should, of course, be taken into consideration that the CMEA is an international organisation with a small, in comparison with the universal international organisations, number of participating States, which are all socialist States and the organisation is based on the principles of socialist internationalism.[289]

6. The Basis and Nature of the International Legal Personality of International Organisations

Up to recent times States had been the only subjects of international law. Semistate entities (free cities, insurgents, belligerents, etc.) were rare and their international legal personality was modelled on the States' pattern. With the development of international organisations more and more of them are becoming subjects of international law.

In this juncture two principal tendencies have developed in legal theory with regard to the problem of international legal personality of international organisations. The first one denied the international legal personality of international organisations because they did not possess the essential characteristics of States. This tendency was dominant in the Soviet international legal literature up to the middle of the 1950s. The growing role of international organisations and their participation in international legal relations have abundantly proved that many international organisations possess international legal personality although in different degrees. In spite of the fact that there are still a few Soviet international lawyers who continue to deny the international legal personality of international organisations, the dispute around this problem in the Soviet legal literature can be regarded as the legacy of history.

Another tendency which is still vivid in the Western international legal literature considers international organisations as subjects of international law identical with or similar to States. This tendency is closely linked with the concept of "inherent jurisdiction" or "inherent competence" of international organisations.

288 E. Ushtor, "Decision-Making in the Council for Mutual Economic Assistance", *RCADI*, Vol. 134 (1974), p. 209.

289 For more detail see *The Council for Mutual Economic Assistance. Principal Legal Problems* (ed. by E. Usenko), Moscow 1975, pp. 87-121 (in Russian).

Professor F. Seyersted's writings may be quoted as an example of the extreme manifestation of this tendency. Professor Seyersted maintained that international organisations have the legal capacity to perform any international act, like States, unless their constituent instruments impose certain limitations.[290]

Although in this extreme form this concept has not fpund many proponents, there is quite a number of Western international lawyers whose position on the question is very close to this concept. They do not fully equate the international legal personality of an international organisation with that of States, but consider that it is based on general international law, not on the constituent instruments, and is comprised of the same elements as the personality of States, although with some limitations.

Some Italian authors (Sereni, Giuliano, Arangio-Ruiz), maintain with some variations that the international legal personality in general and of international organisations in particular can be based only on general international law. A constituent instrument of an international organisation according to them is not by itself able to create a subject of international law. It creates an entity to which the international legal personality may be attributed by general international law.

Professor A. Sereni spoke of an "inability of an agreement to create by itself a subject of international law. . . ."[291] A constituent instrument of an international organisation may have significance only so far as States parties to this agreement "actually have created a de facto entity to which the international law may attribute a quality of subject . . ."[292]

Professor G. Arangio-Ruiz, for his part, maintains that the lack, in the universal society, of the primary organisation and the absence of a norm making it possible for a constituent instrument of international organisation to determine the legal personality of the organisation, excludes the possibility that the legal personality of an association of States derives automatically from an agreement of States.[293]

In his opinion the international legal personality of international organisations derives from the fact that some of them, especially the universal international organisations, maintain relations with other subjects of international law and are subjects of international rights and duties. That means that these organisations meet, although in a very limited degree, the requirements of general international law for being a subject of this system of law, and are really subjects of international law, they have "personalita primaria" (personality of primary degree), like States.[294]

Basically the same idea is expressed by Professor M. Giuliano when he emphasises that international organisations are subjects of international law because general international law provides them with subjective rights and legal obligations.[295]

290 F. Seyersted, "International Personality of Intergovernmental Organizations", *IJIL*, IV (1964), p. 55.

291 A. Sereni, *Diritto internazionale*, Vol. II, Milan, 1960, p. 842.

292 *Ibid.*, p. 843.

293 G. Arangio-Ruiz, *Diritto internazionale e personalità giuridica*, Turin 1971, p. 257.

294 *Ibid.*, pp. 260-262.

295 M. Giuliano, *Diritto internazionale*, Vol. I, Milan 1974, pp. 91-92.

Professor F. Seyersted expressed this point of view in the following terms:

> "It is not the convention containing the constitution of the Organisation (if such a convention exists at all) or the intention of the contracting parties thereto which establishes the international personality of intergovernmental organisations and determines its extent, but general international law . . ."[296]

The same concept underlies the following draft article presented by Professor R.-J. Dupuy in his report to the Institute of International Law entitled "The Application of the Rules of General International Law of Treaties to Agreements Concluded by International Organisations": "Any international organisation may conclude agreements in carrying out its competence or realising its purposes unless the constituent instrument of this organisation provides otherwise."[297]

The above concept does not accurately reflect the reality. Of course in any system of law there is a notion of a subject of this system of law. More than that, there is a general notion of a subject of law which is usually defined as a person or entity possessing rights and duties.

At the same time, in international law as in domestic systems of law of various States, there are different categories of the subject of law. Each of these categories has, alongside the general characteristics of the subject of law, its own complementary characteristics.

States are original subjects of international law in the sense that the very existence of this system of law is impossible without States. States and States only create basic norms of international law which constitute the legal basis for establishing other subjects of international law.

The principle of the sovereign equality of States implies that all States are subjects of international law and have the same amount of international legal personality. "They have equal rights and duties and are equal members of the international community, notwithstanding differences of an economic, social, political or other nature."[298] Article 6 of the Vienna Convention on the Law of Treaties of 1969 says: "Every State possesses the capacity to conclude treaties."

Such is the situation in contemporary international law. It was different in the 19th century when international law under the influence of the imperialist powers recognised an inferior status of some States which were considered outside the circle of "civilised nations".

296 F. Seyersted, "Is the International Personality of Intergovernmental Organisations Valid vis-à-vis Non-Members?", *IJIL*, Vol. 4 (1964), 259.

297 *Annuaire de l'IDI*, 1973, p. 314.

298 Declaration on Principles of International Law of 1970.

States possess a full-size international legal personality which comprises, *inter alia*, the following elements:

1. rights and duties under international law;
2. sovereignty which means supreme power over their respective territories and population;
3. sovereign equality of all States;
4. privileges and immunities of States and their organs;
5. the capacity to participate in the process of creating norms of international law;
6. the capacity to participate in international legal relations;
7. the capacity to bring international claims;
8. the capacity to take enforcement actions under international law;
9. the capacity to bear international responsibility.

The position of international organisations is different. In spite of the fact that many international organisations possess international legal personality, there has not yet developed in general international law a notion of the international organisation as a subject of international law in accordance with which any international organisation would *ipso facto* be a subject of international law equal to any other international organisations, as States are, according to contemporary international law. Or one may imagine eventually several notions of international organisations as subjects of international law, each of these notions comprising international organisations belonging to a certain category of these international entities. General international law, therefore, does not define the international legal personality of international organisations.

In creating international organisations States are legally free to invest them with different amounts of international personality or give no international personality at all. However with the increasing internationalisation and accelerated tempo of life which dictate the creation of effective international organisations, international organisations having no international legal personality at all become rare (for instance, the Nordic Council).

In contrast to the States the immediate legal basis of the international personality of international organisations is not general international law. They are established by agreements between States which, not general international law, constitute the legal basis of their international legal personality.

The frequently cited advisory opinion of the International Court of Justice in the Reparation for Injuries case proceeds in general from this position. The Court stated that in order to answer the question of whether the United Nations has such a nature as involves the capacity to bring international claims "the Court must first inquire whether the Charter has given the Organisation such a position that it possesses, in regard to its members, rights which it is entitled to ask them to respect. In other words, does the Organisation possess international personality".[299]

299 *ICJ Reports* 1949, p. 178.

The International Law Commission also proceeded from the assumption that the primary basis of the international legal personality of an international organisation is its constituent instrument. In 1962 the International Law Commission, when discussing articles on the law of treaties, adopted the following provision: "In the case of international organisations, capacity to conclude treaties depends on the constitution of the organisation concerned."[300] As the Commission later decided to deal with the treaties between States only, this provision was not included in the final draft articles on the law of treaties.

The Soviet doctrine of international law is unanimous in the view that the legal personality of an international organisation is based on its constituent instrument.[301]

But it would also be inaccurate to ignore the role of general international law in this case, and to maintain that the constituent instrument of an international organisation is the sole legal basis of its international legal personality. Both, in their interrelationship, constitute the legal basis of the international legal personality of international organisations. General international law is the basis of international law as a whole, and it is also the legal basis of international organisations. The constituent instruments and the activities of international organisations must fulfil two requirements posed by general international law: (a) the provisions of the constituent instruments of international organisations and their activities must be "consistent with the purposes and principles of the United Nations".[302] This provision of the Charter is, in our opinion, applicable to all international organisations; (b) the provisions of the constituent instrument must not conflict with a peremptory norm of general international law, as otherwise the constituent instrument would be void.[303]

However, the immediate legal basis determining the very existence and scope of the international legal personality of an international organisation is its constituent instrument.

That is why, if States as ipso facto subjects of international law on the basis of general international law are subjects erga omnes, irrespective of recognition, international legal personality of international organisations is binding upon the parties to the respective constituent instruments of these organisations only. It may become binding upon States not members of these organisations as a result of the recognition by these States of the international legal personality of international organisations in each particular case. Such recognition may relate to the legal personality of a given organisation in general or only to individual elements of it (for example, the privileges and immunities of all or only some officials of the organisations). The respective obligations for such a State with respect to the given organisation, of course, arise not from the constituent instrument of this organisation but from a special agreement (clearly or tacitly expressed).

---

300 *ILC Yearbook*, 1962, II, 1964.

301 For more detail see E. Shibaeva, *The Legal Status of Intergovernmental Organizations*, Moscow 1972 (in Russian).

302 Article 52 of the UN Charter.

303 Article 53 of the Vienna Convention on the Law of Treaties of 1969.

States, according to contemporary international law, are always universal subjects of international law, whereas international organisations may be universal or regional subjects of international law. International organisations may become universal subjects of international law as a result of the increasing membership or recognition by third States. The United Nations is a universal subject of international law because almost all States are members of the United Nations and those which are not, as Switzerland, have recognised its international legal personality. United Nations specialised agencies, whose membership is also quasi-universal and whose international legal personality has been recognised by the States which are not their members, are also universal subjects of international law. But the immediate legal basis of the international legal personality of such international organisations at the present stage of the development of international law is the same as any other international organisation. It is different from the legal basis of the international legal personality of States.

The extent and the nature of the international legal personality of international organisations are also different from those of States. All States, irrespective of their powers, have the same international legal personality. They are equal as subjects of international law. However, States as subjects of law in general, can acquire in the course of their relationships supplementary rights and assume supplementary duties, so that the amount of international rights and duties of various States is not the same.

In contrast to the States the amount of international legal personality of various international organisations, as determined by their respective constitutional instruments or supplementary agreements, varies from one organisation to another. There can hardly be two international organisations whose international legal personality is exactly the same. The international legal personality of international organizations differs from that of States not only in its extent, but also in its nature. International organisations possess many of the elements similar to, but not identical with, those of States.

International organisations participate in international legal relations alongside States. But if States may legally act for all purposes (omni modae) the sphere of activities and jurisdictional powers of international organisations are always limited.

International organisations have, like States, the right to bring international claims. But this right is very different from that of States.

International organisations are in many instances empowered by their respective constituent instruments to take law enforcement actions.[304] This power increases with the growing role of international organisations. But this capacity of international organisations differs essentially from the legal capacity of States to take enforcement actions.

As to the international responsibility of international organisations this problem may be considered as in principle resolved. The most authoritative document on this question is so far the Treaty on Principles Governing the Activities of States in the Exploration and Use of Outer Space, including the Moon and Other Celestial Bodies of

304 See J. Combacau, *Le pouvoir de sanction de l'ONU*, Paris 1974; V. Laura F. Pacchie, *La sanzione nel diritto internazionale*, Padua 1974.

1967. The treaty which is but a first step in resolving the problem of the international responsibility of international organisations, has fixed the principle of responsibility of international organisations, taking into account at the same time the difference between international organisations and States. International organisations are not sovereign entities and their principal activities depend on the actions and the co-ordination of the wills of member States. Therefrom the question arises of a joint responsibility of international organisations and their members. Another aspect is that international organisations have no territories and population, they possess no resources which States have, and therefore may be unable in particular cases to repair damage caused by their activities. The treaty on outer space therefore stipulates that in the case of activities in outer space of an international organisation, the responsibility for the application of the treaty bears alongside the international organisation, also the States taking part in these activities. The convention on reparation of damages caused by objects launched into outer space of 1972 proceeds from the same principle.

Two main conclusions may be drawn from the above analysis: the international legal personality of international organisations differs from that of States in all its principal characteristics, viz, the legal basis, nature and extent; in contrast to States, the international legal personality of different international organisations is not the same.

Politics, Law and Force in the Interstate System*

Chapter I The Present Day Interstate System

The role of politics, law and force in a social system depends on the nature of a particular system. It is, therefore, necessary to examine first the nature of the contemporary interstate system.

There are various notions about the international system ranging in scope from an interstate system to society as a whole. I will discuss some of them which, in my opinion, may help understand my own theory of the interstate system.

1. The State of Nature Theory

This theory deals with relations among States only. It emerged when States were virtually the only actors on the international scene so the problem of other actors did not arise.

As I shall show later, principles of interstate relations professed by this theory are to some extent functioning in the present-day interstate system.

As formulated by Hobbes and kept alive to the present day, the essence of this theory is that as soon as there is no central authority above the States they exist in a state of nature, that is, their relations being based on force, or more generally on power. Hobbes proceeded from the assumption that the principal trait in human nature is a striving to dominate, which determines relations not only among individuals, but also among States. Hobbes wrote that "in the first place, I put for a general inclination of all mankind, a perpetual and restless desire of power after power, that ceaseth only in death".[1]

Having described the relations among individuals that are asserted to derive from human nature, Hobbes turns to relations among States. He writes that

> "it is manifest, that during the time men live without a common power to keep them all in awe, they are in that condition which is called war; and such a war, as is of every man, against every man".[2]

---

* This lecture was originally published in Recueil des cours, Tome 219 (1989), pp. 227–396 and is reprinted with kind permission of the Hague Academy of International Law/Académie de droit international de la Haye.

1 *Leviathan or the Matter, Form and Power of a Commonwealth Ecclesiastical and Civil,* Blackwell, Oxford, 1949, p. 64.

2 *Op. cit.*, p. 82.

He then adds:

> "But though there had never been any time, wherein particular men were in a condition of war one against another; yet in all times, kings, and persons of sovereign authority, because of their independency, are in continual jealousies, and in the state and posture of gladiators; having their weapons pointing and their eyes fixed on one another; that is, their forts, garrisons, and guns upon the frontiers of their kingdoms; and continual spies upon their neighbours; which is a posture of war."[3]

The international system has considerably changed since Hobbes, but the state of nature theory persists especially among political scientists. In fact, political realism as well as legal realism are inspired or even based on the Hobbesian state of nature theory. Their guiding idea is *bellum omnium contra omnes* in interstate relations. As the father of political realism theory Professor Hans Morgenthau puts it: "international politics like all politics, is a struggle for power".[4] He adds: "The aspiration for power being the distinguishing element of international politics, as of all politics, international politics is of necessity power politics."[5]

In his widely known book, *Paix et guerre entre les nations,* Raymond Aron considers that so long as sovereign States exist

> "the aim of relations among States appears to be . . . simply their survival as they face the effective threat that is created by the existence of other States . . . In their relations with each other States have not yet left the *state of nature*."[6]

R. J. Art and K. Waltz consider that chaos reigns in interstate relations and therefore there is a constant state of war among States. They say:

> "The reason that statesmen are preoccupied with the use of force is because international politics is anarchic. There exists no central authority above States clothed with the power and the authority to resolve disputes that inevitably arise among them."[7]
> "International relations", they add, are referred to correctly so as a "state of war" . . . There is truth to the old adage: "The best way to keep the peace is just to prepare for war."[8]

3 *Ibid.*, p. 83

4 *Politics among Nations,* New York, Knopf, 1948, p. 25.

5 *Ibid.*, p. 29. 6.

6 *Paix et guerre entre les nations*, Paris, Calmann-Lévy, 1962, p.16

7 "Technology, Strategy and the Use of Force" *in The Use of Force, International Politics and Foreign Policy* (ed. by R. Art and K. Waltz), Lanham, University Press of America, 1983, p. 4.

8 *Ibid.*, p. 7.

In the same vein Professor Marcel Merle writes:

> "But there persists a monumental flaw in the system: in the absence of any constituted power and collectively organized means of sanction States retain in fact the faculty to be their own judges. Thus the state of nature continues to exist behind the increasingly dense screen of customary law."[9]

Happily there are but a few international lawyers who accept the state of nature theory. The most prominent among them is Professor Georg Schwarzenberger. Although he does not use the term "state of nature", his theory is the same. In his book, *Power Politics,* Professor Schwarzenberger asserts that "power politics has been a constant feature of international relations throughout the ages".[10] He elaborated on his concept of power politics in the following way:

> "Power politics may be defined as a system of international relations in which groups consider themselves as ultimate ends; use, at least for vital purposes, the most effective means at their disposal."[11]

In effect, Schwarzenberger derives the unavoidability of power politics from the existence of sovereign States. In his view, relations among sovereign States are inevitably relations of power. He then develops this point as follows: in a situation in which each participant in international relations possesses a power that far exceeds the possibilities of individual persons, "inter-State relations are permeated by an atmosphere of mutual suspicion and never-absent fear of the real intentions of others".[12] The primary concern of each participant in international relations is then with his own self-preservation.[13] "For short, relations on such footing may be described as power politics."[14]

Later, Professor Schwarzenberger's views have changed to some extent, but to some extent only. He went as far as accepting international constitutional law, however, with a considerable reservation.

"The near-universality of the United Nations legal system [he writes], and the character of its fundamental principles as *jus cogens* suggest the treatment of this material in terms of international constitutional law. Yet the consensual character of this *jus cogens* and the whole of the law of international institutions, and even more so the precarious state of the underlying international quasi-order, makes it advisable to stress from the outset the analogous element in the term *international constitutional law.* Without the prefix 'quasi' the term does more justice to the aspiration of the United Nations and its Related Agencies than to the past and contemporary reality."[15]

9 *Sociologie des relations internationales,* Paris, Dalloz, 1976, p. 44.
10 *Power Politics. A Study of World Society,* London, Stevens & Sons Limited, p. 19.
11 *Ibid.,* p. 14.
12 *The Frontiers of International Law,* London, Stevens & Sons Limited, 1962, p. 23.
13 *Ibid.*
14 *Ibid.,* p. 24.
15 *International Constitutional Law,* London, Stevens, 1976, p. 1. 16.

Let us also quote Professor Anthony Carty who, in his book with the intriguing title of *The Decay of International Law?*, says:

> "It is hardly news to international lawyers to be told that a state of nature is a more accurate description of international society than their own vision of an international legal order."[16]

The state of nature theory gives a wrong picture of the present-day interstate system. It considers States as isolated entities possessing absolute sovereignty with no authority whatsoever above them. It was to a great extent time for the XVIIth century. But the contemporary situation is different. States are more and more interrelated and interdependent. There is no absolute sovereignty of States and actually it never existed. Society has a considerably developed international law legally binding upon States. There are international organizations and international organs, though created by agreements among States, but having certain authority over them.

The state of nature theory in a form of a balance of power system theory seems to be prevailing among political scientists even now. However, there are many exceptions as will be shown later.

2. The World Society Theories

The appearance in the world arena of many new actors such as international organizations, powerful transnational corporations was conducive to the emergence of the world society theories. How much social scientists have been influenced by the appearance of new actors on the international scene may be illustrated by the following example. The magazine *Futurist,* in its issue of November-December 1990, published a "summary of the 17 prominent futurists" in which it is stated, *inter alia,* as follows:

> "Corporations and multinationals may be leading actors in the future according to at least half of the futurists. This is because they are more flexible, efficient and adaptable than other institutions. Other more loosely defined, but influential, groups and systems are expected to play an important role in governing the future: the work force, for example, and the international financial system. The groups, such as unions, will play smaller parts. Individuals or groups of individuals, such as women or scientists, may have new and special roles to play in the future."[17]

According to one of these theories there are in the international arena alongside the States many other actors exercising their activities on the same level as States. This approach changes completely the perception of international life.

16 *The Decay of International Law? A Reappraisal of the Limits of Legal Imagination in International Affairs,* Manchester, Manchester University Press, 1986, p. 8.

17 *Futurist,* V. XXIV, 6, 1990, p. 28.

"If States [says Professor M. Banks] were no longer to be treated as the single set of primary actors in the world society, then multiple sets would have to take their place. These would have to be political parties, business firms, ethnic communities, ideological groups and many others – some fully politicized, others apparently less so. If the behaviour of all of these groups was to be understood, then their values would have to be analyzed. Value analysis would therefore cease to focus on international stability, national security, and other items associated only with States, and instead shift to human needs and other basic concern . . . Interaction between groups would have to be analyzed comprehensively, covering all fauns of conflicts and co-operation, so that power politics would become one category, but only one, within the new scheme."[18]

As we see this theory envisages a complete change of international relations and replacement of power politics with other political processes, or at least mitigation of power politics. This would be achieved by emerging multiplicity of conflict instead of it being focused on security and other phenomena connected with States.

A new character of international conflicts would lead to new means of their management. Banks says: "To develop a pluralistic logic of conflict and its efficient management therefore became the principal concern of the world society theorists."[19]

And he continues:

> "So in the world society, forcible conflict-suppressing devices so long employed – power balancing, peacekeeping, hostile intervention – would need to be replaced with other procedures which would not only control conflict symptoms, but also develop the capacity of the world society to become a self-regulating system capable of avoiding destructive conflicts."[20]

Banks is optimistic, saying that the new paradigm

> "offers a vision of the world as a whole combining the empirical and the nonnative. Unlike much of the optimistic forecasting literature, it does not seek to describe a preferred world that does not yet exist. Instead it draws upon elements that already do exist, both in real-world activities and in ideas about them, to compose a new portrait of the world society."[21]

Really, all the components of the world society named by Banks do exist. The problem is whether the analysis of their interaction is correct. In our opinion, it is not. But the problem will be discussed later.

Another theory of world society has been suggested by Professor James Rosenau.

---

18 "Evolution of International Relations Theory", in *Conflict in World Society* (ed. by M. Banks, London), London, School of Economics, 1984, p. 19.

19 *Ibid.*, p. 20.

20 *Ibid.*

21 *Ibid.*, p. 21.

According to Rosenau there is one world comprising two worlds of world politics: multi-centric and state-centric. The author names his theory "conception of global politics as a two world universe".[22]

> "Stated most succinctly, [he says] the pages that follow argue that global politics consists today of two worlds, both of which embrace the same actors, but each of which is highly differentiated by core structures and processes that require the actors to employ very different decision rules to the extent that they move back and forth between the two worlds. As individuals are active in both these personal and professional worlds, so do States, corporations, ethnic groups, international organizations, churches and many other collectivities with transnational aspirations live in two worlds."[23]

This is due to profound socio-economic changes in society. The result enables one "to see nation-states as merely embedded in, rather than presiding over, the complexities of a shrinking, ever more interdependent political universe".[24]

The author suggests to break with the concept that the State is still predominant in international life and accept the concept of a multi-centric system.[25] Rosenau predicts the decay of the State-centric system and the growing preponderance of the multi-centric system. He says:

> "Is not the answer that the combination of technologies and an underlying decentralization has overwhelmed the State system and made it subservient to the complexity and chaos of the repercussive politics that sustain the multi-centric world. The reasoning is persuasive and positive answers to such questions may well be in order. The structures and processes of the multi-centric world are deeply rooted and, as outlined below, they do not seem likely to adjust to the anarchy inherent in the State-centric system. It may even be the case that the State system is already well along the road to decay, so that the coexistence of the two independent worlds of world politics may be merely a transitional phase in global development."[26]

However, the author has to admit that it is too early "to presume that the State-centric system is inexorably disappearing into a more encompassing multi-centric environment".[27]

Rosenau also takes up the problem of self-regulation in a multi-centric system. In his view a multi-centric system has some advantages in this respect in comparison

22 "Patterned Chaos in Global Life: Structure and Process in the Two Worlds of World Politics", in *International Political Science Review*, Vol. 9, No. 1, October 1988, p. 336.

23 *Ibid.*, pp. 329-330

24 *Ibid.*, p. 333.

25 *Ibid.*, p. 329.

26 Rosenau, *op. cit., supra,* footnote 22, pp. 335-336.

27 *Ibid.*, p. 336.

with a State-centric system, though the chaotic nature of the system characteristic of a State-centric system remains in a multi-centric system as well, but in a lesser degree: However, the arguments of the author on this subject are somewhat vague and unconvincing.

"If decentralization provides actors in the multi-centric world with a freedom to initiate a wide range of policies, the peripherality of coercive force to their world has enabled them to pursue their policies with relative abandon. Such force is to no avail for several reasons. An obvious one is that most sovereignty-free actors neither possess the instruments of coercion nor have they the predisposition to attempt to acquire them."[28]

In explaining this assertion he adds:

> "Put in still another way, the implicit legitimacy and equality that serve as organizing principles of the multi-centric world are the functional equivalent of sovereignty in the State-centric world."[29]

The two worlds of world politics overlap. Rosenau writes:

> "The two worlds do have their own structures and processes, and these do derive from different sources, but obviously they are not self-contained . . . What transpires in the State-centric world can have significant consequences for the multi-centric world, and vice versa. Stated differently, since whole systems and subsystems can be actors in both worlds – with States being drawn ever further into the multi-centric world by an intensified interest in expanding their share of world markets and with other actors being drawn into the State-centric world by virtue of their physical presence on the territories of States, the overlap between the two worlds is inherent in their juxtaposition."[30]

States have more and more to adapt themselves to the complexities of the multi-centric world. On the other hand non-State actors who have their headquarters within the jurisdiction of States have to conduct their affairs observing the laws of the respective States.[31]

The conclusion of the author is as follows:

> "Thus it is that the present structures and processes of global life are likely to be more permanent than transitional. Neither of the two worlds of world politics is likely to be overcome by the other. Both seem likely to remain as enduring features of the international scene even as each also tends to foster an ascendency on the part of the other as time passes. The chaos

28 *Ibid.*, p. 343.
29 *Ibid.*, p. 347.
30 *Ibid.*, pp. 354-355.
31 *Ibid.*, p. 335.

> of global life may not only be patterned; it may also unfold in rhythmic cycles."[32]

As a third example of world society theories I shall examine the theory of noosphere. A Soviet natural scientist V. Vernadsky proposed at the beginning of the century a theory that has become known as the theory of noosphere (sphere of Reason). In its contemporary interpretation, mainly by a prominent Soviet scientist N. Moiseev, it has the following principal characteristics.

Activities of men are becoming the main factor of the evolution of the biosphere and the earth as a cosmic object. For further existence of mankind and the biosphere man has to take the responsibility for major evolutionary processes on the planet. This will mark the transition of a biosphere into a new existence directed by Reason. Such a transition will require enormous efforts by mankind. But the way to an epoch of noosphere is open.

N. N. Moiseev points out that:

> "In the course of the whole history of mankind evolution of living material and the biosphere as a whole constituted, in accordance with general laws of evolution, a process of natural self-organization. Of course during the last millenia human reason also took part in this process and influenced it. But up to a certain period this was part of the same elemental self-organization. Now it is no more. Further evolution of the biosphere becomes a purposeful evolution. Its goal is ensuring the future of mankind. Reason has started to regulate this evolution. But to be really regulated by reason this must be the Reason of mankind as a whole.
>
> It means that there must be a transformation of principal mechanisms which determined the evolution of the biosphere during billions of years, there must be its transition to a completely new situation unknown to us, with new principles of evolution, new principles of selection dictated by human reason. This is a sequence of the Vemadsky's idea that man is becoming the principal factor of the evolution of the planet."[33]

In an epoch of transition to the noosphere, says Moiseev, mankind will have essentially to change its own organization.[34]

Moiseev says that:

> "The development of Reason opens the potential possibility of the emergence of such forms of organization of society that are capable of insuring the goal-oriented development of nature and society. Reason may become the main factor of their development and the emergence of an epoch of

32 *Ibid.*, p. 361.

33 *Ecology, Morality and Politics, Questions of Philosophy*, No. 5, 1989, p. 5 (in Russian).

34 *Ibid.*, p. 6.

> noosphere. This will be a radical transformation of all the process of the evolution similar to the emergence of Life and Reason."[35]

Principal characteristics of the noosphere according to Moiseev are the following:

1. The increasing role of Reason in settling human affairs and determining the destiny of mankind.
2. Acceptance by men of an ecological imperative, or in other words the existence of a critical ecological threshold in relation to society and nature that cannot be crossed if mankind wants to survive. A central point of this ecological imperative is the elimination of wars.
3. Acceptance of a moral imperative that is compliance with restraints imposed by the needs of society.
4. Collective resolution of all conflicts arising in society by reasonable compromises.
5. Creation of new social institutions capable of insuring a co-evolution of society and nature. Co-evolution means such a development of society and its influence on the biosphere that not only does not destroy the biosphere, but on the contrary contributes to its further progress and the progress of the human race.

Moiseev states that:

> "The emergence of a noosphere transformation of the biosphere into a sphere of Reason, if it comes at all, is a stage in the evolution of the planet similar to the emergence of Life,. the formation of the biosphere, the appearance of Man and Reason."[36]

The theory of noosphere correctly indicates a growing role of reason in human affairs and especially the necessity of increasing the role of collective reasoning in managing human affairs in general and international affairs in particular to ensure survival.

The world society theories as stated earlier are inspired by speedily growing interaction and interrelation between States and peoples, by increasing the importance on the international arena of new non-State actors.

In general the world society theories make, each in its own way, a contribution to the study of the complex problems of the present-day society and of the interstate system. They examine many new factors influencing the development of society and of the interstate system. Their projects contain elements that should be taken into consideration in international studies.

However, a theory must be based on correct evolution of facts, of their interactions and development. These theories start, in my view, with an unrealistic assessment of the situation in the international arena. The principal question is the role of States.

35 *Justification of Oneness, Questions of Philosophy,* No. 4, 1988, p. 23 (in Russian).

36 *At a Critical Threshold, Questions of Philosophy,* No. 3, October, 1988, p. 170 (in Russian).

If the state of nature theory overestimates the role of States, the world society theories either minimize this role or, as the last theory simply ignore it.

It is true that the behaviour of States in the interstate system is more and more influenced by new factors on which the attention of the world society theories is focused. In this respect these theories are helpful. But it is one thing to say that factors determining behaviour of States have essentially changed and it is quite a different thing to assert that the decisive role of States has diminished radically.

In actual life, in spite of the increasing role on the international scene of non-State actors, decisions on global problems that determine the fate of our civilization are taken by States.

And there are no indications that this situation may drastically change in the foreseeable future.

That is why a denial of the existence of the interstate system is wrong and even dangerous and further study of this system is of great importance.

3. The Notion of International Community

The notion of international community is widely used now in international documents. For instance, in Article 53 of the Vienna Convention on the Law of Treaties of 1969, reference is made to "the international community of States as a whole". We find the term "international community" also in the 1979 Convention Against the Taking of Hostages. The Convention on the Regulation of Antarctic Mineral Resources Activities of 1988 uses the same term as the convention of 1969 on the law of treaties – "the international community as a whole."[37]

It is often used in resolutions of the United Nations General Assembly. The Declaration on the Occasion of the Twenty-fifth Anniversary of the United Nations, approved by the General Assembly on 24 October 1970, states:

> "The international conventions and declarations concluded under its auspices give expression to the moral conscience of mankind and represent humanitarian standards for all members of the international community."

The Declaration on the Principles of International Law concerning Friendly Relations and Co-operation among States in Accordance with the Charter of the United Nations, adopted by the United Nations General Assembly on 24 October 1970, calls for a more effective application of the fundamental principles of international law "within the international community". In the Declaration on the Establishment of a New International Economic Order and in the Charter of Economic Rights and Duties of States adopted by the General Assembly in 1974 the expression "international community" is repeatedly employed.

---

37 *International Legal Materials*, Vol. XXVII, No. 4, 1988, p. 858.

Western literature makes frequent use of the term "international community" in the sense of a community of States. In that connection two separate terms are commonly used, namely "international society" (société internationale) or "international community" (communauté internationale).[38]

Hans Morgenthau, for example, considers it self-evident that international relations are relations among States.[39]

Raymond Aron distinguishes between "international systems" as systems of interstate relations and "international society" encompassing non-interstate relations extending beyond the borders of States.

> "International systems . . . encompass entities that have regular diplomatic relations with each other . . . International systems represent the interstate aspect of society."[40]

He then adds that "transnational society expresses itself in commercial exchanges, the migration of persons, common opinions, organizations that cross national frontiers".[41] At the same time Aron stresses the connection between these two types of relations. He writes:

> "States have concluded numerous agreements, conventions, or treaties, some of which concern above all transnational society, while others concern both transnational society and the international system."[42]

John G. Stoessinger refers to the system of international relations as "the Nation-State System".[43]

Generally, however, Western specialists in international law define the concept of "international community" as including both States and international organizations, that is, they define it in the broad sense of the word.

In his five-volume course on international law, Professor Charles Rousseau (France) writes that by international law he means "a set of rules that apply to the international community".[44] In defining the concept of international relations he stresses that he understands them "in the very general sense of relations among States".[45]

---

38 In Western literature one occasionally comes across debates that are, in our opinion, purely scholastic, as to which of these terms best corresponds to the present state of international relations.

39 See, for example, his *Politics among Nations,* New York, Knopf, 1960; *In Defense of the National Interest,* New York, Knopf, 1951.

40 *Paix et guerre entre les nations,* Paris, Calmann-Lévy, 1962, p. 113.

41 *Ibid.*

42 *Paix et guerre entre les nations,* Paris, Calmann-Lévy, 1962, p. 115.

43 The Might of Nations. World Politics in Our Time, New York, Random House, 1967, p. 7.

44 Droit international public, Vol. I, Paris, Editions Sirey, 1970, p. 13.

45 Ibid., Vol. IV, Paris, 1980, p. 1.

Wilfred Jenks, an English international legal scientist, who worked for many years in the International Labour Organisation and was its Director-General till the end of his life, entitled one of his numerous books Law in the World Community[46].

Professor Alfred Verdross and Professor Bruno Simma (Austria) refer to the "community of States" (Staatengemeinschaft).[47]

Professor Mario Giuliano (Italy) writes that "international law . . . is a part or an aspect of a wider reality . . . which is called international society (società internazionale)". By this he implies "a society of States (società degli Stati)".[48]

Professor Manuel Diez de Velasco Vallejo (Spain) considers that the international community *(Comunidad Internacional)* consists primarily of States, international organizations, and for historical reasons, of certain non-State entities.[49] Under non-State entities he includes, aside from international organizations, the Holy See, the Order of Malta, belligerents, insurgents and national liberation movements.[50]

Professor Cesar Sepulveda (Mexico) also describes the international community as a community of States.[51]

A. Cassese uses interchangeably the terms "world community" and "international community" as meaning a sum total of States.[52]

The term "international political system", in the sense of a system of States, seems to be mostly used in the United States. M. Janis speaks of "the international political system of nation-States".[53] A book by F. S. Northedge has the title *International Political System*.[54] A book by A. M. Scott bears the title *The Functioning of the International Political System*.[55]

But in the recent "Restatement" the term "international community of States" is used.[56]

In the Soviet press the term "international community" is employed very often, primarily in reference to the United Nations which includes practically all the States. In Soviet literature on international relations and international law this term is employed relatively infrequently.

So the notion of international community frequently used now, means a sum total of the States of the earth. This is a useful notion in many respects and in particular when one deals with the notions of general or universal international law.

---

46 *Law in the World Community*, London, Longmans, 1967.

47 Alfred Verdross and Bruno Simma, *Universelles Völkerrecht, Theorie und Praxis*, Berlin (West), Dunker & Humblot, 1967, p. 71.

48 *Diritto internazionale*, Vol. I, Milan, A. Giuffrè Editore, 1974, pp. 8-9.

49 *Instituciones de derecho internacional publico*, Vol. I (6th ed.), Madrid, Editorial Tecnos, 1982, p. 48.

50 *Ibid.*, pp. 232-241.

51 *Derecho internacional* (8th ed.), Mexico, Editorial Porrfia, 1977, pp. 276279.

52 *International Law in a Divided World*, Oxford, Clarendon Press, 1986, pp. 10 ff.

53 *An Introduction to International Law*, Toronto, Little, Brown and Co., 1988, pp. 4 ff.

54 *International Political System*, London, Faber and Faber, 1976.

55 *The Functioning of the International Political System*, New York, Macmillan & Co., 1967.

56 *Restatement of the Law. The Foreign Relations Law of the United States*, American Law Institute Publishers, 1987, p. 16.

4. A New Theory of the Interstate System

As I have shown earlier there are many theories trying to explain complex events in the international arena. I have also stated that most of these theories have contributed one way or another to the understanding of these events. I am going to present my own theory of the interstate system in the hope that it will not be completely useless.

A new theory proceeds from the fact that, in spite of the appearance in the international arena of many new actors, the role of States has not diminished but increased. Indeed, global problems that are the most important and on the resolution of which depends the very existence of mankind may be solved by States only. Of course the behaviour of States is nowadays influenced, as I have stated before, by many new factors that must be taken into consideration.

The second important point of this theory is the following: there is an interstate system embracing States, intergovernmental organizations, nations fighting for their independence (that is, States in the process of emergence), international conferences, associations of States other than international organizations (such as the non-aligned movement, or the Group of 77), various international bodies at the State level (such as international intergovernmental commissions, international courts), international law and other social norms functioning in this system and also relations and interactions between these components.

I have given a similar definition of the concept of "international system" in a paper presented to the annual meeting of the Soviet Association of International Law.[57]

The third important point of this theory is that the interstate system is an integral system. All events in our world and even in the universe may be considered as interrelated and from this point of view any set of things may be considered as a system. However, relations between some phenomena may be considerable, or negligible, or amounting to zero. Relations may be immediate or effected through some intermediate system or systems. A system-approach proceeding from this premise is very often successfully used in different global studies, in the studies of world order, etc.

But there may be another approach when one looks for an integral system.

Now the question is – what is an integral system? I borrow a definition from philosophical studies.

There are dozens of definitions of the concept of "system" in the philosophical literature (V. N. Sadovsky analyses nearly all those that have been most frequently used).[58]

Academician V. G. Afanasyev describes an "integral system" as a

> "totality of objects whose interaction conditions the presence of new integrative qualities that do not exist in its component parts. It is above all in

57 G. I. Tunkin, "XXV syezd KPSS i osnovniye problemy sovetskoi nauki mezhdunarodnogo prava" (The Twenty-fifth Congress of the CPSU and the Basic Problems of the Soviet Science of International Law), in *Sovetsky yezhegoknik mezhdunarodnogo prava 1976*, Moscow, 1978, p. 12.

58 *Osnovaniye obscchei teorii sistem* (The Foundations of General Systems Theory), Moscow, 1974, pp. 93-102.

> this respect that an integral system differs from a simple aggregative system, a simple collection, conglomerate, or a mixture, such as a heap of grain or stones, or accumulations of minerals within the earth whose properties are simple sums of corresponding properties of their component parts."[59]

V. N. Sadovsky notes that

> "specific relations and linkages are established among elements of a set that constitutes a system. It is this which transforms the set of elements into an integrated whole, in which each element is ultimately linked with all others while its properties cannot be understood without considering that linkage. In its turn the overall system's properties are not a mere sum-total of the properties of its component elements but are determined by the presence of specific linkages and relations among them, i.e., are constituted as integrative properties of the overall system. The presence of ties and relations among the system's elements and the resulting integrative properties of the system make possible a relatively autonomous distinct existence and functioning (and in some cases development) of the system."[60]

V. S. Tyukhtin provides the following definition of a system:

> "A system is a set of components of a particular nature that are linked with each other, and have ordered relations and quite specific properties; that set is characterized by a unity that expresses itself in the set's integrative properties and functions."[61]

All components of the interstate system enumerated above interact with each other. States interact with each other, with international organizations, with international law and other social norms, etc. International organizations interact with each other, with States, with international law, etc.

Of all the multiple relations in the interstate system there must be singled out the most important ones that are characteristic of the specific nature of this system. Basic components of the system are States. Relations among States as sovereign entities have a specific character and this is reflected in all the other components and relations within the interstate system.

With the exception of international moral norms all other components of the interstate system are created by States: international organizations, international organs, norms of international law, etc. Qualitative characteristics of interstate relations differentiating them from other international relations is the most important feature of the interstate system.

59 *Sistemnost i obshchestvo* (Systems Approach and Society), Moscow, 1980, p. 24.

60 *Op. cit.*, pp. 83-84.

61 *Otrazheniye, sistemy, kibernetika* (Reflection, Systems, Cybernetics), Moscow, 1972, p. 11.

The interstate system may be called the international State universe in spite of the fact that States are only partially integrated into the system, remaining primarily a part of its environment.

Other essential characteristics of the interstate system are its integral qualities. Integral qualities of an integrated system, as stated earlier, are qualities which do not amount to a sum total of the qualities of its components, but constitute something new resulting from the interaction of the components of the system. The more intensive are these interactions, the higher is the degree of the integral qualities of the system.

The interstate system belongs to a rather decentralized social system. However, with the growing interdependence of States, the intensity of the interactions between all the components of the interstate system is growing and as a result a degree of integral qualities of the system is increasing. This is felt in the global interstate system, and especially in its subsystems that are mainly in international organizations.

Put in another way, the interstate system does not behave like a set of isolated components, first of all as States, but as an integral system. The behaviour of the system is not equal to the arithmetical sum total of the individual actions of its components.

We may take as an example the United Nations, although it should not be equated with the global interstate system. Actions of the United Nations result from interactions of its various components, primarily of States, and are different from the sum total of actions of individual States. They constitute the actions of this international organization as a system.

There is still another aspect of the integral or systemic qualities. Participation in the interstate system influences the behaviour of individual actors. Again, the example of the United Nations may be referred to. The United Nations, as a system, exercises considerable influence on the behaviour of the actors in this system, first of all upon the behaviour of States.

The components of the interstate system enumerated earlier are in constant interrelation and interaction and, taken together, constitute an entity possessing integral qualities. This means that the described set of components is an integral system.

Any definition of an integral system raises the question of its environment.

The interstate system in the sense described above has never been studied. The science of the interstate system is yet to be created. Maybe these lectures will be a contribution to this science. Therefore, the problem of the environment of the interstate system has never been studied as well.

But some interest may present ideas about environment with regard to the system of interstate relations. In Western literature on international relations an opinion has been expressed by some authors that the system of interstate relations embraces all society and therefore its environment, if any, may only be outer space.

Referring to the system of international relations Philippe Braillard states that:

> "...what essentially characterizes this system is not, as in the case of international subsystems, a greater intensity or a specificity of interactions among actors, but the fact that the system's field extends to the entire planet".[62]

62 *Théorie des systèmes et relations internationales,* Brussels, Etablissements Emile Bruylant, 1977, p. 12.

He continues:

> "As one seeks to imagine and analyse the global (planetary) international system the question inevitably arises concerning what constitutes the environment of the system that by definition encompasses all international relations."

He notes that ". . . only a few authors have addressed themselves directly to that question, and the answers that they have offered are widely divergent".[63] Braillard's own view is that "that system's only possible environment is outer space".[64]

Yet if the system's environment is outer space it must include not only the entire human race but also nature.

Referring to both "international relations" and the "international system", Professor Marcel Merle, in his turn, criticizes authors who limit international relations solely to interstate relations.

"Most authors who consider the international system, and who seek to give their definition of it, in fact consider only the system of diplomatic and strategic relations or else of inter-governmental relations . . . The 'international system' is thus defined arbitrarily on the basis of a totality of relations that clearly extend to only a part (even though this may be the most important one but nevertheless only a part) of international relations."[65]

Subsequently he states even more specifically that "international relations include the totality of public and private exchanges that extend beyond national frontiers".[66]

While he does not state this explicitly, Merle comes very close to describing the international system as one that includes all society.

> "If one considers the hypothesis that the international system envelops all relations, all flows, or all exchanges that take place between numberless actors dispersed throughout the planet, one limits oneself to a statement that is almost a tautology."[67]

From Merle's subsequent arguments it becomes more clear that his conception of the international system includes all of human society: in other words, "because of its global as well as closed character, the international system can no longer export its contradictions",[68] and is thus "deprived of all external environment".[69]

63 Philippe Braillard, *op. cit., supra,* footnote 62, p. 126.
64 *Ibid.,* p. 129.
65 *Sociologie des relations internationales,* Paris, Dalloz, 1976, p. 125.
66 *Ibid.,* p. 141
67 *Ibid.,* p. 408.
68 *Ibid.,* p. 413.
69 *Ibid.,* p. 411.

In our view, such conceptions are not valid. It is true that society is a system. This is precisely the way society is viewed by Marxist- Leninist theory.[70] It is also true that modern society is a global system. Academician V. G. Afanasyev notes that

> "being a part of nature and of objectively existing reality, so-ciety as a higher font' of movement of matter endowed with reason constitutes a complex integral system . . .[71]

But society as a system and the interstate system are different phenomena. The interstate system is one of human society's sub-systems. As noted earlier, it includes only relations among States and other relations at that level, the actors who engage in these relations, and other components. Clearly, that is not all of society.

Only some social relations are international, and only some of these are integrated into a global or regional interstate system. Even relations that extend beyond national frontiers, but are not interstate, form only a part of the environment of such systems.

Events within a State that influence its external policies do influence the international system in some way. But one must not forget that domestic events and events in international arenas take place within different systems.

In the Soviet literature on international relations a view has been expressed by V. I. Gantman that the environment of the system of interstate relations includes natural systems and processes, a world socio-economic system, world economic systems, a world process of scientific and technological revolution, a world revolutionary process, a process of ideological struggle, world military strategic factors, different societal systems and processes within various States, politics and political processes, in particular foreign policy.[72]

There are two concepts of environment in the philosophical sense: narrow and wide. According to the wide conception the environment of a system includes all that is outside the system. The narrow conception includes in the environment only those phenomena that have essential relations with the system.

As stated earlier, all objects and processes in the universe are interrelated. Therefore, all of them may be considered as having relations with the system in question. But first, these relations in certain cases may be negligible. Second, some of these relations may reach the system through other intermediary systems and therefore to consider them as exercising an immediate influence on the system under consideration would be incorrect.

The correct notion of the environment of the global interstate system is, in our opinion, the following. The global interstate system is a subsystem of a wider social system – of society as a whole. Society is in interrelation with the nature and

70 See V. P. Kuzmin, *Printsip systemnosti v teorii i metodologii K. Marksa* (The Principle of System Analysis in K. Marx's Theory and Methodology), Moscow, 1980.

71 *Op. cit.*, p. 160.

72 See *System, Structure and Process of Development of Contemporary International Relations*, Moscow, Nauka, 1984, pp. 26-30 (in Russian).

natural factors and societal factors interact. Society influences nature, nature influences society and this influence may be felt in the global interstate system as a component of society. It means that natural phenomena cannot be considered as part of the environment of the global interstate system.

A peculiar character of relations between the global interstate system and its environment is due mainly to the fact that States – the main components of the system – are at the same time part of its environment. States constitute principal channels of communication between the global interstate system and its environment – society as a whole.

The interstate system is an open system, not only in the sense that there is a constant exchange of information between this system and its environment, but also because there is an interpenetration of certain components of the interstate system and the environment.

For instance, international law as a component of the interstate system penetrates into the States' legal systems. This penetration depends on the provisions of the States' constitutions as well as on international law. Human rights may be taken as an example showing that in this field international law penetrates more and more into the sphere of national legal systems.

Norms of national legal systems may sometimes penetrate into the interstate system. Such is the case of the open sea where ships are considered in principle as being under the jurisdiction of a flag State. The same principle is applied to outer-space objects launched from the earth.

If we address the world economy we shall see that international and national regulation are intermingled.

International non-governmental organizations, to a certain extent, penetrate into the interstate systems. Some of them have, for instance, a consultative status in the United Nations and several specialized agencies. In the Charter of Paris for a new Europe the participants stressed the major role that non-governmental organizations, religious and other groups and individuals have played in the achievements of the objectives of the CSCE and expressed their intention to further facilitate their activities for the implementation of the CSCE commitments by the participating States. They stated that these organizations, groups and individuals must be involved in an appropriate way in the activities and new structures of the CSCE.

In such cases they are actors in the interstate system. But, as it has rightly been pointed out by A. Scott, "an actor may or may not be a part of a particular system under study".[73]

In some regional intergovernmental organizations, private corporations and individuals penetrate into these subsystems of the interstate global system. The most advanced example in this sense is the European Communities.

The activities of States and international organizations as components of the interstate system extend more and more frequently outside the interstate system. For instance,

73 *The Functioning of the International Political System*, Macmillan Company, New York, Collier-Macmillan Limited, London, 1967, p. 37.

international treaties on private international law, the number of which is steadily growing, are treaties between components of the interstate system. However, they regulate relations outside this system.

The conclusion is that the interstate system is an open system. At the same time it is an integral system having its own integral qualities and relatively separate from its environment.

It has been proved by philosophical studies that whenever there is an integral system one should not limit one's self to a study of components of the system, and factors influencing the system, though it is indispensable, but also one should study a system as a whole. That is why I suggested several years ago that there should be a science of the interstate system requiring the joint efforts of many social and natural sciences.[74]

The main objective of this science would be a study of changing relationships and interactions among the components of the interstate system, relationships and interactions between the interstate system and its environment, and finding ways and means of a reconstruction of the existing interstate system to make it more adequate to the requirements of a new era in the history of mankind.

The theory of the interstate system distinguishes itself in many respects from other theories about international affairs.

There are authors presenting "possible systems" that may be applied to a study of international affairs. So Professor E. B. Haas writes:

> "Systems . . . refer to ways adopted by outside observers to interpret actions; they are analytical devices scholars use to make the real world understandable to themselves and to their fellow scholars. Systems may stress or slight the empirical world; what matters is that the empirical world need not be aware of the system."[75]

One cannot deny that such studies may help to understand international events, but in essence this method cannot bring satisfactory results.

My method is different; it is a Marxist method – from reality to abstract conclusions. Of course, even authors of "possible systems" are under the influence of reality, whatever their intentions. And in the second case, in trying to find out the existing system and to examine it, an author presents his own vision of things. But still the difference of approach is evident and I believe that my method is more productive.

From the state of nature theory the theory of the interstate system differs greatly by taking into account, at least such is the intention of the author, new realities on the international scene, new actors and other new phenomena. This makes it possible to examine two forms of regulation in the interstate system-balance of power regulation and the regulation based on the co-ordination of the wills of States and effected through international law and organization. (See Chapter VI.)

74 See G. Tunkin, "About the Necessity of a Science of the Interstate System", *Questions of Philosophy*, No. 1, 1987.

75 *Beyond the Nation-State*, Stanford, Stanford University Press, California, 1964, p. 53.

The interstate system differs from the notions of the international community and the system of interstate relations first of all in scope. The system of international relations, or the international community, may be considered as a subsystem of the interstate system as described earlier. Both may be called one-level systems, whereas the interstate system is a multi-level system (different levels of actors and different levels of norms). This difference opens for the theory of the interstate system a possibility to examine not only relations among States but also other components of the system in their interaction.

The interstate system differs from world societies as described by respective theories first of all in scope. It does not embrace all international events which, in my opinion, do not constitute an integral system. The study of all international events taken together is of necessity, whatever the intentions of the authors, a factors study. It certainly contributes, as stated before, to the understanding of international events. However, the study of the interstate system as an integral system is, in my view, a higher level of scientific studies and therefore gives more possibilities for deeper understanding of international events.

Chapter II International Politics and The Creation of Norms of International Law

International politics may be defined as an interaction of foreign policies of States in the interstate system. It is omnipresent in this system. It exercises a decisive influence on the creation and functioning of international law. But being omnipresent, international politics is not omnipotent as will be shown later.

1. General Theory

Norms of international law are created in international political processes. As in the interstate system there are, in principle, no mechanisms that may create for the actors of this system legal norms, as such norms are created by the actors of the system, primarily by States as the principal actors.

The process of creating norms of international law is the co-ordination of the wills of States (on other subjects of international law) concerning the content of the rules of conduct and their recognition as legally binding

In spite of the substantial differences between treaties and customary processes of creating norms of international law they have a common basis, namely the co-ordination of the wills of States or of other subjects of international law.

The creation of norms of international law is a process taking place in the interstate system. This is a politico-legal process that is governed by the norms of international law regarding the creation of the norms of this legal system. It is influenced by many events taking place in the interstate system and in its environment, that is in society as a whole. The environment influences the process of creating norms of international law mainly through States who, being part of the interstate system, are at the same time, and first of all, part of the environment. They bring an influence to the environment in the process of creating norms of international law.

The process of creating norms of international law consists of two stages: co-ordination of the wills of States regarding the content of a rule of conduct and the co-ordination of their wills concerning mutual recognition of the rule as legally binding.

The content of a State's will is its international legal position. It includes the general attitude of a State toward international law, to its progressive development, its concept of international law, its compliance with norms of international law, etc. In other words, the international legal position of a State embraces its position on all questions of international law expressed not only in its declarations, but first of all in its conduct, that is what Guy de Lacharriere called "politique juridique extérieure".[76]

The international legal position of a State, as part of its foreign policy, reflects the national interests of the State that combine real interests of the people of this State and the interests of the ruling classes.

For centuries it has been considered that the "national interests" of a State were its egoistic interests. Such an understanding is no more consistent with contemporary realities. Of course each State has its special legitimate interests that must be respected. But in the contemporary world common interests of mankind, reflecting categorical necessity of solving, by common efforts, global problems menacing the very existence of mankind, should influence more and more the international policy of States and their international legal position. These common interests, by the force of circumstance, have become part and parcel of the "national interests" of States. That is why a new political thinking demands that common interests must prevail over the egoistic interests of States, or at least be co-ordinated with them. This idea was proposed by M. Gorbachev in his article published in *Pravda* on 17 September 1987.

Soon after the Second World War Hans Morgenthau published a book, *In Defense of the National Interest*,[77] in which he professed an idea that the foreign policy of a State should be determined by its national egoistic interests and by nothing else. The book was clearly intended to strike a blow to mondialistic conceptions of world order that were current after the war. Now it is high time to write a book *In Defense of the Interests of Mankind.*

For creating norms of international law, it is not needed that wills of States participating in the norm-creating process be identical. It is only necessary that they be co-ordinated or agreed as far as the content of the rule and its mutual recognition are legally binding.

At the end of the XIXth century H. Triepel, in accordance with the German legal doctrine of the time, argued that only the superior will, in comparison with the wills of subjects of law, may create norms of law for these subjects. According to him, as a result of the agreement between States a new superior will is created, a so-called common will *(Gemeinwille),* resulting from the mixing of identical wills of different States. This common will is the source of the norms of international law.[78]

Some Soviet international lawyers expressed an opinion very close to that of Triepel. So, for instance, Professor L. Alexidze wrote about the existence of a

> "new complex common will different from the wills of States taking part in a process of norm-creating. This new will, resulting from the co-ordination of various wills, is the comparatively independent will of a collectivity of States."[79]

76 *La politique juridique extérieure,* Paris, Economica, 1983.

77 *In Defense of the National Interest,* New York, Knopf, 1951.

78 *Völkerrecht und Landesrecht,* Leipzig, 1899, s. 32.

79 *Some Questions of the Theory of International Law. Peremptory Norms,* Tbilisi, 1982, p. 167 (in Russian).

Professor E. Usenko expressed the following opinion:

> "If by common effort Soviet scholars were able to accept an idea that as a result of the co-ordination of the wills of States a norm of international law expresses one will that may be called a coordinated will, this would be correct and would contribute to the strengthening of international law. This would be a logical development and a summation of the conception of the co-ordination of the wills."[80]

The failure of Triepel's theory to give a proper explanation of the process of creating the norms of international law and their essence is due to an unwarranted application of municipal legal-system notions to the interstate system that is essentially different from a State system. Indeed, in municipal systems, norms of law are created by a State's will that is superior in comparison to the will of the subjects of these legal systems. Norms of international law are created by the co-ordination of the wills of States, but not by some higher will. This is the principal characteristic of the norms of international law that distinguishes them from norms of municipal law.

As to a notion of "common will", one may argue that as soon as the wills of States are co-ordinated with regard to the content of a rule and its acceptance as legally binding, these wills have some common content that may be called common will. But no new will is created as no new subject of the will results from the norm-creating process and a will is always a will of a subject.

The process of creating the norms of international law includes interconditionality of wills which means that a recognition of a rule as a norm of international law is given by a State under the condition that other States participating in the norm-creating process do the same. In other words each State accepting a norm of international law and thereby undertaking a legal obligation to comply with that norm, accepts it under the condition that other participants in the process do the same. This is a principle of reciprocity that is embodied in norms of international law in the process of their creation and which is essential in a process of the functioning of these norms.[81]

What is the relationship between the final outcome of the co-ordination of the wills of States, and their international legal position? Even in the course of a single conference for drafting an international treaty the international legal position of a State may change. It is not uncommon that, at an international conference at which the positions of other States become known, the delegation of a particular State concludes that its initial legal position on issues on the conference agenda calls for adjustment. Of course, even in the initial formulation of a State's international legal position consideration is given to known or assumed legal positions of other States and also to the possible course of the expected negotiations. But international legal positions are formulated by men

80 "The Relationship of International and National (Domestic) Law", *Soviet State and Law,* No. 10, 1984, p. 49 (in Russian).

81 See in this sense B. Simma, *Das Reziprozitätelement in der Entstehung des Völkerrechtsgewohnheitsrecht,* Munich/Salzburg, 1970.

who may fail to take into account all relevant circumstances, commit errors of judgment and base themselves on incorrect assumptions concerning the expected course of the conference. Whenever new circumstances later develop, or new assessments of facts are made, this may change a State's international legal position on the particular issues being discussed. Concessions that may consequently be made in search of a generally acceptable compromise may then result from changes in its international legal position.

So, for instance, at the Vienna conference on diplomatic relations of 1961, the Soviet Union delegation had instructions to vote against a provision contained in the draft convention presented by the International Law Commission regarding the diplomatic status of the representatives of the Pope. It was considered an unjustified privilege and discrimination with regard to other religions. In the course of the conference it became clear that all the delegations, with the exception of the Soviet bloc delegations, would vote for this provision. In these circumstances, as head of the USSR delegation, I asked Moscow to permit the delegation not to vote against the said provision of the convention but to abstain. Permission was given and thereby the position of the Soviet Union on this point was changed.

At the Antarctic conference in Washington in 1959 the conference was blocked by our refusal to agree to a proposal that "the present Treaty does not prevent the use of military personnel or equipment for scientific research or for any other peaceful purposes". As acting head of the USSR delegation I cabled to Moscow three times to obtain permission to accept this proposal. When at last I received this permission and said "yes" at a meeting of the heads of delegations which sat behind closed doors and settled all the thorny problems before convening the plenary meetings where the agreements reached by the heads of delegations were put on record, the discussion of the treaty was actually terminated.

Changes in positions of States participating in conferences intended to adopt international treaties occur very frequently and virtually at any conference.

But concessions in the process of creating norms of international law may also take place without any change in a State's international legal position. A State may accept a compromise in particular issues while continuing to consider that it would be better to act otherwise, and may continue to defend principles and norms that it advocated earlier. Even the acceptance of a compromise proposal as a norm of international law that is mandatory for a given State does not prevent it from continuing to advocate the adoption of a different norm that is more far-reaching than the one that is already accepted. For example, when the Moscow treaty of 1963 banning nuclear weapon tests in the atmosphere, in outer space and under water, was discussed, the Soviet Union argued for a complete prohibition of all nuclear tests. It accepted the compromise proposal concerning the prohibition of nuclear tests in the atmosphere, in outer space and under water, because it felt that such a treaty would serve the cause of peace. But the adoption of the Moscow treaty of 1963 has not changed the position of the Soviet Union with regard to the need for prohibiting all nuclear tests. This is the basis for its continuing efforts to prohibit all nuclear tests and conclude a corresponding treaty.

In creating new norms of international law States appear as sovereign and equal entities. This is why legally their wills are of equal importance. That legal equality is quite important even though it reflects only one aspect of relations among States. It is a major principle of any international conference at which international treaties are being drafted, and it means that States have a right to determine their own international legal position autonomously. When the text of a treaty at an international conference is put to the vote, each State has only one vote.

The legal equality of States in the process of creating norms of international law means that the majority of States cannot create norms which are mandatory for a minority of States and that it does not have the right to seek to impose these norms on other States.

But there is also another aspect of the process of the co-ordination of the wills of States, namely the actual circumstances that basically determine the international legal position of States and that exert a decisive influence on the process of the co-ordination of their wills. These actual circumstances are highly diverse. The process of creating norms of international law takes place in the international system within which various State interests clash and in which the actual role of States in particular issues and their overall influence in the international system is felt.

Thus, in the elaboration of international legal norms bearing on the cessation of the aims race or a reduction in armaments a decisive role is naturally played by States possessing nuclear weapons, since there is no power within the international system that could decree legal norms that would be binding upon those States.

On the other hand, at the Third United Nations Conference on the Law of the Sea, in questions relating to the legal regimes of areas that do not belong to States, an enormous role was played by developing countries because of their great number, even though their own utilization of the world's oceans is inconsiderable.

2. International Politics and the Treaty Process

The influence of politics in the process of creating norms of international law by way of international treaties is evident at all stages of this process.

Even at the preliminary stages of the treaty process the influence of politics is inevitable. Indeed, any reasonable preliminary process has to take into consideration that it is preparing a draft treaty to be submitted to the political decision of States. When, for instance, the International Law Commission prepares draft articles on some subject it is guided not only by considerations of abstract desirability. It is trying to find a balance of interests and foresee how far States may go in their political decisions when discussing these articles.

In the process of the co-ordination of the wills of States, State policies play a decisive role. As stated earlier, the international legal position of a State is part of its foreign policy. A whole treaty process is a politico-legal one.

The decisions of States relating to the content of the rules contained in a treaty, the duration of a treaty, its denunciation and the final decision to accept a treaty as legally binding, all these are political decisions.

From a political, as well as from a legal, point of view the treaty process of creating norms of international law has many advantages over the customary process. It offers possibilities for open discussions so important in reaching a compromise. It is impossible to imagine that, for instance, global problems of today may be solved in the customary manner.

3. International Politics and the Customary Process

The primary question is whether customary norms are also created by the wills of States as conventional norms, or they originate spontaneously without the participation of the wills of States. On the answer to this question depends an answer to the question whether politics take a role in the formation of customary norms. There are two main theories on the subject.

According to the theory of the co-ordination of the wills of States the customary process of creating the norms of international law, though different in form from the conventional process, is essentially the same in nature. In both cases the nature of the processes of norm-creating is the co-ordination of the wills of States.

The customary process, as well as the conventional process, consists of two stages. As a result of uniform practice there may emerge a rule of conduct that is usually followed by the States. This may be usage (a custom not legally binding) or a norm of international comity. At this, the first stage of the co-ordination of the wills of States is terminated. The process may continue in the direction of creating a norm of international law or may stop there for some time or forever.

The second stage of the customary process is the recognition by States of a usage as legally binding, that is, as a norm of international law. This is an expression of the wills by the States. For a usage to become a norm of international law it is not sufficient that one State recognized it as such. At least two or more States should recognize the usage as a norm of international law. This means the coordination of the wills of States regarding recognition of the usage as a norm of international law. This co-ordination of the wills includes, as in the case of conventional norms, the interconditionality of these wills.

It is very important to understand that the co-ordination of the wills of States regarding recognition of usage as a norm of international law happens not instantly, but is a process of the gradual growth of the belief that the usage in question has already become legally binding. It is also of importance to understand that the sphere of validity of a customary norm widens gradually, but the process may begin with only two States.

To become a norm of general international law the customary norm should be accepted by all, or almost all States. The expansion of the sphere of validity of customary norms is a process analogous to that of the expansion of the sphere of validity of conventional norms. States which did not participate in the elaboration of an international treaty, and later acceded to it, and States which did not take part in the formation of a customary norm, but later recognized it as legally binding, are in the same position.

As stated earlier, the creation of customary norms of international law is a process of the co-ordination of the wills of States. But at the first stage of this process a spontaneous element may be present. A State may act the same way without any intention to create a usage or a State may have an intention to create a rule to be followed by others. In both cases a usage may emerge as a result of uniform practice.[82]

An established usage means termination of the first stage of the co-ordination of the wills of States, namely co-ordination of these wills regarding the content of a rule of conduct.

The question arises: what constitutes State practice leading to the creation of a usage? On this point opinion is divided. Professor Bernhardt is certainly right when he says that "it is impossible to enumerate exhaustively the arts or kinds of behaviour which constitute relevant State practice".[83]

It seems indispensable to see a difference between international State practice in general and State practice within the framework of the customary process of creating norms of international law. If the first embraces all the behaviour of States in the international arena, the second includes only those acts, or their absence, that have relevance to the process of creating norms of international law.

The first is much wider than the second. Even some norm-creating State practices such as practices creating political norms or minis of resolutions-recommendations of international organizations are, in principle, not included in the customary process of creating norms of international law, although they influence this process. State practice within the framework of the customary process means practice amounting to the first stage of the co-ordination of the wills of States with regard to the content of a rule of conduct and thereby forming a usage in the relations amongst States. Ignoring this distinction leads some authors to conclusions that any State practice has a significance for the customary process.[84]

It must be State practice expressed in the conduct of State organs, but not practice of private corporations or individuals.

As to the second stage – the recognition of a usage as a legally binding norm – it is evidently an expression of the State's will and therefore a political act. Therefore, in the co-ordination of the wills of States in the process of the formation of the customary norms of international law politics plays the same role as in the process of formation of conventional norms although in a different form.

According to the second theory prevailing in the West many norms of international law originate without the participation of the wills of States. Professor M. Virally stated this theory in the following terms:

"En réalité, le droit coutumier est l'expression des contraintes résultant de la coexistence d'une pluralité d'Etats et de la nécessité ressentie par ceux-ci de conduire leurs relations mutuelles de façon régle . . .

82 See G. Danilenko, "The Theory of International Customary Law", *German Yearbook of International Law,* Vol. 31 (1988), p. 15, whose opinion is very close to this.

83 *Encyclopedia of Public International Law,* Instalment 7 (1984), p. 63.

84 See, for instance, M. Villiger, *Customary International Law and Treaties,* Dordrecht, 1985.

A certaines époques, la pratique a pu être considérée comme l'élément unique du processus coutumier. Une analyse plus fine fait apparaître l'élément *d'opinio* (retrouvée dans la pensée des juristes romains), se founant à son sujet et perinettant de séparer la coutume, juridiquement obligatoire, du simple usage, ou de la courtoisie *(comity)*, observé pour des raisons diverses, mais non juridiques."[85]

This seems to me an accurate presentation of the theory. The first part of the statement relating to the necessity to regulate relations between States may be applicable to international law as a whole. But it states only the social necessity of international law. The second part is important, saying that a usage, that is a uniform practice, becomes a norm of international law when there exists an *opinio juris*.

The notion of *opinio juris* is usually interpreted in a very formal way as something that exists, or does not exist, without examining how *opinio juris* is actually being formed. This leads this theory into an impasse. As Professor J. Kunz noted, on the one hand, practice plus *opinio juris* create a customary norm and, on the other hand, for the emergence of the customary norm it is necessary that States act with a conviction that their actions are in accordance with their legal duties. But as soon as a corresponding customary norm does not yet exist, such a belief has no foundation. "Hence," says Kunz, "the very coming into existence of such a norm would presuppose that the States acted in legal error."[86]

Indeed in a formal approach it is not taken into consideration that *opinio juris*, that is a conviction that a certain rule has become a legal norm, grows gradually, that it is a process in the relations among States.

The essence of the *opinio juris* is that a State recognizes a certain rule as a norm of international law, thereby expressing its will. When other States express their recognition of the rule as a norm of international law, a tacit co-ordination of the wills of States takes place and a usage becomes a legally binding norm.

This interpretation, in my view, corresponds better to the meaning of the provision of the Statute of the International Court of Justice which is a generally recognized statement on the subject and reads as follows: "International custom, as evidence of a general practice accepted as Law" (Art. 38 I, *b* of the Statute). In spite of the deficiencies in its formulation, that have been often noted in legal literature, the core of the content is clear: the practice should be accepted (or recognized) as law, that is, as legally binding, as a norm of international law.

Our interpretation shows that in fact the difference between the two theories discussed earlier is more imaginary than real. In essence both theories recognize that customary norms of international law originate as a result of interstate practice or in other words a usage, and acceptance (or recognition) of this usage as a legally binding norm.

This interpretation leads to a conclusion that the influence of politics in creating norms of international law covers also customary norms, because State practice as

85 "Panorama du droit international contemporain", *Recueil des cours de l'Academie de droit international de La Haye*, Vol. 183 (1983-V), p. 182.

86 "The Nature of Customary International Law", *American Journal of International Law (AJIL)*, Vol. XLII (1953), p. 94.

well as recognition by States of a usage as a norm of international law are both political phenomena.

Thus norms of international law originate in the processes of international politics. But the norm-creating process is not simply a political one, it is a politico-legal process. Norms of international law are created only when there is a political will and the process of creating norms proceeds according to the rules of international law.

One may say that there is the primacy of international politics in the process of creating norms of international law. It is appropriate to recall that Montesquieu considered international law as "loi politique".[87]

4. State Practice and the Development of International Law

This problem is generally covered by the general theory I have discussed in paragraph 1 of the chapter. However, I have decided to examine it separately in view of a recent trend in the doctrine of international law to present some grave violations of international law in its progressive development.

International law, as everything else in the world, is in constant change. But first, this does not mean that international law is something fluid; changes take place in different parts of it as a result of changes in international politics (international practice) which in its turn depends on the development of the international system and society as a whole. Second, it does not mean that changes in international politics bring *ipso facto* changes in international law.

In the theory of international law there is a conception according to which State practice as such is international law as far as customary norms are concerned. Of course, the prevailing theory requires a second element – *opinio juris*. But at the same time this theory insisting that customary norms are created without participation of the wills of States opens the way to various theories that come by a round-about way to a conclusion that State practice is international law. A theory of Professor McDougal belongs to such theories.

The international practice of a State or several States may be a violation of international law. However, according to McDougal's theory as I understand it, one can never say whether a certain act of a State is a violation of international law or a starting point in creating new norms. In the opinion of McDougal, if a certain act of a State which violates existing international law does not meet the powerful resistance of other States it may be considered: *(a)* as lawful; *(b)* or even as changing international law. (See Chapter III.)

As M. Kaplan and N. Katzenbach say:

> "it is this flow of effective decisions by officials invoking international norms that is the substance of international law. We cannot categorically state its content."[88]

87 *De l'esprit des lois*, Paris, Librairie de Lecointe, 1832, tome deuxième, p. 58.

88 *The Political Foundations of International Law*, New York, 1961, p. 28.

There is an element of truth in McDougal's theory as far as the problem in question is concerned. In exceptional cases when an act of a State, contrary to international law, not only meets with no ob jections on the part of other States, but is followed by some of them, it may lead to the creation of new norms of international law. So, for instance, the proclamation of the United States President of 28 September 1945 concerning the continental shelf led to the formation of new norms of international law regarding the continental shelf. These new norms were embodied in the Convention on the Continental Shelf of 1958.

But a situation becomes quite different when an exception is transformed into a rule as is done by the American legal realists. McDougal's very complicated theory means, in fact, that international politics (or practice) in the form of "power processes" not only creates norms of international law but is international law. (See Chapter III.)

Theories equating international State practice with international law may be used and in fact are used to justify any policy including the gravest violations of international law. On the basis of such theories, and especially that of McDougal's theory, attempts are being made to justify the invasion of Grenada in 1983 and Panama in 1989 by the United States although both were the gravest violations of international law. I shall discuss these attempts a little later.

The same is the case as far as the intervention of the Soviet Union in Czechoslovakia in 1958 and the invasion of Afghanistan in 1979 are concerned. Attempts were made by some Soviet international lawyers to justify the intervention in Czechoslovakia by references to the Warsaw Pact provisions. As chief of the legal department of the Ministry of Foreign Affairs of the USSR at the moment I may testify that the Warsaw Pact was drafted in conformity with the norms of international law and contained no provisions that might justify this intervention. But even if there had been such provisions they would have been invalid as derogating from the norms of *jus cogens*.

Attempts to justify the interventions of the United States in Grenada and Panama were based in the final analysis on McDougal's theory and went very far. So Professor d'Amato, confusing State practice with international law, discussed a question "May the United States under international law violate international law?"[89] The question itself is inadmissible for an international lawyer. There is a fundamental principle of international law that has been formulated in the Declaration of Principles of International Law concerning Friendly Relations and Co-operation Among States in Accordance with the Charter of the United Nations of 1970 as follows: "The principle that States shall fulfil in good faith the obligations assumed by them in accordance with the Charter."

The question put by D'Amato is contrary to this principle. But many international lawyers in the United States pay little attention to the principles of international law calling them "generalities". Actually, the principles constitute the core of contemporary international law, they are its fundamental norms. This is the opinion of the International

89 *AJIL* (1987), p. 375.

Court of Justice which, in its judgment in the case concerning the *Delimitation of the Maritime Boundary in the Gulf of Maine Area (Canada v. the United States)* stated:

> "In the Chamber's opinion, the association of the terms 'rules' and 'principles' is no more than the use of a dual expression to convey one and the same idea, since in this context 'principles' clearly means principles of law, that is, it also includes rules of international law in whose case the use of the term 'principles' may be justified because of their more general and more fundamental character."[90]

D'Amato says:

> "This question, which seems on its face to compel its own answer, in fact is not as clear as it appears. To be sure it is perfectly clear with respect to treaties, and maybe a word about that would help set the stage. A treaty is a legal obligation that, under international law, simply cannot be legally violated . . . Where the answer is not clear is the realm of customary international law . . Consider how customary international law has evolved and changed through the centuries. Lacking a real legislature, the system appears to have tolerated changes in customary law as a result of departures from pre-existing norms. Are these departures not also violations[91]?"

D'Amato calls international law a "fluid kind of law"[92] and comes to the following startling conclusions with regard to the American interventions in Grenada and Panama:

> "The US interventions in Panama and, previously, in Grenada, are milestones along the path to a new nonstatist conception of international law that changes previous nonintervention formulas".[93]

And he proceeds:

> "A major customary law development since 1948 was the intervention by the United States in Grenada in 1983, and a second one is the Panamanian intervention of 1989."[94]

I have examined the position of Professor D'Amato based on McDougal's theory in some detail to show to what absurd and dangerous conclusions this theory may lead.

90 *ICJ Reports 1984*, para. 79.
91 81 *AJIL* (1987), p. 376.
92 *Ibid.*, p. 377.
93 84 *AJIL* (1990), p. 517.
94 *Ibid.*, p. 523.

And also because a considerable part of the American international law doctrine is, to a greater or lesser extent, contaminated by this theory.

If one accepted D'Amato's reasonings one could never say whether a clear violation of international law is really a violation or a starting point for creating new norms of international law. One would have to wait years and years to see whether this violation would bring about a change in international law. Although in exceptional cases a violation, as I have stated earlier, may influence the development of international law, exceptions only confirm the old rule *ex injuria non oritur jus.*

D'Amato's position makes international law, as he himself puts it, fluid, depriving it of one of the main characteristics of law, its normativity.

It is worthwhile to remember a judgment of the International Court of Justice in the *Nicaragua v. United States* case. The Court stated:

> "If a State acts in a way prima facie incompatible with a recognized rule, but defends its conduct by appealing to exceptions or justifications contained within the rule itself, then whether or not the State's conduct is in fact justifiable on that basis, the significance of that attitude is to confirm rather than to weaken the rule."[95]

Professor H. Thierry has rightly pointed out:

> "Il y a là un point de droit de grande importance. Si en effet la pratique effective contraire à des normes reconnues était de nature à mettre en cause la validité de ces normes, le droit international dans des domaines tels que ceux de l'emploi de la force ou des droits de l'homme serait vidé de toute substance."[96]

The second problem that should be mentioned in this context is the gap that exists between international politics (and practice) and international law which is analogous to the gap between domestic policy and municipal law.

International law may lag behind international politics or may be ahead of it. The fact is that changes in international politics usually do not immediately exercise their influence on international law. New political situations have to exercise their influence on the positions of States with regard to international law. Then the very process of creating new norms of international law, that is, the process of the co-ordination of the wills of States, takes time. Therefore the influence of international politics may be reflected in international law with some delay. In this case international law is behind international politics.

At the same time norms of international law are created for the future. They not only reflect the existing international politics, but are intended to influence it in a desired direction in the future. In this case, norms of international law go ahead of international politics.

95 *ICJ Reports 1986*, para. 186.

96 "L'évolution du droit international", *Recueil des cours,* Vol. 222 (1990- III), p. 39.

Then there is a problem of relationship between international politics (and practice) as a reality and norms of international law as desiderata. The gap there is also inevitable as reality is always to a greater or lesser extent different from what is desired and planned. And this is not only because there are violations of international law, but also because results intended by States in creating norms of international law and actual results of the realization of these norms are not exactly the same.

However, whatever the gaps are between international politics and practice and international law, they may be bridged only by a way consistent with international law. There is no norm of international law according to which international politics (or practice) is *ipso facto* international law.

5. International Politics, The Resolutions of International Organizations and The Development of International Law

The discussion of the role of politics in the process of creating norms of international law would be incomplete without considering the part that resolutions of international organizations take in this process, because these resolutions are specific channels of the influence of politics on the development of international law.

The increasing role of the resolutions of international organizations in the norm-creating process is generally recognized.

The resolutions of international organizations are adopted by organs of these organizations consisting of States members. The actions of these States within international organizations constitute a part of their policies. Resolutions of international organizations result from the co-ordinations of the wills of States members of respective organizations. They are the acts of these organizations. Whatever the content of the resolutions, the role of politics in their formation cannot be denied.

The resolutions of international organizations, especially the resolutions of the United Nations General Assembly, influence the development of international law in two ways:

1. by creating legally binding norms;
2. by influencing the treaty and customary processes.

a. Legally Binding Resolutions

Legally binding resolutions of international organizations constitute a new process of creating the norms of international law, a new source of this law. Such resolutions actually exist in all international organizations. They concern internal matters of the organizations, such as rules of procedure, budgetary questions, registration of treaties, etc. These norms are part of the law of each international organization.

Now, however, some international organizations create legally binding norms that function beyond the internal activities of these organizations. Some specialized agencies, for instance, adopt regulations that are binding upon member States (the International Postal Union, the International Telecommunication Union, the World Health Organization, the International Civil Aviation Organization, etc.).

The constitutive instruments of international organizations provide for two methods of the entering into force of the regulations: express or tacit consent of the States. The regulations adopted by the Universal Postal Union are subject to ratification; regulations adopted by the International Telecommunication Union are subject to approval by States.

According to the procedure of tacit acceptance a State member is considered as having accepted the regulation and is therefore bound by it, unless during a period fixed by the organization it failed to notify the organization of its refusal to accept the regulation or of its reservations to it. Such is, for instance, the procedure with regard to sanitary regulations adopted by the World Health Organization. In the case of a State's refusal to accept the regulation, the State is not bound by it. In the case of reservations made by a State to a regulation, the question whether the reservations are acceptable is decided by the WHO General Assembly. If the Assembly decides that the reservations are not acceptable, the State that made the reservations is considered as being not bound by the regulation. The procedure of tacit acceptance of the regulations (or rules) exists also in the International Civil Aviation Organization and the World Meteorological Organization.

The question arises as to the nature of these regulations. Some authors consider that the regulations constitute international legislation. W. Friedmann says that the "powers of some international organizations to adopt these regulations are in effect legislative".[97]

Still more categorical is Professor P. Vellas. He writes:

> "Il s'agit ici d'un véritable pouvoir de nature législative; les règlements édictes par l'Organisation sont adoptés en exécution de leur constitution comme les lois étatiques le sont en exécution des constitutions internes."[98]

Professor P. Guggenheim expressed an opinion very close to those just quoted. Referring in particular to the WHO he said:

> "Ce sont surtout les règlements destinés à des situations extérieures qui sont l'expression d'une nouvelle technique de création de règles de droit international, technique qui se rapproche de la procédure législative du droit national."[99]

Thus two arguments are advanced in support of the proposition that international regulations are similar to internal legislation: (a) international regulations are adopted by a procedure analogous to that used in parliaments for adoption of laws; (b) the regulations enter into force immediately.

97 *The Changing Structure of International Law,* London, Stevens & Sons, 1964, p. 280.

98 *Droit international public,* Paris, Librairie générale de droit et de jurisprudence, 1967, p. 210.

99 *Traité de droit international public,* Vol. I, Geneva, Librairie de l'Université, 1967, p. 284.

The first argument is well founded. The regulations are adopted either by plenary or by restricted organs by a majority vote like laws in parliaments. This is an important innovation.

The second argument has also some weight. Regulations, like laws, enter into force without any additional procedure, but in contradistinction to legislation they are subject to tacit acceptance by States. It is also an important innovation.

It is certainly a new technique in creating norms of international law and this technique is likely to develop with the growth of international co-operation in scientific, technological, cultural and other fields.

b. Resolutions-Recommendations and the Treaty Process

The growing number and increasing role of international organizations has led to their having greater influence in international norm-creating processes.

Some resolutions of international organizations may constitute part of the treaty process of creating norms of international law. Such is the position of those resolutions by which international organizations adopt texts of multilateral treaties.

Resolutions serve sometimes as a basis for the treaty process of creating norms of international law. The Universal Declaration of Human Rights adopted by the United Nations General Assembly on 10 December 1948 was a starting point for the treaty process which led to the adoption by the General Assembly in 1966 of two treaties – the international covenants on human rights. The same is true of the Declaration on the Elimination of All Forms of Racial Discrimination adopted by the General Assembly in 1963. The text of the Convention on the Elimination of All Forms of Racial Discrimination was adopted by the General Assembly three years later.

On 13 December 1963 the General Assembly adopted the Declaration of Legal Principles Governing the Activities of States in the Exploration and Use of Outer Space. In a separate resolution the General Assembly stated that

> "consideration should by given to incorporating in international agreement form, in the future as appropriate, legal principles governing the activities of the States in the exploration and use of outer space".

In the practice of the International Labour Organisation recommendations are very often adopted with a view to transforming their norms in the future, with possible modifications, into conventional norms legally binding upon member States.

The treaty process in such cases is not a continuation of the process of fowling recommendatory norms. The latter does not become part of the treaty process. The treaty process starts with the first stage of the co-ordination of the wills of States, that is the co-ordination of the wills concerning a rule of conduct. The parties to a treaty process are not legally bound by a recommendations-resolution which constitutes a starting point for the elaboration of a treaty. The transformation of a recommendatory norm into a treaty norm entails a basic change of its status: it becomes legally binding upon States. It is, therefore, natural that States approach this process with much greater care than they do the formation of recommendatory norms.

If one compares the provisions of the International Convenants on Human Rights of 1966 with the provisions of the Universal Declaration of Human Rights of 1948, the difference is not difficult to see. It is true that in this case the difference is due not only to the fact that in the first instance the States members of the United Nations created recommendatory norms, whereas in the second, legally binding norms of international treaties. In the course of nearly two decades the situation in the world generally and within the United Nations has changed considerably. The correlation of forces in the United Nations in 1966 was materially different from that of 1948. The membership of the Organization doubled between 1948 and 1966, mainly because of the influx of new States born in the process of the liberation of colonial and dependent countries.

As a result of this new situation, the right of self-determination, of which there is no mention at all in the Declaration of 1948, occupies a place of prominence in the covenants on human rights. The provisions of the covenants regarding the right of self-determination are a considerable development of the contents of this principle in comparison with the Charter of the United Nations.

However, the fact that in the second case legally binding norms were being formed also made itself felt. The western States agreed, for instance, to include in the Declaration of 1948 social, economic and cultural rights, such as the right to work, the right to education, the right to social security. However, they were hesitant to make these recommendatory norms full-scale conventional norms. The Western powers insisted on including the provisions regarding economic, social and cultural rights into a separate treaty. An escape clause was included in this covenant to the effect that no immediate realization of the rights recognized in the covenant is required, but that a State party to the covenant "undertakes to take steps . . . to the maximum of its available resources with a view to achieving progressively the full realization of the rights recognized in the present Covenant . . .".

This example is mentioned to prove that the process of creating conventional norms on the basis of recommendatory norms starts with the beginning, that is with co-ordination of the wills of States with regard to the contents of rules of conduct; this process is not a continuation of the process of creating recommendatory norms, and the parties to the treaty process are not legally bound by the recommendatory norms constituting the starting point of the treaty process.

c. Resolutions and the Customary Process

The role of resolutions in the process of forming customary norms of international law is very controversial. The number of normative resolutions of international organizations is growing. In voting for a resolution, States express their approval of certain rules of conduct embodied in the resolution. The question inevitably arises whether the consent, or as I call it, the co-ordination of the wills of States in such a case, has some significance in the framework of the customary process.

In a very abstract way, voting for a resolution may be considered as amounting, especially when there are several identical resolutions, to the first stage of the co-ordination of the wills of States that creates a usage. One may go even further and regard the voting for a resolution as encompassing the second stage of the co-ordination of the wills of States, that is the co-ordination of their wills with regard to recognizing the rules of the resolution as legally binding. This temptation is very great and some authors go, it seems, too far.

To clarify our point of view we shall examine two questions: *(a)* whether resolutions may be considered as evidence of State practice; *(b)* whether they may be considered as evidence of *opinio juris* (or, as I call it, of the second stage of the co-ordination of the wills of States)?

1. The Evidence of State Practice?

The Institute of International Law has for a number of years studied the problem of resolutions of the General Assembly of the United Nations. In comprehensive reports presented to the Institute Professor K. Skubiszewski stated that

> "with the exception of Messrs McDougal and Rosenne, the Members who replied to Question 3 generally admit that the G.A. resolutions can be regarded as evidence of State practice."[100]

As noted earlier there are grounds, when examined in an abstract way, for considering resolutions at least as part of State practice. But do resolutions really conform to or reflect State practice and do States believe that resolutions ought to correspond to or reflect State practice?

A State may vote for a resolution when it reflects its practice, but it may vote for a resolution that does not confoun either to its present practice or to the practice of other States in the sincere hope that the resolution may contribute to changing this practice. However, there are many instances when for political reasons a State votes for a resolution with which its practice is inconsistent and has no intention of changing its practice.

Among members of the Commission of which Professor Skubiszewski was rapporteur, who gave a positive reply to the question whether General Assembly resolutions can be regarded as evidence of State practice, were such eminent scholars as Bindschedler, Blix, Jessup, McWhinney, Monaco, Mosier, do Nascimento e Silva, Rousseau, Schachter, Ustor, Virally and Zemanek. It may well be that they, or some of them, meant State practice in general and in this sense General Assembly resolutions belong to State practice. However, State practice within an international organization is governed by the rules in force in that organization, but not by the rules of customary international law and, therefore, it does not constitute State practice in the framework of the customary process of creating norms of international law.

100 *Annuaire de l'Institut de droit international, Session d' Helsinki,* Vol. 61- I, 1985, p. 93.

2. The Evidence of Opinio Juris?

Quoting Skubiszewski's report again:

> "Messrs McDougal, McWhinney, Monaco, Mosler, do Nascimento e Silva, Schachter, Seyersted, Suy, Ustor, Valticos and Zemanek agree that resolutions can be regarded as evidence of the *opinio juris* (Question 5). Mr. Virally may be included in that majority. Some of these members add different qualifications and explanations. Messrs Bindschedler and Rosenne reply in the negative."[101]

Let us examine this problem more closely. What does *opinio juris* mean? Generally, it is a conviction that a certain rule is legally binding. Can a vote for a resolution be considered as evidence of such a conviction? When voting for a resolution States express their opinion, but it is not *opinio juris.* States vote for a resolution with the conviction that what they adopt is not legally binding (with the exception of resolutions on internal matters which, according to the constitutive instrument of an international organization are legally binding). They are aware that they act within the legal system of an international organization. Virally says that the United Nations General Assembly resolutions "do not constitute the *opinio juris*" but "express an opinion concerning desirable law".[102]

Acceptance of the thesis that voting for a resolution amounts to opinio juris brings us very close to the thesis that resolutions create norms of international law. McDougal and Rosalyn Higgins stop short of accepting this. Speaking of repetitive resolutions, McDougal says: "Repetition could, depending upon various features of the context, create the expectations required for a rule of law."[103]

Rosalyn Higgins has expressed the opinion that "collective acts of States, repeated by and acquiesced in by sufficient numbers with sufficient frequency, eventually attain the status of law."[104] Stating that resolutions of the United Nations General Assembly are not per se binding, Higgins wrote: "But the body of resolutions as a whole, taken as indications of a general customary law, undoubtedly provide a rich source of evidence."[105]

A comparison of the resolutions with the different stages of the customary process discloses some interesting features. This first stage of the customary process brings about the emergence of a usage which is a norm, a rule of conduct, although not an international legal norm. The co-ordination of the wills of States with regard to a rule of conduct as such is terminated. In contrast to the treaty process, it results in the emergence of a living norm which operates, although it is not a norm of law. The second stage consisting of the co-ordination of the wills of States regarding the recognition

101 *Annuaire de l'Institut de droit international,* Vol. 61-I, 1985, p. 94.

102 "Panorama du droit international contemporain", Recueil des cours, Vol. 183 (1983-V), p. 186.

103 Annuaire de l'Institut, Vol. 61-I, 1985, p. 258.

104 The Development of International Law Through the Political Organs of the United Nations, Oxford University Press, 1963, p. 2.

105 Ibid., p. 5.

of this rule as legally binding, that is, as a norm of international law may or may not follow.

Resolutions (normative) terminate the process of the co-ordination of the wills of States resulting in the emergence of recommendatory norms, which, like usages, are living norms. But there is a difference between these two types of norms. A usage is the reflection of States' practice, it is a rule which already operates. Resolutions are recommendations for the future.

As rules of conduct are fixed in a resolution, what can take place afterwards by customary process is the recognition by States of these rules as legally binding. The process of the co-ordination of the wills of States with regard to the recognition of such rules as legally binding does not preclude the possibility of changing these rules. But as the customary process, in contradistinction to the treaty process, does not include negotiations among States, the actual possibility of changing rules set out in recommendatory resolutions is no greater than the possibility of changing customary norms of international law already in existence.

From the above it follows that if norms of recommendatory resolutions become norms of international law by the customary process, such resolutions, as a rule, replace the first stage of the customary process of creating norms of international law. There is still no *opinio juris.* This develops later in the course of practice when States gradually recognize a norm contained in a resolution as legally binding.

There are many instances when certain norms of the United Nations General Assembly resolutions have become or are becoming customary norms of international law. To this category belong certain provisions of the Universal Declaration of Human Rights, certain norms of the United Nations General Assembly resolutions concerning the prohibition of colonialism, racial discrimination, apartheid, etc.

There is no problem when norms of resolutions become norms of international law in a traditional customary way, that is, by way of State practice. One remark is, probably, pertinent: if a State acts in accordance with the provisions of a normative recommendatory resolution this fact does not make such a resolution legally binding upon that State.

There is also the problem of the intentions of States in the course of adopting resolutions of the General Assembly. F. B. Sloan wrote that although as a rule General Assembly resolutions do not create legal obligations, if a State which voted for a resolution intended to bind itself legally, the resolution in this case imposed legal obligation on it.[106]

In voting for a recommendatory resolution members of an international organization create an act of the organization whose legal force depends on the provisions of the constitutive instrument of that organization. Such an act is recommendatory in nature. Recognition by States of recommendatory norms as legally binding is a special process not linked to voting on the resolution and goes beyond the organization itself. Even authors who believe that by voting for a resolution a State may legally

106 See "The Binding Force of a 'Recommendation' of the General Assembly of the United Nations", *British Year Book of International Law,* XXV (1948), 22, 31.

bind itself if such was its intention, as a rule admit that it is not the voting as such, but a different act of a State which makes a resolution legally binding. F. A. Vallat, for example said:

> "Delegations acting without special authority from their governments are limited by the provisions of the Charter. They cannot bind their governments except so far as the Charter allows. If by their votes or their speeches they purport to bind their governments, they do so not by virtue of their position as delegates to the General Assembly but by virtue of some extraneous authority from their governments."[107]

Emphasizing the actions of States by which recommendatory resolutions may become binding upon them, R. Bindschedler points out:

> "When an obligatory character is acquired by a recommendation, we have before us two different legal phenomena, the act of the United Nations remains a recommendation and, more specifically, a not obligatory recommendation. The States have no power to change the legal character of the acts of the Organization. However, to the recommendation, the nature of which does not change, is added a second act, which is a contractual or unilateral acceptance of binding character and which constitutes an obligation. This juridical act of the member State is the foundation of the binding character."[108]

However, to say this is not sufficient. It is true that States, whether members of the organization or not, may recognize norms of recommendatory resolutions as legally binding by customary process and that these actions of States are different from their vote on the resolutions in question. It is, at the same time, of considerable importance to point out that this procedure is outside the respective international organization. It is based not on the constitutive instrument of that organization, but on general international law.

d. Declaratory Resolutions of the United Nations General Assembly

The denomination of a resolution does not in and of itself change the legal status of the resolution. There are no indications in this respect in the United Nations Charter or in the generally accepted practice of the United Nations. There is no doubt, however, that only those resolutions which are considered to be of specific importance are designated

---

107 "The Competence of the United Nations General Assembly", *Collected Courses of the Hague Academy of International Law*, Vol. 97 (1957), p. 230.

108 "La delimitation des competences des Nations Unies", *Recueil des cours*, Vol. 108 (1963-I), pp. 349-350; see in this sense also Ph. Manin, *L'Organisation des Nations Unies et le maintien de la paix*, Paris, Librairie generale de droit et de jurisprudence, 1971, p. 271.

as declarations. But this denomination does not change the recommendatory character of the resolution.

The real problem is posed by those resolutions which are declaratory of existing international law. The declaratory character of a resolution should be expressed in the resolution itself with sufficient clarity. In the 1970 Declaration on Principles of International Law concerning Friendly Relations and Co-operation Among States in accordance with the Charter of the United Nations it is made in the following words: "The principles of the Charter embodied in this Declaration constitute the basic principles of international law . . ."

The term "declaratory" for such a resolution merely conveys its general character. Nobody disputes that the seven principles stated in the Declaration belong to the basic principles of contemporary international law. However, never before had the content of these principles been specified in such detail. There is, therefore, a considerable element of innovation in the Declaration of 1970.

The problem is whether the declaratory character of a resolution makes it binding upon the States which voted for it. The situation is as follows: in the event of a unanimous vote in the General Assembly there is the co-ordination of the wills of member States with regard to recognition of the content of the resolution as expressing international law in force. The question is what is the legal significance of this co-ordination of the wills?

The first possibility is that as soon as the process of the co-ordination of the wills of member States has taken place on the basis of the Charter, it produces those results which are provided for in the Charter, that is, a recommendation. The content of such a recommendation addressed to the member States would be an appeal to consider the principles as formulated in the Declaration as principles of existing international law, therefore as binding upon States.

The interpretation according to which the 1970 declaration on principles of international law is a recommendation has been suggested by some authors.[109]

Another interpretation is based on the assumption that the declaration is an interpretation of the United Nations Charter. Indeed the report of the Committee 11/2 at the San Francisco Conference, which raised no objections at the Conference, contained the following statement:

> "It is to be understood, of course, that if an interpretation by any organ of the organization or by a committee of jurists is not generally acceptable it will be without binding force."[110]

The inference is that an interpretation of the Charter, generally acceptable, is binding upon the members of the United Nations.

109 See, for instance, G. Abi Saab, "The Third World and the Future of the International Legal Order", *Revue egyptienne de droit international,* Vol. 29, 1973, P. 48.

110 *UNCIO,* Vol. XXII, pp. 710-711.

Proceeding from this premise M. Sahovic concluded that the declaration is legally binding as it constitutes an interpretation of the Charter. He says:

> "Since this is the first document after the adoption of the Charter to elaborate its basic principles and fully reaffirm their universal legal force, the unanimous adoption of the Declaration places it in the category of official interpretative acts, whose binding force derives from consensus of all the members of the United Nations."[111]

Schachter expressed essentially the same opinion referring to the 1970 Declaration on Principles of International Law as an example. "To the extent," said Schachter, "that they were interpretation, and agreed by all the member States, they fitted comfortably into an established source of law."[112]

Such a position is justified to a certain extent, as the declaration constitutes an interpretation of the principles of international law embodied in the Charter. But the declaration, as is evident from its text, goes far beyond the interpretation of those principles. The United Nations General Assembly resolution of 1962 (1815 (XVII)) concerning a study to be undertaken of the seven principles, emphasized that this was to be done "with a view to their progressive development and codification".

The Declaration was a considerable development of the principles embodied in the Charter of the United Nations. Therein resides its strength and its weakness. If the Declaration were a simple interpretation, that is, an explanation of the principles of the Charter, it would be of much less value. Actually, the Declaration develops these principles and formulates many new important concrete norms. Therein lies the historical significance of the Declaration and this makes it likely to become "a landmark in the development of international law".[113]

The main problem is whether voting for such a resolution may have an effect within the framework of the customary process of creating norms of international law. There are two elements required for a customary process: co-ordination of the wills of States with regard to the rules of conduct; and the co-ordination of the wills with regard to the recognition of these rules as norms of international law *(opinio juris).*

Logically it may seem that voting for a declaratory resolution, that is, for a resolution stating that the norms enunciated in it are norms of international law in force, should be considered as binding. That is what M. Virally assumed. He said that:

> "a declaration unanimously adopted constitutes, if its content so permits, that consent of the international community which is indispensable for the emergence of a customary norm."[114]

---

111 "Codification of the Legal Principles of Co-existence and the Development of Contemporary International Law", in *Principles of International Law concerning Friendly Relations and Co-operation* (ed. by M. Sahović), Belgrade, 1972, pp. 48-49.

112 "International Law in Theory and Practice", *Collected Courses,* Vol. 178 (1982), p. 113.

113 Resolution 2625 (XXV) of 24 October 1970.

114 *L' Organisation mondiale,* Paris 1972, p. 330.

A. Colliard is, however, more cautious. Discussing the problem of declaratory resolutions of the United Nations General Assembly, he said:

> "One may consider, especially when they have been adopted unanimously or with a few abstentions and a heavy majority in favour, that they express, at a certain moment, a consensus of the member States of the international community on a question.

They resemble, therefore, international custom of which they borrow one element.

The declaratory force is less than the binding force of a treaty, but it nonetheless exists."[115]

There is much truth in these statements. Indeed, it would be absurd if a State voting for a resolution, saying that certain norms of international law are in force, would afterwards express a contrary opinion. But to make declaratory resolutions legally binding there should be a general practice accepted as a norm of international law to the effect that voting in the General Assembly of the United Nations produces an effect outside the Charter, since according to the Charter, even such declaratory resolutions are also recommendations. In other words, there should be a norm of international law according to which voting for such resolutions in the United Nations General Assembly in addition to the results it produces on the basis of the United Nations Charter, has also other consequences, that is, the consequences within the framework of the customary process of creating norms of international law.

There seems to be insufficient evidence at present to maintain that such a norm is in the process of formation, still less that it has already emerged. The practice of the application of the 1970 Declaration on Principles of International Law will demonstrate the position of States on the subject and thereby resolve the problem one way or the other.

However, quite independently of this, the norms of a declaratory resolution, just as any other resolution, may get recognition of States as norms of international law by the customary process. There are indications that this may be happening with regard to the 1970 Declaration on Principles of International Law.

It may be said that resolutions of international organizations influence the processes of creating norms of international law and that this influence is increasing. It means that the influence of politics on the processes of creating norms of international law through these channels is growing.

To sum up, norms of international law are created in world political processes. The creation of these norms is a politico-legal process. A political aspect of this process consists in reaching a balance of interests of States participating in the process. A legal aspect means that a balance of interests achieved may result in creating norms of international law only if it is supplemented by the co-ordination of the wills of States regarding the content of the rules of conduct and their acceptance as legally binding, that is as norms of international law.

115 *Institutions des relations internationales,* Paris, 1974, p. 276.

If, however, a balance of interests is achieved, but there is no coordination of the wills regarding the creation of norms of international law, the result may be a simple political understanding without any obligations. But it may also result in creating political norms that contain obligations, but not of a legal character. (See Chapter V.)

Chapter III International Law and Politics

Norms of international law being created by politics are different from the politics, a social phenomenon that exercises its influence on politics. This is essentially a normative influence. At the same time, as an element of culture, international law also exercises a general influence on politics.

1. The Normative Influence of International Law

The normative character of international law is intrinsic in the very notion of law as a regulatory system. To deny the normative character of international law would mean to consider it as a sum total of social "judgments", "opinions", etc. As Professor S. Alekseev said:

> "Norm of law is not simply one of the variety of social norms, it is specific, essentially most developed, expressing the highest normativity that is characteristic of law."[116]

In the world literature on international law at present there are no authors who openly deny the normative character of international law. However, there are theories that, although not denying openly the normative character of international law, come to that by a round about way. I have in mind primarily the theory of Professor Myres S. McDougal.

McDougal is explicit in expressing his opposition to the view that international law is a system of binding legal norms. In his opinion such a concept of international law leads "too many people to make a sharp and unreal distinction between law and policy", and also considers that "the technical rules, which are said to constitute international law", help decide how one should act.[117]

In his interpretation,

> "international law, at highest level abstraction, is most relevantly conceived as a combination of the two fauns of power indicated above as formal authority conjoined with effective control, all a form of decisions in which

116 *General Theory of Law,* Moscow, 1982, Vol. II, p. 32 (in Russian).

117 "International Law, Power and Policy", *Collected Courses,* Vol. 82, A. W. Sijthoff, Leiden, 1954, p. 141.

> community prescriptions are formulated, invoked, and in fact applied in the promotion of community policies".[118]

The process of "decision-making" is one in which norms of international law are created, interpreted and reinterpreted.[119]

Professor R. Falk (Princeton University) defines international law in the following way:

> "By international law is meant the processes by which national governments and other actors stabilize and revise their interrelations through the assertion of claims and counterclaims about permissible behavior, and through the invocation of rules and procedures to justify their own behavior or condemn the behavior of other governments."[120]

Another disciple of McDougal, Professor M. Barkun (Syracuse University in the United States) states that "all manner of conceptual confusion" results from the fact that "in large measure we continue to construe international law as a coherent corpus of rules which needs only to be applied".[121]

In Barkun's opinion one should reject the traditional view that international law represents a sum total of standards which States must respect.[122] In effect, he calls for abandoning the conception according to which international law exists independently of politics, and for recognizing that its substance is the international policies of States.[123] In short, his conclusion is the same as that of McDougal, namely the confusion or merger of international law with politics.

McDougal asserts that "every application of general rules" of international law "requires the making of policy choices". The need for such a preliminary "making of policy choices" is based on the proposition that a variety of opinions concerning actual behaviour may exist when norms of international law are applied.[124] The conclusion at which McDougal arrives is obvious, namely "that making of policy choices" is a choice of methods of coercion.[125]

What, then, is international law according to McDougal? It is a set of "social prescriptions" that are created and constantly altered in "world power processes" through the mutual presentation by States of claims and counter-claims and that are effectively applied with the help of power. Thus, according to McDougal, international law, while

118 Myres S. McDougal, *op. cit., supra,* footnote 117, p. 181

119 *Ibid.,* pp. 182-183.

120 "The Role of Law in World Society: Present Crisis and Future Prospects", *Towards World Order and Human Dignity. Essays in Honour of Myres S. McDougal,* New York, The Free Press, 1976, p. 150.

121 "International Norms as Facts and Ideals", *American Society of International Law, Proceedings of the 66th Annual Meeting,* Washington, D.C., 1979, p. 41.

122 *Ibid.,* p. 42.

123 *Ibid.,* pp. 43-46.

124 Myres S. McDougal, *op. cit.,* p. 155.

125 *Ibid.*

not vanishing altogether, becomes a "social prescription", created, altered and applied with the help of force.

Recently McDougal vigorously restated his opposition to the normative concept of international law. He said:

> "The conception of international law recommended by Lasswell and his associates makes reference to the totality of this flow of authoritative decision, both constitutive and public order, within the global community: international law is most realistically regarded after the model of the American Legal Realists with respect to the law of any community, as that comprehensive process of authoritative decision by which the members of the larger community of human kind seek to clarify and secure their common interests in the shaping and sharing of all values. The inherited body of rules, described as international law in the positivist frame, with its abundant complementarities, ambiguities and incompletions, has meaning only in so far as it refers to past decision or to the guidance, not command, of future decision."[126]

The difference between the concept of international law as an "inherited body of rules" and the concept according to which international law is "the process of authoritative decision" is enormous.

According to the first concept, which is in full agreement with State practice, there are norms (or rules) of international law that prohibit certain actions by States and norms that authorize certain actions. For instance, the principles (or norm) of non-use of force prohibits the use of force in relations among States. The principle of the freedom of the seas authorizes navigation, air traffic over the high seas, etc., for all States. States are aware of these restrictions and permissions and thereby the norms of international law constitute a legal framework for their policies.

According to the second concept the norms of international law, if they do not disappear altogether, are fluid, uncertain and international law is viewed as something vague, as a "process of authoritative decision" in "world power processes".

The influence of the United States' municipal system of law where courts may, to a certain extent, create law and where law indeed may be considered, again to a certain extent, as a municipal system of law in international law that happens very frequently, is not justified. Municipal law is a component of a State system whereas international law is a component of a different social system – the interstate system.

This is my understanding of McDougal's theory which is a very complex one. To what extent my understanding corresponds to how the author himself understands it, is a different thing. It happens frequently that an author of a theory means one thing, whereas other people understand it differently. There is no doubt that McDougal, as

126 "The Dorsay Comment: a Modest Retrogression", *AJIL*, Vol. 82 (1988), No. 1, pp. 53-54.

most international lawyers, intends to contribute to the rule of law in the international community. Years ago, in 1952, McDougal wrote:

> "In our contemporary disillusionment it is again becoming a fashion to minimize both the role that law presently plays in the world power process and the role that, with more effective organization, it could be made to play in maintaining the values of a free, peaceful and abundant world society."[127]

I believe that McDougal is right in stressing the role of politics in creating norms of international law and in influencing their functioning. But, first, he considers international politics as power processes only and therefore as power politics. In reality there are two elements of international politics: power processes and processes of co-operation, they coexist in the present interstates system and interact. Second, in McDougal's theory international law is so impregnated by power that international law virtually disappears as a specific social phenomenon. This element of McDougal's theory seems to contradict the aim of the author that is increasing the role of international law in international relations.

As to the functioning of international law, according to McDougal a choice of policy should precede a choice of law. In my view, for the rule of law the choice should be vice versa as international law is a legal framework for politics.

These are, in my judgment, the principal contradictions in the theory of McDougal.

When I think of the different theories of international law I become more and more convinced that we all have to re-examine our views in the light of an essentially new situation on the international scene. We have entered a post confrontation era, the picture of international politics has considerably changed. There are new encouraging prospects for increasing the role of international law in the international community. In the light of the new situation and a new thinking we have to re-examine all the problems of international law with a view to making it a more effective means of ensuring the normal functioning of the interstate system, that is the functioning that would enable us to solve global problems and make the life of man more secure, free and prosperous.

2. The Norms of International Law

a. The Norms of International Law as Embodiment of Agreement Among States

As stated earlier norms of international law are created by the coordination of the wills of States (or other subjects of international law) and embody the agreements of these States.

This relates to the acceptance of the contents of the rules and of their recognition as legally binding. They also include reciprocity. (See Chapter II.)

This is a very important feature of the norms of international law, distinguishing them from the norms of municipal law.

127 "Law and Power", quoted from International Law in the Twentieth Century (ed. by Leo Gross), New York, 1969, p. 104.

The creation of norms of international law through the co-ordination of the wills of States characteristic of contemporary international law is of crucial importance for the social nature of these norms.

It ensures to a maximum possible degree that norms of international law embody a balance of interests of the States concerned.

It also ensures as far as possible that norms of general international law – the basis of the whole system of international law – reflect the common interests and values of mankind as a whole.

b. The Norms of International Law as Abstract Rules

In the general theory of law legal norms are usually characterized as non-personalized abstract rules addressed to a number of subjects of law.[128]

This characteristic is fully applicable to the norms of general international law. They are non-personalized, that is, addressed to all the States.

However, the greatest number of norms in the system of international law is particular norms. They may be personalized as well as not personalized. Norms of multilateral treaties with a considerable number of parties are usually of a non-personalized character, that is addressed to all the parties to the treaty.

Bilateral treaties may contain non-personalized as well as personalized norms. For example, the 1987 Soviet-American Treaty on the elimination of intermediate-range and shorter-range missiles incorporates both kinds of norms.

It is clear that non-personalized norms afford a larger latitude for politics than personalized norms.

c. The Legally Binding Character of Norms

As norms of international law regulate the relations primarily among States some authors suggested that they could not be real norms of law because State sovereignty is incompatible with the existence of norms binding upon a sovereign State. There have always been political motives behind such theories.

In the second half of the XIXth century, when German imperialism tried to remove legal obstacles to its expansionist policy, certain prominence was acquired by a theory denying the legal nature of international law. A well-known German jurist, Adolf Lasson, formulated at the time this theory, as follows: "As the legal order of a particular people the State must be fully independent of any external will or law."[129] The so-called norms of international law, Lasson as serted, are merely "rules of wisdom, not norms of law".[130]

Advocates of "political realism" nowadays, which is, in principle, nothing other than a revival of the XIXth-century German theory of *macht politik* (power politics), also

128 See, for instance, S. Alexeev, *General Theory of Law*, Moscow, Juridicheskaya Literatura, Vol. II, 1982, p. 33.

129 *Prinzip und Zukunft des Völkerrechts*, Berlin, Verlag von Wilhelm Hertz, 1871, s. 22.

130 *Ibid.*, s. 49.

come to deny the legal nature of norms of international law. Starting from the premise that relations among States are based on absolute State sovereignty and power, they quite consistently come to a conclusion that in the present state of international relations international law is not and cannot be a genuine law.

In particular, Morgenthau describes modern international law as "primitive", and hence incapable of playing any significant role in international relations.[131]

Raymond Aron in effect concludes that if States are sovereign, then international law is not law.

> "Any theory that has as its point of departure the sovereignty of many States and that in one way or another links law to that sovereignty deprives international law of certain constitutive characteristics of law."[132]

As has been shown earlier, American "legal realism" which negates the normative character of international law thereby denies its legally binding nature.

At present, in my opinion, it may be safely stated that there is a consensus among States and among international lawyers that norms of international law, as all norms of law, are legally binding.

In the Soviet theory of law a norm of law is usually considered as an "authoritative State prescription".[133] Professor Lukashuk has tried to apply this definition to international law.[134] However, it seems that the notion of a legal norm as an "authoritative State prescription" is not quite adequate. Of course in most of the States the norms of law are produced by State organs, that is by the State. But if we take Islamic law or customary law, which is valid in some countries, they have not been created by a State, but they are law. However, this definition is true in the sense that the authority of the State stands behind the law.

In any case that definition of a norm of law is not applicable to international law. Norms of international law are not commands of a superior authority, they embody agreements.

It is worthwhile noting the difference between the process of creating norms of law and the legally binding force of these norms. The process of creating norms of law explains how certain rules of conduct become a part of law, either municipal or international. It does not explain why norms of law are legally binding. Norms of law are legally binding because they are part of a specific social institution consisting of legally binding norms, the institution that has been formed in the course of history. In this sense Professor Berman was right when he said that "law is also history".[135]

---

131 Cf. *Politics among Nations,* New York, Knopf, 1948.

132 *Paix et guerre entre les nations,* pp. 709-710.

133 S. Alexeev, *General Theory of Law,* Moscow, Juridicheskaya Literatura, Vol. II, 1982, p. 34 (in Russian).

134 See *Mechanism of International Legal Regulation,* Kiev, 1980, pp. 5 et seq. (in Russian).

135 "Toward an Integrative Jurisprudence: Politics, Morality, History", *California Law Review,* Vol. 76 (1988), p. 787.

The question so frequently discussed as to why norms of international law are legally binding has never been properly answered. Indeed, to say that they are legally binding because they are an expression of social necessity, of the nature of things, or the embodiment of reason, etc., does contribute to the understanding as to why international law as a social institution is needed, but not why its norms are legally binding. There are other social norms functioning in the interstate system which are binding – moral norms, norms of wisdom, etc. – but they are not *legally* binding.

The answer to the question as to why norms of law are legally binding an only be given historically, that is by tracing the original role and development of the social institution called law. The situation is more or less analogous to the question why man has two eyes set on one side of his head whereas it might have been more reasonable and convenient to locate them in a different way.

The legally binding character of norms of international law distinguishes them from other social norms functioning in the interstate system.

But what does the legally binding character of the norms of international law actually mean? In my view it means that norms of international law fix the legal rights and obligations of the subjects of law. They have the highest binding force of any other norms in the interstate system. States cannot justify violations of international law by references to some other social norms functioning in the interstate system.

The legally binding character of norms of international law means then that in the case of their violation legal sanctions may be applied to the delinquent subject of law.

d. Jus Cogens *and* Jus Dipositivum

The character of the influence of norms of international law on politics depends also on whether these norms belong to the category of *jus cogens* or *jus dispositivum.*

Sometimes there is confusion with regard to this problem: when norms of international law are divided into two groups: mandatory norms and non-mandatory norms. This division is a wrong one. All norms of international law are mandatory, that is binding upon subjects of this system of law. But there are norms from which States may derogate *inter se* by mutual agreement and norms from which such derogation is not permitted. The first constitute *jus dispositivum,* the second – *jus cogens* or peremptory norms.

There was a vivid discussion of the problem whether *jus cogens* exists or even could exist in international law at the International Law Commission and in the literature, as well as at the Vienna Conference on the Law of Treaties in 1968-1969.

The opponents of *jus cogens* based their arguments on the premise that such principles (or norms) were possible only in a well-organized and highly centralized and effective system of law. As international law did not represent such a system of law, it could not contain principles having the character of *jus cogens.* This argument was most vigorously presented by Professor Schwarzenberger who said:

> "Unlike municipal law, international customary law lacks rules of *jus cogens* or international public policy, that is, rules which, by consent, individual subjects of international law may not modify. In fact, *jus cogens,* as

> distinct from *jus dispositivum*, presupposes the existence of an effective *de jure* order, which has at its disposal legislative and judicial machinery, able to formulate rules of public policy, and, in the last resort, can rely on overwhelming physical force."[136]

In spite of divergent opinions on the origin and nature of *jus cogens* the prevailing opinion in the International Law Commission and at the Vienna Conference on the Law of Treaties was that peremptory norms of international law existed. Article 53 of the Vienna convention says:

> "A treaty is void if, at the time of its conclusion, it conflicts with a peremptory norm of general international law. For the purposes of the present Convention, a peremptory norm of general international law is a norm accepted and recognized by the international community of States as a whole as a norm from which no derogation is permitted and which can be modified only by a subsequent norm of general international law having the same character."

I believe that when discussing the problem of *jus cogens* in the International Law Commission we did not fully realize that it was a new approach to international law. Actually the recognition of the existence of *jus cogens* was an element of a new thinking reflecting the realities of a new era in history, the era of a united world, in which global problems acquired crucial importance for mankind as a whole. Hence norms of international law relating to these problems could not be subject to derogation by particular agreements between States. As Professor S. Bastid said:

> "La règle posée par l'article 53 de la Convention de Vienne signifie que, par un traité, deux Etats ne peuvent modifier une norine impérative du droit international général. Autrement dit, on a admis que certaines règles avaient une importance fondamentale dans la vie internationale et qu'il ne pouvait y être porté atteinte par un traité sous peine d'affecter la validite de celui-ci."[137]

It was not a revival of the natural law doctrine. It is true that the text presented by the International Law Commission was susceptible to a different interpretation. At the Vienna conference it was specified that a peremptory norm of international law "is a norm accepted and recognized by the international community of States as a whole". In this formulation Article 53 of the Vienna convention leaves no doubt that peremptory norms of international law are created by the ordinary process of norm-creating in international law that is, as I call it, by the co-ordination of the wills of States. Lord McNair was right in saying that norms of *jus cogens* consisted of "rules which have been accepted either expressly by treaty or tacitly by custom . . ." .[138]

136 See *A Manual of International Law*, London, Stevens, 1967, pp. 29-30.

137 *Les traites dans la vie internatianale*, Paris, Economica, 1865, p. 102.

138 *The Law of Treaties*, London, 1961, pp. 213-214.

However, in the process of creating peremptory norms of international law there is a new element. The co-ordination of the wills of States includes a condition that no derogation from these norms is permitted and that a derogatory agreement will be void. The character of a peremptory norm may be acquired from its very inception, or later by a supplementary co-ordination of the wills of States.

There is no generally accepted list of peremptory norms of international law. But it is of great importance that the definition of *jus cogens* has found its place in the Vienna Convention on the Law of Treaties.

The majority of norms of international law have a character of *jus dispositivum.* From the point of view of the relationship between international law and politics the dispositive norms of international law leave a greater latitude of action for politics than peremptory norms.

3. The Changing International Law in the XXth Century

Evolution of society, international politics, and as a result, evolution of international law is a constant process. Progressive development of international law in its different fields is taking place every day. But from time to time some spectacular events in society as a whole and in international politics bring about such changes in international law that may be called revolutionary. Such transformations have taken place in the course of the XXth century.

As I see it, there have been six major societal events that resulted in great changes in world politics and in international law. First, the Great October Socialist Revolution in Russia. Second, the First World War and the creation of the League of Nations. Third, the Second World War and the creation of the United Nations. Fourth, the collapse of the colonial system. Fifth, the scientific and technological revolutions. Sixth, perestroika in the Soviet Union, the end of the "cold war", and the disappearance of the USSR.

The October Revolution of 1917 in Russia, as all revolutions, had two aspects: a positive and a negative one.

As a truly peoples' revolution it brought into the interstate system new progressive ideas and goals, new political and legal principles, such as the peaceful coexistence of States irrespective of their economic, social and political systems, prohibition of aggressive wars and proclaiming them crimes against humanity, the right of self-determination for all peoples and nations of the world, the new generation of human rights, economic and social rights, etc. These ideas and principles have exercised great influence on the development of world politics and international law and most of them have become principles of contemporary international law.

The October Revolution in Russia was a great revolution, although as far as internal goals of the revolution are concerned they have never been achieved and events have taken a turn basically different from the goals of the revolution. But in spite of that the October Revolution exercised an enormous progressive influence all over the world and will exercise it in the future. The goals of the French Revolution of the XVIIIth century, "liberté, égalité, fraternité" had also not been achieved, but this revolution had enormous influence on the world development in the XIXth century and it is justly called a great revolution.

The negative result of the October Revolution consisted mainly in splitting the world into two opposing socio-economic systems and ideologies. This inevitably led to a confrontation of these systems. The basic idea that nourished this confrontation was a victory of one system over another. Both competing sides were true to this idea.

On the part of the socialist States it had the form of an inevitable victory of socialism and communism all over the world. On the part of the capitalist States it took the form of a rejection of the right of the socialist system to existence and attempts to liquidate it by armed force.

The great idea proclaimed by the October Revolution was the idea of the peaceful coexistence of the new socialist State and the capitalist States. The position of the new Soviet State regarding peaceful co-existence with the capitalist countries was made clear by Lenin in the first days of the revolution. In his speech at the second All-Russia Congress of Soviets of Workers' and Soldiers' Deputies on 8 November 1917, Lenin stated, referring to the treaties of the Tsarist Russia with foreign powers: "We reject all clauses on plunder and violence, but shall welcome all clauses containing provisions on good-neighbourly relations."[139] This position was confirmed in many statements by the Soviet State. So, for instance, a resolution of the Seventh All-Russian Congress of Soviets in December 1919 said: "The Russian Socialist Federated Soviet Republic wishes to live in peace with all peoples."[140] In his statement to the newspaper correspondents of the *Observer* and *Manchester Guardian* in 1922 Lenin pointed out: "We believe that completely friendly relations with both powers (having in mind France and England – G.T.) are wholly possible and constitute our purpose."[141]

Since perestroika started in the Soviet Union and the people obtained freedom of speech, some anti-communist elements in the former USSR and now in the States that were part of it have been trying to paint the history of the Soviet Union only in black colours without giving themselves labour to examine the actual facts. As to peaceful coexistence they present it simply as a negative phenomenon.

Actually, the notion of peaceful coexistence as proclaimed by Lenin consisted of two elements: the practical political element and the ideological element. The first meant "friendly relations", the second – "world revolution". These elements were contradictory. For, practical policy the most important was the first element.

This element contained a new and very important idea. Up to the October Revolution all the States were divided as christian and nonchristian, as civilized and non-civilized, etc. Relations between these groups of States were on different legal and political bases. The core of the first element of the notion of peaceful coexistence was that all States irrespective of their economic and political systems must be on the same legal footing. It contained a seed of the pluralism in the interstate system.

139 Lenin, *On the Foreign Policy of the Soviet State,* Moscow, 1973, p. 17.

140 *Documents of the Foreign Policy of the USSR,* Vol. 2, p. 298.

141 Lenin, *Collected Works,* Vol. 45, p. 237.

The ideological element of peaceful coexistence was in contradiction with its practical political element. It embodied the principle of the victory of the socialist system all over the world and peaceful coexistence was meant as a way of achieving this victory by peaceful means. From the point of view of practical policy this element was of secondary importance, and its influence in the course of time might be mitigated if peaceful coexistence were accepted by the Western powers.

The Western capitalist States proceeding from their main ideological premise that a State which did not recognize private property in the means of production had no right to exist, categorically rejected the Soviet offer of peaceful coexistence. That was a major mistake made by the Western countries which had grave consequences in the future. It is true that later on the Western powers partially accepted peaceful coexistence as a *modus vivendi,* but it was too late.

Anyhow, both sides were guilty of the situation that existed between the First World War and the Second World War and it was characterized by elements of confrontation and elements of peaceful coexistence. The elements of confrontation prevailed and that was the main cause of the Second World War.

This situation decisively affected the development of international law in this period. Indeed, the progressive development of international law depends on the possibility of the co-ordination of the wills of States with regard to problems of international law. Elements of peaceful coexistence in world politics were favourable to progressive development of international law, but the elements of confrontation that prevailed hampered it.

The influence of the October Revolution on world politics and international law was combined with the influence of the First World War and the creation of the League of Nations.

The First World War, for the first time in history, had shown that war does not pay and that both sides suffer. The influence of the October Revolution and the First World War in this field coincided and brought about a strong popular movement for peace and against war.

The creation of the League of Nations aroused hopes that this new international mechanism would ensure lasting peace. Indeed, the creation of the League of Nations was a great innovation. For the first time in modern history a world organization for maintaining international peace and the enforcement, however partial, of international law was established. But the absence of the United States and the Soviet Union from the League, confrontation between States belonging to two opposing systems, and rivalry between the major capitalist countries made the League in most instances powerless.

The contribution of the League in the field of international law was also not very great. However, the Covenant of the League of Nations, though not prohibiting aggressive war, restricted the right of member States to resort to war and provided for sanctions with regard to members who waged war in breach of the Covenant. In this respect the Covenant of the League was a noteworthy step forward in comparison with the Hague conventions on the peaceful settlement of international disputes of 1899 and 1907, which in fact merely contained an appeal "before recourse to arms" to have recourse "as far as circumstances allow" "to good offices or mediation".

In 1923 the Assembly of the League of Nations adopted the draft treaty on mutual assistance that echoed the Soviet Decree on Peace of 8 November 1917 which proclaimed aggressive war as a crime against humanity. The draft said:

> "The High Contracting Parties solemnly declare that aggressive war is an international crime and severally undertake that no one of them will be guilty of its commission."[142]

But this draft never came into force.

In the Declaration on Aggressive War adopted by the League of Nations Assembly in 1927 aggressive war also was classified as an "international crime".

The greatest achievement of this period in the field of international law was the Pact of Paris (the Briand-Kellogg Pact) of 27 August 1928 that introduced into international law the principle of the prohibition of war. Article 1 of the Pact provided:

> "The High Contracting Parties solemnly declare in the names of their respective peoples that they condemn recourse to war for the solution of international controversies, and renounce it as an instrument of national policy in their relations with one another."

Article 2 of the Pact stipulated the obligation of the parties to settle their disputes by peaceful means.

In acceding to the Pact the Government of the USSR pointed out that the Pact did not go far enough, and that, in its view, wars for the purpose of suppressing national liberation movements should be prohibited, as well as such military activities as, for example, blockade, intervention, military occupation of foreign territory, of foreign ports, and so forth.[143]

The principle of the prohibition of war became part of the general international law before the Second World War. The right to wage war had been an important attribute of State sovereignty and therefore the emergence of this principle was an essential limitation of the sovereignty.

Bilateral conventions on the definition of aggression concluded by the Soviet Union with some neighbouring countries in 1933 were also an important contribution to the progressive development of international law. The judgment of the Nuremberg Military Tribunal, based primarily on the principle of the prohibition of war and the responsibility for the violation of this principle, referred as well to these conventions.

142 League of Nations, *Official Journal*, Records of the Fourth Assembly, Plenary Meetings, Special Supplement No. 13 (Geneva, 1923), p. 403.

143 *Izvestia*, 1 September 1928.

The victory of the Allied powers, consisting of capitalist and socialist States, over Nazi Germany and Japan and the creation of the United Nations have greatly changed the world politics that led to important developments in international law. The victory over the aggressors, who intended to replace international law by an animal doctrine of the rule of the world by superior races and guided by these doctrines committed horrible crimes against humanity, gave great impetus to democratic and liberation movements all over the world. Great hopes for a better future inspired not only millions of people, but to a certain extent also governments. This spiritual upheaval in world politics has found its expression in many important international documents, such as the Yalta and Potsdam agreements, the Statutes and Judgments of the Nuremberg and Tokyo Military Tribunals, and especially the Charter of the United Nations.

The Charter of the United Nations is an historic political and legal document, the corner-stone of contemporary international law. It developed the existing fundamental principles of international law, introduced into it new principles of primary importance, such as the non-use of force and the threat of force that was a development of the principle of the prohibition of war, the principle of self-determination of peoples, respect for human rights, etc. If the socialist October Revolution marked the beginning of the transformation of classical international law into a new international law the Charter may be considered as a foundation of this new law.

The Charter also established an international mechanism for law enforcement, more efficient than the mechanism of the League of Nations though covering mainly the part of international law relating to the maintenance of international peace and security.

Unfortunately, the old ideological postulate of the victory of one system over another was soon revived and a new phenomenon entered into world politics – the "cold war". And again, both sides contributed to this situation. The period after the Second World War was marked by a competition of the two tendencies in world politics: the tendency to peaceful coexistence and co-operation on the basis of the United Nations Charter and the confrontation of the two systems in the form of a "cold war". These tendencies coexisted, from time to time one was stronger than the other, but generally confrontation prevailed until the late 1980s.

At the same time the world political situation was changing and new factors influenced more and more world politics and the development of international law.

The collapse of the colonial system brought into the international arena many new States who, since the 1960s, constitute the majority in all the universal international organizations. The membership of the United Nations increased from the original 51 members to about 150 States.

These new States, now equal subjects of international law and members of the international community, had their specific cultures, interests and aspirations. They organized a Non-Aligned Movement as a counterweight to the two opposing military and political blocks: NATO and the Warsaw Pact.

In the field of international law the interests of developing countries were focused mainly on problems of sovereignty over natural resources, and a new international economic order. Generally the developing countries supported all steps aimed at strengthening international peace and security, the progressive development of international law and its codification.

Then came scientific and technological revolutions. These revolutions are changing not only the economic basis of society but society as a whole.

It is true that so far these revolutions have taken place only in the developed countries, but their world-wide influence is felt more and more strongly.

And last but not least, perestroika in the Soviet Union, started by Mikhail Gorbachev in 1985. It was nothing less than a revolution that included liquidation of the totalitarian regime created by Stalin, the introduction of democracy, freedom of speech, reconstruction of the economic system, new political thinking, new foreign policy that led to the liquidation of the confrontation between East and West, stopping the armaments race, etc.

I believe that many in the Soviet Union, including myself, were sure that the totalitarian regime could not last long and that a new revolution was inevitable. But, at the same time, the situation was such that this revolution might be only a revolution from above. This revolution was made by Gorbachev and I am sure that history will name him a "great statesman".

The introduction of democracy in the Soviet Union and the radical change in its foreign policy had important repercussions all over the world. Perestroika changed the face of world politics and created new opportunities for the primacy of international law in politics.

During the electoral campaign of 1992 President Bush stated that the United States had won the "cold war". This statement is certainly in the spirit of the "cold war". It shows how deeply our minds have been, in the course of almost 70 years, permeated with the idea of confrontation and victory of one system, one ideology over another and how difficult it is for a new thinking to completely replace this idea.

According to the new thinking we must consider the end of the "cold war" as a victory of Reason. The initiative in ending the "cold war" belonged to the Soviet Union, personally to Gorbachev. It is true that it was supported by all the major powers.

The coming of democracy, that had never existed either in the Russian Empire or in the Soviet Union, has brought about an upsurge of nationalism. This led to the so-called "Sovereignization", to a super decentralization instead of the former super centralization and finally to the liquidation of the Soviet Union. This was a great disaster for all of its peoples, the main cause of their economic hardships and political turmoil.

Instead of the Union of the Soviet Socialist Republics there have emerged 15 independent States members of the international community and of the United Nations. Some of them are trying to form a Commonwealth of Independent States. But as it seems that even if such a Commonwealth is created, it will not be a State – a subject of international law. It is certainly one of the major events in modern history. What will be the influence of this event on world politics and the development of international law remains to be seen. For the time being the principal successor of the Soviet Union – the Russian Federation – as well as other former Soviet republics, seems to be determined to pursue the foreign policy started by perestroika. An important indication of this is the steps taken recently by the Russian president Boris Yeltzin, in the field of the limitation of armaments and measures intended to further improve the relations of Russia with the United States, Great Britain, France and other countries. As to the attitude of the Russian Federation to international law its Declaration of Rights and Freedoms of Man and Citizen, adopted by the Russian Supreme Soviet on 22 November 1991, may be indicative. I believe that at present the attitude of a State to the international law of human rights is one of the major characteristics of its attitude to international law in general. The Russian declaration of human rights goes even further in protecting human rights than the analogous declaration adopted by the Congress of Peoples Deputies of the USSR on 5 September 1991. Of course, we had many good laws: the Stalin Constitution, the Brezhnev Constitution – both were not bad, but the actual situation was in striking contradiction with these laws.

As a result of the influence of the main developments I have described, international law has undergone in the course of the XXth century a radical transformation: classical international law has become a new, contemporary international law. The name "new" does not, of course, mean that it is a completely new law. In society there is, in a sense, nothing completely new, as everything has its roots in the past. As a French proverb says: "L'histoire se répète." However, there is another French proverb that says: "L'histoire ne se répète jamais." Both are partially true. The first means that everything has its roots in the past, and the second indicates that something new is essentially different from the past.

Already, in the middle of the XXth century, some authors came to the conclusion that the difference between the international law in force and the classical international law was so essential that contemporary international law should be called a new international law. Professor Bobrov of the Leningrad University was probably the first to give this name to contemporary international law.[144]

In 1959 Alvarez published a very important book, *Le droit international nouveau dans ses rapports avec la vie actuelle des peuple.*[145]

Jenks wrote:

> "The developments in the substance of the law of nations which have occurred in the first half of the twentieth century have so transformed the character and content of the international legal system that it can no longer be satisfactorily presented within the framework of the classical exposition of international law".[146]

144 See "The Great October Socialist Revolution and International Law", *Pravovedenie,* No. 1, 1957, p. 87.

145 Paris, Pedone, 1959.

146 *The Common Law of Mankind,* London, Stevens & Sons, 1958, p. 7.

Professor W. Friedmann suggested that: "many profound changes that have affected international law to such an extent that it is today something very different even from what it was a generation ago".[147]

Professor Fenwick entitled his article in the *American Journal of International Law* – "International Law: The Old and the New".[148]

In Europe, with the exception of the Soviet Union, the attitude to a qualification of contemporary international law as a new law has been more cautious and even negative. This is a result of the prevailing purely nonnative approach to international law. As an example one may indicate a very valuable and voluminous treatise on international law by Ch. Rousseau that may be called an encyclopaedia of international law.[149] The author describes the evolution of international law without specifically considering what essential innovations differentiate contemporary international law from classical international law.

Fitzmaurice, confusing theories of natural law with actual international law, came to a conclusion that there is nothing new in contemporary international law. He entitled one of the paragraphs of his report to the Jubilee Session of the Institute of International Law at Rome in 1973 as follows: "Traditional International Law Continues to Remain the Basis for the Future".[150]

It seems, however, that a change has recently taken place in the West European doctrines of international law as far as the distinction between classical and contemporary international law is concerned.

So, when Professor R.-J. Dupuy speaks of "droit relationnel" and "droit institutionnel" he examines essential differences between classical and contemporary international law. He points out:

> "L'erreur de bien des auteurs a été de continuer à raisonner dans l'ancien cadre en ne voyant dans les institutions qu'un élément des relations, sans prendre conscience des transformations qu'elles entraînent dans la structure de la collectivité des Nations."[151]

He continues:

> "En réalité, ce qui frappe, c'est la coexistence, dans l'ordre juridique international, de deux sériès de regles. Certaines, les plus anciennes, sont d'inspiration volontariste, et expriment ce que j'appelle le 'droit relationnel'."

147 *The Changing Structure of International Law,* London, Stevens & Sons, 1964, p. XIII.

148 See Vol. LX (1960), pp. 477-483.

149 See *Droit international public,* Vols. I-V, Paris, 1970-1983.

150 "The Future of Public International Law and of the International Legal System in the Circumstances of Today", Institut de droit international, *Livre du Centenaire, Evolution et perspectives du droit international,* Editions S. Karger S.A., Basle, 1973.

151 "Communauté internationale et disparité de développement", *Recueil des cours,* Vol. 165 (1979-IV), p. 46.

and the other rules that "relèvent d'un système non plus relationnel, mais institutionnel".[152]

One may agree or disagree with this evaluation of the changes in international law, but it is evident that this is an attempt to find the difference between the old and the new international law.

Professor A. Cassese examines "classical" or "traditional" international law and "modern" international law.[153] According to Cassese: "In the international community two different patterns in law, one traditional, the other modern, live side by side."[154]

Some 30 years ago Professor W. Friedmann expressed a similar idea, but in a somewhat different form. According to Friedmann

> "international law is today essentially divided between an international law of coexistence and an international law of cooperation, and that different perspectives and principles apply to these two fields . . .".[155]

To some extent it is true, as many norms of classical international law continue to exist and many new important principles and norms have emerged. But there is one international law, or better, one system of international law, the core of which is the fundamental principle of international law. This is a system and the norms of classical international law have become part of this system, which is a new system. Therefore, the norms inherited from classical international law are norms of classical law only from the point of view of their origin.

The examination of the actual state of international law at the beginning and at the end of the XXth century shows that classical international law has undergone in the course of the century fundamental transformations that have essentially changed its normative content and its role in society. As Professor Gross has pointed out:

> "Looking back over its history it would be difficult to find a period in which international law has made greater strides and has undergone a more significant transformation than in the twentieth century."[156]

Of course, it is not so important whether one calls international law now in force a "new" international law or simply contemporary international law. But it is of considerable theoretical and practical importance to see an essential difference between contemporary and classical international law.

This difference is considerable in all branches of international law. The fundamental principles of international law that constitute its core and have the greatest importance from the point of view of ensuring international peace and security, have undergone

152 *Ibid.*

153 *International Law in a Divided World,* Oxford, Clarendon Press, 1990, p. 23.

154 *Ibid.*, p. 39.

155 *The Changing Structure of International Law,* London, Stevens, 1964, p. 297.

156 "Preface", *International Law in the Twentieth Century,* New York, The American Society of International Law, 1969, p. VII.

a cardinal change. Such principles and institutions of classical international law that were of crucial importance as "the right of a State to wage war", "the right of the victor", "*debellatio*", "humanitarian intervention", etc., ceased to exist. Instead, new important principles of a quite different nature have emerged, such as the prohibition of the threat or use of force, the peaceful settlement of international disputes, the responsibility of States and even individuals for aggressive war and crimes against humanity, the principle of equal rights and self-determination of peoples, the principle of peaceful coexistence and cooperation. But probably the most promising change constitutes the principle of respect for human rights and fundamental freedoms. If, for centuries, international law had to do only with States, leaving human beings to a discretionary power of States, new international law ensures more and more the protection of the rights of individuals. It is true that the international defence of human rights is still in most instances not very effective, but it is getting stronger.

At the same time old democratic principles of international law, such as the principles of the sovereign equality of States, non-intervention, strict observance of international obligations and others have been further developed, have become stronger.

As I have stated before, changes have taken place in all the branches of international law.[157] Many new branches of international law have emerged which are indispensable for regulating new spheres of international relations, such as the international outer space law, the international law of the environment, the law of disarmament, the law of international organizations, etc.

In many instances the appearance of new branches of international law, such as for instance outer space law, or the essential changes in some parts of international law were due mainly to the progress of science and technology. As R.-J. Dupuy and D. Vignes pointed out with regard to the law of the sea:

> "Today, the radical change in the law of the sea is the result, precisely, of the huge progress made in maritime technology, and of the multiplicity and diversification of the actors in the theatre of operations."[158]

Classical international law authorized States to use aimed force and wage war against each other. This right was considered as the most important element of State sovereignty. International law legally justified, with some exceptions, the rule of force in international relations. Contemporary international law prohibits resort to war, prohibits the use or threat of force in interstate relations. This difference between contemporary and classical international law is fundamental.

Classical international law recognized two equal states of relations among members of the international community: a state of peace and a state of war. Usually, a half of the treatise on international law was devoted to the law of peace and the other half to the

157 For more detail see G. Tunkin, *Theory of International Law,* Cambridge, Mass., Harvard University Press, 1974.

158 *A Handbook on the Law of the Sea,* Martinus Nijhoff Publishers, 1991, p. XLVI.

law of war. Generally a greater part was given to the law of war. In the famous treatise by Grotius entitled *De Jure Belli ac Pacis* (1625) the law of war was put first. The spirit of public conscience of the time was, though somewhat cynically, expressed by Nietzsche who said: "Ihr soll Frieden lieben als Mittel zu neuen Kriegen. Und den kurzen Frieden mehr als den Langen."[159] (You must love peace as a means of a new war. And a short peace more than a long one.)

In contemporary international law the situation is different. A state of war has ceased to be a "normal" state of relations between States. There is no law of war in the old sense of the term as the right of a State to wage war does not exist any more. But as wars still occur, there remains that part of the old law of war that deals with the conduct of military operations. It has been considerably transformed especially after the Second World War to make wars less cruel. However, sometimes the old name "law of war" remains.[160]

In classical international law all parties to a war were on an equal legal footing. According to the contemporary international law one party, the aggressor, has committed the gravest breach of international law, having unleashed a war, and is waging the war in violation of law. Classical international law permitted any State not party to a war to enter the war on any side. Contemporary international law prohibits an aggressor State to join in waging war, but gives all States the right to render every assistance to a victim of aggression (the right of collective self-defence).

As stated before the elimination of the "right of a State to wage war" and the emergence of the principle of the non-use of force and threat of force has led to the liquidation of many other institutions of classical international law linked to the use of force, such as the "right of the victor", *"debellatio"*, etc. Victory gives no rights. Iraq, after occupying Kuwait in 1991, proclaimed its annexation. This would have been legal under classical international law, but is a crime according to contemporary international law.

Classical international law contained institutes that were instruments of colonial domination. It legalized the acquisition of territories of the so-called uncivilized peoples and colonial oppression. Under contemporary international law colonialism is prohibited.

There is also a very important difference between classical and contemporary international law in the field of norm-creating. Norms of classical international law were created by a small group of the most powerful States and all other States were compelled by the force of circumstances, or even by force, to comply with them. Norms of contemporary international law are created by the co-ordination of the wills of all the States. They reflect the common interests of these States and the balance of their particular interests.

General international law, that is, law of the interstate system, is a common legal space for all States. It is a kind of common language of States. It is also a legal framework for international politics.

159 *Also sprach Zarathustra*, Leipzig, 1902, s. 67.

160 See, for instance, I. D. DeLupis, *The Law of War*, Cambridge University Press, 1987.

As to particular norms of international law, they may reflect specific interests of various groups of States and on the basis of agreements between them, may derogate from the dispositive norms of international law. But contemporary international law also contains peremptory norms (norms of *jus cogens)* from which no such derogation is permitted. Peremptory norms guarantee a much greater unity of contemporary international law in comparison to classical international law.

Summing up, we may say that contemporary international law is essentially different from classical international law. And whether one calls it a "new" or simply contemporary international law, this difference should not be ignored.

4. International Law as a Restraint and Support for Politics

At the first glance international law appears as only a restraint for international politics. And it is partially true. Nonnative restraint is an essential characteristic of law in general and international law in particular.

Nobody denies nowadays that international law exists and functions. As soon as it is law, it means restraint for its subjects because legal norms are binding upon them. As stated earlier, international law is a legal framework for international politics.

But at the same time international law is a means of, or support for, international politics. Approximately the same idea was expressed by Professor Virally in the following terms: "Depending upon what it is used for (law – G.T.), a subject of law sees the system of law as directed against it or as being at its service."[161]

According to P. Corbett, international law, if it is to regulate relations among States, cannot be a support for politics. Corbett said:

> "International law, if it is to regulate, must operate as a limitation upon, rather than a tool of, national aims and practice. If it is an objective regulating device, it cannot at the same time be subservient to the passing purposes of governments."[162]

But the dual role of international law, as of many other societal phenomena, is a reality. It is, of course, a general proposition that should be specified.

Rules of general international law as non-personalized norms contain, as a rule, reciprocal rights and duties of the subjects of international law. That means that generally a right is coupled with a duty and vice versa. So, the right of navigation on the high seas is coupled with the duty to respect other States' rights to such navigation; the right to exercise a State's powers on its own territory is coupled with a duty to respect the same right of other States. The duty not to use force or the threat of force in international relations is coupled with the right to demand that other States comply with this duty;

161 "Le phénomène juridique", *Revue du droit public et de la science politique en France et à l'étranger,* LXXXII (1966), p. 11.

162 *Law in Diplomacy,* Princeton, Princeton University Press, 1959, p. 101.

the obligation (or duty) to ensure diplomatic privileges and immunities on the territory of a State is coupled with the right of that State to demand that another State or States also ensure diplomatic privileges and immunities to its own diplomats, etc.

So, when a State must fulfil its obligations under international law, this law is a restraint for its foreign policy and for international politics in general and when a State exercises its rights under international law, this law is a support for its policy and for international politics in general. It does not mean at all that law becomes "subservient" to States' policies, it remains the law on which States rely in their actions.

But in international law there are also norms providing for rights without duties or duties without rights. So, in the case of an illegal action by one State against another, an injured State has a right to take certain measures in accordance with international law. There are no duties of this State, whereas a State which committed a wrongful act has in this case no rights but only duties to submit itself to sanctions.

In the case of the gravest violation of international law – an armed attack – all the States have a right to assist the victim of aggression and an obligation not to render assistance to an aggressor State. But a right of collective self-defence means a right, not a duty, to give help to a victim of aggression. An obligation to render assistance in such a case may exist if it is stipulated by a treaty or if there is an appropriate decision of the Security Council of the United Nations. It means that to help or not to help a victim of aggression is left, in many instances, to the political decision of States.

International law may play its dual role of restraint and support for politics only in the fields of international relations covered by it. However, in this sense, there is always a disproportion between international law and international relations. International law always lags behind international relations in some fields and at the same time it is always ahead of international relations in other fields. (See paragraph 5 below.) Professor V. N. Likhachev of the Kazan University is partially right in saying that "lacunae in international law as well as in municipal law are not accidental".[163]

Judge Lachs has rightly pointed out:

> "Où finit la politique, où commence le droit? C'est une question que l'on a souvent posée; mais qui de nos jours vise fréquemment un faux problème, car entre les nations il y a très peu de questions juridiques qui n'aient un aspect politique, et très peu de questions politiques qui ne comportent d'élément juridique. Les unes et les autres se mêlent inextricablement."[164]

One might nowadays go even a little further and say that all political questions among States have their legal aspect because there are no absolute lacunae in contemporary international law. Fundamental principles of international law and some other norms cover all relations among States in the sense that States in all their relations must comply

163 See *Identification of Lacunae in International Law,* Kazan University, 1989, p. 22 (in Russian).

164 "Le droit international, l'ordre mondial et les Nations Unies", in *Le droit des peuples à disposer d'eux-même. Mélanges Charles Chaumont,* Paris, Pedone, 1984, p. 386.

with them. But in many instances it is not sufficient to make decisions on the basis of international law if there are no specific norms that may be applied. Unfortunately, but understandably, it is the case with the most important problems and because of that the most difficult problems of contemporary international relations.

The first example is disarmament and limitation of armaments. Much has been done in recent decades to cover by international legal regulations some of the problems of limitation of armaments, to stop the arms race. But there are still so many problems to be covered by international law. The fact is that according to general international law a State, with the limitations stipulated by international treaties entered into by this State, is its own judge as to types and amount of armaments it may possess. A progressive idea of limiting States' armaments by reasonable sufficiency has so far found no embodiment in international law.

In fact, not only the problem of the limitation of armaments but all global problems, such as the problems of the environment, food, health, terrorism, etc., are not sufficiently covered by international law.

It means that in these fields international politics functions without sufficient legal restraint and support. However, one should not forget that in this case non-legal norms that function in the interstate system may play a substantial role. (See Chapter V.)

But alongside that in the areas covered by international law, international politics meets with different degrees of restraint and therefore with different possibilities of using international law as a support.

As stated earlier in international law there are two types of norms: peremptory norms or *jus cogens* and dispositive norms or *jus dispositivum.* (See Chapter II.) From the point of view of legal restraint for international politics these two types of norms differ considerably. Most of the norms of international law are of the dispositive type, that is they allow States, by an agreement amongst them, to deviate from norms of general international law. That means that these norms leave much greater discretion for international politics than peremptory norms, from which no derogation is permitted. That also means that dispositive norms render in general lesser support for international politics.

There is also a type of international law norms that gives rights to States but defines very loosely the extent of these rights. This is first of all the case of responsibility of States under international law. A grave responsibility of States for international crimes may be considered as firmly established in the contemporary international law. But there is no strict definition as to what measures may be taken in cases of different crimes, as is the case with the criminal codes of States. Let us take the aggression of Iraq against Kuwait in 1990. There is no doubt that the United Nations, in the name of the international community, had the right to impose sanctions against Iraq. There is also no doubt that these sanctions might include the use of military force and other necessary measures. But what concrete measures may be used is not defined by international law and therefor is left to political decision, to politics.

Such political decisions based on international law have, however, some limits. In the case of aggression at least one limit definitely exists – this is the inadmissibility of *debellatio* that is a complete liquidation of an aggressor State. Generally, international law leaves less latitude for politics than classical international law, but still this latitude is too great. Speedy progressive development of international law in the field of State responsibility is urgently needed. The codification and progressive development of international law in this area is now one of the principal topics in the work of the International Law Commission.

In some other areas of international law it leaves to politics a certain latitude of decision, but indicates what concrete decisions may be taken. So, for instance, according to the Vienna Convention on the Law of Treaties of 1969 (Article 60) in the case of a material breach of a multilateral treaty by one of the parties, the other parties may, by unanimous agreement, suspend the operation of the treaty in whole or in part or to teHninate it either in the relations between themselves and the defaulting State, or as between all of the parties, etc. The choice is left to a political decision of the States concerned.

So the legal restraints for politics set up by international law vary from one area of international law to another. In general even contemporary international law leaves too much to the political decisions of States or of international organizations.

5. The Stabilizing and Creative Role of International Law

History is accelerating its pace. Society as a whole, and the interstate system as part of it, changes much more rapidly than in the past.

How does this situation influence the role of international law? From the point of view of the dynamics of the interstate system the role of international law may be either stabilizing or creative.

Centuries of relatively slow development of society and the interstate system have favoured the view that international law plays mainly, if not exclusively, a stabilizing, conservative role. It is also of importance that this stabilizing role is more visible. International law, as law in general, is associated primarily with restraints for actions rather than with something that facilitates activities of subjects of law. This view persists, especially among political scientists.

In particular, Morgenthau states that "any legal order tends to be primarily a static social force".[165] He also states that international law is responsible for the fact that in many cases diplomacy suffers a defeat. He writes:

> "The old diplomacy has failed, it is true, but so has the new one. The new diplomacy has failed and was bound to fail, for its legalistic tools have no access to the political problems to be solved."[166]

---

165 *Politics among Nations,* New York, Knopf, 1948, p. 87.

166 *Politics in the Twentieth Century,* Vol. I, *The Decline of Democratic Politics,* Chicago, The University of Chicago Press, 1962, p. 358.

Another prominent representative of "political realism", George Kennan, a former Ambassador of the United States to the USSR, went much further in criticizing the "legalistic-moralistic approach to international problems" in the early 1950s. In his opinion, international law is not only unsuitable as a means for solving international problems but efforts to use it for that purpose are actually harmful. He describes international law as a "legal strait jacket" that impedes the free play of forces in the international arena.

> "The national State pattern is not, should not be, and cannot be a fixed and static thing. By nature it is an unstable phenomenon in a constant state of change and flux. History has shown that the will and the capacity of individual peoples to contribute to their world environment is constantly changing. It is only logical that the organizational forms (and what else are such things as borders and government?) should change with them. The function of a system of international relationships is not to inhibit this process of change by imposing a legal strait jacket upon it but rather to facilitate it; to ease its transitions, to temper the asperities to which it often leads, to isolate and moderate the conflicts to which it gives rise, and to see that these conflicts do not assume forms too unsettling for international life in general. But this is a task for diplomacy, in the most old-fashioned sense of the term. For this law is too abstract, too inflexible, too hard to adjust to the demands of the unpredictable and the unexpected."[167]

A slightly more balanced view has been expressed by Professor R. Falk who stated:

> "The focus upon international law as a world order perspective should also not be taken as an automatic endorsement of the beneficial role played by law . . . My analysis takes it for granted that to the extent that change rather than stability is of prime concern, law tends to function in a regressive fashion."

However he adds:

> "The legal system also can and does function in a positive fashion; under appropriate circumstances it can facilitate consensus formation in a fragmented world community"[168]

In the radically new conditions in the world the role of international law should be re-examined. Law, either national or international, always plays a double role: stabilizing

167 See *American Diplomacy 1900-1950,* Chicago, A. Mentor Book, 1951, p. 85.

168 "The Role of Law in World Society: Present Crisis and Future Prospects", in *Toward World Order and Human Dignity. Essays in Honor of Myers S. McDougal* (ed. W. M. Reisman and B. Weston), New York, The Free Press, 1976, p. 149.

and creative, though the degree of the first and of the second role may differ. Actually any rule of law is intended to preserve something and to facilitate it to attain new objectives.

In creating norms of international law States act purposefully and their wills are co-ordinated not only with regard to a technical rule of conduct, but also with regard to the aim of this rule. The degree of the co-ordination of the wills with regard to the aim of the rule may not only be less clear but also less perfect than the degree of the co-ordination of the wills with regard to a rule of conduct as such, but it is there.

This is one of the reasons why the results intended in the process of the creation of norms of international law very often are only partially achieved in the process of the functioning of these norms.

The principal and most comprehensive role of international law consists in ensuring normal functioning of the interstate system. Of course, this role is exercised in conjunction with politics. But as far as international law is concerned it is aimed at ensuring not only an equilibrium of the system in a static form, but at ensuring a dynamic equilibrium. That is the only way to facilitate the normal functioning of the system. The development of the interstate system cannot be stopped, if international law tried to stop it it would be simply rejected by the system. To ensure a dynamic equilibrium of the interstate system international law must play a double role: to conserve the system, that is to be a stabilizing factor, and to facilitate its development, that is to be a creative factor.

In the course of time one and the same norm may play a predominantly stabilizing or a predominantly creative role. So, before the United Nations emerged States had to adopt norms of international law according to which this organization should be created and function. Norms of the United Nations Charter, which are norms of international law, had to play a creative role. The United Nations was established according to the Charter provisions. But as soon as the United Nations appeared the norms of the Charter started to play a double role: they had to ensure a dynamic equilibrium of the organization. In other words they had to ensure stability of the organization and at the same time to be a basis for its development, that is to facilitate this development.

One can hardly accept a widely current interpretation of the Charter in the United Nations as a kind of ideal rather than as a binding legal document. Expressing this attitude W. Rogers says: "The Charter, in short, is an ideal. It is universally embraced as an inspiration."[169]

Of course, every legal norm, in some sense, is an ideal, an inspiration, as it may be viewed as an image of a desired behaviour. But, and it is of major importance, it is a legally binding norm.

Thousands of international treaties play a creative role, establishing new relations among States in certain spheres of their relations. At the same time they play a stabilizing role by putting relations among parties on a stable legal footing.

169 "The Principles of Force, the Force of Principles", in *Right v. Might. International Law and the Use of Force*, New York, Council of Foreign Relations Press, 1989, p. 107.

The creative role of international law has not been properly studied. In fact very few international lawyers speak of it. Judge Lachs has rightly pointed out:

> "Car si nous devons admettre la nécessité du changement (et il va sans dire que toute innovation comporte des elements de changement), c'est au droit qu'il appartiendra de fournir le cadre protecteur dans lequel l'innovation peut déployer ses effets en renforçant l'ossature de l'ordre mondial."[170]

Examining the role of international law in establishing a new international economic order Judge Bedjaoui said:

> "On voudrait assigner ainsi au droit international, en tant que tel, un objectif de transformation de la société internationale. C'est là une tâche neuve pour le droit international qui était confiné jusqu'ici dans une fonction de sauvegarde d'un certain type de rapports internationaux non encore purgés de leur contenu inégalitaire et impérialiste."[171]

I would like to stress that both eminent international lawyers accept a creative role of international law. Although one can hardly agree in full with their opinions. The opinion of Judge Lachs is incomplete as it indicates only a protective role of international law in the case of innovations. But international law may initiate innovations, of course in conjunction with politics and in a certain sense as a means of politics.

Bedjaoui speaks of a creative role of international law as a new phenomenon. As stated earlier, in my view, international law has always played both roles – creative and stabilizing

Now I come to the question put at the beginning of this paragraph. An accelerated pace of history has greatly increased the creative role of international law. And a creative role of international law as a means of peaceful change is growing. (See Chapter VI.)

170 "Le droit international, l'ordre mondial et les Nations Unies", in *Le droit des peuples à disposer d'eux-mêmes. Mélanges Charles Chaumont,* Paris, Pedone, 1984, p. 393.

171 *Pour un nouvel ordre economique international,* Unesco, 1979, p. 114.

Chapter IV International Law and Force

1. The Historical Background

Two giants – law and force – have been fighting each other since time immemorial. Law tried to limit the recourse to force though it needed force, as law must be enforceable.

As Pascal, a famous French scholar and writer of the XVIIIth century, stated: "La justice sans la force est impuissante; la force sans la justice est tyrannique" (justice without force is helpless, force without justice is tyrannical).[172]

Local and sporadic attempts to limit the recourse to force by States have been made since the very appearance of States. They usually took the form of bilateral treaties of "eternal friendship", "eternal peace", etc. It is known now that such treaties were concluded more than five thousand years ago.[173]

But it would be wrong to suggest that international law has always been a means to limit the recourse to force.

It would, as well, be wrong to assert that peoples have always striven for peace and that only their rulers forced them to go to war. But it is true, however, as Lori Damrosch says, that "throughout history, decisions to go to war have been made by a handful of individuals in powerful positions".[174] I would even say that in many instances such fateful decisions have been taken by a single individual.

There is no doubt that peace has always been a predominant desire of peoples. But from time to time a considerable part of the people eagerly supported their rulers in wars against other people. Examples are many: the invasions by the Huns, the invasions by the Mongols, etc. Even in modern history: the aggressive wars of Napoleon and Hitler were actively supported by a considerable part of the population of France and Germany respectively.

Science has not yet given a proper explanation to this phenomenon. One thing seems to be certain: as man is a starting point for all societal events, much depends on the nature of man. What has happened to human nature? Academician I. Frolov has pointed out:

> "Today, as never before, mankind acutely examines itself and sometimes, as if for the first time, opens Man: not without happy astonishment and even with admiration, and frequently with bitter disappointment."[175]

172 *Pensées* (ed. Leon Brunschvig), S. V, 298.

173 Baskin and D. Feldman, *History of International Law*, Moscow, 1990, p. 15 (in Russian).

174 *AJIL*, Vol. 85 (1991), p. 92.

175 *About Man and Humanism*, Moscow, 1989, p. *17* (in Russian).

Speaking of scientific and technological revolutions Frolov says: "Will it bring about a change of man, of his biology, genetics, and his psychological qualities?"[176]

There are two parts of human nature which are closely interlocked: animal and societal. We find this idea in the works of Kant and even in those of Aristotle. The animal nature that makes itself felt, *inter alia,* in the use of force and in violence in general, had existed for millions of years before the societal nature appeared. There is no doubt that societal nature has been gaining ground at the expense of animal nature. But recent events in Yugoslavia and on the territory of the former Soviet Union have shown once again how easily animal nature, in the form of nationalism and ethnic hatred, may revive and how it may be used by skilful politicians as a means of satisfying their lust for political power.

Societal conditions in general exercise a considerable influence on human nature as a whole but certainly they affect more the societal part of it whereas the animal element is influenced more by natural processes. At the same time natural processes affecting biological processes in man through them influence the societal nature of man. It seems that science does not yet know enough how conditions in biospheric and cosmic events influence human nature. The idea expressed by Kenneth Clark seems not at all absurd. He says:

> "There have been times in the history of man when the earth seems suddenly to have grown warmer or more radio-active. I don't put that forward as a scientific proposition, but the fact remains that three or four times in history man has made a leap forward that would have been unthinkable under ordinary evolutionary conditions."[177]

Societal conditions conducive to the use of force in interstate relations consisted mainly in the fact that violence and war paid off. Rulers gained by conquering other people, the wealthy classes also gained by plundering other nations, and even the poor of a victorious State might get something as a result of victory. Such situations existed during the course of the entire history of man until recently.

In these conditions international law could do no more than to leave the use of force to the discretion of States and to legitimize what had been achieved by force. In spite of sporadic attempts to limit the use of force, international law in general was a law of force, a means of force. Treaties creating military alliances, that is treaties for preparing new wars, played a principal role in international politics.

In contemporary history the first general steps to limit the use of force in relations among States in the form of war were made at the end of the XIXth century. Up to that time the use of force was considered as an unlimited prerogative of a sovereign State. It is, therefore, understandable that the 1899 and 1907 Hague conventions on the pacific

176 *Ibid.*, p. 21.

177 *Civilisation*, Penguin Books, 1987, p. 36.

settlement of international disputes contained only a recommendation, "when possible", to refrain from using force and to have recourse to peaceful means of settling disputes. "With a view to obviating as far as possible recourse to force in the relations between States," says Article 1 of the 1907 Hague Convention, "the Contracting Powers agree to use their efforts to ensure the pacific settlement of international differences." Article 2 of this Convention provided an obligation "in case of serious disagreement or dispute, before an appeal to arms, . . . to have recourse as far as circumstances allow to the good offices or mediation of one or more friendly Powers".

The Covenant of the League of Nations went significantly further in limiting the use of force in the interstate relations. The Covenant did not prohibit recourse to war. But in a case of conflict States members of the League were bound to settle their differences by arbitration or judicial means. If one of the parties involved was not satisfied with the decision of an arbitral tribunal or of the court it might, not before three months after the decision, have recourse to war. So, if the Hague conventions of 1899 and 1907 only recommended to States that before starting a war they should settle their difference by peaceful means, the Covenant made such a recourse to peaceful means obligatory. Only the Pact of Paris of 1928 prohibited recourse to war. (See Chapter III, paragraph 2).

2. The United Nations Charter and the Use of Force

As I mentioned earlier, the victory of the Allied Powers over Nazi Germany and imperialist Japan brought about an upheaval of a world-wide movement for peace and democracy. And this made it possible to adopt the Charter of the United Nations. If the Charter introduced revolutionary innovations into international law in general the most important of them was the prohibition of the threat or use of force in interstate relations. Paragraph 4 of Article 2 of the Charter was formulated as follows:

> "All Members shall refrain in their international relations from the threat or use of force against the territorial integrity or political independence of any State, or in any other manner inconsistent with the principles of the United Nations."

Paragraph 3 of Article 2 obligates States to settle their international disputes by peaceful means in such a manner that international peace and security, and justice, are not endangered.

It would, of course, be more logical to put paragraph 4 before paragraph 3, as was done in the Pact of Paris. Paragraph 4 is broader than paragraph 3: it prohibits recourse to the threat or use of force not only in cases of disputes, but also in cases where there are no disputes.

The importance of the principle of the non-use of force can hardly be overestimated. It seems, however, that the magnitude of what was done in international law in 1945 was not immediately realized even by many prominent international lawyers. So

H. Kelsen examined paragraphs 3 and 4 of Article 2 under the title "The Obligation of Pacific Settlement of Conflicts".[178]

The eminent Soviet international lawyer S. Krylov who took part in the drafting of the Charter, did not single out the principle of nonuse of force. In a 1947 manual on international law edited by V. Durdenevsky and S. Krylov, Professor Krylov said only this:

> "The Charter of the United Nations excludes completely the recourse to war as a means of settling a dispute or conflict among States. Members of the Organizations involved in a dispute, the continuation of which is likely to endanger the maintenance of international peace and security, must resolve such a dispute by peaceful means of their choice."[179]

As time went on the revolutionary character of the principle became more and more evident. It was stressed by States and by international lawyers. In the Declaration of 1987 the United Nations General Assembly stated

> "the urgent need to enhance the effectiveness of the principle that States shall refrain from the threat or use of force in order to contribute to the establishment of lasting peace and security for all States".

The special committee of the General Assembly established in 1962 to draft a declaration on principles of international law stated in one of its reports that the principle of the non-use of force and threat of force was "the corner-stone of the contemporary international legal order and of the co-operation, friendly relations, and peaceful coexistence of States".[180]

In the doctrine of international law all over the world, in spite of some controversies concerning the precise content of the principle of the non-use of force and the threat of force, the dominant opinion is that this principle is the greatest innovation in international law and the most important one.

Special significance of the principle of non-use of force has been consistently stressed in the Soviet literature on international law.[181]

Stressing the importance of the principle of the non-use of force Professor Henkin says:

> "For the first time, nations tried to bring within the realm of law these ultimate political tensions and interests that had long been deemed beyond the control of the law."[182]

178 See *The Law of the United Nations,* London, Stevens & Sons, 1951, p. 90.

179 *International Law,* Moscow, Jurizdat, 1947, p. 482 (in Russian).

180 *Report of the Special Committee on Principles of International Law Concerning Friendly Relations and Cooperation among States,* Doc. No. A/6799 (XXII), para. 29.

181 See, for instance, G. Tunkin, *Fundamentals of International Law,* Moscow, 1956; R. Bobrov, *Principal Problems of the Theory of International Law,* Moscow, International Relations, 1968 (in Russian).

182 *How Nations Behave. Law and Foreign Policy,* New York, Columbia University Press, 1968, p. 137.

Professor Virally points out:

> "Ce n'est plus seulement la guerre qui est interdite, comme dans le Pacte de Paris, mais tout usage de la force dans les rapports internationaux, fût-ce même sous la forme d'une simple menace. Le droit de faire la guerre disparaît totalement comme attribut de la souveraineté étatique et, avec lui, le droit de recourir à la force. C'est là un changement radical par rapport à l'état du droit antérieur."[183]

In the words of a political scientist, W. Rogers:

> "The norms of Articles 2 (4) and 51 of the United Nations Charter are the central geo-political issue of our time – whether limits on the threat or use of force constitute a basic organizing principle of relations between States in the modern world."[184]

The content of the principle of non-use of force or threat of force was specified in the Declaration on Principles of International Law concerning Friendly Relations and Co-operation among States in Accordance with the Charter of the United Nations adopted by the United Nations General Assembly in 1970. Although a resolution of the General Assembly, this declaration was a step in the development of international law. The declaration was adopted by consensus. It has no legal consequences, but is of factual importance. The provisions of the declaration it seems are entering by and by into international law by the customary way. (See Chapter II.) It is therefore worthwhile quoting the principle as formulated in the declaration in full.

"Every State has the duty to refrain in its international relations from the threat or use of force against the territorial integrity or political independence of any State, or in any other manner inconsistent with the purposes of the United Nations. Such a threat or use of force constitutes a violation of international law and the Charter of the United Nations and shall never be employed as a means of settling international issues.

A war of aggression constitutes a crime against the peace, for which there is responsibility under international law.

In accordance with the purposes and principles of the United Nations, States have the duty to refrain from propaganda for wars of aggression.

Every State has the duty to refrain from the threat or use of force to violate existing international boundaries of another State or as a means of solving international disputes, including territorial disputes and problems concerning frontiers of States.

Every State likewise has the duty to refrain from the threat or use of force to violate international lines of demarcation, such as armistice lines, established by or pursuant to an international agreement to which it is a party or which it is otherwise bound to

183 See *La Charte des Nations Unies* (eds. J.-P. Cot and A. Pellet), Paris, Economica, 1985, p. 114.

184 "The Principle of Force, the Force of Principles", *Right v. Might. International Law and the Use of Force*, New York, Council on Foreign Relations, 1989, p. 95.

respect. Nothing in the foregoing shall be construed as prejudicing the positions of the parties concerned with regard to the status and effects of such lines under their spatial regimes or as affecting their temporary character.

States have a duty to refrain from acts of reprisal involving the use of force.

Every State has the duty to refrain from any forcible action which deprives the peoples referred to in the elaboration of the principle of equal rights and self-detemination of their right to self-determination and freedom and independence.

Every State has the duty to refrain from organizing or encouraging the organization of irregular forces or armed bands, including mercenaries, for incursion into the territory of another State.

Every State has the duty to refrain from organizing, instigating, assisting or participating in acts of civil strife or terrorist acts in another State or acquiescing in organized activities within its territory directed towards the commission of such acts, when the acts referred to in the present paragraph involve a threat or use of force.

The territory of a State shall not be the object of military occupation resulting from the use of force in contravention of the provisions of the Charter. The territory of a State shall not be the object of acquisition by another State resulting from the threat or use of force. No territorial acquisition resulting from the threat or use of force shall be recognized as legal. Nothing in the foregoing shall be construed as affecting:

(a) Provisions of the Charter or any international agreement prior to the Charter regime and valid under international law; or
(b) The powers of the Security Council under the Charter.

All States shall pursue in good faith negotiations for an early conclusion of a universal treaty on general and complete disarmament under effective international control and strive to adopt appropriate measures to reduce international tension and strengthen confidence among States.

All States shall comply in good faith with their obligations under the generally recognized principles and rules of international law with respect to the maintenance of international peace and security, and shall endeavour to make the United Nations security system based upon the Charter more effective.

Nothing in the foregoing paragraphs shall be construed as enlarging or diminishing in any way the scope of the provisions of the Charter concerning cases in which the use of force is lawful."

The definition of aggression adopted by the General Assembly in 1974 enumerates, not exhaustively, for the guidance of the Security Council, characteristics of "the most serious and dangerous form of the illegal use of force".

The principle of non-use of force and threat of force is a rule of general international law binding upon all the States. It may be considered as firmly established, although there are some controversies to which I'll come later.

It is also generally accepted that the term "force" in the Charter means armed force. But there is good reason to believe that new norms are at the stage of formation according to which the use of non-military force should also be prohibited if such acts are directed against essential rights of any State. It seems to me that such norms may be deduced from the system of the fundamental principles of contemporary international law. In the preambles of the declaration on the principles of international law of 1970 and of the declaration on the enhancement of the effectiveness of the principle of non-use of force of 1987, there is an identical paragraph

"reaffirming the duty of States to refrain in their international relations from military, political, economic or any other form of coercion aimed against the political independence or territorial integrity of any State".

It means that States consider the corresponding rules as necessary and the doctrine of international law might help to formulate these rules.

Even in today's international law there are some norms prohibiting the use of non-armed force in specific cases. So the principle of non-intervention prohibits the use of non-military force of any kind for intervening in the domestic affairs of other States. As formulated in the declaration on principles of international law of 1970 this prohibition includes the following:

> "No State may use or encourage the use of economic, political or any other type of measures to coerce another State in order to obtain from it the subordination of the exercise of its sovereign rights and to secure from it advantages of any kind."

The principle of non-use of force has two exceptions; the use of force in accordance with the right of self-defence (see paragraph 3 below) and the use of force by the United Nations. (See paragraph 5 below.)

The right of self-defence is stated in Article 51 of the Charter in the following terms:

> "Nothing in the present Charter shall impair the inherent right of individual or collective self-defence if an armed attack occurs against a member of the United Nations, until the Security Council has taken measures necessary to maintain international peace and security."

As in all the principles of the Charter, the right of self-defence is now a principle of general international law. In comparison with classical international law, where this right was not strictly defined, now the right of self-defence is limited to cases of armed attack.

The right of self-defence in contemporary international law is a field of great legal battles immediately linked to international politics.

3. The Political Implications of Articles 2 (4) and 51 of the Charter and Legal Controversies

The prohibition of the threat or use of force in relations among States has far-reaching political implications. In all the preceding history, force had been a dominant factor in world politics. Now the use of force in world politics is prohibited. It meant logically if not legally that power politics became contrary if not to the letter, but at least to the spirit of international law. The prohibition of the use of force indicates the necessity of putting an end to the armaments race and starting to limit States' armaments.

How could such a norm of international law menacing traditional policies, especially policies of great powers, have been accepted by all the States including the great Powers? As I have stated earlier it was due to a great spiritual upheaval in the aftermath of the terrible Second World War.

But after the adoption of the Charter and as time went on and power politics became again the dominant element of world politics, efforts to revive pre-Charter international law concerning the use of force were inevitable. Such efforts have taken various forms, but their essence was as one: to find loopholes in order to legally justify the use of force to the maximum possible degree.

Direct assaults on Article 2 (4) have been undertaken mainly by political realists. They proceed from an assumption that in a society of sovereign States there can be no other world politics, but politics based on relations of power, and therefore any attempt to limit the use of force in relations among States is futile. The inference was that Article 2 (4) of the Charter could not function and that former international law would actually work.

In criticizing political realists I do not mean at all that their analyses of international relations have no positive elements. Unfortunately, they are nearer to the actual situation than many international lawyers who are tempted to present legal rules as identical to factual situations. But international political scientists everywhere, including Soviet political scientists, are guilty of ignoring in their analyses many factors in international life including international law, and thereby presenting an incorrect picture of international realities.

This is of specific importance with regard to the use of force in international relations. A typical example is a book under the editorship of the two well-known political scientists Robert J. Art and Kenneth N. Waltz, *The Use of Force. Military Power and International Politics* (University Press of America, 1988). The use of force in international relations is discussed here without even mentioning international law. The father of the contemporary international political science in the United States, Professor Hans Morgenthau, wrote:

> "The aspiration for power being the distinguishing element of international politics, as all politics, international politics is of necessity power politics."[185]

It follows that any attempts to prohibit the use of force in international politics are contrary to the very nature of interstate relations and therefore fruitless.

185 See *Politics Among Nations*, New York, Knopf, 1948, p. 29.

R. Aron was more explicit:

> "I tried [he wrote] to determine what constitutes the distinctive nature of international or interstate relations, and I concluded that it rests in the legitimacy or legality of the use of military force."[186]

M. Merle, a jurist and political scientist, has rightly pointed out: "Certes, la connaissance des règles de droit est toujours nécessaire et même indispensable à qui veut comprendre une société".[187] It looks strange that at the same time Merle asserts that "le recours à la force demeure légitime dans les rapports entre Etats".[188]

International lawyers who are trying to widen the possibilities to justify the use of force by States in international relations advance different legal arguments in support of their positions.

Some base their arguments on a fallacious theory (see paragraph 4 below) that the Charter of the United Nations being an international treaty did not change international law and therefore the right of States to use force remains as it was in classical international law. Many prominent Western international lawyers divided international law even after the adoption of the Charter in two parts: the law of the United Nations and general international law. Proceeding from this assumption, Kelsen, for instance, said:

> "General international law authorizes the State, the individual member of the international community, to resort, in case of a violation of its rights, to reprisals or war against that State which is responsible for the violation."[189]

Such a theory might have some justification at that time when only 51 States were members of the United Nations. But now, when practically all the States are members of the world organization and the principles of the Charter have acquired recognition as principles of general international law, it is untenable.

There is an attempt to prove that Article 2 (4) is simply invalid because it was part of the system of collective security as envisaged in the Charter. As soon as the system does not work, say the partisans of this opinion, Article 2 (4) cannot work as well, and therefore we have come back to the classical international law.

So Professor Reisman says:

> "The net result of the ineffectiveness of the Charter regime for general enforcement might be more accurately described as a partial revival of a unilateral *jus ad bellum*."[190]

186 *Politics and History*, London, Collier Macmillan Publishers, 1979, p. 171.

187 *Sociologie des relations internationales* (2e ed.), Paris, Dalloz, 1976, p. 45.

188 *Ibid.*, p. 32.

189 See "Collective Security and Collective Self-Defence Under the Charter of the United Nations", *AJIL*, XLII (1948), p. 783.

190 "The Emperor Has no Clothes. Article 2 (4) and the Use of Force in Contemporary International Law", *United Nations for a Better World*, New Delhi, 1986, p. 10.

Reisman qualifies the statement by saying that

> "appraisals of the resort to coercion by States cannot simply invoke Article 2 (4) and condemn them, but must test the permissibility or lawfulness of the action concerned by reference to a number of factors, including the objective for which and the contingency under which coercion is being applied."[191]

In other words the lawfulness of the use of force may be justified by many non-legal factors and Article 2 (4) may be pushed aside especially if a purpose is good. It reminds us of an old Latin saying: salus populi suprema lex. By this slogan dictators throughout history justified their tyrannical rule. In this case it would justify a tyranny of force in relations among States.

A very pessimistic view is also expressed by Professor Combacau who, like Reisman, puts forward the following arguments:

> "The international community no longer believes in the system of the Charter, because the collective guarantee, in exchange for which its members had renounced their individual right to resort to force, does not work, and no real substitute for it has been found . . . Whatever the official pretence, and perhaps the legal situation, the international community is in fact back where it was before 1945."[192]

The arguments to which I have just referred are invalid. Principles enumerated in Article 2 of the United Nations Charter are not only principles of the United Nations Organization, but principles of general international law as I have stated previously. Their legal validity cannot, therefore, be limited to the system of enforcement envisaged in the Charter. If one proceeded from the assumption that rules of international law are valid only in the case if there existed a system for their enforcement, then almost all international law should be considered legally invalid and not true law.

Attempts to erode the principle of the non-use of force more frequently take the form of extending the scope of the right of self-defence.

Some authors consider that Article 51 of the Charter simply confirms the existing right of self-defence. So Professor J. N. Moore has argued that Article 51 of the Charter does not restrict "the preexisting right of defence under customary law".[193] And instead of the words "armed attack", Moore uses the words "aggressive attack" that open a possibility to widen the sense of the term "armed attack", or rather to replace it by a quite different and vaguer notion.

191 *Ibid.*

192 "The Exception of Self-Defence in U.N. Practice", *The Current Legal Regulation of the Use of Force* (ed. by A. Cassese), Dordrecht, Martinus Nijhoff Publishers, 1986, p. 32.

193 "The Secret War in Central America and the Future of World Order", *AJIL*, 80 (1986), p. 82.

There is also an attempt to prove that Article 51 did not change the pre-existing right of self-defence because this Article speaks of "the inherent right of individual and collective self-defence".

Both arguments are invalid. Article 51 has changed the institution of self-defence that existed in classical international law because the provisions of this Article have become part of the contemporary general international law. As to the notion of "inherent" rights such an argument is nothing other than an appeal to theories of natural law. Everything in society is changing and the notion of "inherent" rights must be understood as rights considered as inalienable in the course of a certain period of history. We now consider the right to liberty of a person as an "inherent" right of every man. But in ancient Greece, or in Rome, when slavery existed, slaves did not have such a right. According to classical international law the right of a State to wage war against another State was considered as an "inherent" right of every State. But in the XXth century States relinquished this right and on the basis of agreement accepted the norm of international law prohibiting war and later the norm prohibiting the use of force in their mutual relations.

One of the devices to widen the possibility of using force is the theory of humanitarian intervention. The right of a State to use force in certain cases "to protect life and property" of its citizens abroad existed in classical international law. Some authors maintain that such a right exists now as well (Waldock, Bowett, D'Amato, and some others). With the increasing importance of the international defence of human rights some authors go very far. So, for instance, Reisman speaks of a right of a State to use force to overthrow a despotic government in another country.[194]

In the light of Article 2 (4) of the Charter the right of a humanitarian intervention can hardly be proved. But it may well be that the right of the United Nations to use force against a State committing grave violations of human rights is emerging. Indeed, grave violations of human rights may well be considered by the Security Council as a threat to the peace because in the contemporary world they may constitute a real threat to international peace and security.

Putting aside political influences that are almost visible in all attempts to widen possibilities of the use of force, I would like to examine the major theoretical errors in these attempts.

The first is an outdated division of international law on customary and conventional international law, whereas it should be divided in general and particular international law or rather rules of international law as a system should be divided in general rules and particular rules. (See paragraph 4 below.)

The second is the erroneous understanding of the relationship between State practice and international law. Practice, as such, does not automatically change international law. It must be accepted by States as law. (See Chapter II, paragraph 4.)

194 See Reisman in the *AJIL*, No. 3 (1984).

The third, a wrong interpretation of the relationship between Article 2 (4) of the Charter and Article 51. Article 2 (4) of the Charter contains a general prohibition of the use of force in interstate relations whereas Article 51 deals with the most dangerous use of force – an armed attack, and for this case it makes an exception a kind of a *lex specialis.* And only in this specific case does it permit the use of force by a State, the victim of an armed attack or by any other State against an aggressor State.

Article 51 does not cover Article 2 (4) of the Charter as implicitly asserts N. Rostow speaking of a "defensive use of force" allegedly allowed by Article 51.[195] Article 51 permits the use of force only in the case of an armed attack.

In conclusion I. would like to state once again that the appearance of the principle of the non-use of force or threat of force was the most important event in the history of international law. This principle constitutes a great contribution to human civilization.

4. The United Nations Charter and Contemporary General International Law

As follows from what I have said above the attempts to erode the principle of non-use of force are based on a division of international law in conventional and customary law. This division reflects the modes of creation of norms: conventional and customary. The sphere of validity of norms of international law is reflected in the notions of general and particular norms.

In the Western doctrine of international law and in the doctrine of developing countries borrowed from the Western literature the dominant conception is that general international law is customary law only and the term customary is used as synonymous to the term general.

There are two approaches to this problem: first it is based on a conceptual premise that treaties are not sources of international law. Second, it proceeds from the assumption that as soon as there are no international treaties to which all the States are parties, therefore general international law is, in fact, customary law only.

I'll quote only a few examples of the first theory which, in my opinion, has its roots in the Anglo-American municipal legal systems. Professor D. O'Connell argued that international law as a whole "is customary law".[196] "It is quite incorrect," he wrote, "to speak of treaties as 'sources' of international law. They are no more than the contracts between the parties . . . ".[197]

In his contribution to the *Livre du centenaire de l'Institut de droit international* Fitzmaurice said:

> "We shall, for the present purposes, treat conventional treaty as being law, and shall not insist on our view, expressed elsewhere, that except where in

195 "Nicaragua and the Law of Self-Defence Revisited", *Yale Journal of International Law, 11* (1986), p. 454.
196 *International Law,* London, Stevens & Sons, 1965, p. 4.
197 *Ibid.*, p. 22.

> the nature of codification, it is not so, any more than the private contract is 'law'."[198]

Proceeding from this position Fitzmaurice, being rapporteur on the law of treaties in the International Law Commission, stubbornly insisted that the Commission should draft a "Code" to be approved by the United Nations General Assembly, but not a convention, as conventions are not sources of international law or at least of general international law. Only when Fitzmaurice left for the International Court of Justice and Professor Waldock became the British member of the Commission and special rapporteur on the law of treaties, in 1961, during my presidency in the Commission, the Commission adopted a decision to draft not a "Code", but a convention. The work on this draft was completed in 1966 and the convention on the law of treaties was adopted at the conference in 1969. The convention works and there is no doubt that it will soon become part of general international law.

As Professor C. J. Warbrick of Durham University pointed out, the view that international treaties are not a source of international law is "widely held among British international lawyers".[199]

The position according to which international treaties are not a source of international law contradicts the very nature of this law. It reflects the notions of some municipal legal systems. But the interstate system is not a State. International law is created by subjects of this legal system. That means that there is not only general, but also particular international law created by some States only and binding upon these States. Then general international law binding upon all the States consists of peremptory and dispositive norms. The latter are more numerous. Dispositive norms permit States to derogate from them by concluding treaties and thereby creating *lex specialis.*

In spite of that, the traditional dogma that general international law is customary law only and conventional international law is a particular law persists even now and not only in the Anglo-American doctrine.

I. Brownlie speaks of "customary (or general) international Law".[200]

Professor Suzanne Bastid is of the opinion that "a treaty may change customary norm. On the other hand it may be a basis for creating a customary norm."[201]

In the same vein Professor M. Boss writes:

> "A special type of State practice to be mentioned in the context of custom is treaty practice. Treaty practice, indeed, is of some relevance to the creation

198 See, "The Future of Public International Law and of the International Legal System in the Circumstances of Today", Institut de droit international, *Livre du centenaire,* Basle, Editions S. Karger, 1973, para. 4, footnote, at p. 200.

199 "The Theory of International Law: Is There an English Contribution?", *Perestroika and International Law* (ed. by W. Butler), Dordrecht, Martinus Nijhoff Publishers, 1990, pp. 46-47.

200 "Problems concerning the Unity of International Law", *International Law in the Time of Its Codification. Essays in Honour of Roberto Ago,* Milan, Dott. A. Giuffrè Editore, 1987, 1, p. 154.

201 *Les traité dans la vie internationale,* Paris, Economica, 1985, p. 167.

> of custom, for as provided in Article 38 of the Vienna Convention on the Law of Treaties 'nothing in Articles 34 to 37 precludes a rule set forth in a treaty from becoming binding upon a third State as a customary rule of international law, recognized as such.'"[202]

In the opinion of Giuliano there are "norms of general or customary international law and norms of particular or conventional international law".[203]

It is only regrettable, but not unexpected, that the International Court of Justice has also contributed to the maintenance of this outdated doctrine. In its otherwise historic judgment in the *Nicaragua v. United States* case the Court said:

> "Where two States agree to incorporate a particular rule in a treaty, their agreement suffices to make that rule a legal one binding upon them; but in the field of customary international law, the shared view of the parties as to the content of what they regarded as the rule is not enough. The Court must satisfy itself that the existence of the rule in the *opinio juris* of States is confirmed by practice."[204]

One may find similar pronouncements in other judgments of the Court.[205]

The essence of this theory is that any international treaty with regard to customary international law is nothing more than a practice that requires *opinio juris* to become part of the general international law. Therefore, according to this theory, principles of the Charter of the United Nations to which practically all States are parties are not principles of general international law, and to become such they must be confirmed by *opinio juris*. So the members of the United Nations had to put in doubt their recognition of the principles of the Charter as generally binding when they ratified the Charter and to prove this recognition for the second time by their subsequent practice. Is it not absurd? It is one of the many examples of when a theory correct in the past becomes incorrect under the new circumstances.

In an age when general multilateral treaties tend to be a kind of international legislation, this theory is not only fallacious, but reactionary. It is the result of an outdated concept of relationship between customary, conventional and general international law.

It is also rooted in the premise that there is a basic difference in the creation of customary and conventional norms of international law, namely that conventional norms are created by the wills of States, or in other words, by agreement, but customary norms emerge spontaneously without participation of the wills of States. I have shown in Chapter II, above, that it is not so. There is, of course, a difference in creating customary and conventional norms, but it is not a radical difference. Conventional, as

202 *A Methodology of International Law,* Amsterdam, North Holland, 1984, p. 67.

203 *Diritto internazionale,* Milan, t. 1, 1974, p. 235.

204 *ICJ Reports 1986,* Case concerning *Military and Paramilitary Activities in and against Nicaragua,* para. 183.

205 See, for instance, *ICJ Reports 1969,* para. 70.

well as customary, norms are created by the co-ordination of the wills of States. Their binding force, in principle, is the same. A treaty may change customary norms.

The second theory does not deny the possibility of international treaties being part of general international law but, in my view, it does not take into consideration all the complexities of contemporary international law and therefore considers as part of general international law only those treaties to which all, or almost all, States are parties.

Kelsen wrote in 1952:

> "The term 'general international law' designates norms of international law which are valid for all the States of the world, whereas the term 'particular international law' designates norms of international law valid only for certain States. General international law is, as a matter of fact, customary law. As treaties are in principle binding upon the contracting parties, and there is no treaty concluded by or adhered to by all the States of the world, there is only customary, not conventional general international law."[206]

The words "as a matter of fact" mean that Kelsen did not exclude that norms of general international law might be of conventional character, but at the time there were no treaties to which all the States were parties.

Such a factual situation was still more evident at the time of Vattel who wrote: "As soon as it is evident that a treaty binds only the contracting parties, conventional international law is not general but particular law."[207]

Lauterpacht, in the eighth edition of Oppenheim, took one step forward saying:

> "*Universal* international law is created when all or practically all the members of the *Family of Nations* are parties to these treaties . . . Many law-making treaties have been concluded which contain *general* international law because the majority of States, including the leading Powers, are parties to them."[208]

Lauterpacht, therefore, recognized that there are treaty norms in general international law. As I have said it was a step forward but not a sufficient step. Present day general international law contains not only norms of treaties to which all, or almost all, States are parties, but also norms of many other treaties as I shall show later on.

As to the possibility of treaty norms being changed by customary methods, opinion differs. I expressed my opinion on the subject in 1962 in the following terms:

"Cases when a treaty is changed by a customary way are relatively rare, because treaties as a rule contain provisions for their denunciation and amendment. But legally such an amendment is possible by the consent of all the parties."[209]

---

206 *Principles of International Law,* New York, Rhinehart & Company, 1952, p. 188.

207 *Law of Nations* (in Russian), Moscow, 1960, para. 24.

208 L. Oppenheim, *International Law,* ed. by H. Lauterpacht, 8th ed., London, Longmans, 1955, p. 28.

209 See *Questions of Theory of International Law,* Moscow, Juridicheskaya Literatura, 1962, p. 111. French ed. *Droit international public. Problêmes theoriques,* Paris, Pedone, p. 94.

Now I would make only one amendment to this opinion of mine: cases of changing provisions of a treaty by subsequent practice are very frequent, especially as far as bilateral treaties are concerned.

The question was thoroughly examined by the International Law Commission. As a result the Commission adopted the following article: "A treaty may be modified by subsequent practice in the application of the treaty establishing the agreement of the parties to modify its provisions."[210]

As one of the partisans of this article I saw in it some useful elements: *(a)* not any practice may modify the provisions of a treaty; *(b)* it should be a practice accepted by all the parties to the treaty as changing its provisions *(opinio juris).*

And in fact it was an agreed opinion of the Commission. In its comments to the article the Commission pointed out:

> "in formulating the rule in this way the Commission intended to indicate that the subsequent practice, even if every party might not itself have actively participated in the practice, must be such as to establish the agreement of the parties as a whole to the modification in question".[211]

It may well be that the Commission went too far and frightened the conference by its sweeping proposal. The proposal was rejected by the conference on the law of treaties of 1968-1969. It is certainly regrettable that this problem was left unsettled by the convention on the law of treaties of 1969. As stated earlier in State practice, cases of changing the provisions of a treaty by subsequent practice of its application, that is, by a customary way, are not rare and nobody considers them as unlawful. On the other hand, it is doubtful that there is a rule of international law according to which any change of treaty provisions is permitted or that such an unlimited rule is advisable *de lege ferenda.*

That is why an opinion of F. Capotorti that "there is a general norm that a treaty may be amended by the subsequent practice of the parties,"[212] cannot be accepted without reservation.

Partisans of the concept according to which general international law is customary law only, refer sometimes to the usefulness of this concept from the point of view of the stability of international law. They argue that international treaties may be terminated by States whereas customary norms may be amended only by State practice accepted as law. There is a grain of truth in this assertion. But it is generally admitted that customary norms may be amended or abrogated by treaties. Then there are general international treaties that do not contain provisions on their termination. The number of such treaties grows. According to the Vienna convention on the law of treaties:

---

210 *ILC Yearbook,* 1966, 11, p. 236.

211 *Ibid.*

212 "Sul valore della prassi applicativa dei trattati secondo la Convention de Vienna", *Mélanges in Honour of R. Ago, 1,* p. 206.

> "A treaty which contains no provision regarding its termination and which does not provide for denunciation or withdrawal is not subject to denunciation or withdrawal unless:
>
> (a) it is established that the parties intended to admit the possibility of denunciation or withdrawal; or
>
> (b) a right of denunciation or withdrawal may be implied by the nature of the treaty." (Article 56)"

General international treaties concluded in recent decades, with the exception of treaties on the limitation of armaments, contain no provision on termination, denunciation or withdrawal. Such treaties with regard to their stability are in fact on the same level as customary norms.

Some authors argue that treaty norms are rigid whereas customary norms are more flexible.[213]

It is also true to a certain extent only. If there is a norm of international law admitting, within certain limits, the amendment of a treaty by subsequent practice of its application, this objection against conventional norms practically vanishes.

At the same time one should not lose sight of the fact that conventional norms are more precise than customary norms. It is their great advantage in comparison with customary norms.

The foregoing conceptions do not take sufficiently into consideration that there is now a new situation in international law. The growing number of general multilateral treaties is intended to change existing general international law and in fact is changing it. First, these treaties foresee the participation of all States. Second, when not all States are parties to these treaties they become, by and by, binding upon non-participating States by the customary way. The Vienna convention of 1969 contains the following provision on the subject:

> "Nothing in Articles 34 to 37 precludes a rule set forth in a treaty from becoming binding upon a third State as a customary rule of international law, recognized as such." (Article 38.)

The words "recognized as such" were added at the Conference on the Law of Treaties and introduce a small amount of confusion, but still the sense of the article remains clear enough, namely that provisions of a treaty may become binding upon non-participating States by the customary way.

Nowadays such examples are numerous, although this process of expanding the sphere of application of a treaty may take years. One example is the Vienna convention on diplomatic relations of 1961. It was adopted at the conference in 1961 and entered

213 See, for instance, M. Seara Vasquez, *Derecho internacional publico*, Mexico, Editorial Porrua, 1976, p. 63; Nguyen Quoc Dinh, P. Daillier, A. Pellet, *Droit international public* (3e ed.), Paris, Librairie générale de droit et de jurisprudence, 1987, pp. 292-310.

into force in 1964. Up till now not all the States are parties to this convention, but I doubt that there may be a State that would say that the provisions of this convention are not generally binding.

But the Vienna convention of 1961 contains not only previously existing norms of international law. It has many new rules. For instance, according to this convention diplomatic privileges and immunities are extended, with few exceptions, to members of administrative and technical staff of a diplomatic mission.

What is the situation in the case when provisions of a treaty become binding upon non-participating States by the customary way? For the States parties to a treaty the norms are conventional, but for States non-parties, customary. I suggested long ago to call such norms "mixed norms". What is of importance is that in a case of interpretation such customary norms should, in my view, be interpreted in the context of the treaty.

During my membership of the International Law Commission from 1957 to 1967 I never noticed any doubt among the members of the Commission that we were called upon to prepare draft articles intended to be part of general international law. And the Commission never used the terms "general international law" and "customary international law" as synonymous.

Summing up I may say that general international law consists of customary as well as conventional norms and with the progress of codification the number of conventional norms will grow.

Some Western authors have slowly abandoned the outdated concept that general international law is customary law only. I have already quoted Lauterpacht who accepted as part of the general international law those treaties to which all or almost all States are parties. It was a step forward. Somewhat vague, but still in this vein, was the position of A. Verdross who had to change his views on the subject. I believe that each scholar has to change his views if he, as a result of new research or new facts, comes to a conclusion that his former opinion was inexact or wrong. I therefore regret that some scholars stick to their views when they become obsolete and consider it as not decent to change them.

In his *Völkerrecht* of 1959 Verdross strictly distinguished the general international law and the Charter of the United Nations as a treaty and therefore particular international law.[214] In 1973 he said, regarding the Charter: "It may be considered as a universal constitution because it has a tendency to become almost universa1."[215]

This point of view is close to that of Lauterpacht, quoted earlier.

Of course this position is, as I have said before, a step forward in comparison with the prevailing position according to which norms of a treaty as such can never be norms of general international law. But is it not time for Western international lawyers to examine whether this prevailing position that has existed since the XVIIth century accurately reflects the present-day situation and whether it favours the progressive development of international law and its effectiveness?

214 See *Völkerrecht*, Vienna, Springer Verlag, 1959, p. 555.

215 *Die Quellen des universellen Völkerrechts*, Freiburg, Verlag Rombac, 1973, p. 21.

5. The Use Of Force By The United Nations

The Charter of the United Nations says:

> "*We the Peoples of the United Nations determined* . . .
> to unite our strength to maintain international peace and security, and
> to ensure, by the acceptance of principles and the institution of methods,
> that armed force shall not be used, save in the common interest."

As stated earlier, by accepting the Charter States have drastically limited their right to use force in mutual relations. At the same time they have given to the United Nations much greater competence to use force against individual States than the competence possessed by the League of Nations and the right to use force left to the States.

This was an historic step forward in increasing the regulatory capacity of the interstate system. (See Chapter VI.) The fact is that the use of force by the United Nations is one of the important elements of its regulatory capacity. But as soon as the United Nations is the most important subsystem of the interstate system, the increasing regulatory capacity of the United Nations means increasing the regulatory capacity of the interstate system as a whole.

The Security Council has the authority to use force in a variety of situations. Article 39 of the Charter says:

> "The Security Council shall determine the existence of any threat to the peace, breach of the peace, or act of aggression and shall make recommendations, or decide what measures shall be taken in accordance with. Articles 41 and 42 to maintain or restore international peace and security."

Article 41 indicates measures "not involving the use of armed force" that may be taken by the Security Council to give effect to its decisions. Article 42 gives the Security Council the authority to take decisions to use force against a delinquent State when it considers that "measures provided for in Article 41 would be inadequate or have proved to be inadequate". So the Security Council is not bound first to apply Articles 40 and 41. It may adopt a decision to apply Article 42 as a first step.

Article 39 is much wider than Article 51. Article 51 allows States to use force only in the case of an armed attack. Article 39 permits the United Nations to use force not only in cases of a breach of the peace or an act of aggression that evidently implies the use of armed force. The United Nations may also use force in the case of "any threat to the peace".

On the other hand, Article 2 (4), containing the general prohibition of the use of force by States, is wider than Article 39, because not every use of force constitutes a threat to the peace, a breach of the peace or an act of aggression, and therefore not every illegal use of force falls under the competence of the Security Council. There may be border incidents involving the use of force which are not covered by Article 39 of the Charter.

Therefore, States may use force only in the case of an armed attack; the United Nations may use force even when there was no use of force by States and no violation of international law. On the other hand the competence of the United Nations to use force does not cover all cases of illegitimate use of force.

Article 43 of the Charter provides that member States shall make available to the Security Council armed forces in accordance with special agreements to be concluded between the Security Council and individual members. Such agreements have not been concluded.

The Charter contains the necessary safeguards that the United Nations forces be used "in the common interest". A decision to use force may be adopted by the vote of at least nine members in favour, including five permanent members of the Council, or if none of the permanent members votes against. As Th. Frank and F. Patel point out

"the new system vests that responsibility in the Security Council, a body where the most divergent interests and perspectives of humanity are represented and where five of fifteen members have a veto power".[216]

Deficiencies of the system are well known. In some instances the Security Council cannot take the necessary measures because of the veto power. But what else can be suggested? It seems that there is nothing in this world without deficiencies: nothing is perfect.

I am not discussing here the problem of the peace-keeping forces of the United Nations. It is a separate problem, and a great achievement of mankind. Though not directly mentioned in the Charter, the establishment of such forces may be considered as falling under the implied competence of the Security Council.

Because of the cold war that followed the Second World War, the provisions of the Charter regarding the use of force by the United Nations, the implementation of which required the agreement of the permanent members of the Council, did not work and many thought that they were dead for ever. But the end of the cold war made these provisions work. The encouraging example was the use of force by the United Nations against Iraq in 1991.

This action raised, however, some questions.

The first question is whether the Security Council could use aimed force without previous agreements with the States as provided for in Article 43 of the Charter? I believe that in this situation the Security Council could not adopt a decision on the use of force binding upon the members, but could adopt a recommendation as was the case with Iraq.[217]

The next problem concerns the conduct of the operations of the United Nations forces. According to Articles 46 and 47, plans for the operation of armed force are made by the Security Council with the assistance of the Military Staff Committee. This Committee must be responsible, under the Security Council, for the strategic direction of the armed forces. In this case the Military Staff Committee was not activated. It may be considered as a kind of deviation from the strict letter of the Charter, but certainly

216 See "UN Police Action in Lieu of War: 'The Old Order Changeth'", *AJIL* 85 (1991), p. 74.

217 See in this sense D. W. Bowett, *United Nations Forces,* London, Stevens & Sons, 1964, p. 277.

not an essential deviation. The Military Staff Committee, according to the Charter, is an organ of the Security Council. The authority for the conduct of a military operation is vested not in the Committee, but in the Security Council, and therefore the Security Council might use this authority directly, if the situation so requires, although this should not be a rule but only an exception justified by a specific situation. In the case of Iraq such a situation, I believe, existed. The Military Staff Committee had not yet been revived, and the situation required immediate action. One may hope that with the end of the cold war the Military Staff Committee will be revived.

The use of force by the United Nations against Iraq has also raised the thorny question of the relationship between the right of individual and collective self-defence and the authority of the Security Council. According to Article 51 of the Charter this right may be used "until the Security Council has taken measures necessary to maintain international peace and security". If the Security Council did not take the necessary measures the right of self-defence continues to exist.[218]

The main problem is this: when the Security Council has taken measures, who is to decide whether these measures are "measures necessary to maintain international peace and security" or are they "insufficient"? Whether States involved may argue that measures taken by the Security Council are insufficient and therefore they will continue to exercise their right of self-defence? This is a very important question. I believe that according to Article 51 of the Charter the question whether measures taken by the Security Council are "measures necessary to maintain international peace and security" is for the Security Council to decide. The involved States have, of course, the right to ask the Security Council to reconsider its decision or decisions concerning the measures taken.

In the case of Iraq the resolution of the Security Council concerning the use of force was too broad, actually giving to the United States a very great latitude of action. This experience shows that in the future decisions of the Security Council should be more precise and especially that the machinery for such actions provided by the Charter must function. The changed world situation has created sufficient opportunities for a more strict application of the provisions of the Charter.

The recent decision of the Security Council concerning sanctions against Libya for the refusal by the Libyan Government to extradite two of its officials suspected of terrorist activities (the blowing up of an American airliner in 1988) to be tried, raises the question of an evolution of the notion of a "threat to the peace" that gives the Security Council the right to impose sanctions including the use of armed force. When the United Nations Charter was drafted there was actually no international terrorism and therefore the drafters could not have had in mind that the Security Council would deal with such a problem as international terrorism. Since then the situation has changed and in 1972 the General Assembly expressed its concern over the growing acts of international terrorism.

218 See in this sense Th. Frank and F. Patel, *op. cit.*, p. 63. They speak, however, of a revival of the right of self-defence whereas there is simply a continuation of the exercise of this right.

Regrettably, there are some States that organize, support or encourage international terrorism.[219]

The Charter does not give a definition of a "threat to the peace", leaving it to the judgment of the Security Council to evaluate a situation in each particular case. The decision of the Security Council concerning sanctions against Libya seems to indicate that the Security Council considers international terrorism in general as constituting a threat to the peace. There are sufficient reasons for that, but this should be applied in the future to all States. Of course the Security Council, as well as the International Court of Justice, is not a legislative body, but there is no doubt that its decisions have very great weight and may accelerate the formation of new norms of international law, in this case a norm according to which international terrorism is an international crime for which there is responsibility of individuals and States under international law. Such a norm, in my view, is in *statu nascendi* if not already an acting norm.

There are good reasons to argue that the time has come when grave violations of human rights should also be considered by the Security Council as a threat to the peace. The International Law Commission suggested in its draft articles on State responsibility that such violations constitute an international crime.[220]

219 See E. Lachov, *Terrorism and Interstate Relations*, Moscow, International Relations, 1991.
220 *ILC Yearbook*, 1980, Vol. II, part II, p. 32.

Chapter V Non-Legal Norms in the Interstate System

Alongside with the norms of international law there are non-legal norms functioning in the interstate system. They are of different kinds. I am going to examine only the most important, to which belong political norms, norms of resolution-recommendations of international organizations and moral norms.

The role of non-legal norms in the interstate system is growing due to a number of factors:

(a) International law is never able to follow step by step the development of a situation in the interstate system so that there are always some international relations not covered or not sufficiently covered by it. It is especially visible now.

(b) Non-legal norms are more flexible, they do not impose strict obligations and, with regard to political and the recommendatory norms, States are in many cases ready to accept them whereas they hesitate to accept legal norms.

(c) There is a growing belief that international politics should conform not only to norms of international law, but also to non-legal norms.

Non-legal norms contribute to the regulatory capacity of the interstate system.

1. Political Norms

Political norms are a relatively new phenomenon. The attention of scholars has been attracted to them actually only after the signing of the Final Act of the Conference on Security and Co-operation in Europe in 1975.

Political norms are the most numerous and the most important of all the non-legal norms functioning in the interstate system. In their nature they are closer to norms of international law than other nonlegal norms. Political norms may be found in many international documents, such as joint communiqués, joint declarations of States, etc.

In the United States international documents, such as the Helsinki Final Act, are often called "non-binding agreements".[221] The term is certainly not appropriate as

221 See, for instance, "The Twilight Existence of Nonbinding International Agreements", 71 *AJIL* (1977), p. 296.

it stresses a non-binding character of such agreements which is not the case. And Schachter himself spoke later of a "non-legal commitment".[222]

L. Henkin, although using the term "non-binding agreements" actually means "non-legally binding". So speaking of the Helsinki Final Act he points out:

> "All parties to the Helsinki Accord agreed that it was not to be legally binding . . . yet all the participants also appeared careful not to stress the non-binding character of the Accord."[223]

According to the theory of the co-ordination of the wills of States, political norms are also the result of such a co-ordination of the wills of States. This co-ordination consists, as in the case of the norms of international law, of two stages: *(a)* the co-ordination of the wills regarding the substance of the rules of behaviour; *(b)* the co-ordination of the wills regarding the binding force of these rules. The first stage is analogous to the first stage of the process of creating norms of international law. The second stage, however, is basically different. In the case of international law it is a co-ordination of the wills with regard to a legally binding character of the rules of conduct. In the case of political norms it is a co-ordination of the wills of States with regard to non-legal, but still binding, force. But in both cases the process of the co-ordination of the wills of States includes the inter-conditionality of wills, reflected in the fact that the consent of a State to recognize a particular political norm as binding is given on the condition of analogous consent by another or other States (the principle of reciprocity).

So two conclusions may be drawn. Political norms, as well as norms of international law, are created by political processes and both are the result of the co-ordination of the wills of States.

Second: political norms as well as norms of international law contain international obligations. The last paragraph of the Helsinki Final Act is formulated as follows:

> "Wherefore, the undersigned High Representatives of the participating States, mindful of the high political significance which they attach to the results of the Conference, and declaring their determination to act in accordance with the provisions contained in the above texts, have subscribed their signatures below."

We find the analogous statement in the Charter of Paris for a New Europe of 21 November 1990.

The problem is what is the nature of obligations contained in political norms and what is the difference between these obligations and legal obligations.

222 "International Law in Theory and Practice", 178 *Collected Courses*, p. 130.

223 "International Law, Politics, Values and Functions", 216 *Collected Courses*, 1989, p. 225.

Professor I. Lukashuk has defined an international political norm as a "politically binding rule of conduct in interstate relations that is created, carried out and ensured by political means"[224]

4. This definition, however, does not show the specificity of political norms as norms of international law are also created, carried out and ensured by political means.

A thorough examination of the difference between legal obligations and political obligations (engagements politiques) has been undertaken by Professor Virally. In a report to the Institut de droit international entitled "Difference Between International Texts Possessing Legal Significance and Texts not Possessing Such a Significance" Virally has given a remarkable analysis of the nature of political obligations.[225]

According to Virally, political obligations "are genuine obligations" and that States in relation to which such commitments have been adopted have every reason to expect that the promised behaviour will in fact be observed and may therefore demand it.[226]

The basis of political obligations, in his opinion, is the moral principle of good faith according to which the word given to another State must be respected. "Good faith," says Virally, "fulfils in respect of purely political obligations the same role it takes with regard to legal obligations."[227]

Professor O. Schachter also takes the view that the basis of political obligations is the principle of good faith, but the good faith as a principle of international law rather than a moral principle. He states:

> "I believe it is fair to say that States entering into a non-legal commitment generally view it as a political (or moral) obligation and intend to carry it out in good faith. Other parties or other States concerned have reason to expect such compliance and rely upon it. What we must deduce from it, I submit, is that the political texts which express commitments and positions of one kind or another are governed by the general principle of good faith. Moreover, since good faith is an accepted general principle of international law, it is appropriate and even necessary to apply it in its legal sense."[228]

A widely discussed problem of the basis of obligations with regard to international law as well as with regard to political norms is based on the theory of natural law. Actually political norms, as well as norms of international law, are societal phenomena having their characteristics that have developed in the course of history and which have their roots in the needs of society and emerged to meet these needs. The appearance of political norms has been necessitated by the growing volume of interstate relations,

224 "International Political Norms in the Period of Detente", *Soviet State and Law*, 1976, No. 8, p. 107.

225 See "La distinction entre textes internationaux ayant une portée juridique dans les relations mutuelles entre leurs auteurs et textes qui en sont dépourvus", *Annuaire de l' Institut de droit international*, Vol. 60 (I), 1963.

226 *Ibid.*, p. 336.

227 *Ibid.*

228 *Op. cit.*, p. 130.

some of which are not regulated or not sufficiently regulated by international law. That is why under the title "basis of obligations" the discussion is actually focused on the problem of a "nature of obligations", or a nature of specific norms.

As has been stated earlier the nature of political norms is not legal. In this case it may be either political or moral or both. The moral element in the form of good faith is present in all international norms that result from the co-ordination of the wills of States, that is in norms of international law and in political norms. But if it were the only element of political norms, then they would be nothing else but moral norms which they are not. They do contain a political element.

The question therefore is what is the essence of this political element in the nature of political norms. I believe that this political element may be defined as political expediency and political wisdom.

This differentiates political norms from norms of international law. It makes political norms more flexible as political expediency and wisdom of political decisions change with the change of circumstances.

With regard to the norms of international law the Vienna convention on the law of treaties of 1969 has a very rigid rule to ensure the compliance of States with their obligations. It states:

> "A fundamental change of circumstances which has occurred with regard to those existing at the time of the conclusion of a treaty, and which was not foreseen by the parties, may not be invoked as a ground for terminating or withdrawing from the treaty." (Article 62.)

Considering the essence of political norms, a conclusion may be drawn that this rule is not applicable to political norms. To some extent it has already been stated by Virally who said:

> "It seems that in practice political commitments are always taken in the light of the existing political situation at the time when they are assumed, and, normally, with the reservation of 'political difficulty', i.e., difficulties pertaining to changes in international circumstances that make it more difficult to fulfil these commitments (for example, disturbances in the international monetary system, or a political or economic crisis), or even changes of a domestic character (economic recession, political troubles, and even simple changes in a political majority)."[229]

And Virally has come to the following conclusion that is, in my opinion, largely correct:

> "Thus, the clause rebus sic stantibus and the state of necessity in case of political norms are taken into consideration in much greater measure than in international law."[230]

229 *Op. cit.*, p. 338.
230 *Ibid.*

Referring to Virally's arguments Professor Schachter says:

> "Probably the most important consideration is that the purely political, non-legal instruments allow for change or abrogation in the event political circumstances change. By making it clear that an arrangement or commitment is political and not legal, there is an implied understanding that it is based on the existing political situation and consequently that any alteration in that situation would be a sufficient ground to abandon the commitment."[231]

Of course, not any change of circumstances may justify non-fulfilment of a political obligation. A change should be considerable and seriously affect the expediency of the obligation and the wisdom of its fulfilment.

The next question is the problem of pressure upon States to make them comply with political obligations and sanctions in case of violations of political obligations. It is a moot point. If we take the most important example, that is the Helsinki Final Act, we will not find there any provisions regarding sanctions or pressures. Theoretically at least one point seems clear: non-compliance of a State with a political norm gives another or other parties a right not to comply with the respective political norm with regard to a defaulting State.

Virally expressed an opinion that in the case of the non-fulfilment of a *purely political accord* other participants in the accord may consider such conduct as unfriendly or even hostile. In such a case it would be justified to take against a defaulting State all measures of retorsion, such as diplomatic representations, protests, recall of diplomats, postponement of diplomatic visits, interruption of on-going negotiations, suspension of co-operation in various fields, or suspension of diplomatic or commercial relations, etc.[232]

Virally's reasoning seems, logical. It actually means that in the case of violations of political norms individual States are authorized to take the same measures they may take in case of violations of norms of international law. But there is not yet State practice accepted as law to confirm these conclusions.

Within the framework of the Helsinki process new procedures and mechanisms are developing to ensure compliance with agreed provisions. They may be defined as discussions at appropriate international forums, persuasion, assistance and collective political and moral pressures.

A few examples from the Helsinki process may clarify the issue.

At the various meetings held in the course of the Helsinki process the participating States created a great number of political norms on the basis of the Helsinki Final Act, specifying and developing its provisions. They have also devised procedures and institutions intended to ensure the compliance of States with the adopted norms.

As stated in the Vienna Concluding Document of 15 January 1989, the participating States examined in detail the fulfilment of the Helsinki Final Act and of the Madrid

231 *Op. cit.*, p. 126.
232 *Op. cit.*, p. 338.

Concluding Document. Different opinions have been expressed regarding the fulfilment of these obligations. Encouraging developments have been noted in many fields. At the same time serious shortcomings in the realization of these documents have been criticized. An open and frank discussion concerning the application and respect of the principles of the Final Act took place and preoccupation was expressed concerning serious violations of some of these principles.

At the Copenhagen Meeting in 1990 the participating States held a review of the implementation of their commitments in the field of the human dimension. They concluded that the degree of compliance with the commitments contained in the relevant provisions of the CSCE documents had shown a fundamental improvement. They also expressed the view that further steps were required for the full realization of their commitments relating to the human dimension.

At the Moscow meeting of the Conference on the Human Dimension of the CSCE in 1991 views were expressed by the participating States on the implementation of their commitments in the field of the human dimension. They considered that the degree of compliance with the commitments contained in the relevant provisions of the CSCE documents had shown further substantial improvement since the Copenhagen Meeting. At the same time, they stated that in spite of considerable progress made, serious threats to and violations of the CSCE principles and provisions continue to exist. In particular, they deplored acts of discrimination, hostility and violence against persons or groups on national, ethnic or religious grounds.

The development of the CSCE process shows that such forums characterized by an exchange of views, persuasion and political and moral pressures are giving good results especially in the field of the human dimension.

But more sophisticated procedures and institutions are also *emerging* within the framework of the CSCE. Important institutional arrangements were agreed upon at the Paris Conference on Security and Co-operation in November 1990. They include the creation of the following institutions:

(1) Periodical meetings of heads of State and government.
(2) A Council consisting of ministers of foreign affairs of the participating States. The Council will provide the central forum for regular political consultations within the CSCE process.
(3) A Committee of senior officials to prepare the meetings of the Council and to carry out its decisions.
(4) A Secretariat at Prague.
(5) A Conflict Prevention Centre in Vienna to assist the Council in reducing the risk of conflict.
(6) An Office for Free Elections in Warsaw to facilitate contacts and the exchange of information on elections within participating States.

There are some other procedures and mechanisms provided for in the CSCE documents, such as the exchange of information on problems of the human dimension, the creation of a list of experts who may be invited to assist an inviting State in the resolution of questions relating to the human dimension, etc.

These mechanisms are beginning to function.

Some of the similar procedures have developed within other associations of States that are not international organizations, such as the Non-Aligned Movement, the "Group of 77" and others.

A conclusion may be drawn that with regard to political norms new procedures and mechanisms are developing intended to ensure the compliance of States with these norms. These procedures and mechanisms are in many respects different from those that exist in international law.

A very important problem is that of relationship between norms of international law and political norms. Virally actually takes the view that political obligations must prevail over legal obligations. He writes:

> "Good faith on which all political commitments rest requires that such commitments also carry renunciation of reference to legal arguments that could, in some cases, in effect deprive them of all substance."[233]

As an example of such reference to international law he cites a possibility of invoking the principle of non-intervention that could impede implementation of specific political obligations.

This argument is, however, not valid. As has been stated before a moral element in the form of good faith is present in all international norms that are created by the co-ordination of the wills of States, that is in norms of international law as well as in political norms. But in the norms of international law a dominant element is legal, the essence of which is embodied in the principle that States must strictly fulfil their obligations under international law. Exceptions allowed are extremely rare and consequences of violations of these norms are severe.

As to political norms these obligations to comply with them are more loose and flexible and sanctions in case of violations are less severe. So it would be correct to say that the norms of international law are more binding than political norms. It is a general proposition.

Then there are in international law two kinds of norms: peremptory norms *(jus cogens)* and dispositive norms *(jus dispositivum).* The relationship of political norms with these two kinds of norms is different. States cannot derogate from peremptory norms in their mutual relations even by agreement. By implication political norms cannot derogate from peremptory norms of international law. As to the dispositive norms of international law the situation is different. States may derogate from dispositive norms by concluding a treaty that creates norms of international law valid between the parties to the treaty, but deviating from the norms of general international law. It is logical, to suggest that political norms may also deviate from dispositive norms of international law.

This situation reflects generally the relationship between international politics and international law.

---

233 *Op. cit.*, p. 347.

2. The Recommendatory Resolutions of the International Organizations

Resolutions of the international organizations may be divided into two groups: legally binding resolutions and resolutions-recommendations. (See Chapter II, paragraph 5 *(a)*.)

The number of resolutions-recommendations is very great. This is a new phenomenon in the interstate system. It is therefore understandable that the world science of international law has recently paid much attention to this phenomenon, and especially to resolutions- recommendations of the most important international organization – the United Nations. I shall also deal mainly with these resolutions.

There is no doubt that resolutions-recommendations play a certain regulatory role in the interstate system, they influence the behaviour of States and contribute to the regulatory capacity of the system.

With regard to these resolutions the main problem is what is their nature and especially their "binding quality".[234] But first, one should not confuse, as happens frequently, legal effects or legal consequences of resolutions of international organizations with the nature of these resolutions. Legal effects may result from resolutions as simple legal fact. Legal fact is usually defined as an event producing an effect in law.[235] Therefore, a resolution that has no legal element at all may have a legal effect or legal consequences.

With regard to the binding quality or binding force of the resolutions of the United Nations General Assembly several opinions have been expressed.

To begin with there are two extreme positions. According to the first one, recommendatory resolutions of the General Assembly, or at least some of them, are legally binding upon members of the United Nations. This point of view is held mainly by international lawyers from the developing countries that constitute a majority in all the international organizations and are therefore interested in enhancing the role of the United Nations General Assembly.

Judge Elias (Nigeria) was strongly of the opinion that resolutions of the General Assembly are binding upon member States. He argued as follows:

> "It seems clear that, as far as General Assembly recommendations in respect of nine specifically enumerated matters in Article 18 (2) are concerned, its 'decisions' in the form of 'recommendations' are binding upon all concerned once they have been adopted by a two-thirds majority. As regards all other matters within the competence of the Assembly, a simple majority is all that is required by Article 18 (2) of the Charter."[236]

234 R. Higgins, "The Role of Resolutions of International Organisations in the Process of Creating Norms in the International System", *International Law and the International System* (ed. by W. E. Butler), Martinus Nijhoff Publishers, 1987, p. 23.

235 See J. Salmon, "Le fait dans l'application du droit international", *Recueil des cours,* Vol. 175 (1982).

236 *Africa and the Development of International Law,* Leiden, A. W. Sijthoff, Oceana Publications Inc., New York, 1972, p. 71.

This interpretation of Article 18 (2) of the Charter is entirely unjustified. Article 18 (2) does not deal with the legal quality of the resolutions of the General Assembly. It regulates only one question, namely how resolutions on different matters within the competence of the General Assembly are adopted. Decisions "on important questions" include matters on which the General Assembly may adopt legally binding decisions (e.g., the admission of new members to the United Nations, the suspension of rights and privileges of individual members, budget questions), and matters with regard to which the General Assembly may adopt only recommendations (e.g., resolutions on maintaining international peace and security, on disarmament, on the development of international law).

But Elias goes much further. He argues that:

> "if there is unanimity in the Assembly during the vote all are bound, provided the subject falls within its competence. If the vote is divided then those States that vote for a particular resolution by the requisite majority, are bound on the ground of consent and estoppel. Those that abstain are also bound on the ground of acquiescence and tacit consent since an abstention is not a negative vote; while those that vote against the resolution should be regarded as bound by the democratic principle that the majority view should always prevail where the vote has been truly free and fair and the requisite majority has been secured."[237]

So according to Elias all resolutions of the United Nations General Assembly are binding upon the members of the United Nations. Actually Elias asserts that the General Assembly has a legislative power which is evidently not the case.

Some other authors from the developing countries, not going as far as Elias, still try to prove that the General Assembly resolutions have a legally binding force. O.Y. Assamoah expressed an opinion that declarations of the United Nations General Assembly are agreements among States and as such are legally binding.[238] As soon as declarations are also resolutions, such an assertion actually means that all resolutions of the General Assembly are legally binding upon all States that have voted for them.

P. K. Menon (India) has chosen another way to come to the same conclusion. In his opinion, the United Nations General Assembly is a body whose members are sovereign States and their representatives in the Assembly may bind respective States. If these representatives vote for a resolution the States that they represent become "parties to the code of conduct resolved by the General Assembly."[239] It is true that Menon is a little vague as he does not say expressly that this code of conduct is legally binding.

237 *Ibid.*, pp. 74-75.

238 *The Legal Significance of the Declarations of the General Assembly of the United Nations,* The Hague, Martinus Nijthoff, 1966, pp. 66-67.

239 "United Nations Special Committee and Decolonisation", *Indian Journal of International Law,* 9 (1969), p. 27.

These examples may show how in interpreting an international treaty one may go away from the treaty if no attention is paid to the text of the treaty and fundamental principles of international law, but is guided by abstract considerations. The authors of the opinions I have just quoted reject in the name of democracy the most important principle of democracy – the principle of *good faith* as a moral principle and corresponding fundamental principle of international law – the principle *pacta sunt servanda* (treaties must be fulfilled in good faith). The United Nations Charter is an international treaty and according to international law "every treaty in force is binding upon the parties to it and must be performed by them in good faith". (Article 26 of the Vienna Convention on the Law of Treaties of 1969.)

The points of view I have just enumerated have no support in the United Nations Charter and indeed their authors do not even try to base their positions on the provisions of the Charter.

According to some very authoritative international lawyers such as Verdross and Bastid, resolutions of the General Assembly have only political and moral weight. This seems to be a prevailing opinion among Western international lawyers. Professor Verdross wrote:

"If on the basis of the United Nations Charter the General Assembly can address only recommendations to States, such resolutions can be neither binding nor semi-binding."[240]

Professor Bastid is of the opinion that recommendatory resolutions of international bodies "possess only political significance".[241]

The Soviet international lawyers G. Dmitrieva and I. Lukashuk are also of the opinion that General Assembly resolutions have "moral and political force".[242]

In my view there is no doubt that resolutions of the General Assembly possess political and moral power, but as I shall try to show later this characteristic does not exhaust the nature of these resolutions.

Between these two extreme positions there are at least two intermediate positions.

The first of these intermediate positions is represented by Lauterpacht and stated as follows:

> "Although on proper occasions they (General Assembly resolutions – G.T.) provide a legal authorization for Members determined to act upon them individually or collectively they do not create a legal obligation to comply with them."[243]

If this statement is correct resolutions of the General Assembly convey a right to act according to these resolutions and therefore a legal obligation to respect this right. It is

240 "Kann die Generalversammlung der Vereinten Nationen das Voelkerrecht weiterbilden", *Zeitschrift für auslandisches Offentliches Recht und Völkerrecht,* 26 (1966), s. 693.

241 *Droit international public. Le droit des organisations internationales,* Paris, 1969-1970 (mimeo), fasc. 1, p. 91.

242 See "The Role of the UN General Assembly Resolutions in the International Norm-Making", *Indian Journal of International Law,* 28 (1988), p. 240.

243 *ICJ Reports 1955,* Advisory Opinion of 7 June 1955, p. 115.

a quality of a legal norm. That would mean that the General Assembly has some legislative power which is not the case.

As representatives of the second intermediate position I'll quote Professors Malintoppi and Virally. Malintoppi points out that the basic obligation of a member State of an international organization is to co-operate in achieving the organization's objectives. This is why the recommendations are adopted. A member of an organization which does not carry out its recommendations thus fails to carry out its duty.[244]

The same arguments are presented by Virally to prove that recommendations of the United Nations General Assembly "are not deprived of legal significance"[245].

Formerly I was also of the opinion that "there is a certain element of legal obligation in recommendatory resolutions of international organizations"[246].

These arguments relate, however, to the legal basis of recommendations, but not to the nature of recommendations. The means of achieving the aims of an organization may not necessarily be only legal although they must be based on legal norms. Recommendations of the United Nations General Assembly have their legal basis in the Charter and general international law, but themselves are not legal or semi-legal. The same is the case with political actions undertaken by the United Nations organs: based on legal norms and necessary for achieving the aims of the organization, they are not legal in nature.

A correct solution of the problem of the nature of normative resolutions-recommendations of international organizations can be found on the basis of the theory of the co-ordination of the wills of States. Recommendations of international organizations are the result of the co-ordination of the wills of States members in accordance with a statute of an organization. And in the case of recommendations the wills of member States, are directed to create recommendations, recommendatory norms of behaviour.

These norms possess a certain power. From many definitions of "power" let us take one given by Bertrand Russell: "Power may be defined as the production of intended effects."[247]

As stated earlier resolutions have a political power. As emanating from a very authoritative body they exercise a certain political influence upon States as do many other non-normative actions of international organizations.

But what is specific for resolutions-recommendations is their *recommendatory power.* This power is based on the Charter of the United Nations. Recommendatory resolutions create neither legal nor political nor moral obligations to act in accordance with them. They recommend to act in a certain way, but in the case of any recommendation, those to whom it is addressed may act in accordance with it or not. But in contradistinction to Lauterpacht, I am of the opinion that a resolution-recommendation does not create legal justification for those who act in accordance with it. It means that a resolution-recommendation must conform to international

244 A. Malintoppi, *Le raccomandazioni internazionali,* Milan, Dott. A. Giuffrè, 1958.

245 M. Virally, *L' Organisation mondiale,* Paris, Armand Colin, 1972, p. 187.

246 G. Tunkin, *Law and Force in the International System,* Moscow, Progress Publishers, 1985, p. 125.

247 *Power,* London, Unwin Books, 1963, p. 25.

law as it cannot change it, and a State acting upon a resolution-recommendation must not violate international law.

As to the real influence of the resolutions of the United Nations General Assembly the Declaration on the Occasion of the Twenty- fifth Anniversary of the United Nations (Resolution 2627 XXV) may be going too far in saying that:

> "the international conventions and resolutions concluded under its (the United Nations G.T.) auspices give expression to the moral conscience of mankind and represent humanitarian standards for all members of the international community".

But there is no doubt that the influence of resolutions-recommendations especially those of the United Nations General Assembly in the contemporary world is multi-sided and great.

In a general way they help to create an atmosphere of mutual understanding and co-operation. In spite of the fact that most of the General Assembly resolutions are not fully implemented they influence the behaviour of States sometimes in an imperceptible way. Thereby they perform a regulatory role but as soon as they are recommendations their real and potential influence on States' behaviour varies very much depending on the content of the resolutions. In other words the more a resolution reflects the common interests of the members of the organization and therefore the more the vote for it approaches unanimity, the more chances there are that States will act in accordance with it. The practical conclusion is that no State or group of States should try to get their draft resolution passed at all costs, but to seek the most possible consensus. Of course, too-great a number of resolutions adopted by the United Nations General Assembly, as well as by many other international organizations, diminish their actual effectiveness.

3. International Moral Norms

International moral norms, in contradistinction to norms of international law and norms of recommendatory resolutions of international organizations, are not created by States. They are part of the peoples' consciousness, judgments about what is good and what is bad in international politics. Dmitrieva correctly points out that international morality "contains a rich historical experience of international relations, embodied in moral ideas, outlooks, principles and norms."[248]

There are different systems of moral norms: religious, ethnic, class, etc. But there are also moral norms common to mankind as a whole. Marxism, although putting too much stress on class morality, has at the same time recognized the primary importance of international morality. So, for instance, Marx in his "Inaugural Address to the Working Men's International Association" (1864) called upon the working class to "vindicate

248 "Morality and International Law", *International Relations*, Moscow, 1991, p. 11.

the simple laws of morality and justice, which ought to govern the relations of private individuals, as the rules paramount of the intercourse of nations."[249]

In the Decree on Peace, Lenin started his definition of the right of self-determination of the peoples with the words – "in accordance with the legal consciousness of democrats in general."[250]

Norms of international morality reflect common aims and values of mankind as they are seen by the peoples of the entire world. This is certainly a vague phenomenon, but it exists as such.

International moral norms, as everything in the world, have changed in the course of history as to their content and sphere of validity. In antiquity, and even later, slavery was considered as a natural phenomenon. Now, it is an international crime. With growing communications between the peoples of the earth the number of commonly accepted moral norms will certainly be increasing.

With regard to States, moral norms constitute an objective reality not depending on the wills of States. They are considered by mankind nowadays as morally binding upon States. The moral obligations of States are based on the conscience of the peoples of the world. If norms of international law have legal sanctions enforced by States or international organizations, and embrace different measures including the use of force against a defaulting State, moral norms have only social sanctions in the faun of condemnation by public opinion. In some cases such sanctions may be sufficiently effective, but generally they are less effective than legal sanctions.

Probably the most dangerous, though not completely false theory in our days, is the political realism theory. According to it, morality and international law have no place in international politics. As Art and Waltz put it:

> ". . . States in anarchy cannot afford to be moral. The possibility for moral behaviour rests upon the existence of an effective government that can deter and punish illegal actions. In anarchy there is no government, hence there are no laws. International law reflects merely the prevailing consensus among States about their common self-interests. Such 'laws' are followed only when useful to States. They are violated, usually with impunity, whenever States find it inexpedient to observe them. If there is neither government nor laws, then there can be no concept of legal rights. So States have a 'right' only to what they can achieve by their own efforts. No State has a legal or moral right to exist or to prosper, only the 'right' to do all that is in its power to do."[251]

I discuss political realism mainly in Chapter VI. Here I only say that the starting point, that is, the state of anarchy in the interstate system, is wrong though not completely

249 K. Marx and F. Engels, *Selected Works in Three Volumes,* Vol. 2, Moscow, Progress Publishers, 1976, p. 18.

250 *On the Foreign Policy of the Soviet State,* Moscow, Progress Publishers, 1973, p. 12.

251 See "Technology, Strategy and the Use of Force", *The Use of Force. International Politics and Foreign Policy* (ed. by Art and Waltz), Lanham, University Press of America, 1983, p. 6.

wrong. As a result the opinion on the role of international law and international morality is incorrect, though not entirely incorrect. It is incorrect because, as a matter of fact, moral norms influence behaviour of States as States and their ruling elites are forced to pay attention to public opinion, at least in the democratic States. It is not completely incorrect, as in most cases the influence of moral norms is small.

On the other hand there are theories rooted in the theories of natural law that exaggerate the role of international morality with regard to international law and international politics. A considerable part of the world doctrine of international law holds the view that morality is a basis of international law.

The problem of relationship between international morality and international law is of considerable importance, first of all because there are tendencies to justify violations of international law by references to moral norms.

International law and international morality are two separate systems of norms functioning in the interstate system. They interact and influence each other, but no one of them depends on the other.

To say that morality is the basis of international law is a kind of logical simplification. Moral norms influence the international legal position of States and thereby influence international law. One may speak of a moral obligation of States to make international law conform to international morality. But the international legal position of a State is influenced by many factors (see Chapter II) and among them by moral considerations that are usually not decisive.

As a rule, international morality goes ahead of international law and very often moral norms become norms of international law, or more correctly, they appear in international law norms analogous to norms of international morality and to a considerable extent as a result of the influence of international morality on the development of international law.

Examples of the appearance of new norms of international law analogous to norms of international morality and under the considerable influence of international morality are many. I shall quote only the most important: the prohibition of the use of force and threat of force in interstate relations, the Nuremberg principles, the prohibition of apartheid, the prohibition of colonialism, etc.

On the other hand, international law in many cases stimulates the development and strengthens international morality. There is no doubt that the principal document of contemporary international law – the United Nations Charter – has an enormous influence on international morality.

The position of norms of international law with regard to international morality varies. Some of them embody norms of international morality wholly or partially, others are neutral or semi-neutral.

As Lauterpacht pointed out:

> "like any other law, international law is to a large extent the expression of dictates of morality."[252]

252 *International Law. Collected Papers* (ed. by E. Lauterpacht), *1 General Works,* Cambridge University Press, 1970, p. 46.

Soviet scholars, in particular Levin, Lukashuk and Dmitrieva, stressed the legal-moral character of the fundamental principles of contemporary international law.[253]

However, the greatest number of norms of international law are neutral or semi-neutral with regard to morality. So, a number of norms of international diplomatic law are morally neutral: the norms on the establishment of diplomatic missions, the appointment of ambassadors and personnel of a mission and so on. Norms of diplomatic law concerning privileges and immunities may be considered morally semi-neutral as foreign ambassadors and personnel of a diplomatic mission should be considered as guests of a receiving country.

Most important in the relationship between international law and morality is that violations of international law cannot be morally justified. The principle of fulfilling in good faith international obligations is one of the fundamental principles of international law and at the same time a principle of international morality. Any violation of international law is, above all, a violation of the said principle of international law. Consequently, a violation of international law is always a violation of the moral principle of *good faith.*

253 See D. Levin, *The Principle of Peaceful Settlement of International Disputes,* Moscow, 1977; I. Lukashuk, "Morality and International Law", *Indian Journal of International Law,* Vol. 14 (1974); G. Dmitrieva, *op. cit.*

Chapter VI Increasing Regulatory Capacity of the Interstate System

1. The Notion of the Regulatory Capacity of the Interstate System. Two Models of the Interstate System

The global interstate system is a comparatively new phenomenon. It actually appeared in the second half of the XXth century.

Any integrated system has its regulatory capacity. An integrated system without regulation is impossible: it would be chaos and would disintegrate. There are different definitions of regulation as there are different definitions of any societal event. According to Kaplan:

> "regulation is the process by means of which a system attempts to maintain or preserve its identity over time as it adapts to changing conditions. Integrative and disintegrative actions are also regulatory in character."[254]

Kaplan defines the regulatory capacity of a system as follows: "Let capacity be defined as a measure of the responses a system is able to make that compensate for potential disturbances of the system's equilibrium."[255] This definition is quoted by Haas.[256] As a whole it seems to me a satisfactory definition. However, it would be better if one word is added to read: "the system's *dynamic* equilibrium" as this capacity should not only help the system to maintain the existing equilibrium but also to make the system capable of development, that is of changing equilibrium.

The interstate system is a social system, different from State systems. There is no such central and powerful authority that exists in every organized contemporary State system. As Professor I. Claude has pointed out "the presence of sovereignty in the States accounts for its absence in the system".[257]

The absence of sovereignty in the interstate system does not mean an absence of order. In this system, as in any system, there are elements of anarchy and elements of order, but the degree of anarchy and the degree of order in the interstate system is

254 *System and Process in International Politics,* New York, 1957, p. 89.

255 *Ibid.*

256 See *Beyond the Nation State,* Stanford, Stanford University Press, 1964, p. 58.

257 *States and the Global System, Politics, Law and Organization,* New York, St. Martin Press, 1988, p. 2.

different from those in the State systems. The degree of anarchy in the interstate system is higher than in State systems.

The interstate system possesses a regulatory capacity, but it is generally agreed that this capacity is inadequate. Merle rightly calls the interstate system "un système dépourvu de régulation adéquate".[258] (A system having no adequate regulation.) However, this capacity is growing. The regulatory means of the interstate system are politics, norms, first of all norms of international law, and power including military force.

As stated earlier, politics is omnipresent: it stands behind the law as well as behind power or force. According to what outweighs in politics – law or force – one may speak of two conceptual models of the interstate system: the balance-of-power model and the rule of law, or as I would prefer, the primacy of international law model.

As I understand it, a conceptual model of the interstate system is a part of a *Weltanschaung* or general outlook, a general vision of the interstate system, or, in other words, a part of an ideology.

At present in the West, and now also in Russia, it is *a la mode* to say that international relations should be made free of ideological influences. But it is impossible. Ideology, as a background of a State's foreign policy, will always be there. A man, and the policy of a State is made by men, makes a decision that he finds reasonable, but what he considers reasonable depends to a bigger or lesser degree, depending on the circumstances, on his general outlook, that is, on his ideology. But an ideology is only a background of policy decisions. It should not dominate in interstate politics as being a very general and goal dominated phenomenon, it cannot reflect an ever-changing situation, whereas policy should and can do it. As Haas pointed out "the ideological bias is exposed by close attention to the end result of functional development postulated by the observer as being desirable".[259]

Two models of the interstate system coexist in the present day interstate system and not only in world politics as a whole, but also in the policies of one and the same State. But the difference between them is enormous. One may say that there is a constant fight between them, it is a fight between power politics and politics based on the Charter of the United Nations, the politics of primacy of international law.

I believe that it is generally true to say that the balance-of-power model and politics corresponding to it reflect primarily the animal part of the nature of man, whereas the primacy of the international law model and corresponding politics reflect the societal part of the nature of man.

2. The Balance-of-Power Model of the Interstate System

It is usually considered that the balance of power system emerged after the Treaty of Westphalia in 1648.[260] The book by Grotius, *De Jure Belli ac Pacis Libri Tres,* contains no notion of balance of power politics. On the contrary Grotius says:

258 *Sociologie des relations internationales,* Paris, Dalloz, 1976, p. 418.

259 *Op. cit.,* p. 85.

260 See A. Vagst and D. Vagst, "The Balance of Power in International Law: a History of an Idea", *AJIL,* Vol. 73 (1979).

> "The opinion of some authors that under the law of nations it is allowed to use arms against growing menacing force which when reaching enormous dimensions may cause damage is wholly unacceptable."[261]

The balance of power model of the interstate system is based on the assumption that in a society of sovereign States, with no central authority over States, relations among them are inevitably based on power, first of all on military strength. The father of contemporary political realism, Professor Hans Morgenthau, taking as a starting point the Hobbesian ideas stated: "The tendency to dominate, in particular, is an element of all human associations and local political organizations, to the State."[262] His conclusion was that "international politics, like all politics, is a struggle for power".[263] And he added:

> "aspiration for power being the distinguishing element of international politics, as of all politics, international politics is of necessity power politics."[264]

This is the foundation of the balance of power model which is considered as a law of the development of the interstate system.[265]

According to this, model power takes the primary regulatory role in the interstate system. As Haas points out:

> "in the balance-of-power system integration was achieved by the balancing nation's playing its proper role, that of balancing the system so as to prevent the hegemony of any one alliance or State"[266].

The balance-of-power system has been probed by mankind for centuries. It has always brought about an arms race and wars. War is an essential element of the balance-of-power system because there force remains the main regulatory means.

This model is in crying contradiction with contemporary international law. It suffices to say that the balance-of-power system is based on the threat or use of force, whereas both are prohibited by contemporary international law.

Political realists, in accordance with their principal thesis about the dominant role of power in the interstate system, assert that international law means very little, if at all. (See Chapter I.) Legal realists, that is McDougal and his associates, come actually to the same conclusion. Professor Reisman states:

261 *De Jure Belli ac Pacis Libri Tres,* Lib. 2, para. XVII, transl. by Saccetti, Moscow, Gosurizdat, 1950.

262 *Politics Among Nations,* New York, Knopf, 1948, p. 32.

263 *Ibid.,* p. 25.

264 *Ibid.,* p. 29.

265 See in more detail G. Tunkin, *Law and Force in the International System,* Moscow, Progress Publishers, 1983.

266 E. Haas, *op. cit.,* p. 59.

> "If international law were working as it is supposed to be working, McDougal and his associates would have been among the first to use it in that fashion. The system was not working before World War I, it was not working in the interim period, it was not working and did not stave off the violence during World War II, and it has hardly minimized the peril of the high expectation of violence since then."[267]

If such is the case it is necessary to abandon nonnative international law and to replace it by "a process of making authoritative choices or decisions".[268]

But it is politics, not law. To degrade international law down to international politics is to deprive it of its purpose as law, that is of its role as a regulatory device used by men for centuries.

Both political and legal realists forget that alongside with the politics, reflecting a balance of power model, there exists in the interstate system another type of politics – politics based on the primacy of the international law model. These two types of politics, as stated earlier, coexist in the contemporary interstate system.

It would be suicidal for mankind to penult the balance of power model to function without restraint. As Boyle points out:

> "The present danger is Machiavellian power politics. The only antidote is international law and organizations. In a thermonuclear age, human kind's existential choice is stark, ominous, and compelling."[269]

The only way to survival is to harness power politics by international law and international organization.

3. The Primacy of the International Law Model

The idea of the primacy of international law in politics was advanced by M. Gorbachev in 1987.[270] It was the result of a new situation in the world and of new political thinking: "the core of which is recognition of the priority of general humanitarian values"[271].

The idea, however, was not elaborated and I am going to present it as how I understand it. The first question is what is the difference between the primacy of international law in politics and the old notion of the rule of law in international relations? The rule of law was understood as the compliance by States with international law. This idea

267 *Proceedings of Seventy-Ninth Annual Meeting, American Society of International Law,* "McDougal's Jurisprudence: Utility, Influence, Controversy", New York, 1985, p. 273.

268 *Ibid.*

269 Francis Anthony Boyle, *World Politics and International Law,* Durham Duke University Press, 1985, p. 295.

270 See "Possibility and Guarantees of a Safe World", *Pravda,* 17 September 1987.

271 *Perestroika and a New Thinking,* Moscow, Political Literature, 1987, p. 149 (in Russian).

is incorporated in the notion of the primacy of international law in politics, and indeed is the core of the new notion.

But the notion of the primacy of international law in politics is much wider than the rule of law in international relations.

Proceeding from the recognition of the priority of the general humanitarian values it means that all international politics should be in conformity with international law. This implies that international law embodies to a maximum possible degree the general humanitarian values.[272]

For this, first of all, it is necessary that international law covers all the important problems of world politics. It may be that there is excellent compliance with international law, but it would not amount to the primacy of international law in politics if international law covers only a part of the international problems, leaving to States the liberty to frame their policies with regard to problems not covered by international law.

Of course, law cannot and should not cover all the problems of life. I mean, therefore, only that international law should cover all the essential international problems. But even this is hardly possible as such essential problems arise from day to day and international law is simply unable to completely catch up with this development. So the notion is a relative one, but still very important.

Classical international law was certainly far enough from covering all the essential problems of world politics. Even contemporary international law is not ready for that, although the progress in the course of the XXth century has been remarkable. (See Chapter III.) As stated earlier, actually all the new global problems are not sufficiently covered by contemporary international law. It means that the task of the progressive development of international law is now more vital than ever before.

The primacy of international law model does not propose that international law should be the only means of normative regulation in the interstate system. Other social norms in the interstate system will also function. (See Chapter V.) Political regulation as such will play a considerable part, but it will be based more on international law than at present.

The use of force is also not excluded. Force, as stated before, is needed to support international law and especially to ensure international peace and security. In this domaine international law has made a gigantic step forward by prohibiting the threat or use of force. The use of armed force is permitted only by the United Nations. As to States, they may use force only in the case of "an aimed attack". (Article 51 of the Charter.)

The idea of the primacy of international law had found its expression in the Charter of the United Nations, although its formulation there is not quite clear. In the Preamble to the Charter it is stated that the United Nations will strive "to establish conditions under which justice and respect for the obligations arising from treaties and other sources of international law can be maintained".

272 See in this sense V. Vereshetin and R. Mullerson, "Primacy of International Law in World Politics", *Soviet State and Law*, 7, 1989, p. 4.

The formulation of the Helsinki Act is more precise. As stated there: "The participating States will fulfil in good faith their obligations under international law . . ."

In the primacy of the international law model the role of non-legal norms will certainly be more important than at present as higher compliance with international law will bring about an atmosphere of higher mutual confidence in relations among States and therefore increase compliance with other international understandings.

From what I have said, the following conclusion may be drawn: the primacy of international law model comprises two stages. The first stage is the rule of law in international relations. It is indispensable for survival and it may be achieved in the near future.

As Professor B. Weston has rightly pointed out:

> "Rededication to the world rule of law and co-operation in this Age of Nuclear Anxiety is not a matter of choice. It is quite simply a matter of survival."[273]

The final goal is the primacy of international law in politics. It will require more time and much more effort to achieve.

4. International Mechanisms of the Functioning of International Law

Under the functioning of international law I understand the regulatory influence of this system of law. This influence is exercised first of all directly without any mechanisms. The very existence of norms of international law influences the subjects of this system and to some extent forces them to comply with these norms. In most instances norms of international law exercise their influence this way, which is almost invisible. That is why so little attention is paid to this type of functioning of international law.

The second type of functioning is the functioning through specific mechanisms that ensure compliance. These mechanisms of functioning may be either: *(a)* international, or *(b)* municipal. International mechanisms are provided by international law, municipal – by legal systems of various States. Municipal mechanisms are of great importance, but of course international mechanisms play the greatest role and I shall limit my analysis to the international mechanisms only.

International mechanisms of the functioning of international law may be divided into three categories: (1) mechanisms of settling international disputes; (2) mechanisms of international control; (3) mechanisms of law enforcement.

All these mechanisms are created by agreements among States.

International mechanisms are put into action mainly by the principal components of the interstate system, that is by States and international organizations, but in exceptional cases, also by individuals and private corporations.

273 "Reagan Administration versus International Law", *Journal of International Law*, Reserve University, 19 (1987), p. 29.

(a) The International Mechanisms for Settling International Disputes

They are one of the oldest institutions of international law. Contemporary international law provides for many such mechanisms, and obligates States to use only them. The principle of the peaceful settlement of disputes is one of the fundamental principles of contemporary international law and is applicable to all disputes. There are many international mechanisms for the settling of international disputes. Article 33 of the United Nations Charter enumerates the following: negotiation, enquiry, mediation, conciliation, arbitration, judicial settlement, resort to regional agencies or arrangements, or other peaceful means chosen by the parties. One should add the growing role of international organizations, especially of the United Nations, in the settling of international disputes, especially when a dispute becomes a hot spot.

The mechanisms enumerated in Article 33 of the Charter constitute a kind of a chain in which each consecutive link is nearer to the principle *nemo judex in causa sua.* The existing mechanisms for settling international disputes leave the primary role to the parties to a dispute. It is the reflection of the specificity of the interstate system. In principle, according to general international law, each State is permitted in the case of a dispute to act according to its own judgment and to take measures not prohibited by international law. But at the same time, the progress has been remarkable if one takes into consideration that measures which a State may take exclude the use of armed force.

It should also be taken into consideration that alongside general international law that leaves States to decide in each particular case which mechanism of settlement to choose, there is a network of obligations on the basis of particular international treaties to use specific mechanisms.

The most frequently used mechanism for settling international disputes is negotiation. The advantages of this mechanism are evident. It is flexible, it gives an opportunity to the parties to present their case, to exchange views, to discuss, to move step by step to an agreement. As G. Geamanu has rightly pointed out: "If one examines the practice of States one may state that negotiations take the dominant part among methods used by States to settle their conflicts."[274]

After the mechanism of negotiation, where the parties to a dispute only take part, there follows a range of mechanisms with the growing influence of third parties. To ensure the rule of law in the interstate system the objective must be that all international disputes not settled by negotiation should be settled by the use of mechanisms with the participation of third parties. This has already been agreed to by the States participating in the Conference on Security and Cooperation in Europe. As stated in the Charter of Paris for a New Europe of 1990:

> "... We undertake to seek new forms of co-operation in this area, in particular a range of methods for the peaceful settlement of disputes, including mandatory third-party involvement."

274 "Théorie et pratique des négociations en droit international", *Recueil des cours,* Vol. 166 (1980), p. 416.

But there is still no such norm of general international law. The international mechanisms with the third-party involvement are divided into two rather different parts: *(a)* mechanisms where the final decision is left to the States concerned; *(b)* mechanisms where the final decision is made by a third party. The first part includes good offices, mediation and conciliation. They play a very important role in international relations. The United Nations undertook a special study of these mechanisms and in 1989 the General Assembly decided to bring the results of these studies to the attention of States. The document annexed to this resolution is called "Resort to a commission of good offices, mediation and conciliation within the United Nations". It seems, however, that this document contains very little that is new.[275]

There is, in practice, an enormous number of different permanent and ad hoc commissions, provided for in the treaties, especially in bilateral treaties for settling disputes among States.

But up to now States were reluctant to accept more sophisticated mechanisms for settling international disputes where the final decision does not belong to the parties involved, that is arbitration and judicial procedures. The reason is obvious: the acceptance of compulsory arbitral or judicial procedures means further restrictions of State sovereignty and States are always very cautious about that. Arbitral procedure is more easily accepted by States as it gives the parties involved in a dispute the freedom to decide which sources an arbitral tribunal must apply and also a considerable role in choosing the members of a tribunal.

The situation with the judicial procedure is entirely different. A dispute is left to a court to decide. The parties involved in a dispute do not influence the composition of a court. As to the International Court of Justice, a State involved in a dispute and having no member of its nationality among the judges of the Court may appoint a judge *ad hoc* who has the same status as the other judges. To decide what sources of international law should be applied is a competence of the Court. Only about 50 States have accepted the compulsory jurisdiction of the International Court of Justice. Among the permanent members of the Security Council only Great Britain is bound by the compulsory jurisdiction of the Court. The Soviet Union and China have made no declarations accepting the compulsory jurisdiction of the Court. France and the United States have withdrawn their declarations on compulsory jurisdiction. The situation is absurd. The international community urgently requires a greater role of the International Court of Justice.

In the past there were weighty reasons for some States to be cautious about accepting the compulsory jurisdiction of the Court. They were, in my judgment, of three kinds. The first related to the composition of the Court. The majority of judges were nationals of Western countries and belonged to the old conservative school. The second reason related to the state of international law. There were many uncertainties which made it

275 See R. Lavalle, "The Amical Dispute Settlement Scheme Brought to the Attention of States by the United Nations General Assembly in 1989: A Critical Commentary", *Austrian Journal of Public and International Law,* 42 (1991), pp. 163-179.

possible that judgments of the Court might be influenced by ideological considerations or by different positions on some questions of international law. For instance, in relations between the USSR and Japan there were many fishery disputes connected with the limit of the territorial sea. The USSR insisted on the 12-mile limit of the territorial sea, whereas Western countries, as well as Japan, held the position that according to international law such a limit was three miles. How could the Soviet Union agree to present such cases to the Court when it was clear in advance that the majority of judges would base their opinion on the three-mile limit of the territorial sea and vote against the Soviet Union. The third reason was the cold war and mutual suspicions. If to single out the Soviet Union, the important role played by the cult of State sovereignty was dictated by the cult of Stalin. Being the Chief of the Treaty and Legal Department of the Ministry of Foreign Affairs for 13 years, I tried to mitigate this position, but could not do very much. It was so simple and easy, when you did not want to accept some proposal at an international forum, to say that it was contrary to State sovereignty.

Now the situation is different. The composition of the Court has changed. Western judges do not have a majority in the Court any more and it is also of importance that they are modern international lawyers. The number of uncertainties in international law has greatly diminished. And it is probably most important that, since 1985, the international climate has radically changed for the better.

In accordance with the new foreign policy of the USSR connected with perestroika and a new political thinking, it was logical that in 1987 Gorbachev announced a new position of the Soviet Union with regard to the International Court of Justice. He made a call for the general acceptance of the compulsory jurisdiction of the Court on mutually agreed conditions and first of all the acceptance of this jurisdiction by the permanent members of the Security Council. Some reservations made by the Soviet Union to international treaties were withdrawn. The Ministry of Foreign Affairs of the USSR started consultations on the subject with the ministries of other permanent members of the Security Council. I have no doubt that the Russian Ministry of Foreign Affairs will continue these efforts.

Anyhow, the prestige of the International Court of Justice is growing. The number of cases presented to the Court has increased considerably. One may be cautiously optimistic about the future role of the International Court.

(b) The Mechanisms of International Control

The mechanisms of international control over the fulfilment by States of their international obligations is a comparatively recent phenomenon. The legal basis of this mechanism is the international treaties or decisions of international organizations. As it exists now it is applied only to international treaties and, in some cases, to resolutions of international organizations. In most cases the control is exercised by international organizations and international organs.

International mechanisms of control are developing as a separate institution, but they also fulfil to a certain extent the function of law enforcement, as the very existence of international control exercises a certain pressure upon States to fulfil their international obligations. Some authors consider international control as a kind of law enforcement.[276]

W. Morawiecki, referring to Symonides, gives the following, to my mind, acceptable definition of international control:

> "Under control one understands various actions having the aim to ascertain the actual situation and determine to what extent it corresponds to a certain legal norm."[277]

Cassese points out that in many instances international control does not terminate by stating fulfilment or non fulfilment of international obligations, but also includes recommendations to a defaulting State to rectify the situation.[278]

International control is an important means of increasing the effectiveness of international law. Experience has shown that the more the important and difficult problems are regulated, the more international control is indispensable.[279]

So far international control has been exercised with regard to some treaties only. There is no international control over fulfilment by States of their obligations arising from customary norms of international law.

Some authors are of the opinion that there are two types of international control: administrative and judicial. Charpentier even considers the difference between these two types as very important.[280]

It seems that there is a confusion of two things which have certain similarities, but are essentially different. A court is called to take up a case when there is an alleged violation of international law. International control is exercised regardless of the fact whether there are allegations of violations or not. It is potentially a permanent action. The task of a court is to verify whether an alleged violation has really taken place and to decide what measures must be taken. The task of an international control is to verify whether the international obligations of States are fulfilled or not and to state it.

Special mechanisms of international control are created within or outside the international organizations. A pioneer in this field was the International Labour Organisation. In 1927 it established a committee of experts on the application of conventions adopted by the ILO. Since then many other international organizations have assumed controlling functions over fulfilment by States of their obligations deriving from treaties concluded under the auspices of these organizations (UNESCO, WHO, IMO, etc). Attention should also be drawn to the fact that a growing number of international treaties recently concluded contain provisions on international control.

---

276 See, for instance, Doris Konig, *Durchsetzung internationaler Bestands und Umweltschutzvorschriften auf Hoher See im Interesse der Staatengemeinschaft,* Berlin, Duncker & Humblot, 1990.

277 *Functions of an International Organisation* (in Russian), Moscow, Progress Publishers, 1976, p. 175.

278 *Il controllo internazionale,* Milan, Giuffrè Editore, 1971, p. 175.

279 See in this sense I. Kotlyarov, *International Control with the Use of Cosmic Means* (in Russian), Moscow, International Relations, 1981, pp. 14 et seq.

280 "Le contrôle des organisations internationales de l'execution des obligations des Etats", *Recueil des cours,* Vol. 182 (1983), p. 154.

Mechanisms of international control may be divided into two categories: the report system and the inspection system. But very often the tern "international inspection" is used as a general term covering all kinds of international control.[281] But it seems useful for practical purposes to distinguish between the report system and the inspection system.

The report system is widely used. It consists in the presentation of reports by States parties to an international treaty to an international organization or international organ. These reports are examined by the international organization or international organ which usually makes general conclusions about the implementation of conventions or even names defaulting States. The inspection system may be considered as going further than the report system. It is intended to deal not only with reports but also with the verification of facts, including on-site inspection, inspection from the air, from satellites, etc.

An example of a very sophisticated report system is a system existing in the International Labour Organisation. Briefly, it consists in the presenting of reports by governments on the implementation of ratified conventions and to some extent also on the implementation of non-ratified conventions and even recommendations. The reports of the governments are studied by the commission of experts that presents its report to the General Conference of the ILO. The commission of experts, and later the commission of the Conference and the General Conference itself, enumerates cases of non-fulfilment of obligations by certain States in the form of observations. The defaulting States are put on a "special list". As N. Valticos points out that although corresponding organs of the ILO severally stated that these observations are not a sanction, still "this 'special list' is considered by the interested States as a kind of moral sanction".[282]

This system is a very important means of ensuring the fulfilment by States of their obligations, especially those derived from international labour conventions. On this subject Valticos says:

> "General study of the results of the functioning of the mechanisms of control has shown that during the period of 30 years they are certainly positive, because in more than 60 per cent of cases where the organs of control have found divergencies, necessary measures have been taken to eliminate completely or partially the divergencies indicated."[283]

Being for some years a member of the ILO commission of experts I know how Governments react to observations made by the ILO organs and fully subscribe to the Valticos statement.

Many international treaties contain provisions regarding the presentation of reports by States parties to these treaties concerning fulfilment of their obligations under the

281 See, for instance, *L'inspection internationale* (ed. G. Fischer and D. Vignes), ,Brussels, Bruylant, 1976.

282 Droit international du travail, Paris, Dalloz, 1970, p. 569.

283 Op. cit., p. 579.

treaties. Provisions concerning the presentation of reports exist in such important international treaties as the International Covenants on Human Rights, the Convention on the Elimination of all Forms of Racial Discrimination, and many others.

As stated earlier, the inspection system goes further than the report system. The inspection system may be divided into three categories: inspection by international organizations, State inspection under the supervision of an international organization and mutual State inspection.

The International Atomic Energy Agency may be an example of an inspection by an international organization. It has its own inspectors who exercise on-site inspections and report to the IAEA. It may be considered as the most advanced international inspection because it is conducted by an impartial body. As Charpentier points out:

> "Un contrôle international ne peut être convenablement assuré que s'il échappe non seulement à l'Etat soumis à l'obligation mais également à l'Etat bénéficiaire, il faut donc qu'il soit confié à un tiers."[284]

This is generally true, but in certain cases mutual inspection may not be less effective than any other.

State inspection under international supervision is made by State inspectors. Usually the aim, region and time of inspection are decided by a State that intends to inspect. Rules of the inspection are laid down by an international commission. The report of the experts is presented to their respective government which has to forward a report to an international commission.

As an example of mutual State inspection one may take the Antarctic Treaty of 1959. I recall that at the Antarctic conference we agreed without much discussion on the article concerning mutual inspection. According to this article, all the regions of Antarctica, including all stations, all marine and air ships, are open to inspection by inspectors appointed by any of the parties to the treaty. This provision is functioning very well and has exercised considerable influence upon other treaties concluded afterwards.

Mutual inspection has been thoroughly elaborated in the Soviet-American treaties of 1987 and 1981 on medium-range and strategic missiles.

There are many other forms of international inspection. The conferences to review the operation of a treaty provided for in the Nuclear Non-Proliferation Treaty of 1968, in the Treaty on the Prohibition of the Emplacement of Nuclear Weapons and Other Weapons of Mass Destruction on the Seabed and the Ocean Floor and in the Subsoil Thereof of 1971, and in the Convention on the Prohibition of the Development, Production and Stockpiling of Bacteriological (Biological) and Toxic Weapons and on Their Destruction of 1972, may be considered as a kind of international inspection. New forms of international inspection that I have described in Chapter V, paragraph 1, are functioning within the framework of the CSCE.

---

284 *Op. cit.*, p. 161.

There is no doubt that a new important institution of international control is gaining ground. The time seems to be ripe for the creation within the framework of the United Nations of a control body to supervise the functioning of general multilateral treaties which are the principal means for the reconstruction of the interstate system. The activities of such a body might promote the compliance of States with general multilateral treaties, and mutual confidence among States.

(c) The International Mechanisms of Law Enforcement

The weakest point of international law is the absence of any effective mechanisms of law enforcement. Law enforcement, in a broad sense, consists of two kinds of measures: preventive measures and *post factum* measures. Preventive measures have the task of exercising pressures upon States to make them comply with norms of international law. The *post factum* measures have a character of sanctions in a broad sense of the term.

Mechanisms of international control may be considered as belonging, or being very close, to the first category. International mechanisms for settling international disputes at their highest level (arbitral tribunals and international courts) may be considered as belonging to the second category.

However, in a narrow sense, international mechanisms of law enforcement are only those mechanisms which deal with *post factum* cases, that is with cases of violations of international law and which exercise the necessary pressures upon a defaulting State to make it comply with sanctions.

The first question that may arise is whether at all one may speak of mechanisms of law enforcement in the interstate system, considering that States are sovereign entities and there is no such central authority that exists in a State. Such a question was raised by Professors Fischer and Vignes even with regard to international inspection.[285] It is a relevant question. In classical international law such mechanisms did not exist. Their appearance in contemporary international law has been a great step forward in increasing the regulatory capacity of the interstate system.

In classical international law only States could take enforcement measures, including the use of force and war, although war was not so much an enforcement measure as a means of the rule of force. Classical international law admitted "unrestricted self-help".[286]

Even contemporary international law leaves to States a considerable latitude in applying measures of enforcement, but it prohibits the use of force and the threat of force. Measures that may be taken according to the right of self-defence in the case of an armed attack constitute an exception. (See Chapter IV.)

By agreements among States a considerable part of law enforcement competence was given to the international organizations. Actually, all international organizations

285 "Existe-t-il une fonction d'inspection dans la societe internationale?", *L'inspection internationale*, Brussels, Bruylant, 1976, p. 7.

286 O. Young, *Compliance in the International System, International Law. A Contemporary Perspective* (ed. Falk, Kratochwil, Mendlovitz), Boulder, Westview Press, 1985, p. 108.

now have competence to take enforcement measures in the field of their activities without the use of armed force.

The only exception is the United Nations. Measures that may be taken by the United Nations on decisions of the Security Council even exceed the range of law enforcement. The law enforcement measures, including the use of armed force and the threat of force, may be taken according to Chapter VII of the Charter in the case "of any threat to the peace, breach of the peace or act of aggression". Law enforcement action may be taken by the Security Council against a party that "fails to perform the obligations incumbent upon it under a judgment rendered by the Court". (Article 94.) But such measures may be taken by the Security Council only upon the demand of the other party. Then the Security Council is not "the automatic law-enforcement agency of the Court".[287] The Security Council "may, if it deems necessary, make recommendations or decide upon measures to be taken to give effect to the judgment". (Article 94 of the Charter.)

The question arises whether Article 39 of the United Nations Charter goes beyond the law enforcement measures. Law enforcement measures are applied in cases of violations of international law. There must, therefore, be a State or States that violated international law. But it may well be that a threat to the peace may arise when no State has violated international law. Under Article 39 even in such cases the Security Council may take the necessary measures, but they will not be strictly speaking law-enforcement measures.

The further development of the international mechanisms of law enforcement depends on the development of international organizations and primarily on the strengthening of the United Nations.

287 Sh. Rosenne, *The Law and Practice of the International Court*, Leiden, Sijthoff, Vol. 1, 1965, p. 150.

Chapter VII Some Thoughts About the Future of the Interstate System

1. General Remarks

As defined by the *Encyclopaedia Britannica*, futurology is "the study of current trends in order to forecast future developments".[288]

The human mind never limits itself to analysis of the present, but tries to discover the future. An accelerated pace of history in the second half of the XXth century has increased the desire of man to know what will happen tomorrow. The result was extensive research in the field of futurology. Considerable work has been done by political scientists. Comprehensive analysis of their theories has been done in Russia by G. Shahnazarov.[289]

A grandiose project under the title "Toward a New Civilization" is being started under the leadership of Shahnazarov in the framework of the Gorbachev Foundation.

Considerable research about the future of the interstate system, international law and international organization has been carried out by international lawyers, especially in the United States.[290]

I embark on this perilous enterprise with some trepidation. To speak of the future means to speak of what does not exist. But as I have just said, the human mind cannot resist the temptation to try to foresee what will happen tomorrow. More than that. Man is forced to think of the next days, to plan his existence. But every forecast has an element of dreaming.

Mankind has many dreams embodied in tales, in folklore in general, in religions, in different projects for a better world. Even law, a societal institution considered by many as excluding any imagination, contains an element of dreaming. It envisages desired situations, but desired is something that does not exist, and is to some extent a dream. Without a dream, mankind cannot exist. There is much truth in the words of Anatole France who said in a somewhat imaginative way:

---

288 *Encyclopaedia Britannica,* Vol. 5 (15th ed.), 1990, p. 63.

289 See *Socialism and the Future,* Moscow, Nauka, 1983.

290 See, in particular, S. Mendlovitz (ed.), *Legal and Political Problems of World Order,* New York, 1962; *The Strategy of World Order* (ed. R. Falk, S. Mendlovitz), New York, 1966; *Toward a Just World Order* (ed. R. Falk, S. Kim, S. Mendlovitz), Boulder, Westview Press, 1982; *International Law. A Contemporary Perspective* (ed. R. Falk, F. Kratochwil, S. Mendlovitz), Boulder, Westview Press, 1985.

> "J'aime la vérité. Je crois que l'humanité en a besoin; mais certes elle a bien plus grand besoin encore du mensonge qui la flatte, la console, lui donne des espérances infinies. Sans le mensonge, elle périrait de désespoir et d'ennui."[291]
> (I love the truth. I believe that it is necessary for mankind; but certainly mankind needs still more a dream that flatters and consoles it and gives it unlimited hopes. Without the dream mankind would perish of despair and boredom.)

The development of science is almost completely unpredictable. But science may predict when it starts from existing tendencies. However, unforseeable events may cancel all forecasts. Who, for instance, could foresee the consequences of perestroika in the Soviet Union, for the Soviet Union itself and for the entire world?

With all these caveats in mind I'll present my brief remarks on the future of the interstate system, international law and international organization.

The interstate system, as everything in the world, is changing. Now it is in a critical period of its development. In the second half of the XXth century science and technology have made a spectacular leap ahead, that is changing all aspects of society, although in different degrees. It is true that the tremendous progress in science and technology has taken place only in the developed countries, but its influence is global. All this is well known. It is also generally agreed that a transformation of the existing interstate system to make it conform to the changed society as a whole is necessary.

As to what kind of transformation it should be there are three main points of view. According to the opinion of the federalists this transformation must consist in the abolition of sovereign States and the creation of a world federation. The advocates of world society theories envisage a mixed world society where States and private corporations act, and are on the same level. Others take the view that the only possible and even desirable way is that of combining a strong international organization with the existence of sovereign States.

I believe that the last approach is the correct one, if one considers the existing tendencies. Of course, nobody can predict what the world will be like in the year 5000 or even in the year 3000. It may well happen that the Marxist dream of a classless and stateless society, which is so close to religious teachings, may become a reality. Scientific forecasts can be made only for the foreseeable future.

To speak of the future of the interstate system one should, in my view, start from the following postulates.

Any transformation of the interstate system is possible only on the basis of agreement among States. In the world of today an attempt to change the interstate system by force is suicide for mankind. This *categorical imperative* is usually ignored by the futurologists.

This means that for transforming the interstate system a common understanding is needed relating first of all to goals, actors and the means of such a transformation. And, in my opinion, mankind has already achieved in this field much more than is generally thought.

291 *La vie en fleur,* Moscow, Editions en langues étrangères, 1948, p. 193.

2. The Goals

Common goals relating to the interstate system reflect a common outlook. Such common global goals may emerge only as a result of considerable global economic and spiritual integration. This process is going on and now with the disappearance of the ideological confrontation will be accelerated. With the growing integration and increasing number of global problems, common goals will also become more numerous.

Common goals are of great importance as they are a kind of ideological background of States' policies. However, their influence should not be overestimated. In real life, people, as well as States, espousing good ideas often commit bad actions. Therefore, as far as a normative regulation in the interstate system is concerned it is of great importance that common goals be reflected in concrete norms of behaviour.

People in general, and ruling elites in particular usually reach the heights of global common goals in times of crisis. As preliminary steps to contemporary common goals were the Hague Peace Conferences of 1899 and 1907 when the threat of a great war became visible; the Covenant of the League of Nations as a result of the greatest war in history up to that time. Then after the horrible Second World War it was the Charter of the United Nations that embodied common goals which will live for a long time.

These goals may be summarized as follows:

(1) Elimination of war.
(2) Primacy of common human values and problems.
(3) Respect for human rights.
(4) Primacy of international law in politics.
(5) Promotion of social progress and better standards of life in larger freedom.

With the collapse of the colonial system and the appearance of sovereign States all over the world a real global interstate system emerged. The scientific and technological revolutions have drastically changed the situation. All these have created new global problems and new common goals, such as the conservation of the natural environment, the development of underdeveloped countries, etc.

Many of these common goals have already found, to a considerable degree, expression in concrete principles and norms of international law. Some, as stated earlier, very little. An enormous task is ahead: to translate the agreed common goals into concrete principles and norms of international law.

3. The Actors and Means

According to the tendencies visible at present, one may predict the following developments.

States will remain the principal actors in the interstate system for a long time. They will create on the basis of agreement norms of general international law and also political and recommendatory norms. They will create international intergovernmental organizations also on the basis of agreement.

The solution of global problems on which depends the fate of civilization may be achieved also only on the basis of agreement among States. The part of the international organization in the solution of these problems will depend on agreement among States as well. In general, the functioning of the interstate system will depend mainly on the behaviour of States. There are no indications that the primary role of States in the interstate system will change considerably.

The role of international organizations in the interstate system is increasing and this process will continue.

The inevitable development of general integration in the world will necessitate the creation of new international organizations and the expansion of their competence.

The growing competence of international organizations requires some reorientation with regard to supranationality. If in the past there prevailed a cult of State sovereignty, in recent decades public opinion is changing, especially in the developed countries. The example is the development of the European Community, which is tending to become a European Union.

At the same time, as Professor Anand says:

> "the newly independent States are extremely sensitive to any infringement of their independence, and are attached to their sovereignty with all the freshness and warmth of their national sentiments."[292]

A recent upsurge of nationalism as a result of the cult of State sovereignty has taken place on the territory of the former Soviet Union and also Yugoslavia. The immediate consequences of this are disastrous for the peoples of these countries. From the point of view of historical development, they have been thrown back.

In the present international organizations there are inter-state and supra-state elements. In his book on supranationality, Lindeiner-Wildau sets up four minimum conditions for supranationality: (a) decisions are taken by a majority vote; (b) persons – members of a supranational organ must be independent of States; (c) decisions must have automatic binding force for States; (d) an organization must have direct powers over individuals.[293]

However, there are different degrees of supranationality. The present general international organizations are essentially inter-state organizations, but actually all of them contain, as I have already said, an element of supranationality. Some decisions are taken by a majority vote and are directly binding upon member States.

If we take the United Nations, there is a considerable supranationality element. On a number of questions relating mainly to the internal life of the organization (budgetary questions, the election of nonpermanent members of the Security Council, the admission of new members to the United Nations, the suspension of the rights and privileges

292 *International Law and the Developing Countries*, New Delhi, Banyan Publications, 1986, p. 90.
293 *La supranationalité en tant que principe de droit*, A. W. Sijthoff, Leiden, 1970, pp. 46-58.

of members, etc.), the General Assembly takes decisions binding upon States members. On the most important questions the Security Council may take by a majority vote decisions binding upon all member States. (Article 25 of the United Nations Charter.) Paralysed for many years by the atmosphere of confrontation, and with the cardinal change of the situation in the world, relative provisions of the Charter start to operate. Recent examples are decisions of the Security Council with regard to Iraq and Libya.

Nowadays some new politicians in the former Soviet Union, who hardly have any idea of what sovereignty really means declare with aplomb that a State possesses sovereignty or not, as if sovereignty were something immutable and untouchable. I have already shown that all the history of international law, although it is based on State sovereignty, has been a gradual limitation of this sovereignty. State sovereignty, as individual freedom, is always limited.

It is inevitable that the settlement of global problems will be regulated more and more by international law and on its basis also by international organizations. This course is dictated by reason as well as by the imperative of survival. This means that a reasonable limitation of State sovereignty and the increasing competence of international organizations are necessary, inevitable and desirable.

The element of human dimension in international law will certainly grow further. It is already generally accepted that the dignity and welfare of a human being is the final goal of the State, international law and the international organization. Of course the realities of life are far from these sacred goals.

Nations, ethnic groups, non-governmental organizations and private corporations will be covered more and more by public international law and by that part of private international law that consists of the norms created by international treaties. Their rights and duties will be determined not only by municipal legal systems, but more and more by legal norms based on agreements among States. They will have greater access to international bodies to defend their rights. At the same time they will be more than at present subjects of international responsibility.

However, there are no indications that individuals and private cor porations will be on the same level in the interstate system as States, still less that corporations will play a leading role in this system.

In general, a collective regulation in the interstate system on the basis of agreement among States, by means of international law, international organization, political and recommendatory norms will greatly diminish the role of the unilateral actions of States in this system.

The use of force in the interstate system will be more limited. It will be used only on the basis of decisions of a principal international organization. The right of self-defence will be further restricted.

Whatever the dangers of comparison between interstate systems and municipal systems, the development of the interstate systems will in some respects resemble the historic development of municipal systems. Although the multiplicity of international organizations in the future is inevitable experience has shown that there will be one principal international organization. The competence of such an organization will include the most important and general problems of international life. This does not mean that the role of the specialized international organizations should be underestimated.

It seems more than probable that such a principal international organization of the future will be the United Nations. The years after perestroika in the Soviet Union and the radical changes in the international atmosphere have shown that the United Nations is capable of performing its main functions effectively. There is no doubt that an increase in its supranationality will be necessary and that would mean some amendment of the Charter. But it must be all well thought out and agreed to by members of the United Nations. Hasty decisions, or decisions imposed by a majority on a minority of the United Nations, may only cause great damage and delay the adoption of decisions dictated by the interests of mankind.

There is no doubt that this will be the way to the primacy of international law in politics, as an element of the rule of Reason. (See Chapter VI, paragraph 3.)

With all that, one should not forget that the interstate system is a subsystem of society and the development of society as a whole will be decisive for the development of the interstate system.

Index of Names

Entries below are based, where appropriate, on the Library of Congress transliteration system, short form, with minor emendations and may vary from versions printed in the text.

C

G

H

I

J

K

L

M

N

O

P

Q

R

S

T

U

V

W

Y

Z